PHILIP'S

MODERN SCHOOL ATLAS

96TH EDITION

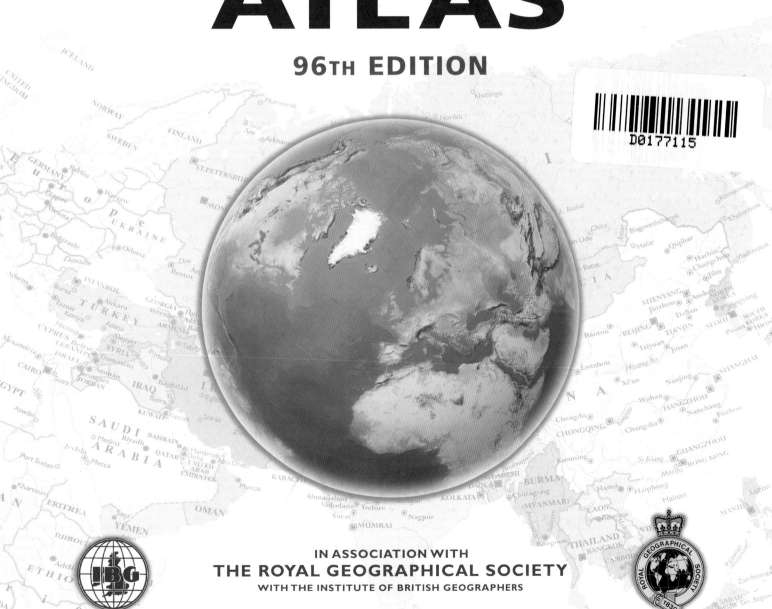

IN ASSOCIATION WITH
THE ROYAL GEOGRAPHICAL SOCIETY
WITH THE INSTITUTE OF BRITISH GEOGRAPHERS

MAP SYMBOLS

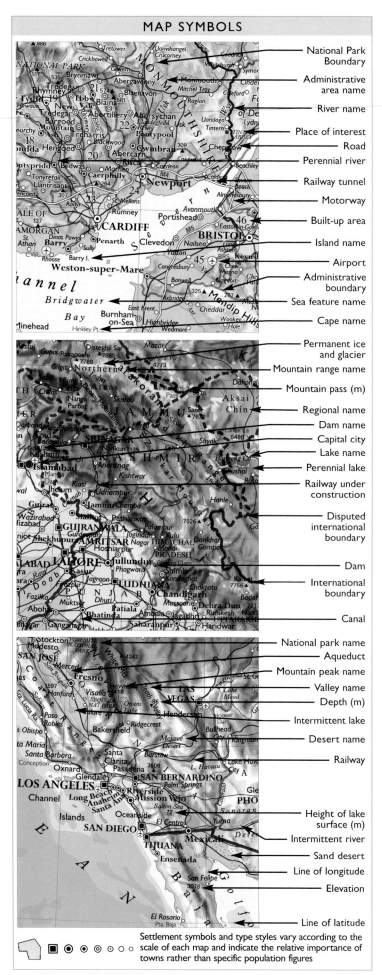

- National Park Boundary
- Administrative area name
- River name
- Place of interest
- Road
- Perennial river
- Railway tunnel
- Motorway
- Built-up area
- Island name
- Airport
- Administrative boundary
- Sea feature name
- Cape name
- Permanent ice and glacier
- Mountain range name
- Mountain pass (m)
- Regional name
- Dam name
- Capital city
- Lake name
- Perennial lake
- Railway under construction
- Disputed international boundary
- Dam
- International boundary
- Canal
- National park name
- Aqueduct
- Mountain peak name
- Valley name
- Depth (m)
- Intermittent lake
- Desert name
- Railway
- Height of lake surface (m)
- Intermittent river
- Sand desert
- Line of longitude
- Elevation
- Line of latitude

Settlement symbols and type styles vary according to the scale of each map and indicate the relative importance of towns rather than specific population figures

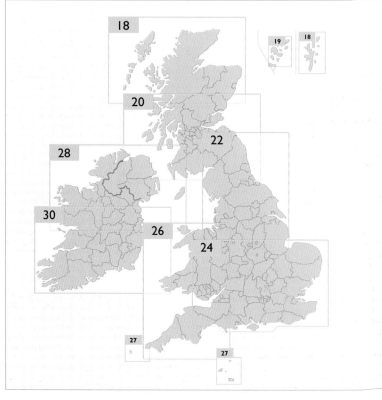

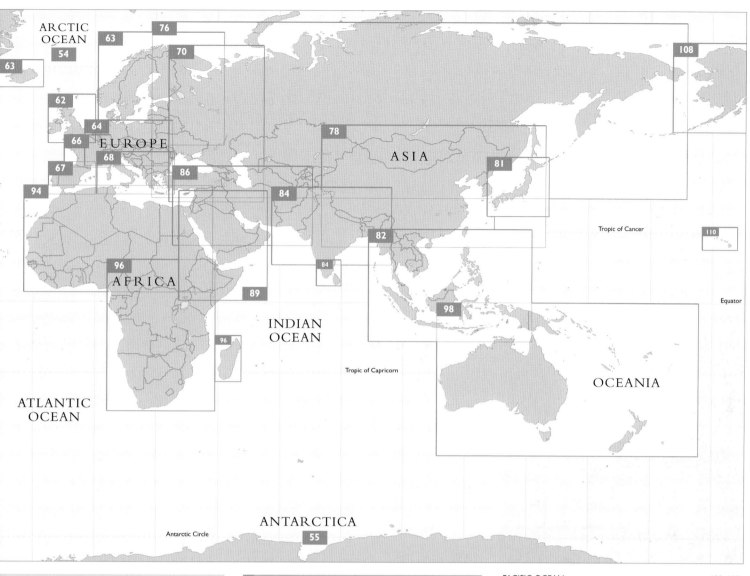

CONTENTS

:ALE, LATITUDE AND LONGITUDE 4
:AP PROJECTIONS 5

REMOTE SENSING   **6–16**

:TRODUCTION 6–7
:OLOUR COMPOSITES 8
:GETATION AND LANDFORMS 9
:OBAL MONITORING 10–11
:VIRONMENTAL MONITORING 12–13
:OLOGICAL INTERPRETATION 14
:NTHETIC APERTURE RADAR 15
:E URBAN ENVIRONMENT 16

UNITED KINGDOM AND IRELAND   **17–48**

:ORTHERN SCOTLAND 18–19
:UTHERN SCOTLAND 20–21
:ORTHERN ENGLAND 22–23
:UTH AND SOUTH-EAST ENGLAND 24–25
:ALES AND SOUTH-WEST ENGLAND 26–27
:LAND – NORTH 28–29
:LAND – SOUTH 30–31
: AND IRELAND: GEOLOGY 32
: AND IRELAND: RELIEF OF LAND 33
: AND IRELAND: CLIMATE 34–35
: AND IRELAND: ENVIRONMENT 36–37
: AND IRELAND: AGRICULTURE, INDUSTRY
:AND TRADE 38–39
: AND IRELAND: ENERGY 40–41
: AND IRELAND: TRANSPORT AND TOURISM 42–43
: AND IRELAND: COUNTIES AND REGIONS 44–45
: AND IRELAND: POPULATION TRENDS 46–47
: AND IRELAND: STANDARDS OF LIVING 48

THE WORLD   **49–122**

THE WORLD: RELIEF OF LAND 50–51
THE WORLD: COUNTRIES 52–53
ARCTIC OCEAN AND ANTARCTICA 54–55
EUROPE: RELIEF OF LAND 56
EUROPE: COUNTRIES 57
EUROPE: CLIMATE AND BIOMES 58
EUROPE: POPULATION 59
EUROPEAN UNION 60–61
UK AND IRELAND 62
SCANDINAVIA AND THE BALTIC LANDS 63
CENTRAL EUROPE 64–65
FRANCE 66
SPAIN AND PORTUGAL 67
ITALY AND THE BALKAN STATES 68–69
EASTERN EUROPE AND TURKEY 70–71
ASIA: RELIEF OF LAND 72
ASIA: COUNTRIES 73
ASIA: CLIMATE AND BIOMES 74
ASIA: POPULATION AND WEALTH 75
RUSSIA AND NORTHERN ASIA 76–77
CHINA AND THE FAR EAST 78–79
CHINA: INDUSTRY AND HYDROELECTRICITY 80
JAPAN 81
SOUTH-EAST ASIA 82–83
SOUTH ASIA 84–85
THE MIDDLE EAST 86–87
THE MIDDLE EAST: OIL AND WATER 88
ARABIA AND THE HORN OF AFRICA 89
AFRICA: RELIEF OF LAND 90
AFRICA: COUNTRIES 91
AFRICA: CLIMATE AND BIOMES 92
AFRICA: POPULATION AND WEALTH 93
NORTHERN AFRICA 94–95
CENTRAL AND SOUTHERN AFRICA 96–97
OCEANIA 98–99
OCEANIA: CLIMATE AND POPULATION 100–101

PACIFIC OCEAN 102–103
NORTH AMERICA: RELIEF OF LAND 104
NORTH AMERICA: COUNTRIES 105
NORTH AMERICA: CLIMATE AND BIOMES 106
NORTH AMERICA: POPULATION AND WEALTH 107
CANADA 108–109
UNITED STATES 110–111
NORTH-EAST UNITED STATES AND THE ST LAWRENCE 112–113
MEXICO, CENTRAL AMERICA AND THE CARIBBEAN 114–115
CARIBBEAN: HURRICANES 116
SOUTH AMERICA: RELIEF OF LAND 117
SOUTH AMERICA: CLIMATE AND BIOMES 118
SOUTH AMERICA: POPULATION AND WEALTH 119
SOUTH AMERICA 120–121
SOUTH-EAST BRAZIL 122

WORLD THEMES   **123–160**

THE WORLD: VOLCANOES AND EARTHQUAKES 124–125
THE WORLD: TEMPERATURE AND OCEAN CURRENTS 126
THE WORLD: PRESSURE, WINDS AND PRECIPITATION 127
THE WORLD: CLIMATE 128–129
THE WORLD: CLIMATE CHANGE 130–131
THE WORLD CLIMATE STATISTICS 132–133
THE WORLD: BIOMES 134–135
THE WORLD: AGRICULTURE 136–137
THE WORLD: ENERGY AND MINERALS 138–139
THE WORLD: INDUSTRY AND TRADE 140–141
THE WORLD: TRAVEL AND TOURISM 142–143
THE WORLD: STANDARDS OF LIVING 144–145
THE WORLD: POPULATION DISTRIBUTION 146–147
THE WORLD: POPULATION TRENDS 148–149
THE WORLD: LANGUAGES AND RELIGION 150
THE WORLD: INTERNATIONAL ORGANIZATIONS 151
THE WORLD: HUMAN CONCERNS 152–153
THE WORLD: SOCIAL AND ECONOMIC STATISTICS 154–159
THE WORLD: PHYSICAL DIMENSIONS 160

INDEX   **161–184**

SCALE

The scale of a map is the relationship of the distance between two points shown on the map and the distance between the same two points on the Earth's surface. For instance, 1 inch on the map represents 1 mile on the ground, or 10 kilometres on the ground is represented by 1 centimetre on the map.

Instead of saying 1 centimetre represents 10 kilometres, we could say that 1 centimetre represents 1 000 000 centimetres on the map. If the scale is stated so that the same unit of measurement is used on both the map and the ground, then the proportion will hold for any unit of measurement. Therefore, the scale is usually written 1:1 000 000. This is called a 'representative fraction' and usually appears at the top of the map page, above the scale bar.

Calculations can easily be made in centimetres and kilometres by dividing the second figure in the representative fraction by 100 000 (i.e. by deleting the last five zeros). Thus at a scale of 1:5 000 000, 1 cm on the map represents 50 km on the ground. This is called a 'scale statement'. The calculation for inches and miles is more laborious, but 1 000 000 divided by 63 360 (the number of inches in a mile) shows that 1:1 000 000 can be stated as 1 inch on the map represents approximately 16 miles on the ground.

Many of the maps in this atlas feature a scale bar. This is a bar divided into the units of the map – miles and kilometres – so that a map distance can be measured with a ruler, dividers or a piece of paper, then placed along the scale bar, and the distance read off. To the left of the zero on the scale bar there are usually more divisions. By placing the ruler or dividers on the nearest rounded figure to the right of the zero, the smaller units can be counted off to the left.

The map extracts below show Los Angeles and its surrounding area at six different scales. The representative fraction, scale statement and scale bar are positioned above each map. Map 1 is at 1:27 000 and is the largest scale extract shown. Many of the individual buildings are identified and most of the streets are named, but at this scale only part of central Los Angeles can be shown within the given area. Map 2 is much smaller in scale at 1:250 000. Only a few important buildings and streets can be named, but the whole of central Los Angeles is shown. Maps 3, 4 and 5 show how greater areas can be depicted as the map scale decreases, down to Map 6 at 1:35 000 000. At this small scale, the entire Los Angeles conurbation is depicted by a single town symbol and a large part of the south-western USA and part of Mexico is shown.

The scales of maps must be used with care since large distances on small-scale maps can be represented by one or two centimetres. On certain projections scale is only correct along certain lines, parallels or meridians. As a general rule, the larger the map scale, the more accurate and reliable will be the distance measured.

1 1 : 27 000 — 1 cm on the map represents 0.27 km on the ground

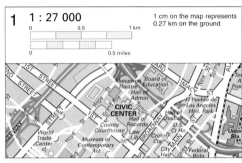

2 1 : 250 000 — 1 cm on the map represents 2.5 km on the ground

3 1 : 2 500 000 — 1 cm on the map represents 25 km on the ground

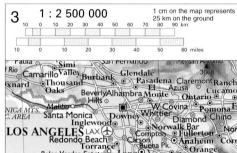

4 1 : 6 000 000 — 1 cm on the map represents 60 km on the ground

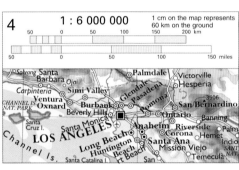

5 1 : 12 000 000 — 1 cm on the map represents 120 km on the ground

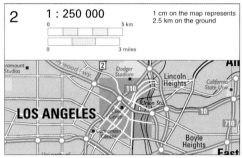

6 1 : 35 000 000 — 1 cm on the map represents 350 km on the ground

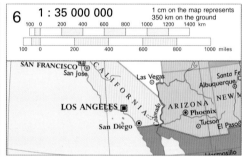

LATITUDE AND LONGITUDE

Accurate positioning of individual points on the Earth's surface is made possible by reference to the geometric system of latitude and longitude.

Latitude is the distance of a point north or south of the Equator measured at an angle with the centre of the Earth, whereby the Equator is latitude 0 degrees, the North Pole is 90 degrees north and the South Pole 90 degrees south. Latitude parallels are drawn west–east around the Earth, parallel to the Equator, decreasing in diameter from the Equator until they become a point at the poles. On the maps in this atlas the lines of latitude are represented by blue lines running across the map in smooth curves, with the degree figures in blue at the sides of the maps. The degree interval depends on the scale of the map.

Lines of longitude are meridians drawn north–south, cutting the lines of latitude at right angles on the Earth's surface and intersecting with one another at the poles. Longitude is measured by an angle at the centre of the Earth from the prime meridian (0 degrees), which passes through Greenwich in London. It is given as a measurement east or west of the Greenwich Meridian from 0 to 180 degrees. The meridians are normally drawn north–south vertically down the map, with the degree figures in blue in the top and bottom margins of the map.

In the index each place name is followed by its map page number, its letter-figure grid reference, and then its latitude and longitude. The unit of measurement is the degree, which is subdivided into 60 minutes. An index entry states the position of a place in degrees and minutes. The latitude is followed by N(orth) or S(outh) and the longitude E(ast) or W(est).

For example:
Helston, U.K.   27 G3   50 7N   5 17W
Helston is on map page 27, in grid square G3, and is 50 degrees 7 minutes north of the Equator and 5 degrees 17 minutes west of Greenwich.

McKinley, Mt., U.S.A.   108 B4   63 4N   151 0W
Mount McKinley is on map page 108, in grid square B4, and is 63 degrees 4 minutes north of the Equator and 151 degrees west of Greenwich.

HOW TO LOCATE A PLACE OR FEATURE

The two diagrams (left) show how to estimate the required distance from the nearest line of latitude or longitude on the map page, in order to locate a place or feature listed in the index (such as Helston in the UK and Mount McKinley in the USA, as detailed in the above example).

In the left-hand diagram there are 30 minutes between the lines and so to find the position of Helston an estimate has to be made: 7 parts of the 30 minutes north of the 50 0N latitude line, and 17 parts of the 30 minutes west of the 5 0W longitude line.

In the right-hand diagram it is more difficult to estimate because there is an interval of 10 degrees between the lines. In the example of Mount McKinley, the reader has to estimate 3 degrees 4 minutes north of 60 0N and 1 degree west of 150 0W.

MAP PROJECTIONS

A map projection is the systematic depiction of the imaginary grid of lines of latitude and longitude from a globe on to a flat surface. The grid of lines is called the 'graticule' and it can be constructed either by graphical means or by mathematical formulae to form the basis of a map. As a globe is three dimensional, it is not possible to depict its surface on a flat map without some form of distortion. Preservation of one of the basic properties listed below can only be secured at the expense of the others and thus the choice of projection is often a compromise solution.

Correct area
In these projections the areas from the globe are to scale on the map. This is particularly useful in the mapping of densities and distributions. Projections with this property are termed 'equal area', 'equivalent' or 'homolographic'.

Correct distance
In these projections the scale is correct along the meridians, or, in the case of the 'azimuthal equidistant', scale is true along any line drawn from the centre of the projection. They are called 'equidistant'.

Correct shape
This property can only be true within small areas as it is achieved only by having a uniform scale distortion along both the 'x' and 'y' axes of the projection. The projections are called 'conformal' or 'orthomorphic'.

Map projections can be divided into three broad categories – **'azimuthal'**, **'conic'** and **'cylindrical'**. Cartographers use different projections from these categories depending on the map scale, the size of the area to be mapped, and what they want the map to show.

AZIMUTHAL OR ZENITHAL PROJECTIONS

These are constructed by the projection of part of the graticule from the globe on to a plane tangential to any single point on it. This plane may be tangential to the equator (equatorial case), the poles (polar case) or any other point (oblique case). Any straight line drawn from the point at which the plane touches the globe is the shortest distance from that point and is known as a 'great circle'. In its 'gnomonic' construction any straight line on the map is a great circle, but there is great exaggeration towards the edges and this reduces its general uses. There are five different ways of transferring the graticule on to the plane and these are shown below. The diagrams below also show how the graticules vary, using the polar case as the example.

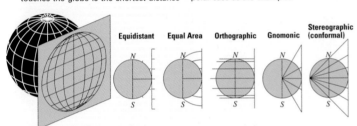

Polar case
The polar case is the simplest to construct and the diagram on the right shows the differing effects of all five methods of construction, comparing their coverage, distortion, etc, using North America as the example.

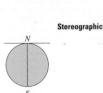

Oblique case
The plane touches the globe at any point between the Equator and poles. The oblique orthographic uses the distortion in azimuthal projections away from the centre to give a graphic depiction of the Earth as seen from any desired point in space.

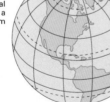

Equatorial case
The example shown here is Lambert's Equivalent Azimuthal. It is the only projection which is both equal area and where bearing is true from the centre.

CONICAL PROJECTIONS

These use the projection of the graticule from the globe on to a cone which is tangential to a line of latitude (termed the 'standard parallel'). This line is always an arc and scale is always true along it. Because of its method of construction, it is used mainly for depicting the temperate latitudes around the standard parallel, i.e. where there is least distortion. To reduce the distortion and include a larger range of latitudes, the projection may be constructed with the cone bisecting the surface of the globe so that there are two standard parallels, each of which is true to scale. The distortion is thus spread more evenly between the two chosen parallels.

Bonne
This is a modification of the simple conic, whereby the true scale along the meridians is sacrificed to enable the accurate representation of areas. However, scale is true along each parallel but shapes are distorted at the edges.

Albers Conical Equal Area
This projection uses two standard parallels. The selection of these relative to the land area to be mapped is very important. It is equal area and is especially useful for large land masses oriented east–west, such as the USA.

CYLINDRICAL AND OTHER WORLD PROJECTIONS

This group of projections are those which permit the whole of the Earth's surface to be depicted on one map. They are a very large group of projections and the following are only a few of them. Cylindrical projections are constructed by the projection of the graticule from the globe on to a cylinder tangential to the globe. Although cylindrical projections can depict all the main land masses, there is considerable distortion of shape and area towards the poles. One cylindrical projection, Mercator, overcomes this shortcoming by possessing the unique navigational property that any straight line drawn on it is a line of constant bearing ('loxodrome'). It is used for maps and charts between 15° either side of the Equator. Beyond this, enlargement of area is a serious drawback, although it is used for navigational charts at all latitudes.

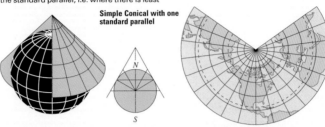

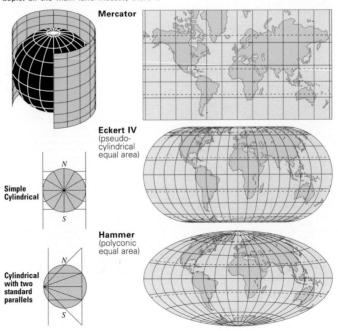

The first satellite to monitor our environment systematically was launched as long ago as April 1961. It was called TIROS-1 and was designed specifically to record atmospheric change. The first of the generation of Earth resources satellites was Landsat-1, launched in July 1972.

The succeeding decades have seen a revolution in our ability to survey and map our global environment. Digital sensors mounted on satellites now scan vast areas of the Earth's surface day and night. They collect and relay back to Earth huge volumes of geographical data which is processed and stored by computers.

Satellite imagery and remote sensing

Continuous development and refinement, and freedom from national access restrictions, have meant that sensors on these satellite platforms are increasingly replacing surface and airborne data-gathering techniques. Twenty-four hours a day, satellites are scanning and measuring the Earth's surface and atmosphere, adding to an ever-expanding range of geographic and geophysical data available to help us identify and manage the problems of our human and physical environments. Remote sensing is the science of extracting information from such images.

Satellite orbits

Most Earth-observation satellites (such as the Landsat, SPOT and IRS series) are in a near-polar, Sun-synchronous orbit (*see diagram opposite*). At altitudes of around 700–900 km the satellites revolve around the Earth approximately every 100 minutes and on each orbit cross a particular line of latitude at the same local (solar) time. This ensures that the satellite can obtain coverage of most of the globe, replicating the coverage typically within 2–3 weeks. In more recent satellites, sensors can be pointed sideways from the orbital path, and 'revisit' times with high-resolution frames can thus be reduced to a few days.

Exceptions to these Sun-synchronous orbits include the geostationary meteorological satellites, such as Meteosat. These have a 36,000 km high orbit and rotate around the Earth every 24 hours, thus remaining above the same point on the Equator.

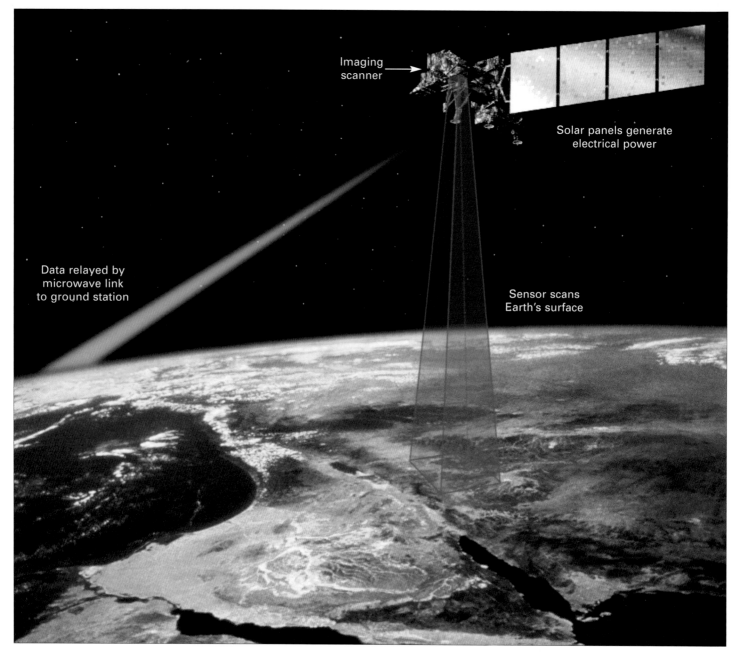

Imaging scanner

Solar panels generate electrical power

Data relayed by microwave link to ground station

Sensor scans Earth's surface

Landsat-7
This is the latest addition to the Landsat Earth-observation satellite programme, *orbiting at 705 km above the Earth. With onboard recorders, the satellite can store data until it passes within range of a* *ground station. Basic geometric and radiometric corrections are then applied before distribution of the imagery to users.*

These satellites acquire frequent images showing cloud and atmospheric moisture movements for almost a full hemisphere.

In addition, there is the Global Positioning System (GPS) satellite 'constellation', which orbits at a height of 20,200 km, consisting of 24 satellites. These circle the Earth in six different orbital planes, enabling us to fix our position on the Earth's surface to an accuracy of a few centimetres. Although developed for military use, this system is now available to individuals through hand-held receivers and in-car navigation systems. The other principal commercial uses are for surveying and air and sea navigation.

Digital sensors

Early satellite designs involved images being exposed to photographic film and returned to Earth by capsule for processing, a technique still sometimes used today. However, even the first commercial satellite imagery, from Landsat-1, used digital imaging sensors and transmitted the data back to ground stations (*see diagram opposite*).

Passive, or optical, sensors record the radiation reflected from the Earth for specific wavebands. Active sensors transmit their own microwave radiation, which is reflected from the Earth's surface back to the satellite and recorded. The SAR (Synthetic Aperture Radar) Radarsat images on page 15 are examples of the latter.

Whichever scanning method is used, each satellite records image data of constant width but potentially several thousand kilometres in length. Once the data has been received on Earth, it is usually split into approximately square sections or 'scenes' for distribution.

Spectral resolution, wavebands and false-colour composites

Satellites can record data from many sections of the electromagnetic spectrum (wavebands) simultaneously. Since we can only see images made from the three primary colours (red, green and blue), a selection of any three wavebands needs to be made in order to form a picture that will enable visual interpretation of the scene to be made. When any combination other than the visible bands are used, such as near or middle infrared, the resulting image is termed a 'false-colour composite'. An example of this is shown on page 8.

The selection of these wavebands depends on the purpose of the final image – geology, hydrology, agronomy and environmental requirements each have their own optimum waveband combinations.

GEOGRAPHIC INFORMATION SYSTEMS

A Geographic Information System (GIS) enables any available geospatial data to be compiled, presented and analysed using specialized computer software.

Many aspects of our lives now benefit from the use of GIS – from the management and maintenance of the networks of pipelines and cables that supply our homes, to the exploitation or protection of the natural resources that we use. Much of this is at a regional or national scale and the data collected from satellites form an important part of our interpretation and understanding of the world around us.

GIS systems are used for many aspects of central planning and modern life, such as defence, land use, reclamation, telecommunications and the deployment of emergency services. Commercial companies can use demographic and infrastructure data within a GIS to plan marketing strategies, identifying where their services would be most needed, and thus decide where best to locate their businesses. Insurance companies use GIS to determine premiums based on population distribution, crime figures and the likelihood of natural disasters, such as flooding or subsidence.

Whatever the application, all the relevant data can be prepared in a GIS so that a user can extract and display the information of particular interest on a map, or compare it with other material in order to help analyse and resolve a specific problem. From analysis of the data that has been acquired it is often possible to use a GIS to create a computer 'model' of possible future situations and see what impact various actions may have. A GIS can also monitor change over time, aiding the interpretation of long term trends.

A GIS may also use satellite data to extract useful information and map large areas, which would otherwise take many man-years using other methods. For applications such as hydrocarbon and mineral exploration, forestry, agriculture, environmental monitoring and urban development, these developments have made it possible to undertake projects on a global scale unheard of before.

To find out more about how GIS works and how it affects our lives, why not go the Ordnance Survey's Mapzone website at: http://mapzone.ordnancesurvey.co.uk/mapzone/giszone.html

SELECTED REMOTE SENSING SATELLITES

Year Launched	Satellite	Country	Pixel Size (Resolution)
Passive Sensors (Optical)			
1972	Landsat-1 MSS	USA	80 m
1978	NOAA AVHRR	USA	1.1 km
1981	Cosmos TK-350	Russia	10 m
1982	Landsat-4 TM	USA	30 m
1986	SPOT-1	France	10 / 20 m
1988	IRS-1A	India	36 / 72 m
1989	Cosmos KVR-1000	Russia	2 m
1991	IRS-1B	India	36 / 72 m
1995	IRS-1C	India	5.8 / 23.5 m
1997	IRS-1D	India	5.8 / 23.5 m
1999	Landsat-7 ETM	USA	15 / 30 m
1999	UoSAT-12	UK	10 / 32 m
1999	IKONOS-2	USA	1.0 / 4 m
1999	ASTER	USA	15 m
2000	Hyperion	USA	30 m
2000	EROS-A1	International	1.8 m
2001	Quickbird	USA	0.61 / 2.4 m
2002	SPOT-5	France	2.5 / 5 / 10 m
2002	DMC AlSat-1	Algeria (UK)	32 m
2003	DMC UK	UK	32 m
2003	DMC NigeriaSat-1	Nigeria (UK)	32 m
2003	DMC BilSat	Turkey (UK)	32 m
2003	OrbView-3	USA	1.0 / 4 m
2004	Formosat-2	Taiwan	2.0 / 8 m
2004	KOMPSAT-2	South Korea	1.0 / 4 m
2006	ALOS PRISM & AVNIR	Japan	2.5 m
2007	Worldview-1	USA	0.5 m
2008	GeoEye	USA	0.4 m
Active Sensors (Synthetic Aperture Radar)			
1991	ERS-1	Europe	25 m
1992	JERS-1	Japan	18 m
1995	ERS-2	Europe	25 m
1995	Radarsat	Canada	8–100 m
2002	ENVISAT	Europe	25 m
2006	ALOS PALSAR	Japan	10 m
2007	Radarsat-2	Canada	3 m
2007	TERRASAR-X	Germany	1 m
2007	COSMO-SkyMed	Italy	1 m

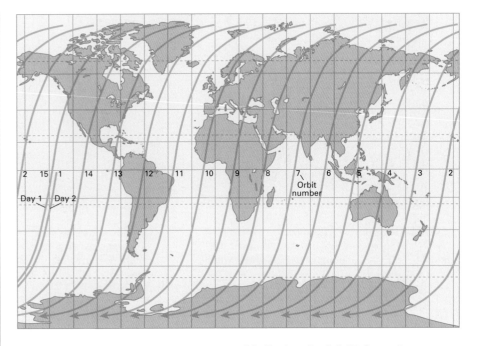

Satellite orbits
Landsat-7 makes over 14 orbits per day in its Sun-synchronous orbit. During the full 16 days of a repeat cycle, coverage of the areas between those shown is achieved.

Natural-colour and false-colour composites
These images show the salt ponds at the southern end of San Francisco Bay, which now form the San Francisco Bay National Wildlife Refuge. They demonstrate the difference between 'natural colour' (*top*) and 'false colour' (*bottom*) composites.

The top image is made from visible red, green and blue wavelengths. The colours correspond closely to those one would observe from an aircraft. The salt ponds appear green or orange-red due to the colour of the sediments they contain. The urban areas appear grey and vegetation is either dark green (trees) or light brown (dry grass).

The bottom image is made up of near-infrared, visible red and visible green wavelengths. These wavebands are represented here in red, green and blue, respectively. Since chlorophyll in healthy vegetation strongly reflects near-infrared light, this is clearly visible as red in the image.

False-colour composite imagery is therefore very sensitive to the presence of healthy vegetation. The bottom image thus shows better discrimination between the 'leafy' residential urban areas, such as Palo Alto (south-west of the Bay) from other urban areas by the 'redness' of the trees. The high chlorophyll content of watered urban grass areas shows as bright red, contrasting with the dark red of trees and the brown of natural, dry grass. *(EROS)*

Western Grand Canyon, Arizona, USA
This false-colour image shows in bright red the sparse vegetation on the limestone plateau, including sage, mesquite and grasses. Imagery such as this is used to monitor this and similar fragile environments. The sediment-laden river, shown as blue-green, can be seen dispersing into Lake Mead to the north-west. Side canyons cross the main canyon in straight lines, showing where erosion along weakened fault lines has occurred. *(EROS)*

Ayers Rock and Mt Olga, Northern Territory, Australia
These two huge outliers are the remnants of Precambrian mountain ranges created some 500 million years ago and then eroded away. Ayers Rock (*seen at right*) rises 345 m above the surrounding land and has been a part of Aboriginal life for over 10,000 years. Their dramatic coloration, caused by oxidized iron in the sandstone, attracts visitors from around the world. *(EROS)*

Mount St Helens, Washington, USA
A massive volcanic eruption on 18 May 1980 killed 60 people and devastated around 400 sq km of forest within minutes. The blast reduced the mountain peak by 400 m to its current height of 2,550 m, and volcanic ash rose some 25 km into the atmosphere. The image shows Mount St Helens eight years after the eruption in 1988. The characteristic volcanic cone has collapsed in the north, resulting in the devastating 'liquid' flow of mud and rock. *(EROS)*

Niger Delta, West Africa
The River Niger is the third longest river in Africa after the Nile and Congo. Deltas are by nature constantly evolving sedimentary features and often contain many ecosystems within them. In the case of the Niger Delta, there are also vast hydro-carbon reserves beneath it with associated wells and pipelines. Satellite imagery helps to plan activity and monitor this fragile and changing environment. *(EROS)*

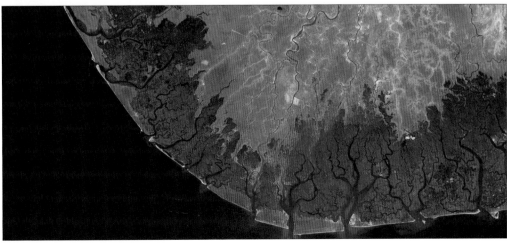

Europe at night

This image was derived as part of the Defense Meteorological Satellite Program. The sensor recorded all the emissions of near-infrared radiation at night, mainly the lights from cities, towns and villages. Note also the 'lights' in the North Sea from the flares of the oil production platforms. This project was the first systematic attempt to record human settlement on a global scale using remote sensing. *(© Fugro-NPA)*

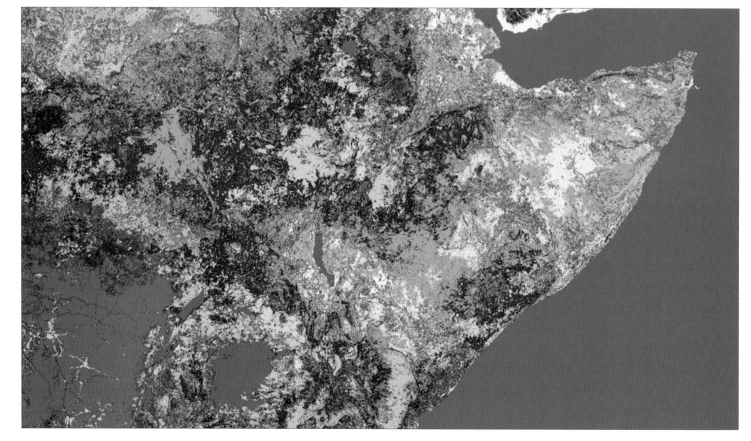

World Land Cover

The European Space Agency's (ESA) GlobCover project between 2004 and 2006 has produced the first complete global land cover data down to a resolution of 300 metres. It is an ongoing process and differentiates between 22 different land cover types, including croplands, wetlands, forests, artificial surfaces, water and snow. This will allow scientists to perform much more accurate research and prediction on sustainable environmental management, humanitarian issues and climate change modelling. *(© ESA/ESA GlobCover Project, led by MEDIAS-France)*

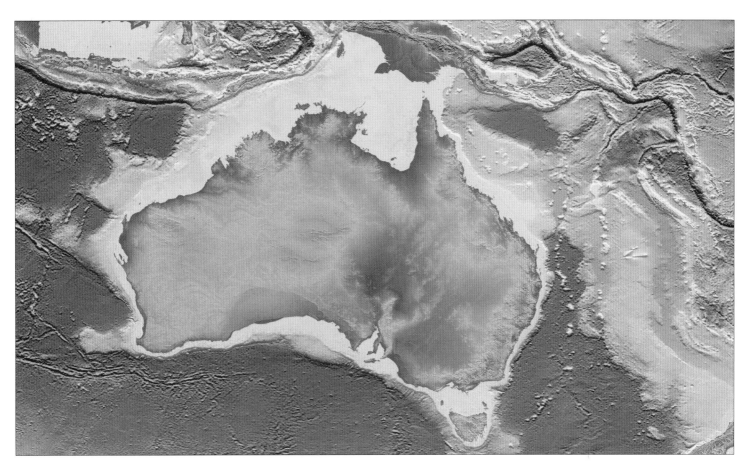

Mapping the Ocean Floors
The accurate global mapping of whole ocean floors has only been possible since the advent of satellite radar altimetry. From a precisely known orbit microwave pulses measure the ocean surface. The effects of tides, waves and currents can mathematically be removed from these measurements and the resultant ocean surface shape reflects that of the ocean floor beneath due the gravitational effects of the water over the sea floor topography. However for large scale navigational charts shipboard echo soundings are still used. (© Fugro-NPA)

Weather monitoring
Geostationary and polar orbiting satellites monitor the Earth's atmospheric movements, giving us an insight into the global workings of the atmosphere and permitting us to predict weather change. (NASA image courtesy GOES Project Science Office)

Tropical Cyclone 'Billy'
On Christmas Day 2008 the storm approaches Western Australia from the Indian Ocean. Such images aid in monitoring the development and track of weather systems. (Jeff Schmaltz, MODIS Rapid Response Team at NASA Goddard Space Flight Center)

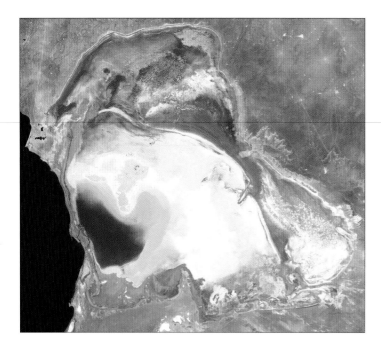

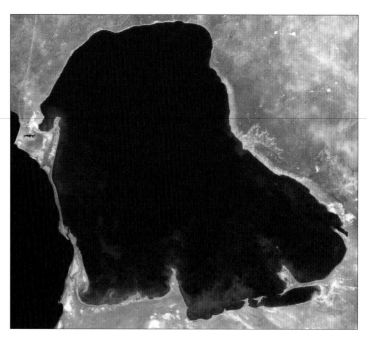

Kara-Bogaz-Gol, Turkmenistan
The Kara-Bogaz-Gol (*above, left and right*) is a large, shallow lagoon joined by a narrow, steep-sided strait to the Caspian Sea. Evaporation makes it one of the most saline bodies of water in the world. Believing the Caspian sea level was falling, the strait was dammed by the Soviet Union in 1980 with the intention of conserving the water to sustain the salt industry. However, by 1983 it had dried up completely (*above left*), leading to widespread wind-blown salt, soil poisoning and health problems downwind to the east. In 1992 the Turkmenistan government began to demolish the dam to re-establish the flow of water from the Caspian Sea (*above right*). Satellite imagery has helped to monitor and map the Kara-Bogaz-Gol as it has fluctuated in size. *(EROS)*

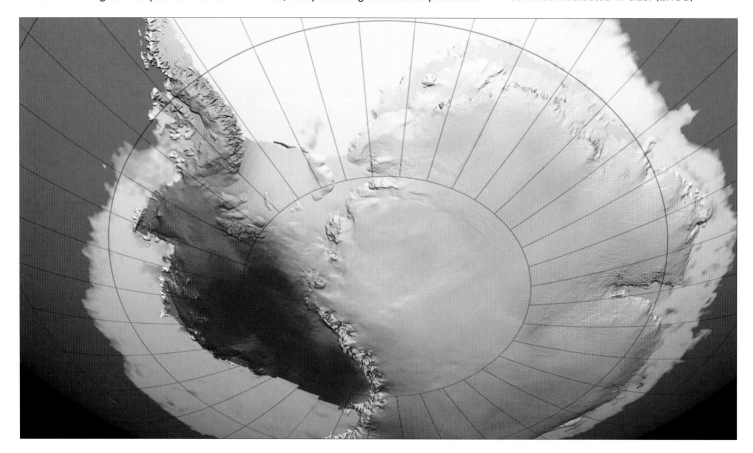

Antarctic warming
Antarctica was generally considered to be less affected by global warming than the Arctic, but gathering data was difficult because of its isolation. This false-colour image however displays the results of scientific analysis of 50 years of temperature recordings between 1957–2007. Temperature records for the early years, before satellite data was available, are extrapolated from ground weather station records. The darker orange tones indicate the highest temperature rise, showing that western Antarctica, including the peninsula, has warmed most during this period. *(Image courtesy Trent Schindler, NASA Goddard Space Flight Center Scientific Visualization)*

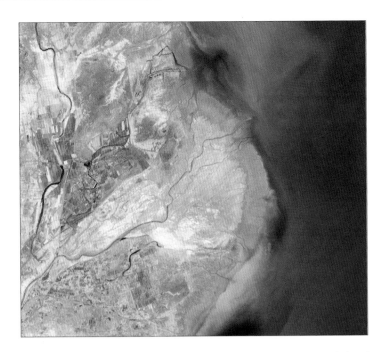

Yellow River Delta

The image on the left was captured in 1979, whilst the one on the right was obtained in 2000. They both cover exactly the same area of the Yellow River (Huang He) Delta in China, as can be seen from the course of the river in the top left hand corner. Much further upstream, the river erodes large amounts of sediment as it cuts through soft plateaux in its upper course. It carries this load until it deposits it at its mouth, as it slows to meet the sea. Notice as well how much other change has taken place on the land over the same period. *(NASA image created by Jesse Allen, using Landsat data provided by the United States Geological Survey)*

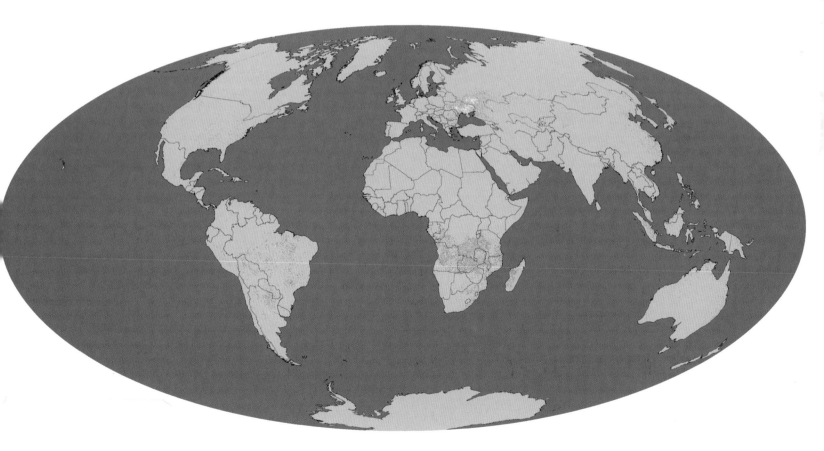

World Fires

This image shows all the fires worldwide which were burning during August 2008, whether they were man-made, to clear ground for crops, for example, or occurs naturallly from, say, lightning strikes. The orange tint indicates where fires are at their fiercest. Over any given year the areas affected by the fires move with the seasons, February being the month with most fires in the tropics. Acquiring this data from satellites allows efficient management of scarce resources in remote and environmentally threatened areas. *(NASA image by Reto Stockli and Jesse Allen using data courtesy the MODIS Land Science Team at NASA Goddard Space Flight Center)*

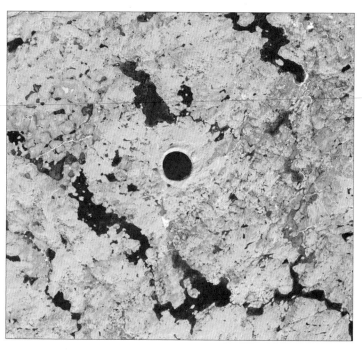

Sichuan Basin, China
The north-east/south-west trending ridges in this image are anticlinal folds developed in the Earth's crust as a result of plate collision and compression. Geologists map these folds and the lowlands between them formed by synclinal folds, as they are often the areas where oil or gas are found in commercial quantities. The river shown in this image is the Yangtze, near Chongqing. *(China RSGS)*

Pingualuit Crater
The circular feature is a meteorite crater in the Ungava Peninsula, Québec, formed by an impact over 1.4 million years ago. It is 3.4 km wide and the lake within is 264 m deep. The lake has no link to any water sources and has been formed only by rain and snow. Thus the water is very pure and among the world's clearest and least saline. Sediments at the bottom have been unaffected by ice sheets and are important for scientific research. *(© Fugro-NPA)*

Wadi Hadhramaut, Yemen
Yemen is extremely arid – however, in the past it was more humid and wet, enabling large river systems to carve out the deep and spectacular gorges and dried-out river beds (*wadis*) seen in this image. The erosion has revealed many contrasting rock types. The image has been processed to exaggerate this effect, producing many shades of red, pink and purple, which make geological mapping easier and more cost-effective. *(EROS)*

Zagros Mountains, Iran
These mountains were formed as Arabia collided with Southern Eurasia. The upper half of this colour-enhanced image shows an anticline that runs east–west. The dark grey features are called *diapirs*, which are bodies of viscous rock salt that are very buoyant and sometimes rise to the surface, spilling and spreading out like a glacier. The presence of salt in the region is important as it stops oil escaping to the surface. *(EROS)*

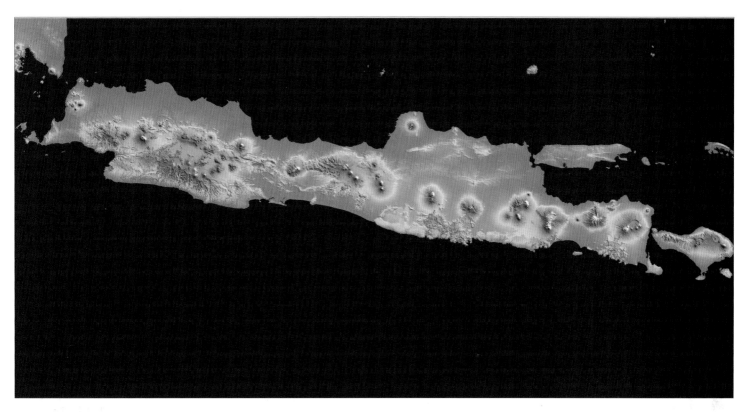

Topographic Survey

In February 2000 the Shuttle Radar Topography Mission (SRTM) was launched. Over 11 days, using specially developed radar equipment, it captured the topography of 80% of the earth's land area at high resolution. This was the first time that this had been done on a consistent basis globally and for many inaccessible areas was the first survey. The volcanic cones of the Indonesian islands of Java and Bali are clearly visible. *(© Fugro-NPA)*

Environmental Monitoring

Synthetic Aperture Radar (SAR) uses microwaves to penetrate cloud and needs no solar illumination, so is ideal for monitoring remote and difficult areas. In the middle of this image the David Glacier in Antarctica is seen flowing to the sea. Here it floats onwards and is known as the Drygalski Ice Tongue. At its end, a tabular iceberg is breaking off, or calving, whilst to the right is part of a 120km long iceberg which almost collided with it. *(© ESA)*

Lidar Surveying.

Lasers based on aircraft or satellites can be used to scan surface elevations to an accuracy of a few centimetres. This extract from a survey of the whole of London shows the City of London (from St Paul's Cathedral in the north-west to the Tower of London and Tower Bridge in the south-east. The very narrow and deep urban canyons and atriums in this area clearly demonstrate the advantages of airborne laser scanning (Lidar), which only requires a single line-of-sight to obtain precise measurements. A basic variant of this technology has been used for several years from satellites to acquire elevation profiles of the surface of Mars. Sensors capable of more detailed scanning are currently under development for Earth-orbiting satellites. *(Precision Terrain Surveys Ltd – www.precisionterrain.com)*

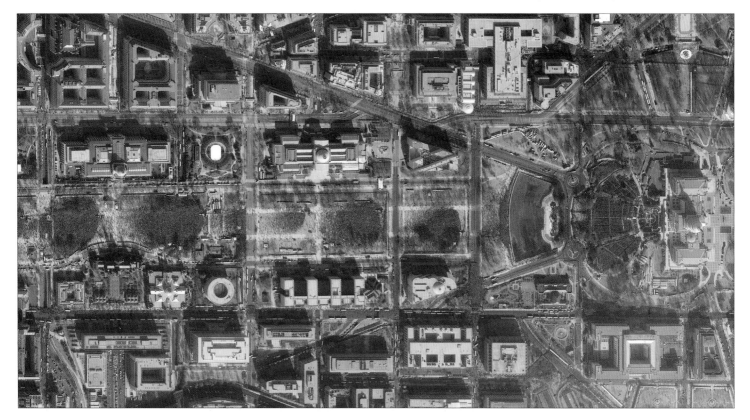

Washington DC, January 20th, 2009

Modern satellite and sensor technology now mean that imagery goes down to resolutions of less than 0.5m. Thus human beings become visible for the first time on commercially available imagery. On this image, crowds can clearly be seen gathering on the Mall in the early morning sunshine leading up to Barrack Obama's inauguration. The large building on the right with blue roofs is the U.S. Capitol. *(Image courtesy GeoEye)*

SHETLAND ISLANDS
on same scale

ATLANTIC OCEAN

SHETLAND

Lerwick

Fair Isle

Lewis

WESTERN ISLES

North Uist

Benbecula

South Uist

Barra

Outer Hebrides

Skye

HIGHLAND

Inner Hebrides

Sea of the Hebrides

ORKNEY ISLANDS
on same scale

NORTH SEA

1: 1 000 000

HIGHLAND

Ardnamurchan
Pt. of Ardnamurchan
Moidart
L. Moidart
Shona I.
Kilchoan
Ben Hiant 527
Mingary
Acharacle
Salen
Strontian
888
Corran
Onich
Fort William
1342 Ben Nevis
Kinlochleven
Glencoe
Glen Coe
Blackwater Res.
Rannoch Station
L. Laidon
L. Treig
1148 Ben Alder
L. Ericht
L. Errochty
Kinloch Rannoch
L. Rannoch
1081 Schieh
Keltneyb
Fearnan

Coll
Clabhach
Arinagour
Caliach Pt.
Calgary
Dervaig
Tobermory
Drimnin
Morvern
Sunart
Ardgour
Kingairloch
L. Sunart
Claggan
Lochaline
L. Leven
Ballachulish
Appin
1148 Bidean nam Bian
Clach Leathad
Glen Etive
Rannoch Moor
1098
Rannoch
Glen Lyon
Ben Lawers 1214

Tiree
Caoles
Treshnish Is.
Scarinish
Hynish B.
Hynish
Gometra
Ulva
Oskamull
Salen
Lochdon
Kerrera
Oban
Connel
Taynuilt
Ben Cruachan 1126
KILCHURN CASTLE
Dalmally
Ben Lui 1130
Tyndrum
Crianlarich
1174 Lochearnhead
L. Earn
Breadalbane
1079
1074 Ben Donich
Killin
Ardchyle

ATLANTIC

Passage of Tiree
L. Frisa
L. Tuath
Mull
Ben More 966
L. na Keal
L. Scridain
Ross of Mull
Fionnphort
Iona
IONA ABBEY
Bunessan
Staffa
FINGAL'S CAVE
91
Torran Rocks

OCEAN

Dubh Artach
Colonsay
Scalasaig
Oronsay
Passage of Oronsay
Rubh a' Mhail
Ardnave Pt.
Coul Pt.
Bruichladdich
Port Charlotte
Islay
Bowmore
Ben Bheigeir 490
Portnahaven
Rhinns Pt.
Laggan B.
Port Ellen
The Oa
Ardbeg
Mull of Oa

Jura
Paps of Jura 784
Feolin Ferry
Craighouse
Sound of Islay
Port Askaig
Ballygrant
Bridgend
Kilberry
Gigha
Garvellachs
Luing
Scarba
G. of Corryvreckan
Kinuachdrachd
Ardlussa

Firth of Lorn
Seil
Bolvicar
L. Melfort
Kilmelford
L. Avich
Ford
Kilmartin
Ardrishaig
Lochgilphead
Crinan Canal
Knapdale
Whitehouse
West L. Tarbert
Clachan
L. Caolisport
Kilberry
Tayinloan
Killean
Glenbarr
Carradale
Saddell
Kintyre
Machrihanish Bay
Machrihanish
Earadale Pt.
Campbeltown
Southend
Johnston's Pt.
Sanda I.
Mull of Kintyre
Cnoc Moy 446

ARGYLL AND BUTE

L. Awe
Kilchrenan
Cladich
L. Fyne
Inveraray
Furnace
Strachur
Cowal
Otter Ferry
Tighnabruaich
Kames
Port Bannatyne
Rothesay
Bute
Kingarth
Sd. of Bute
Kilfinan
Colintraive
Skipness
Claonaig
Lochranza
Pirnmill
Corrie
Goat Fell 874
Brodick
Arran
Lamlash
Blackwaterfoot
Holy I.
Kilchenzie
Dippen
Pladda

Loch Lomond
L. Katrine
The Trossachs
LOCH LOMOND & THE TROSSACHS NATIONAL PARK
Ben Ime 1011
Arrochar
Tarbet
578
Ben Lomond 973
Luss
Balloch
779
L. Goil
L. Eck
Lochgoilhead
Garelochhead
Faslane
Gare L.
Helensburgh
Rosneath
Cove
Kilcreggan
Gourock
Greenock
Port Glasgow
Dunoon
Innellan
Wemyss Bay
Skelmorlie
Largs
Fairlie
Millport
Cumbrae Is.
West Kilbride
Ardrossan
Saltcoats
Stevenston
Irvine

STIRLING
Callander
Aberfoyle
Drymen
Buchlyvie
Kippen
Gartmore
Balmaha
Killearn
Strathblane
Milngavie
Bearsden
Clydebank
GLASGOW
Paisley
Johnstone
Barrhead
Rutherglen
East Kilbride
Hamil
Dumbarton
Alexandria
Erskine
Renfrew
Neilston
Beith
Dalry
Kilbirnie
Lochwinnoch
Kilwinning
Kilmaurs
Kilmarnock
Galston
Darvel
Newmilns
Stewarton
Dunlop

NORTH AYRSHIRE
Cunninghame
KYLE
EAST AYRSHIRE
Troon
Barassie
Monkton
Prestwick
Ayr
Tarbolton
Mauchline
Muirkirk
Sorn
Catrine
Auchinleck
Cumnock
New Cumnock
AYRSHIRE
Maybole
Patna
Dalmellington
SOUTH AYRSHIRE
Carrick
Dailly
Girvan
Barr
Pinwherry
Ballantrae
Barrhill
Colmonel
Lendalfoot
Bennane Hd.
Beneraird 439

IRELAND
Caldaff
Inishowen Hd.
Malin Hd.
Greencastle
Moville
Magilligan Pt.
Portstewart
Portrush
Portballintrae
Bushmills
GIANT'S CAUSEWAY
DUNLUCE CASTLE
Ballintoy
Ballycastle
Fair Hd.
Rathlin I.
Benbane Hd.
The Skerries
Downhill
Coleraine
Ballybogy
Ballymoney
Derrykeighan
Dervock
Armoy
Knocklayd 517
BONAMARGY CASTLE
Ballyvoy
Cushendun
Runabay Hd.
Cushendall
Red B.
Glenariff
Mountains of Antrim
Garron Pt.

LONDONDERRY (DERRY)
Claudy
Feeny
Dungiven
Swatragh
Kilrea
Garvagh
Ballykelly
Limavady
Ringsend
Crossgare
Macosquin
Carrowkeel
Lough Foyle
Bellarena
Magilligan

Sperrin Mts
Sawel Mt. 683
Draperstown
Moneymore
Magherafelt
Castledawson
TYRONE
Cookstown
Pomeroy
Tullaghoge
Creggan
Carrickmore
Ballinderry
Coogh
Ballyronan
The Loup
Lough Neagh
Crumlin
Glenavy

NORTHERN IRELAND
ANTRIM
Rasharkin
Clogh
Cloughmills
Broughshane
Ballymena
Kells
Connor
Moorfields
Randalstown
Antrim
Templepatrick
Ballyclare
Doagh
Ballynure
Glengormley
Newtownabbey
BELFAST
Holywood
Bangor
Donaghadee
Millisle
Groomsport
Copeland I.
Belfast Lough
Carrickfergus
Greenisland
Whitehead
Black Hd.
I. Magee
Larne
Larne Lough
Glynn
Ballycarry
Carncastle
Agnews Hill 476
Glenoe

North Channel
269
123
Corsewall Pt.
The Rhins
Kirkcolm
Cairnryan
Stranraer
Leswalt
Lochans
Stoneykirk
Portpatrick
Port Logan
Sandhead
Drummore
Mull of Galloway
Burrow Hd.
Isle of Whithorn
Whithorn
Luce Bay
Port William
Wigtown Bay
Sorbie
Garlieston
Whauphill
The Machars
Kirkinner
Wigtown
Newton Stewart
Minnigaff
GLENLUCE ABBEY
New Luce
Glenluce
Kirkcowan
Creetown
Gatehouse of Fleet
Kirkcudbright
Borgue
Ringford
Laurieston
Clatteringshaws L.
New Galloway
L. Ken
GALLOWAY
DUMFRIES
Rhinns of Kells
Merrick 844
710
Carsphairn
Glentrool Village
Cairnsmore of Fleet
331
796
781
Firth of Clyde
Ailsa Craig 334
Culzeran Castle
Kirkoswald
Turnberry
Crosshill
Kirkmichael
Straiton
Drumohn
Dunure
Heads of Ayr
Colmonell

Projection : Conical with two standard parallels

West from Greenwich

Key to Scottish unitary authorities on map

2 DUNDEE CITY
3 WEST DUNBARTONSHIRE
4 EAST DUNBARTONSHIRE
5 CITY OF GLASGOW
6 INVERCLYDE
7 RENFREWSHIRE
8 EAST RENFREWSHIRE

9 NORTH LANARKSHIRE
10 FALKIRK
11 CLACKMANNANSHIRE
12 WEST LOTHIAN
13 CITY OF EDINBURGH
14 MIDLOTHIAN

NORTH SEA

1:1 000 000

COPYRIGHT PHILIP'S

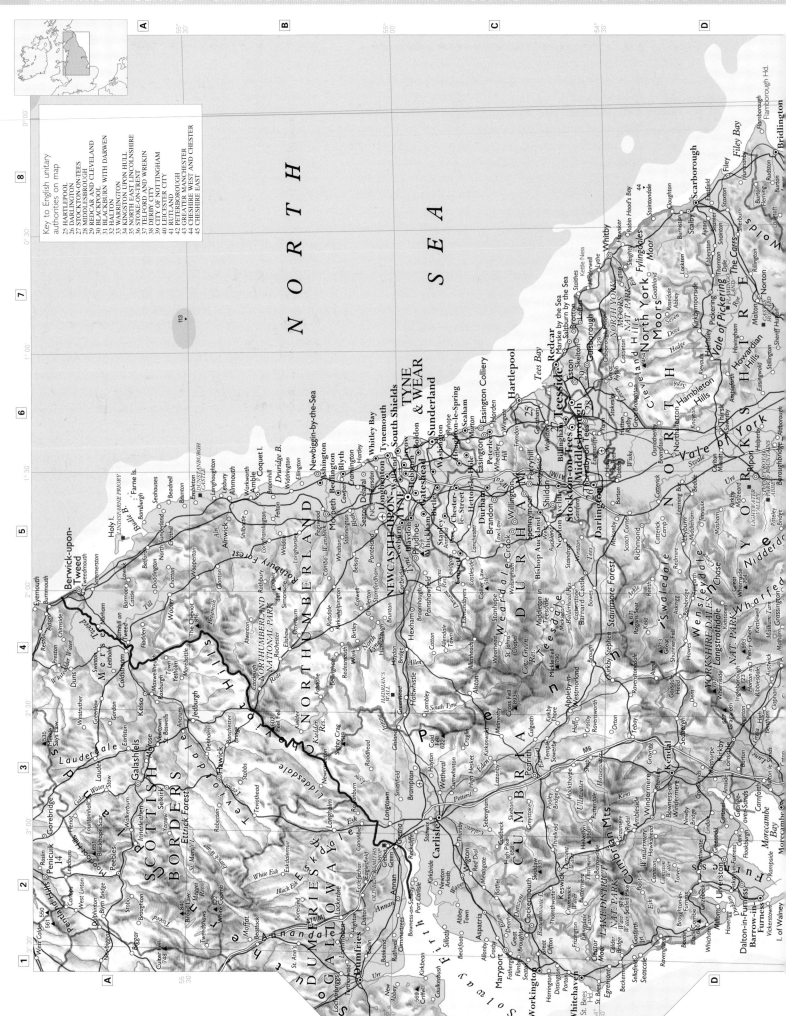

Key to English unitary authorities on map

25 HARTLEPOOL
26 DARLINGTON
27 STOCKTON-ON-TEES
28 MIDDLESBROUGH
29 REDCAR AND CLEVELAND
30 BLACKPOOL
31 BLACKBURN WITH DARWEN
32 HALTON
33 WARRINGTON
34 KINGSTON UPON HULL
35 NORTH EAST LINCOLNSHIRE
36 STOKE-ON-TRENT
37 TELFORD AND WREKIN
38 DERBY CITY
39 CITY OF NOTTINGHAM
40 LEICESTER CITY
41 RUTLAND
42 PETERBOROUGH
43 GREATER MANCHESTER
44 CHESHIRE WEST AND CHESTER
45 CHESHIRE EAST

NORTH   SEA

Projection : Conical with two standard parallels

1:1 000 000

Projection : Conical with two standard parallels

West from Greenwich

Key to English unitary authorities on map
37 TELFORD AND WREKIN
38 DERBY CITY
39 CITY OF NOTTINGHAM
40 LEICESTER CITY
41 RUTLAND
42 PETERBOROUGH
43 MILTON KEYNES
44 LUTON
45 NORTH SOMERSET
46 CITY OF BRISTOL
47 BATH AND NORTH EAST SOMERSET
48 SWINDON
49 READING
50 WOKINGHAM
51 WINDSOR AND MAIDENHEAD
52 SLOUGH
53 BRACKNELL FOREST
54 THURROCK
55 SOUTHEND-ON-SEA
56 MEDWAY
59 POOLE
60 BOURNEMOUTH
61 SOUTHAMPTON
62 PORTSMOUTH
63 BRIGHTON AND HOVE
64 BEDFORD
65 CENTRAL BEDFORDSHIRE

Key to Welsh unitary authorities on map
16 NEATH PORT TALBOT
17 BRIDGEND
18 RHONDDA CYNON TAFF
19 MERTHYR TYDFIL
20 CAERPHILLY
21 BLAENAU GWENT
22 TORFAEN
23 CARDIFF
24 NEWPORT

COPYRIGHT PHILIP'S

1:1 000 000

5   0   10   20   30   40   50 km

5   0   5   10   15   20   25   30   35 miles

East from Greenwich

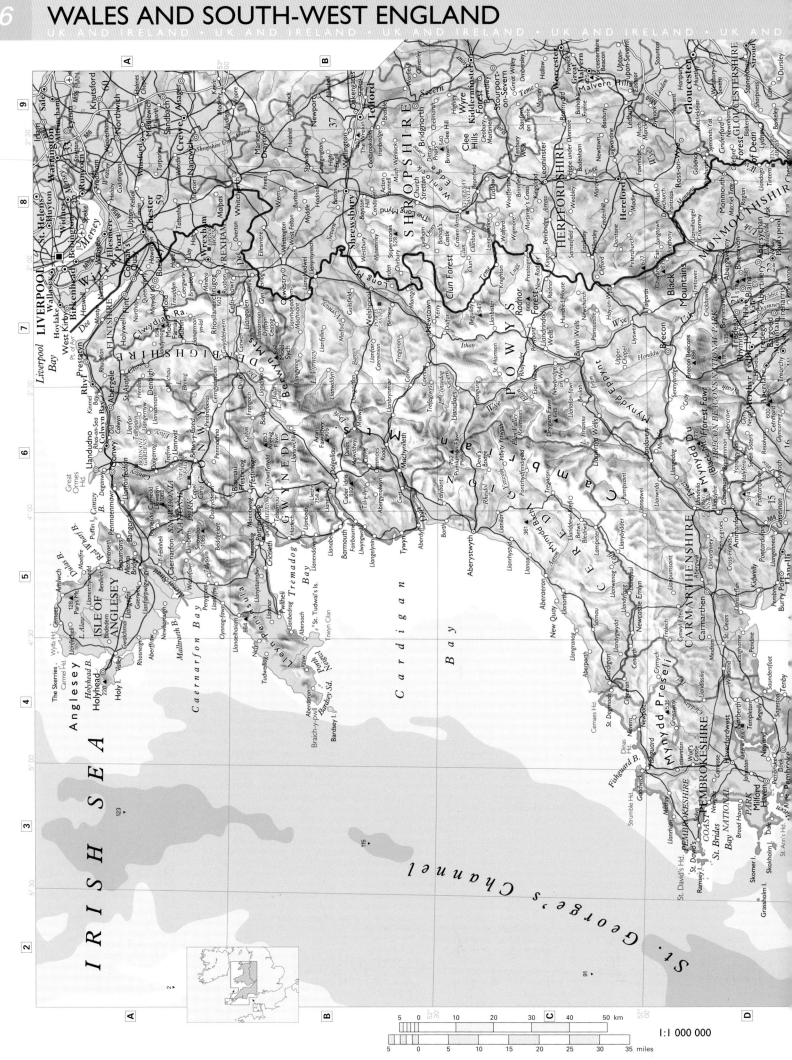

1 : 1 000 000

Key to Welsh unitary
authorities on map

15 SWANSEA
16 NEATH PORT TALBOT
17 BRIDGEND
18 RHONDDA CYNON TAFF
19 MERTHYR TYDFIL
20 CAERPHILLY
21 BLAENAU GWENT
22 TORFAEN
23 CARDIFF
24 NEWPORT

ISLES OF
SCILLY
on same scale

Isles of Scilly

Key to English unitary
authorities on map

32 HALTON
33 WARRINGTON
37 TELFORD AND WREKIN
45 NORTH SOMERSET
46 CITY OF BRISTOL
47 BATH AND NORTH EAST SOMERSET
57 PLYMOUTH
58 TORBAY
59 WEST CHESHIRE AND CHESTER
60 EAST CHESHIRE

CHANNEL
ISLANDS
on same scale

FRANCE

Passage de la Déroute

Jersey

CHANNEL ISLANDS

Guernsey

COPYRIGHT PHILIP'S

Projection: Conical with two standard parallels

1:1 000 000

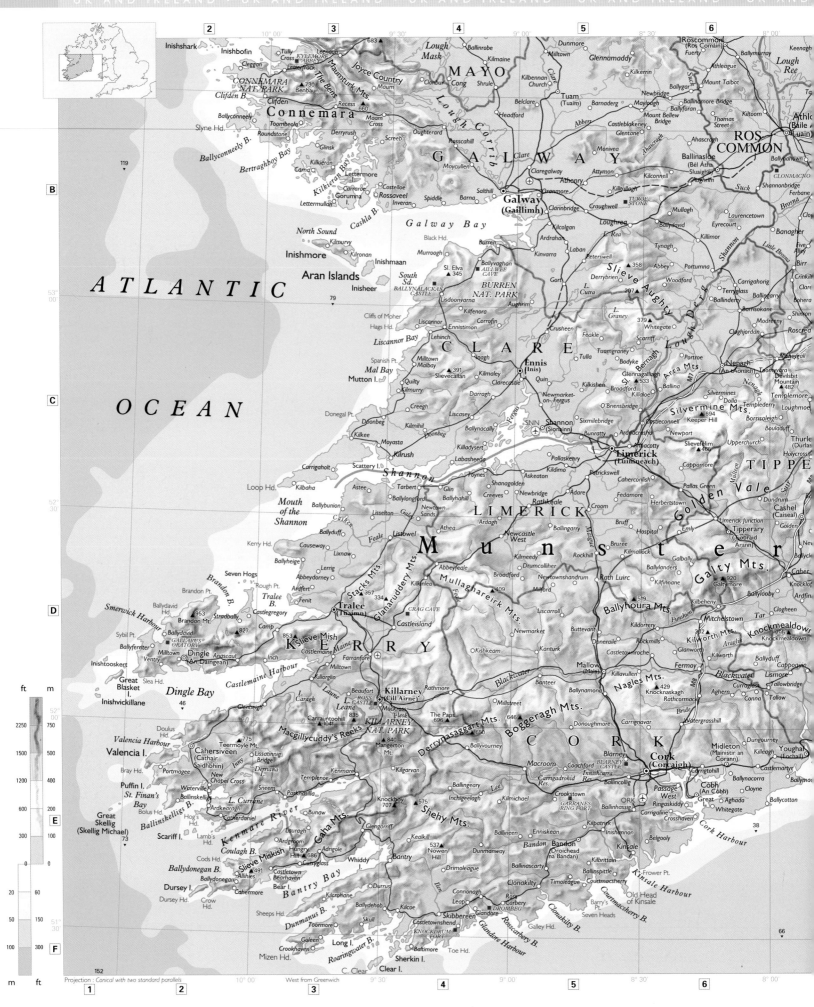

COPYRIGHT PHILIP'S

1:1 000 000

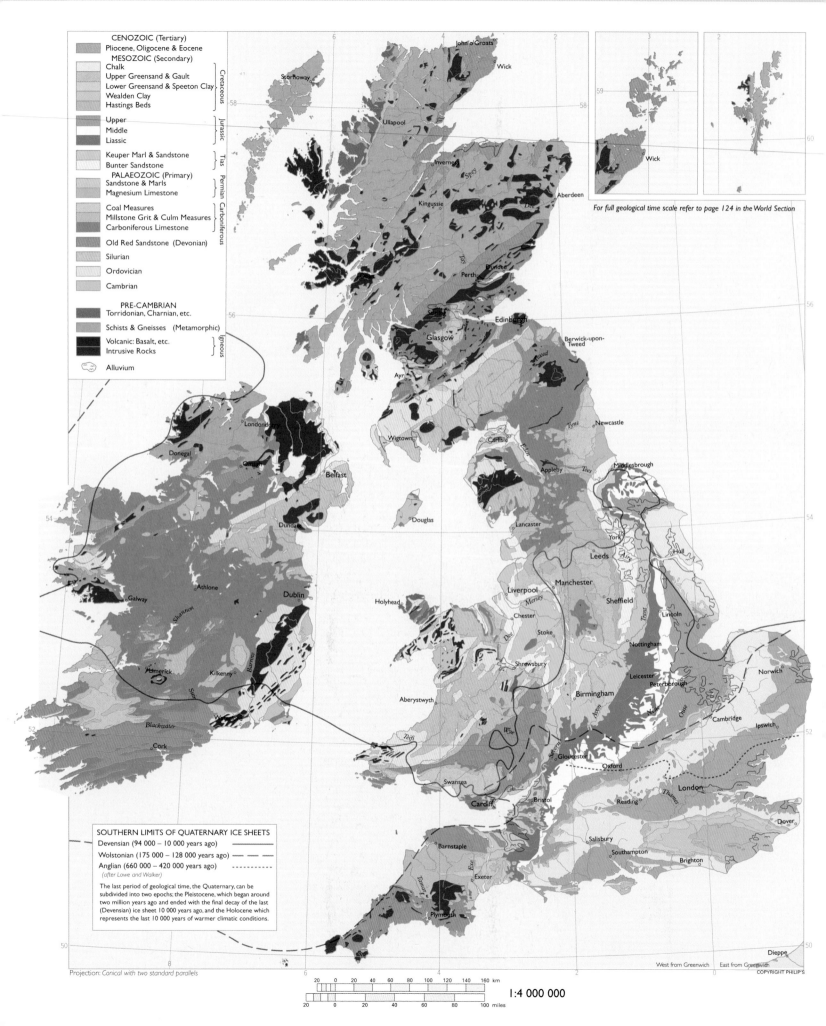

CENOZOIC (Tertiary)
Pliocene, Oligocene & Eocene
MESOZOIC (Secondary)
Chalk
Upper Greensand & Gault
Lower Greensand & Speeton Clay
Wealden Clay
Hastings Beds
— Cretaceous

Upper
Middle
Liassic
— Jurassic

Keuper Marl & Sandstone
Bunter Sandstone
— Trias

PALAEOZOIC (Primary)
Sandstone & Marls
Magnesium Limestone
— Permian

Coal Measures
Millstone Grit & Culm Measures
Carboniferous Limestone
— Carboniferous

Old Red Sandstone (Devonian)
Silurian
Ordovician
Cambrian

PRE-CAMBRIAN
Torridonian, Charnian, etc.
Schists & Gneisses (Metamorphic)
Volcanic: Basalt, etc.
Intrusive Rocks
— Igneous

Alluvium

For full geological time scale refer to page 124 in the World Section

SOUTHERN LIMITS OF QUATERNARY ICE SHEETS
Devensian (94 000 – 10 000 years ago) ———
Wolstonian (175 000 – 128 000 years ago) — — —
Anglian (660 000 – 420 000 years ago) ·········
(after Lowe and Walker)

The last period of geological time, the Quaternary, can be
subdivided into two epochs; the Pleistocene, which began around
two million years ago and ended with the final decay of the last
(Devensian) ice sheet 10 000 years ago, and the Holocene which
represents the last 10 000 years of warmer climatic conditions.

Projection: *Conical with two standard parallels*

West from Greenwich   East from Greenwich
COPYRIGHT PHILIP'S

20 0 20 40 60 80 100 120 140 160 km
20 0 20 40 60 80 100 miles

1:4 000 000

Projection: Conical with two standard parallels

COPYRIGHT PHILIP'S

West from Greenwich 0 East from Greenwich

1:4 000 000

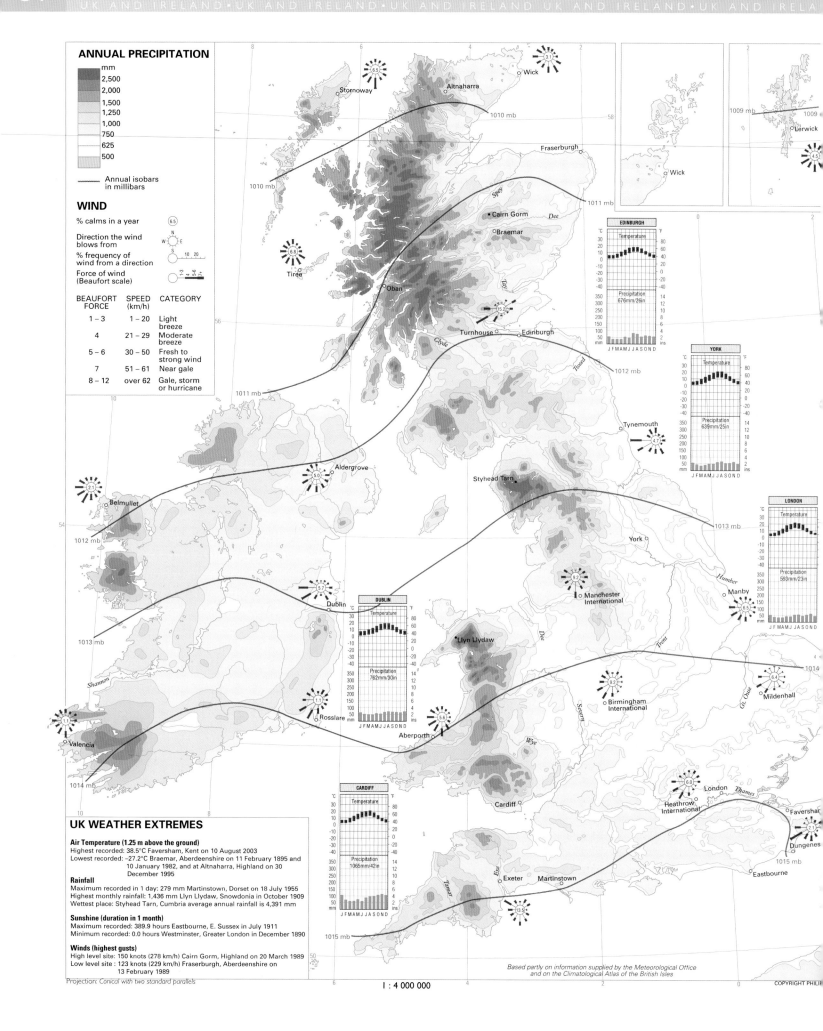

ANNUAL PRECIPITATION

mm
2,500
2,000
1,500
1,250
1,000
750
625
500

—— Annual isobars
in millibars

WIND

% calms in a year ⬤ 6.5

Direction the wind
blows from

% frequency of
wind from a direction

Force of wind
(Beaufort scale)

BEAUFORT FORCE	SPEED (km/h)	CATEGORY
1 – 3	1 – 20	Light breeze
4	21 – 29	Moderate breeze
5 – 6	30 – 50	Fresh to strong wind
7	51 – 61	Near gale
8 – 12	over 62	Gale, storm or hurricane

UK WEATHER EXTREMES

Air Temperature (1.25 m above the ground)
Highest recorded: 38.5°C Faversham, Kent on 10 August 2003
Lowest recorded: –27.2°C Braemar, Aberdeenshire on 11 February 1895 and
　　　　　　　　10 January 1982, and at Altnaharra, Highland on 30
　　　　　　　　December 1995

Rainfall
Maximum recorded in 1 day: 279 mm Martinstown, Dorset on 18 July 1955
Highest monthly rainfall: 1,436 mm Llyn Llydaw, Snowdonia in October 1909
Wettest place: Styhead Tarn, Cumbria average annual rainfall is 4,391 mm

Sunshine (duration in 1 month)
Maximum recorded: 389.9 hours Eastbourne, E. Sussex in July 1911
Minimum recorded: 0.0 hours Westminster, Greater London in December 1890

Winds (highest gusts)
High level site: 150 knots (278 km/h) Cairn Gorm, Highland on 20 March 1989
Low level site: 123 knots (229 km/h) Fraserburgh, Aberdeenshire on
　　　　　　　13 February 1989

Projection: Conical with two standard parallels

I : 4 000 000

Based partly on information supplied by the Meteorological Office
and on the Climatological Atlas of the British Isles

COPYRIGHT PHILIP

Climate station graphs labelled: EDINBURGH (Precipitation 676mm/26in), YORK (Precipitation 639mm/25in), LONDON (Precipitation 593mm/23in), DUBLIN (Precipitation 762mm/30in), CARDIFF (Precipitation 1065mm/42in)

JANUARY TEMPERATURE

Actual surface temperature

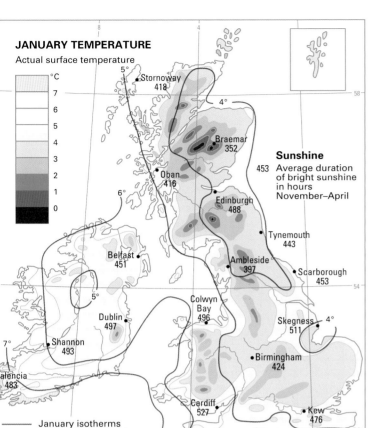

°C
7
6
5
4
3
2
1
0

Sunshine

453 Average duration
of bright sunshine
in hours
November–April

—— January isotherms
reduced to sea-level
° Celsius

Stornoway 418
Braemar 352
Oban 416
Edinburgh 488
Tynemouth 443
Belfast 451
Ambleside 397
Scarborough 453
Colwyn Bay 496
Dublin 497
Skegness 511
Shannon 493
Birmingham 424
Valencia 483
Cardiff 527
Kew 476
Bournemouth 593
Newquay 575

JULY TEMPERATURE

Actual surface temperature

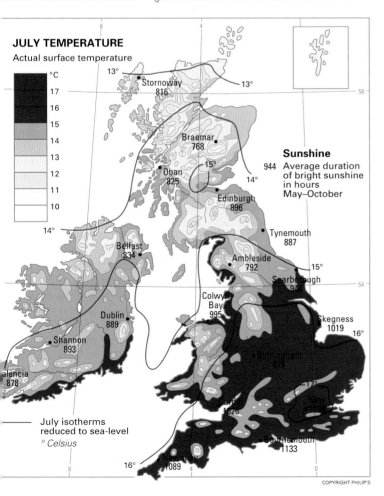

°C
17
16
15
14
13
12
11
10

Sunshine

944 Average duration
of bright sunshine
in hours
May–October

—— July isotherms
reduced to sea-level
° Celsius

Stornoway 816
Braemar 768
Oban 825
Edinburgh 896
Tynemouth 887
Belfast 834
Ambleside 792
Scarborough 943
Colwyn Bay 995
Dublin 889
Skegness 1019
Shannon 893
Birmingham 975
Valencia 878
Cardiff 1026
Kew 1039
Bournemouth 1133
Newquay 1089

COPYRIGHT PHILIP'S

CHANGES IN UK RAINFALL PATTERNS

Annual percentage change
in precipitation, 1914-2007

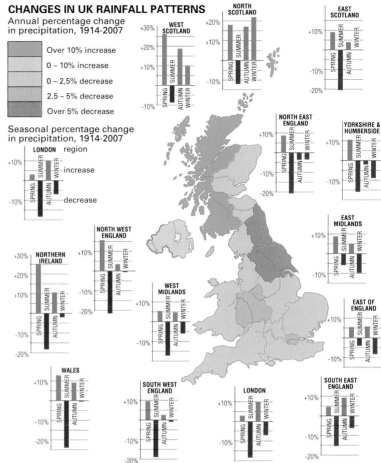

Over 10% increase
0 – 10% increase
0 – 2,5% decrease
2.5 – 5% decrease
Over 5% decrease

Seasonal percentage change
in precipitation, 1914-2007
region
increase
decrease

(Regional bar charts: WEST SCOTLAND, NORTH SCOTLAND, EAST SCOTLAND, LONDON, NORTH EAST ENGLAND, YORKSHIRE & HUMBERSIDE, NORTH WEST ENGLAND, NORTHERN IRELAND, WEST MIDLANDS, EAST MIDLANDS, EAST OF ENGLAND, WALES, SOUTH WEST ENGLAND, LONDON, SOUTH EAST ENGLAND — each showing SPRING, SUMMER, AUTUMN, WINTER)

CHANGES IN SUMMER AND WINTER RAINFALL 1874–2005

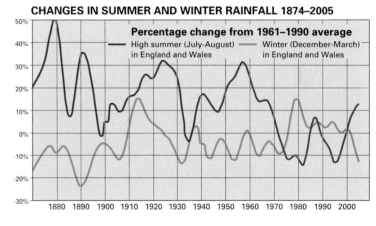

Percentage change from 1961–1990 average

—— High summer (July–August) in England and Wales
—— Winter (December–March) in England and Wales

CHANGES IN AVERAGE SURFACE TEMPERATURE 1850–2007

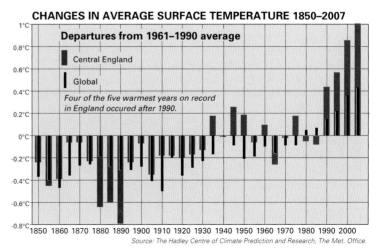

Departures from 1961–1990 average

▮ Central England

▮ Global

Four of the five warmest years on record in England occured after 1990.

Source: The Hadley Centre of Climate Prediction and Research, The Met. Office.

WATER SUPPLY

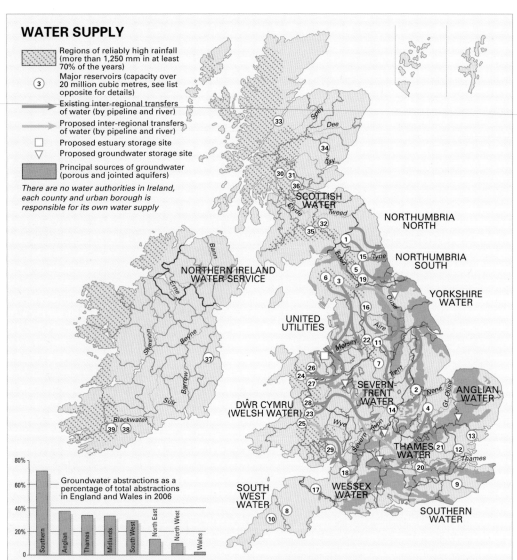

Regions of reliably high rainfall (more than 1,250 mm in at least 70% of the years)

③ Major reservoirs (capacity over 20 million cubic metres, see list opposite for details)

→ Existing inter-regional transfers of water (by pipeline and river)

→ Proposed inter-regional transfers of water (by pipeline and river)

☐ Proposed estuary storage site

▽ Proposed groundwater storage site

Principal sources of groundwater (porous and jointed aquifers)

There are no water authorities in Ireland, each county and urban borough is responsible for its own water supply

Groundwater abstractions as a percentage of total abstractions in England and Wales in 2006

(bar chart: Southern, Anglian, Thames, Midlands, South West, North East, North West, Wales)

MAJOR RESERVOIRS (with capacity in million m)

England
1	Kielder Reservoir	198
2	Rutland Water	123
3	Haweswater	85
4	Grafham Water	59
5	Cow Green Reservoir	41
6	Thirlmere	41
7	Carsington Reservoir	36
8	Roadford Reservoir	35
9	Bewl Water Reservoir	31
10	Colliford Lake	29
11	Ladybower Reservoir	28
12	Hanningfield Reservoir	27
13	Abberton Reservoir	25
14	Draycote Water	23
15	Derwent Reservoir	22
16	Grimwith Reservoir	22
17	Wimbleball Lake	21
18	Chew Valley Lake	20
19	Balderhead Reservoir	20
20	Thames Valley (linked reservoirs)	
21	Lea Valley (linked reservoirs)	
22	Longendale (linked reservoirs)	

Wales
23	Elan Valley
24	Llyn Celyn
25	Llyn Brianne
26	Llyn Brenig
27	Llyn Vyrnwy
28	Llyn Clywedog
29	Llandegfedd Reservoir

Scotland
30	Loch Lomond
31	Loch Katrine
32	Megget Reservoir
33	Loch Ness
34	Blackwater Reservoir
35	Daer Reservoir
36	Carron Valley Reservoir

Ireland
37	Poulaphouca Reservoir
38	Inishcarra Reservoir
39	Carrigadrohid Reservoir

WATER SUPPLY IN THE UK

Total water abstraction in England and Wales in 200 was approximately 58,000 million litres a day.
The pie graph represents the almost 19,000 million litres a day that were supplied by the water service and supply companies in the U.K. in 2006.

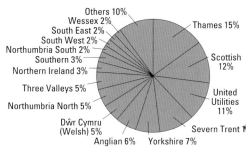

Others 10%
Wessex 2%
South East 2%
South West 2%
Northumbria South 2%
Southern 3%
Northern Ireland 3%
Three Valleys 5%
Northumbria North 5%
Dŵr Cymru (Welsh) 5%
Anglian 6%
Yorkshire 7%
Severn Trent
United Utilities 11%
Scottish 12%
Thames 15%

WASTE RECYCLING

The percentage of household waste recycled in 2007

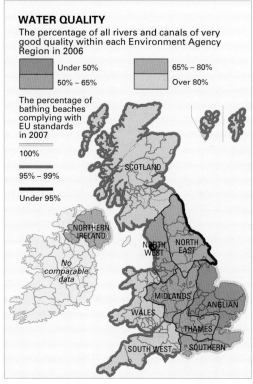

| Over 35% | 25 – 30% |
| 30 – 35% | Under 25% |

WATER QUALITY

The percentage of all rivers and canals of very good quality within each Environment Agency Region in 2006

| Under 50% | 65% – 80% |
| 50% – 65% | Over 80% |

The percentage of bathing beaches complying with EU standards in 2007

100%
95% – 99%
Under 95%

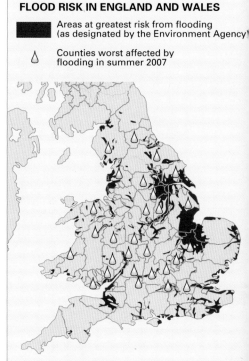

FLOOD RISK IN ENGLAND AND WALES

■ Areas at greatest risk from flooding (as designated by the Environment Agency)

◊ Counties worst affected by flooding in summer 2007

EU AIR QUALITY

Greenhouse gas emissions in thousand tonnes

	Sulphur dioxide			Nitrogen oxides		
	1975	1990	2005	1975	1990	2005
Austria	–	90	26	–	221	237
Belgium/Lux.	–	105	146	–	172	285
Denmark	418	183	22	182	270	184
Finland	–	260	69	–	290	177
France	3,329	1,200	465	1,608	1,487	1,412
Germany	3,325	5,633	560	2,532	3,033	1,447
Greece	–	–	529	–	338	332
Ireland	**186**	**187**	**70**	**60**	**128**	**124**
Italy	3,250	1,682	496	1,499	2,041	1,112
Netherlands	386	204	62	447	575	325
Portugal	178	286	214	104	216	289
Spain	–	2,205	1,359	–	1,247	1,529
Sweden	–	169	40	–	411	181
United Kingdom	**5,310**	**3,754**	**706**	**2,365**	**2,731**	**1,619**

SOILS

- Calcareous brown earth
- Brown earth
- Acid brown earth
- Podsol
- Peaty podsol
- Grey-brown podsol
- Gley
- Basin peat and alluvial gleys
- Peaty gley and blanket peat

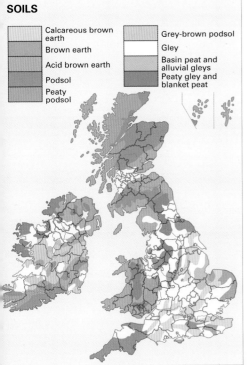

NATURAL VEGETATION

The plant cover associated with a particular environment if it was unaffected by human activity

- Oak
- Beech and oak
- Ash and oak
- Birch and oakwood
- Scots pine
- Heath, moorland, water meadows, fen, bog and marsh

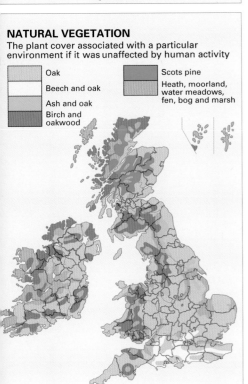

ACID RAIN

Average acidity of precipitation in the UK (pH scale)

- 4.29 and under (most acidic)
- 4.30 – 4.39
- 4.40 – 4.49
- 4.50 – 4.59
- 4.60 – 4.69
- 4.70 – 4.79
- 4.80 and over (least acidic)

ESAs
Environmentally Sensitive Areas in the UK

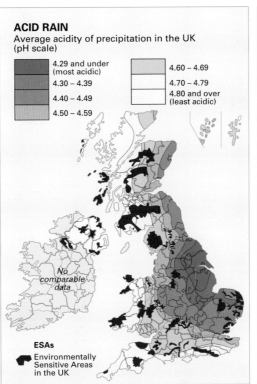

No comparable data

GREENHOUSE GAS EMISSIONS*

CO₂ emissions in tonnes per capita 2006

- Over 20
- 14 – 20
- 10 – 14
- 8 – 10
- 6 – 8
- Under 6

*Includes emissions from transport except ships and aircraft.
Emissions from power generation are allocated to the end user.

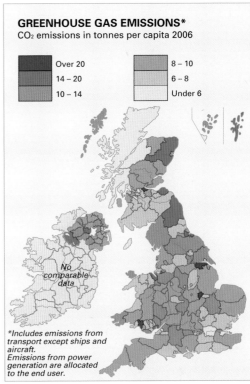

No comparable data

CONSERVATION

- National Parks
- Areas of Outstanding Natural Beauty
- National Scenic Areas
- Forest Parks, Regional Parks in Scotland and Special Protected Areas
- Green Belts (and the urban areas they surround)
- Heritage Coast (England and Wales)/Coastal Conservation Zones (Scotland)

✱ World Heritage Sites in the UK and Ireland

Other designated UK sites not shown:
St. Kilda, Outer Hebrides
Henderson I., South Pacific Ocean
Gough I. and Inaccessible I., South Atlantic Ocean
St. George, Bermuda

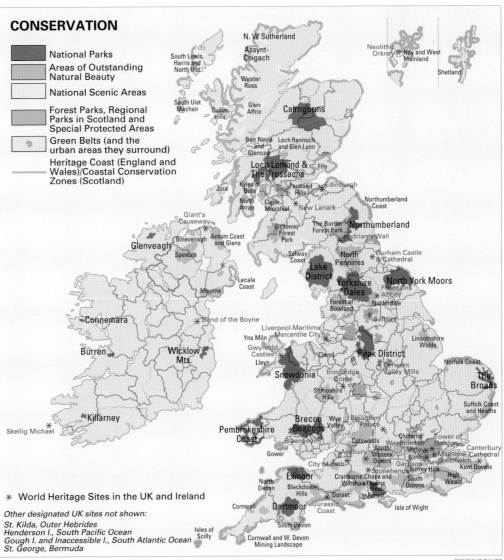

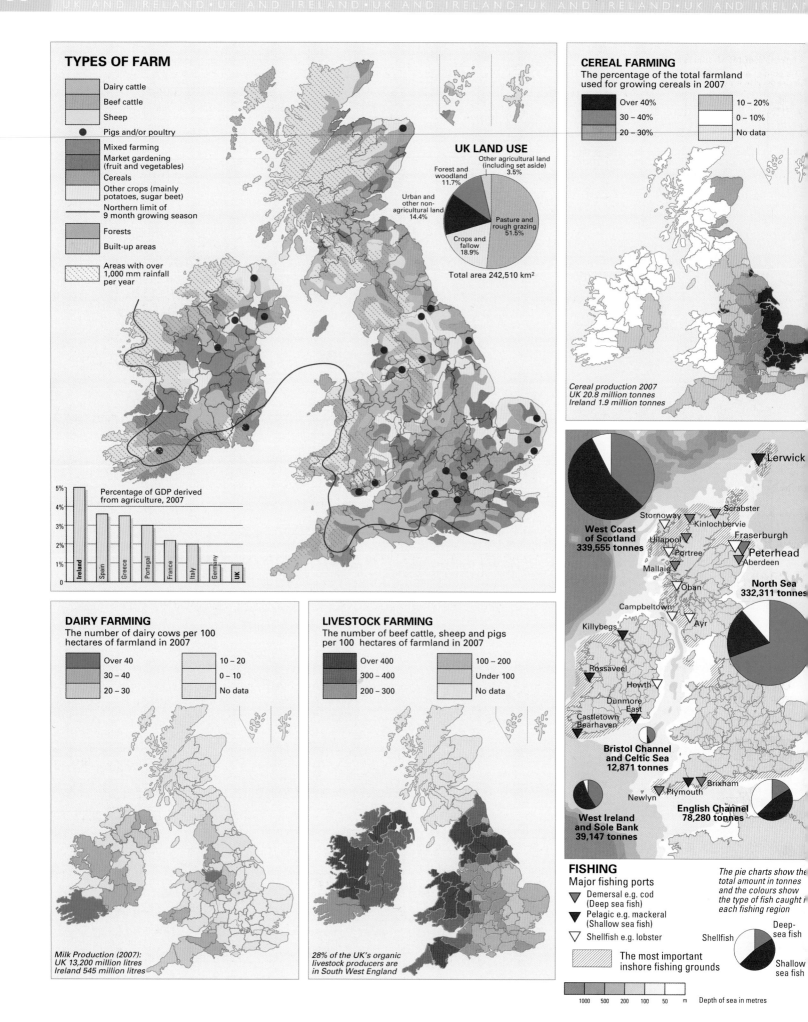

TYPES OF FARM

- Dairy cattle
- Beef cattle
- Sheep
- ● Pigs and/or poultry
- Mixed farming
- Market gardening (fruit and vegetables)
- Cereals
- Other crops (mainly potatoes, sugar beet)
- Northern limit of 9 month growing season
- Forests
- Built-up areas
- Areas with over 1,000 mm rainfall per year

UK LAND USE

Forest and woodland 11.7%
Other agricultural land (including set aside) 3.5%
Urban and other non-agricultural land 14.4%
Pasture and rough grazing 51.5%
Crops and fallow 18.9%

Total area 242,510 km²

Percentage of GDP derived from agriculture, 2007

5%, 4%, 3%, 2%, 1%, 0

Ireland, Spain, Greece, Portugal, France, Italy, Germany, UK

CEREAL FARMING

The percentage of the total farmland used for growing cereals in 2007

- Over 40%
- 30 – 40%
- 20 – 30%
- 10 – 20%
- 0 – 10%
- No data

Cereal production 2007
UK 20.8 million tonnes
Ireland 1.9 million tonnes

DAIRY FARMING

The number of dairy cows per 100 hectares of farmland in 2007

- Over 40
- 30 – 40
- 20 – 30
- 10 – 20
- 0 – 10
- No data

Milk Production (2007):
UK 13,200 million litres
Ireland 545 million litres

LIVESTOCK FARMING

The number of beef cattle, sheep and pigs per 100 hectares of farmland in 2007

- Over 400
- 300 – 400
- 200 – 300
- 100 – 200
- Under 100
- No data

28% of the UK's organic livestock producers are in South West England

FISHING

Major fishing ports

- ▼ Demersal e.g. cod (Deep sea fish)
- ▼ Pelagic e.g. mackeral (Shallow sea fish)
- ▽ Shellfish e.g. lobster

The pie charts show the total amount in tonnes and the colours show the type of fish caught in each fishing region

- Shellfish
- Deep-sea fish
- Shallow sea fish

The most important inshore fishing grounds

1000 500 200 100 50 m Depth of sea in metres

West Coast of Scotland 339,555 tonnes

North Sea 332,311 tonnes

Bristol Channel and Celtic Sea 12,871 tonnes

English Channel 78,280 tonnes

West Ireland and Sole Bank 39,147 tonnes

Lerwick
Stornoway
Scrabster
Kinlochbervie
Ullapool
Fraserburgh
Portree
Peterhead
Mallaig
Aberdeen
Oban
Campbeltown
Ayr
Killybegs
Rossaveel
Howth
Dunmore East
Castletown Bearhaven
Newlyn
Plymouth
Brixham

EMPLOYMENT IN SERVICES

The percentage of the workforce employed in the service industry in 2007

- Over 85%
- 80 – 85%
- 75 – 80%
- 70 – 75%
- Under 70%

EMPLOYMENT IN MANUFACTURING

The percentage of the workforce employed in manufacturing in 2007

- Over 20%
- 16 – 20%
- 14 – 16%
- 12 – 14%
- 10 – 12%
- Under 10%

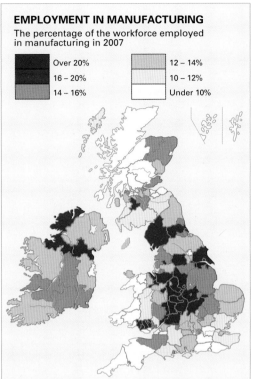

MOTOR MANUFACTURING IN ENGLAND AND WALES

- ■ Car manufacturing sites
- ▨ Commercial vehicle manufacturing sites
- □ Selected engine manufacturing sites

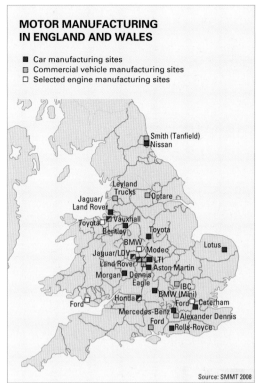

Source: SMMT 2008

CHANGES IN EMPLOYMENT IN THE UK

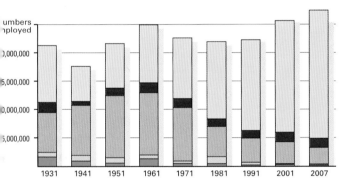

Employment by industry

- Services
- Transport
- Manufacturing
- Mining & energy supply
- Agriculture, forestry & fishing

MANUFACTURING OUTPUT IN THE UK

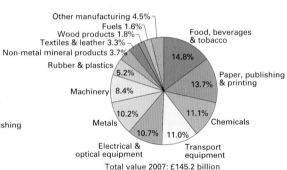

- Other manufacturing 4.5%
- Fuels 1.6%
- Wood products 1.8%
- Textiles & leather 3.3%
- Non-metal mineral products 3.7%
- Rubber & plastics 5.2%
- Machinery 8.4%
- Metals 10.2%
- Electrical & optical equipment 10.7%
- Transport equipment 11.0%
- Chemicals 11.1%
- Paper, publishing & printing 13.7%
- Food, beverages & tobacco 14.8%

Total value 2007: £145.2 billion

UK FOREIGN TRADE

TOP TEN TRADING PARTNERS One container represents 1% of the total value of imports or 1% of the total value of exports in 2007

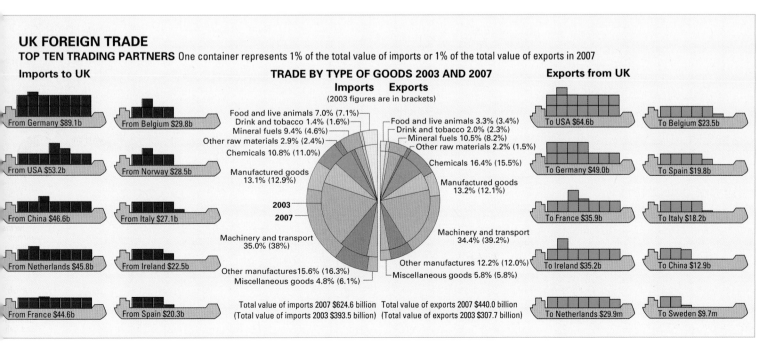

Imports to UK

- From Germany $89.1b
- From Belgium $29.8b
- From USA $53.2b
- From Norway $28.5b
- From China $46.6b
- From Italy $27.1b
- From Netherlands $45.8b
- From Ireland $22.5b
- From France $44.6b
- From Spain $20.3b

TRADE BY TYPE OF GOODS 2003 AND 2007

Imports   Exports

(2003 figures are in brackets)

Imports:
- Food and live animals 7.0% (7.1%)
- Drink and tobacco 1.4% (1.6%)
- Mineral fuels 9.4% (4.6%)
- Other raw materials 2.9% (2.4%)
- Chemicals 10.8% (11.0%)
- Manufactured goods 13.1% (12.9%)
- Machinery and transport 35.0% (38%)
- Other manufactures 15.6% (16.3%)
- Miscellaneous goods 4.8% (6.1%)

Exports:
- Food and live animals 3.3% (3.4%)
- Drink and tobacco 2.0% (2.3%)
- Mineral fuels 10.5% (8.2%)
- Other raw materials 2.2% (1.5%)
- Chemicals 16.4% (15.5%)
- Manufactured goods 13.2% (12.1%)
- Machinery and transport 34.4% (39.2%)
- Other manufactures 12.2% (12.0%)
- Miscellaneous goods 5.8% (5.8%)

2003
2007

Total value of imports 2007 $624.6 billion
(Total value of imports 2003 $393.5 billion)

Total value of exports 2007 $440.0 billion
(Total value of exports 2003 $307.7 billion)

Exports from UK

- To USA $64.6b
- To Belgium $23.5b
- To Germany $49.0b
- To Spain $19.8b
- To France $35.9b
- To Italy $18.2b
- To Ireland $35.2b
- To China $12.9b
- To Netherlands $29.9m
- To Sweden $9.7m

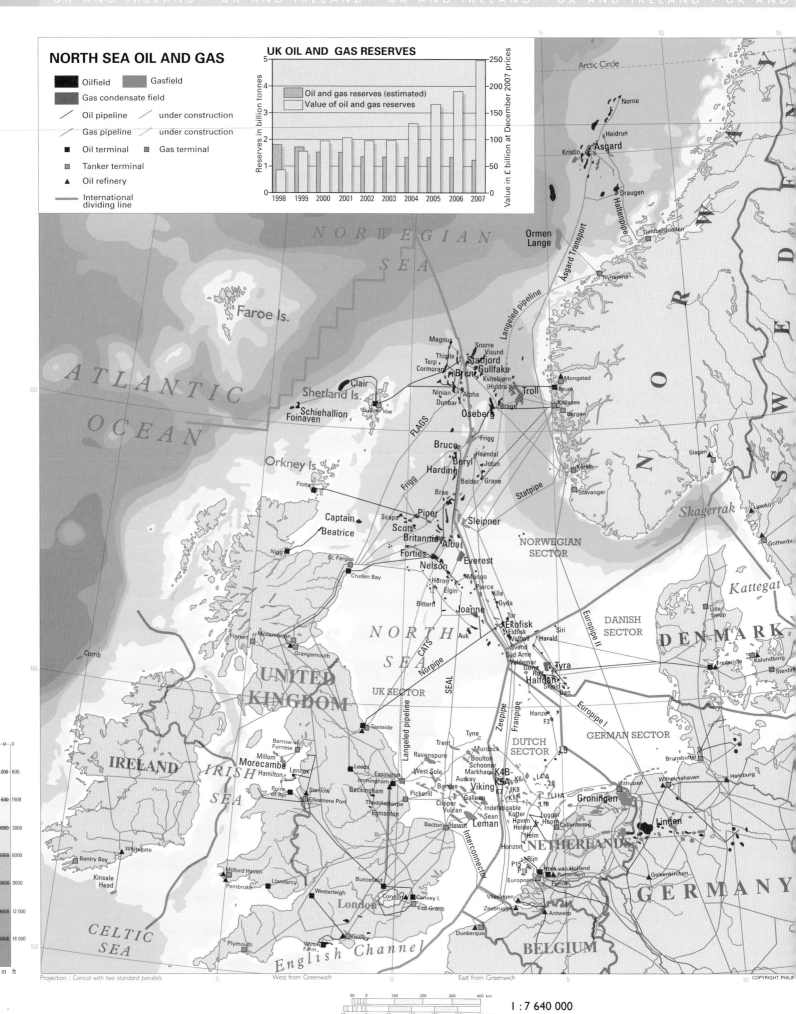

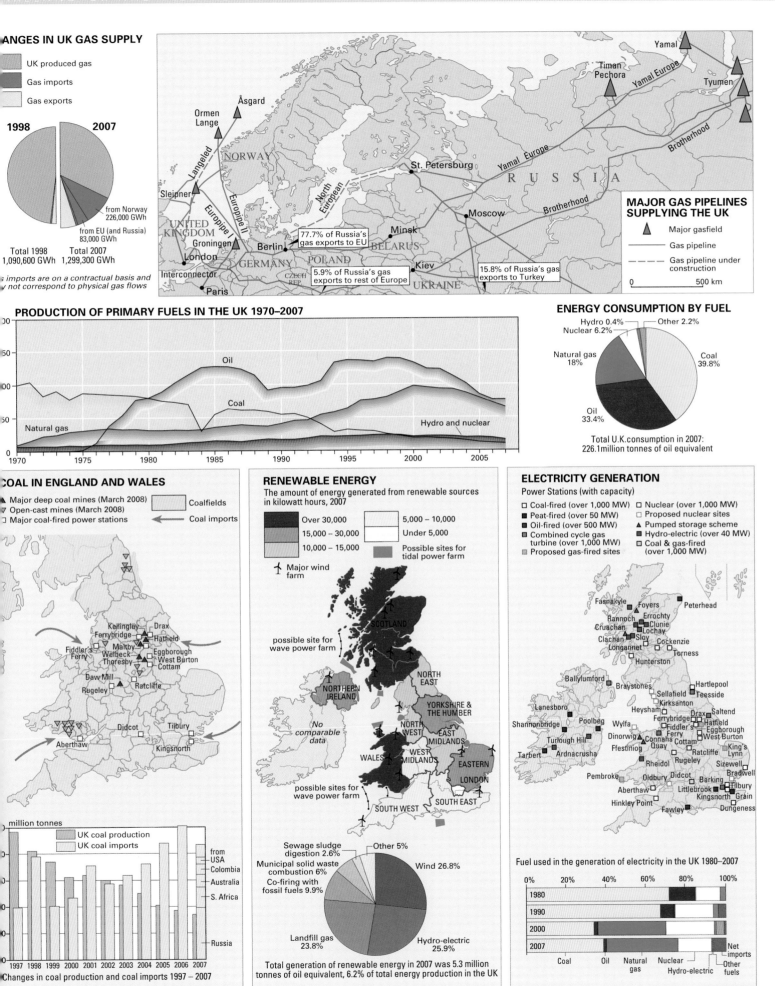

CHANGES IN UK GAS SUPPLY

- UK produced gas
- Gas imports
- Gas exports

1998 **2007**

from Norway 226,000 GWh
from EU (and Russia) 83,000 GWh

Total 1998 1,090,600 GWh
Total 2007 1,299,300 GWh

Gas imports are on a contractual basis and may not correspond to physical gas flows

MAJOR GAS PIPELINES SUPPLYING THE UK

- Major gasfield
- Gas pipeline
- Gas pipeline under construction

0 500 km

Yamal, Timan Pechora, Yamal Europe, Tyumen, Ormen Lange, Åsgard, NORWAY, Brotherhood, Langeled, St. Petersburg, RUSSIA, Europipe I, Europipe II, Yamal Europe, Sleipner, North European, Moscow, Groningen, UNITED KINGDOM, Berlin, Minsk, BELARUS, London, GERMANY, POLAND, Kiev, Interconnector, CZECH REP, UKRAINE, Paris

77.7% of Russia's gas exports to EU
5.9% of Russia's gas exports to rest of Europe
15.8% of Russia's gas exports to Turkey

PRODUCTION OF PRIMARY FUELS IN THE UK 1970–2007

Oil, Coal, Natural gas, Hydro and nuclear
1970 1975 1980 1985 1990 1995 2000 2005

ENERGY CONSUMPTION BY FUEL

Hydro 0.4%, Other 2.2%, Nuclear 6.2%, Natural gas 18%, Coal 39.8%, Oil 33.4%

Total U.K. consumption in 2007: 226.1 million tonnes of oil equivalent

COAL IN ENGLAND AND WALES

- Major deep coal mines (March 2008)
- Open-cast mines (March 2008)
- Major coal-fired power stations
- Coalfields
- Coal imports

Kellingley, Drax, Ferrybridge, Hatfield, Fiddler's Ferry, Maltby, Welbeck, Eggborough, Thoresby, West Burton, Cottam, Daw Mill, Ratcliffe, Rugeley, Aberthaw, Didcot, Tilbury, Kingsnorth

million tonnes
- UK coal production
- UK coal imports
from USA, Colombia, Australia, S. Africa, Russia
1997 1998 1999 2000 2001 2002 2003 2004 2005 2006 2007
Changes in coal production and coal imports 1997 – 2007

RENEWABLE ENERGY

The amount of energy generated from renewable sources in kilowatt hours, 2007

- Over 30,000
- 15,000 – 30,000
- 10,000 – 15,000
- 5,000 – 10,000
- Under 5,000
- Possible sites for tidal power farm
- Major wind farm

SCOTLAND, NORTHERN IRELAND, NORTH EAST, YORKSHIRE & THE HUMBER, NORTH WEST, EAST MIDLANDS, WALES, WEST MIDLANDS, EASTERN, LONDON, SOUTH WEST, SOUTH EAST
possible site for wave power farm
No comparable data

Sewage sludge digestion 2.6%, Other 5%, Municipal solid waste combustion 6%, Co-firing with fossil fuels 9.9%, Wind 26.8%, Landfill gas 23.8%, Hydro-electric 25.9%

Total generation of renewable energy in 2007 was 5.3 million tonnes of oil equivalent, 6.2% of total energy production in the UK

ELECTRICITY GENERATION

Power Stations (with capacity)
- Coal-fired (over 1,000 MW)
- Peat-fired (over 50 MW)
- Oil-fired (over 500 MW)
- Combined cycle gas turbine (over 1,000 MW)
- Proposed gas-fired sites
- Nuclear (over 1,000 MW)
- Proposed nuclear sites
- Pumped storage scheme
- Hydro-electric (over 40 MW)
- Coal & gas-fired (over 1,000 MW)

Fasnakyle, Foyers, Peterhead, Rannoch, Errochty, Cruachan, Clunie, Lochay, Clachan, Sloy, Cockenzie, Longannet, Torness, Hunterston, Ballylumford, Braystones, Hartlepool, Lanesboro, Sellafield, Teesside, Heysham, Kirksanton, Shannonbridge, Poolbeg, Wylfa, Ferrybridge, Drax, Saltend, Turlough Hill, Dinorwig, Fiddler's Ferry, Hatfield, Eggborough, Tarbert, Ardnacrusha, Connahs Quay, Cottam, West Burton, Ffestiniog, Ratcliffe, King's Lynn, Rheidol, Rugeley, Sizewell, Pembroke, Oldbury, Didcot, Bradwell, Aberthaw, Littlebrook, Barking, Hinkley Point, Fawley, Kingsnorth, Tilbury, Grain, Dungeness

Fuel used in the generation of electricity in the UK 1980–2007
0% 20% 40% 60% 80% 100%
1980, 1990, 2000, 2007
Coal, Oil, Natural gas, Nuclear, Hydro-electric, Net imports, Other fuels

COPYRIGHT PHILIP'S

ROADS AND FERRIES

Motorways
Other main roads
Principal car ferry routes

Average 24 hour flow of vehicles for major sections of motorway network. Figures are given in thousands for 2006

RAILWAYS

Electrified lines
Other main lines
Channel Tunnel
High-speed rail link

Furthest distances from London reached within a journey time of

	3 hours	6 hours
1950	▲	●
2005	▲	●

CHANNEL TUNNEL AND HIGH-SPEED RAIL LINKS IN EUROPE

Estimated journey times between London and other European cities

1990 Best time achievable using existing networks
2002 Opening of Channel Tunnel in 1994 and completion of high-speed links in Europe
2008 Journey time on completion of high speed link from London to Folkestone

MEANS OF TRANSPORTATION WITHIN THE UK

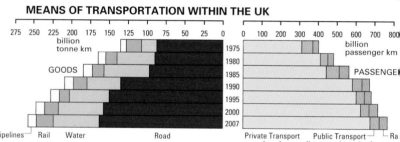

GOODS — Pipelines Rail Water Road
PASSENGER — Private Transport (cars) Public Transport (buses and coaches) Rail

SEAPORTS

Goods traffic by port in thousand tonnes (2007)

50,000
25,000
10,000
5,000

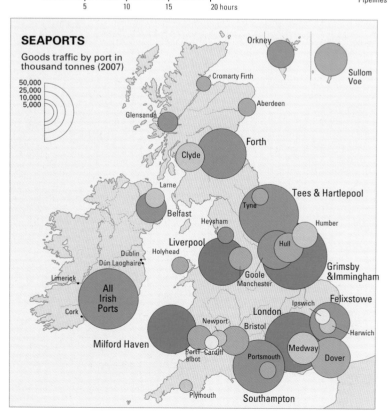

AIRPORTS

Passenger traffic in thousands (2007)

60,000
30,000
5,000
1,000

(34.6%) International Passengers as a percentage of the total for selected airports

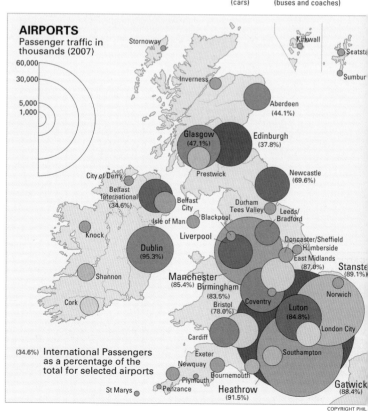

COPYRIGHT PHIL

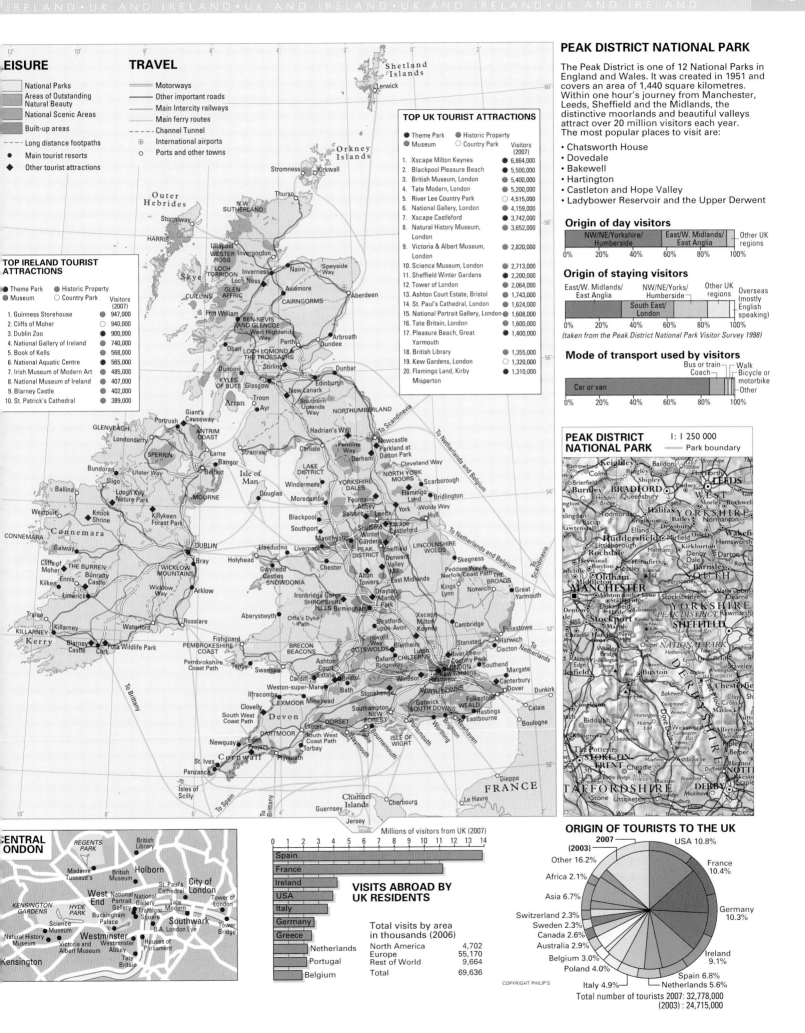

LEISURE

- National Parks
- Areas of Outstanding Natural Beauty
- National Scenic Areas
- Built-up areas
- Long distance footpaths
- ● Main tourist resorts
- ◆ Other tourist attractions

TRAVEL

- Motorways
- Other important roads
- Main Intercity railways
- Main ferry routes
- Channel Tunnel
- ⊕ International airports
- ○ Ports and other towns

TOP IRELAND TOURIST ATTRACTIONS

● Theme Park ● Historic Property
● Museum ○ Country Park

		Visitors (2007)
1.	Guinness Storehouse	● 947,000
2.	Cliffs of Moher	○ 940,000
3.	Dublin Zoo	● 900,000
4.	National Gallery of Ireland	● 740,000
5.	Book of Kells	● 568,000
6.	National Aquatic Centre	● 565,000
7.	Irish Museum of Modern Art	● 485,000
8.	National Museum of Ireland	● 407,000
9.	Blarney Castle	● 402,000
10.	St. Patrick's Cathedral	● 389,000

TOP UK TOURIST ATTRACTIONS

● Theme Park ● Historic Property
● Museum ○ Country Park

		Visitors (2007)
1.	Xscape Milton Keynes	● 6,864,000
2.	Blackpool Pleasure Beach	● 5,500,000
3.	British Museum, London	● 5,400,000
4.	Tate Modern, London	● 5,200,000
5.	River Lee Country Park	○ 4,515,000
6.	National Gallery, London	● 4,159,000
7.	Xscape Castleford	● 3,742,000
8.	Natural History Museum, London	● 3,652,000
9.	Victoria & Albert Museum, London	● 2,820,000
10.	Science Museum, London	● 2,713,000
11.	Sheffield Winter Gardens	● 2,200,000
12.	Tower of London	● 2,064,000
13.	Ashton Court Estate, Bristol	● 1,743,000
14.	St. Paul's Cathedral, London	● 1,624,000
15.	National Portrait Gallery, London	● 1,608,000
16.	Tate Britain, London	● 1,600,000
17.	Pleasure Beach, Great Yarmouth	● 1,400,000
18.	British Library	● 1,355,000
19.	Kew Gardens, London	○ 1,320,000
20.	Flamingo Land, Kirby Misperton	● 1,310,000

PEAK DISTRICT NATIONAL PARK

The Peak District is one of 12 National Parks in England and Wales. It was created in 1951 and covers an area of 1,440 square kilometres. Within one hour's journey from Manchester, Leeds, Sheffield and the Midlands, the distinctive moorlands and beautiful valleys attract over 20 million visitors each year. The most popular places to visit are:

- Chatsworth House
- Dovedale
- Bakewell
- Hartington
- Castleton and Hope Valley
- Ladybower Reservoir and the Upper Derwent

Origin of day visitors

NW/NE/Yorkshire/Humberside — East/W. Midlands/East Anglia — Other UK regions

Origin of staying visitors

East/W. Midlands/East Anglia — NW/NE/Yorks/Humberside — Other UK regions — Overseas (mostly English speaking) — South East/London

(taken from the Peak District National Park Visitor Survey 1998)

Mode of transport used by visitors

Car or van — Coach — Bus or train — Walk — Bicycle or motorbike — Other

PEAK DISTRICT NATIONAL PARK   1: 1 250 000   — Park boundary

VISITS ABROAD BY UK RESIDENTS

Millions of visitors from UK (2007)

Spain, France, Ireland, USA, Italy, Germany, Greece, Netherlands, Portugal, Belgium

Total visits by area in thousands (2006)

North America	4,702
Europe	55,170
Rest of World	9,664
Total	69,636

ORIGIN OF TOURISTS TO THE UK

2007 (2003)

- USA 10.8%
- France 10.4%
- Germany 10.3%
- Ireland 9.1%
- Spain 6.8%
- Netherlands 5.6%
- Italy 4.9%
- Poland 4.0%
- Belgium 3.0%
- Australia 2.9%
- Canada 2.6%
- Sweden 2.3%
- Switzerland 2.3%
- Asia 6.7%
- Africa 2.1%
- Other 16.2%

Total number of tourists 2007: 32,778,000
(2003): 24,715,000

CENTRAL LONDON

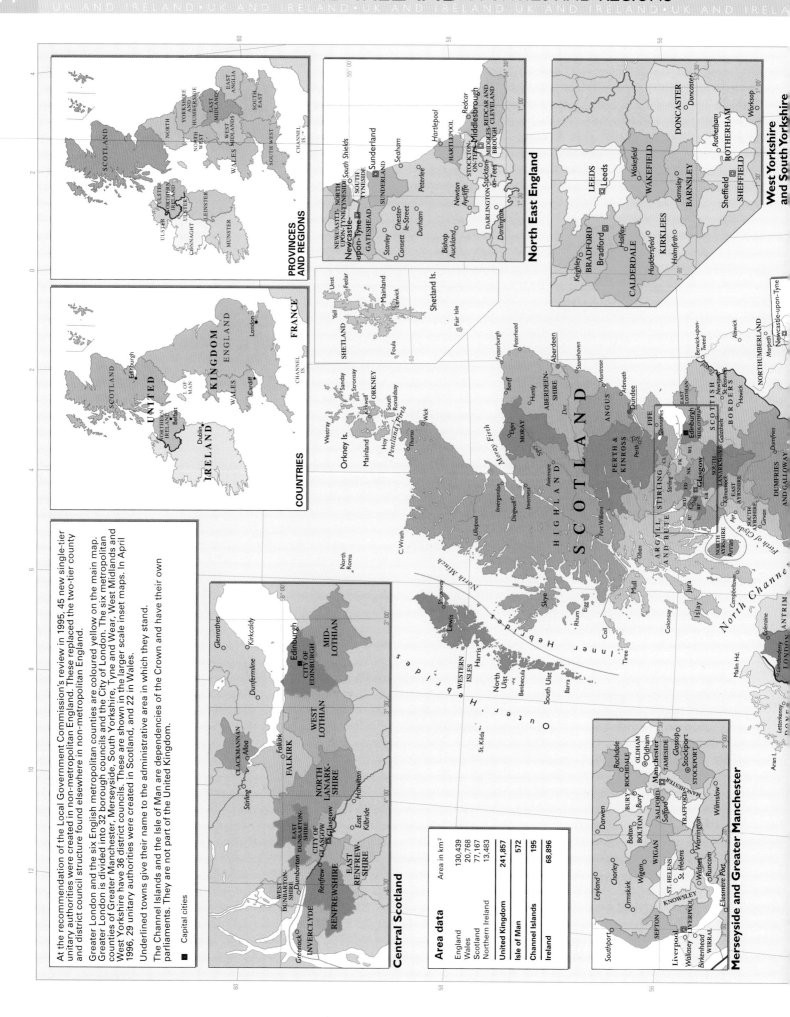

At the recommendation of the Local Government Commission's review in 1995, 45 new single-tier unitary authorities were created in non-metropolitan England. These replaced the two-tier county and district council structure found elsewhere in non-metropolitan England.

Greater London and the six English metropolitan counties are coloured yellow on the main map. Greater London is divided into 32 borough councils and the City of London. The six metropolitan counties of Greater Manchester, Merseyside, South Yorkshire, Tyne and Wear, West Midlands and West Yorkshire have 36 district councils. These are shown in the larger scale inset maps. In April 1996, 29 unitary authorities were created in Scotland, and 22 in Wales.

Underlined towns give their name to the administrative area in which they stand.

The Channel Islands and the Isle of Man are dependencies of the Crown and have their own parliaments. They are not part of the United Kingdom.

■ Capital cities

PROVINCES AND REGIONS

COUNTRIES

North East England

West Yorkshire and South Yorkshire

Central Scotland

Merseyside and Greater Manchester

Area data

	Area in km²
England	130,439
Wales	20,768
Scotland	77,167
Northern Ireland	13,483
United Kingdom	**241,857**
Isle of Man	572
Channel Islands	195
Ireland	68,896

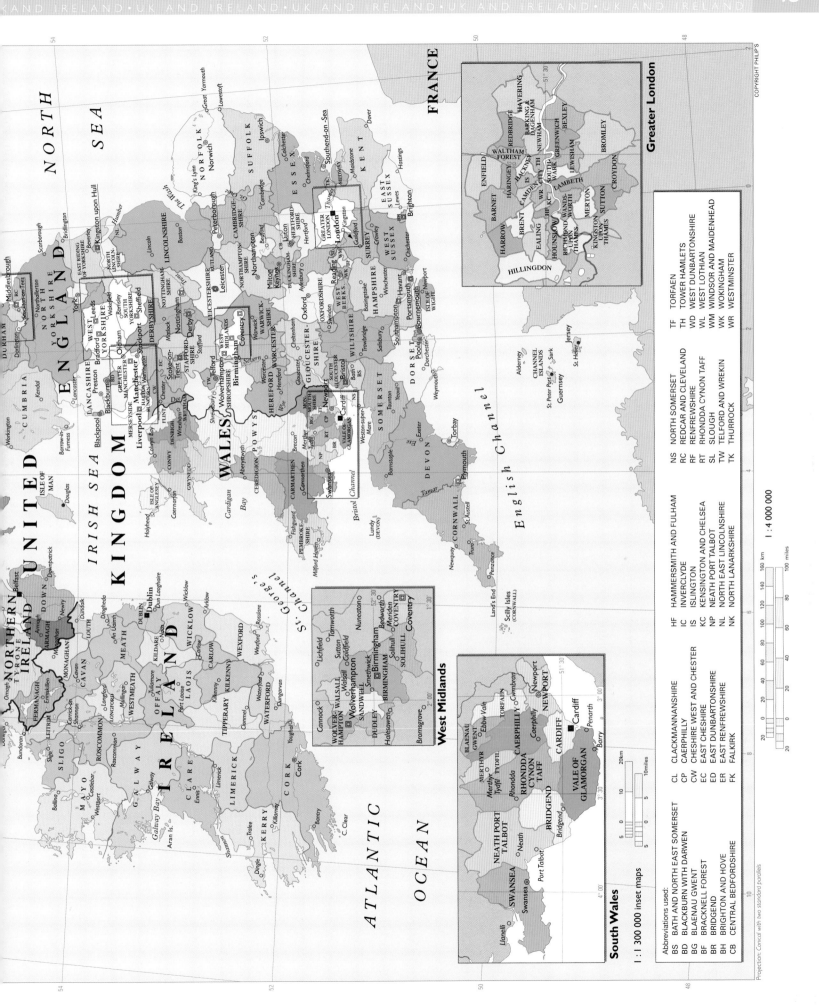

Greater London

NORTH SEA

UNITED KINGDOM

NORTHERN IRELAND

IRELAND

ATLANTIC OCEAN

ENGLAND

WALES

IRISH SEA

St. George's Channel

English Channel

FRANCE

COPYRIGHT PHILIP'S

West Midlands

South Wales
1 : 1 300 000 inset maps

Projection: Conical with two standard parallels

1 : 4 000 000

Abbreviations used:

BS	BATH AND NORTH EAST SOMERSET	CL	CLACKMANNANSHIRE	
BD	BLACKBURN WITH DARWEN	CP	CAERPHILLY	
BG	BLAENAU GWENT	CW	CHESHIRE WEST AND CHESTER	
BF	BRACKNELL FOREST	EC	EAST CHESHIRE	
BR	BRIDGEND	ED	EAST DUNBARTONSHIRE	
BH	BRIGHTON AND HOVE	ER	EAST RENFREWSHIRE	
CB	CENTRAL BEDFORDSHIRE	FK	FALKIRK	

HF	HAMMERSMITH AND FULHAM	NS	NORTH SOMERSET
IC	INVERCLYDE	RC	REDCAR AND CLEVELAND
IS	ISLINGTON	RF	RENFREWSHIRE
KC	KENSINGTON AND CHELSEA	RT	RHONDDA CYNON TAFF
NP	NEATH PORT TALBOT	SL	SLOUGH
NL	NORTH EAST LINCOLNSHIRE	TW	TELFORD AND WREKIN
NK	NORTH LANARKSHIRE	TK	THURROCK

TF	TORFAEN
TH	TOWER HAMLETS
WD	WEST DUNBARTONSHIRE
WL	WEST LOTHIAN
WM	WINDSOR AND MAIDENHEAD
WK	WOKINGHAM
WR	WESTMINSTER

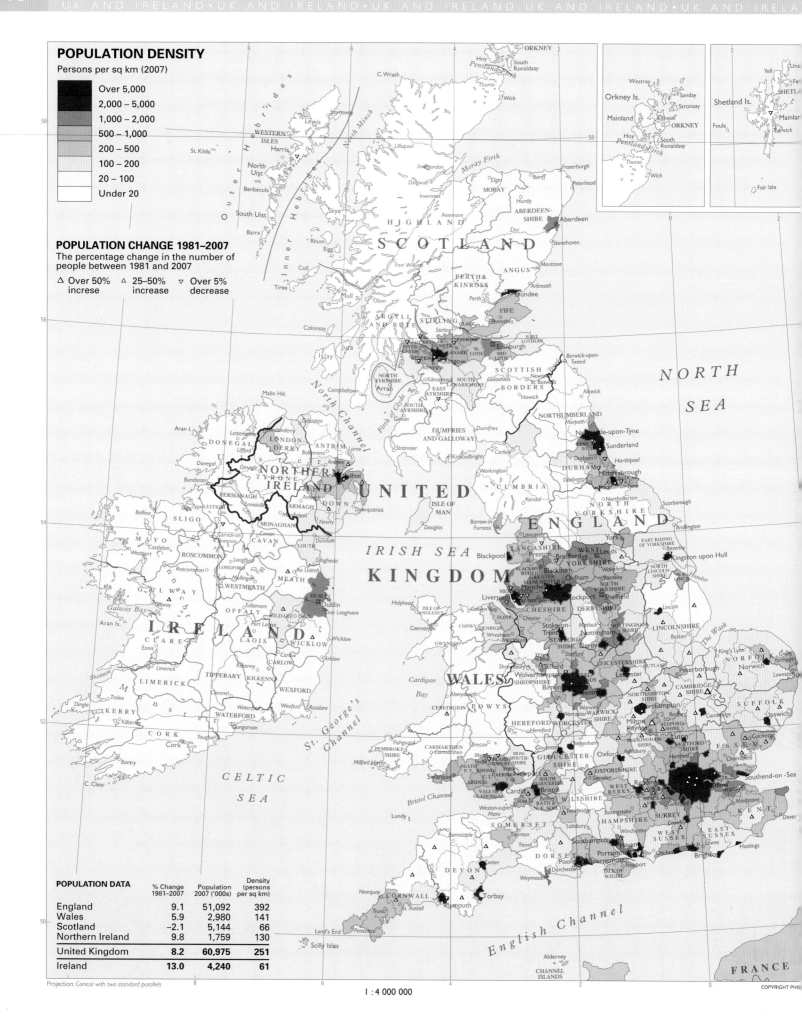

POPULATION DENSITY

Persons per sq km (2007)

- Over 5,000
- 2,000 – 5,000
- 1,000 – 2,000
- 500 – 1,000
- 200 – 500
- 100 – 200
- 20 – 100
- Under 20

POPULATION CHANGE 1981–2007

The percentage change in the number of people between 1981 and 2007

△ Over 50% increse   △ 25–50% increase   ▽ Over 5% decrease

POPULATION DATA	% Change 1981–2007	Population 2007 ('000s)	Density (persons per sq km)
England	9.1	51,092	392
Wales	5.9	2,980	141
Scotland	-2.1	5,144	66
Northern Ireland	9.8	1,759	130
United Kingdom	8.2	60,975	251
Ireland	13.0	4,240	61

Projection: Conical with two standard parallels

1 : 4 000 000

POPULATION DENSITY IN 1891

Persons per sq km

- Over 1,000
- 500 – 1,000
- 200 – 500
- 100 – 200
- 50 – 100
- 25 – 50
- Under 25

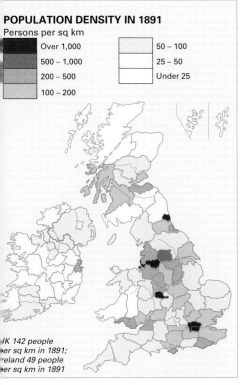

JK 142 people
er sq km in 1891;
eland 49 people
er sq km in 1891

ETHNIC GROUPS

Ethnic minorities as a percentage of total
population in 2003

- Over 30%
- 10 – 30%
- 5 – 10%
- 0 – 5%

Ethnic minority groups

- Indian/ Pakistani/ Bangladeshi
- W. Indian/ African
- Other

77 000 Total number of ethnic minority people in each region

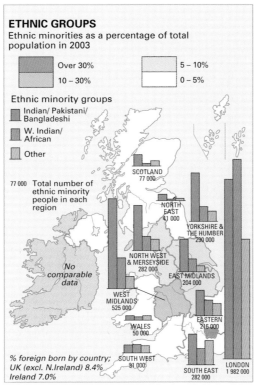

SCOTLAND 77 000
NORTH EAST 41 000
YORKSHIRE & THE HUMBER 290 000
NORTH WEST & MERSEYSIDE 282 000
EAST MIDLANDS 204 000
WEST MIDLANDS 525 000
WALES 50 000
EASTERN 216 000
SOUTH WEST 91 000
SOUTH EAST 282 000
LONDON 1 982 000

No comparable data

% foreign born by country;
UK (excl. N.Ireland) 8.4%
Ireland 7.0%

MIGRATION

The difference between the number moving in and
the number moving away per 1,000 inhabitants 2007*

- Over 10 moved in
- 5 – 10 moved in
- 0 – 5 moved in
- 0 – 5 moved away
- 5 – 10 moved away
- Over 10 moved away

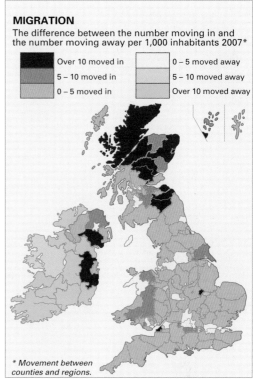

* Movement between
counties and regions.

NATURAL POPULATION CHANGE

The difference between the number of births and the
number of deaths per thousand inhabitants in 2007

- Over 7.5 more births
- 5 – 7.5 more births
- 2.5 – 5 more births
- 0 – 2.5 more births
- 0 – 2.5 more deaths
- Over 2.5 more deaths

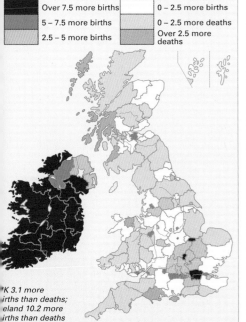

K 3.1 more
irths than deaths;
eland 10.2 more
irths than deaths

YOUNG PEOPLE

The percentage of the population
under 15 years old in 2007

- Over 21%
- 20 – 21%
- 19 – 20%
- 18 – 19%
- 17 – 18%
- Under – 17%

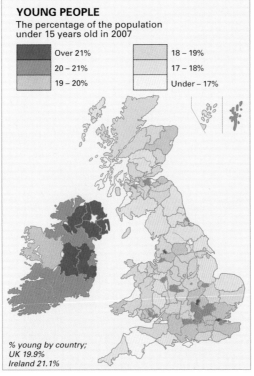

% young by country;
UK 19.9%
Ireland 21.1%

OLD PEOPLE

The percentage of the population
over pensionable age* in 2007

- Over 26%
- 24 – 26%
- 22 – 24%
- 20 – 22%
- 18 – 20%
- Under 18%

*Pensionable age is
65 for males, 60 for
females

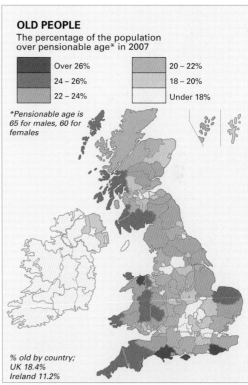

% old by country;
UK 18.4%
Ireland 11.2%

K VITAL STATISTICS (1900–2007)

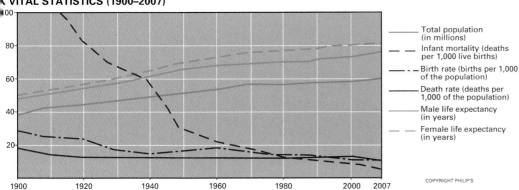

- Total population (in millions)
- Infant mortality (deaths per 1,000 live births)
- Birth rate (births per 1,000 of the population)
- Death rate (deaths per 1,000 of the population)
- Male life expectancy (in years)
- Female life expectancy (in years)

COPYRIGHT PHILIP'S

AGE STRUCTURE OF THE UK

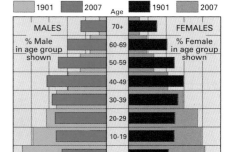

1901 2007 Age 1901 2007

MALES
% Male in age group shown

FEMALES
% Female in age group shown

70+
60-69
50-59
40-49
30-39
20-29
10-19
0-9

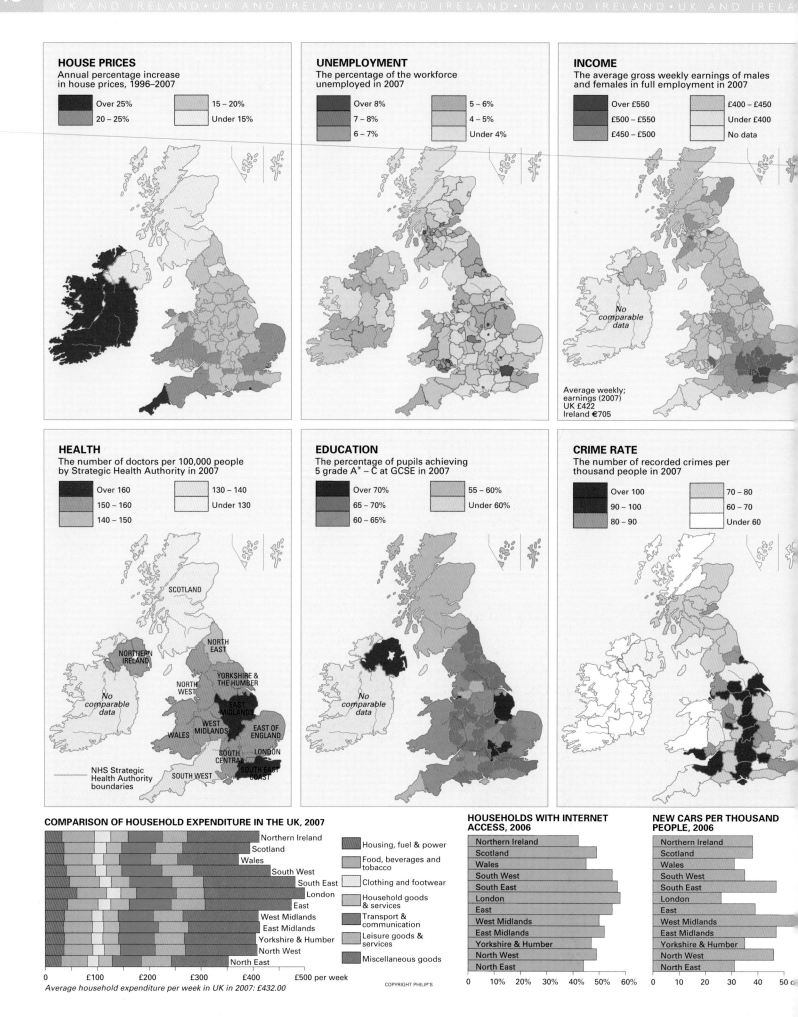

HOUSE PRICES
Annual percentage increase
in house prices, 1996–2007

- Over 25%
- 20 – 25%
- 15 – 20%
- Under 15%

UNEMPLOYMENT
The percentage of the workforce
unemployed in 2007

- Over 8%
- 7 – 8%
- 6 – 7%
- 5 – 6%
- 4 – 5%
- Under 4%

INCOME
The average gross weekly earnings of males
and females in full employment in 2007

- Over £550
- £500 – £550
- £450 – £500
- £400 – £450
- Under £400
- No data

No comparable data

Average weekly;
earnings (2007)
UK £422
Ireland €705

HEALTH
The number of doctors per 100,000 people
by Strategic Health Authority in 2007

- Over 160
- 150 – 160
- 140 – 150
- 130 – 140
- Under 130

SCOTLAND

NORTHERN IRELAND

NORTH EAST

YORKSHIRE & THE HUMBER

NORTH WEST

No comparable data

EAST MIDLANDS

WEST MIDLANDS

WALES

EAST OF ENGLAND

SOUTH CENTRAL

LONDON

SOUTH WEST

SOUTH EAST COAST

— NHS Strategic
Health Authority
boundaries

EDUCATION
The percentage of pupils achieving
5 grade A* – C at GCSE in 2007

- Over 70%
- 65 – 70%
- 60 – 65%
- 55 – 60%
- Under 60%

No comparable data

CRIME RATE
The number of recorded crimes per
thousand people in 2007

- Over 100
- 90 – 100
- 80 – 90
- 70 – 80
- 60 – 70
- Under 60

COMPARISON OF HOUSEHOLD EXPENDITURE IN THE UK, 2007

Northern Ireland
Scotland
Wales
South West
South East
London
East
West Midlands
East Midlands
Yorkshire & Humber
North West
North East

- Housing, fuel & power
- Food, beverages and tobacco
- Clothing and footwear
- Household goods & services
- Transport & communication
- Leisure goods & services
- Miscellaneous goods

0   £100   £200   £300   £400   £500 per week

Average household expenditure per week in UK in 2007: £432.00

COPYRIGHT PHILIP'S

HOUSEHOLDS WITH INTERNET ACCESS, 2006

Northern Ireland
Scotland
Wales
South West
South East
London
East
West Midlands
East Midlands
Yorkshire & Humber
North West
North East

0   10%   20%   30%   40%   50%   60%

NEW CARS PER THOUSAND PEOPLE, 2006

Northern Ireland
Scotland
Wales
South West
South East
London
East
West Midlands
East Midlands
Yorkshire & Humber
North West
North East

0   10   20   30   40   50 c

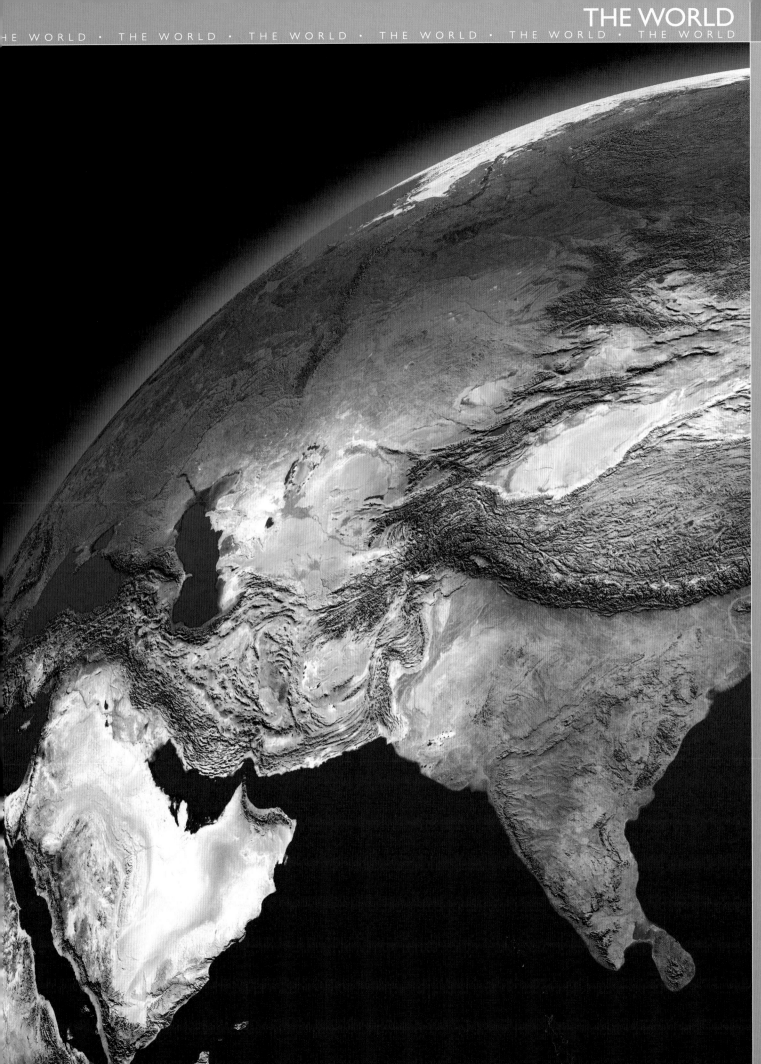

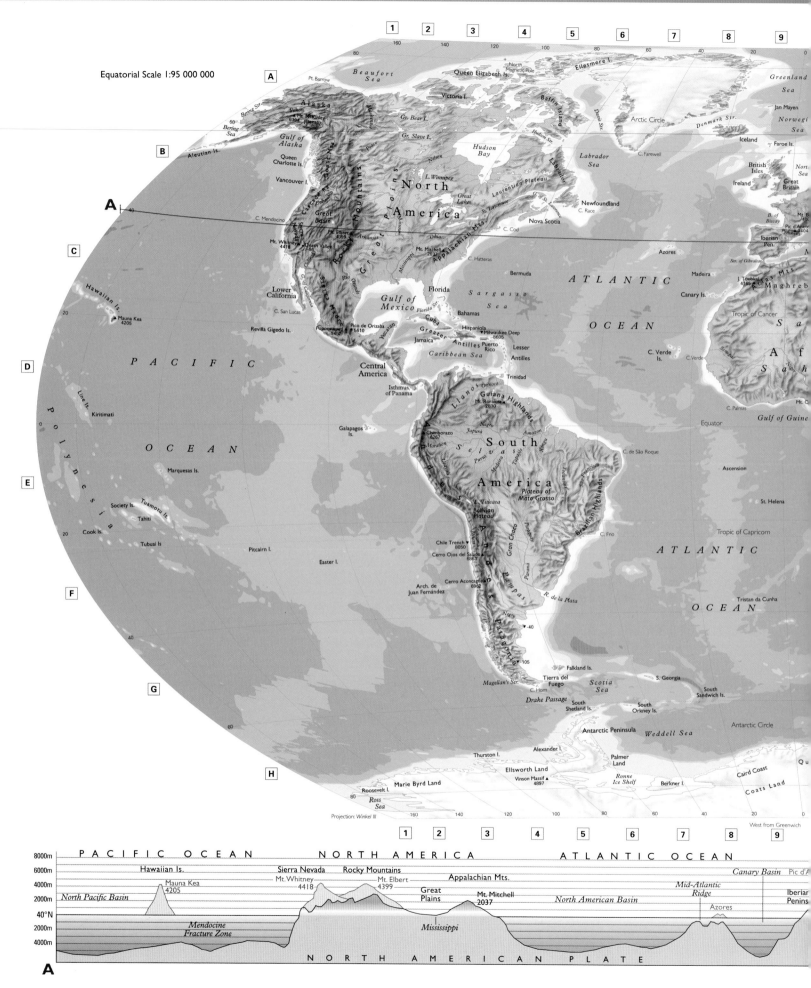

Equatorial Scale 1:95 000 000

Projection: Winkel III

West from Greenwich

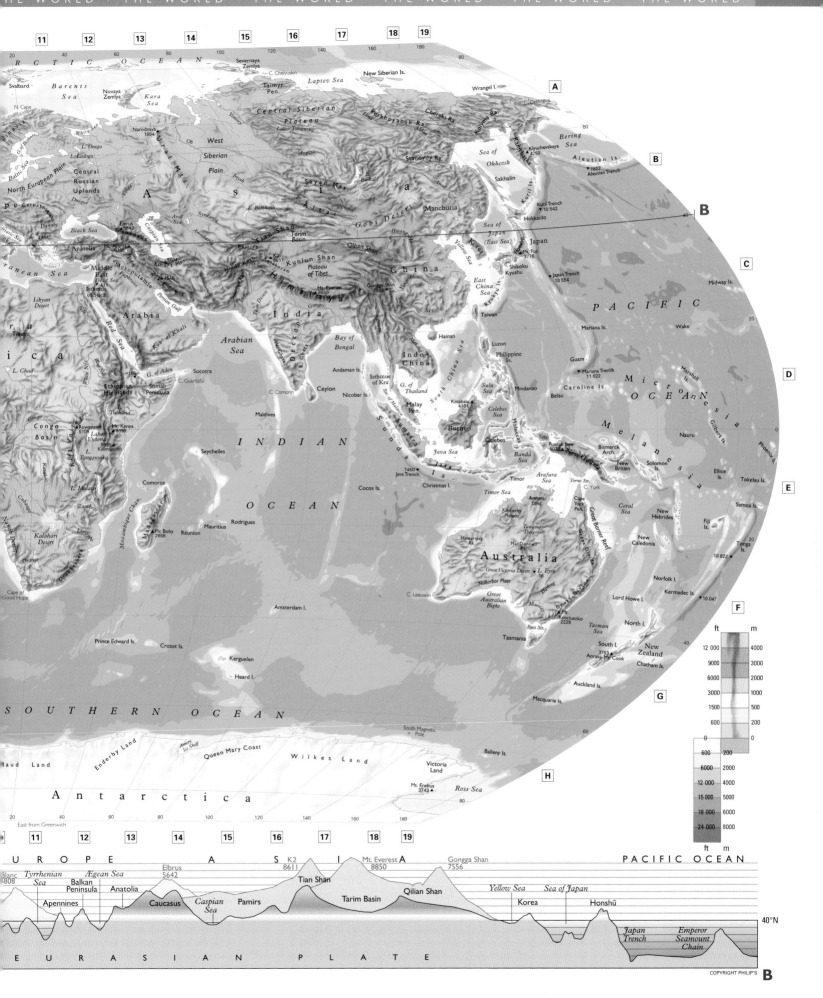

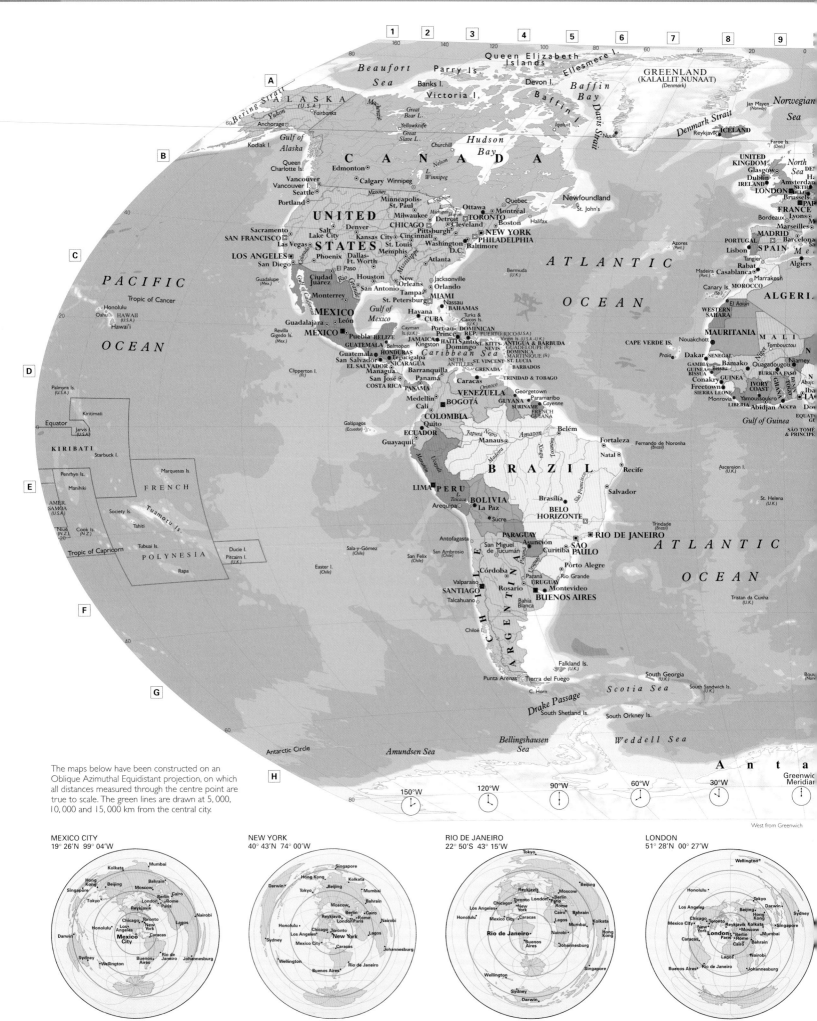

The maps below have been constructed on an Oblique Azimuthal Equidistant projection, on which all distances measured through the centre point are true to scale. The green lines are drawn at 5,000, 10,000 and 15,000 km from the central city.

West from Greenwich

MEXICO CITY
19° 26'N 99° 04'W

NEW YORK
40° 43'N 74° 00'W

RIO DE JANEIRO
22° 50'S 43° 15'W

LONDON
51° 28'N 00° 27'W

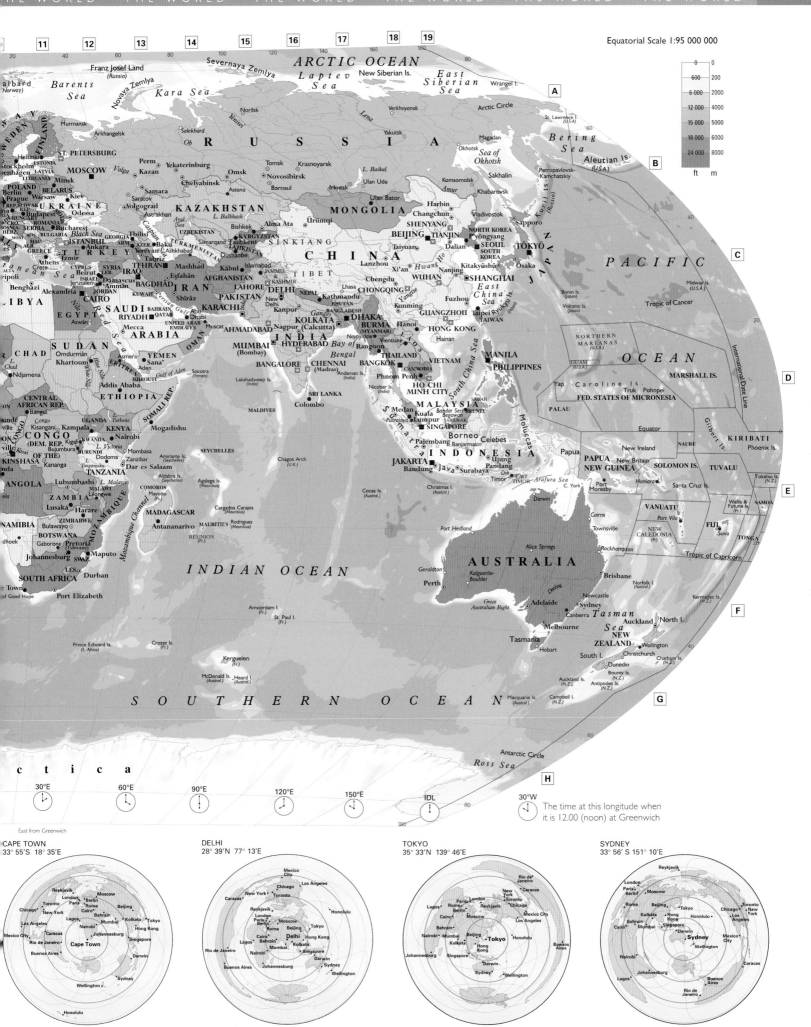

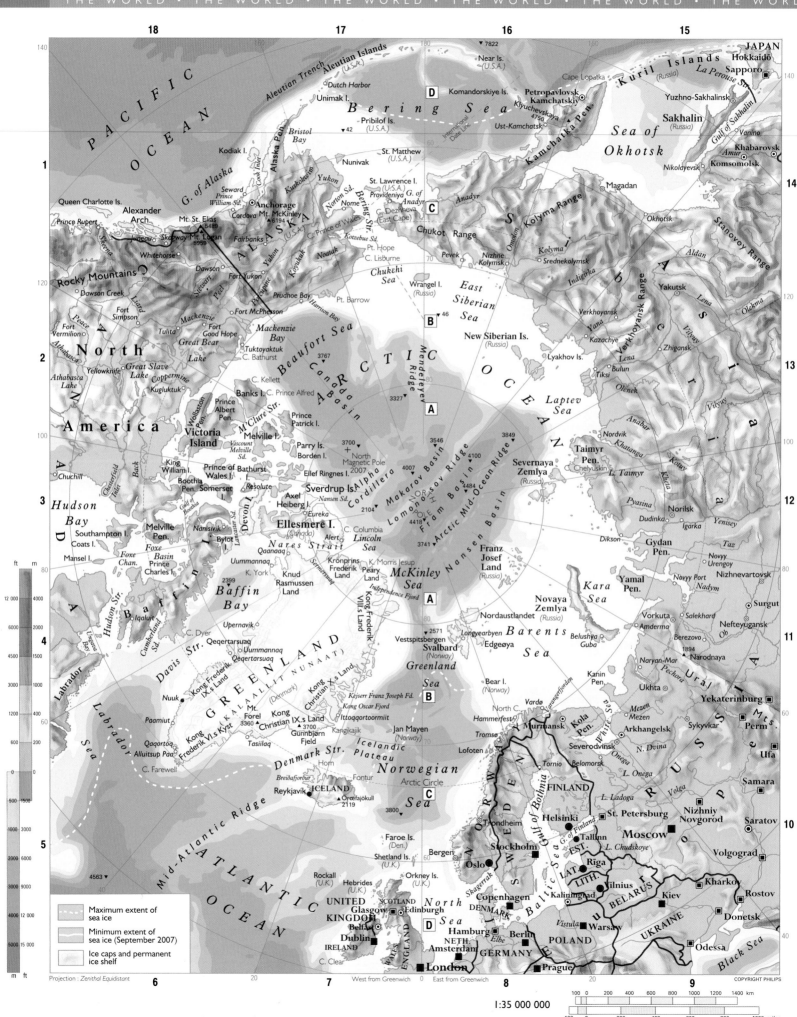

Projection: Zenithal Equidistant

Maximum extent of sea ice

Minimum extent of sea ice (September 2007)

Ice caps and permanent ice shelf

1:35 000 000

COPYRIGHT PHILIPS

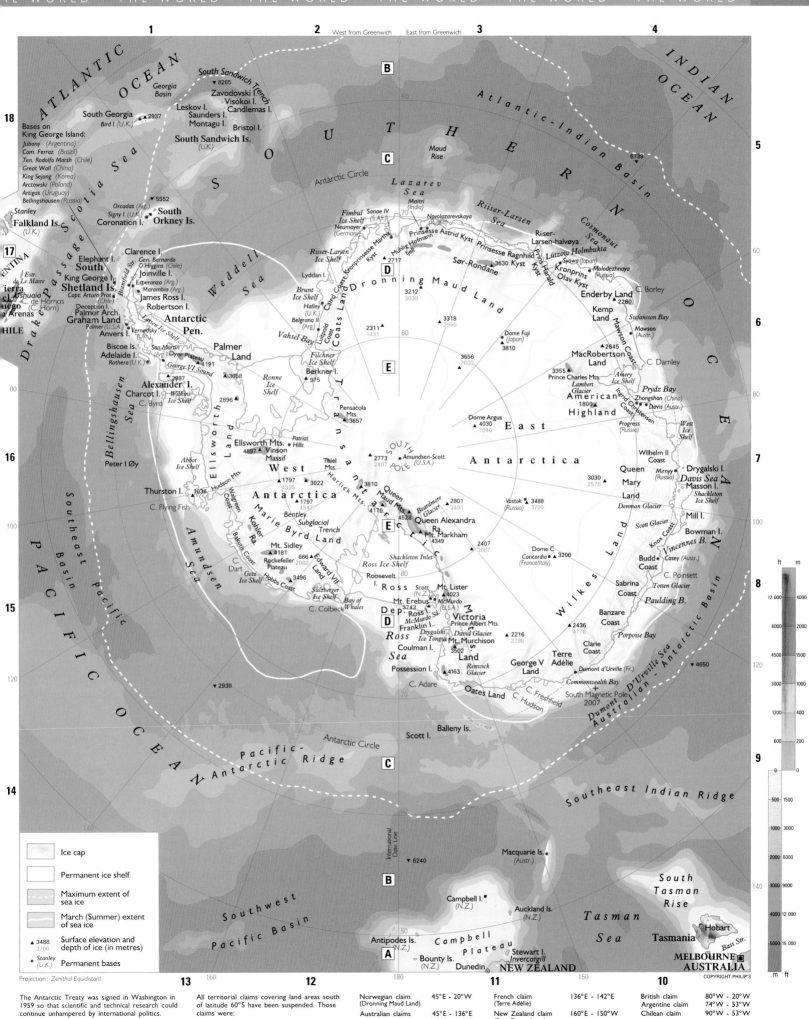

Projection : Zenithal Equidistant

Legend:
- Ice cap
- Permanent ice shelf
- Maximum extent of sea ice
- March (Summer) extent of sea ice
- ▲3488 / 3700   Surface elevation and depth of ice (in metres)
- • *Stanley* (U.K.)   Permanent bases

Bases on King George Island:
Jubany (Argentina)
Com. Ferraz (Brazil)
Ten. Rodolfo Marsh (Chile)
Great Wall (China)
King Sejong (Korea)
Arctowski (Poland)
Artigas (Uruguay)
Bellingshausen (Russia)

The Antarctic Treaty was signed in Washington in 1959 so that scientific and technical research could continue unhampered by international politics.

All territorial claims covering land areas south of latitude 60°S have been suspended. Those claims were:

Norwegian claim (Dronning Maud Land)	45°E – 20°W
Australian claims	45°E – 136°E
	142°E – 160°E
French claim (Terre Adélie)	136°E – 142°E
New Zealand claim (Ross Dependency)	160°E – 150°E
British claim	80°W – 20°W
Argentine claim	74°W – 53°W
Chilean claim	90°W – 53°W

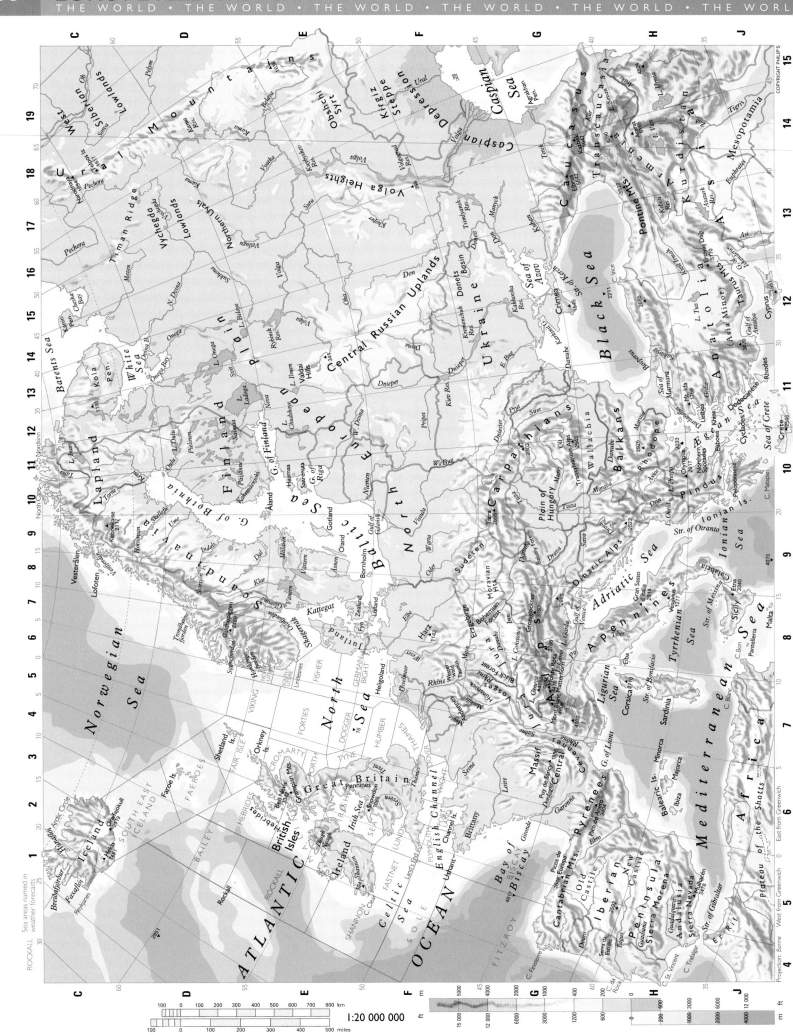

1:20 000 000

Projection: Bonne

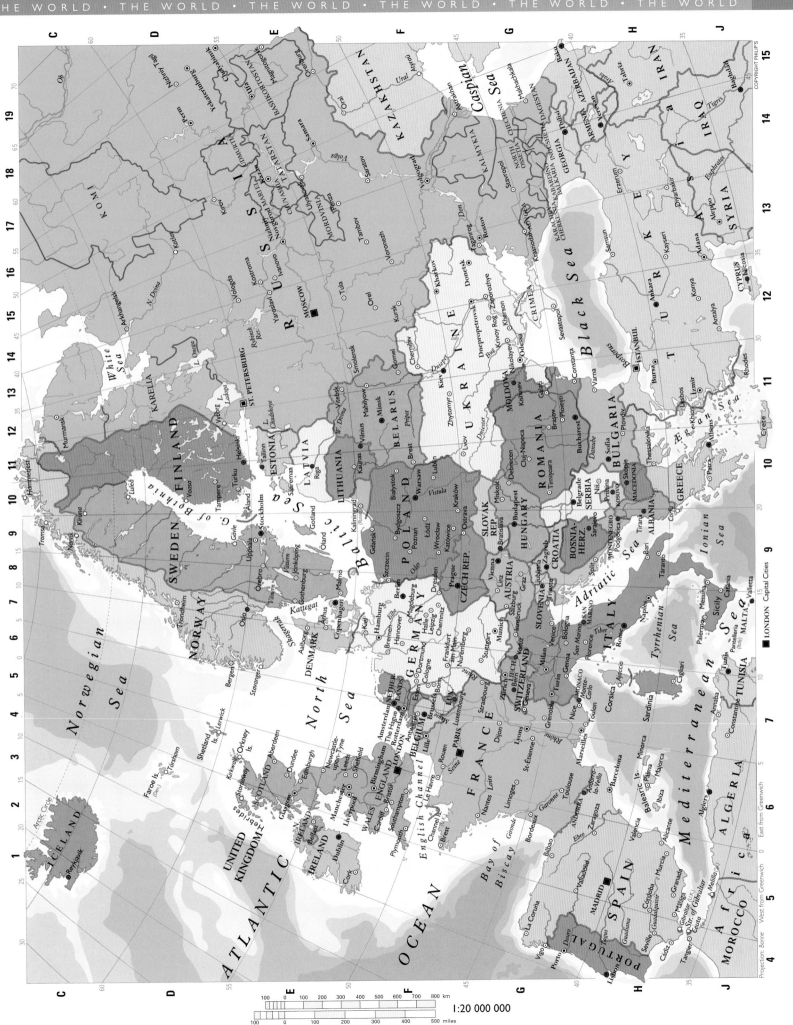

Projection: Bonne   West from Greenwich   0   East from Greenwich

100 0 100 200 300 400 500 600 700 800 km

1:20 000 000

100 0 100 200 300 400 500 miles

■ LONDON Capital Cities

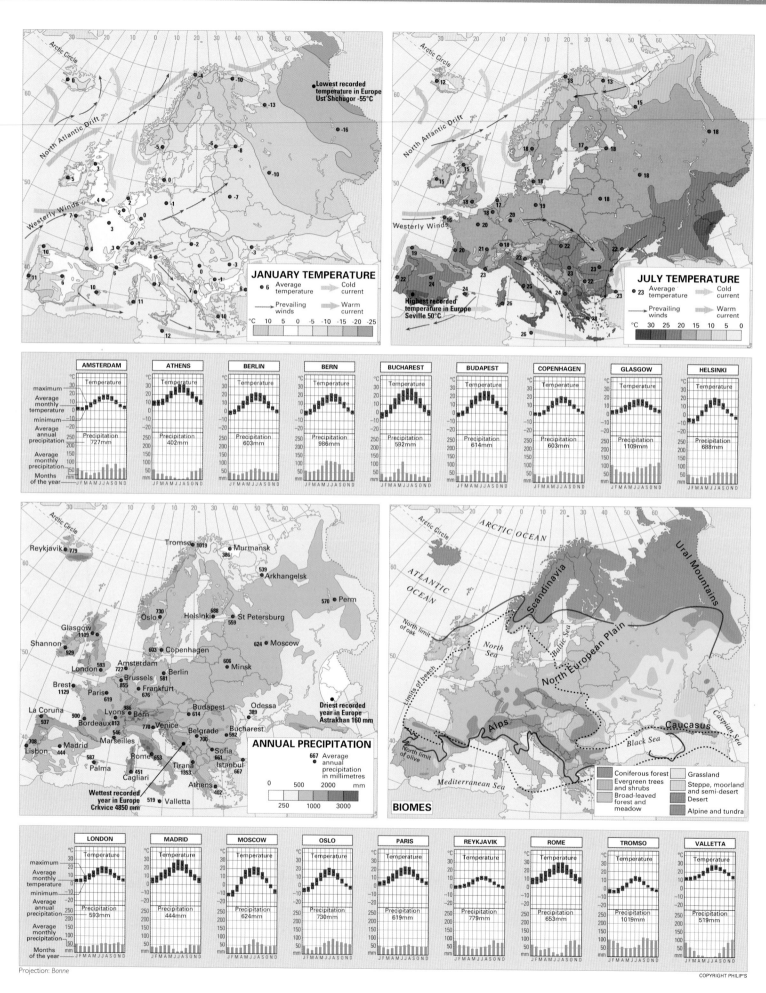

JANUARY TEMPERATURE
Lowest recorded temperature in Europe Ust'Shchugor -55°C

- 6 Average temperature
- → Prevailing winds
- ⇒ Cold current
- ⇒ Warm current

°C 10 5 0 -5 -10 -15 -20 -25

JULY TEMPERATURE
Highest recorded temperature in Europe Seville 50°C

- 23 Average temperature
- → Prevailing winds
- ⇒ Cold current
- ⇒ Warm current

°C 30 25 20 15 10 5 0

Climate graphs (top row): AMSTERDAM (Precipitation 727mm), ATHENS (Precipitation 402mm), BERLIN (Precipitation 603mm), BERN (Precipitation 986mm), BUCHAREST (Precipitation 592mm), BUDAPEST (Precipitation 614mm), COPENHAGEN (Precipitation 603mm), GLASGOW (Precipitation 1109mm), HELSINKI (Precipitation 688mm)

ANNUAL PRECIPITATION

Tromsø 1019, Murmansk 386, Reykjavik 779, Arkhangelsk 539, Perm 570, Oslo 730, Helsinki 688, St Petersburg 559, Glasgow 1109, Shannon 929, Moscow 624, Copenhagen 603, London 593, Amsterdam 727, Berlin 581, Minsk 606, Brussels 855, Frankfurt 676, Brest 1129, Paris 619, Lyons 813, Bern 986, Budapest 614, Odessa 389, La Coruña 900, Bordeaux 813, Venice 770, Belgrade 700, Bucharest 592, Marseilles 546, Sofia 661, Lisbon 708, Madrid 444, Rome 653, Istanbul 667, Palma 451, Tirana 1353, Cagliari, Athens 402, Valletta 519

Driest recorded year in Europe Astrakhan 160 mm

Wettest recorded year in Europe Crkvice 4850 mm

- 667 Average annual precipitation in millimetres

0   500   2000   mm
250   1000   3000

BIOMES

Arctic Circle, ARCTIC OCEAN, ATLANTIC OCEAN, Scandinavia, Ural Mountains, North limit of oak, Baltic Sea, North European Plain, North Sea, Limits of beech, Alps, Caucasus, Caspian Sea, Black Sea, North limit of olive, Mediterranean Sea

- Coniferous forest
- Evergreen trees and shrubs
- Broad-leaved forest and meadow
- Grassland
- Steppe, moorland and semi-desert
- Desert
- Alpine and tundra

Climate graphs (bottom row): LONDON (Precipitation 593mm), MADRID (Precipitation 444mm), MOSCOW (Precipitation 624mm), OSLO (Precipitation 730mm), PARIS (Precipitation 619mm), REYKJAVIK (Precipitation 779mm), ROME (Precipitation 653mm), TROMSO (Precipitation 1019mm), VALLETTA (Precipitation 519mm)

Each graph: maximum / Average monthly temperature / minimum / Average annual precipitation / Average monthly precipitation / Months of the year

Projection: Bonne

COPYRIGHT PHILIP'S

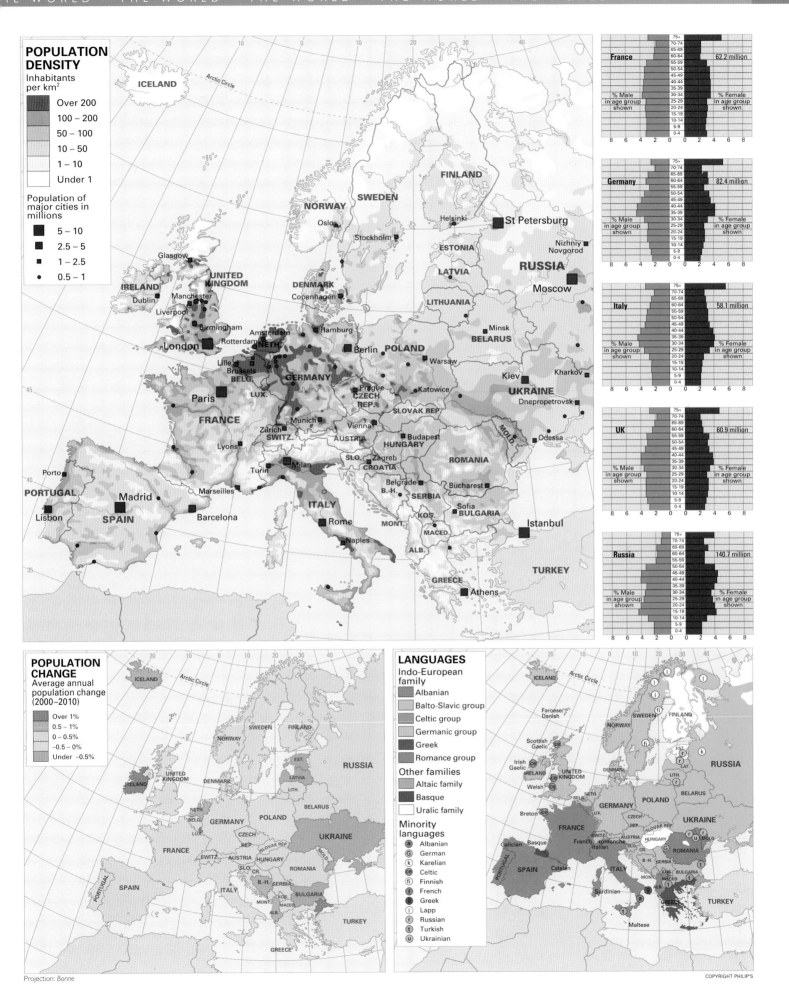

POPULATION DENSITY
Inhabitants per km²
- Over 200
- 100 – 200
- 50 – 100
- 10 – 50
- 1 – 10
- Under 1

Population of major cities in millions
- 5 – 10
- 2.5 – 5
- 1 – 2.5
- 0.5 – 1

POPULATION CHANGE
Average annual population change (2000–2010)
- Over 1%
- 0.5 – 1%
- 0 – 0.5%
- −0.5 – 0%
- Under −0.5%

LANGUAGES
Indo-European family
- Albanian
- Balto-Slavic group
- Celtic group
- Germanic group
- Greek
- Romance group

Other families
- Altaic family
- Basque
- Uralic family

Minority languages
- (a) Albanian
- (G) German
- (k) Karelian
- (ce) Celtic
- (fi) Finnish
- (f) French
- (g) Greek
- (l) Lapp
- (r) Russian
- (t) Turkish
- (u) Ukrainian

Age-sex pyramids:
- France 62.2 million
- Germany 82.4 million
- Italy 58.1 million
- UK 60.9 million
- Russia 140.7 million

Projection: Bonne

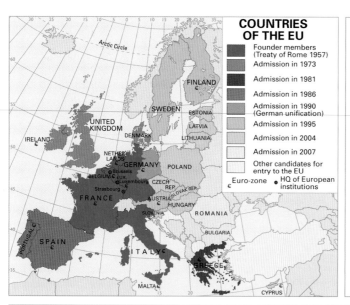

COUNTRIES OF THE EU

- Founder members (Treaty of Rome 1957)
- Admission in 1973
- Admission in 1981
- Admission in 1986
- Admission in 1990 (German unification)
- Admission in 1995
- Admission in 2004
- Admission in 2007
- Other candidates for entry to the EU
- Euro-zone
- ● HQ of European institutions

EU COUNTRY COMPARISONS	Population (thousands)	Annual Income (US$ per capita)
Germany	82,370	34,400
France	62,200	33,800
United Kingdom	60,944	35,300
Italy	58,145	31,000
Spain	40,491	33,700
Poland	38,501	16,200
Romania	22,247	11,100
Netherlands	16,645	38,600
Greece	10,723	30,500
Portugal	10,677	21,800
Belgium	10,404	36,500
Czech Republic	10,221	24,400
Hungary	9,931	19,500
Sweden	9,045	36,900
Austria	8,206	39,000
Bulgaria	7,263	11,800
Denmark	5,485	37,400
Slovakia	5,455	19,800
Finland	5,245	35,500
Ireland	4,156	55,600
Lithuania	3,565	16,700
Latvia	2,245	17,700
Slovenia	2,008	27,300
Estonia	1,308	21,800
Cyprus	793	24,600
Luxembourg	486	80,800
Malta	404	23,200
Total EU 2008 (27 countries)	**491,021**	**30,181**

REGIONS OF THE EU

Austria (States) — A
1. Niederösterreich
2. Oberösterreich
3. Burgenland
4. Kärnten
5. Salzburg
6. Steiermark
7. Tirol
8. Wien
9. Vorarlberg

Belgium (Regions) — B
1. Bruxelles
2. Vlaanderen
3. Wallonie

Bulgaria (Regions) — BU
1. Severen tsentralen
2. Severoiztochen
3. Severozapaden
4. Yugoiztochrn
5. Yugozapaden
6. Yuzhen tsentralen

Cyprus (member state with no corresponding division) — CY

Czech Republic (Kraj) — CZ
1. Jihovychod
2. Jihozapad
3. Moravskoslezsko
4. Praha
5. Severovychod
6. Severozapad
7. Stredni Cechy
8. Stredni Morava

Denmark (member state with no corresponding division) — DK

Estonia (member state with no corresponding division) — EE

Finland (Provinces) — FIN
1. Åland
2. Itä-Suomi
3. Väli-Suomi
4. Pohjois-Suomi
5. Uusimaa (Suuralue)
6. Etelä-Suomi

France (Regions) — F
1. Alsace
2. Aquitaine
3. Auvergne
4. Bourgogne
5. Bretagne
6. Centre
7. Champagne-Ardenne
8. Corse
9. Franche-Comté
10. Ile-de-France
11. Languedoc-Roussillon
12. Limousin
13. Loire (Pays de la)
14. Lorraine
15. Midi-Pyrénées
16. Nord-Pas-de-Calais
17. Normandie (Basse-)
18. Normandie (Haute-)
19. Picardie
20. Poitou-Charentes
21. Provence-Alpes-Côte d'Azur
22. Rhône-Alpes

Germany (Länder) — D
1. Baden-Württemberg
2. Niedersachsen
3. Bayern
4. Berlin
5. Brandenburg
6. Bremen
7. Hamburg
8. Hessen
9. Mecklenburg-Vorpommern
10. Nordrhein-Westfalen
11. Rheinland-Pfalz
12. Saarland
13. Sachsen
14. Sachsen-Anhalt
15. Schleswig-Holstein
16. Thüringen

Greece (Regions) — EL
1. Anatoliki Makedonia kai Thraki
2. Kriti
3. Voreio Aigaio
4. Notio Aigaio
5. Epiros
6. Attiki
7. Sterea Ellas
8. Dytiki Ellas
9. Ionioi Nisoi
10. Dytiki Makedonia
11. Kentriki Makedonia
12. Peloponnese
13. Thessaly

Hungary (Megyék) — HU
1. Del-Alfold
2. Del-Dunantul
3. Eszak-Alfold
4. Eszak-Magyarorszag
5. Kozep-Dunantul
6. Kozep-Magyarorszag
7. Nyugat-Dunantul

Ireland (Provinces) — IRL
1. Border, Midlands & Western
2. Southern & Eastern

Italy (Regions) — I
1. Abruzzo
2. Basilicata
3. Calàbria
4. Campánia
5. Emilia-Romagna
6. Friuli-Venézia Giulia
7. Lazio
8. Liguria
9. Lombardia
10. Marche
11. Molise
12. Umbria
13. Piemonte
14. Puglia
15. Sardegna
16. Sicília
17. Toscana
18. Trentino-Alto Adige
19. Valle d'Aosta
20. Véneto

Latvia (member state with no corresponding division) — L

Lithuania (member state with no corresponding division) — L

Luxembourg (member state with no corresponding division) — L

Malta (member state with no corresponding division) — MT

Netherlands (Regions) — NL
1. Noord-Nederland
2. Oost-Nederland
3. West-Nederland
4. Zuid-Nederland

Poland (Voivodships) — PL
1. Dolnośląskie
2. Kujawsko-Pomorskie
3. Łódzkie
4. Lubelskie
5. Lubuskie
6. Małopolskie
7. Mazowieckie
8. Opolskie
9. Podkarpackie
10. Podlaskie
11. Pomorskie
12. Śląskie
13. Swietokrzyskie
14. Warmińsko-Mazurskie
15. Wielkopolskie
16. Zachodniopomorskie

Portugal (Autonomous regions) — P
1. Alentejo
2. Algarve
3. Centro
4. Lisboa-Vale do Tejo
5. Norte

Romania (Regions) — RO
1. Bucureşti
2. Centru
3. Nord-Est
4. Nord-Vest
5. Sud
6. Sud-Est
7. Sud-Vest
8. Vest

Slovak Republic (Kraj) — SK
1. Bratislavsky Kraj
2. Stredne Slovensko
3. Vychodne Slovensko
4. Zapadne Slovensko

Slovenia (member state with no corresponding division) — SI

Spain (Autonomous communities) — E
1. Andalucía
2. Aragon
3. Asturias
4. Islas Baleares
5. País Vasco
6. Islas Canarias
7. Cantabria
8. Castilla y Léon
9. Castilla-La Mancha
10. Cataluña
11. Extremadura
12. Galicia
13. Madrid
14. Murcia
15. Navarra
16. Rioja (La)
17. Valencia

Sweden (Regions) — S
1. Stockholm
2. Östra Mellansverige
3. Sydsverige
4. Västsverige
5. Norra Mellansverige
6. Mellersta Norrland
7. Övre Norrland
8. Småland med öarna

United Kingdom (Government Office Regions) — UK
1. North East
2. North West
3. Yorkshire & The Humber
4. East Midlands
5. West Midlands
6. Eastern
7. London
8. South East
9. South West
10. Wales
11. Scotland
12. Northern Ireland

Projection: Bonne

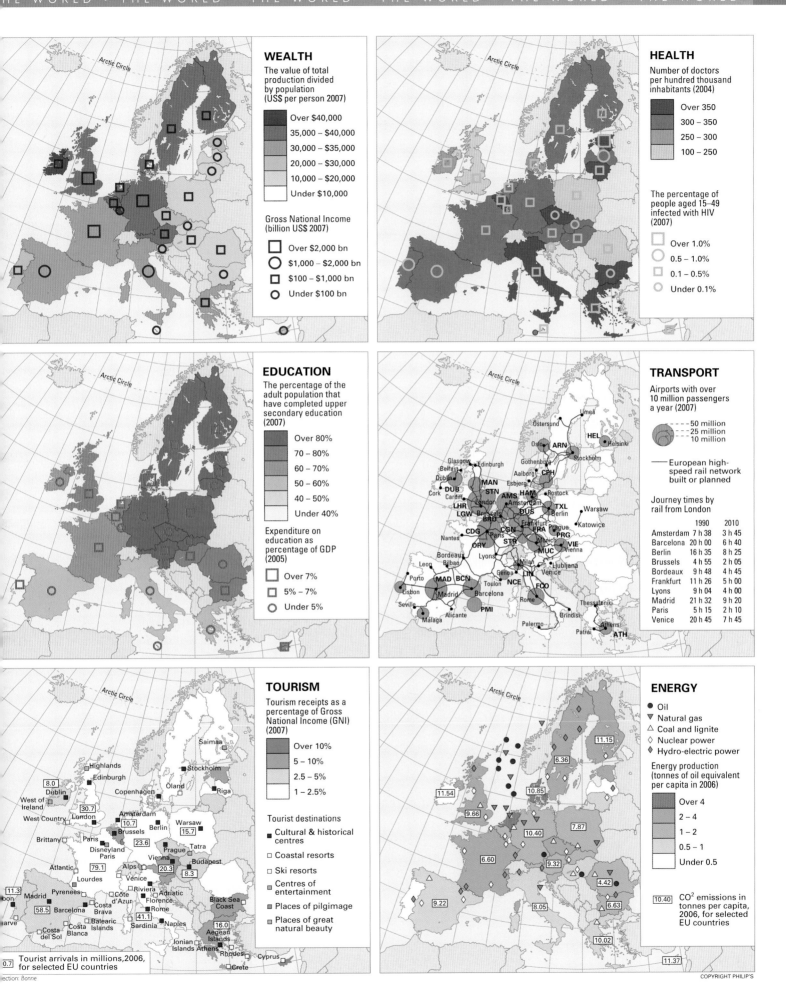

WEALTH

The value of total production divided by population (US$ per person 2007)

- Over $40,000
- 35,000 – $40,000
- 30,000 – $35,000
- 20,000 – $30,000
- 10,000 – $20,000
- Under $10,000

Gross National Income (billion US$ 2007)

- Over $2,000 bn
- $1,000 – $2,000 bn
- $100 – $1,000 bn
- Under $100 bn

HEALTH

Number of doctors per hundred thousand inhabitants (2004)

- Over 350
- 300 – 350
- 250 – 300
- 100 – 250

The percentage of people aged 15–49 infected with HIV (2007)

- Over 1.0%
- 0.5 – 1.0%
- 0.1 – 0.5%
- Under 0.1%

EDUCATION

The percentage of the adult population that have completed upper secondary education (2007)

- Over 80%
- 70 – 80%
- 60 – 70%
- 50 – 60%
- 40 – 50%
- Under 40%

Expenditure on education as percentage of GDP (2005)

- Over 7%
- 5% – 7%
- Under 5%

TRANSPORT

Airports with over 10 million passengers a year (2007)

- 50 million
- 25 million
- 10 million

European high-speed rail network built or planned

Journey times by rail from London

	1990	2010
Amsterdam	7 h 38	3 h 45
Barcelona	20 h 00	6 h 40
Berlin	16 h 35	8 h 25
Brussels	4 h 55	2 h 05
Bordeaux	9 h 48	4 h 45
Frankfurt	11 h 26	5 h 00
Lyons	9 h 04	4 h 00
Madrid	21 h 32	9 h 20
Paris	5 h 15	2 h 10
Venice	20 h 45	7 h 45

TOURISM

Tourism receipts as a percentage of Gross National Income (GNI) (2007)

- Over 10%
- 5 – 10%
- 2.5 – 5%
- 1 – 2.5%

Tourist destinations

- Cultural & historical centres
- Coastal resorts
- Ski resorts
- Centres of entertainment
- Places of pilgimage
- Places of great natural beauty

Tourist arrivals in millions, 2006, for selected EU countries

ENERGY

- Oil
- Natural gas
- Coal and lignite
- Nuclear power
- Hydro-electric power

Energy production (tonnes of oil equivalent per capita in 2006)

- Over 4
- 2 – 4
- 1 – 2
- 0.5 – 1
- Under 0.5

10.40 CO_2 emissions in tonnes per capita, 2006, for selected EU countries

ection: Bonne

ICELAND
on same scale

1:10 000 000

Projection: Conical with two standard parallels

COPYRIGHT PHILIP'S

Projection: Conical with two standard parallels

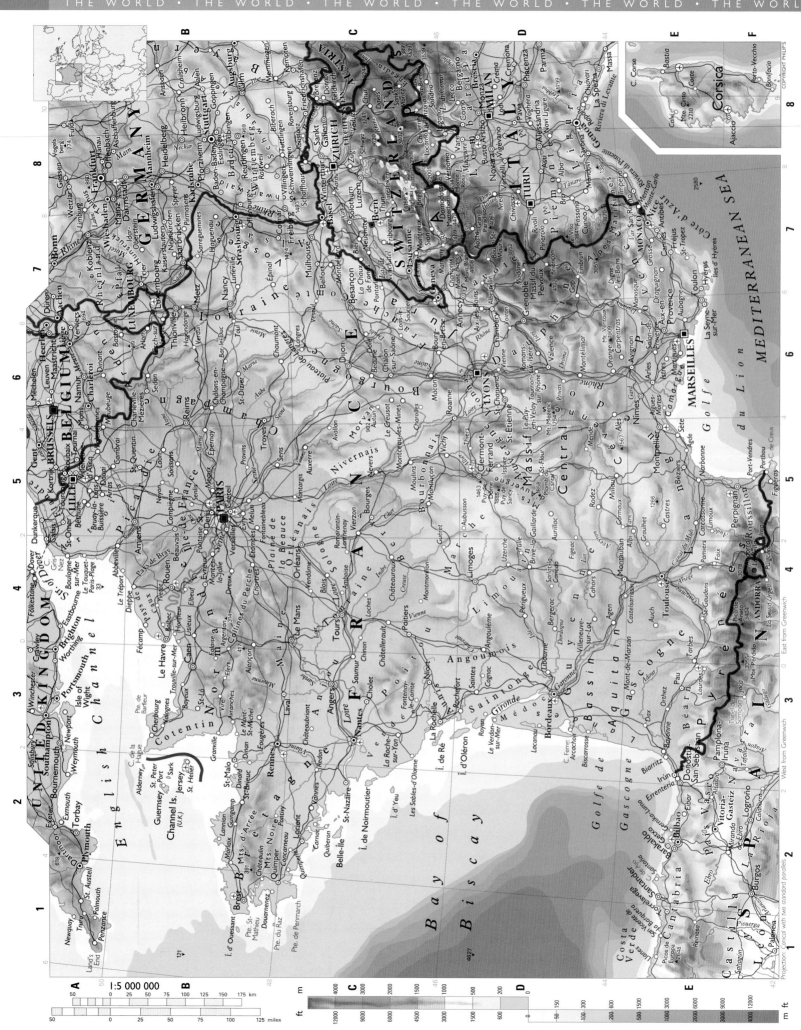

1:5 000 000

Projection: Conical with two standard parallels

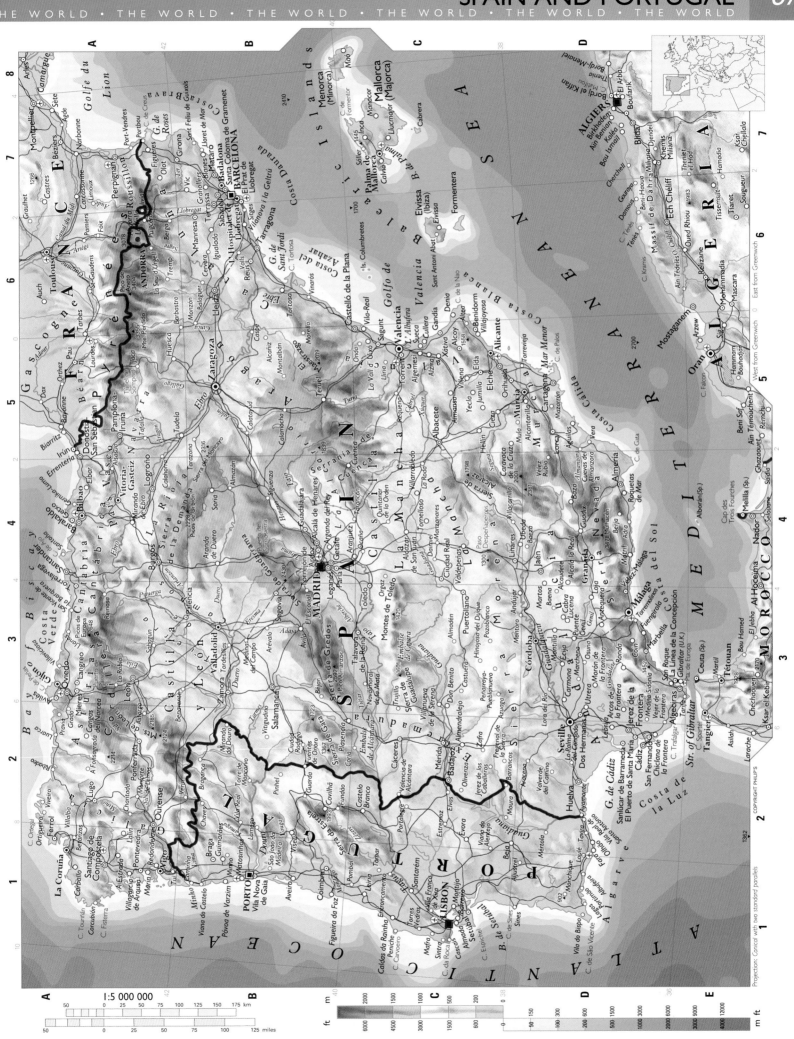

Projection: Conical with two standard parallels

1:5 000 000

COPYRIGHT PHILIP'S

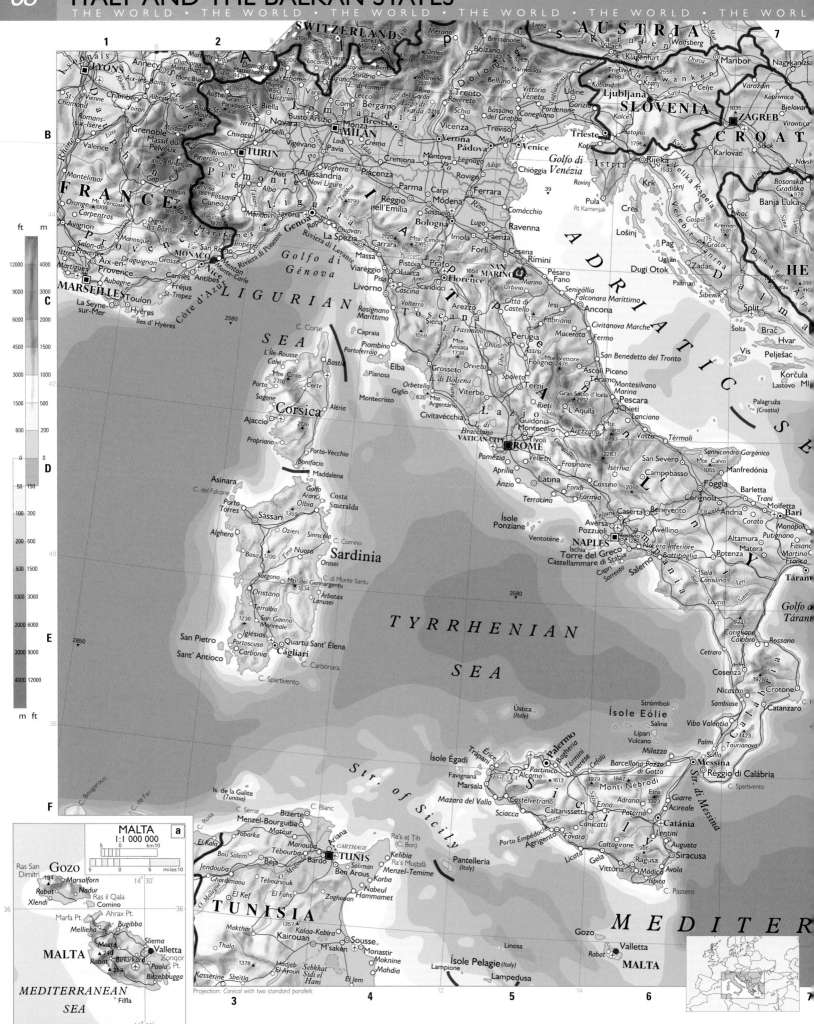

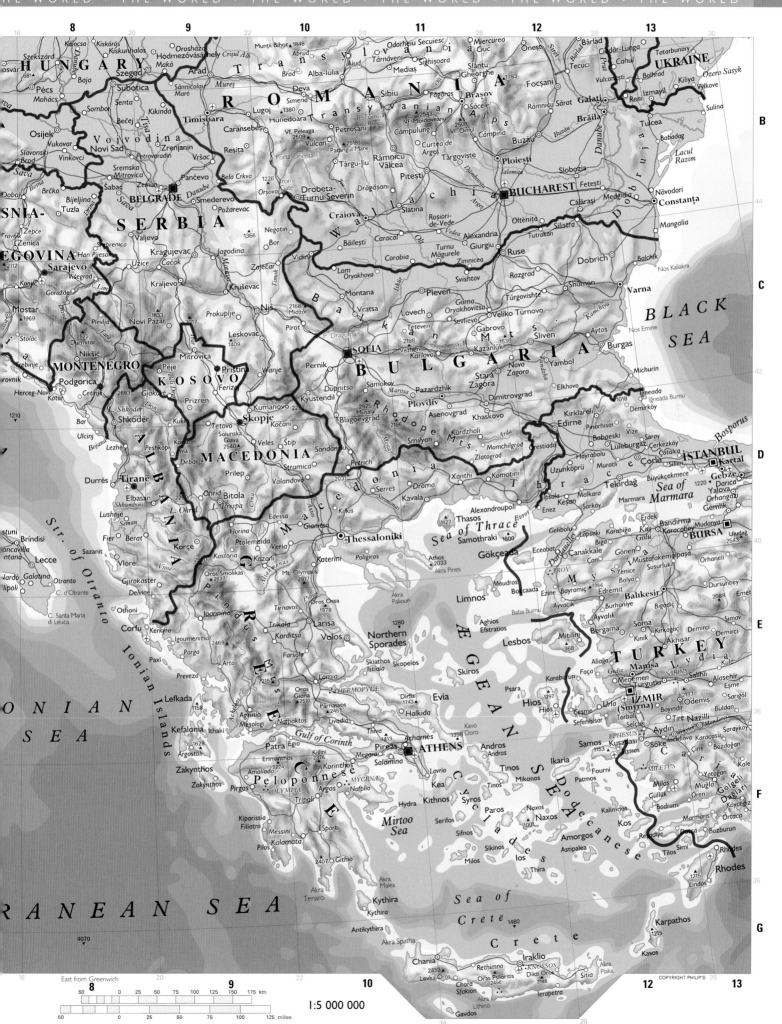

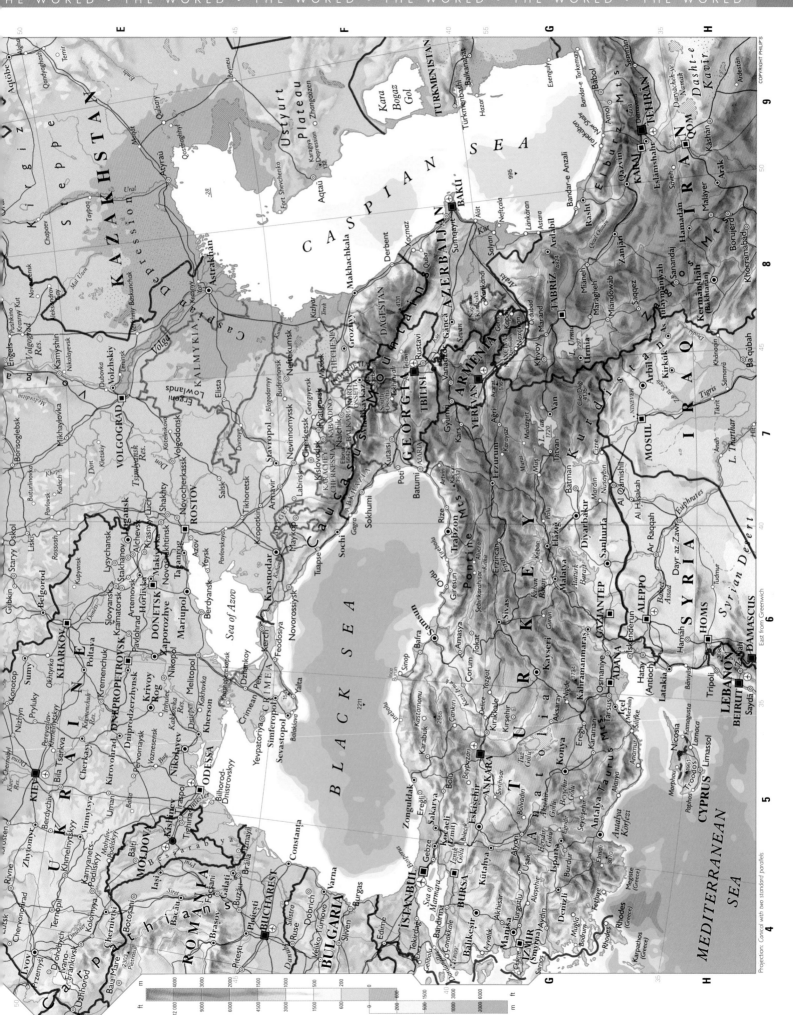

1:50 000 000

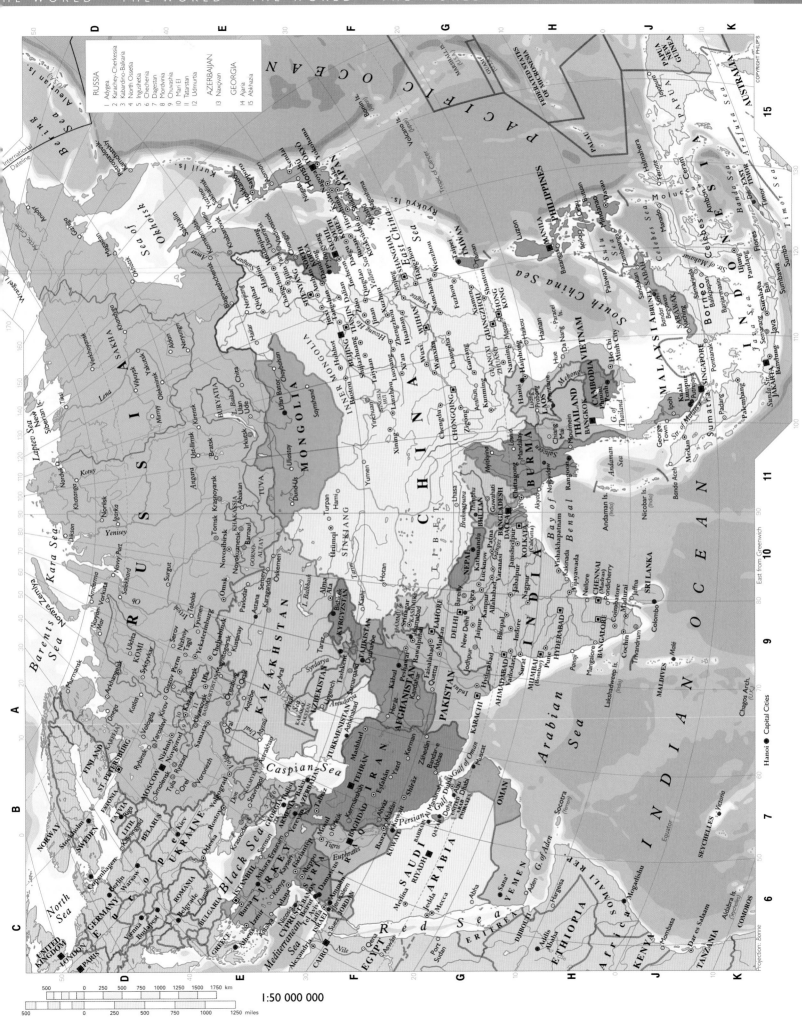

RUSSIA
1 Adygea
2 Karachey–Cherkessia
3 Kabardino–Balkana
4 North Ossetia
5 Ingushetia
6 Chechenia
7 Dagestan
8 Mordvinia
9 Chuvashia
10 Mari El
11 Tatarstan
12 Udmurtia

AZERBAIJAN
13 Naxçıvan

GEORGIA
14 Ajaria
15 Abkhazia

1:50 000 000

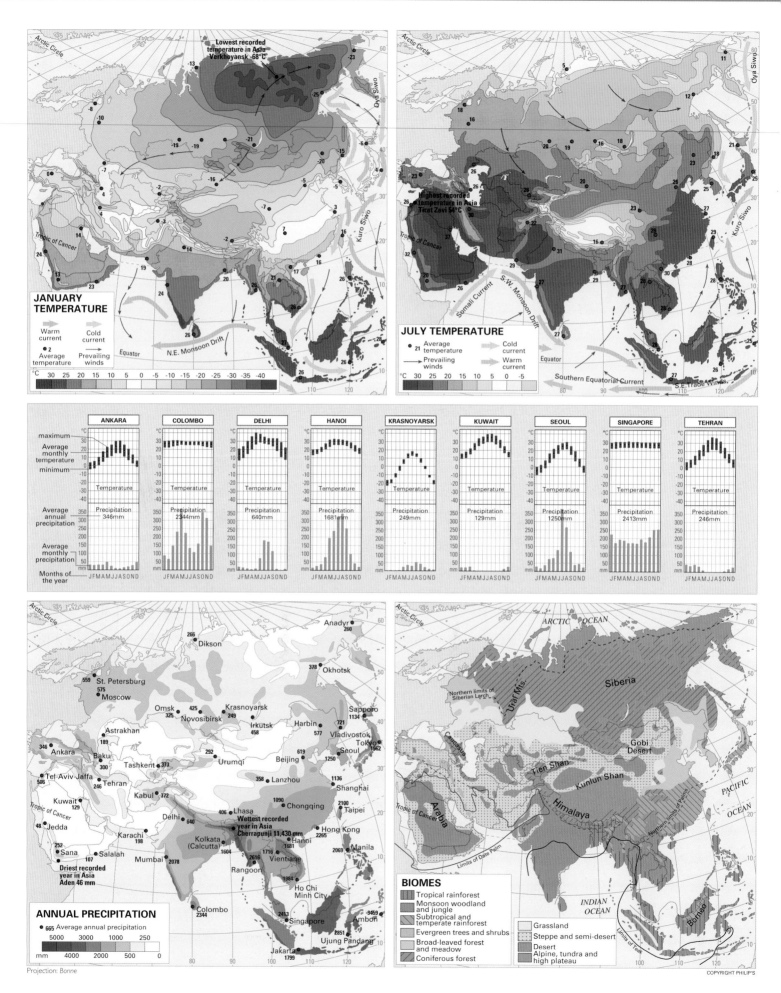

JANUARY TEMPERATURE

Lowest recorded temperature in Asia Verkhoyansk -68°C

Warm current
Cold current
Average temperature
Prevailing winds

°C 30 25 20 15 10 5 0 -5 -10 -15 -20 -25 -30 -35 -40

N.E. Monsoon Drift
Equator
Tropic of Cancer
Arctic Circle
Oya Siwo
Kuro Siwo

JULY TEMPERATURE

Highest recorded temperature in Asia Tirat Zevi 54°C

Average temperature
Cold current
Prevailing winds
Warm current

°C 30 25 20 15 10 5 0 -5

Somali Current
S.W. Monsoon Drift
Southern Equatorial Current
S.E. Trade Winds
Tropic of Cancer
Equator
Arctic Circle
Oya Siwo
Kuro Siwo

Climate graphs (maximum / Average monthly temperature / minimum / Average annual precipitation / Average monthly precipitation / Months of the year JFMAMJJASOND):

- **ANKARA** — Temperature; Precipitation 346mm
- **COLOMBO** — Temperature; Precipitation 2344mm
- **DELHI** — Temperature; Precipitation 640mm
- **HANOI** — Temperature; Precipitation 1681mm
- **KRASNOYARSK** — Temperature; Precipitation 249mm
- **KUWAIT** — Temperature; Precipitation 129mm
- **SEOUL** — Temperature; Precipitation 1250mm
- **SINGAPORE** — Temperature; Precipitation 2413mm
- **TEHRAN** — Temperature; Precipitation 246mm

ANNUAL PRECIPITATION

Dikson 266
Anadyr 260
Okhotsk 378
St. Petersburg 559
Moscow 575
Omsk 425
Novosibirsk 325
Krasnoyarsk 249
Irkutsk 458
Sapporo 1134
Harbin 577
Vladivostok 619
Tokyo 1562
Seoul 1250
Astrakhan 189
Ankara 346
Baku
Tashkent 300
373
Urumqi 292
Beijing 619
Shanghai 1136
Tel-Aviv-Jaffa 506
Tehran 246
Kabul 372
Lanzhou 358
Lhasa 406
Chongqing 1090
Taipei 2100
Kuwait 129
Delhi 640
Wettest recorded year in Asia Cherrapunji 11,430 mm
Hong Kong 2265
Jedda 48
Karachi 198
Kolkata (Calcutta) 1604
Hanoi 1681
Manila 2069
Sana 252
Salalah 107
Mumbai 2078
Rangoon 2616
Vientiane 1716
Driest recorded year in Asia Aden 46 mm
Ho Chi Minh City 1984
Colombo 2344
Singapore 2413
Ambon 3459
Ujung Pandang 2851
Jakarta 1799

665 Average annual precipitation

5000 3000 1000 250
mm 4000 2000 500 0

Projection: Bonne

BIOMES

ARCTIC OCEAN
Northern limits of Siberian Larch
Ural Mts.
Siberia
Caucasus
Tien Shan
Gobi Desert
Kunlun Shan
Himalaya
Arabia
Northern limits of Palms
Limits of Date Palm
Limits of Teak
Tropic of Cancer
PACIFIC OCEAN
INDIAN OCEAN
Borneo

Tropical rainforest
Monsoon woodland and jungle
Subtropical and temperate rainforest
Evergreen trees and shrubs
Broad-leaved forest and meadow
Coniferous forest
Grassland
Steppe and semi-desert
Desert
Alpine, tundra and high plateau

COPYRIGHT PHILIP'S

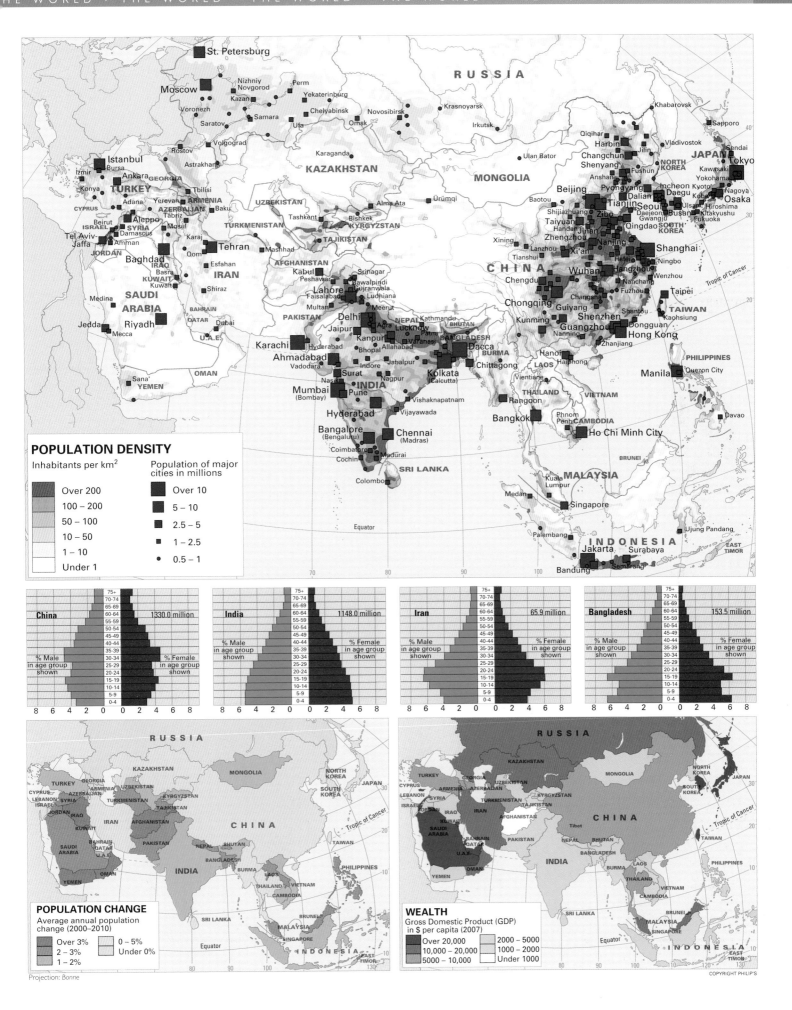

POPULATION DENSITY

Inhabitants per km²

- Over 200
- 100 – 200
- 50 – 100
- 10 – 50
- 1 – 10
- Under 1

Population of major cities in millions

- Over 10
- 5 – 10
- 2.5 – 5
- 1 – 2.5
- 0.5 – 1

China — 1330.0 million

India — 1148.0 million

Iran — 65.9 million

Bangladesh — 153.5 million

POPULATION CHANGE
Average annual population change (2000–2010)

- Over 3%
- 2 – 3%
- 1 – 2%
- 0 – 5%
- Under 0%

WEALTH
Gross Domestic Product (GDP) in $ per capita (2007)

- Over 20,000
- 10,000 – 20,000
- 5000 – 10,000
- 2000 – 5000
- 1000 – 2000
- Under 1000

Projection: Bonne

COPYRIGHT PHILIP'S

RUSSIA
1 Adygea
2 Karachey-Cherkessia
3 Kabardino-Balkaria
4 North Ossetia
5 Ingushetia
6 Chechenia
7 Dagestan
8 Mordvinia
9 Chuvashia
10 Mari El
11 Tatarstan
12 Udmurtia
13 Khakassia

AZERBAIJAN
14 Naxçivan

GEORGIA   UKRAINE
15 Ajaria   17 Crimea
16 Abkhazia

Projection: Conical Orthomorphic with two standard parallels

East from Greenwich

OCEAN

Severnaya Zemlya

Ostrov Komsomolets

Ostrov Oktyabrskoy Revolyutsii

965

Ostrov Bolshevik

Vilkitski Strait   C. Chelyuskin

Byrranga Ra.

Taimyr

Peninsula   Nordvik

1146

621

L. Taimyr

Laptev Sea

New Siberian Islands

Ostrova Delonga

3800

Ostrov Faddeyevskiy

Ostrov Novaya Sibir

Lyakhov Islands   Ostrov Kotelny

Dmitri Laptev Str.

East Siberian Sea

Wrangel I.

Chukchi Sea

C. Dezhneva (East C.)

Uelen

533

1194

Ust Chaun   Pevek

Chukot Range

1843   1853

Ambarchik   Chersky

Nizhne Kolymsk

Bilibino

Egvekinot

Providenya

1046

Gulf of Anadyr

Beringovskiy

St. Lawrence I. (USA)

Bering Sea

Norilsk   Talnakh

1591

Gory Putorana

1678

1341

Kayak

Volochanka   Kheta

Khatanga

Novorybnoye

Khatanga

Pyasina

Ust Olenek

Tit-Ary   Tiksi

Saskylakh

Olenek   Anabar

Bulun

Zhilinda

Ust Kuyga

Kazachye

Chokurdakh

Indigirka

Srednekolymsk

Kolyma

Zyryanka

Khonuu

Oloy

Bolshoy

1792

Omolon

Paren   Gizhiga

2453

Koryak Range

Ossora   Ostrov Karaginskiy

Tilichiki   Ostrov

Kavacha

Ust Kamchatsk

Klyuchi   Gora

4750

4649

Komandorskiye Ostrova

Nikolskoye   755

Kamchatka Peninsula

3621   3456

Petropavlovsk-Kamchatskiy

2359

Vilyuchinsk

Severnaya   2185

Deputatskiy

Yana

Verkhoyansk

2389   Batagay

Gora Chen   Ust-Nera

2547   3147

Teskan   Omsukchan

Orotukan

Susuman   Yagodnoye

Ust-Omchug

Magadan

Palatka

Ola

2559   Ust-Maya

Yessey

1071

Noginsk   Tura

Lower Tunguska

Yukta

Yerbogachen

599

Lensk

Vitim

R   U   S   S

Vilyuy   Vilyuysk   Verkhnevilyuysk

Nyurba   Sinsk

Mirnyy   Suntar

Olekminsk

S   A   K   H   A

Namtsy   Nizhniy

Yakutsk   Bestyakh

Pokrovsk

Amga   Amga

Tommot   Aldan

Aldan   2254

Neryungri   Nogornyy

2246

Chumikan

Nelkan   Ayan   Shantar Is.

Dzhugdzur Range   1906

Okha   Sakhalin

Noglik

Aleksandrovsk-Sakhalinskiy

1609   Gora Lopatina

Sea of Okhotsk

1780

Okhotsk

Ust Khayryuzovo

Tigil

Palana

Shelikhov Gulf

Sredinnyy Range

50

Oktyabrskiy   Severo-

Ozernovskiy

Ostrov Paramushir

Ostrov Onekotan

1816

Kuril Islands

Ostrov Simushir   1539

Ostrov Urup   1426

Ostrov Iturup   1589

Ostrov Kunashir

1319

Yartsevo   1104

Yeniseysk   Lesosibirsk

Kodinsk   Boguchany

Angara   Chuna

Achinsk   Kansk   Zelenogorsk   Ilanskiy

Krasnoyarsk   Krasnoyarsk Res.

Artemovsk

Sayan Mountains   Minusinsk   2922

Abakan   Sayanogorsk

Turan   Kyzyl

Toora-Khem

Av-Dovurak   UVA   Samagaltay

Kyzyl-Khem

Erzin

TUVA

Yeniseysk   Severo-Yeniseyskiy

962

Udachnyy

Aykhal

Chernyshevskiy

Yuktra

Kuyumba   Mutoray

Vanavara

Stony Tunguska

Kezhma

Ust-Ilimsk

Makarovo   Korshunovo

Zheleznogorsk-Ilimskiy

Tayshet   Ust-Kut

Magistralnyy

Nizhneudinsk   Tulun

Zima   Zalari

Cheremkhovo   Usolye Sibirskoye

Angarsk   Irkutsk

1509   Lena

Bratsk   Bratsk Res.

495

1840

Severobaykalsk

Taksimo

Karalon   Chara   2999   Olekma   Aldan

Neryungri   Stanovoy Range   Uda   2371

Tynda   Zeya Zeya Res.   Selemdzha

Skovorodino   Ushumun

Magdagachi   Narsk

Mogocha   1908

Chita   Shilka   Nerchinsk   Sretensk

Bukachacha   2840   Shilka

Amazar   Amur

Jagdachi   Shimanovsk

Gulian   Svobodnyy   Belogorsk   Zavitinsk   Progress

Blagoveshchensk   Heihe

Nenjiang   Bei'an   Komsomolsk-na-Amur   2078

Chegdomyn   Obluchye

Birobidzhan   Smidovich

Khabarovsk

Hegang   JIAMUSI

Dalnerechensk

Bikin

Lesozavodsk

Spassk Dalniy   Arsenev

Kavalerovo   Dalnegorsk   3659

Ussuriysk   Artem

Vladivostok   Nakhodka   Partizansk

Kraskino   Yanji

Sikhote Alin Ra.

Amgu   Terney

Amur

Nikolayevsk-na-Amur

Lazarev   Tatar Str.

Nelma   Sovetskaya Gavan

Nevelsk   Kholmsk   Yuzhno-Sakhalinsk

Gornozavodsk   Krilon

La Perouse Str.   Wakkanai   Rebun

Rumoi   Otaru   SAPPORO

Hokkaido   Hakodate

2290   Obihiro   Kushiro

Ostrov Tsuning   Ostrov Kunashir

Mombetsu

Abashiri   Nemuro

R   Baykal   BUR.   Ulan-Ude   Petrovsk-Zabaykalskiy   Khilok

Tayshet   Bayandai   Ulyukhan

Munku-Sardyk   3491   Slyudyanka   Kabansk

Hövsgöl Nuur   Hatgal

Mondy

Hangayn Nuruu

3905

617

Döröö Nuur

Uliastay   Tsetserleg

Altay   Bayanhongor   Arvayheer

4266

4885

Hami

Gaxun Nur

BAOTOU   HOHHOT   ZHANGJIAKOU

Dalandzadgad

Choyr

Mandalgovi   Buyant-Uhaa   Erenhot

Xilinhot   1949   Linxi

Gobi

Ulan Bator   Hentiyn Nuruu   Öndörhaan   Baruun-Urt

Choybalsan   Tamsagbulag

MONGOLIA   (Aerhtai Shan)   G   O   B   I

CHINA

Chengde

BEIJING   TANGSHAN

Yingkou   DALIAN

CHIFENG   CHINA

SHENYANG   ANSHAN

JINXI   FUSHUN

Dandong

NORTH KOREA

PYONGYANG   NAMPO   INCHEON   SEOUL   SOUTH KOREA

DAEJON   DAEGU   BUSAN   GWANGJU

Hamhüng   Wönsan

Kimch'aek   2744

Ch'öngjin

Songhua Hu

CHANGCHUN   JILIN   Vladivostok

Siping   Tonghua

FUYU   Manchuria   MUDANJIANG

QIQIHAR   DAQING   Yichun   HARBIN   JIXI

Baicheng   Suihua   Songhua Jiang

Zalantun   Fuyu

Yakeshi   Nenjiang

Hailar   Nen Jiang

Great Khingan Mts

Zabaykalsk   Yakeshi

Manzhouli   Hulun Nur

Borzya   2519

Aginskoye   Olovyannaya

Baley   Krasnokamensk

Sherlovaya Gora

Karymskoye   Shilka

Sea of Japan (East Sea)

Honshū   Niigata   Akita   Aomori   Hachinohe

Kanazawa   Toyama

JAPAN   KOBE   KYOTO   OSAKA

COPYRIGHT PHILIP'S

100 0 100 200 300 400 500 600 700 800 km

1:20 000 000

100 0 100 200 300 400 500 miles

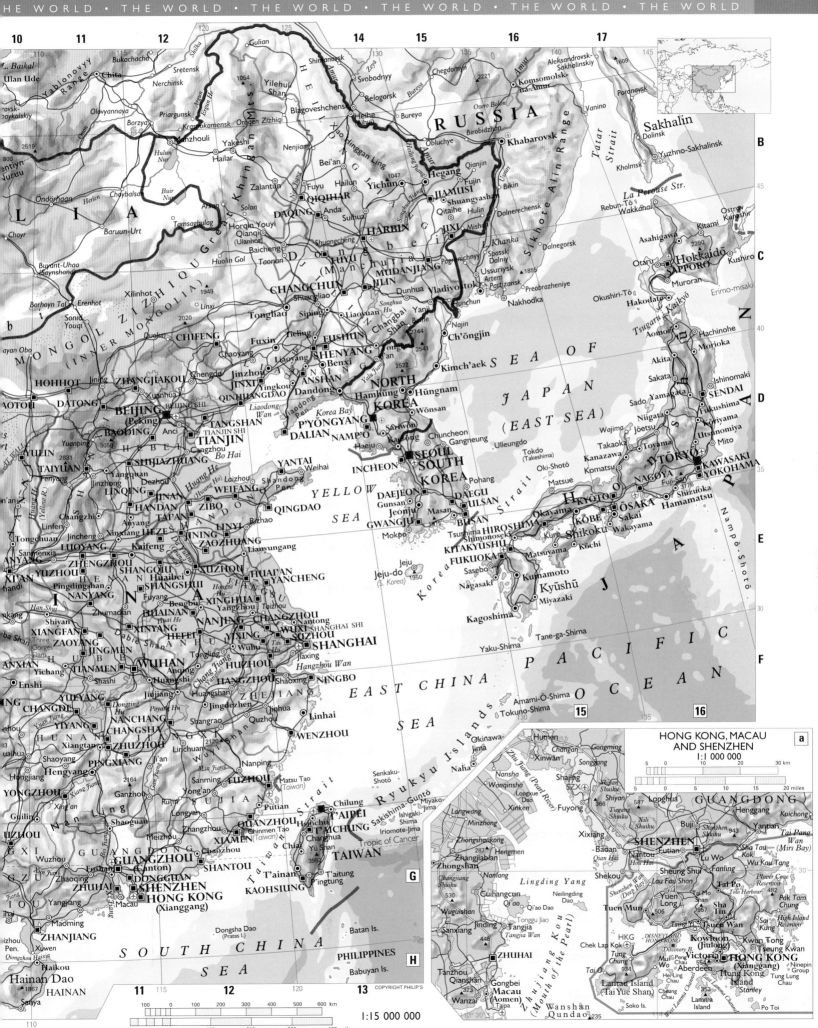

EMPLOYMENT IN INDUSTRY

Industrial population by province in millions

8 6 4 2 1 0.5

The percentage of the total workforce employed in industry (2003)

- Over 30%
- 20% – 30%
- 10% – 20%
- Under 10%

Provinces labelled: HEILONGJIANG, JILIN, SINKIANG, INNER MONGOLIA, LIAONING, BEIJING, GANSHU, NINGXIA HUI, HEBEI, TIANJIN, SHANDONG, QINGHAI, SHANXI, SHAANXI, HENAN, JIANGSU, TIBET, SICHUAN, CHONGQING, HUBEI, ANHUI, SHANGHAI, ZHEJIANG, HUNAN, JIANGXI, GUIZHOU, FUJIAN, YUNNAN, GUANGXI ZHUANGZU, GUANGDONG, MACAU, HONG KONG, HAINAN

CHINA'S SHARE OF WORLD MANUFACTURING
(for selected goods)

Textiles — China 24.3%, USA 19.2%, India 12.4%, Finland 3.5%
World total (2006): 23,300,00 tonnes

Paper — China 11.3%, Japan 9.0%, Germany 6.1%, Finland 4.2%, S. Korea 3.0%
World total (2006): 336,800,000 tonnes

Cement — China 43.7%, India 5.9%, USA 4.7%, Japan 3.5%, S. Korea 3.1%
World total (2006): 1,970,000,000 tonnes

Coal — China 39.5%, USA 16.2%, India 7.4%, Australia 6.2%, Russia 4.9%
World total (2006): 7,080,000,000 tonnes

Hydroelectricity — China 14.4%, Canada 11.7%, USA 8.6%, Russia 5.8%
World total (2006): 2,997 kWh

Aluminium — China 27.7%, Russia 11.0%, Canada 9.1%, Australia 5.7%
World total (2006): 33,700,00 tonnes

Steel — China 40.8%, Japan 11.2%, USA 9.5%, Russia 6.8%, S. Korea 4.7%
World total (2006): 1,037,000,000 tonnes

TV and Radios — China 49.7%, Turkey 9.9%, Malaysia 6.5%, Portugal 5.6%, USA 5.4%
World total (2006): 151,622 units

Sulphuric Acid — China 43.8%, Russia 11.4%, Japan 8.5%, India 7.9%, Brazil 7.9%
World total (2006): 760,900,000 tonnes

INDUSTRIAL DEVELOPMENT

Core regions
- Industrial regions
- ● Major centres for industry and services
- ●• Other industrial centres
- ○ Centres for iron and steel and chemicals
- ▨ Rapidly developing coastal regions
- ■ Special Economic Zones (SEZ)
- ▼ Special Administrative Regions (SAR) 'One country, two systems'

Peripheral regions
- Densely populated and industrialized peripheral region
- Peripheral region with traditional heavy industry
- Remote undeveloped region
- ← Direction of future growth
- — Important rail links

Direction of foreign investment
- ← Hong Kong ← Taiwan
- ← Japan ← South Korea

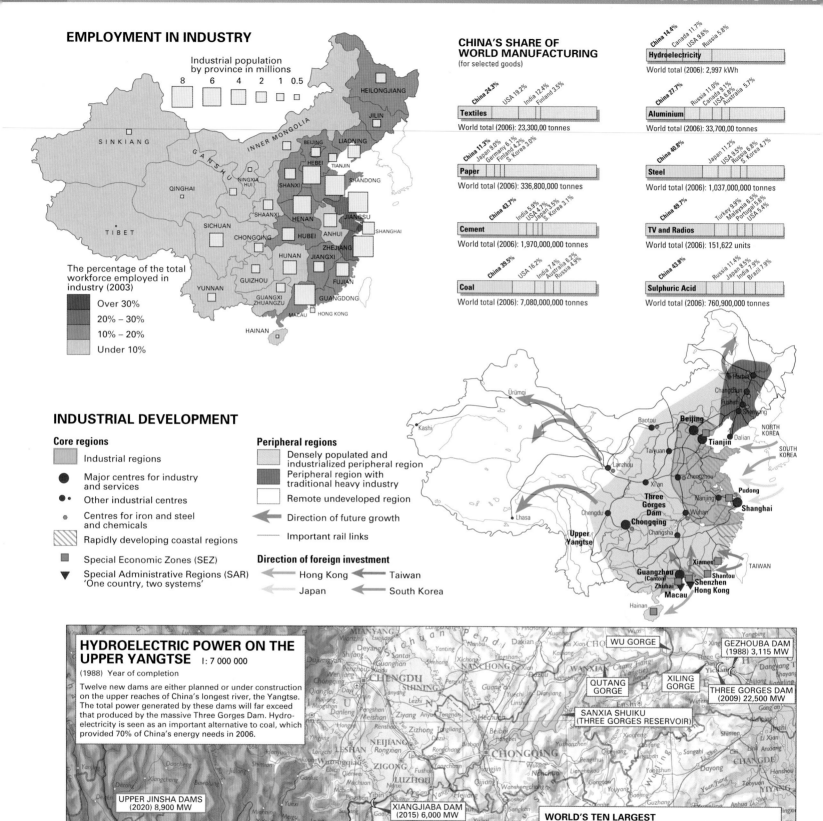

Map labels: Ürümqi, Kashi, Baotou, Beijing, Changchun, Fushun, Shenyang, NORTH KOREA, Tianjin, Dalian, SOUTH KOREA, Taiyuan, Lanzhou, Zhengzhou, Xian, Pudong, Three Gorges Dam, Nanjing, Shanghai, Chengdu, Wuhan, Chongqing, Changsha, Upper Yangtse, Lhasa, Xiamen, TAIWAN, Guangzhou (Canton), Shantou, Zhuhai, Shenzhen, Macau, Hong Kong, Hainan

HYDROELECTRIC POWER ON THE UPPER YANGTSE 1: 7 000 000

(1988) Year of completion

Twelve new dams are either planned or under construction on the upper reaches of China's longest river, the Yangtse. The total power generated by these dams will far exceed that produced by the massive Three Gorges Dam. Hydroelectricity is seen as an important alternative to coal, which provided 70% of China's energy needs in 2006.

Dam labels:
- WU GORGE
- GEZHOUBA DAM (1988) 3,115 MW
- QUTANG GORGE
- XILING GORGE
- THREE GORGES DAM (2009) 22,500 MW
- SANXIA SHUIKU (THREE GORGES RESERVOIR)
- UPPER JINSHA DAMS (2020) 8,900 MW
- LIYUAN DAM
- MIDDLE JINSHA DAMS (2018) 21,150 MW
- XIANGJIABA DAM (2015) 6,000 MW
- XILUODU DAM (2015) 12,600 MW
- LIANGJIAREN DAM
- AHAI DAM
- HUTIAOXIA DAM
- JINANQIAO DAM
- GUANYINGYAN DAM
- BAIHETAN DAM (2015) 14,000 MW
- LONGKAIKOU DAM
- LUDILA DAM
- WUDONGDE DAM (2015) 7,400 MW

WORLD'S TEN LARGEST HYDROELECTRIC POWER STATIONS
(1986) Year of completion

1. Three Gorges Dam, China (2009) 22,500 MW
2. Itaipu, Brazil/Paraguay (2003) 14,000 MW
3. Guri, Venezuela (1986) 10,200 MW
4. Tucuruí, Brazil (1984) 8,370 MW
5. Sayano Shushenskaya, Russia (1989) 6,400 MW
7. Grand Coulee, USA (1942) 6,809 MW
7. Krasnoyarskaya, Russia (1972) 6,000 MW
8. Robert-Bourassa, Canada (1981) 5,616 MW
9. Churchill Falls, Canada (1971) 5,429 MW
10. Longtan Dam, China (2009) 6,300 MW

COPYRIGHT PHILIP'S

VOLCANOES AND EARTHQUAKES

○ Epicentres of earthquakes greater than 7 on the Richter Scale (since AD 1600)

Plate boundary

▲ Destructive plate boundary (plates colliding)

→ Direction of movement

Volcanic regions

▲ Active volcanoes

Coasts vulnerable to tsunamis

NORTH AMERICAN PLATE

EURASIAN PLATE

PACIFIC PLATE

PHILIPPINE PLATE

Rausu-Dake
Me-Akan-Dake
Tokachi-Dake
Iwate-San
Chōkai-San
Zao-San
Bandai-San
Nantai-San
Asama-Yama
Fuji-San
Haku-San
Mihara-Yama
Aso-San
Unzen-Dake
Sakurajima

Hokkaidō

Wakkanai
Rebun-Tō
Rishiri-Tō
Teshio
Embetsu
Haboro
Shibetsu
Rumoi
Takikawa
Nayoro
Kitami
Asahigawa
Daisetsu-Zan 2290
Tokachi-Dake 2077
Esashi
Otoineppu
Ōmu
Mombetsu
Yūbetsu
Engaru
Abashiri-Wan
Abashiri
Rausu-Dake 1661
Shari
Shibecha
Akkeshi
Nemuro
Nakashibetsu
Kunashir
Kushiro
Honbetsu
Hiroo
Poroshiri-Dake 2052
Obihiro
Tomakomai
Muroran
Samani
Erimo-misaki
SAPPORO
Otaru
Ebetsu
Bibai
Iwamizawa
Atsuta
Iwanai
Suttsu
Setana
Yakumo
Okushiri-Tō
Esashi
Matsumae
Hakodate
Esan-Misaki
Shiriya-Zaki
Kamui-Misaki
Nikotu-Ko
Toya-Ko
Uchiura-Wan
Ishikari-Wan

Honshū

Ohata
Mutsu
Mutsu-Wan
Aomori
Kanagi
Goshogawara
Hirosaki
Odate
Towada
Hakkoda-San 1585
Hachinohe
Kuji
Iwaizumi
Noshiro
Oga
Oga-Hantō
Akita
Iwate-San 2041
Morioka
Miyako
Omagari 1914
Hanamaki
Kamaishi
Honjō
Chōkai-San 2230
Ichinoseki
Kesennuma
Sakata
Furukawa
Tsuruoka
Mogami 1980
Ishinomaki
Yamagata
SENDAI
Sendai-Wan
Niigata
Sado
Ryōtsu
Aikawa
Shibata
Fukushima
Higashiazuma-San 2024
Sōma
Haranomachi
Niitsu
Aizuwakamatsu
Kōriyama
Sanjo
Sukagawa
Iwaki
Nagaoka
Tōkamachi
Kitaibaraki
Hitachi
Takada
Tajima 2578
Tanakura
Suzu-Misaki
Suzu-Wan
Wajima
Nanao
Himi
Toyama-Wan
Toyama
Nagano
Maebashi
Kiryū
Utsunomiya
Mito
Takaoka
Asama-Yama 2542
Takasaki
Oyama
Tsuchiura
Kanazawa
Hodaka-Dake 3190
Matsumoto
Kumagaya
SAITAMA
Komatsu
Haku-San 2702
Takayama 3063
Ina
Kawagoe
Kawaguchi
Funabashi
Chiba
Fukui
Kōfu 3192
TOKYO
Kawasaki
Ichihara
Takefu
Gifu
Kiso-Gawa
Fuji-San 3776
Odawara
YOKOHAMA
Yokosuka
Tsuruga
Ōgaki
Ichinomiya
Shizuoka
Numazu
Itō
Tsuyama
Fukuchiyama
Ayabe
NAGOYA
Toyota
Okazaki
Toyohashi
Iwata
Hamamatsu
Matsusaka
Tateyama
Nojima-Zaki
Ō-Shima
Izu-Shotō
Nii-Jima
Miyake-Jima
Kōbe
OSAKA
KYŌTO
Ōtsu
Yokkaichi
Higashiōsaka
Amagasaki
Izumi-Sano
Ise-Wan
Daiō-Misaki
Wakayama 1915
Owase
Tanabe
Shingū
Kushimoto
Shio-no-Misaki
Irō-Zaki
Suruga-Wan
Miyake-Jima
Hachijō-Jima
Aoga-Shima

Shikoku

Matsue
Yonago
Tottori 1712
Toyoka
Izumo
Ōda
Hamada
Masuda
Maizuru
Wakasa-Wan
Kyō-ga-Saki
Biwa-Ko
HIROSHIMA
Fukuyama
Kure
Marugame
Takamatsu
Naruto
Awaji-Shima
Tokushima
Okayama
Himeji
Fuchū
Yamaguchi
Iwakuni
Ube
Hofu
Tokuyama
Shimonoseki
Hagi
Hiji
KITAKYŪSHŪ
Nōgata
Buzen
Imabari
Ikeda 1955
Anan
Mugi
Kōchi
Muroto
Muroto-Misaki
Tosa-Wan
Nakamura
Sukumo
Ashizuri-Zaki
Uwajima
Yawatahama
Matsuyama
Tanabe
Kii Channel
Inland Sea
Chūgoku-Sanchi

Kyūshū

FUKUOKA
Karatsu
Imari
Saga
Kurume
Ōmuta
Yatsushiro
Kumamoto 1787
Unzen-Dake 1360
Isahaya
Nagasaki
Sasebo
Gotō-Rettō
Fukue-Shima
Amakusa-Shotō
Ushibuka
Minamata
Miyazaki
Miyakonojō
Nobeoka
Hyūga
Saiki
Ōita
Beppu
Kanoya
Ibusuki
Kagoshima
Sakurajima 1118
Makurazaki
Koshikijima-Rettō
Sata-Misaki
Sendai
Kanoya
Iki
Tsushima (Japan)

SOUTH KOREA

Yeongdeok
Pohang
ULSAN
Ulleungdo (S. Korea)
Tokdo (Takeshima)
Korea Strait

SEA OF JAPAN (EAST SEA)

JAPAN

PACIFIC OCEAN

Oki-Shotō (Japan)

8412
9076

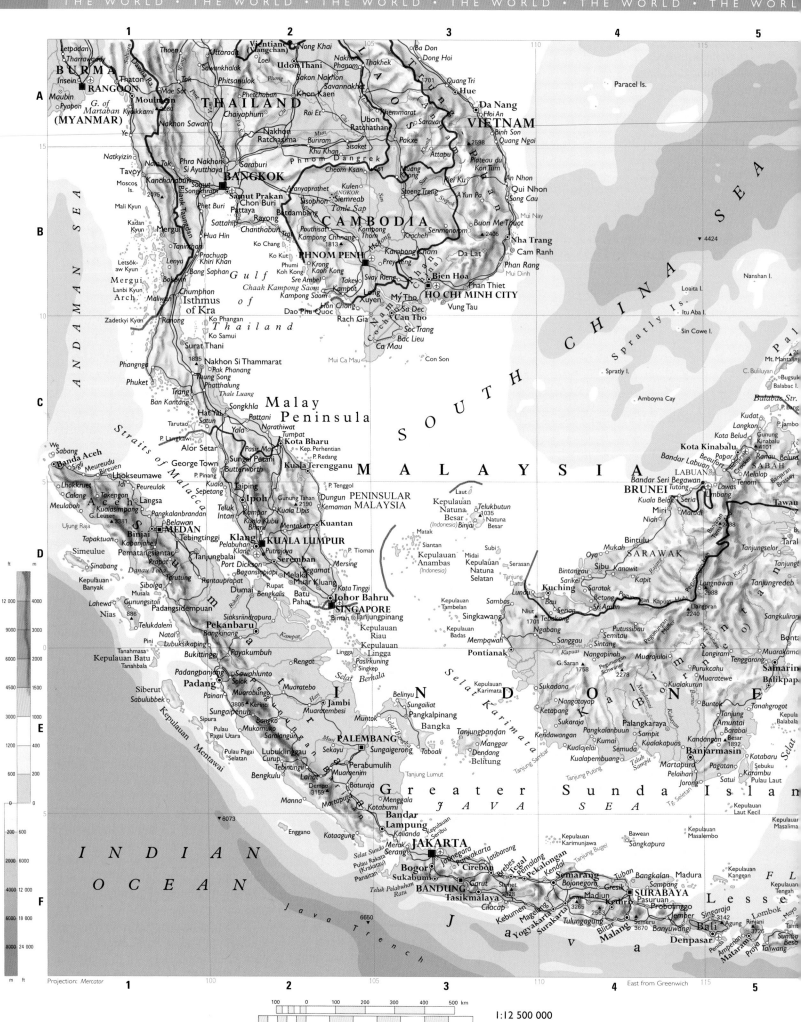

Projection: Mercator

1:12 500 000

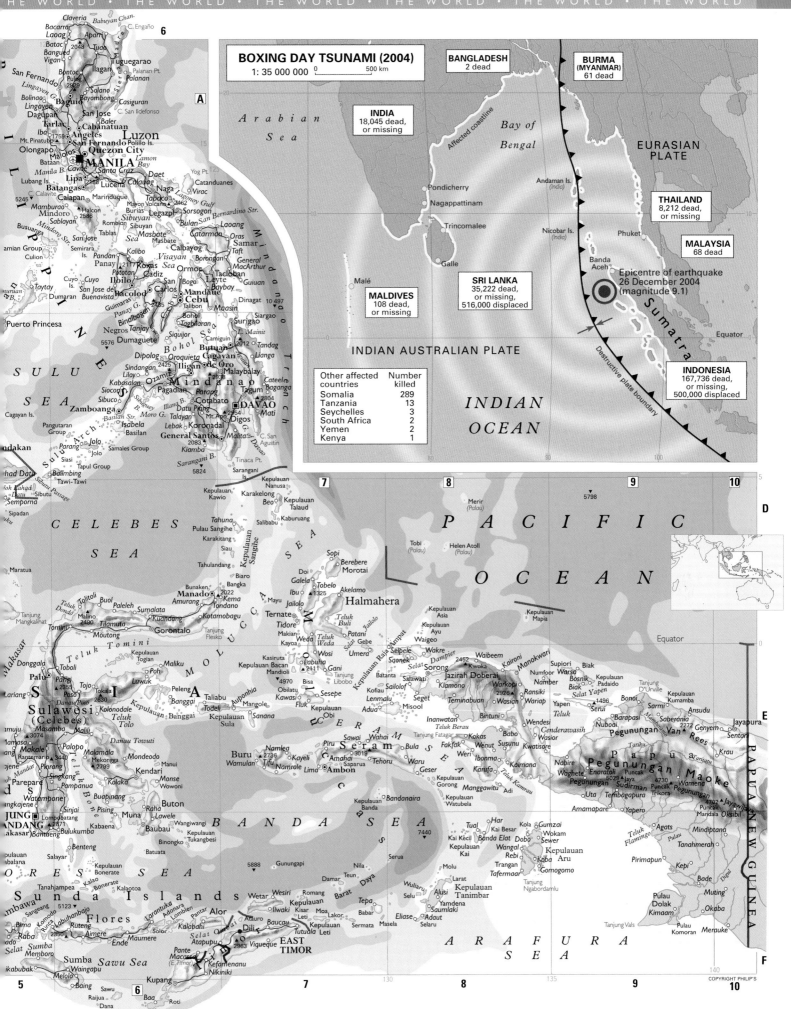

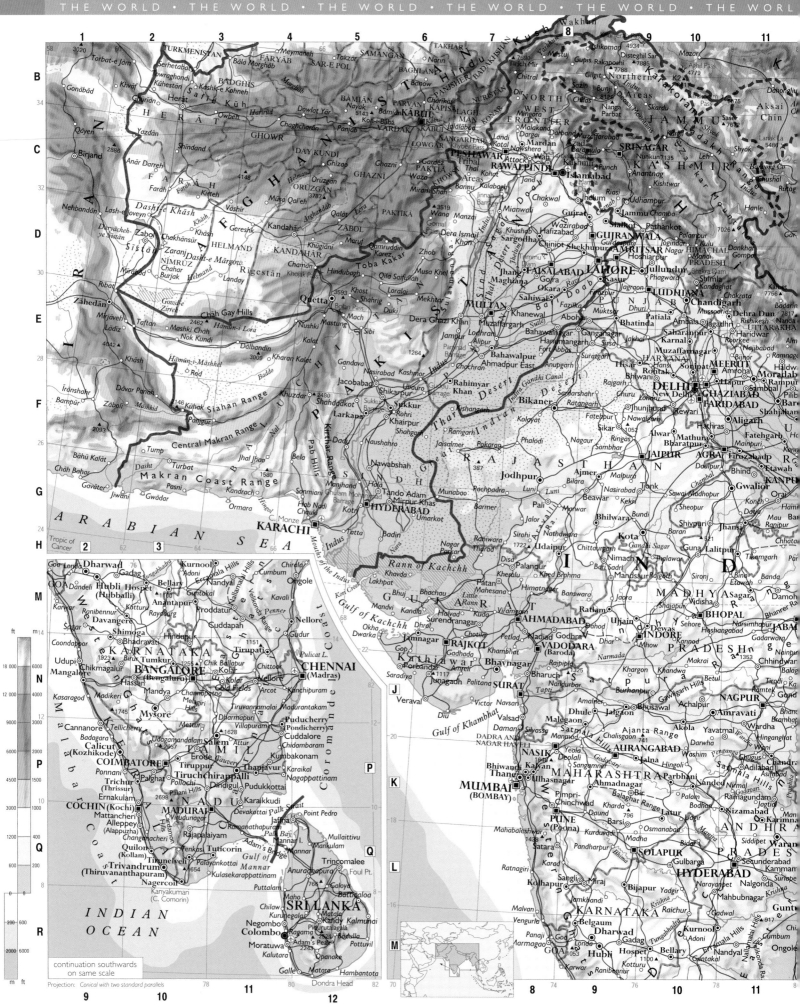

continuation southwards
on same scale

Projection: Conical with two standard parallels

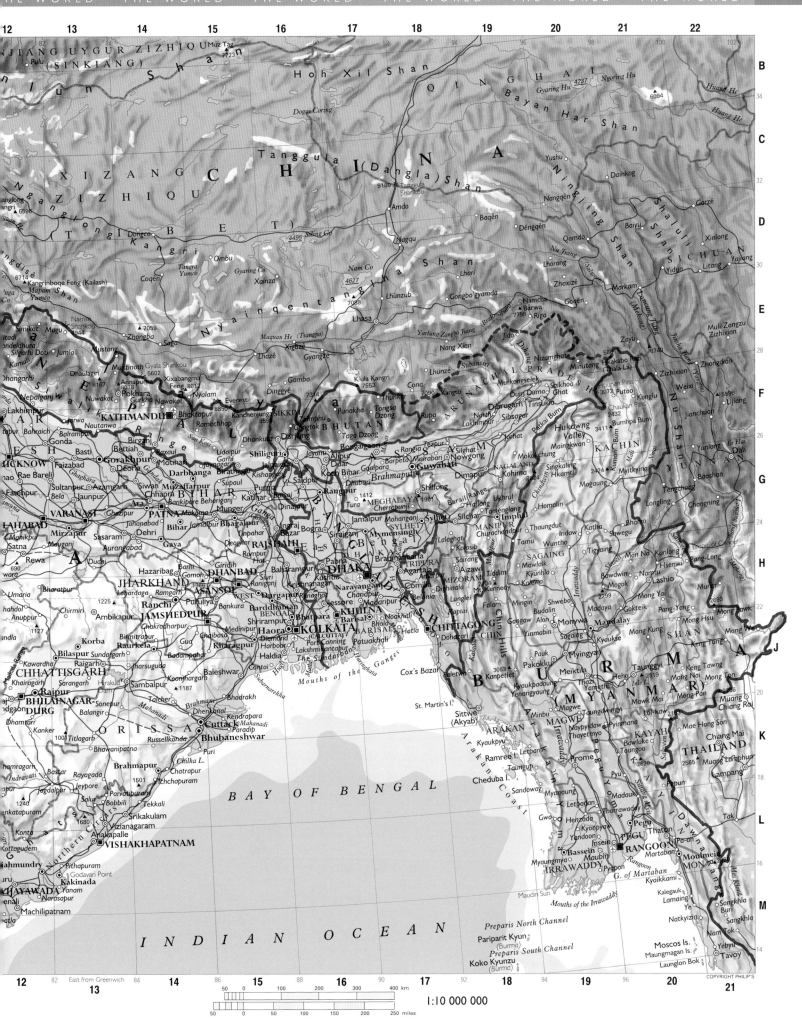

BAY OF BENGAL

INDIAN OCEAN

1:10 000 000

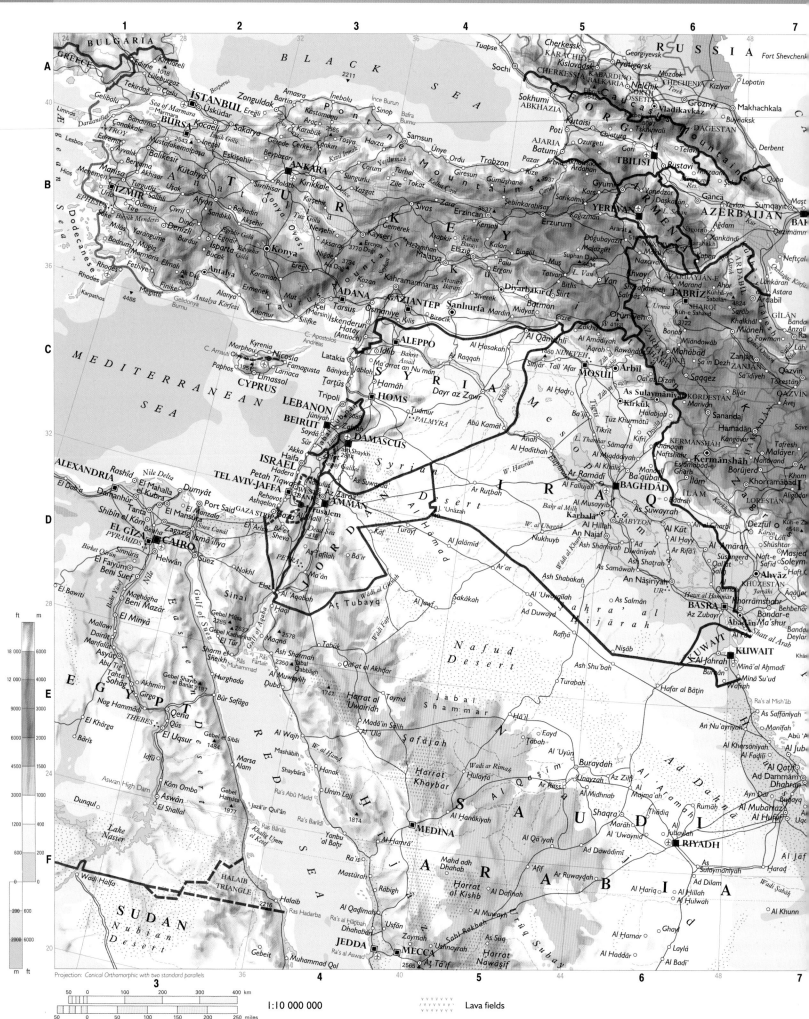

Projection: Conical Orthomorphic with two standard parallels

1:10 000 000

v v v v v Lava fields

50   0   100   200   300   400 km
50   0   50   100   150   200   250 miles

ft   m
18 000 6000
12 000 4000
9000   3000
6000   2000
4500   1500
3000   1000
1200   400
600   200
0   0
200   600
2000   6000
m   ft

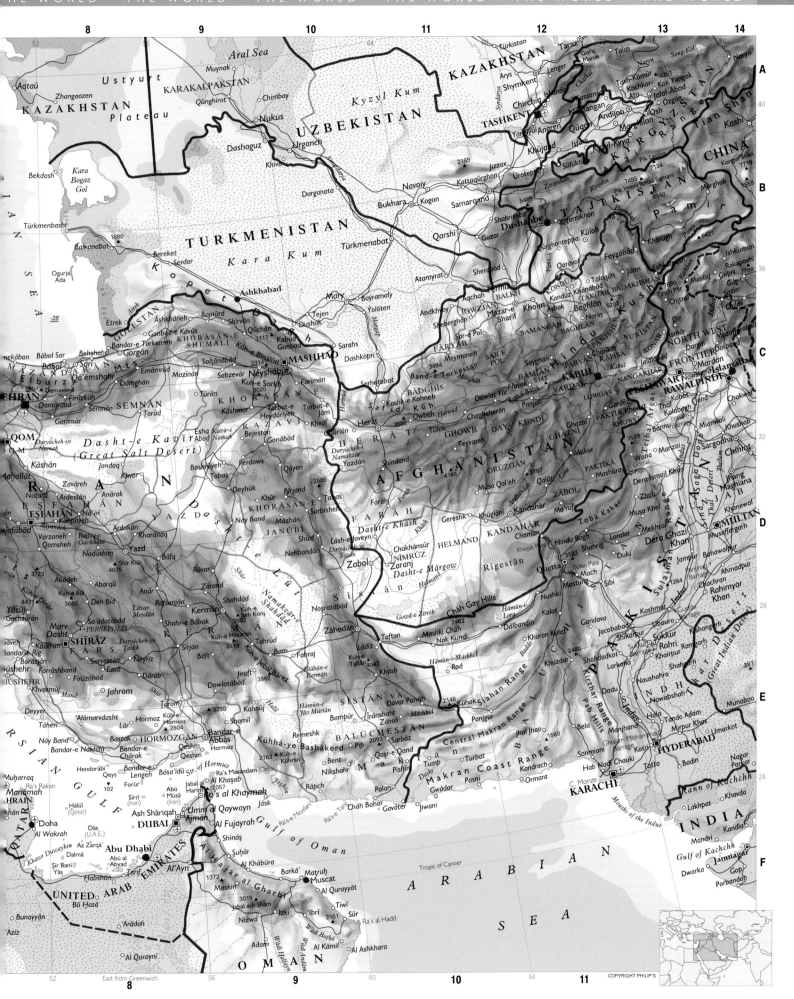

WATER RESOURCES

◄ RIYADH, SAUDI ARABIA

This false-colour image shows the Saudi Arabian capital, at the top left-hand corner of the image, in its desert setting, situated almost at the geographical centre of the kingdom. With a population of over 5 million people, water supply is of prime importance. Most of it is drawn from underground aquifers. To the south-east, the green circles are in fact fields, irrigated by centre-pivot irrigation systems.

▨	Deep fossil-water aquifer
⌣	Dam
•	Major desalination plant
—	Freshwater pipeline
– – –	Proposed pipeline
··········	Freshwater aqueduct

Average annual rainfall

▨	Over 1,000 mm
▨	500 – 1,000 mm
▨	250 – 500 mm
▨	Under 250 mm

OIL AND GAS RESOURCES

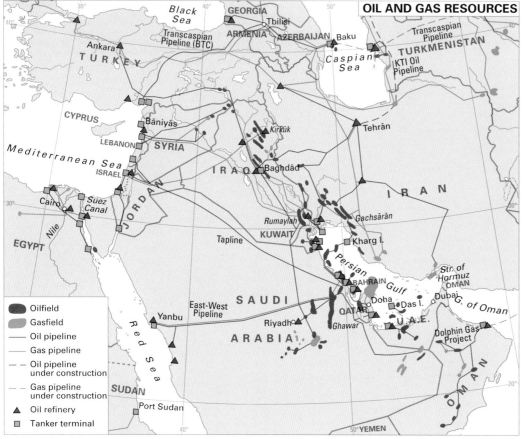

⬤	Oilfield
⬤	Gasfield
—	Oil pipeline
—	Gas pipeline
– –	Oil pipeline under construction
– –	Gas pipeline under construction
▲	Oil refinery
▪	Tanker terminal

Top 10 oil producers
(thousand barrels per day 2007)

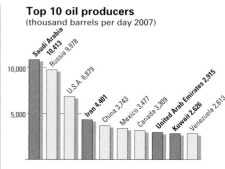

Saudi Arabia **10,413**
Russia 9,978
U.S.A. 6,879
Iran **4,401**
China 3,743
Mexico 3,477
Canada 3,309
United Arab Emirates **2,915**
Kuwait **2,626**
Venezuela 2,613

Oil production by region

South & Central America 8%
Middle East **31%**
Europe & Eurasia **22%**
North America 17%
Africa 12%
Asia/Pacific 10%

World production (2007)
81.5 million barrels per day

Oil reserves by region

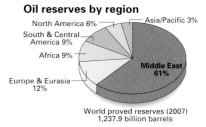

North America 6%
Asia/Pacific 3%
South & Central America 9%
Africa 9%
Middle East **61%**
Europe & Eurasia 12%

World proved reserves (2007)
1,237.9 billion barrels

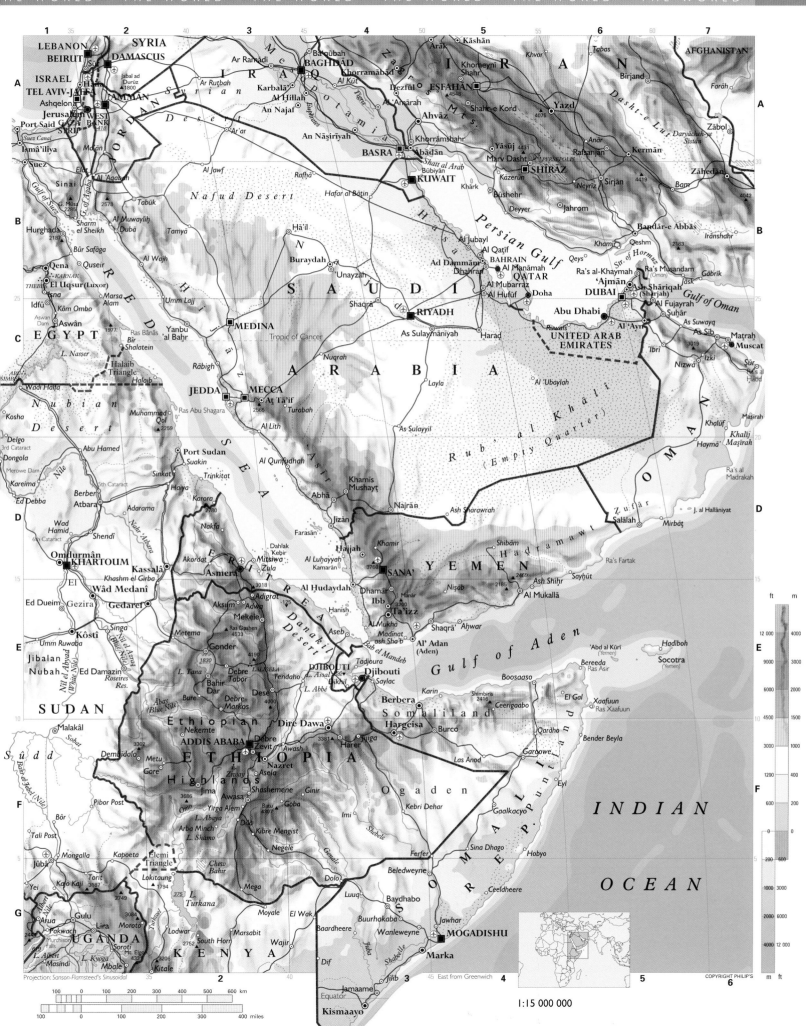

Projection: Sanson-Flamsteed's Sinusoidal

East from Greenwich

COPYRIGHT PHILIP'S

1:15 000 000

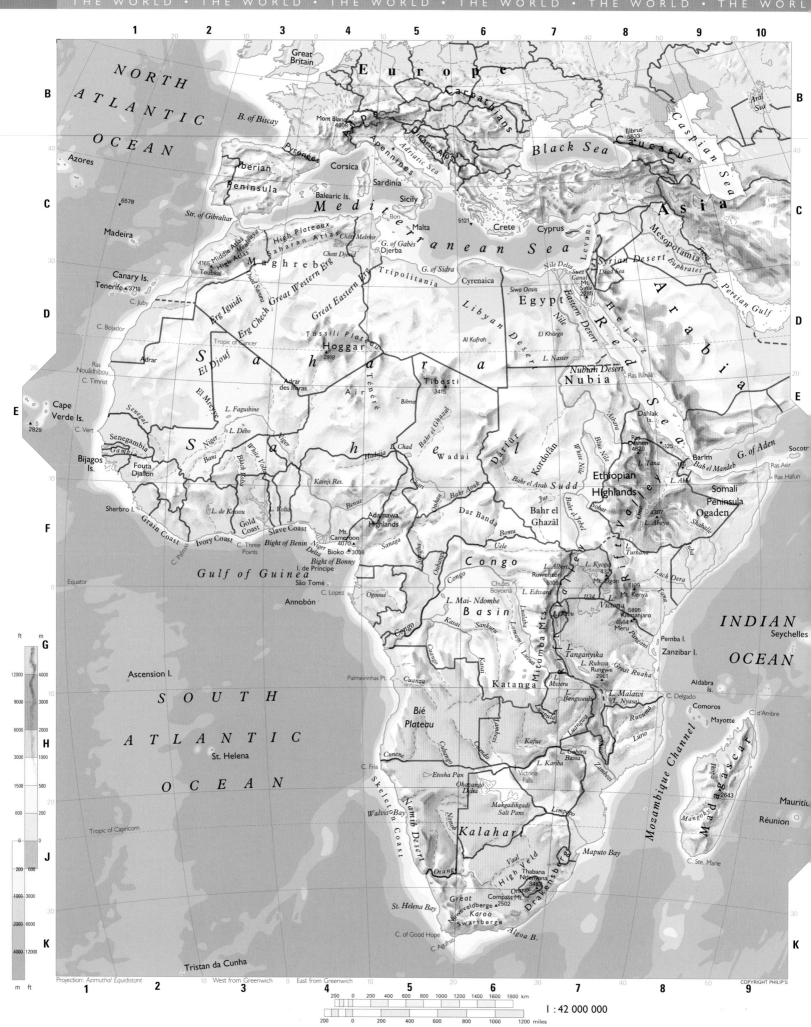

1 : 42 000 000

COPYRIGHT PHILIP'S

Projection: Azimuthal Equidistant

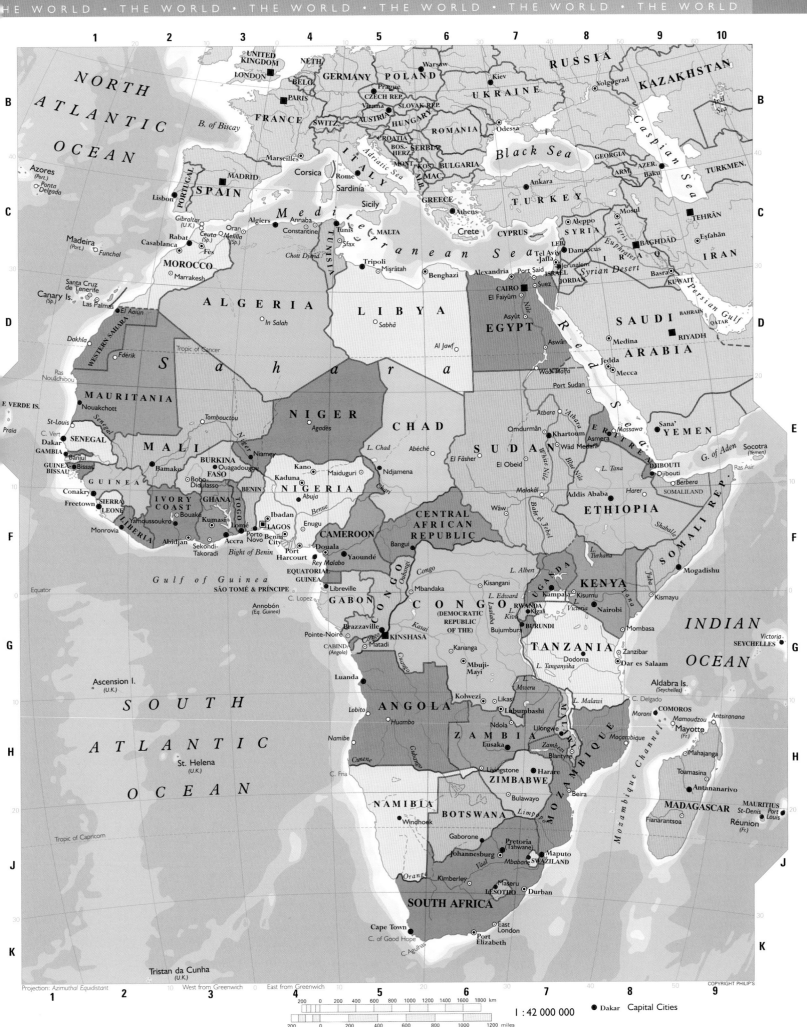

NORTH

ATLANTIC

OCEAN

Azores
(Port.)
○ Ponta
Delgada

RUSSIA

UNITED
KINGDOM
■ LONDON
NETH
BELG
■ PARIS
FRANCE
B. of Biscay

GERMANY POLAND
○ Warsaw
Prague CZECH REP.
Vienna SLOVAK REP.
SWITZ. AUSTRIA HUNGARY
CROATIA
BOS.-
HERZ.
SERBIA
MONT. KOS.
MAC.
● Kiev
○ Volgograd
UKRAINE
○ Odessa
ROMANIA
BULGARIA
Black Sea

KAZAKHSTAN
Aral
Sea
Caspian Sea

Marseilles ○
Corsica
Rome ●
Sardinia
Italy
Adriatic Sea
GREECE
● Athens
Crete

● Ankara
TURKEY
CYPRUS

GEORGIA
ARM. AZER.
● Baku
TURKMEN.

■ MADRID
SPAIN
Lisbon ●
PORTUGAL
Gibraltar
(U.K.)
Ceuta
(Sp.)
Melilla
(Sp.)
Rabat ●
Casablanca ●
Fès ○
MOROCCO
Marrakech ○

Algiers ●
Oran ○
Annaba ○
Constantine ○
Tunis ●
Sfax ○
TUNISIA
Mediterranean Sea
MALTA
Tripoli ●
Mişrātah ○
Benghazi ○

Alexandria ●
Port Said ○
Cairo ■
El Faiyûm ○
Suez ○
ISRAEL
Tel Aviv
-Jaffa
Jerusalem ●
LEB.
Damascus ●
Aleppo ○
Mosul ○
SYRIA
Tigris
Euphrates
BAGHDAD ■
IRAQ
Eşfahān ○
IRAN
TEHRĀN ■

Madeira
(Port.)
○ Funchal

Canary Is.
(Sp.)
Santa Cruz
de Tenerife ○
Las Palmas ○

Tropic of Cancer
In Salah ○
ALGERIA
Sabhā ○
LIBYA
Al Jawf ○
EGYPT
Asyût ○
Aswân ○
Nile
Wâdi Halfa ○
Red Sea
Medina ○
Jedda ○
Mecca ○
SAUDI
ARABIA
BAHRAIN
QATAR
RIYADH ■
Basra ●
KUWAIT ●
Persian Gulf

El Aaiún ○
Dakhla ○
WESTERN SAHARA
Fdérik ○
Ras
Nouâdhibou

Sahara

C. VERDE IS.
St-Louis ○
C. Vert
Dakar ●
GAMBIA
Banjul ●
GUINEA-
BISSAU ● Bissau

MAURITANIA
Nouakchott ●
Senegal
SENEGAL
MALI
Bamako ●
GUINEA
Conakry ●
Freetown ●
SIERRA
LEONE
LIBERIA
Monrovia ●

Tombouctou ○
NIGER
Agadès ○
Niamey ●
BURKINA
FASO
Ouagadougou ●
Bobo-
Dioulasso ○
Kano ○
Kaduna ○
IVORY
COAST
Yamoussoukro ●
Bouaké ○
GHANA
Kumasi ○
TOGO
BENIN
Lomé ●
Accra ●
Porto
Novo ●
NIGERIA
Abuja ●
Ibadan ○
Lagos ■
Benin
City ○
Enugu ○
Benue
CAMEROON
Douala ○
Yaoundé ●

L. Chad
CHAD
Abéché ○
Ndjamena ●
Maiduguri ○
Chari
CENTRAL
AFRICAN
REPUBLIC
Bangui ●

SUDAN
El Fâsher ○
El Obeid ○
Khartoum ●
Omdurmân ●
Wâd Medani ○
Atbara ○
White Nile
Blue Nile
Malakâl ○
Wâw ○
Bahr el Jebel
L. Tana

ERITREA
Massawa ○
Asmera ●
Djibouti ●
DJIBOUTI
Berbera ○
SOMALILAND
Addis Ababa ●
ETHIOPIA
Harer ○

Sana'
YEMEN
G. of Aden
Ras Asir
Socotra
(Yemen)

SÃO TOMÉ & PRÍNCIPE
EQUATORIAL
GUINEA
Rey Malabo ●
Gulf of Guinea
Bight of Benin
Port
Harcourt ○

Equator
GABON
Libreville ●
C. Lopez
Annobón
(Eq. Guinea)

CONGO
Mbandaka ○
CONGO
(DEMOCRATIC
REPUBLIC
OF THE)
Kisangani ○
Oubangui
L. Albert
L. Edward
UGANDA
Kampala ●
RWANDA
Kigali ●
L. Kivu
BURUNDI
Bujumbura ●
L. Victoria
Kisumu ○
KENYA
Nairobi ●
Mombasa ○
Juba
L. Turkana
SOMALI REP.
Mogadishu ●
Kismayu ○

Brazzaville ●
Pointe-Noire ○
KINSHASA ■
Matadi ○
CABINDA
(Angola)
Kasai
Kananga ○
Mbuji-
Mayi ○
L. Tanganyika
TANZANIA
Dodoma ●
Dar es Salaam ●
Zanzibar ○
INDIAN
OCEAN
SEYCHELLES
Victoria ●

Luanda ●
ANGOLA
Lobito ○
Namibe ○
Huambo ○
Cuanza
Kwango
Kolwezi ○
Likasi ○
Lubumbashi ○
Ndola ○
L. Mweru
ZAMBIA
Lusaka ●
Lilongwe ●
MALAWI
L. Malawi
Blantyre ○
Livingstone ○
Zambezi
Moroni ●
COMOROS
Mamoudzou ○
Mayotte
(Fr.)
Antsiranana ○
Mahajanga ○
Moçambique ○
Aldabra Is.
(Seychelles)
C. Delgado
Mozambique Channel

SOUTH
ATLANTIC
OCEAN
St. Helena
(U.K.)
Ascension I.
(U.K.)
C. Fria
Cunene
NAMIBIA
Windhoek ●
BOTSWANA
Gaborone ●
Okavango
ZIMBABWE
Harare ●
Bulawayo ○
Beira ○
MOZAMBIQUE
Limpopo
Toamasina ○
Antananarivo ●
MADAGASCAR
Fianarantsoa ○
MAURITIUS
St-Denis ● Port
Louis
Réunion
(Fr.)

Tropic of Capricorn
Orange
Vaal
SOUTH AFRICA
Pretoria
(Tshwane) ●
Johannesburg ●
Mbabane ●
SWAZILAND
Maputo ●
Maseru ●
LESOTHO
Durban ●
Kimberley ○
Cape Town ●
C. of Good Hope
C. Agulhas
East
London ○
Port
Elizabeth ●

Projection: Azimuthal Equidistant
West from Greenwich   East from Greenwich
COPYRIGHT PHILIP'S

200 0 200 400 600 800 1000 1200 1400 1800 km
200 0 200 400 600 800 1000 1200 miles
1 : 42 000 000
● Dakar Capital Cities

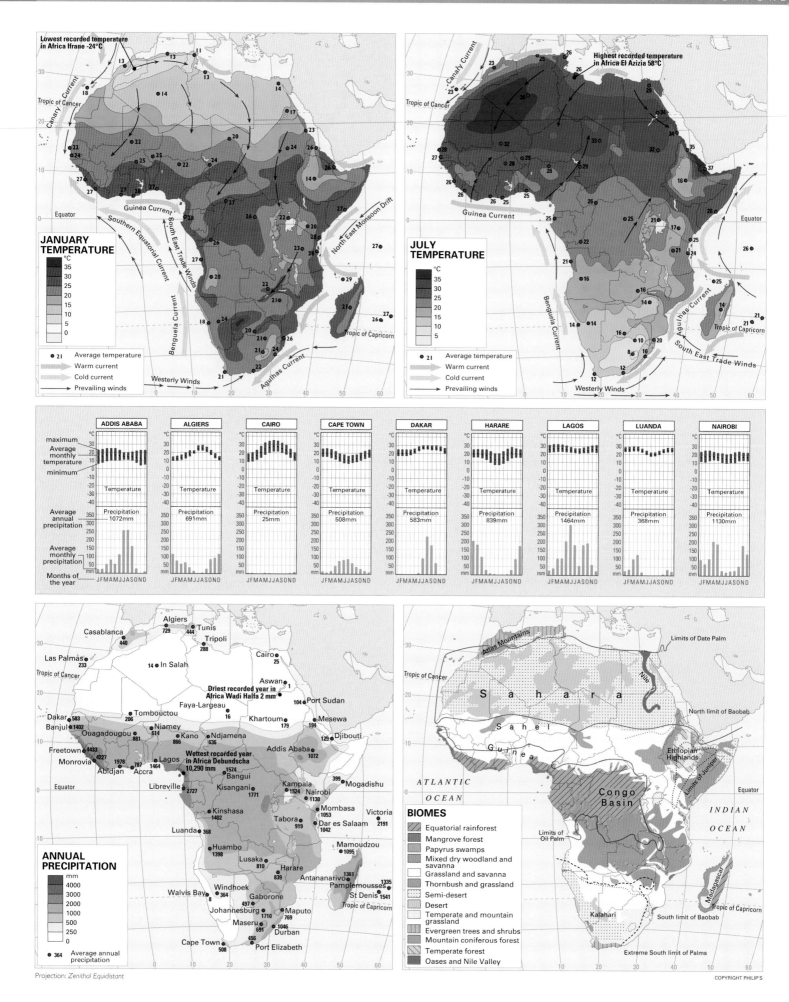

JANUARY TEMPERATURE
°C
35
30
25
20
15
10
5
0

Lowest recorded temperature in Africa Ifrane -24°C

• 21 Average temperature
Warm current
Cold current
Prevailing winds

JULY TEMPERATURE
°C
35
30
25
20
15
10
5

Highest recorded temperature in Africa El Azizia 58°C

• 21 Average temperature
Warm current
Cold current
Prevailing winds

ADDIS ABABA — Temperature — Precipitation 1072mm
ALGIERS — Temperature — Precipitation 691mm
CAIRO — Temperature — Precipitation 25mm
CAPE TOWN — Temperature — Precipitation 508mm
DAKAR — Temperature — Precipitation 583mm
HARARE — Temperature — Precipitation 839mm
LAGOS — Temperature — Precipitation 1464mm
LUANDA — Temperature — Precipitation 368mm
NAIROBI — Temperature — Precipitation 1130mm

maximum
Average monthly temperature
minimum
Average annual precipitation
Average monthly precipitation
Months of the year

ANNUAL PRECIPITATION
mm
4000
3000
2000
1000
500
250
• 364 Average annual precipitation

Driest recorded year in Africa Wadi Halfa 2 mm
Wettest recorded year in Africa Debundscha 10,290 mm

BIOMES
Equatorial rainforest
Mangrove forest
Papyrus swamps
Mixed dry woodland and savanna
Grassland and savanna
Thornbush and grassland
Semi-desert
Desert
Temperate and mountain grassland
Evergreen trees and shrubs
Mountain coniferous forest
Temperate forest
Oases and Nile Valley

Limits of Date Palm
North limit of Baobab
Limits of Oil Palm
South limit of Baobab
Extreme South limit of Palms
Limits of Juniper

Projection: Zenithal Equidistant

COPYRIGHT PHILIP'S

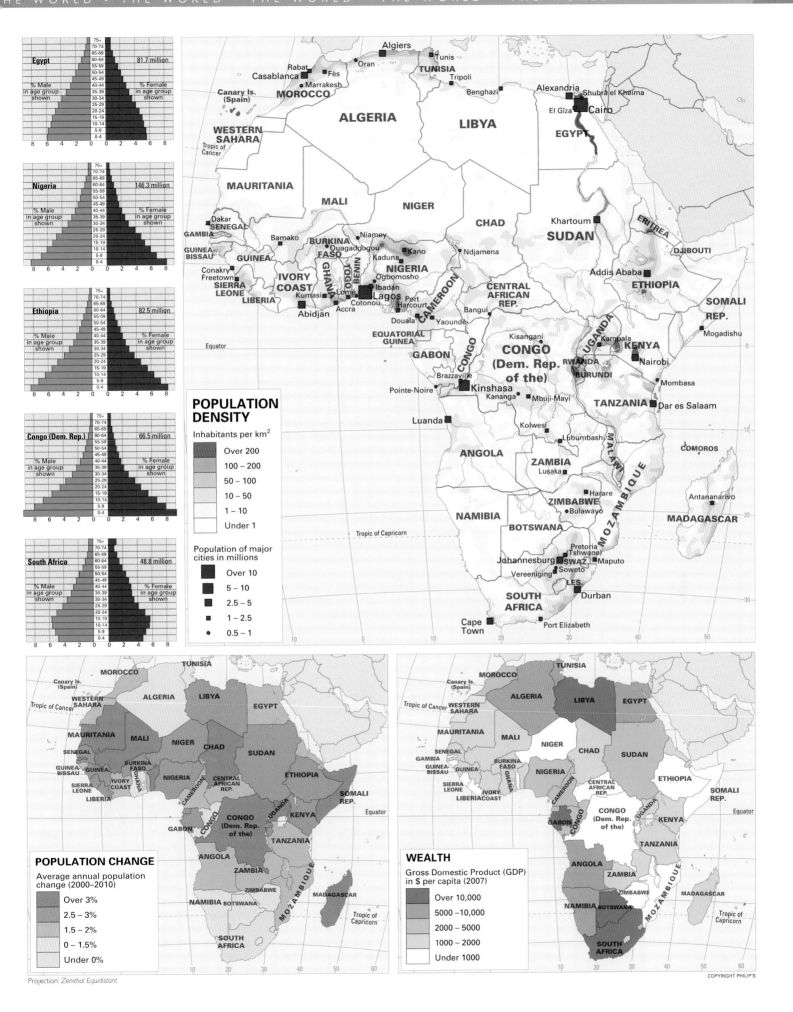

Egypt 81.7 million
% Male in age group shown / % Female in age group shown

Nigeria 146.3 million
% Male in age group shown / % Female in age group shown

Ethiopia 82.5 million
% Male in age group shown / % Female in age group shown

Congo (Dem. Rep.) 66.5 million
% Male in age group shown / % Female in age group shown

South Africa 48.8 million
% Male in age group shown / % Female in age group shown

POPULATION DENSITY

Inhabitants per km²

- Over 200
- 100 – 200
- 50 – 100
- 10 – 50
- 1 – 10
- Under 1

Population of major cities in millions

- Over 10
- 5 – 10
- 2.5 – 5
- 1 – 2.5
- 0.5 – 1

POPULATION CHANGE

Average annual population change (2000–2010)

- Over 3%
- 2.5 – 3%
- 1.5 – 2%
- 0 – 1.5%
- Under 0%

Projection: *Zenithal Equidistant*

WEALTH

Gross Domestic Product (GDP) in $ per capita (2007)

- Over 10,000
- 5000 – 10,000
- 2000 – 5000
- 1000 – 2000
- Under 1000

COPYRIGHT PHILIP'S

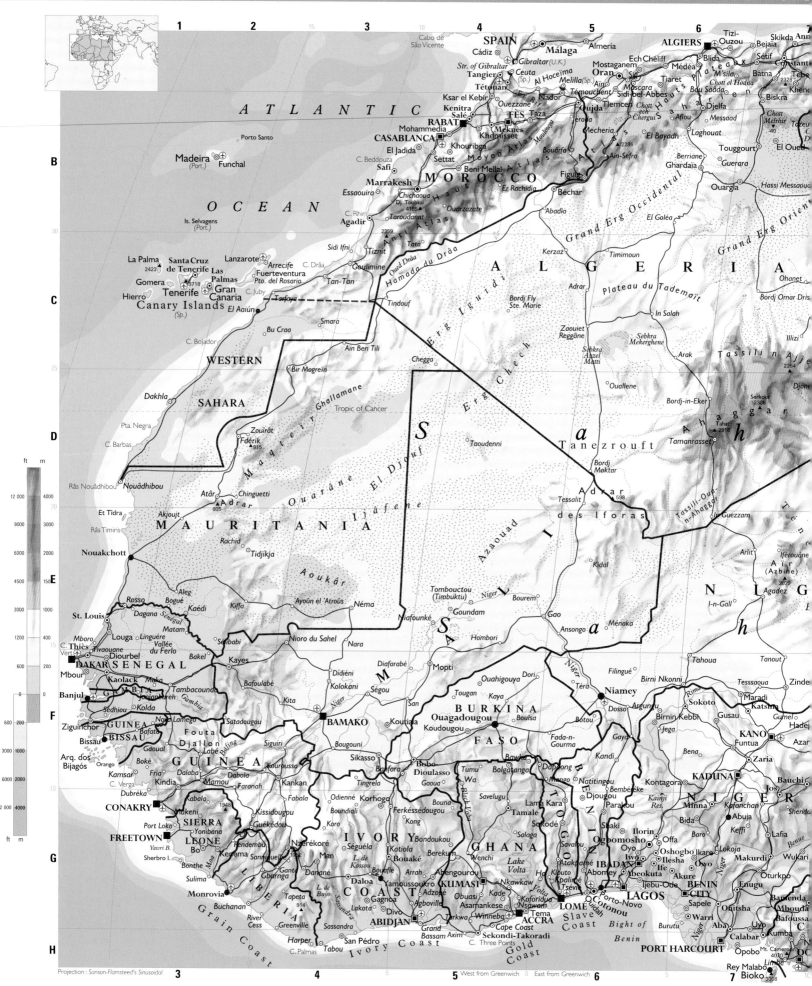

Projection : Sanson-Flamsteed's Sinusoidal

West from Greenwich   East from Greenwich

1:15 000 000

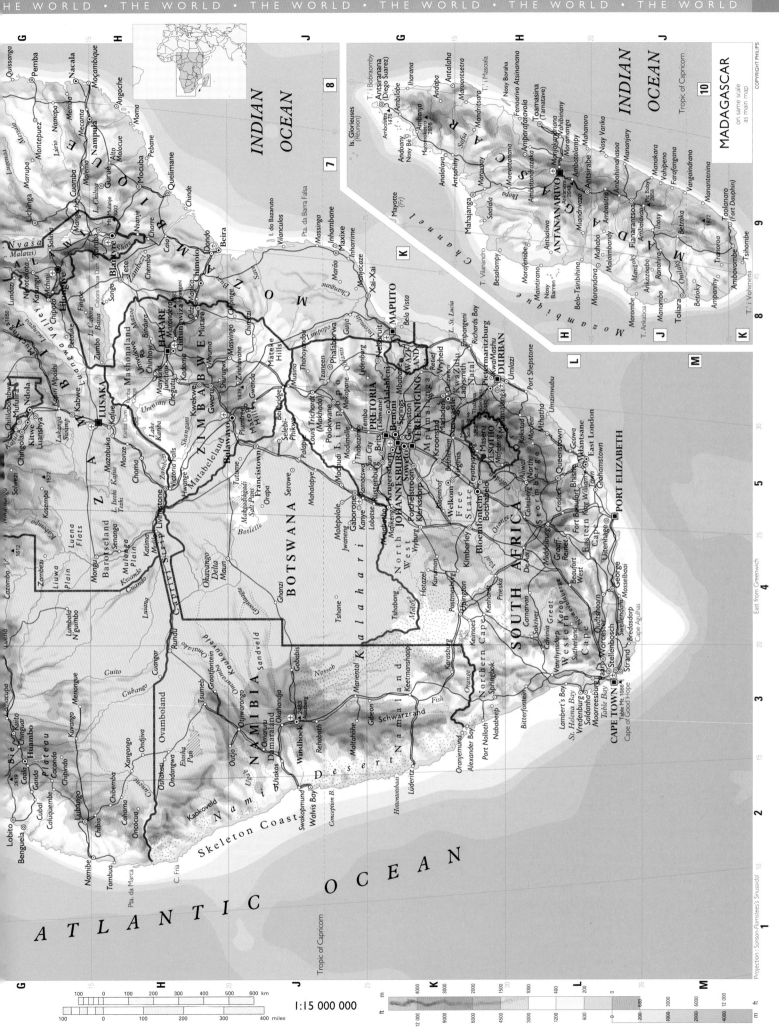

MADAGASCAR
on same scale
as main map

INDIAN OCEAN

INDIAN OCEAN

ATLANTIC OCEAN

Projection: Sanson-Flamsteed's Sinusoidal

1:15 000 000

COPYRIGHT PHILIPS

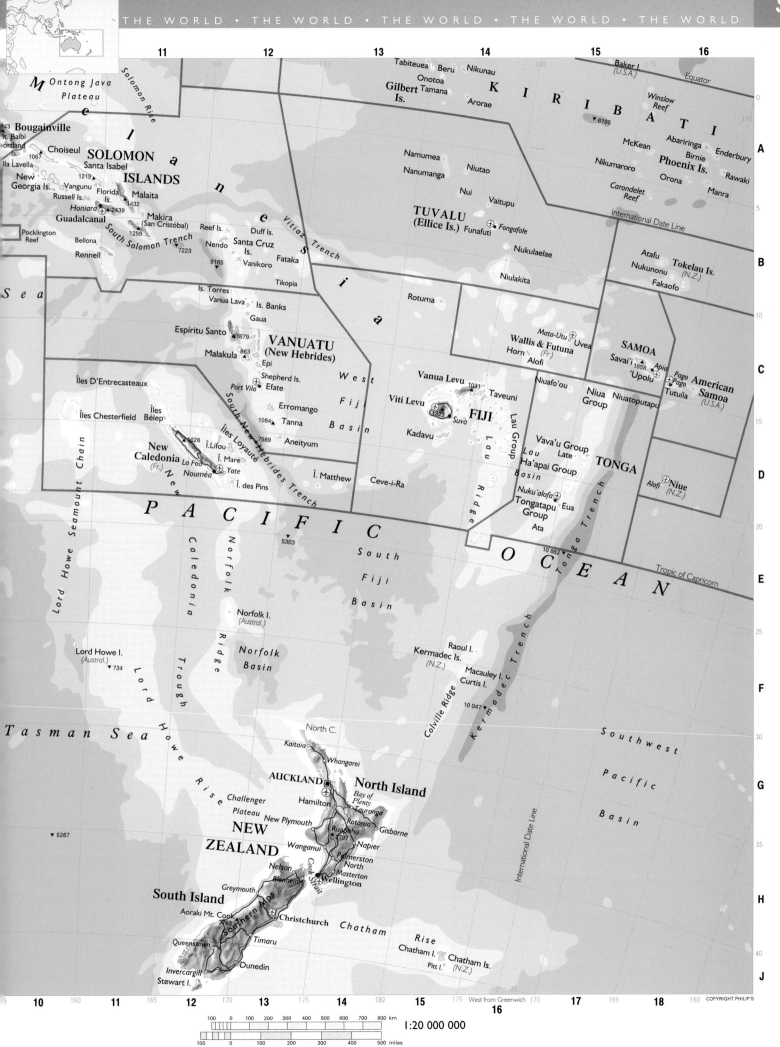

1:20 000 000

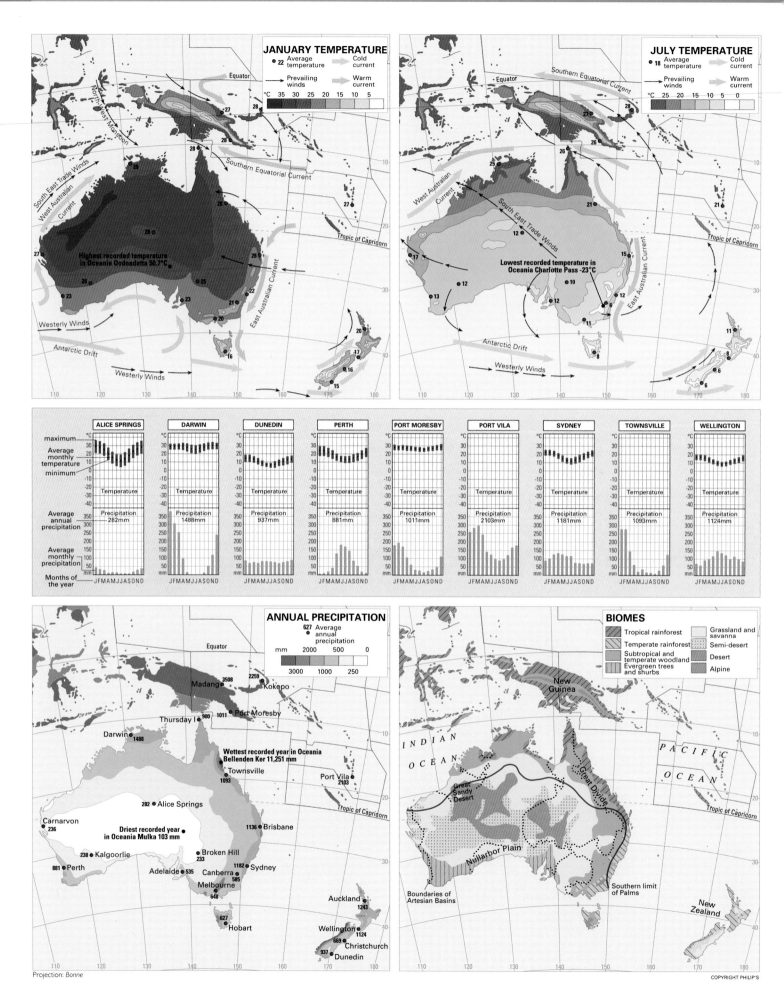

JANUARY TEMPERATURE

- 22 Average temperature
- Prevailing winds
- Cold current
- Warm current

°C 35 30 25 20 15 10 5

Equator

North-West Monsoon

South East Trade Winds

West Australian Current

Southern Equatorial Current

Tropic of Capricorn

Highest recorded temperature in Oceania Oodnadatta 50.7°C

East Australian Current

Westerly Winds

Antarctic Drift

Westerly Winds

JULY TEMPERATURE

- 18 Average temperature
- Prevailing winds
- Cold current
- Warm current

°C 25 20 15 10 5 0

Southern Equatorial Current

Equator

West Australian Current

South East Trade Winds

Lowest recorded temperature in Oceania Charlotte Pass -23°C

East Australian Current

Tropic of Capricorn

Antarctic Drift

Westerly Winds

ALICE SPRINGS
Temperature
Precipitation 282mm

DARWIN
Temperature
Precipitation 1488mm

DUNEDIN
Temperature
Precipitation 937mm

PERTH
Temperature
Precipitation 881mm

PORT MORESBY
Temperature
Precipitation 1011mm

PORT VILA
Temperature
Precipitation 2103mm

SYDNEY
Temperature
Precipitation 1181mm

TOWNSVILLE
Temperature
Precipitation 1093mm

WELLINGTON
Temperature
Precipitation 1124mm

maximum
Average monthly temperature
minimum

Average annual precipitation

Average monthly precipitation

Months of the year   J F M A M J J A S O N D

ANNUAL PRECIPITATION

- 627 Average annual precipitation

mm 2000 500 0
3000 1000 250

Equator

Madang 3508
Kokopo 2259
Thursday I 900
Port Moresby 1011
Darwin 1488

Wettest recorded year in Oceania Bellenden Ker 11,251 mm

Townsville 1093
Port Vila 2103

Alice Springs 282

Carnarvon 236

Driest recorded year in Oceania Mulka 103 mm

Brisbane 1136

Kalgoorlie 238
Broken Hill 233
Perth 881
Adelaide 535   Canberra 585   Sydney 1182
Melbourne 648

Tropic of Capricorn

Auckland 1243

Hobart 627

Wellington 1124
Christchurch 669
Dunedin 937

BIOMES

- Tropical rainforest
- Temperate rainforest
- Subtropical and temperate woodland
- Evergreen trees and shrubs
- Grassland and savanna
- Semi-desert
- Desert
- Alpine

New Guinea

INDIAN OCEAN

PACIFIC OCEAN

Great Sandy Desert

Great Divide

Nullarbor Plain

Tropic of Capricorn

Boundaries of Artesian Basins

Southern limit of Palms

New Zealand

Projection: Bonne

COPYRIGHT PHILIP'S

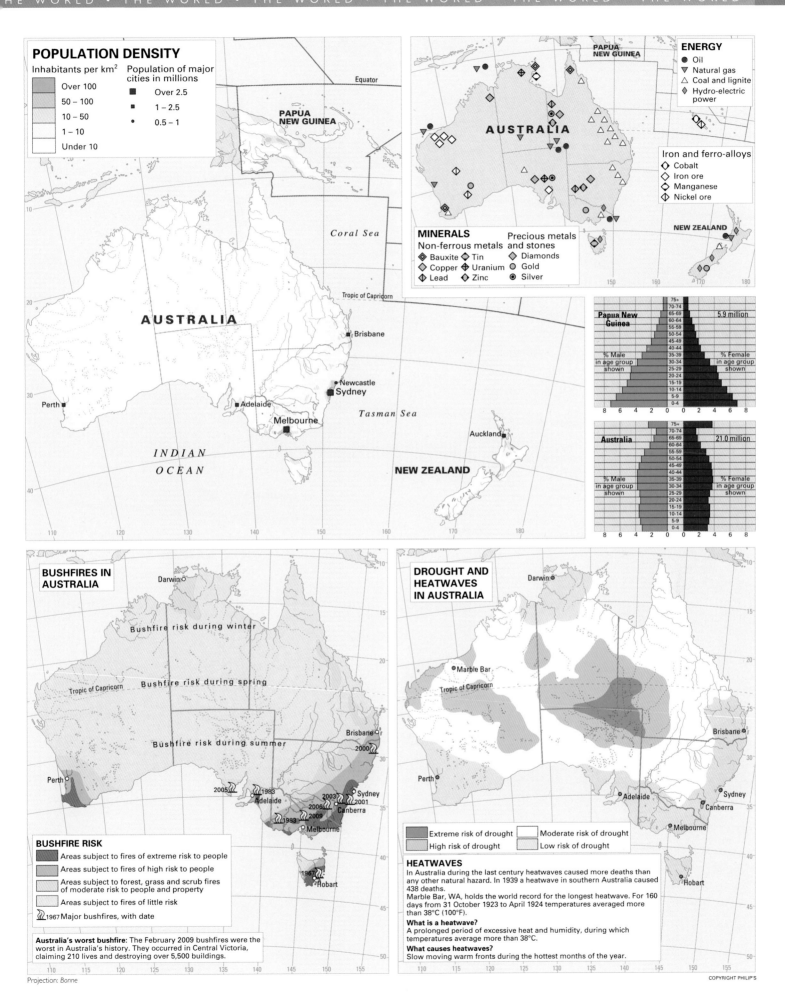

POPULATION DENSITY

Inhabitants per km²

- Over 100
- 50 – 100
- 10 – 50
- 1 – 10
- Under 10

Population of major cities in millions
- ■ Over 2.5
- ■ 1 – 2.5
- • 0.5 – 1

ENERGY

- ● Oil
- ▼ Natural gas
- △ Coal and lignite
- ◆ Hydro-electric power

Iron and ferro-alloys
- ◇ Cobalt
- ◇ Iron ore
- ◇ Manganese
- ◇ Nickel ore

MINERALS
Non-ferrous metals
- ◆ Bauxite   ◆ Tin
- ◆ Copper   ◆ Uranium
- ◆ Lead   ◆ Zinc

Precious metals and stones
- ◇ Diamonds
- ○ Gold
- ◉ Silver

Papua New Guinea — 5.9 million
% Male in age group shown / % Female in age group shown

Australia — 21.0 million
% Male in age group shown / % Female in age group shown

BUSHFIRES IN AUSTRALIA

Bushfire risk during winter

Bushfire risk during spring

Bushfire risk during summer

2000, 2005, 1983, 2003, 2001, Sydney, 2006, Canberra, 2009, 1983, Melbourne, 1967, Hobart

BUSHFIRE RISK
- Areas subject to fires of extreme risk to people
- Areas subject to fires of high risk to people
- Areas subject to forest, grass and scrub fires of moderate risk to people and property
- Areas subject to fires of little risk
- 〰1967 Major bushfires, with date

Australia's worst bushfire: The February 2009 bushfires were the worst in Australia's history. They occurred in Central Victoria, claiming 210 lives and destroying over 5,500 buildings.

Projection: Bonne

DROUGHT AND HEATWAVES IN AUSTRALIA

- Extreme risk of drought
- High risk of drought
- Moderate risk of drought
- Low risk of drought

HEATWAVES

In Australia during the last century heatwaves caused more deaths than any other natural hazard. In 1939 a heatwave in southern Australia caused 438 deaths.

Marble Bar, WA, holds the world record for the longest heatwave. For 160 days from 31 October 1923 to April 1924 temperatures averaged more than 38°C (100°F).

What is a heatwave?
A prolonged period of excessive heat and humidity, during which temperatures average more than 38°C.

What causes heatwaves?
Slow moving warm fronts during the hottest months of the year.

COPYRIGHT PHILIP'S

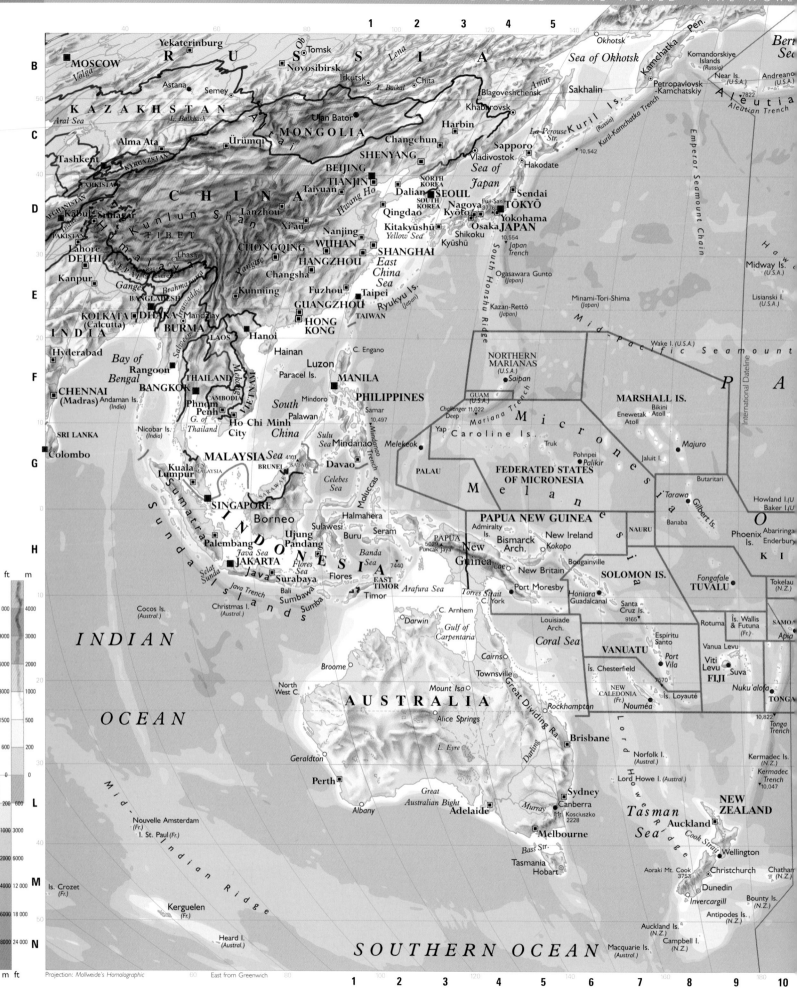

ALASKA
(U.S.A.)
Anchorage
6959
Juneau
Bristol Bay
Gulf of Alaska
Prince of Wales I.
(U.S.A.) Prince Rupert
Queen Charlotte Is.
(Canada)
Is . (U.S.A.)

C A N A D A

B

Edmonton
Calgary
Vancouver
Vancouver I.
Victoria
Seattle
Regina
Winnipeg
L. Winnipeg
Newfoundland

N O R T H

Portland
Boise
Minneapolis
L. Superior
Québec
Montréal
Ottawa
St. Lawrence
St. John's

C

ROCKY
Snake
Missouri
L. Michigan
Toronto
L. Huron
Detroit
Buffalo
L. Ontario
Boston
L. Erie

Salt Lake City
Denver
CHICAGO
Pittsburgh
Cincinnati
NEW YORK
PHILADELPHIA
Baltimore
Washington D.C.

A T L A N T I C

C. Mendocino
Sacramento
SAN FRANCISCO
4418
UNITED STATES
Kansas City
St. Louis
Memphis
Appalachian Mts.

D

6741
Colorado
Oklahoma City
Atlanta
C. Hatteras

LOS ANGELES
Phoenix
Dallas
Jacksonville
Bermuda
(U.K.)

San Diego
Ciudad Juárez
Houston
Mississippi
Sargasso Sea

Guadalupe
(Mex.)
Baja California
San Antonio
New Orleans
Monterrey
Gulf of Mexico
Miami
BAHAMAS

E

Tropic of Cancer
M E X I C O
Golfo de California

O C E A N

C. San Lucas
Havana
CUBA
West Indies

Honolulu
O'ahu
4205
HAWAI'I
(U.S.A.)
Hawai'i
Guadalajara
MEXICO
5610
Puebla
Mérida
Yucatan Channel
JAMAICA
HAITI
DOMINICAN REP.
8605
Leeward Is.

Is. de Revillagigedo
(Mex.)
Acapulco
BELIZE
Kingston
PUERTO RICO
(U.S.A.)
7680

F

C I F I C

GUATEMALA
Guatemala
HONDURAS
Caribbean Sea
BARBADOS
Windward Is.

I. Clipperton
(Fr.)
San Salvador
EL SALVADOR
Managua
NICARAGUA
Barranquilla
San José
Maracaibo
Caracas

North West Christmas I. Ridge
Palmyra Is.
(U.S.A.)
Teraina
COSTA RICA
Colón
PANAMA
Panamá
Orinoco
VENEZUELA

Tabuaeran
Kiritimati
I. del Coco
(Costa Rica)
Medellín
Bogotá

G

Jarvis I.
(U.S.A.)
Equator
I. de Malpelo
(Colombia)
COLOMBIA

B A T I E
Malden I.
Starbuck I.
Galápagos
(Ecuador)
Quito
ECUADOR

E A N
Line Is.
Guayaquil
C. Paliñas
Amazonas
BRAZIL

H

Tongareva
Pukapuka
Manihiki
Vostok I.
Caroline I.
(Millennium I.)
Flint I.
Iquitos
Trujillo

Suwarrow Is.
6369
PERU

J

Société
Papeete
Tahiti
Cuzco
L. Titicaca
6550
Nevada Ancohuma

Cook Is.
(N.Z.)
FRENCH POLYNESIA
Tuamotu
Arequipa
6866
La Paz
BOLIVIA

Rarotonga
Mururoa
Peru-
Arica

Australo
Seamount Chain
Tropic of Capricorn
Iquique
Chile

K

Henderson I.
8050
Trench
Antofagasta
PARAGUAY
Asunción

Pitcairn I.
(U.K.)
Sala-y-Gómez
(Chile)
San Ambrosio
(Chile)
San Miguel de Tucumán

Rapa
I. de Pascua
(Chile)
Pórto Alegre

Arch. de
Juan Fernández
(Chile)
Córdoba
Aconcagua
6962
Rosario
URUGUAY

L

Valparaíso
SANTIAGO
BUENOS AIRES
Montevideo
Río de la Plata

Concepción
ARGENTINA

Chile Rise

SOUTH

M

Pacific-Antarctic Ridge
ATLANTIC

6212
OCEAN

N

Falkland Is.
(U.K.)
Punta Arenas
Magellan's Str.
Tierra del Fuego
South Georgia
(U.K.)
C. Horn

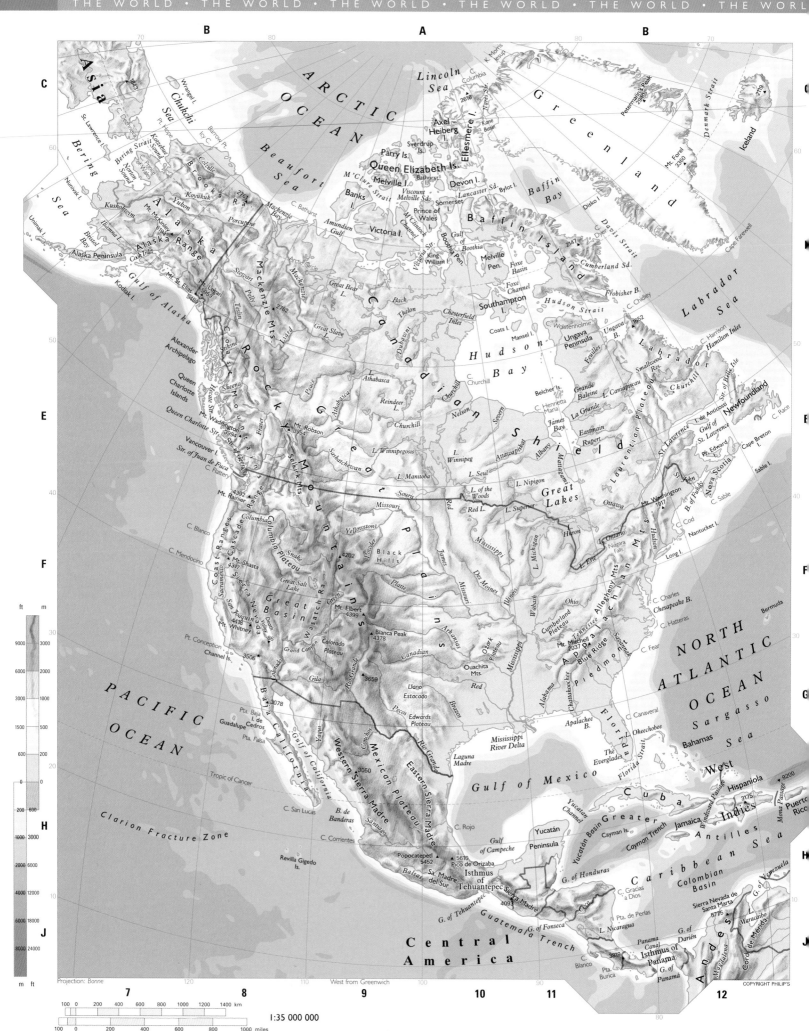

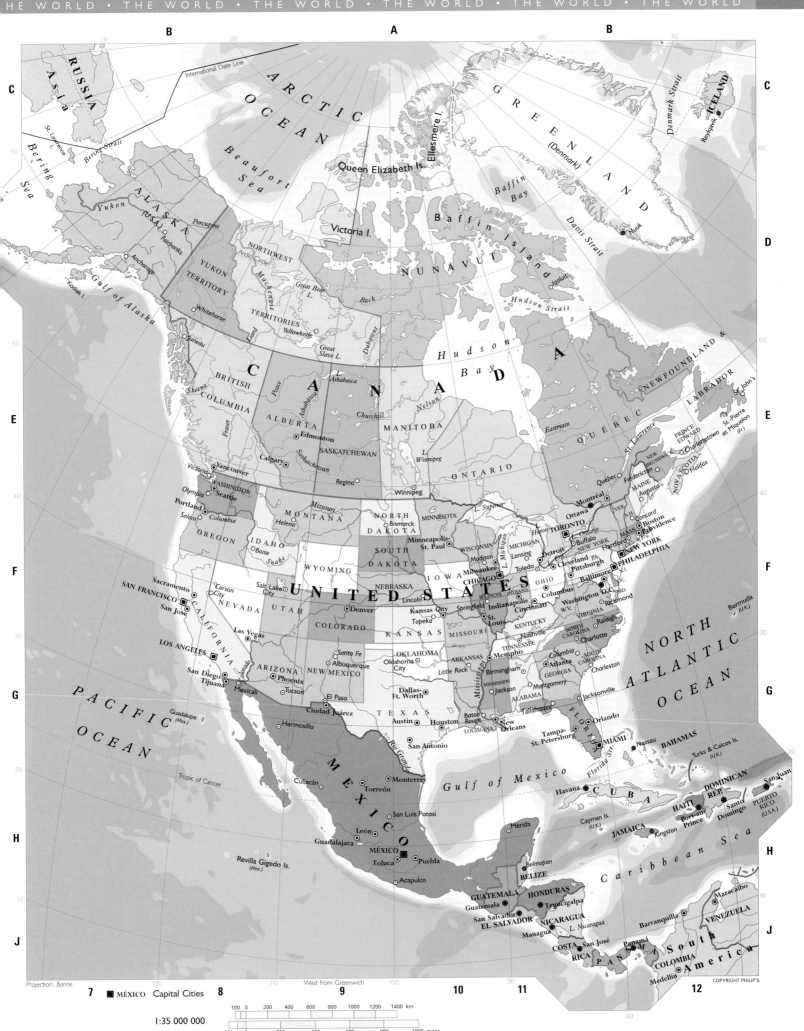

Projection: Bonne

7 ■ MÉXICO Capital Cities 8

1:35 000 000

COPYRIGHT PHILIP'S

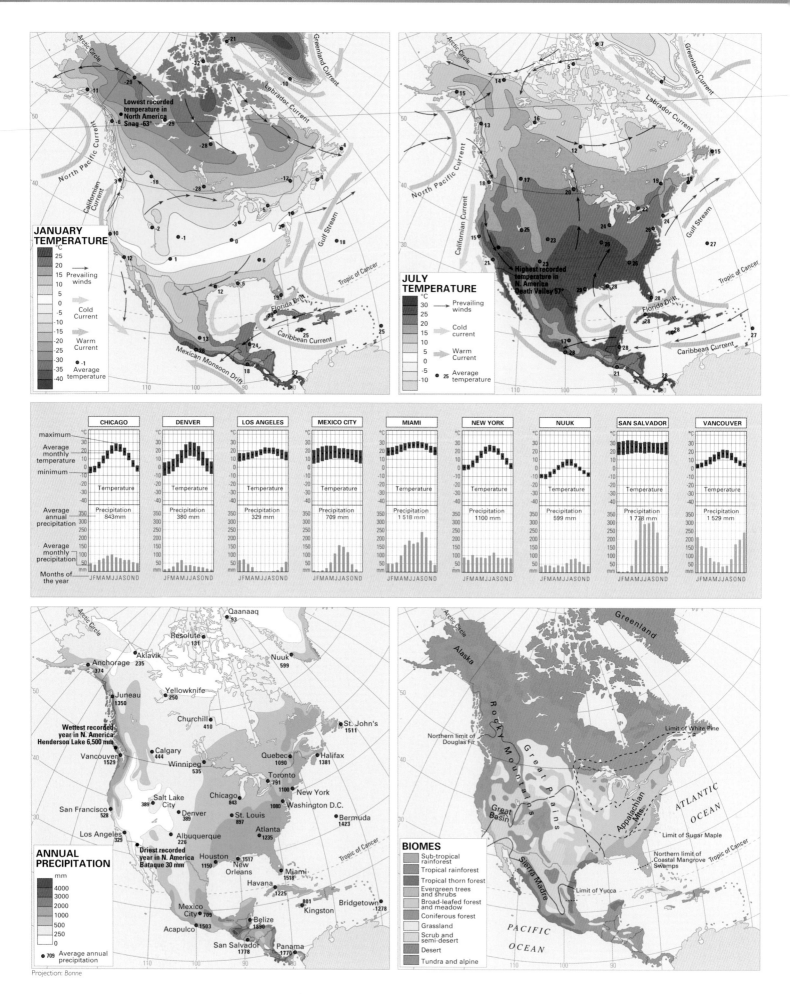

JANUARY TEMPERATURE

°C
25
20
15
10
5
0
-5
-10
-15
-20
-25
-30
-35
-40

→ Prevailing winds
⇨ Cold Current
⇨ Warm Current
• -1 Average temperature

Lowest recorded temperature in North America Snag -63°

JULY TEMPERATURE

°C
30
25
20
15
10
5
0
-5
-10

→ Prevailing winds
⇨ Cold current
⇨ Warm Current
• 25 Average temperature

Highest recorded temperature in N. America Death Valley 57°

CHICAGO	DENVER	LOS ANGELES	MEXICO CITY	MIAMI	NEW YORK	NUUK	SAN SALVADOR	VANCOUVER
Temperature	Temperature	Temperature	Temperature	Temperature	Temperature	Temperature	Temperature	Temperature
Precipitation 843mm	Precipitation 380 mm	Precipitation 329 mm	Precipitation 709 mm	Precipitation 1 518 mm	Precipitation 1100 mm	Precipitation 599 mm	Precipitation 1 778 mm	Precipitation 1 529 mm

maximum
Average monthly temperature
minimum

Average annual precipitation
Average monthly precipitation
Months of the year

ANNUAL PRECIPITATION

mm
4000
3000
2000
1000
500
250
0

• 709 Average annual precipitation

Wettest recorded year in N. America Henderson Lake 6,500 mm

Driest recorded year in N. America Bataque 30 mm

Qaanaaq 93
Resolute 131
Aklavik
Anchorage 235
Anchorage 374
Juneau 1350
Yellowknife 250
Nuuk 599
Churchill 410
St. John's 1511
Calgary 444
Vancouver 1529
Quebec 1090
Halifax 1381
Winnipeg 535
Toronto 791
Chicago 843
New York 1080
Salt Lake City 389
Denver 389
St. Louis 897
Washington D.C.
San Francisco 528
Atlanta 1235
Bermuda 1423
Los Angeles 329
Albuquerque 226
Houston 1150
New Orleans
Miami 1518
Havana 1225
Mexico City 709
Kingston 801
Bridgetown 1278
Acapulco 1503
Belize 1890
San Salvador 1778
Panama 1770

Projection: Bonne

BIOMES

- Sub-tropical rainforest
- Tropical rainforest
- Tropical thorn forest
- Evergreen trees and shrubs
- Broad-leafed forest and meadow
- Coniferous forest
- Grassland
- Scrub and semi-desert
- Desert
- Tundra and alpine

Greenland
Alaska
Rocky Mountains
Great Plains
Great Basin
Sierra Madre
Appalachian Mts.
ATLANTIC OCEAN
PACIFIC OCEAN

Northern limit of Douglas Fir
Limit of White Pine
Limit of Sugar Maple
Northern limit of Coastal Mangrove Swamps
Limit of Yucca

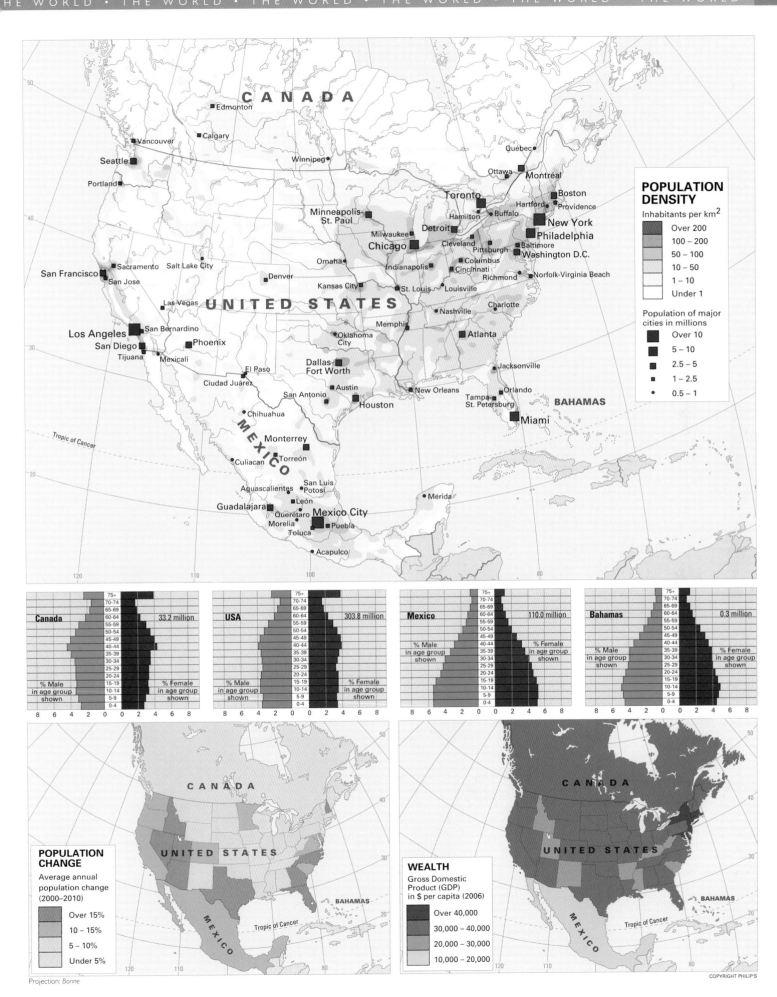

POPULATION DENSITY

Inhabitants per km²

Over 200
100 – 200
50 – 100
10 – 50
1 – 10
Under 1

Population of major cities in millions

Over 10
5 – 10
2.5 – 5
1 – 2.5
0.5 – 1

Canada — 33.2 million

USA — 303.8 million

Mexico — 110.0 million

Bahamas — 0.3 million

% Male in age group shown   % Female in age group shown

POPULATION CHANGE

Average annual population change (2000–2010)

Over 15%
10 – 15%
5 – 10%
Under 5%

Projection: Bonne

WEALTH

Gross Domestic Product (GDP) in $ per capita (2006)

Over 40,000
30,000 – 40,000
20,000 – 30,000
10,000 – 20,000

COPYRIGHT PHILIP'S

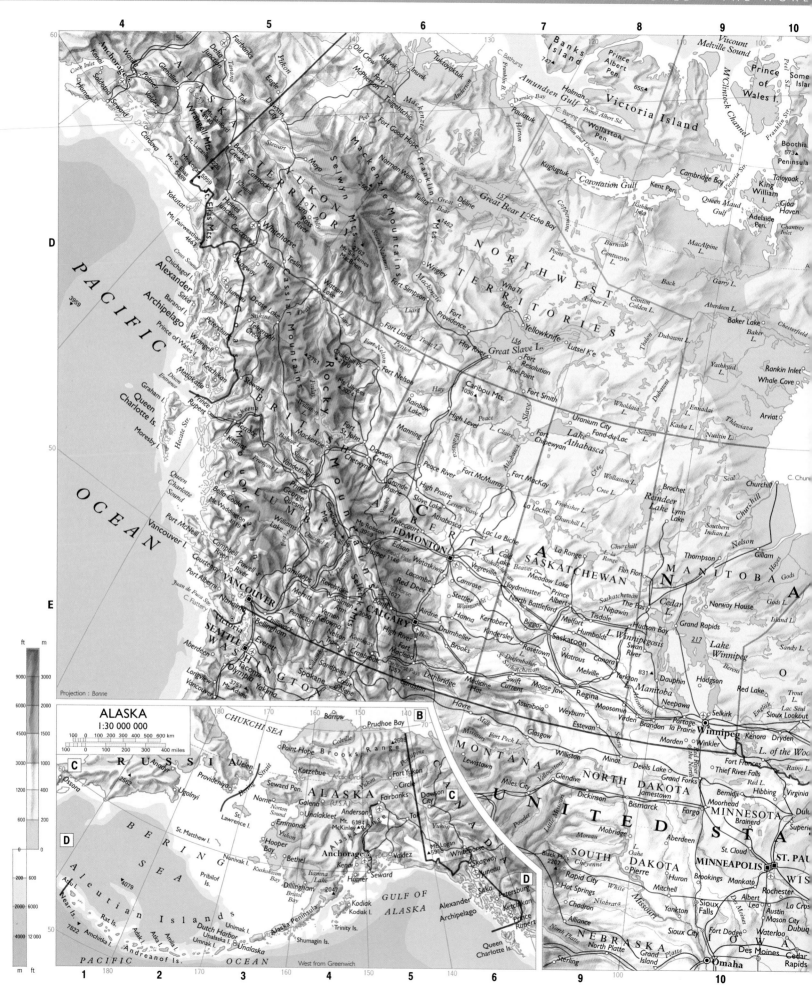

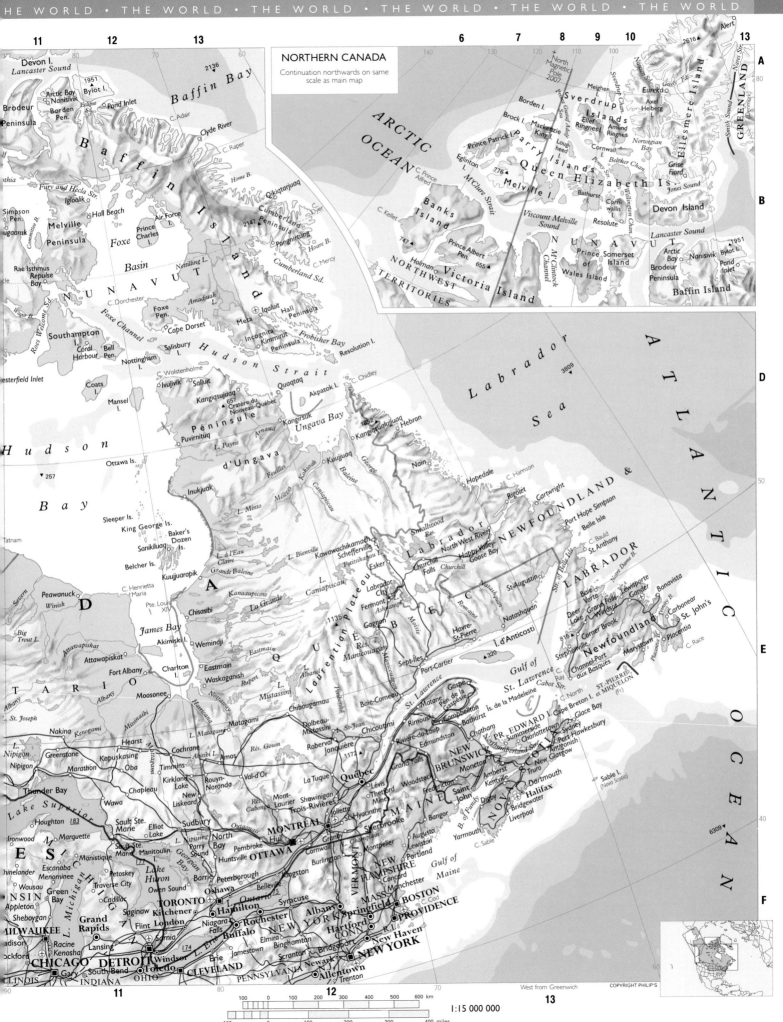

NORTHERN CANADA

Continuation northwards on same
scale as main map

1:15 000 000

COPYRIGHT PHILIP'S

West from Greenwich

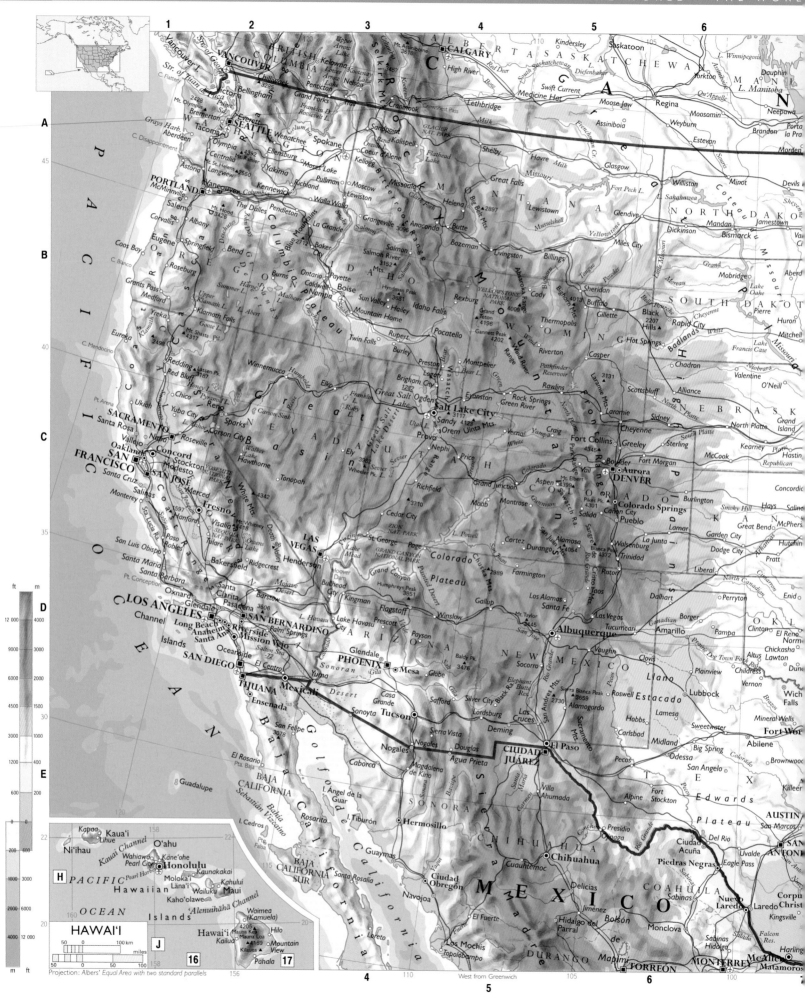

HAWAI'I

Projection: Albers' Equal Area with two standard parallels

1:12 000 000

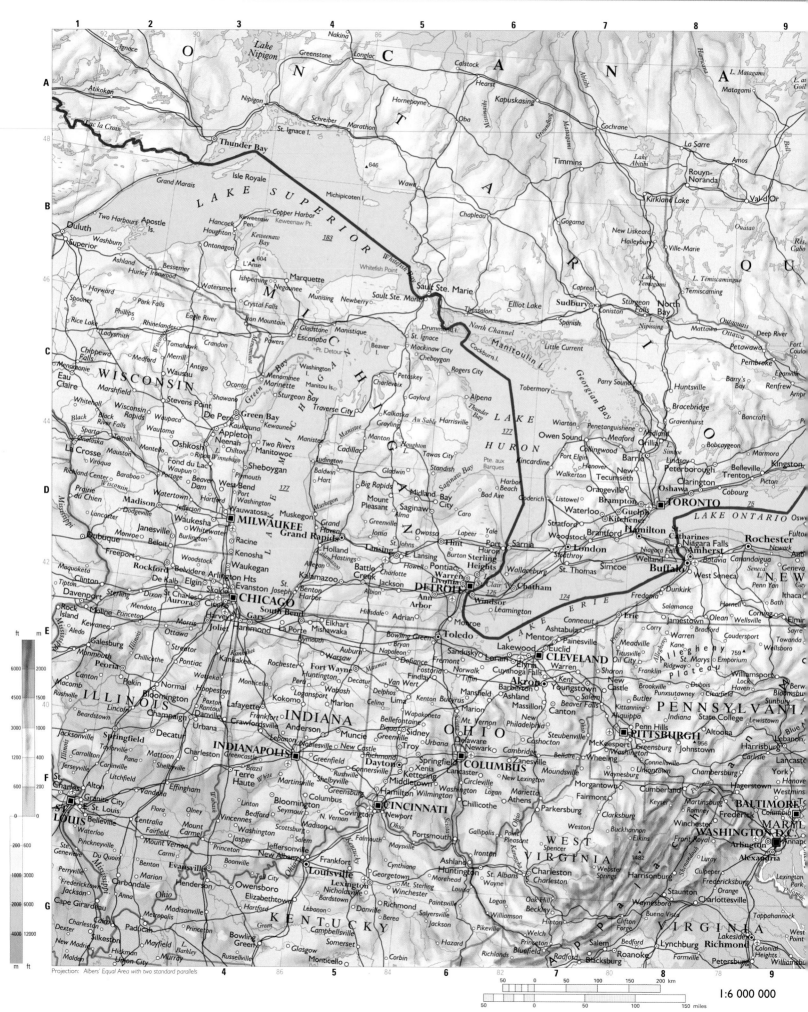

Projection: Albers' Equal Area with two standard parallels

1:6 000 000

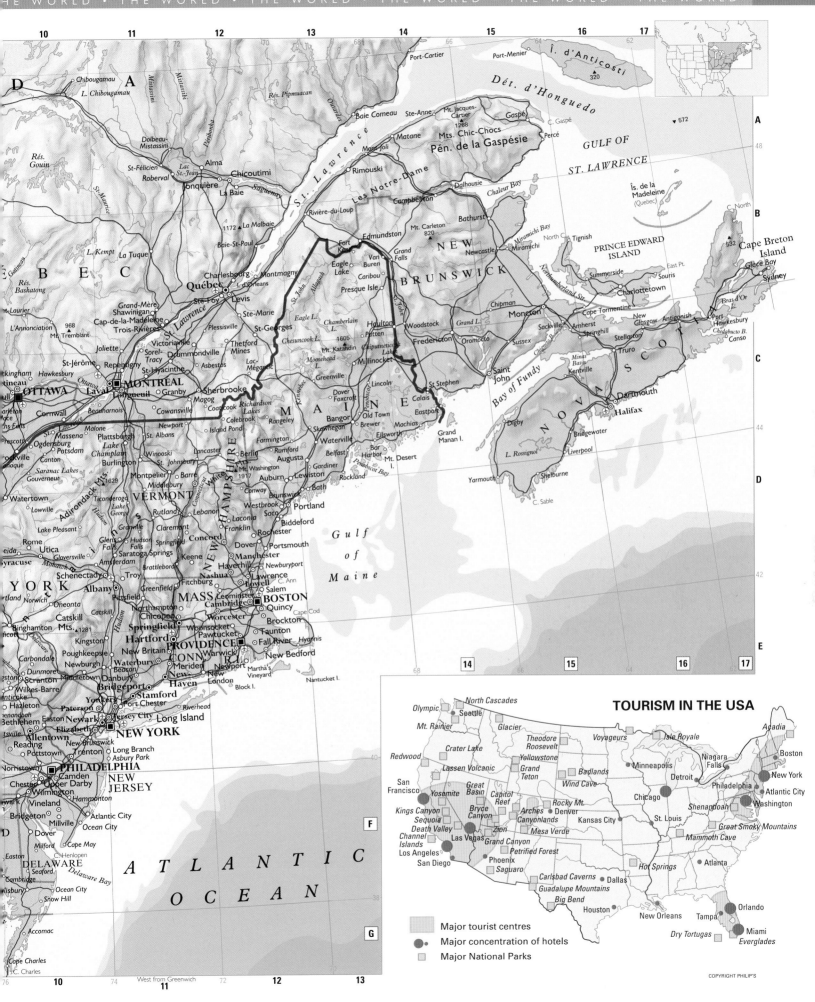

TOURISM IN THE USA

Olympic
North Cascades
Seattle
Mt. Rainier
Crater Lake
Redwood
Lassen Volcanic
San Francisco
Yosemite
Kings Canyon
Sequoia
Death Valley
Channel Islands
Los Angeles
San Diego
Glacier
Theodore Roosevelt
Yellowstone
Grand Teton
Great Basin
Bryce Canyon
Zion
Grand Canyon
Phoenix
Saguaro
Voyageurs
Badlands
Wind Cave
Rocky Mt.
Denver
Arches
Canyonlands
Capitol Reef
Mesa Verde
Petrified Forest
Carlsbad Caverns
Guadalupe Mountains
Big Bend
Minneapolis
Chicago
Kansas City
St. Louis
Dallas
Houston
New Orleans
Isle Royale
Detroit
Hot Springs
Atlanta
Dry Tortugas
Tampa
New Orleans
Acadia
Boston
Niagara Falls
New York
Philadelphia
Atlantic City
Washington
Shenandoah
Great Smoky Mountains
Mammoth Cave
Orlando
Miami
Everglades

Major tourist centres

Major concentration of hotels

Major National Parks

COPYRIGHT PHILIP'S

JAMAICA
1:3 000 000

CARIBBEAN SEA

JAMAICA

GUADELOUPE AND MARTINIQUE
1:2 000 000

GUADELOUPE (Fr.)

MARTINIQUE (Fr.)

PACIFIC OCEAN

Projection : Bonne

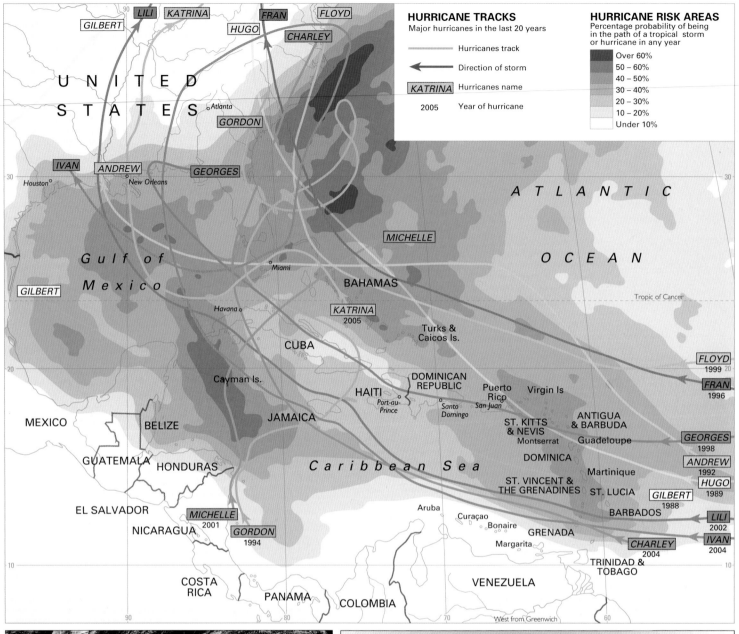

HURRICANE TRACKS
Major hurricanes in the last 20 years

————	Hurricanes track
⟵	Direction of storm
KATRINA	Hurricanes name
2005	Year of hurricane

HURRICANE RISK AREAS
Percentage probability of being in the path of a tropical storm or hurricane in any year

- Over 60%
- 50 – 60%
- 40 – 50%
- 30 – 40%
- 20 – 30%
- 10 – 20%
- Under 10%

▲ Hurricane Katrina hit the USA's Gulf Coast on 29th August 2005. It was the costliest and one of the five deadliest hurricanes ever to strike the United States. This satellite image shows the storm approaching the US coastline.

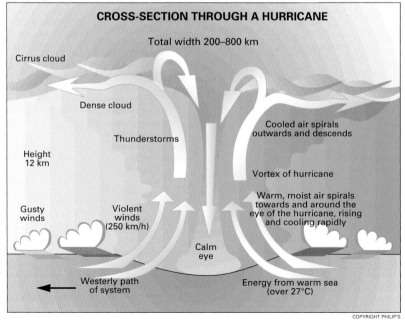

CROSS-SECTION THROUGH A HURRICANE

Total width 200–800 km

Cirrus cloud

Dense cloud

Thunderstorms

Cooled air spirals outwards and descends

Vortex of hurricane

Height 12 km

Warm, moist air spirals towards and around the eye of the hurricane, rising and cooling rapidly

Gusty winds

Violent winds (250 km/h)

Calm eye

Westerly path of system

Energy from warm sea (over 27°C)

COPYRIGHT PHILIP'S

Projection: Lambert's Azimuthal Equal Area

1:35 000 000

COPYRIGHT PHILIP'S

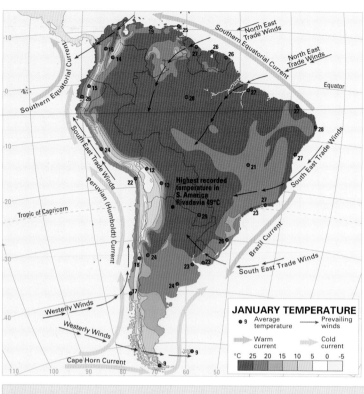

JANUARY TEMPERATURE

Highest recorded temperature in S. America Rivadavia 49°C

- 9 Average temperature
- → Prevailing winds
- Warm current
- Cold current

°C 25 20 15 10 5 0 -5

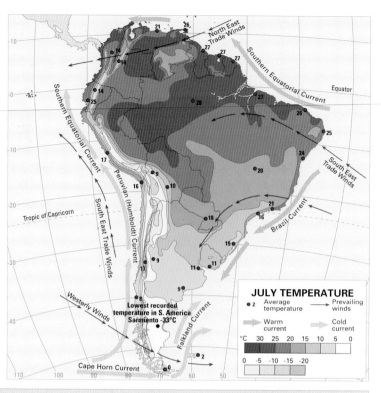

JULY TEMPERATURE

Lowest recorded temperature in S. America Sarmiento -33°C

- 2 Average temperature
- → Prevailing winds
- Warm current
- Cold current

°C 30 25 20 15 10 5 0
0 -5 -10 -15 -20

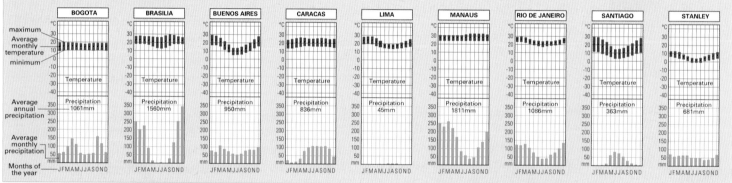

| BOGOTA | BRASILIA | BUENOS AIRES | CARACAS | LIMA | MANAUS | RIO DE JANEIRO | SANTIAGO | STANLEY |

maximum
Average monthly temperature
minimum

Temperature

Average annual precipitation

Average monthly precipitation

Months of the year

Precipitation 1061mm — Precipitation 1560mm — Precipitation 950mm — Precipitation 836mm — Precipitation 45mm — Precipitation 1811mm — Precipitation 1086mm — Precipitation 363mm — Precipitation 681mm

JFMAMJJASOND

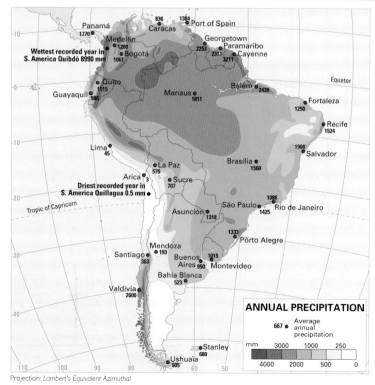

Panamá 1770
Medellín 1200
Caracas 836
Port of Spain 1384
Georgetown 2253
Paramaribo 2311
Cayenne 3211
Bogotá 1061
Wettest recorded year in S. America Quibdó 8990 mm
Quito 1115
Guayaquil 986
Manaus 1811
Belém 2439
Fortaleza 1250
Recife 1524
Lima 45
La Paz 575
Arica 3
Sucre 707
Driest recorded year in S. America Quillagua 0.5 mm
Salvador 1900
Brasília 1560
São Paulo 1086
Rio de Janeiro 1425
Asunción 1318
Pôrto Alegre 1333
Mendoza 193
Santiago 363
Buenos Aires 950
Montevideo 1015
Bahía Blanca 523
Valdivia 2600
Stanley 680
Ushuaía 505

ANNUAL PRECIPITATION

- 667 Average annual precipitation

mm 3000 1000 250
4000 2000 500 0

Guiana Highlands

Amazon Basin

South limit of wild rubber

Andes

Atacama Desert

Brazilian Highlands

PACIFIC OCEAN

South limit of Quebracho

Pampas

ATLANTIC OCEAN

Patagonia

BIOMES

- Tropical rainforest
- Tropical thorn forest
- Temperate rainforest
- Evergreen trees and shrubs
- Grassland and savanna
- Semi-desert
- Desert
- Alpine and high plateau

Projection: Lambert's Equivalent Azimuthal

COPYRIGHT PHILIP'S

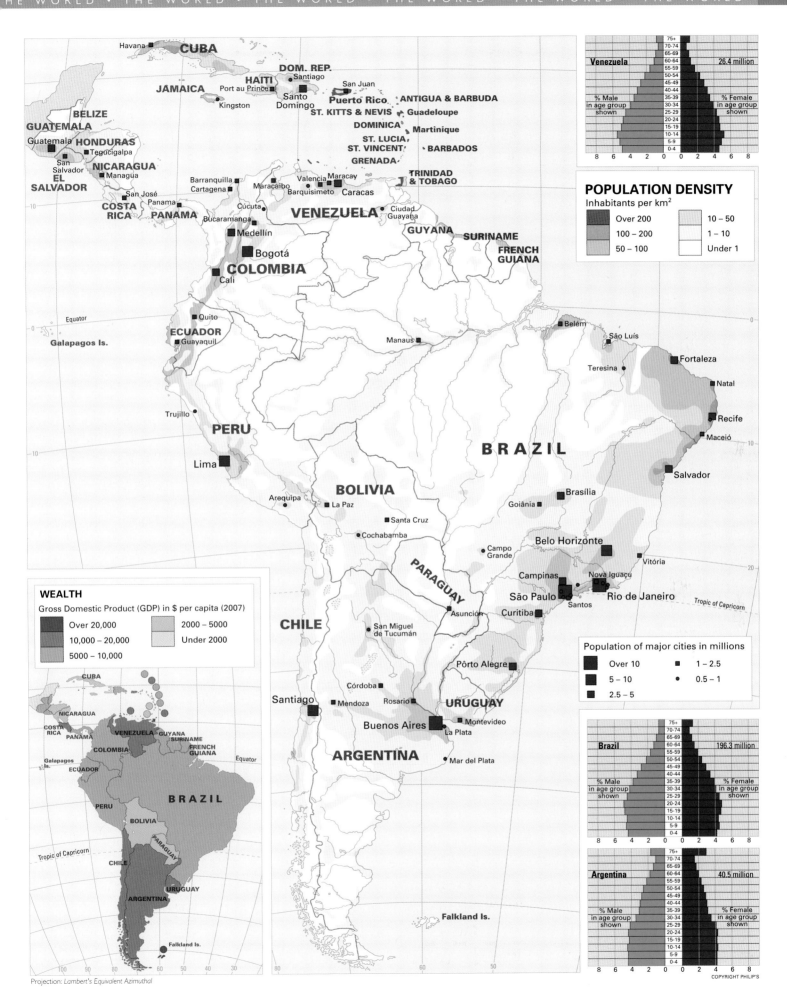

Venezuela 26.4 million

75+
70-74
65-69
60-64
55-59
50-54
45-49
40-44
35-39
30-34
25-29
20-24
15-19
10-14
5-9
0-4

% Male in age group shown
% Female in age group shown

8 6 4 2 0 0 2 4 6 8

POPULATION DENSITY
Inhabitants per km²

Over 200
100 – 200
50 – 100
10 – 50
1 – 10
Under 1

WEALTH
Gross Domestic Product (GDP) in $ per capita (2007)

Over 20,000
10,000 – 20,000
5000 – 10,000
2000 – 5000
Under 2000

Population of major cities in millions

Over 10
5 – 10
2.5 – 5
1 – 2.5
0.5 – 1

Brazil 196.3 million

75+
70-74
65-69
60-64
55-59
50-54
45-49
40-44
35-39
30-34
25-29
20-24
15-19
10-14
5-9
0-4

% Male in age group shown
% Female in age group shown

8 6 4 2 0 0 2 4 6 8

Argentina 40.5 million

75+
70-74
65-69
60-64
55-59
50-54
45-49
40-44
35-39
30-34
25-29
20-24
15-19
10-14
5-9
0-4

% Male in age group shown
% Female in age group shown

8 6 4 2 0 0 2 4 6 8

Projection: Lambert's Equivalent Azimuthal

COPYRIGHT PHILIP'S

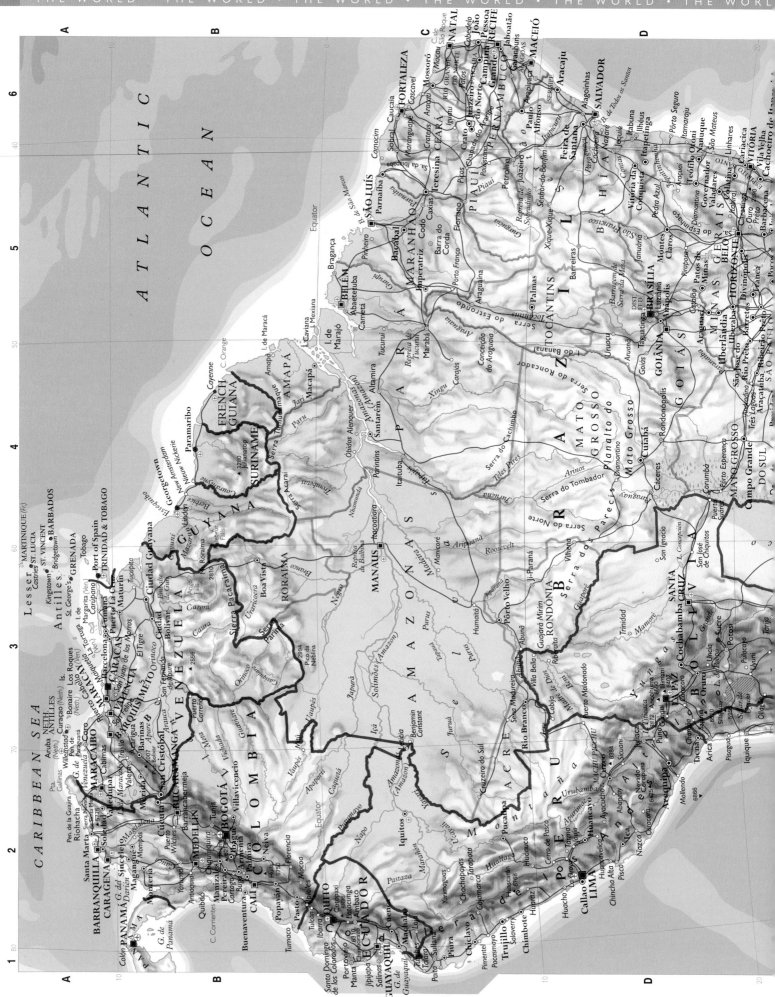

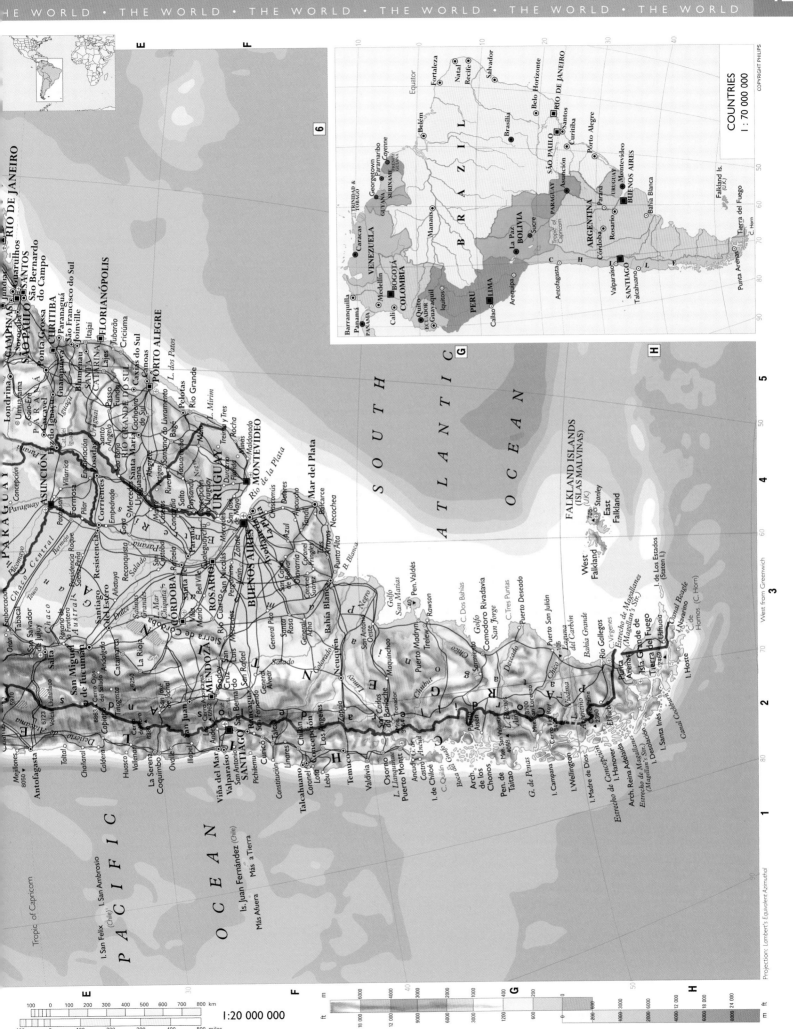

COUNTRIES
1 : 70 000 000

COPYRIGHT PHILIPS

Projection: Lambert's Equivalent Azimuthal

1:20 000 000

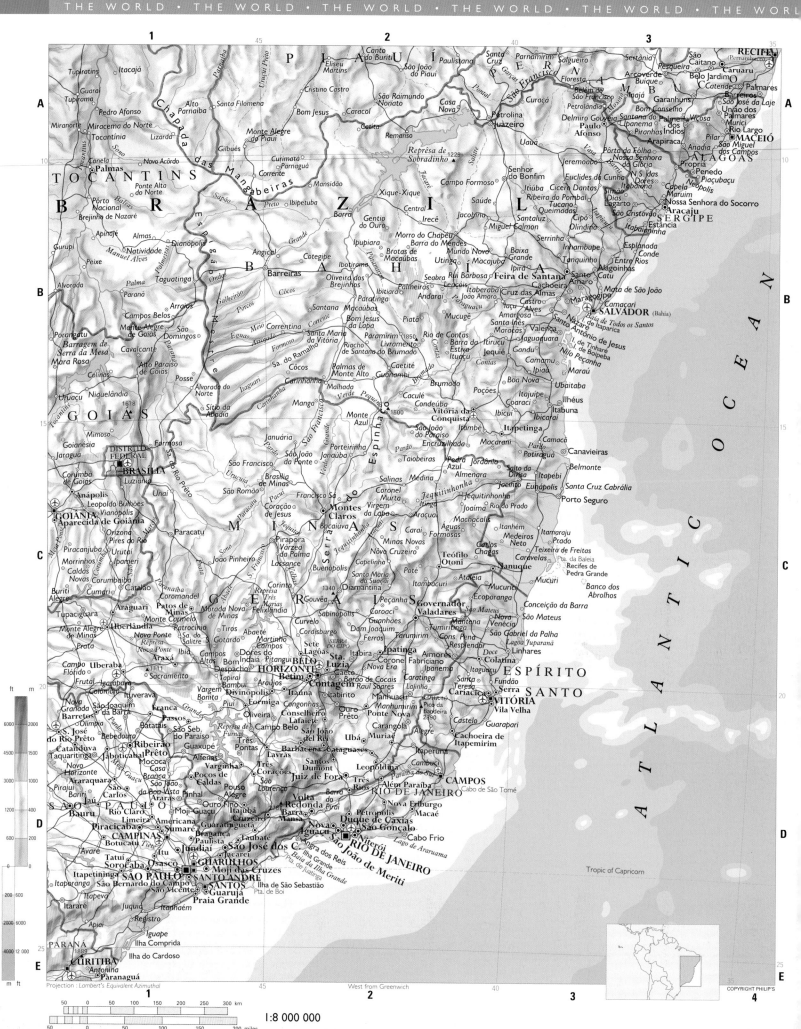

Projection : Lambert's Equivalent Azimuthal

West from Greenwich

COPYRIGHT PHILIP'S

50   0   50   100   150   200   250   300 km
50   0   50   100   150   200 miles

1:8 000 000

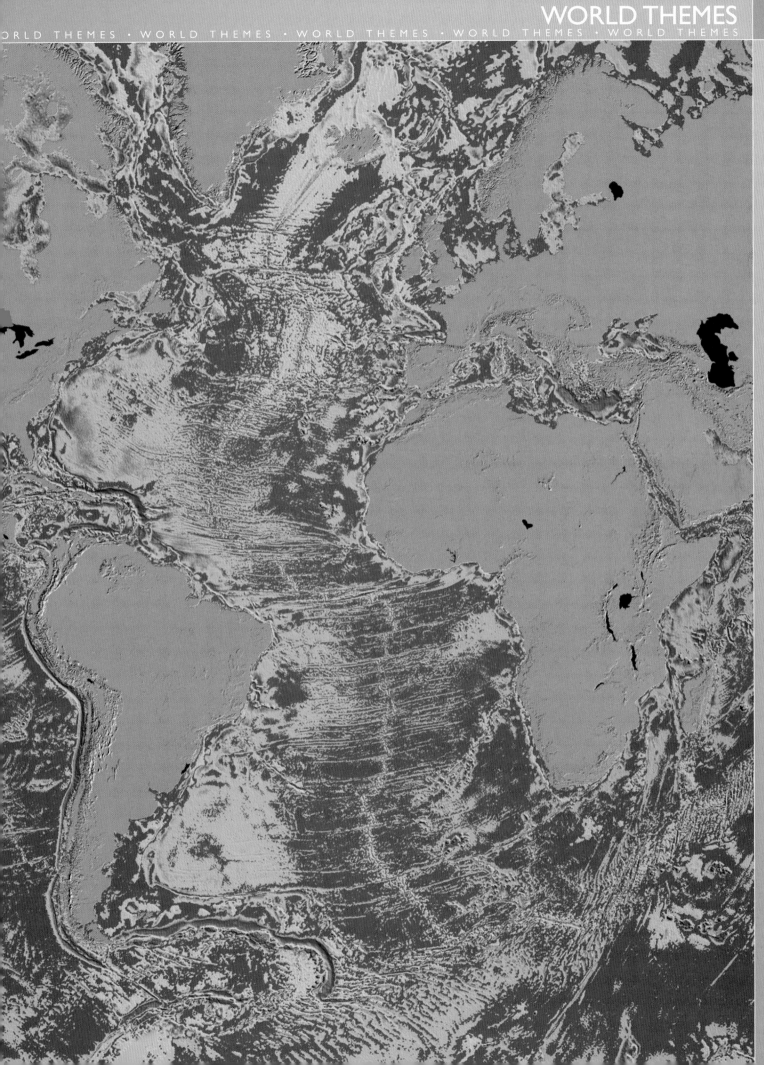

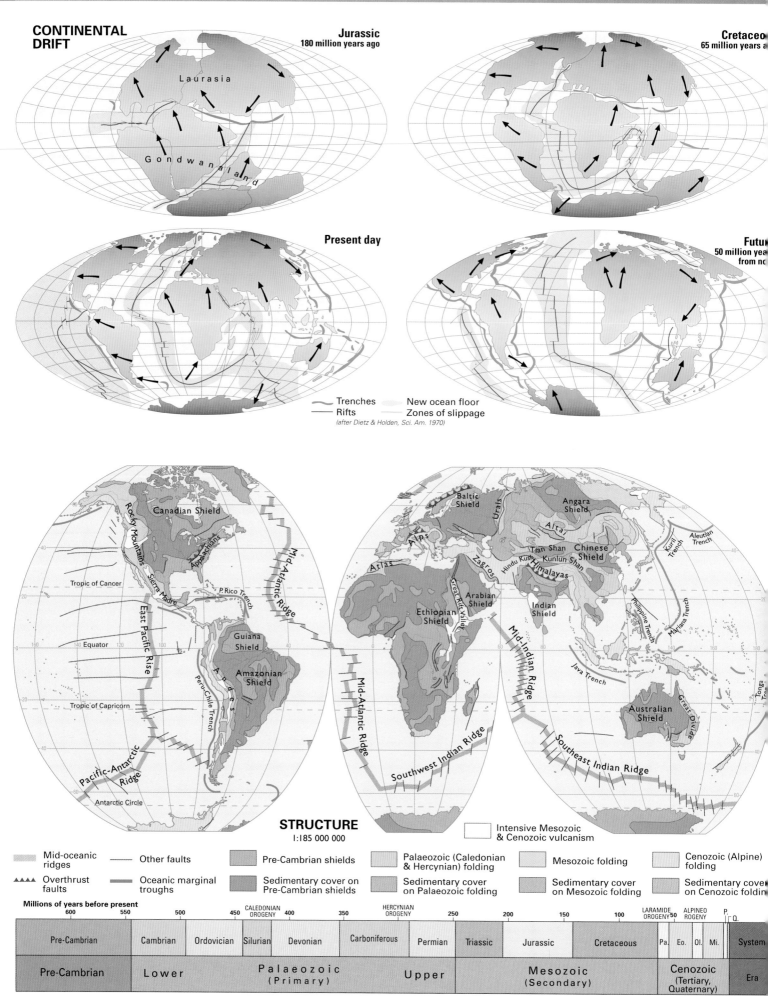

CONTINENTAL DRIFT

Jurassic
180 million years ago

Laurasia

Gondwanaland

Cretaceo
65 million years a

Present day

Futu
50 million yea
from no

Trenches   New ocean floor
Rifts   Zones of slippage
(after Dietz & Holden, Sci. Am. 1970)

STRUCTURE
1:185 000 000

Canadian Shield
Rocky Mountains
Appalachians
Tropic of Cancer
Sierra Madre
East Pacific Rise
P. Rico Trench
Equator
Guiana Shield
Andes
Amazonian Shield
Peru-Chile Trench
Tropic of Capricorn
Mid-Atlantic Ridge
Pacific-Antarctic Ridge
Antarctic Circle

Baltic Shield
Urals
Angara Shield
Alps
Altai
Tian Shan
Chinese Shield
Atlas
Zagros
Hindu Kush
Kunlun Shan
Himalayas
Kuril Trench
Aleutian Trench
Great Rift Valley
Arabian Shield
Indian Shield
Ethiopian Shield
Philippine Trench
Mariana Trench
Mid-Indian Ridge
Java Trench
Mid-Atlantic Ridge
Australian Shield
Great Divide
Tonga Trench
Southwest Indian Ridge
Southeast Indian Ridge

Intensive Mesozoic
& Cenozoic vulcanism

Mid-oceanic ridges
Overthrust faults
Other faults
Oceanic marginal troughs
Pre-Cambrian shields
Sedimentary cover on Pre-Cambrian shields
Palaeozoic (Caledonian & Hercynian) folding
Sedimentary cover on Palaeozoic folding
Mesozoic folding
Sedimentary cover on Mesozoic folding
Cenozoic (Alpine) folding
Sedimentary cover on Cenozoic foldin

Millions of years before present

600	550	500	450 CALEDONIAN OROGENY	400	350	HERCYNIAN OROGENY	250	200	150	100	LARAMIDE OROGENY 50	ALPINEO ROGENY	P.	
Pre-Cambrian	Cambrian	Ordovician	Silurian	Devonian	Carboniferous	Permian	Triassic	Jurassic	Cretaceous		Pa.	Eo.	Ol.	Mi.	System
Pre-Cambrian	Lower		Palaeozoic (Primary)			Upper		Mesozoic (Secondary)			Cenozoic (Tertiary, Quaternary)			Era

System names in Cenozoic era: Q. = Quaternary   Mi. = Miocene   Eo. = Eocene
P. = Pliocene   Ol. = Oligocene   Pa. = Palaeocen

VOLCANOES AND PLATE TECTONICS

1:185 000 000   ▨ 'Ring of Fire'   ═══ Constructive boundary (plates moving apart)   ▲▲▲ Destructive boundary (plates colliding)   ─── Conservative boundary (plates sliding past each other)   7.2 ↙ Direction of movement along plate boundaries (cm/year)

○ Submarine volcanoes   ✦ Geysers   △ Land volcanoes active since 1700

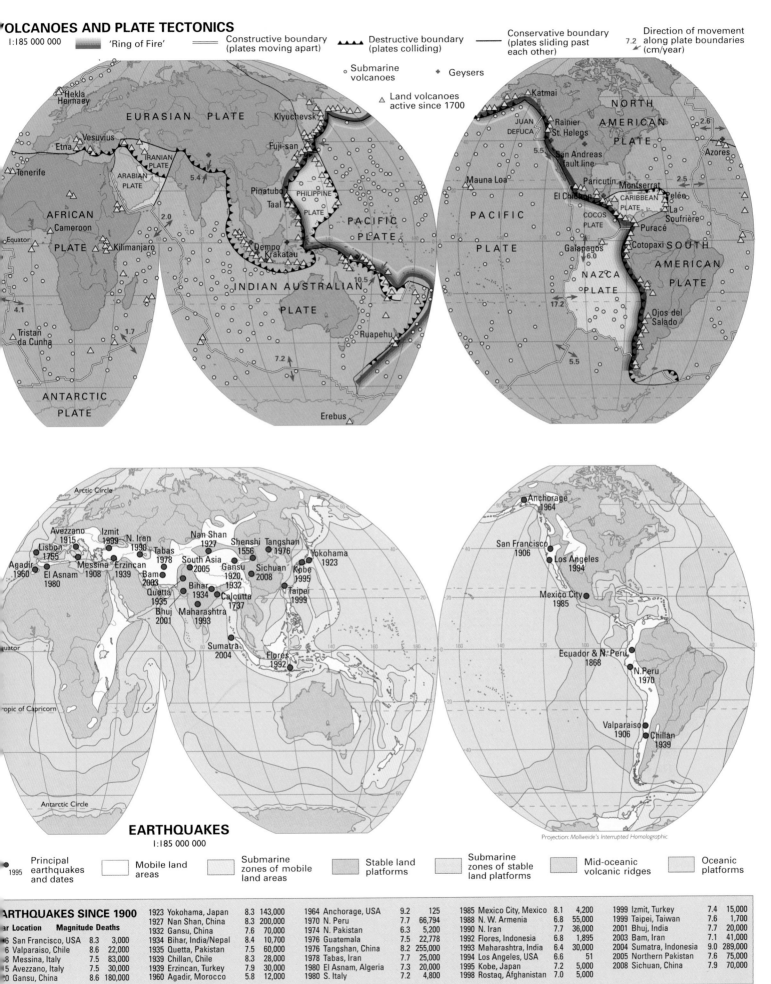

EARTHQUAKES
1:185 000 000

● 1995 Principal earthquakes and dates   ▢ Mobile land areas   ▨ Submarine zones of mobile land areas   ▨ Stable land platforms   ▨ Submarine zones of stable land platforms   ▨ Mid-oceanic volcanic ridges   ▨ Oceanic platforms

Projection: Mollweide's Interrupted Homolographic

EARTHQUAKES SINCE 1900										
Year Location	Magnitude	Deaths	Location	Mag.	Deaths	Location	Mag.	Deaths	Location	Mag.	Deaths
1906 San Francisco, USA	8.3	3,000	1923 Yokohama, Japan	8.3	143,000	1964 Anchorage, USA	9.2	125	1985 Mexico City, Mexico	8.1	4,200	1999 Izmit, Turkey	7.4	15,000
1906 Valparaiso, Chile	8.6	22,000	1927 Nan Shan, China	8.3	200,000	1970 N. Peru	7.7	66,794	1988 N. W. Armenia	6.8	55,000	1999 Taipei, Taiwan	7.6	1,700
1908 Messina, Italy	7.5	83,000	1932 Gansu, China	7.6	70,000	1974 N. Pakistan	6.3	5,200	1990 N. Iran	7.7	36,000	2001 Bhuj, India	7.7	20,000
1915 Avezzano, Italy	7.5	30,000	1934 Bihar, India/Nepal	8.4	10,700	1976 Guatemala	7.5	22,778	1992 Flores, Indonesia	6.8	1,895	2003 Bam, Iran	7.1	41,000
1920 Gansu, China	8.6	180,000	1935 Quetta, Pakistan	7.5	60,000	1976 Tangshan, China	8.2	255,000	1993 Maharashtra, India	6.4	30,000	2004 Sumatra, Indonesia	9.0	289,000
			1939 Chillan, Chile	8.3	28,000	1978 Tabas, Iran	7.7	25,000	1994 Los Angeles, USA	6.6	51	2005 Northern Pakistan	7.6	75,000
			1939 Erzincan, Turkey	7.9	30,000	1980 El Asnam, Algeria	7.3	20,000	1995 Kobe, Japan	7.2	5,000	2008 Sichuan, China	7.9	70,000
			1960 Agadir, Morocco	5.8	12,000	1980 S. Italy	7.2	4,800	1998 Rostaq, Afghanistan	7.0	5,000			

COPYRIGHT PHILIP'S

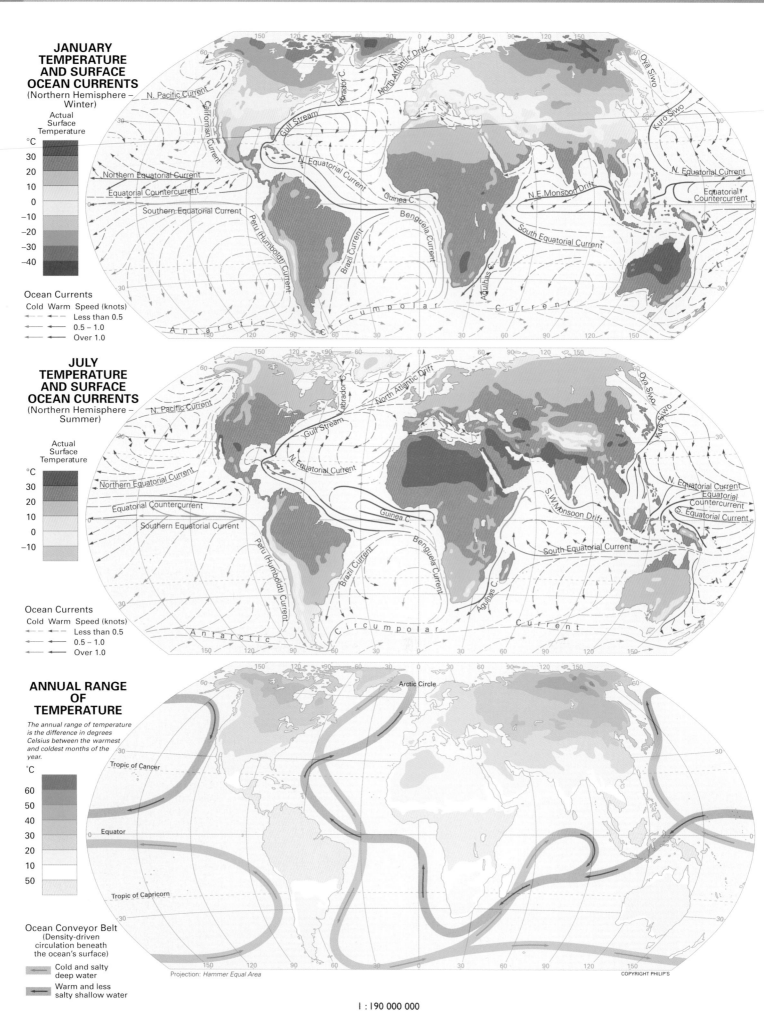

JANUARY TEMPERATURE AND SURFACE OCEAN CURRENTS
(Northern Hemisphere – Winter)

Actual Surface Temperature

°C
30
20
10
0
−10
−20
−30
−40

Ocean Currents
Cold Warm Speed (knots)
Less than 0.5
0.5 – 1.0
Over 1.0

JULY TEMPERATURE AND SURFACE OCEAN CURRENTS
(Northern Hemisphere – Summer)

Actual Surface Temperature

°C
30
20
10
0
−10

Ocean Currents
Cold Warm Speed (knots)
Less than 0.5
0.5 – 1.0
Over 1.0

ANNUAL RANGE OF TEMPERATURE

The annual range of temperature is the difference in degrees Celsius between the warmest and coldest months of the year.

°C
60
50
40
30
20
10
50

Ocean Conveyor Belt
(Density-driven circulation beneath the ocean's surface)

Cold and salty deep water

Warm and less salty shallow water

Projection: Hammer Equal Area

COPYRIGHT PHILIP'S

1 : 190 000 000

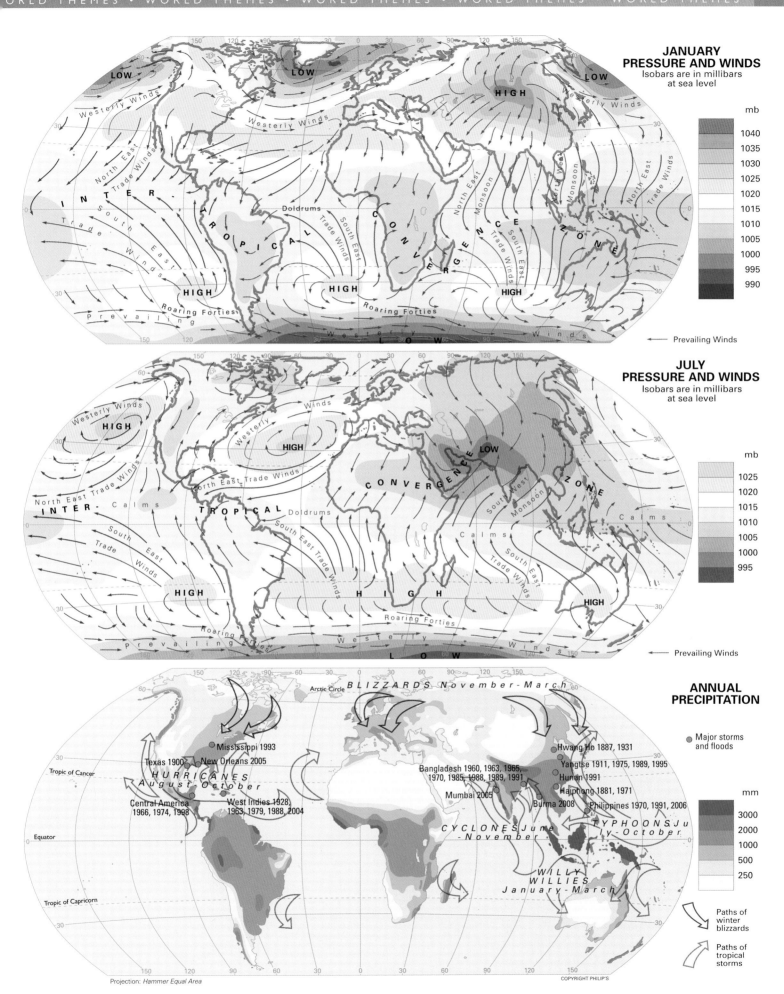

JANUARY PRESSURE AND WINDS

Isobars are in millibars at sea level

mb

1040
1035
1030
1025
1020
1015
1010
1005
1000
995
990

← Prevailing Winds

JULY PRESSURE AND WINDS

Isobars are in millibars at sea level

mb

1025
1020
1015
1010
1005
1000
995

← Prevailing Winds

ANNUAL PRECIPITATION

● Major storms and floods

mm

3000
2000
1000
500
250

Paths of winter blizzards

Paths of tropical storms

Mississippi 1993
Texas 1900
New Orleans 2005
HURRICANES August - October
Central America 1966, 1974, 1998
West Indies 1928, 1963, 1979, 1988, 2004

BLIZZARDS November - March

Hwang Ho 1887, 1931
Yangtse 1911, 1975, 1989, 1995
Bangladesh 1960, 1963, 1965, 1970, 1985, 1988, 1989, 1991
Hunan 1991
Mumbai 2005
Haiphong 1881, 1971
Burma 2008
Philippines 1970, 1991, 2006

CYCLONES June - November

TYPHOONS July - October

WILLY WILLIES January - March

Projection: Hammer Equal Area

COPYRIGHT PHILIP'S

KEY TO CLIMATE REGIONS MAP

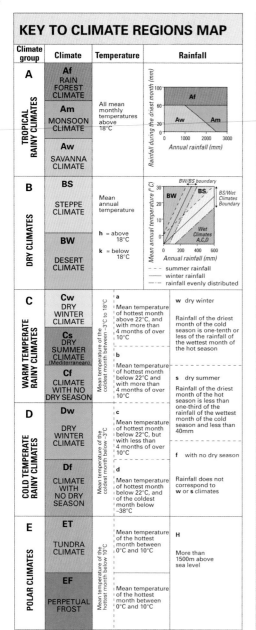

Climate group	Climate	Temperature	Rainfall
A TROPICAL RAINY CLIMATES	**Af** RAIN FOREST CLIMATE	All mean monthly temperatures above 18°C	*Rainfall during the driest month (mm)* — graph: Af, Aw, Am; Annual rainfall (mm)
	Am MONSOON CLIMATE		
	Aw SAVANNA CLIMATE		
B DRY CLIMATES	**BS** STEPPE CLIMATE	Mean annual temperature h = above 18°C k = below 18°C	graph: BW/BS boundary, BW, BS, BS/Wet Climates Boundary, Wet Climates A,C,D; Mean annual temperature (°C); Annual rainfall (mm); --- summer rainfall; — winter rainfall; -·- rainfall evenly distributed
	BW DESERT CLIMATE		
C WARM TEMPERATE RAINY CLIMATES	**Cw** DRY WINTER CLIMATE	*Mean temperature of the coldest month between −3°C to 18°C*	**a** Mean temperature of hottest month above 22°C, and with more than 4 months of over 10°C
			w dry winter — Rainfall of the driest month of the cold season is one-tenth or less of the rainfall of the wettest month of the hot season
	Cs DRY SUMMER CLIMATE (Mediterranean)		**b** Mean temperature of hottest month below 22°C and with more than 4 months of over 10°C
	Cf CLIMATE WITH NO DRY SEASON		**s** dry summer — Rainfall of the driest month of the hot season is less than one-third of the rainfall of the wettest month of the cold season and less than 40mm
D COLD TEMPERATE RAINY CLIMATES	**Dw** DRY WINTER CLIMATE	*Mean temperature of the coldest month below −3°C*	**c** Mean temperature of hottest month below 22°C, but with less than 4 months of over 10°C
			f with no dry season
	Df CLIMATE WITH NO DRY SEASON		**d** Mean temperature of hottest month below 22°C, and of the coldest month below −38°C — Rainfall does not correspond to **w** or **s** climates
E POLAR CLIMATES	**ET** TUNDRA CLIMATE	*Mean temperature of the hottest month below 10°C* — Mean temperature of the hottest month between 0°C and 10°C	**H** More than 1500m above sea level
	EF PERPETUAL FROST		Mean temperature of the hottest month between 0°C and 10°C

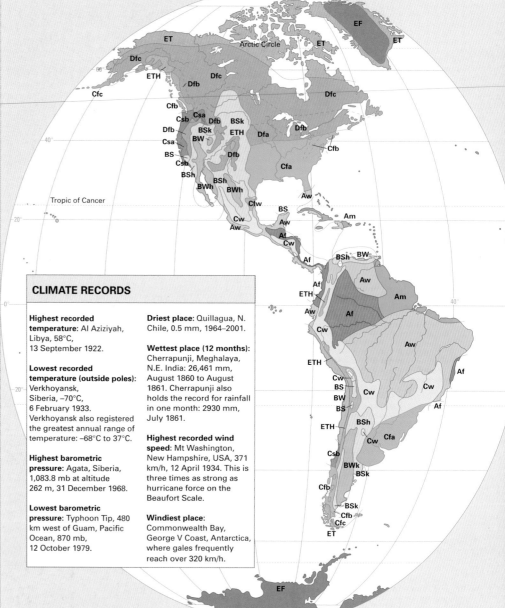

Tropic of Cancer

Arctic Circle

Projection: Interrupted Mollweide's Homolographic

CLIMATE RECORDS

Highest recorded temperature: Al Aziziyah, Libya, 58°C, 13 September 1922.

Lowest recorded temperature (outside poles): Verkhoyansk, Siberia, −70°C, 6 February 1933. Verkhoyansk also registered the greatest annual range of temperature: −68°C to 37°C.

Highest barometric pressure: Agata, Siberia, 1,083.8 mb at altitude 262 m, 31 December 1968.

Lowest barometric pressure: Typhoon Tip, 480 km west of Guam, Pacific Ocean, 870 mb, 12 October 1979.

Driest place: Quillagua, N. Chile, 0.5 mm, 1964–2001.

Wettest place (12 months): Cherrapunji, Meghalaya, N.E. India: 26,461 mm, August 1860 to August 1861. Cherrapunji also holds the record for rainfall in one month: 2930 mm, July 1861.

Highest recorded wind speed: Mt Washington, New Hampshire, USA, 371 km/h, 12 April 1934. This is three times as strong as hurricane force on the Beaufort Scale.

Windiest place: Commonwealth Bay, George V Coast, Antarctica, where gales frequently reach over 320 km/h.

THE MONSOON   1:90 000 000

Monthly rainfall

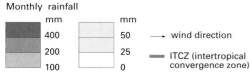

mm		mm	
400		50	→ wind direction
200		25	∿ ITCZ (intertropical convergence zone)
100		0	

In early March, which normally marks the end of the subcontinent's cool season and the start of the hot season, winds blow outwards from the mainland. But as the overhead sun and the ITCZ move northwards, the land is intensely heated, and a low-pressure system develops. The south-east trade winds, which are drawn across the Equator, change direction and are sucked into the interior to become south-westerly winds, bringing heavy rain. By November, the overhead sun and the ITCZ have again moved southwards and the wind directions are again reversed. Cool winds blow from the Asian interior to the sea, losing any moisture on the Himalayas before descending to the coast.

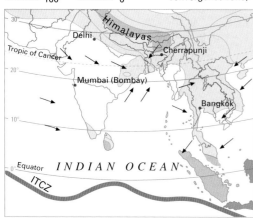

March – Start of the hot, dry season, the ITCZ is over the southern Indian Ocean.

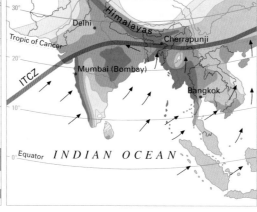

July – The rainy season, the ITCZ has migrated northwards; winds blow onshore.

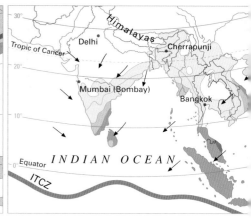

November – The ITCZ has returned south, the offshore win are cool and dry.

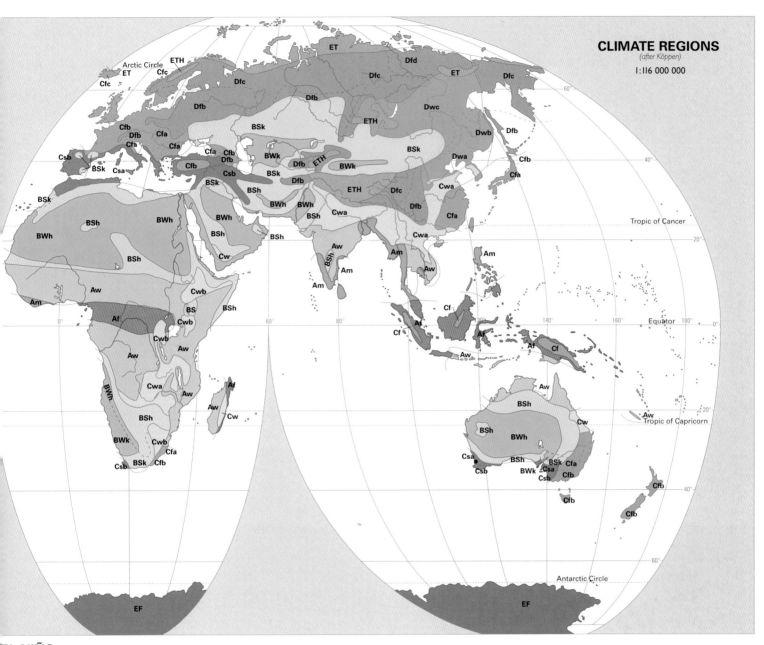

CLIMATE REGIONS
(after Köppen)

1:116 000 000

EL NIÑO

In a normal year, south-easterly trade winds drive surface waters westwards off the coast of South America, drawing cold, nutrient-rich water up from below. In an El Niño year, warm water from the west Pacific suppresses upwelling in the east, depriving the region of nutrients. The water is warmed by as much as 7°C, disturbing the tropical atmosphere circulation. During an intense El Niño, the south-east trade winds change direction and become equatorial westerlies, resulting in climatic extremes in many regions of the world, such as drought in parts of Australia and India, and heavy rainfall in south-eastern USA.

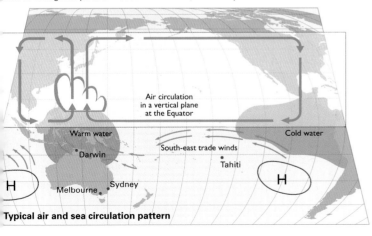

Typical air and sea circulation pattern

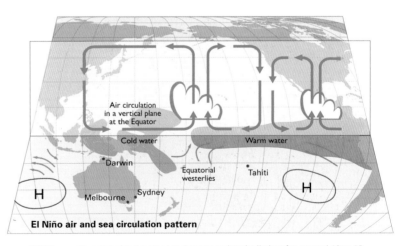

El Niño air and sea circulation pattern

El Niño events occur about every 4 to 7 years and typically last for around 12 to 18 months. El Niño usually results in reduced rainfall across northern and eastern Australia. This can lead to widespread and severe drought, as well as increased temperatures and bushfire risk. However, each El Niño event is unique in terms of its strength as well as its impact. It is measured by the Southern Oscillation Index (SOI) and the changes in ocean temperatures.

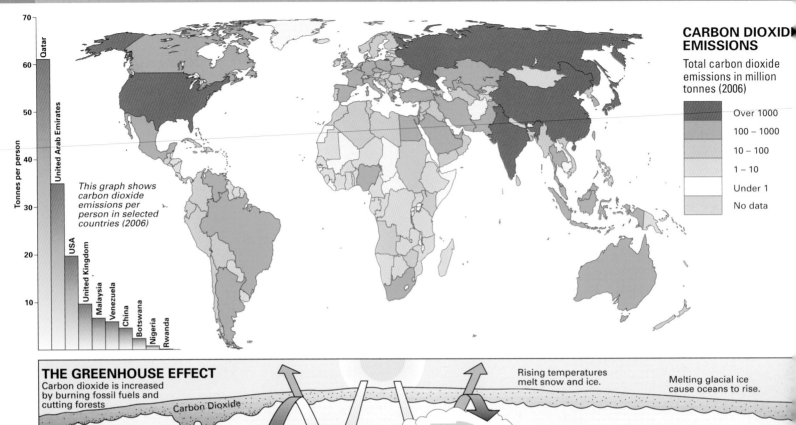

CARBON DIOXIDE EMISSIONS

Total carbon dioxide emissions in million tonnes (2006)

- Over 1000
- 100 – 1000
- 10 – 100
- 1 – 10
- Under 1
- No data

This graph shows carbon dioxide emissions per person in selected countries (2006)

Tonnes per person

Qatar
United Arab Emirates
USA
United Kingdom
Malaysia
Venezuela
China
Botswana
Nigeria
Rwanda

THE GREENHOUSE EFFECT

Carbon dioxide is increased by burning fossil fuels and cutting forests

Carbon Dioxide

Rising temperatures melt snow and ice.

Melting glacial ice cause oceans to rise.

The carbon dioxide traps the heat being reflected from the Earth, although some heat is lost.

The warming increases water vapour in the air, leading to even greater absorption of heat.

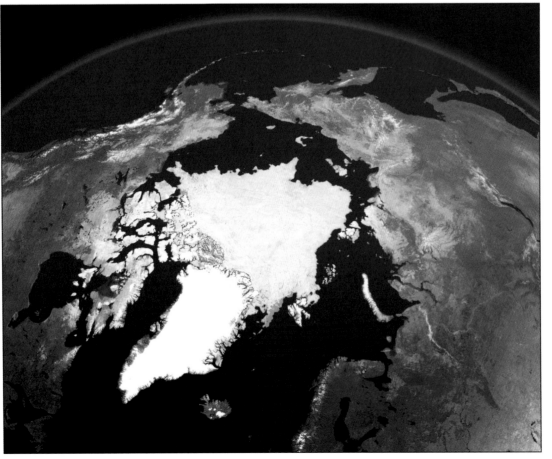

Arctic Ice Cap

This image shows the extent of sea-ice in the Arctic in September 2008. The sea-ice area expands and contracts seasonally and September, at the end of the northern hemisphere summer, represents its smallest extent. The year 2008 showed the biggest reduction in sea-ice since satellite surveillance began in 1979 and this is believed to be related to climate change and global warming. Although dramatic, the sea-ice itself is thought to be quite thin, on average about 3 m (10 ft) thick. Even large reductions would not in themselves involve any sea-level change since the ice is floating and displaces the sea water. One by-product of this is the opening-up of clear sea. This would enable shipping in the northern hemisphere to move between the Atlantic and Pacific Oceans using the much shorter routes around the north coasts of Canada and of Russia, rather than heading south to do this.

PREDICTED CHANGE IN TEMPERATURE

The difference between actual annual average surface air temperature, 1960–90, and predicted annual average surface air temperature, 2070–2100. This map shows the predicted increase, assuming a 'medium growth' of the global economy and assuming that no measures to combat the emission of greenhouse gases are taken.

5 – 10°C warmer

3 – 5°C warmer

2 – 3°C warmer

1 – 2°C warmer

0 – 1°C warmer

Source: The Hadley Centre of Climate Prediction and Research, The Met. Office.

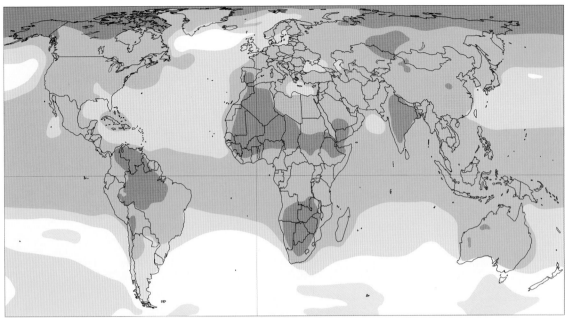

PREDICTED CHANGE IN PRECIPITATION

The difference between actual annual average precipitation, 1960–90, and predicted annual average precipitation, 2070–2100. It should be noted that these predicted annual mean changes mask quite significant seasonal detail.

Over 2 mm more rain per day

1 – 2 mm more rain per day

0.5 – 1 mm more rain per day

0.2 – 0.5 mm more rain per day

no change

0.2 – 0.5 mm less rain per day

0.5 – 1 mm less rain per day

1 – 2 mm less rain per day

Over 2 mm less rain per day

DESERTIFICATION AND DEFORESTATION

Existing deserts and dry areas

Areas with a high risk of desertification

Areas with a moderate risk of desertification

Former extent of rainforest

Existing rainforest

Deforestation 2000–2005

	Annual Actual Loss
Brazil	34,660 sq km
Indonesia	14,478 sq km
Russia	5,322 sq km
Mexico	2,600 sq km
Papua New Guinea	2,502 sq km

	% Loss 1990-2005
Nigeria	79%
Vietnam	78%
Cambodia	58%
Sri Lanka	35%
Indonesia	31%

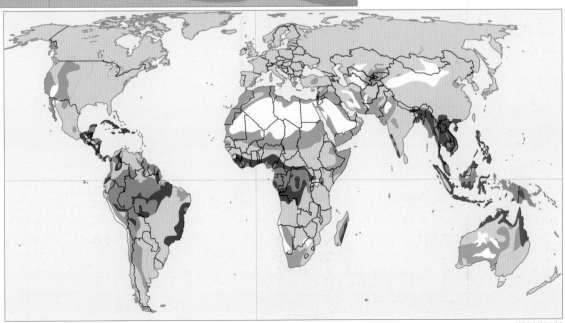

Projection: Eckert IV

COPYRIGHT PHILIP'S

		Jan	
Addis Ababa, Ethiopia 2,410 m			Height of meteorological station above sea level in metres
Temperature	Daily max. °C	23	Average monthly maximum temperature in degrees Celsius
	Daily min. °C	6	Average monthly minimum temperature in degrees Celsius
	Average monthly °C	14	Average monthly temperature in degrees Celsius
Rainfall	Monthly total mm	13	Average monthly precipitation in millimetres
Sunshine	Hours per day	8.7	Average daily duration of bright sunshine per month in hours

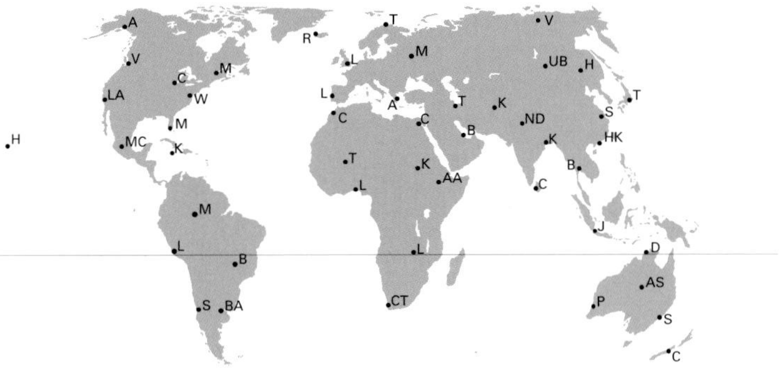

Addis Ababa, Ethiopia 2,410 m		Jan	Feb	Mar	Apr	May	June	July	Aug	Sept	Oct	Nov	Dec	Year
Temperature	Daily max. °C	23	24	25	24	25	23	20	20	21	22	23	22	23
	Daily min. °C	6	7	9	10	9	10	11	11	10	7	5	5	8
	Average monthly °C	14	15	17	17	17	16	16	15	15	15	14	14	15
Rainfall	Monthly total mm	13	35	67	91	81	117	247	255	167	29	8	5	1,115
Sunshine	Hours per day	8.7	8.2	7.6	8.1	6.5	4.8	2.8	3.2	5.2	7.6	6.7	7	6.4

Alice Springs, Australia 580 m		Jan	Feb	Mar	Apr	May	June	July	Aug	Sept	Oct	Nov	Dec	Year
Temperature	Daily max. °C	35	35	32	27	23	19	19	23	27	31	33	35	28
	Daily min. °C	21	20	17	12	8	5	4	6	10	15	18	20	13
	Average monthly °C	28	27	25	20	15	12	12	14	18	23	25	27	21
Rainfall	Monthly total mm	44	33	27	10	15	13	7	8	7	18	29	38	249
Sunshine	Hours per day	10.3	10.4	9.3	9.2	8	8	8.9	9.8	10	9.7	10.1	10	9.5

Anchorage, USA 183 m		Jan	Feb	Mar	Apr	May	June	July	Aug	Sept	Oct	Nov	Dec	Year
Temperature	Daily max. °C	–7	–3	0	7	13	18	19	17	13	6	–2	–6	–6
	Daily min. °C	–15	–12	–9	–2	4	8	10	9	5	–2	–9	–14	–2
	Average monthly °C	–11	–7	–4	3	9	13	15	13	9	2	–5	–10	–4
Rainfall	Monthly total mm	20	18	13	11	13	25	47	64	64	47	28	24	374
Sunshine	Hours per day	2.4	4.1	6.6	8.3	8.3	9.2	8.5	6	4.4	3.1	2.6	1.6	5.4

Athens, Greece 107 m		Jan	Feb	Mar	Apr	May	June	July	Aug	Sept	Oct	Nov	Dec	Year
Temperature	Daily max. °C	13	14	16	20	25	30	33	33	29	24	19	15	23
	Daily min. °C	6	7	8	11	16	20	23	23	19	15	12	8	14
	Average monthly °C	10	10	12	16	20	25	28	28	24	20	15	11	18
Rainfall	Monthly total mm	62	37	37	23	23	14	6	7	15	51	56	71	402
Sunshine	Hours per day	3.9	5.2	5.8	7.7	8.9	10.7	11.9	11.5	9.4	6.8	4.8	3.8	7.3

Bahrain City, Bahrain 2 m		Jan	Feb	Mar	Apr	May	June	July	Aug	Sept	Oct	Nov	Dec	Year
Temperature	Daily max. °C	20	21	25	29	33	36	37	38	36	32	27	22	30
	Daily min. °C	14	15	18	22	25	29	31	32	29	25	22	16	23
	Average monthly °C	17	18	21	25	29	32	34	35	32	29	25	19	26
Rainfall	Monthly total mm	18	12	10	9	2	0	0	0	0	0.4	3	16	70
Sunshine	Hours per day	5.9	6.9	7.9	8.8	10.6	13.2	12.1	12	12	10.3	7.7	6.4	9.5

Bangkok, Thailand 10 m		Jan	Feb	Mar	Apr	May	June	July	Aug	Sept	Oct	Nov	Dec	Year
Temperature	Daily max. °C	32	33	34	35	34	33	32	32	32	31	31	31	33
	Daily min. °C	20	23	24	26	25	25	25	24	24	24	23	20	24
	Average monthly °C	26	28	29	30	30	29	28	28	28	28	27	26	28
Rainfall	Monthly total mm	9	30	36	82	165	153	168	183	310	239	55	8	1,438
Sunshine	Hours per day	8.2	8	8	10	7.5	6.1	4.7	5.2	5.2	6.1	7.3	7.8	7

Brasilia, Brazil 910 m		Jan	Feb	Mar	Apr	May	June	July	Aug	Sept	Oct	Nov	Dec	Year
Temperature	Daily max. °C	28	28	28	28	27	27	27	29	30	29	28	27	28
	Daily min. °C	18	18	18	17	15	13	13	14	16	18	18	18	16
	Average monthly °C	23	23	23	22	21	20	20	21	23	24	23	22	22
Rainfall	Monthly total mm	252	204	227	93	17	3	6	3	30	127	255	343	1,560
Sunshine	Hours per day	5.8	5.7	6	7.4	8.7	9.3	9.6	9.8	7.9	6.5	4.8	4.4	7.2

Buenos Aires, Argentina 25 m		Jan	Feb	Mar	Apr	May	June	July	Aug	Sept	Oct	Nov	Dec	Year
Temperature	Daily max. °C	30	29	26	22	18	14	14	16	18	21	25	28	22
	Daily min. °C	17	17	16	12	9	5	6	6	8	10	14	16	11
	Average monthly °C	23	23	21	17	13	10	10	11	13	15	19	22	16
Rainfall	Monthly total mm	79	71	109	89	76	61	56	61	79	86	84	99	950
Sunshine	Hours per day	9.2	8.5	7.5	6.8	4.9	3.5	3.8	5.2	6	6.8	8.1	8.5	6.6

Cairo, Egypt 75 m		Jan	Feb	Mar	Apr	May	June	July	Aug	Sept	Oct	Nov	Dec	Year
Temperature	Daily max. °C	19	21	24	28	32	35	35	35	33	30	26	21	28
	Daily min. °C	9	9	12	14	18	20	22	22	20	18	14	10	16
	Average monthly °C	14	15	18	21	25	28	29	28	26	24	20	16	22
Rainfall	Monthly total mm	4	4	3	1	2	1	0	0	1	1	3	7	27
Sunshine	Hours per day	6.9	8.4	8.7	9.7	10.5	11.9	11.7	11.3	10.4	9.4	8.3	6.4	9.5

Cape Town, South Africa 44 m		Jan	Feb	Mar	Apr	May	June	July	Aug	Sept	Oct	Nov	Dec	Year
Temperature	Daily max. °C	26	26	25	23	20	18	17	18	19	21	24	25	22
	Daily min. °C	15	15	14	11	9	7	7	7	8	10	13	15	11
	Average monthly °C	21	20	20	17	14	13	12	12	14	16	18	20	16
Rainfall	Monthly total mm	12	19	17	42	67	98	68	76	36	45	12	13	505
Sunshine	Hours per day	11.4	10.2	9.4	7.7	6.1	5.7	6.4	6.6	7.6	8.6	10.2	10.9	8.4

Casablanca, Morocco 59 m		Jan	Feb	Mar	Apr	May	June	July	Aug	Sept	Oct	Nov	Dec	Year
Temperature	Daily max. °C	17	18	20	21	22	24	26	26	26	24	21	18	22
	Daily min. °C	8	9	11	12	15	18	19	20	18	15	12	10	14
	Average monthly °C	13	13	15	16	18	21	23	23	22	20	17	14	18
Rainfall	Monthly total mm	78	61	54	37	20	3	0	1	6	28	58	94	440
Sunshine	Hours per day	5.2	6.3	7.3	9	9.4	9.7	10.2	9.7	9.1	7.4	5.9	5.3	7.9

Chicago, USA 186 m		Jan	Feb	Mar	Apr	May	June	July	Aug	Sept	Oct	Nov	Dec	Year
Temperature	Daily max. °C	1	2	6	14	21	26	29	28	24	17	8	2	15
	Daily min. °C	–7	–6	–2	5	11	16	20	19	14	8	0	–5	–6
	Average monthly °C	–3	–2	2	9	16	21	24	23	19	13	4	–2	4
Rainfall	Monthly total mm	47	41	70	77	96	103	86	80	69	71	56	48	844
Sunshine	Hours per day	4	5	6.6	6.9	8.9	10.2	10	9.2	8.2	6.9	4.5	3.7	7

Christchurch, New Zealand 5 m		Jan	Feb	Mar	Apr	May	June	July	Aug	Sept	Oct	Nov	Dec	Year
Temperature	Daily max. °C	21	21	19	17	13	11	10	11	14	17	19	21	16
	Daily min. °C	12	12	10	7	4	2	1	3	5	7	8	11	7
	Average monthly °C	16	16	15	12	9	6	6	7	9	12	13	16	11
Rainfall	Monthly total mm	56	46	43	46	76	69	61	58	51	51	51	61	669
Sunshine	Hours per day	7	6.5	5.6	4.7	4.3	3.9	4.1	4.7	5.6	6.1	6.9	6.3	5.5

Colombo, Sri Lanka 10 m		Jan	Feb	Mar	Apr	May	June	July	Aug	Sept	Oct	Nov	Dec	Year
Temperature	Daily max. °C	30	31	31	31	30	30	29	29	30	29	29	30	30
	Daily min. °C	22	22	23	24	25	25	25	25	25	24	23	22	24
	Average monthly °C	26	26	27	28	28	27	27	27	27	27	26	26	27
Rainfall	Monthly total mm	101	66	118	230	394	220	140	102	174	348	333	142	2,368
Sunshine	Hours per day	7.9	9	8.1	7.2	6.4	5.4	6.1	6.3	6.2	6.5	6.4	7.8	6.9

Darwin, Australia 30 m		Jan	Feb	Mar	Apr	May	June	July	Aug	Sept	Oct	Nov	Dec	Year
Temperature	Daily max. °C	32	32	33	33	33	31	31	32	33	34	34	33	33
	Daily min. °C	25	25	25	24	23	21	19	21	23	25	26	26	24
	Average monthly °C	29	29	29	29	28	26	25	26	28	29	30	29	28
Rainfall	Monthly total mm	405	309	279	77	8	2	0	1	15	48	108	214	1,466
Sunshine	Hours per day	5.8	5.8	6.6	9.8	9.3	10	9.9	10.4	10.1	9.4	9.6	6.8	8.6

Harbin, China 175 m		Jan	Feb	Mar	Apr	May	June	July	Aug	Sept	Oct	Nov	Dec	Year
Temperature	Daily max. °C	–14	–9	0	12	21	26	29	27	20	12	–1	–11	9
	Daily min. °C	–26	–23	–12	–1	7	14	18	16	8	0	–12	–22	–3
	Average monthly °C	–20	–16	–6	6	14	20	23	22	14	6	–7	–17	3
Rainfall	Monthly total mm	4	6	17	23	44	92	167	119	52	36	12	5	577
Sunshine	Hours per day	6.4	7.8	8	7.8	8.3	8.6	8.6	8.2	7.2	6.9	6.1	5.7	7.5

Hong Kong, China 35 m		Jan	Feb	Mar	Apr	May	June	July	Aug	Sept	Oct	Nov	Dec	Year
Temperature	Daily max. °C	18	18	20	24	28	30	31	31	30	27	24	20	25
	Daily min. °C	13	13	16	19	23	26	26	26	25	23	19	15	20
	Average monthly °C	16	15	18	22	25	28	28	28	27	25	21	17	23
Rainfall	Monthly total mm	30	60	70	133	332	479	286	415	364	33	46	17	2,265
Sunshine	Hours per day	4.7	3.5	3.1	3.8	5	5.4	6.8	6.5	6.6	7	6.2	5.5	5.3

Honolulu, Hawaii 5 m		Jan	Feb	Mar	Apr	May	June	July	Aug	Sept	Oct	Nov	Dec	Year
Temperature	Daily max. °C	26	26	26	27	28	29	29	29	30	29	28	26	28
	Daily min. °C	19	19	19	20	21	22	23	23	23	22	21	20	21
	Average monthly °C	23	22	23	23	24	26	26	26	26	26	24	23	24
Rainfall	Monthly total mm	96	84	73	33	25	8	11	23	25	47	55	76	556
Sunshine	Hours per day	7.3	7.7	8.3	8.6	8.8	9.1	9.4	9.3	9.2	8.3	7.5	6.2	8.3

Jakarta, Indonesia 10 m		Jan	Feb	Mar	Apr	May	June	July	Aug	Sept	Oct	Nov	Dec	Year
Temperature	Daily max. °C	29	29	30	31	31	31	31	31	31	31	30	29	30
	Daily min. °C	23	23	23	24	24	23	23	23	23	23	23	23	23
	Average monthly °C	26	26	27	27	27	27	27	27	27	27	27	26	27
Rainfall	Monthly total mm	300	300	211	147	114	97	64	43	66	112	142	203	1,799
Sunshine	Hours per day	6.1	6.5	7.7	8.5	8.4	8.5	9.1	9.5	9.6	9	7.7	7.1	8.1

Kabul, Afghanistan 1,791 m		Jan	Feb	Mar	Apr	May	June	July	Aug	Sept	Oct	Nov	Dec	Year
Temperature	Daily max. °C	2	4	12	19	26	31	33	33	30	22	17	8	20
	Daily min. °C	–8	–6	1	6	11	13	16	15	11	6	1	–3	5
	Average monthly °C	–3	–1	6	13	18	22	25	24	20	14	9	3	12
Rainfall	Monthly total mm	28	61	72	117	33	1	7	1	0	1	37	14	372
Sunshine	Hours per day	5.9	6	5.7	6.8	10.1	11.5	11.4	11.2	9.8	9.4	7.8	6.1	8.5

Khartoum, Sudan 380 m		Jan	Feb	Mar	Apr	May	June	July	Aug	Sept	Oct	Nov	Dec	Year
Temperature	Daily max. °C	32	33	37	40	42	41	38	36	38	39	35	32	37
	Daily min. °C	16	17	20	23	26	27	26	25	25	25	21	17	22
	Average monthly °C	24	25	28	32	34	34	32	30	32	32	28	25	30
Rainfall	Monthly total mm	0	0	0	1	7	5	56	80	28	2	0	0	179
Sunshine	Hours per day	10.6	11.2	10.4	10.8	10.4	10.1	8.6	8.6	9.6	10.3	10.8	10.6	10.2

Kingston, Jamaica 35 m		Jan	Feb	Mar	Apr	May	June	July	Aug	Sept	Oct	Nov	Dec	Year
Temperature	Daily max. °C	30	30	30	31	31	32	32	32	32	31	31	31	31
	Daily min. °C	20	20	20	21	22	24	23	23	23	23	22	21	22
	Average monthly °C	25	25	25	26	26	28	28	28	27	27	26	26	26
Rainfall	Monthly total mm	23	15	23	31	102	89	38	91	99	180	74	36	801
Sunshine	Hours per day	8.3	8.8	8.7	8.7	8.3	7.8	8.5	8.5	7.6	7.3	8.3	7.7	8.2

		Jan	Feb	Mar	Apr	May	June	July	Aug	Sept	Oct	Nov	Dec	Year
Kolkata (Calcutta), India	5m													
Temperature	Daily max. °C	27	29	34	36	35	34	32	32	32	32	29	26	31
	Daily min. °C	13	15	21	24	25	26	26	26	26	23	18	13	21
	Average monthly °C	20	22	27	30	30	30	29	29	29	28	23	20	26
Rainfall	Monthly total mm	10	30	34	44	140	297	325	332	253	114	20	5	1,604
Sunshine	Hours per day	8.6	8.7	8.9	9	8.7	5.4	4.1	4.1	5.1	6.5	8.3	8.4	7.1
Lagos, Nigeria	40m													
Temperature	Daily max. °C	32	33	33	32	31	29	28	28	29	30	31	32	31
	Daily min. °C	22	23	23	23	23	22	22	21	22	22	23	22	22
	Average monthly °C	27	28	28	28	27	26	25	24	25	26	27	27	27
Rainfall	Monthly total mm	28	41	99	99	203	300	180	56	180	190	63	25	1,464
Sunshine	Hours per day	5.9	6.8	6.3	6.1	5.6	3.8	2.8	3.3	3	5.1	6.6	6.5	5.2
Lima, Peru	120m													
Temperature	Daily max. °C	28	29	29	27	24	20	20	19	20	22	24	26	24
	Daily min. °C	19	20	19	17	16	15	14	14	14	15	16	17	16
	Average monthly °C	24	24	24	22	20	17	17	16	17	18	20	21	20
Rainfall	Monthly total mm	1	1	1	1	5	5	8	8	8	3	3	1	45
Sunshine	Hours per day	6.3	6.8	6.9	6.7	4	1.4	1.1	1	1.1	2.5	4.1	5	3.9
Lisbon, Portugal	77m													
Temperature	Daily max. °C	14	15	17	20	21	25	27	28	26	22	17	15	21
	Daily min. °C	8	8	10	12	13	15	17	17	17	14	11	9	13
	Average monthly °C	11	12	14	16	17	20	22	23	21	18	14	12	17
Rainfall	Monthly total mm	111	76	109	54	44	16	3	4	33	62	93	103	708
Sunshine	Hours per day	4.7	5.9	6	8.3	9.1	10.6	11.4	10.7	8.4	6.7	5.2	4.6	7.7
London (Kew), UK	5m													
Temperature	Daily max. °C	6	7	10	13	17	20	22	21	19	14	10	7	14
	Daily min. °C	2	2	3	6	8	12	14	13	11	8	5	4	7
	Average monthly °C	4	5	7	9	12	16	18	17	15	11	8	5	11
Rainfall	Monthly total mm	54	40	37	37	46	45	57	59	49	57	64	48	593
Sunshine	Hours per day	1.7	2.3	3.5	5.7	6.7	7	6.6	6	5	3.3	1.9	1.4	4.3
Los Angeles, USA	30m													
Temperature	Daily max. °C	18	18	18	19	20	22	24	24	24	23	22	19	21
	Daily min. °C	7	8	9	11	13	15	17	17	16	14	11	9	12
	Average monthly °C	12	13	14	15	17	18	21	21	20	18	16	14	17
Rainfall	Monthly total mm	69	74	46	28	3	3	0	0	5	10	28	61	327
Sunshine	Hours per day	6.9	8.2	8.9	8.8	9.5	10.3	11.7	11	10.1	8.6	8.2	7.6	9.2
Lusaka, Zambia	1,154m													
Temperature	Daily max. °C	26	26	26	27	25	23	23	26	29	31	29	27	27
	Daily min. °C	17	17	16	15	12	10	9	11	15	18	18	17	15
	Average monthly °C	22	22	21	21	18	17	16	19	22	25	23	22	21
Rainfall	Monthly total mm	224	173	90	19	3	1	0	1	1	17	85	196	810
Sunshine	Hours per day	5.1	5.4	6.9	8.9	9	9	9.1	9.6	9.5	9	7	5.5	7.8
Manaus, Brazil	45m													
Temperature	Daily max. °C	31	31	31	31	31	31	32	33	34	34	33	32	32
	Daily min. °C	24	24	24	24	24	24	24	24	24	25	25	24	24
	Average monthly °C	28	28	28	27	28	28	28	29	29	29	29	28	28
Rainfall	Monthly total mm	278	278	300	287	193	99	61	41	62	112	165	220	2,096
Sunshine	Hours per day	3.9	4	3.6	3.9	5.4	6.9	7.9	8.2	7.5	6.6	5.9	4.9	5.7
Mexico City, Mexico	2,309m													
Temperature	Daily max. °C	21	23	26	27	26	25	23	24	23	22	21	21	24
	Daily min. °C	5	6	7	9	10	11	11	11	11	9	6	5	8
	Average monthly °C	13	15	16	18	18	18	17	17	17	16	14	13	16
Rainfall	Monthly total mm	8	4	9	23	57	111	160	149	119	46	16	7	709
Sunshine	Hours per day	7.3	8.1	8.5	8.1	7.8	7	6.2	6.4	5.6	6.3	7	7.3	7.1
Miami, USA	2m													
Temperature	Daily max. °C	24	25	27	28	30	31	32	32	31	29	27	25	28
	Daily min. °C	14	15	16	19	21	23	24	24	24	22	18	15	20
	Average monthly °C	19	20	21	23	25	27	28	28	27	25	22	20	24
Rainfall	Monthly total mm	51	48	58	99	163	188	170	178	241	208	71	43	1,518
Sunshine	Hours per day	7.7	8.3	8.7	9.4	8.9	8.5	8.7	8.4	7.1	6.5	7.5	7.1	8.1
Montreal, Canada	57m													
Temperature	Daily max. °C	−6	−4	2	11	18	23	26	25	20	14	5	−3	11
	Daily min. °C	−13	−11	−5	2	9	14	17	16	11	6	0	−9	3
	Average monthly °C	−9	−8	−2	6	13	19	22	20	16	10	3	−6	7
Rainfall	Monthly total mm	87	76	86	83	81	91	98	87	96	84	89	89	1,047
Sunshine	Hours per day	2.8	3.4	4.5	5.2	6.7	7.7	8.2	7.7	5.6	4.3	2.4	2.2	5.1
Moscow, Russia	156m													
Temperature	Daily max. °C	−6	−4	1	9	18	22	24	22	17	10	1	−5	9
	Daily min. °C	−14	−16	−11	−1	5	9	12	9	4	−2	−6	−12	−2
	Average monthly °C	−10	−10	−5	4	12	15	18	16	10	4	−2	−8	4
Rainfall	Monthly total mm	31	28	33	35	52	67	74	74	58	51	36	36	575
Sunshine	Hours per day	1	1.9	3.7	5.2	7.8	8.3	8.4	7.1	4.4	2.4	1	0.6	4.4
New Delhi, India	220m													
Temperature	Daily max. °C	21	24	29	36	41	39	35	34	34	34	28	23	32
	Daily min. °C	6	10	14	20	26	28	27	26	24	17	11	7	18
	Average monthly °C	14	17	22	28	33	34	31	30	29	26	20	15	25
Rainfall	Monthly total mm	25	21	13	8	13	77	178	184	123	10	2	11	665
Sunshine	Hours per day	7.7	8.2	8.2	8.7	9.2	7.9	6	6.3	6.9	9.4	8.7	8.3	8
Perth, Australia	60m													
Temperature	Daily max. °C	29	30	27	25	21	18	17	18	19	21	25	27	23
	Daily min. °C	17	18	16	14	12	10	9	9	10	11	14	16	13
	Average monthly °C	23	24	22	19	16	14	13	13	15	16	19	22	18
Rainfall	Monthly total mm	8	13	22	44	128	189	177	145	84	58	19	13	900
Sunshine	Hours per day	10.4	9.8	8.8	7.5	5.7	4.8	5.4	6	7.2	8.1	9.6	10.4	7.8
Reykjavik, Iceland	18m													
Temperature	Daily max. °C	2	3	5	6	10	13	15	14	12	8	5	4	8
	Daily min. °C	−3	−3	−1	1	4	7	9	8	6	3	0	−2	3
	Average monthly °C	0	0	2	4	7	10	12	11	9	5	3	1	5
Rainfall	Monthly total mm	89	64	62	56	42	42	50	56	67	94	78	79	779
Sunshine	Hours per day	0.8	2	3.6	4.5	5.9	6.1	5.8	5.4	3.5	2.3	1.1	0.3	3.7
Santiago, Chile	520m													
Temperature	Daily max. °C	30	29	27	24	19	15	15	17	19	22	26	29	23
	Daily min. °C	12	11	10	7	5	3	3	4	6	7	9	11	7
	Average monthly °C	21	20	18	15	12	9	9	10	12	15	17	20	15
Rainfall	Monthly total mm	3	3	5	13	64	84	76	56	31	15	8	5	363
Sunshine	Hours per day	10.8	8.9	8.5	5.5	3.6	3.3	3.3	3.6	4.8	6.1	8.7	10.1	6.4
Shanghai, China	5m													
Temperature	Daily max. °C	8	8	13	19	24	28	32	32	27	23	17	10	20
	Daily min. °C	−1	0	4	9	14	19	23	23	19	13	7	2	11
	Average monthly °C	3	4	8	14	19	23	27	27	23	18	12	6	15
Rainfall	Monthly total mm	48	59	84	94	94	180	147	142	130	71	51	36	1,136
Sunshine	Hours per day	4	3.7	4.4	4.8	5.4	4.7	6.9	7.5	5.3	5.6	4.7	4.5	5.1
Sydney, Australia	40m													
Temperature	Daily max. °C	26	26	25	22	19	17	17	18	20	22	24	25	22
	Daily min. °C	18	19	17	14	11	9	8	9	11	13	16	17	14
	Average monthly °C	22	22	21	18	15	13	12	13	16	18	20	21	18
Rainfall	Monthly total mm	89	101	127	135	127	117	117	76	74	71	74	74	1,182
Sunshine	Hours per day	7.5	7	6.4	6.1	5.7	5.3	6.1	7	7.3	7.5	7.5	7.5	6.8
Tehran, Iran	1,191m													
Temperature	Daily max. °C	9	11	16	21	29	30	37	36	29	24	16	11	22
	Daily min. °C	−1	1	4	10	16	20	23	23	18	12	6	1	11
	Average monthly °C	4	6	10	15	22	25	30	29	23	18	11	6	17
Rainfall	Monthly total mm	37	23	36	31	14	2	1	1	1	5	29	27	207
Sunshine	Hours per day	5.9	6.7	7.5	7.4	8.6	11.6	11.2	11	10.1	7.6	6.9	6.3	8.4
Timbuktu, Mali	269m													
Temperature	Daily max. °C	31	35	38	41	43	42	38	35	38	40	37	31	37
	Daily min. °C	13	16	18	22	26	27	25	24	24	23	18	14	21
	Average monthly °C	22	25	28	31	34	34	32	30	31	31	28	23	29
Rainfall	Monthly total mm	0	0	0	1	4	20	54	93	31	3	0	0	206
Sunshine	Hours per day	9.1	9.6	9.6	9.7	9.8	9.4	9.6	9	9.3	9.5	9.5	8.9	9.4
Tokyo, Japan	5m													
Temperature	Daily max. °C	9	9	12	18	22	25	29	30	27	20	16	11	19
	Daily min. °C	−1	−1	3	4	13	17	22	23	19	13	7	1	10
	Average monthly °C	4	4	8	11	18	21	25	26	23	17	11	6	14
Rainfall	Monthly total mm	48	73	101	135	131	182	146	147	217	220	101	61	1,562
Sunshine	Hours per day	6	5.9	5.7	6	6.2	5	5.8	6.6	4.5	4.4	4.8	5.4	5.5
Tromsø, Norway	100m													
Temperature	Daily max. °C	−2	−2	0	3	7	12	16	14	10	5	2	0	5
	Daily min. °C	−6	−6	−5	−2	1	6	9	8	5	1	−2	−4	0
	Average monthly °C	−4	−4	−3	0	4	9	13	11	7	3	0	−2	3
Rainfall	Monthly total mm	96	79	91	65	61	59	56	80	109	115	88	95	994
Sunshine	Hours per day	0.1	1.6	2.9	6.1	5.7	6.9	7.9	4.8	3.5	1.7	0.3	0	3.5
Ulan Bator, Mongolia	1,305m													
Temperature	Daily max. °C	−19	−13	−4	7	13	21	22	21	14	6	−6	−16	4
	Daily min. °C	−32	−29	−22	−8	−2	7	11	8	2	−8	−20	−28	−11
	Average monthly °C	−26	−21	−13	−1	6	14	16	14	8	−1	−13	−22	−4
Rainfall	Monthly total mm	1	1	2	5	10	28	76	51	23	5	5	2	209
Sunshine	Hours per day	6.4	7.8	8	7.8	8.3	8.6	8.6	8.2	7.2	6.9	6.1	5.7	7.5
Vancouver, Canada	5m													
Temperature	Daily max. °C	6	7	10	14	17	20	23	22	19	14	9	7	14
	Daily min. °C	0	1	3	5	8	11	13	12	10	7	3	2	6
	Average monthly °C	3	4	6	9	13	16	18	17	14	10	6	4	10
Rainfall	Monthly total mm	214	161	151	90	69	65	39	44	83	172	198	243	1,529
Sunshine	Hours per day	1.6	3	3.8	5.9	7.5	7.4	9.5	8.2	6	3.7	2	1.4	5
Verkhoyansk, Russia	137m													
Temperature	Daily max. °C	−47	−40	−20	−1	11	21	24	21	12	−8	−33	−42	−8
	Daily min. °C	−51	−48	−40	−25	−7	4	6	1	−6	−20	−39	−50	−23
	Average monthly °C	−49	−44	−30	−13	2	12	15	11	3	−14	−36	−46	−16
Rainfall	Monthly total mm	7	5	5	4	5	25	33	30	13	11	10	7	155
Sunshine	Hours per day	0	2.6	6.9	9.6	9.7	10	9.7	7.5	4.1	2.4	0.6	0	5.4
Washington, D.C., USA	22m													
Temperature	Daily max. °C	7	8	12	19	25	29	31	30	26	20	14	8	19
	Daily min. °C	−1	−1	2	8	13	18	21	20	16	10	4	−1	9
	Average monthly °C	3	3	7	13	19	24	26	25	21	15	9	4	14
Rainfall	Monthly total mm	84	68	96	85	103	88	108	120	100	78	75	75	1,080
Sunshine	Hours per day	4.4	5.7	6.7	7.4	8.2	8.8	8.6	8.2	7.5	6.5	5.3	4.5	6.8

Tropical Rain Forest
Tall broadleaved evergreen forest, trees 30–50m high with climbers and epiphytes forming continuous canopies. Associated with wet climate, 2–3000mm precipitation per year and high temperatures 24–28°C. High diversity of species, typically 100 per ha, including lianas, bamboo, palms, rubber, mahogany. Mangrove swamps form in coastal areas.

This diagram shows the highly stratified nature of the tropical rain forest. Crowns of trees form numerous layers at different heights and the dense shade limits undergrowth.

Temperate Deciduous and Coniferous Forest
A transition zone between broadleaves and conifers. Broadleaves are better suited to the warmer, damper and flatter locations.

Coniferous Forest (Taiga or Boreal)
Forming a large continuous belt across Northern America and Eurasia with a uniformity in tree species. Characteristically trees are tall, conical with short branches and wax-covered needle-shaped leaves to retain moisture. Cold climate with prolonged harsh winters and cool summers where average temperatures are under 0°C for more than six months of the year Undergrowth is sparse with mosses and lichens. Tree species include pine, fir, spruce, larch, tamarisk.

Mountainous Forest, mainly Coniferous
Mild winters, high humidity and high levels of rainfall throughout the year provide habitat for dense needle-leaf evergreen forests and the largest trees in the world, up to 100m, including the Douglas fir, redwood and giant sequoia.

High Plateau Steppe and Tundra
Similar to arctic tundra with frozen ground for the majority of the year. Very sparse ground coverage of low, shallow-rooted herbs, small shrubs, mosses, lichens and heather interspersed with bare soil.

Arctic Tundra
Average temperatures are 0°C, precipitation is mainly snowfall and the ground remains frozen for 10 months of the year. Vegetation flourishes when the shallow surface layer melts in the long summer days. Underlying permafrost remains frozen and surface water cannot drain away, making conditions marshy. Consists of sedges, snow lichen, arctic meadow grass, cotton grasses and dwarf willow.

Polar and Mountainous Ice Desert
Areas of bare rock and ice with patches of rock-strewn lithosols, low in organic matter and low water content. In sheltered patches only a few mosses, lichens and low shrubs can grow, including woolly moss and purple saxifrage.

Subtropical and Temperate Rain Forest
Precipitation, which is less than in the Tropical Rain Forest, falls in the long wet season interspersed with a season of reduced rainfall and lower temperatures. As a result there are fewer species, thinner canopies, fewer lianas and denser ground level foliage. Vegetation consists of evergreen oak, laurel, bamboo, magnolia and tree ferns.

Monsoon Woodland and Open Jungle
Mostly deciduous trees, because of the long dry season and lower temperature Trees can reach 30m but are sparser than in the rain forests. There is le competition for light and thick jungle vegetation grows at lower levels. Hig species diversity includes lianas, bamboo, teak, sandalwood, sal and banya

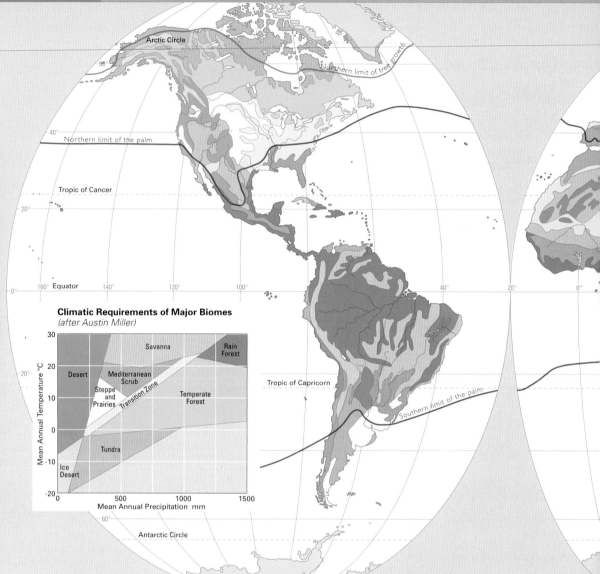

Climatic Requirements of Major Biomes
(after Austin Miller)

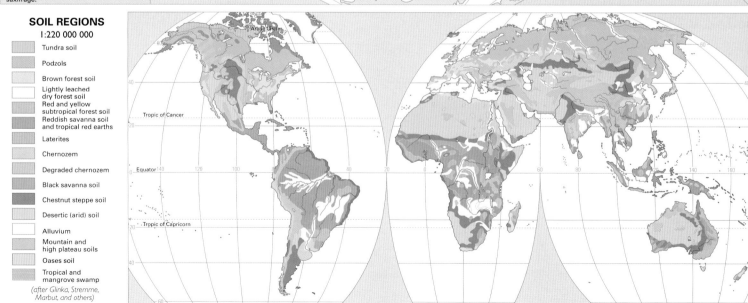

SOIL REGIONS
1:220 000 000

- Tundra soil
- Podzols
- Brown forest soil
- Lightly leached dry forest soil
- Red and yellow subtropical forest soil
- Reddish savanna soil and tropical red earths
- Laterites
- Chernozem
- Degraded chernozem
- Black savanna soil
- Chestnut steppe soil
- Desertic (arid) soil
- Alluvium
- Mountain and high plateau soils
- Oases soil
- Tropical and mangrove swamp

(after Glinka, Stremme, Marbut, and others)

Projection: Interrupted Mollweide's Homolographic

ubtropical and Temperate Woodland, Scrub and Bush
ast clearings with woody shrubs and tall grasses. Trees are fire-resistant and
ther deciduous or xerophytic because of long dry periods. Species include
ucalyptus, acacia, mimosa and euphorbia.

Tropical Savanna with Low Trees and Bush
Tall, coarse grass with enough precipitation to support a scattering of short
deciduous trees and thorn scrub. Vegetation consists of elephant grass, acacia,
palms and baobob and is limited by aridity, grazing animals and periodic fires;
trees have developed thick, woody bark, small leaves or thorns.

Tropical Savanna and Grassland
Areas with a hot climate and long dry season. Extensive areas of tall grasses
often reach 3.5m with scattered fire and drought resistant bushes, low trees
and thickets of elephant grass. Shrubs include acacia, baobab and palms.

BIOMES
Classified by Climax Vegetation
1:116 000 000

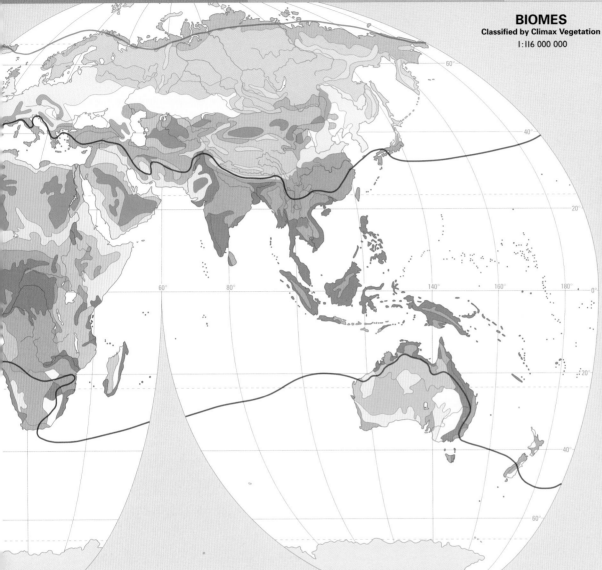

Dry Semi-desert with Shrub and Grass
Xerophytic shrubs with thin grass cover and few trees, limited by a long dry season and short, hot, rainy period. Sagebrush, bunch grass and acacia shrubs are common.

Desert Shrub
Scattered xerophytic plants able to withstand daytime extremes in temperature and long periods of drought. There is a large diversity of desert flora such as cacti, yucca, tamarisk, hard grass and artemisia.

Desert
Precipitation less than 250mm per year. Vegetation is very sparse, mainly bare rock, sand dunes and salt flats. Vegetation comprises a few xerophytic shrubs and ephemeral flowers.

Dry Steppe and Shrub
Semi-arid with cold, dry winters and hot summers. Bare soil with sparsely distributed short grasses and scattered shrubs and short trees. Species include acacia, artemisia, saksaul and tamarisk.

Temperate Grasslands, Prairie and Steppe
Continuous, tall, dense and deep-rooted swards of ancient grasslands, considered to be natural climax vegetation as determined by soil and climate. Average precipitation 250–750mm, with a long dry season, limits growth of trees and shrubs. Includes Stipa grass, buffalo grass, blue stems and loco weed.

Mediterranean Hardwood Forest and Scrub
Areas with hot and arid summers. Sparse evergreen trees are short and twisted with thick bark, interspersed with areas of scrub land. Trees have waxy leaves or thorns and deep root systems to resist drought. Many of the hardwood forests have been cleared by man, resulting in extensive scrub formation – maquis and chaparral. Species found are evergreen oak, stone pine, cork, olive and myrtle.

Temperate Deciduous Forest and Meadow
Areas of relatively high, well-distributed rainfall and temperature favourable for forest growth. The Tall broadleaved trees form a canopy in the summer, but shed their leaves in the winter. The undergrowth is sparse and poorly developed, but in the spring, herbs and flowers develop quickly. Diverse species, with up to 20 per ha, including oak, beech, birch, maple, ash, elm, chestnut and hornbeam. Many of these forests have been cleared for urbanization and farming.

SOIL DEGRADATION
1:220 000 000

Areas of Concern
- Areas of serious concern
- Areas of some concern
- Stable terrain
- Non-vegetated land

Causes of soil degradation (by region)
- Grazing practices
- Other agricultural practices
- Industrialization
- Deforestation
- Fuelwood collection

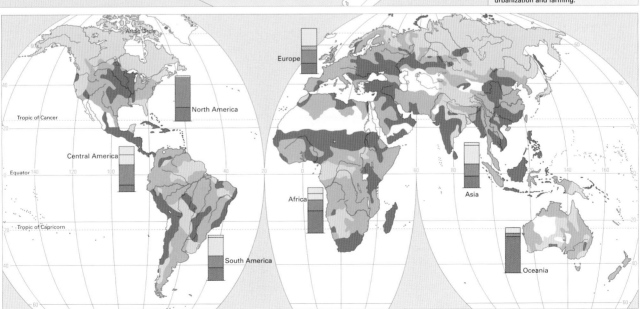

(after Wageningen)

AGRICULTURAL PRODUCTION

Staple Crops

Wheat

China 17.2%, India 11.4%, USA 9.5%, Russia 7.4%, France 5.8%, Canada 4.5%, Germany 3.7%

World total (2006): 605,946,000 tonnes

Rice

China 29.0%, India 21.5%, Indonesia 8.6%, Bangladesh 6.9%, Vietnam 6.9%, Thailand 5.6%, Burma 4.0%

World total (2006): 634,606,000 tonnes

Cassava

Nigeria 20.2%, Brazil 11.8%, Thailand 10.0%, Indonesia 8.8%, Congo (D.R.) 6.6%, Mozambique 5.1%

World total (2006): 226,337,000 tonnes

Barley

Russia 13.3%, Germany 8.8%, Ukraine 8.3%, France 7.6%, Canada 7.0%, Turkey 7.0%

World total (2006): 136,209,000 tonnes

Maize

USA 38.5%, China 20.9%, Brazil 6.1%

World total (2006): 695,228,000 tonnes

Potatoes

China 22.3%, Russia 12.2%, India 7.6%, USA 6.3%, Ukraine 6.2%

World total (2006): 315,100,000 tonnes

Soybeans

USA 39.6%, Brazil 23.6%, Argentina 18.3%, China 7.0%

World total (2006): 221,501,000 tonnes

Millet

India 31.8%, Nigeria 24.2%, Niger 10.1%, China 5.7%

World total (2006): 31,781,000 tonnes

Animal Products

Milk

India 14.6%, China 5.6%, Russia 4.8%, Pakistan 4.8%, Germany 4.4%

World total (2006): 653,789,000 tonnes

Eggs

China 40.8%, USA 8.6%, India 4.2%, Japan 4.0%

World total (2006): 62,089,000 tonnes

Chicken

USA 21.7%, China 14.6%, Brazil 11.9%, Mexico 3.4%, India 2.7%

World total (2006): 73,088,000 tonnes

Beef and Veal

USA 19.5%, Brazil 12.7%, China 11.8%, Argentina 4.9%, Australia 3.1%, Russia 2.9%

World total (2006): 61,033,000 tonnes

Pigmeat

China 49.9%, USA 9.0%, Germany 4.4%, Spain 3.1%, Brazil 2.9%

World total (2006): 106,383,000 tonnes

Sugars

Sugar Cane

Brazil 32.7%, India 20.2%, China 7.2%, Mexico 3.6%, Thailand 3.4%, Pakistan 3.2%

World total (2006): 1,393,365,000 tonnes

Sugar Beet

Russia 12.0%, France 11.7%, USA 11.3%, Ukraine 8.7%, Germany 8.1%, Turkey 5.6%, Poland 4.5%, Italy 4.2%

World total (2006): 256,407,000 tonnes

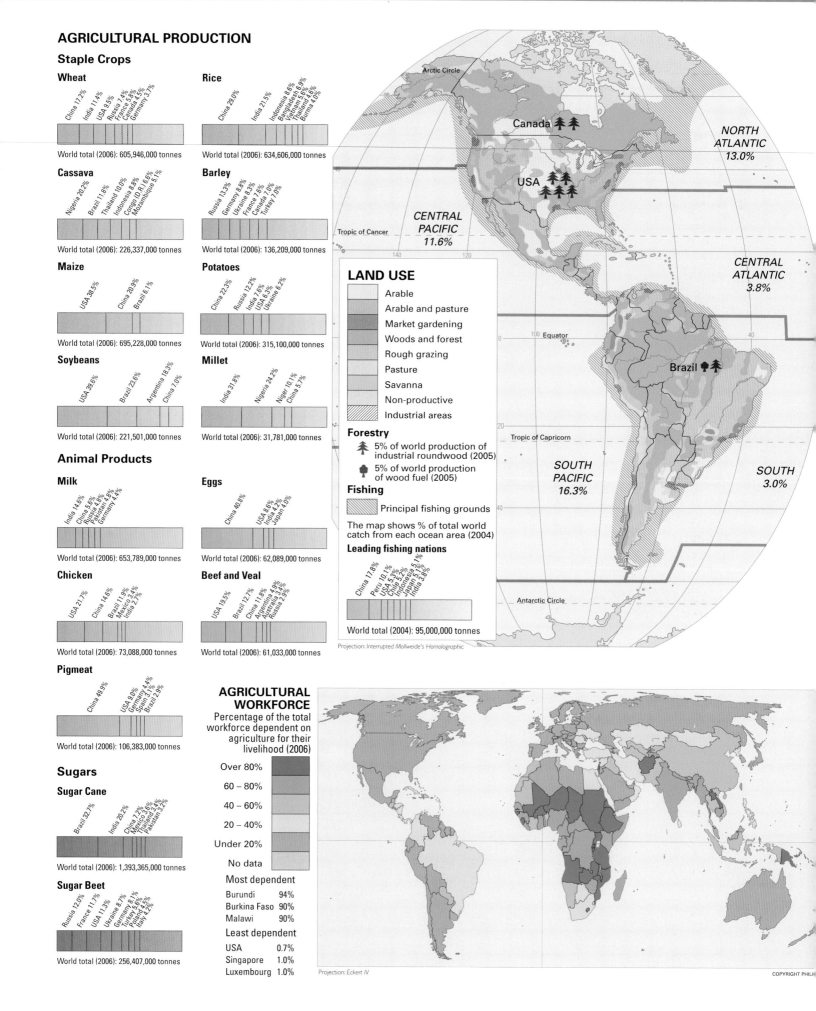

LAND USE

- Arable
- Arable and pasture
- Market gardening
- Woods and forest
- Rough grazing
- Pasture
- Savanna
- Non-productive
- Industrial areas

Forestry

🌲 5% of world production of industrial roundwood (2005)

🌳 5% of world production of wood fuel (2005)

Fishing

Principal fishing grounds

The map shows % of total world catch from each ocean area (2004)

Leading fishing nations

China 17.8%, Peru 10.1%, USA 5.3%, Chile 5.2%, Indonesia 5.1%, Japan 5.1%, India 3.8%

World total (2004): 95,000,000 tonnes

Projection: Interrupted Mollweide's Homolographic

NORTH ATLANTIC 13.0%

CENTRAL PACIFIC 11.6%

CENTRAL ATLANTIC 3.8%

SOUTH PACIFIC 16.3%

SOUTH 3.0%

Canada, USA, Brazil

AGRICULTURAL WORKFORCE

Percentage of the total workforce dependent on agriculture for their livelihood (2006)

- Over 80%
- 60 – 80%
- 40 – 60%
- 20 – 40%
- Under 20%
- No data

Most dependent

Burundi 94%
Burkina Faso 90%
Malawi 90%

Least dependent

USA 0.7%
Singapore 1.0%
Luxembourg 1.0%

Projection: Eckert IV

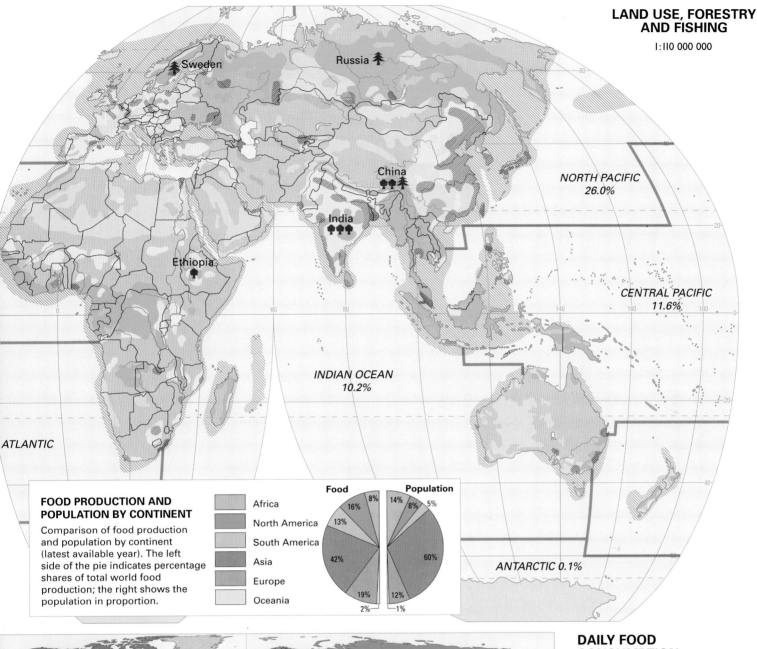

LAND USE, FORESTRY AND FISHING

1:110 000 000

NORTH PACIFIC
26.0%

CENTRAL PACIFIC
11.6%

INDIAN OCEAN
10.2%

ATLANTIC

ANTARCTIC 0.1%

FOOD PRODUCTION AND POPULATION BY CONTINENT

Comparison of food production and population by continent (latest available year). The left side of the pie indicates percentage shares of total world food production; the right shows the population in proportion.

Africa
North America
South America
Asia
Europe
Oceania

Food

8%
16%
13%
42%
19%
2%

Population

14%
8%
5%
60%
12%
1%

DAILY FOOD CONSUMPTION

Average daily food intake in calories per person (2003)

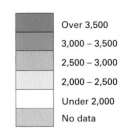

Over 3,500
3,000 – 3,500
2,500 – 3,000
2,000 – 2,500
Under 2,000
No data

Top 5 countries		Bottom 5 countries	
USA	3,774	Eritrea	1,513
Portugal	3,741	Afghanistan	1,539
Greece	3,721	Congo (Dem. Rep.)	1,599
Luxembourg	3,701	Somalia	1,628
Austria	3,673	Burundi	1,648

UK 3,412

In 2008, the United Nations estimated that 923 million people were undernourished.

Projection: Eckert IV

ENERGY PRODUCTION BY REGION
Each square represents 1% of world primary energy production (2007)

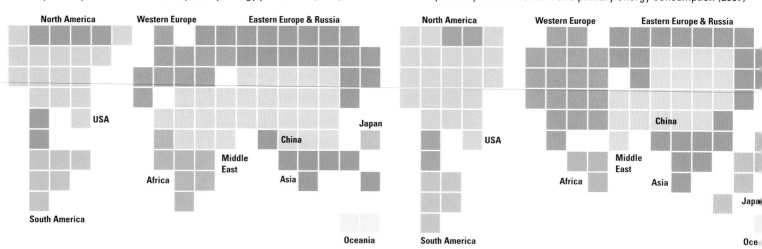

North America
Western Europe
Eastern Europe & Russia
USA
Japan
China
Middle East
Africa
Asia
South America
Oceania

ENERGY CONSUMPTION BY REGION
Each square represents 1% of world primary energy consumption (2007)

North America
Western Europe
Eastern Europe & Russia
China
USA
Middle East
Africa
Asia
Japa
South America
Oce

ENERGY BALANCE
Difference between primary energy production and consumption in millions of tonnes of oil equivalent (MtOe) 2007

↑ Energy surplus in MtOe

Over 35 surplus
1 – 35 surplus
1 deficit – 1 surplus (approx. balance)
1 – 35 deficit
Over 35 deficit

↓ Energy deficit in MtOe

Fossil fuel production
	Principal	Secondary
Oilfields	●	●
Gasfields	▼	▼
Coalfields	△	△

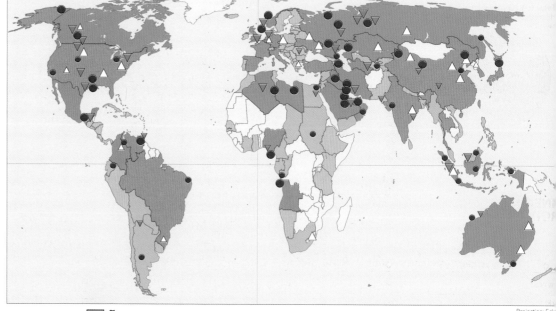

Projection: Ecke

OIL RESERVES
World oil reserves by region and country, thousand million tonnes (2006)

Abbreviations used:
Al:	Algeria	No:	Norway
Au:	Australia	Po:	Poland
Br:	Brazil	Ru:	Russia
Cn:	China	SA:	Saudi Arabia
In:	Indonesia	S Af:	South Africa
Iq:	Iraq	UAE:	United Arab Emirates
Ka:	Kazakhstan	Uk:	Ukraine
Li:	Libya	USA:	United States of America
Ni:	Nigeria		
		Ve:	Venezuela

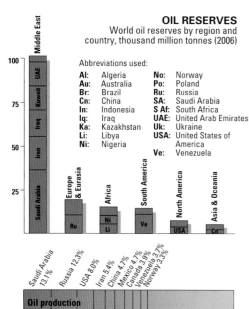

Middle East
UAE
Kuwait
Iraq
Iran
Saudi Arabia
Europe & Eurasia
Ru
Africa
Ni
Li
South America
Ve
North America
USA
Asia & Oceania
Cn

Oil production
World total (2006): 3,914,000,000 tonnes

Saudi Arabia 13.1%, Russia 12.3%, USA 8.0%, Iran 5.4%, China 4.7%, Mexico 4.7%, Canada 3.3%, Venezuela 3.7%, Norway 3.3%

GAS RESERVES
World natural gas reserves by region and country, thousand million tonnes of oil equivalent (2006)

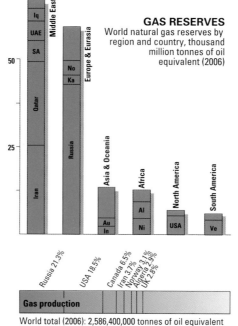

Middle East
Iq
UAE
SA
Qatar
Iran
Europe & Eurasia
No
Ka
Russia
Asia & Oceania
Au
In
Africa
Al
Ni
North America
USA
South America
Ve

Gas production
World total (2006): 2,586,400,000 tonnes of oil equivalent

Russia 21.3%, USA 18.5%, Canada 6.5%, Iran 3.7%, Norway 3.1%, Algeria 2.9%, UK 2.8%

COAL RESERVES
World coal reserves by region and country, thousand million tonnes (2006, including lignite)

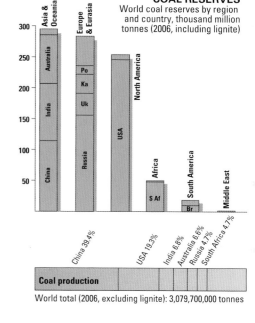

Asia & Oceania
Australia
India
China
Europe & Eurasia
Po
Ka
Uk
Russia
North America
USA
Africa
S Af
South America
Br
Middle East

Coal production
World total (2006, excluding lignite): 3,079,700,000 tonnes

China 39.4%, USA 19.3%, India 6.8%, Australia 6.6%, Russia 4.7%, South Africa 4.7%

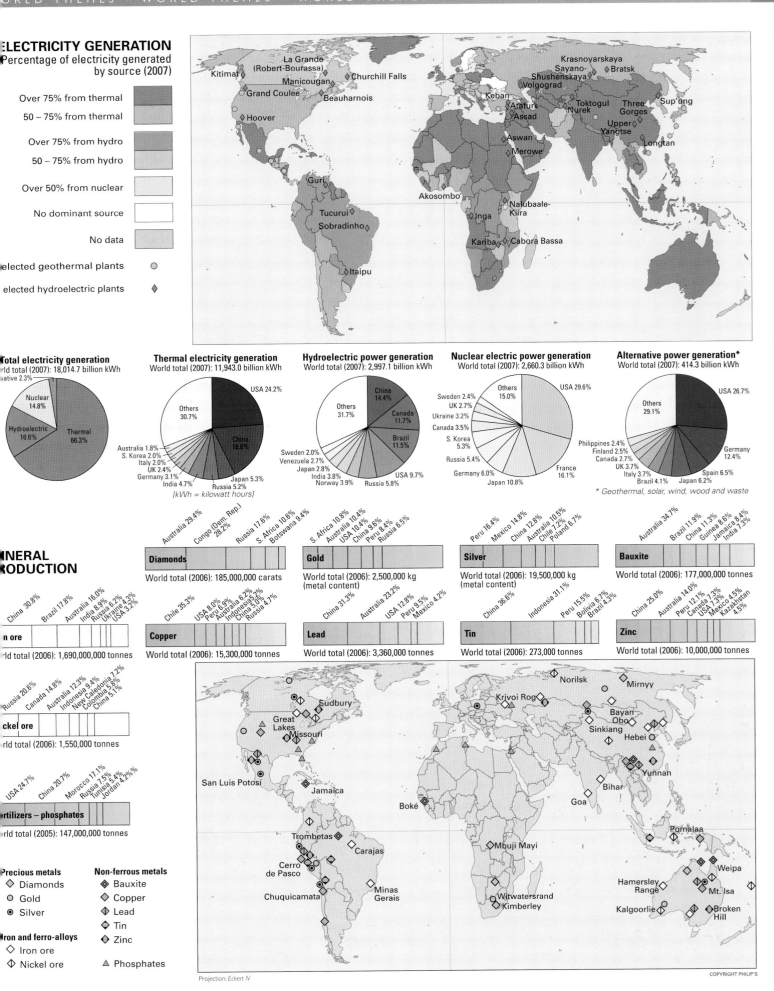

ELECTRICITY GENERATION

Percentage of electricity generated by source (2007)

- Over 75% from thermal
- 50 – 75% from thermal
- Over 75% from hydro
- 50 – 75% from hydro
- Over 50% from nuclear
- No dominant source
- No data
- ○ elected geothermal plants
- ◆ elected hydroelectric plants

Total electricity generation
rld total (2007): 18,014.7 billion kWh

- native 2.3%
- Nuclear 14.8%
- Hydroelectric 16.6%
- Thermal 66.3%

Thermal electricity generation
World total (2007): 11,943.0 billion kWh

- USA 24.2%
- China 18.6%
- Others 30.7%
- Australia 1.8%
- S. Korea 2.0%
- Italy 2.0%
- UK 2.4%
- Germany 3.1%
- India 4.7%
- Russia 5.2%
- Japan 5.3%

[kWh = kilowatt hours]

Hydroelectric power generation
World total (2007): 2,997.1 billion kWh

- China 14.4%
- Canada 11.7%
- Brazil 11.5%
- Others 31.7%
- Sweden 2.0%
- Venezuela 2.7%
- Japan 2.8%
- India 3.8%
- Norway 3.9%
- Russia 5.8%
- USA 9.7%

Nuclear electric power generation
World total (2007): 2,660.3 billion kWh

- USA 29.6%
- Others 15.0%
- Sweden 2.4%
- UK 2.7%
- Ukraine 3.2%
- Canada 3.5%
- S. Korea 5.3%
- Russia 5.4%
- Germany 6.0%
- Japan 10.8%
- France 16.1%

Alternative power generation*
World total (2007): 414.3 billion kWh

- USA 26.7%
- Others 29.1%
- Germany 12.4%
- Spain 6.5%
- Japan 6.2%
- Brazil 4.1%
- Italy 3.7%
- UK 3.7%
- Canada 2.7%
- Finland 2.5%
- Philippines 2.4%

* Geothermal, solar, wind, wood and waste

Diamonds
World total (2006): 185,000,000 carats
- Australia 29.4%
- Congo (Dem. Rep.) 28.2%
- Russia 17.6%
- S. Africa 10.6%
- Botswana 9.4%

Gold
World total (2006): 2,500,000 kg (metal content)
- S. Africa 10.8%
- Australia 10.4%
- USA 10.4%
- China 9.6%
- Peru 8.4%
- Russia 6.5%

Silver
World total (2006): 19,500,000 kg (metal content)
- Peru 16.4%
- Mexico 14.8%
- China 12.8%
- Australia 10.5%
- Chile 7.2%
- Poland 6.7%

Bauxite
World total (2006): 177,000,000 tonnes
- Australia 34.7%
- Brazil 11.9%
- China 11.3%
- Guinea 8.6%
- Jamaica 8.4%
- India 7.3%

Copper
World total (2006): 15,300,000 tonnes
- Chile 35.3%
- USA 8.0%
- Peru 6.9%
- Australia 6.2%
- Indonesia 5.5%
- China 5.0%
- Russia 4.7%

Lead
World total (2006): 3,360,000 tonnes
- China 31.3%
- Australia 23.2%
- USA 12.8%
- Peru 9.5%
- Mexico 4.2%

Tin
World total (2006): 273,000 tonnes
- China 36.6%
- Indonesia 31.1%
- Peru 15.5%
- Bolivia 6.7%
- Brazil 4.3%

Zinc
World total (2006): 10,000,000 tonnes
- China 25.0%
- Australia 14.0%
- Peru 12.1%
- Canada 7.3%
- USA 7.3%
- Mexico 4.5%
- Kazakhstan 4.5%

INERAL RODUCTION

n ore
rld total (2006): 1,690,000,000 tonnes
- China 30.8%
- Brazil 17.8%
- Australia 16.0%
- India 8.9%
- Russia 6.2%
- Ukraine 4.3%
- USA 3.2%

ckel ore
rld total (2006): 1,550,000 tonnes
- Russia 20.6%
- Canada 14.8%
- Australia 12.3%
- Indonesia 9.4%
- New Caledonia 7.2%
- Colombia 5.8%
- China 5.1%

rtilizers – phosphates
rld total (2005): 147,000,000 tonnes
- USA 24.7%
- China 20.7%
- Morocco 17.1%
- Russia 7.5%
- Tunisia 5.4%
- Jordan 4.2%

Precious metals
- ◇ Diamonds
- ○ Gold
- ◉ Silver

Iron and ferro-alloys
- ◇ Iron ore
- ◇ Nickel ore

Non-ferrous metals
- ◈ Bauxite
- ◇ Copper
- ◆ Lead
- ◇ Tin
- ◇ Zinc
- △ Phosphates

Projection: Eckert IV

COPYRIGHT PHILIP'S

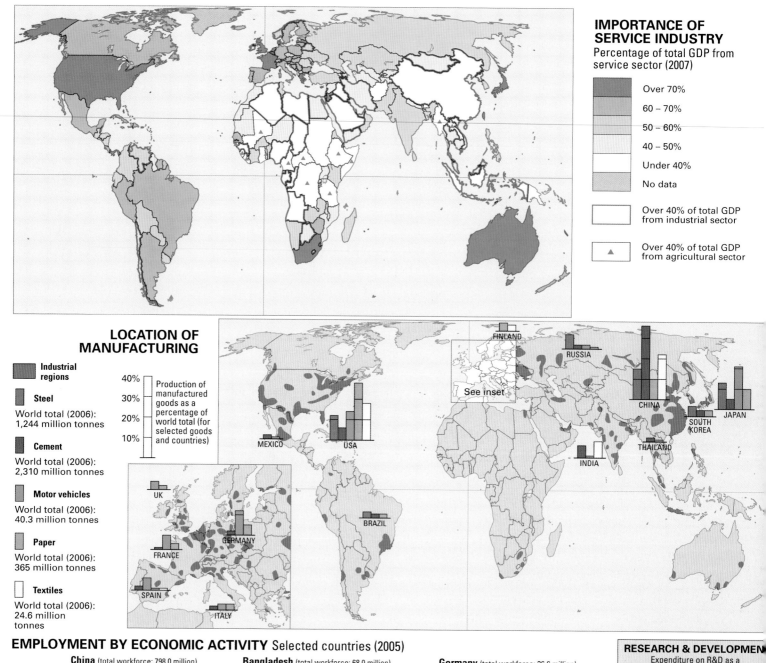

IMPORTANCE OF SERVICE INDUSTRY
Percentage of total GDP from service sector (2007)

- Over 70%
- 60 – 70%
- 50 – 60%
- 40 – 50%
- Under 40%
- No data
- Over 40% of total GDP from industrial sector
- ▲ Over 40% of total GDP from agricultural sector

LOCATION OF MANUFACTURING

- **Industrial regions**
- **Steel**
  World total (2006): 1,244 million tonnes
- **Cement**
  World total (2006): 2,310 million tonnes
- **Motor vehicles**
  World total (2006): 40.3 million tonnes
- **Paper**
  World total (2006): 365 million tonnes
- **Textiles**
  World total (2006): 24.6 million tonnes

40% / 30% / 20% / 10% — Production of manufactured goods as a percentage of world total (for selected goods and countries)

FINLAND, RUSSIA, CHINA, SOUTH KOREA, JAPAN, See inset, MEXICO, USA, THAILAND, INDIA, BRAZIL
UK, GERMANY, FRANCE, SPAIN, ITALY

EMPLOYMENT BY ECONOMIC ACTIVITY Selected countries (2005)

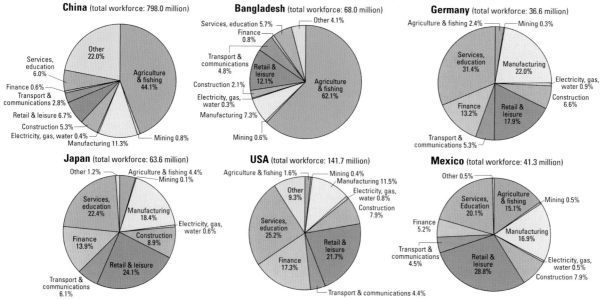

China (total workforce: 798.0 million)
- Other 22.0%
- Agriculture & fishing 44.1%
- Services, education 6.0%
- Finance 0.6%
- Transport & communications 2.8%
- Retail & leisure 6.7%
- Construction 5.3%
- Electricity, gas, water 0.4%
- Manufacturing 11.3%
- Mining 0.8%

Bangladesh (total workforce: 68.0 million)
- Services, education 5.7%
- Other 4.1%
- Finance 0.8%
- Transport & communications 4.8%
- Retail & leisure 12.1%
- Construction 2.1%
- Agriculture & fishing 62.1%
- Electricity, gas, water 0.3%
- Manufacturing 7.3%
- Mining 0.6%

Germany (total workforce: 36.6 million)
- Agriculture & fishing 2.4%
- Mining 0.3%
- Services, education 31.4%
- Manufacturing 22.0%
- Electricity, gas, water 0.9%
- Construction 6.6%
- Finance 13.2%
- Retail & leisure 17.9%
- Transport & communications 5.3%

Japan (total workforce: 63.6 million)
- Other 1.2%
- Agriculture & fishing 4.4%
- Mining 0.1%
- Services, education 22.4%
- Manufacturing 18.4%
- Electricity, gas, water 0.6%
- Finance 13.9%
- Construction 8.9%
- Retail & leisure 24.1%
- Transport & communications 6.1%

USA (total workforce: 141.7 million)
- Agriculture & fishing 1.6%
- Mining 0.4%
- Manufacturing 11.5%
- Electricity, gas, water 0.8%
- Construction 7.9%
- Other 9.3%
- Services, education 25.2%
- Retail & leisure 21.7%
- Finance 17.3%
- Transport & communications 4.4%

Mexico (total workforce: 41.3 million)
- Other 0.5%
- Services, Education 20.1%
- Agriculture & fishing 15.1%
- Mining 0.5%
- Finance 5.2%
- Manufacturing 16.9%
- Transport & communications 4.5%
- Retail & leisure 28.8%
- Electricity, gas, water 0.5%
- Construction 7.9%

RESEARCH & DEVELOPMEN
Expenditure on R&D as a percentage of GDP (2005)

Country	Percentage
Israel	4.7
Sweden	3.9
Finland	3.5
Japan	3.2
South Korea	3.0
Switzerland	2.9
Iceland	2.8
USA	2.7
UK	2.6
Taiwan	2.5
Germany	2.5
Denmark	2.4
Austria	2.4
Singapore	2.4
France	2.1
Canada	2.0
Australia	1.8
Belgium	1.8
Netherlands	1.8
Luxembourg	1.6
Slovenia	1.5
Norway	1.5
Czech Republic	1.4
China	1.3
Ireland	1.3

WORLD TRADE
Percentage share of total
world exports by value (2007)

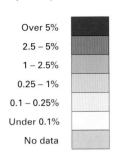

Over 5%

2.5 – 5%

1 – 2.5%

0.25 – 1%

0.1 – 0.25%

Under 0.1%

No data

The members of 'G8', the inner circle
of OECD, account for more than half
the total. The majority of nations
contribute less than one quarter of 1%
to the worldwide total of exports;
EU countries account for 35%; the
Pacific Rim nations over 50%.

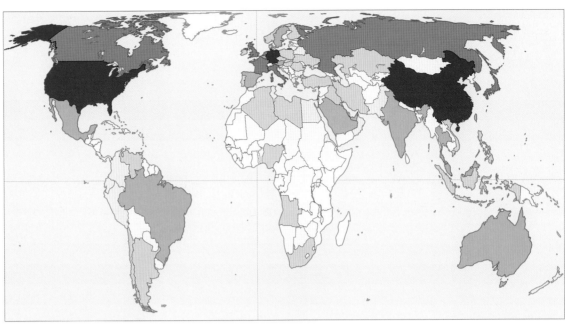

AJOR EXPORTS Leading manufactured items and their exporters

Motor Vehicles
World total (2007): US$ 2,706,511 million

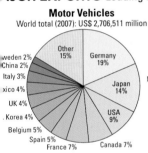

Other 15%, Germany 19%, Japan 14%, USA 9%, Canada 7%, France 7%, Spain 5%, Belgium 5%, . Korea 4%, UK 4%, xico 4%, Italy 3%, China 2%, weden 2%

Telecommunications Gear
World total (2007): US$ 577,845 million

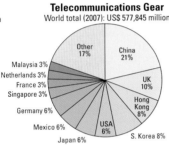

Other 17%, China 21%, UK 10%, Hong Kong 8%, S. Korea 8%, USA 6%, Japan 6%, Mexico 6%, Germany 6%, Singapore 3%, France 3%, Netherlands 3%, Malaysia 3%

Petrol Products
World total (2007): US$ 1,031,202 million

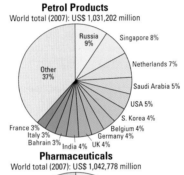

Russia 9%, Singapore 8%, Netherlands 7%, Saudi Arabia 5%, USA 5%, S. Korea 4%, Belgium 4%, Germany 4%, UK 4%, India 4%, Bahrain 3%, Italy 3%, France 3%, Other 37%

Computers
World total (2007): US$ 236,396 million

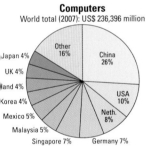

Other 16%, China 26%, USA 10%, Neth. 8%, Germany 7%, Singapore 7%, Malaysia 5%, Mexico 5%, Korea 4%, land 4%, UK 4%, Japan 4%

Electrical Components
World total (2007): US$ 4,187,042 million

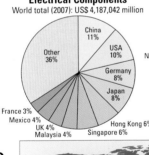

Other 36%, China 11%, USA 10%, Germany 8%, Japan 8%, Hong Kong 6%, Singapore 6%, Malaysia 4%, UK 4%, Mexico 4%, France 3%

Pharmaceuticals
World total (2007): US$ 1,042,778 million

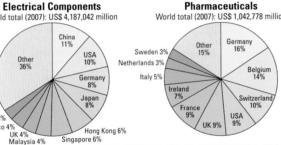

Other 15%, Germany 16%, Belgium 14%, Switzerland 10%, USA 9%, UK 9%, France 9%, Ireland 7%, Italy 5%, Netherlands 3%, Sweden 3%

Top Container Ports
Total container traffic,
in million TEU (2007)
('TEU' stands for Twenty-foot
Equivalent Unit, the equivalent
of a standard container)

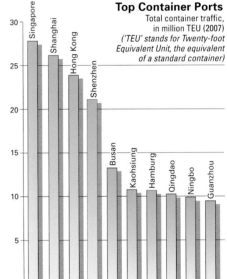

Singapore, Shanghai, Hong Kong, Shenzhen, Busan, Kaohsiung, Hamburg, Qingdao, Ningbo, Guanzhou

INTERNET AND TELECOMMUNICATIONS
Percentage of total population
using the Internet (2007)

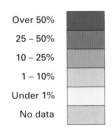

Over 50%

25 – 50%

10 – 25%

1 – 10%

Under 1%

No data

Telecommunications

Trade in office machines
and telecom equipment,
percentage of world total
(2007)

IMPORT EXPORT

40%

30%

20%

10%

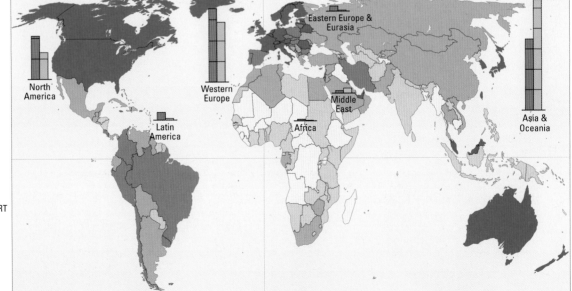

North America, Latin America, Western Europe, Eastern Europe & Eurasia, Middle East, Africa, Asia & Oceania

Projection: *Eckert IV*

COPYRIGHT PHILIP'S

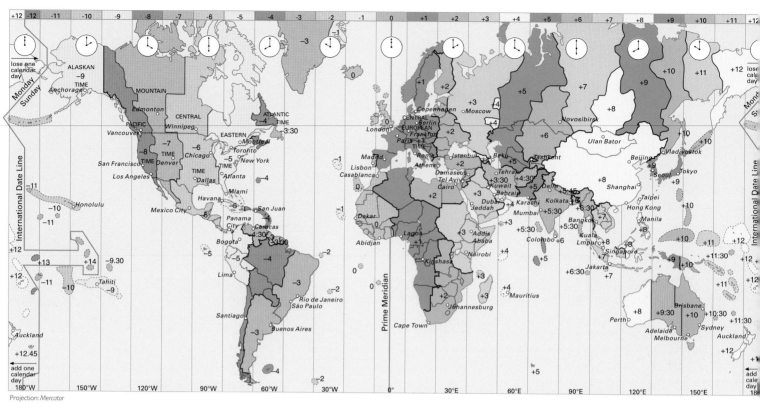

Projection: Mercator

TIME ZONES

Zones using UT (Universal Time)

Zones behind UT (Universal Time)

Zones ahead of UT (Universal Time)

Half-hour zones

10   Hours behind or ahead of UT (Universal Time)

International boundaries

Time zone boundaries

Actual solar time, when it is noon at Greenwich, is shown at the top of the map.

Time-zone boundaries

International Date Line

Note: Certain time zones are affected by the incidence of daylight saving time in countries where it is adopted.
UT (Universal Time) has replaced GMT (Greenwich Mean T

AIR TRAVEL

Major airports
Number of passengers (international and domestic 2007)

○ Over 50 million
○ 25 – 50 million
○ 15 – 25 million
○ 10 – 15 million

Total world passenger traffic

Africa 3%
Middle East 2%
Latin America & Caribbean 6%
North America 37%
Asia Pacific 21%
Europe 31%

Total world passenger traffic (2007)
4,480 million

Traffic in passenger kilometres
Passengers carried (international and local) multiplied by distance flown from airport of origin (2007)

over 100 billion
50 – 100 billion
20 – 50 million
Under 20 billion

Projection: Peirce

WORLD'S BUSIEST AIRPORTS

Total passengers in millions (2007)

1. Atlanta Hartsfield-Jackson (ATL)	89.4
2. Chicago O'Hare (ORD)	76.2
3. London Heathrow (LHR)	68.1
4. Tokyo Haneda (HND)	66.8
5. Los Angeles (LAX)	61.9
6. Paris Charles de Gaulle (CDG)	59.9
7. Dallas-Fort Worth (DFW)	59.8
8. Frankfurt (FRA)	54.2
9. Beijing Capital (PEK)	53.6
10. Madrid Barajas (MAD)	52.1
11. Denver (DEN)	49.9
12. Amsterdam Schiphol (AMS)	47.8
13. New York John F. Kennedy (JFK)	47.7
14. Hong Kong (HKG)	47.0
15. Las Vegas McCarran (LAS)	47.0
16. Houston George Bush (IAH)	43.0
17. Phoenix Sky Harbor (PHX)	42.2
18. Bangkok Suvarnabhumi (BKK)	41.2
19. Singapore Changi (SIN)	36.7
20. Orlando (MCO)	36.5

UNESCO WORLD HERITAGE SITES 2007

Total sites = 851 (660 cultural, 166 natural and 25 mixed)

Region	Cultural sites	Natural sites	Mixed sites
Africa	39	35	3
Arab States	59	3	1
Asia & Pacific	119	46	9
Europe & North America	380	57	10
Latin America & Caribbean	81	35	3

Some sites are trans-boundary, therefore the total figures may not add up

TOURIST EARNINGS

Countries receiving the most from overseas tourism, US$ million (2006)

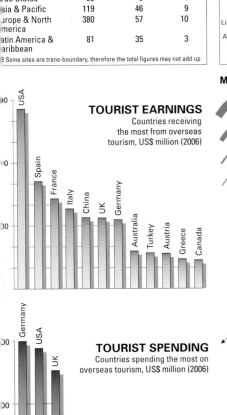

TOURIST SPENDING

Countries spending the most on overseas tourism, US$ million (2006)

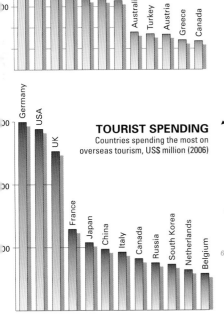

IMPORTANCE OF TOURISM

Tourism receipts as a percentage of Gross National Income (2005)

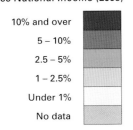

- 10% and over
- 5 – 10%
- 2.5 – 5%
- 1 – 2.5%
- Under 1%
- No data

Tourist arrivals in millions (2006)

France	79.1
Spain	58.5
USA	51.1
China	49.6
Italy	41.1
UK	30.7

Europe at larger scale

Destinations
- Cultural & historical centres
- Coastal resorts
- Ski resorts
- Centres of entertainment
- Places of pilgrimage
- Places of great natural beauty
- Other tourist destinations

Movement of tourists
- More than 10 million
- 5 – 10 million
- 3 – 5 million
- Less than 3 million

TOURIST DESTINATIONS
Projection: Peirce

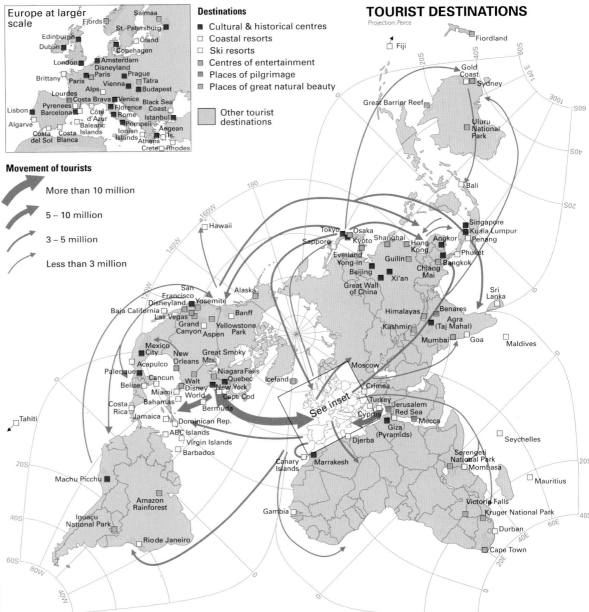

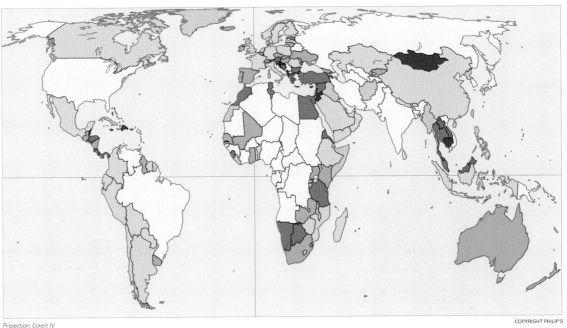

Projection: Eckert IV

COPYRIGHT PHILIP'S

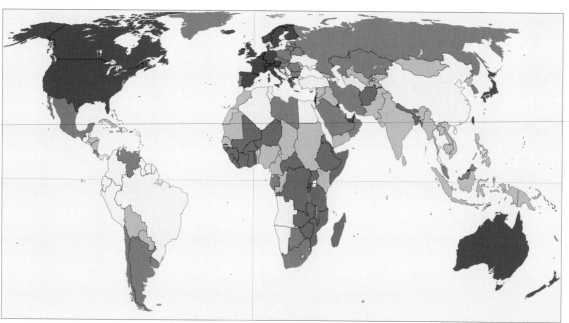

WEALTH

The value of total production divided by the population (the Gross Domestic Product per capita, in 2007)

 Over 250% of world average

100 – 250% of world average

World average U$10,000

50 – 100% of world average

15 – 50% of world average

Under 15% of world average

No data

Top 5 countries		Bottom 5 countries	
Lux'bourg	$80,800	Congo (D. Rep.)	$300
Norway	$55,600	Liberia	$500
Kuwait	$55,300	Zimbabwe	$500
UAE	$55,200	Comoros	$600
Singapore	$48,900	Guinea-Bissau	$600

UK $35,000

WATER SUPPLY

The percentage of total population with access to safe drinking water (2004)

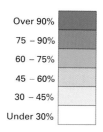
Over 90%

75 – 90%

60 – 75%

45 – 60%

30 – 45%

Under 30%

Least well-provided countries

Afghanistan	13%
Ethiopia	22%
Western Sahara	26%
Papua New Guinea	39%
Cambodia	41%
Somalia	42%

One person in eight in the world has no access to a safe water supply.

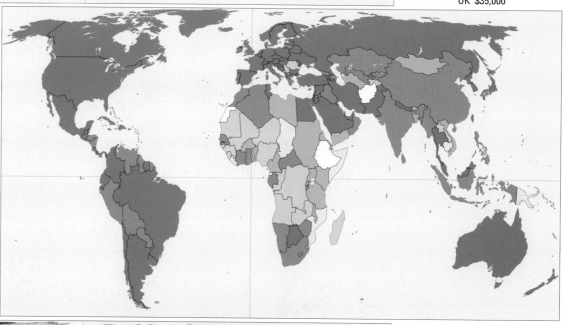

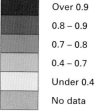

HUMAN DEVELOPMENT

The Human Development Index (HDI), calculated by the UN Development Programme (UNDP), gives a value to countries using indicators of life expectancy, education and standards of living in 2005. Higher values show more developed countries.

Over 0.9

0.8 – 0.9

0.7 – 0.8

0.4 – 0.7

Under 0.4

No data

Highest values		Lowest values	
Norway	0.968	Sierra Leone	0.336
Iceland	0.968	Burkina Faso	0.370
Australia	0.962	Niger	0.374
Canada	0.961	Guinea-Bissau	0.374
Ireland	0.959	Mali	0.380

UK 0.946

Projection: *Eckert IV*

HEALTH CARE

Number of qualified doctors
per 100,000 people (2004)

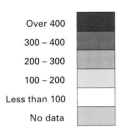

Over 400

300 – 400

200 – 300

100 – 200

Less than 100

No data

Countries with the most and least
doctors per 100,000 people

Most doctors		Least doctors	
Cuba	591	Malawi	2
Monaco	581	Tanzania	2
Belarus	455	Mozambique	3
Belgium	449	Ethiopia	3
Estonia	448	Burundi	3

UK = 230 doctors

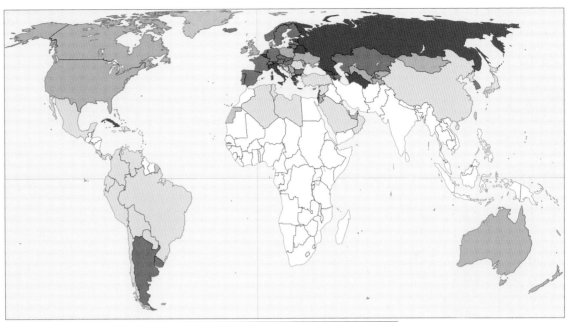

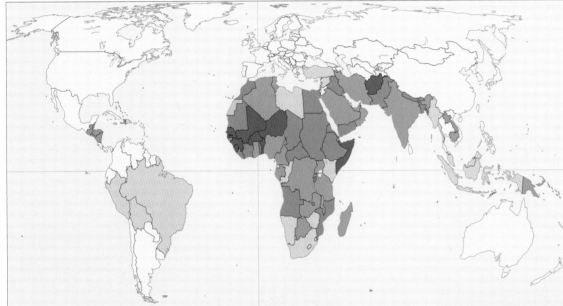

ILLITERACY

Percentage of adult total
population unable to read or
write (2005)

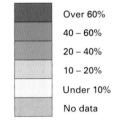

Over 60%

40 – 60%

20 – 40%

10 – 20%

Under 10%

No data

Countries with the highest
and lowest illiteracy rates

Highest (%)		Lowest (%)	
Burkina Faso	87	Australia	0
Niger	83	Denmark	0
Mali	81	Finland	0
Sierra Leone	69	Liechtenstein	0
Guinea	64	Luxembourg	0

UK 1%

GENDER DEVELOPMENT INDEX (GDI)

The Gender Development Index (GDI) shows
economic and social differences between
men and women by using various UNDP
indicators (2005). Countries with higher
values of GDI have more equality between
men and women.

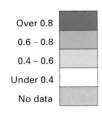

Over 0.8

0.6 – 0.8

0.4 – 0.6

Under 0.4

No data

Highest values		Lowest values	
Iceland	0.962	Sierra Leone	0.320
Australia	0.960	Niger	0.355
Norway	0.957	Guinea-Bissau	0.355
Canada	0.956	Burkina Faso	0.354

UK = 0.944

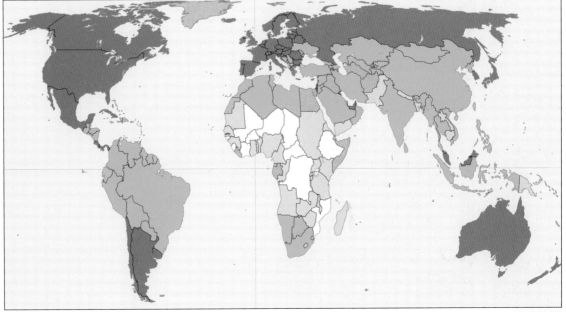

Projection: *Eckert IV*

COPYRIGHT PHILIP'S

AGE DISTRIBUTION PYRAMIDS

The bars represent the percentage of the total population (males plus females) in each age group. Developed countries such as New Zealand have populations spread evenly across age groups and usually a growing percentage of elderly people. Developing countries such as Kenya have the great majority of their people in the younger age groups, about to enter their most fertile years.

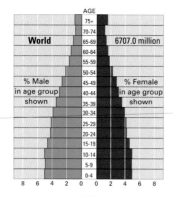

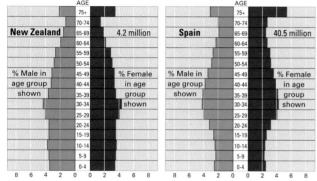

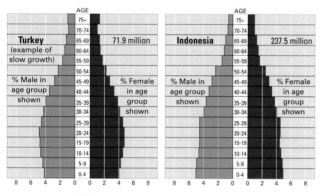

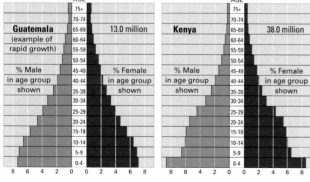

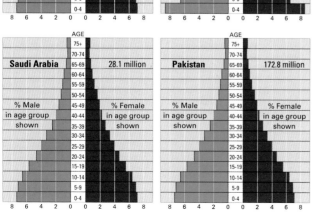

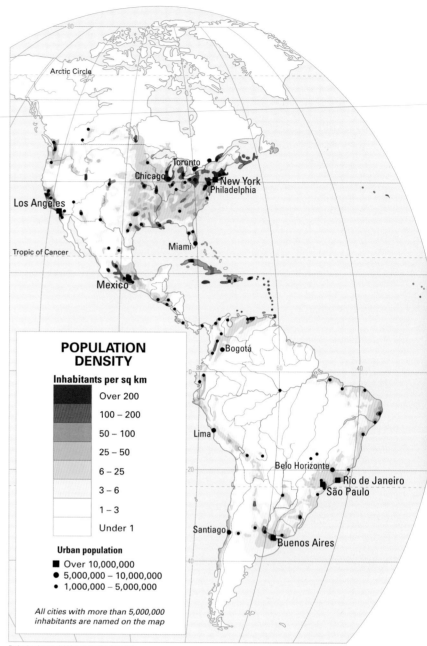

POPULATION DENSITY

Inhabitants per sq km

- Over 200
- 100 – 200
- 50 – 100
- 25 – 50
- 6 – 25
- 3 – 6
- 1 – 3
- Under 1

Urban population

- ■ Over 10,000,000
- ● 5,000,000 – 10,000,000
- • 1,000,000 – 5,000,000

All cities with more than 5,000,000 inhabitants are named on the map

Projection: Interrupted Mollweide's Homolographic

POPULATION CHANGE 1930–2020   Population totals are in millions

Figures in italics represent the percentage average annual increase for the period shown

	1930	1930–1960	1960	1960–1990	1990	1990–2020	2020
World	2,013	1.4%	3,019	1.9%	5,292	1.4%	8,062
Africa	1551	2.0%	2811	2.9%	6482	2.7%	1,441
North America	3512	1.3%	9921	1.1%	7644	0.6%	3277
Latin America*	91,07	1.8%	81,66	2.4%	83,10	1.6%	194,6
Asia	3355	1.5%	9425	2.1%	8498	1.4%	8051
Europe	1017	0.6%	1621	0.6%	2728	0.1%	4373
Oceania	6	1.4%	4	1.8%	8	1.1%	43
CIS†		0.7%		1.0%		0.6%	

* South America plus Central America, Mexico and the West Indies
† Commonwealth of Independent States, formerly the USSR

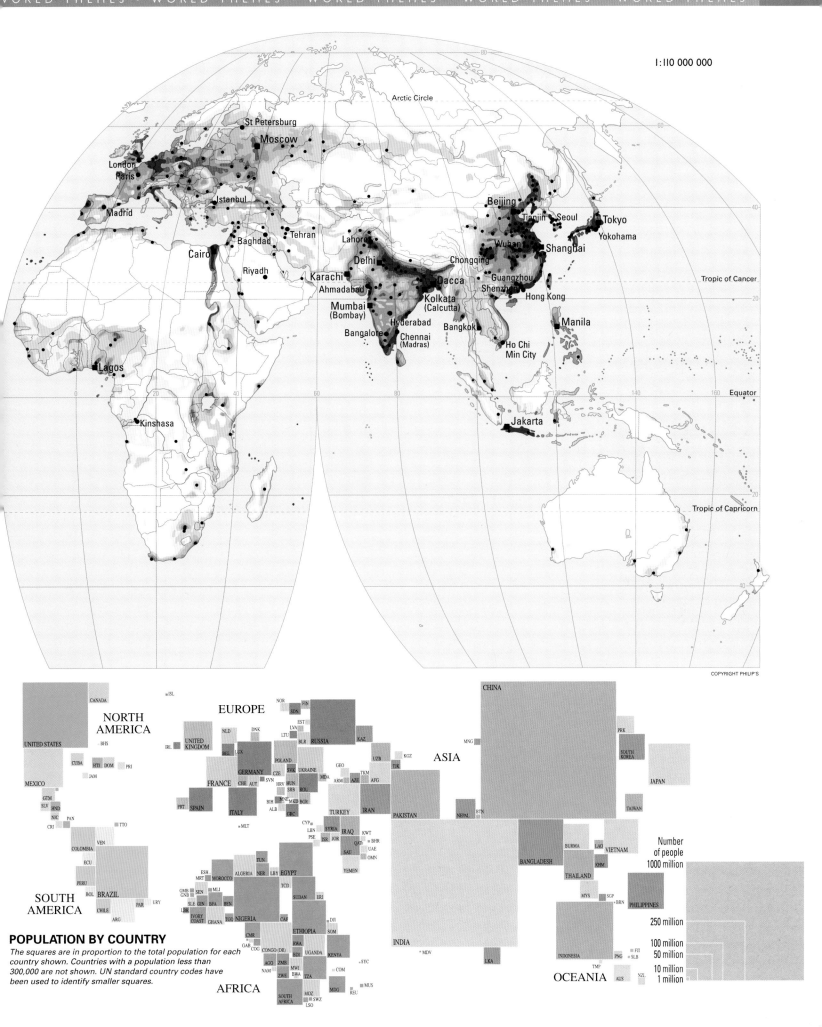

1:110 000 000

Arctic Circle

St Petersburg
Moscow
London
Paris
Madrid
Istanbul
Cairo
Baghdad
Tehran
Riyadh
Beijing
Tianjin
Seoul
Tokyo
Yokohama
Wuhan
Shanghai
Lahore
Delhi
Chongqing
Karachi
Dacca
Guangzhou
Ahmadabad
Shenzhen
Kolkata
(Calcutta)
Hong Kong
Mumbai
(Bombay)
Hyderabad
Bangkok
Manila
Bangalore
Chennai
(Madras)
Ho Chi
Min City
Lagos
Kinshasa
Jakarta

Tropic of Cancer

Equator

Tropic of Capricorn

COPYRIGHT PHILIP'S

POPULATION BY COUNTRY

The squares are in proportion to the total population for each country shown. Countries with a population less than 300,000 are not shown. UN standard country codes have been used to identify smaller squares.

NORTH AMERICA
UNITED STATES
CANADA
BHS
CUBA   HTI DOM PRI
MEXICO   JAM
GTM
SLV HND
NIC   PAN
CRI   TTO

SOUTH AMERICA
COLOMBIA
VEN
ECU
PERU
BOL BRAZIL
CHILE   URY
PAR
ARG

EUROPE
ISL
NOR FIN
SDN
EST
LVA
NLD DNK
LTU
IRL UNITED   BLR RUSSIA
KINGDOM
BEL LUX
POLAND   KAZ
GERMANY   SVK UKRAINE
CZE
CHE AUT SVN HRV HUN
FRANCE   SRB ROU
BIH MNE MKD
PRT SPAIN   ALB BGR
ITALY   GRC
MLT
CYP
LBN SYRIA IRAQ
PSE ISR JOR
TUN
ESH   ALGERIA NER LBY EGYPT
MRT MOROCCO
GMB MLI   TCD
GNB SEN   SUDAN ERI
SLE GIN BFA BEN
LBR
IVORY TGO
COAST GHANA NIGERIA CAF
CMR   DJI
GAB CONGO (DR) ETHIOPIA SOM
COG   RWA
BDI UGANDA KENYA
AGO ZMB   COM
NAM   MWI
ZWE BWA TZA
MOZ MDG
SOUTH SWZ REU
AFRICA LSO MUS

ASIA
CHINA
MNG
PRK
SOUTH
KOREA
JAPAN
TAIWAN
KGZ
UZB
GEO   TKM
ARM AZE TJK
MDA   AFG
TURKEY IRAN
PAKISTAN
NEPAL BTN
KWT
BHR
QAT
UAE
SAU
OMN
YEMEN
INDIA
MDV
LKA
BANGLADESH
BURMA LAO VIETNAM
THAILAND KHM
MYS SGP
BRN PHILIPPINES
INDONESIA PNG FJI
SLB
TMP
OCEANIA AUS NZL

Number of people
1000 million

250 million

100 million
50 million

10 million
1 million

AFRICA

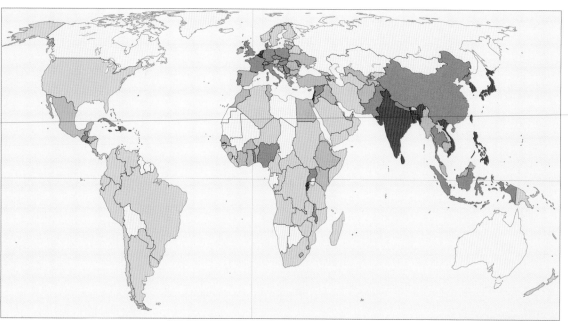

POPULATION DENSITY BY COUNTRY

Density of people per square kilometre (2008)

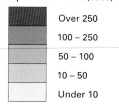

	Over 250
	100 – 250
	50 – 100
	10 – 50
	Under 10

Most and least densely populated countries

Most		Least	
Monaco	16,818	Chad	0.8
Singapore	6,650	W. Sahara	1.5
Gaza Strip	4,167	Mongolia	1.9
Maldives	1,286	Namibia	2.5
Malta	1,227	Australia	2.7

(UK = 249 people per square km)

POPULATION CHANGE

The projected population change for the years 2004–2050

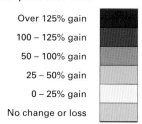

	Over 125% gain
	100 – 125% gain
	50 – 100% gain
	25 – 50% gain
	0 – 25% gain
	No change or loss

Based on estimates for the year 2050, below are listed the ten most populous nations in the world, in millions:

India	1,628	Pakistan	295
China	1,437	Bangladesh	280
USA	420	Brazil	221
Indonesia	308	Congo (Dem. Rep.)	181
Nigeria	307	Ethiopia	171

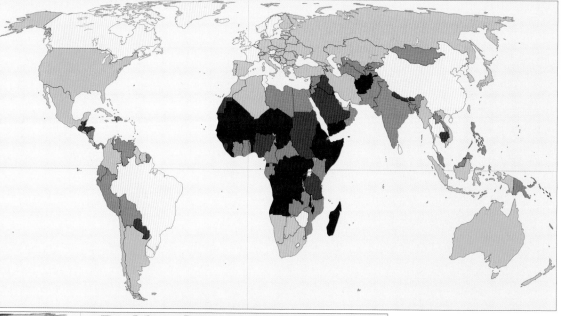

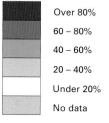

URBAN POPULATION

Percentage of total population living in towns and cities (2005)

	Over 80%
	60 – 80%
	40 – 60%
	20 – 40%
	Under 20%
	No data

Countries that are the most and least urbanized (%)

Most urbanized		Least urbanized	
Singapore	100	Burundi	10
Kuwait	97	Bhutan	11
Belgium	97	Trinidad & Tob.	12

UK 89.6

In 2008, for the first time in history, more than half the world's population lived in urban areas.

Projection: *Eckert IV*

COPYRIGHT PHILIP'S

INFANT MORTALITY

Number of babies who died under the age of one, per 1,000 live births (2007)

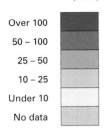

- Over 100
- 50 – 100
- 25 – 50
- 10 – 25
- Under 10
- No data

Countries with the highest and lowest child mortality

Highest		Lowest	
Angola	184	Singapore	2
Sierra Leone	158	Sweden	3
Afghanistan	157	Hong Kong (China)	3
Liberia	150	Japan	3
Niger	117	Iceland	3

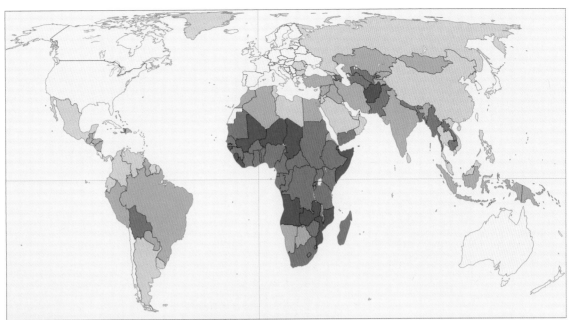

LIFE EXPECTANCY

The average expected lifespan of babies born in 2007

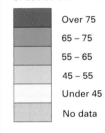

- Over 75
- 65 – 75
- 55 – 65
- 45 – 55
- Under 45
- No data

Countries with the highest and lowest life expectancy at birth in years

Highest		Lowest	
Andorra	83.5	Mozambique	36.5
San Marino	81.2	Botswana	37.1
Japan	80.8	Zimbabwe	37.1
Singapore	80.2	Zambia	37.3
Australia	79.9	Angola	38.6

UK 78.7 years

FAMILY SIZE

Children born per woman (2007)

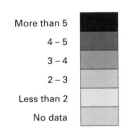

- More than 5
- 4 – 5
- 3 – 4
- 2 – 3
- Less than 2
- No data

Countries with the largest and smallest family size

Largest		Smallest	
Mali	7.4	Hong Kong	1.0
Niger	7.4	Singapore	1.1
Uganda	6.8	Taiwan	1.1
Somalia	6.7	Lithuania	1.2
Afghanistan	6.6	Czech Rep.	1.2

UK = 1.7 children

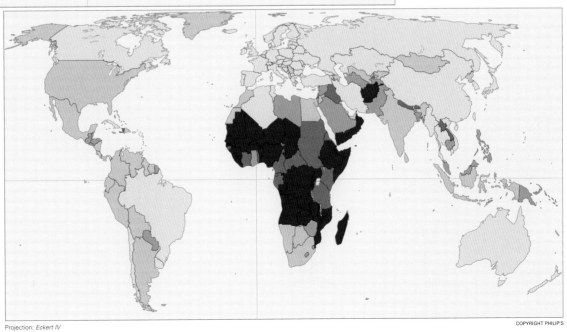

Projection: *Eckert IV*

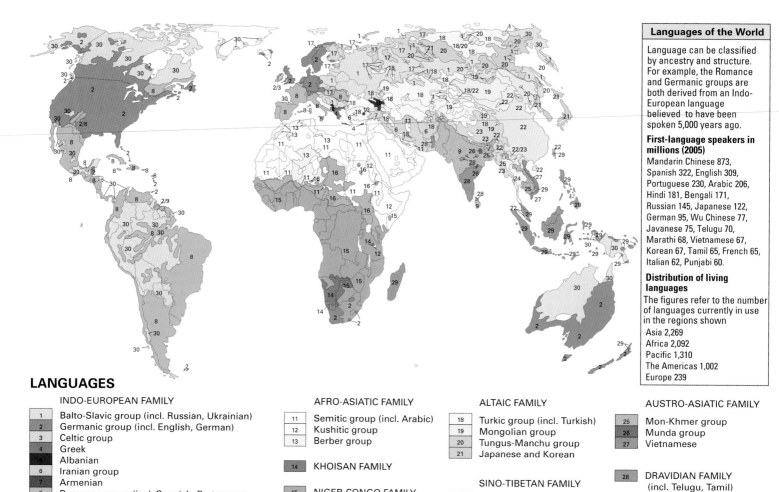

Languages of the World

Language can be classified by ancestry and structure. For example, the Romance and Germanic groups are both derived from an Indo-European language believed to have been spoken 5,000 years ago.

First-language speakers in millions (2005)
Mandarin Chinese 873, Spanish 322, English 309, Portuguese 230, Arabic 206, Hindi 181, Bengali 171, Russian 145, Japanese 122, German 95, Wu Chinese 77, Javanese 75, Telugu 70, Marathi 68, Vietnamese 67, Korean 67, Tamil 65, French 65, Italian 62, Punjabi 60.

Distribution of living languages
The figures refer to the number of languages currently in use in the regions shown
Asia 2,269
Africa 2,092
Pacific 1,310
The Americas 1,002
Europe 239

LANGUAGES

INDO-EUROPEAN FAMILY
1 Balto-Slavic group (incl. Russian, Ukrainian)
2 Germanic group (incl. English, German)
3 Celtic group
4 Greek
5 Albanian
6 Iranian group
7 Armenian
8 Romance group (incl. Spanish, Portuguese, French, Italian)
9 Indo-Aryan group (incl. Hindi, Bengali, Urdu, Punjabi, Marathi)
10 CAUCASIAN FAMILY

AFRO-ASIATIC FAMILY
11 Semitic group (incl. Arabic)
12 Kushitic group
13 Berber group
14 KHOISAN FAMILY
15 NIGER-CONGO FAMILY
16 NILO-SAHARAN FAMILY
17 URALIC FAMILY

ALTAIC FAMILY
18 Turkic group (incl. Turkish)
19 Mongolian group
20 Tungus-Manchu group
21 Japanese and Korean

SINO-TIBETAN FAMILY
22 Sinitic (Chinese) languages (incl. Mandarin, Wu, Yue)
23 Tibetic-Burmic languages
24 TAI FAMILY

AUSTRO-ASIATIC FAMILY
25 Mon-Khmer group
26 Munda group
27 Vietnamese
28 DRAVIDIAN FAMILY (incl. Telugu, Tamil)
29 AUSTRONESIAN FAMILY (incl. Malay-Indonesian, Javanese)
30 OTHER LANGUAGES

RELIGIONS

▲ Roman Catholicism
Orthodox and other Eastern Churches
● Protestantism
Sunni Islam
Shiite Islam
Buddhism
Hinduism
Confucianism
★ Judaism
Shintoism
Tribal Religions

Religious Adherents

Religious adherents in millions (2006)

Christianity	2,100	Hindu	900
Roman Catholic	1,050	Chinese folk	394
Protestant	396	Buddhism	376
Orthodox	240	Ethnic religions	300
Anglican	73	New religions	103
Others	341	Sikhism	23
Islam	1,070	Spiritism	15
Sunni	940	Judaism	14
Shi'ite	120	Baha'i	7
Others	10	Confucianism	6
Non-religious/		Jainism	4
Agnostic/Atheist	1,100	Shintoism	4

United Nations

Created in 1945 to promote peace and co-operation and based in New York, the United Nations is the world's largest international organization, with 192 members and an annual budget of US $2.1 billion (2007). Each member of the General Assembly has one vote, while the five permanent members of the 15-nation Security Council – China, France, Russia, UK and USA – hold a veto. The Secretariat is the UN's principal administrative arm. The 54 members of the Economic and Social Council are responsible for economic, social, cultural, educational, health and related matters. The UN has 16 specialized agencies – based in Canada, France, Switzerland and Italy, as well as the USA – which help members in fields such as education (UNESCO), agriculture (FAO), medicine (WHO) and finance (IFC). By the end of 1994, all the original 11 trust territories of the Trusteeship Council had become independent.

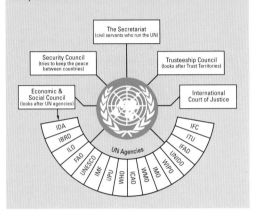

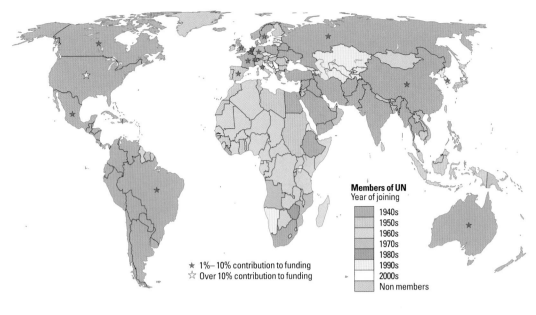

Members of UN
Year of joining
- 1940s
- 1950s
- 1960s
- 1970s
- 1980s
- 1990s
- 2000s
- Non members

★ 1% – 10% contribution to funding
☆ Over 10% contribution to funding

MEMBERSHIP OF THE UN In 1945 there were 51 members; by the end of 2006 membership had increased to 192 following the admission of East Timor, Switzerland and Montenegro. There are 2 independent states which are not members of the UN – Taiwan and the Vatican City. All the successor states of the former USSR had joined by the end of 1992. The official languages of the UN are Chinese, English, French, Russian, Spanish and Arabic.

FUNDING The UN regular budget for 2007 was US$ 2.1 billion. Contributions are assessed by the members' ability to pay, with the maximum 24% of the total (USA's share), the minimum 0.01%. The European Union pays over 37% of the budget.

PEACEKEEPING The UN has been involved in 65 peacekeeping operations worldwide since 1948.

International Organizations

ACP African-Caribbean-Pacific (formed in 1963). Members have economic ties with the EU.

APEC Asia-Pacific Economic Co-operation (formed in 1989). It aims to enhance economic growth and prosperity for the region and to strengthen the Asia-Pacific community. APEC is the only intergovernmental grouping in the world operating on the basis of non-binding commitments, open dialogue, and equal respect for the views of all participants. There are 21 member economies.

ARAB LEAGUE (formed in 1945). The League's aim is to promote economic, social, political and military co-operation. There are 22 member nations.

ASEAN Association of South-east Asian Nations (formed in 1967). Cambodia joined in 1999.

AU The African Union replaced the Organization of African Unity (formed in 1963) in 2002. Its 53 members represent over 94% of Africa's population. Arabic, French, Portuguese and English are recognized as working languages.

COLOMBO PLAN (formed in 1951). Its 25 members aim to promote economic and social development in Asia and the Pacific.

COMMONWEALTH The Commonwealth of Nations evolved from the British Empire. Pakistan was suspended in 1999, and Zimbabwe in 2002. In response to its continued suspension, Zimbabwe left the Commonwealth in December 2003. Pakistan was reinstated in 2004, but Fiji Islands was suspended in December 2006 following a military coup. It now comprises 16 Queen's realms, 31 republics and 6 indigenous monarchies, giving a total of 53 member states.

EU European Union (evolved from the European Community in 1993). Cyprus, the Czech Republic, Estonia, Hungary, Latvia, Lithuania, Malta, Poland, the Slovak Republic and Slovenia joined the EU in May 2004; Bulgaria and Romania joined in January 2007. The other members are Austria, Belgium, Denmark, Finland, France, Germany, Greece, Ireland, Italy, Luxembourg, Netherlands, Portugal, Spain, Sweden and the UK – together these 27 countries aim to integrate economies, co-ordinate social developments and bring about political union.

LAIA Latin American Integration Association (1980). Its aim is to promote freer regional trade.

NATO North Atlantic Treaty Organization (formed in 1949). It continues after 1991 despite the winding up of the Warsaw Pact. Bulgaria, Estonia, Latvia, Lithuania, Romania, the Slovak Republic and Slovenia became members in 2004.

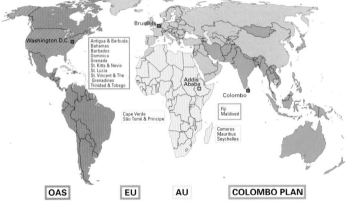

| OAS | EU | AU | COLOMBO PLAN |

OAS Organization of American States (formed in 1948). It aims to promote social and economic co-operation between developed countries of North America and developing nations of Latin America.

OECD Organization for Economic Co-operation and Development (formed in 1961). It comprises 30 major free-market economies. Poland, Hungary and South Korea joined in 1996, and the Slovak Republic in 2000. 'G8' is its 'inner group' of leading industrial nations, comprising Canada, France, Germany, Italy, Japan, Russia, UK and USA.

OPEC Organization of Petroleum Exporting Countries (formed in 1960). It controls about three-quarters of the world's oil supply. Gabon left the organization in 1996.

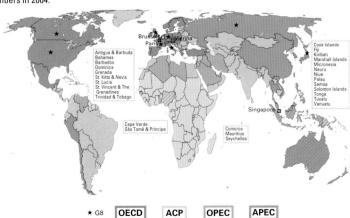

★ G8 | OECD | | ACP | | OPEC | | APEC |

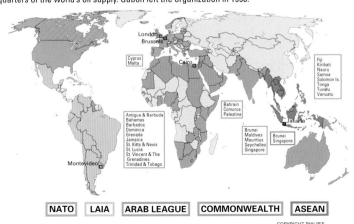

| NATO | | LAIA | | ARAB LEAGUE | | COMMONWEALTH | | ASEAN |

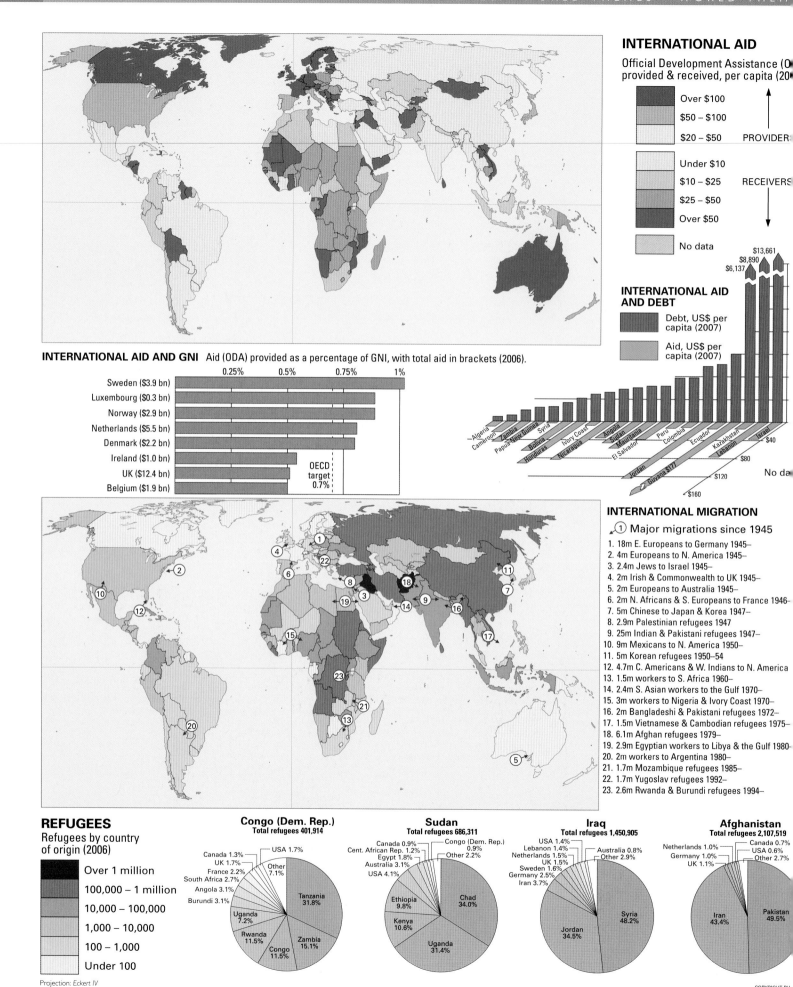

INTERNATIONAL AID

Official Development Assistance (O
provided & received, per capita (20

- Over $100
- $50 – $100   PROVIDER
- $20 – $50

- Under $10
- $10 – $25   RECEIVERS
- $25 – $50
- Over $50

- No data

INTERNATIONAL AID AND GNI

Aid (ODA) provided as a percentage of GNI, with total aid in brackets (2006).

	0.25%	0.5%	0.75%	1%
Sweden ($3.9 bn)				
Luxembourg ($0.3 bn)				
Norway ($2.9 bn)				
Netherlands ($5.5 bn)				
Denmark ($2.2 bn)				
Ireland ($1.0 bn)				
UK ($12.4 bn)		OECD target 0.7%		
Belgium ($1.9 bn)				

INTERNATIONAL AID AND DEBT

- Debt, US$ per capita (2007)
- Aid, US$ per capita (2007)

$13,661
$8,890
$6,137

Algeria, Cameroon, Zambia, Papua New Guinea, Syria, Honduras, Bolivia, Nicaragua, Ivory Coast, El Salvador, Angola, Sudan, Mauritania, Jordan $177, Guyana, Peru, Colombia, Ecuador, Kazakhstan, Lebanon, Israel

$40, $80, $120, $160

No da

INTERNATIONAL MIGRATION

① Major migrations since 1945

1. 18m E. Europeans to Germany 1945–
2. 4m Europeans to N. America 1945–
3. 2.4m Jews to Israel 1945–
4. 2m Irish & Commonwealth to UK 1945–
5. 2m Europeans to Australia 1945–
6. 2m N. Africans & S. Europeans to France 1946–
7. 5m Chinese to Japan & Korea 1947–
8. 2.9m Palestinian refugees 1947
9. 25m Indian & Pakistani refugees 1947–
10. 9m Mexicans to N. America 1950–
11. 5m Korean refugees 1950–54
12. 4.7m C. Americans & W. Indians to N. America
13. 1.5m workers to S. Africa 1960–
14. 2.4m S. Asian workers to the Gulf 1970–
15. 3m workers to Nigeria & Ivory Coast 1970–
16. 2m Bangladeshi & Pakistani refugees 1972–
17. 1.5m Vietnamese & Cambodian refugees 1975–
18. 6.1m Afghan refugees 1979–
19. 2.9m Egyptian workers to Libya & the Gulf 1980–
20. 2m workers to Argentina 1980–
21. 1.7m Mozambique refugees 1985–
22. 1.7m Yugoslav refugees 1992–
23. 2.6m Rwanda & Burundi refugees 1994–

REFUGEES

Refugees by country of origin (2006)

- Over 1 million
- 100,000 – 1 million
- 10,000 – 100,000
- 1,000 – 10,000
- 100 – 1,000
- Under 100

Congo (Dem. Rep.)
Total refugees 401,914

Canada 1.3% — USA 1.7%
UK 1.7%
France 2.2% — Other 7.1%
South Africa 2.7%
Angola 3.1%
Burundi 3.1%
Tanzania 31.8%
Uganda 7.2%
Rwanda 11.5%
Congo 11.5%
Zambia 15.1%

Sudan
Total refugees 686,311

Canada 0.9% — Congo (Dem. Rep.) 0.9%
Cent. African Rep. 1.2% — Other 2.2%
Egypt 1.8%
Australia 3.1%
USA 4.1%
Ethiopia 9.8%
Kenya 10.6%
Chad 34.0%
Uganda 31.4%

Iraq
Total refugees 1,450,905

USA 1.4% — Australia 0.8%
Lebanon 1.4% — Other 2.9%
Netherlands 1.5%
UK 1.5%
Sweden 1.6%
Germany 2.5%
Iran 3.7%
Syria 48.2%
Jordan 34.5%

Afghanistan
Total refugees 2,107,519

Netherlands 1.0% — Canada 0.7%
Germany 1.0% — USA 0.6%
UK 1.1% — Other 2.7%
Iran 43.4%
Pakistan 49.5%

Projection: *Eckert IV*

COPYRIGHT PH

ARMED CONFLICTS

Armed conflict since 1994

Countries with at least one armed conflict between 1994 and mid-2008

Countries in the top half of the Human Developement Index (HDI)

Countries in the bottom half of the HDI

MAJOR WARS SINCE 1900	
War	**Total deaths**
Second World War (1939–45)	55,000,000
First World War (1914–18)	8,500,000
Korean War (1950–53)	4,000,000
Congolese Civil War (1998–)	3,800,000
Vietnam War (1965–73)	3,000,000
Sudanese Civil War (1983–2000)	2,000,000

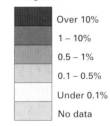

SPREAD OF HIV/AIDS

Percentage of adults (15 – 49 years) living with HIV/AIDS (2007)

- Over 10%
- 1 – 10%
- 0.5 – 1%
- 0.1 – 0.5%
- Under 0.1%
- No data

Total number of adults and children living with HIV/AIDS by region (2007)

Human Immunodeficiency Virus (HIV) is passed from one person to another and attacks the body's defence against illness. It develops into the Acquired Immunodeficiency Syndrome (AIDS) when a particularly severe illness, such as cancer, takes hold. The pandemic started just over 20 years ago and by 2007 33 millon people were living with HIV or AIDS.

(Map labels: North America 1,200,000 · Caribbean 230,000 · Latin America 1,700,000 · Western Europe 730,000 · Eastern Europe & Central Asia 1,500,000 · North Africa & Middle East 380,000 · Sub-Saharan Africa 22,000,000 · East Asia 740,000 · South & South-east Asia 4,200,000 · Oceania 74,000)

TRAFFIC IN DRUGS

Countries producing illegal drugs

- Cannabis
- Opium poppy
- Coca leaves
- Cocaine
- Amphetamines ■

Major routes of drug trafficking

- Opium
- Coca leaves
- Cocaine
- Heroin
- Cannabis
- Amphetamines (usually used within producing countries)
- Conflicts relating to drug trafficking ✸

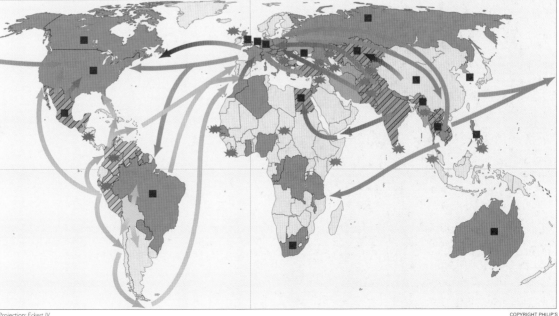

Projection: *Eckert IV*

COPYRIGHT PHILIP'S

	POPULATION							WEALTH					TRADE		
	Total population (millions 2008)	Population density (persons per km² 2008)	Life expectancy (years 2008)	Population change (average annual percentage 2008)	Birth rate (births per thousand people 2008)	Death rate (deaths per thousand people 2008)	Urban population (percentage of total 2006)	Gross National Income (million US$ 2007)	Gross National Income per capita (PPP US$ 2007)	GDP from agriculture (percentage of GDP 2007)	GDP from industry (percentage of GDP 2007)	GDP from services (percentage of GDP 2007)	Imports (US$ per capita 2008)	Exports (US$ per capita 2008)	Tourism receipts (US$ per capita 2005)
Afghanistan	32.7	51	44	2.6	46	20	22	10,137	250	31.0	26.0	43.0	148	10	
Albania	3.6	126	78	0.5	15	5	45	10,456	6,580	20.6	19.9	59.5	1,346	393	2
Algeria	33.8	14	74	1.2	17	5	63	122,465	7,640	8.1	62.5	29.4	1,091	2,221	
Angola	12.5	10	38	2.1	44	24	53	43,635	4,400	9.3	65.9	24.8	1,220	5,806	
Argentina	40.5	15	74	1.1	18	7	90	238,853	12,990	9.2	34.1	56.7	1,479	1,802	
Armenia	3.0	100	72	-0.1	13	8	64	7,925	5,900	17.2	36.4	46.4	1,182	408	
Australia	21.0	3	82	1.2	13	7	88	755,795	33,340	2.5	26.4	71.1	8,914	8,519	8
Austria	8.2	98	79	0.1	9	10	66	355,088	38,140	1.9	30.6	67.5	22,366	19,915	1,8
Azerbaijan	8.2	94	66	0.7	18	8	52	21,872	6,260	6.0	62.6	31.4	914	4,668	
Bahamas	0.3	22	66	0.6	17	9	90	4,476	14,920	3.0	7.0	90.0	8,003	2,247	6,8
Bahrain	0.7	1,080	75	1.3	17	4	96	14,022	34,310	0.3	43.6	56.1	22,343	27,386	1,2
Bangladesh	153.5	1,066	63	2.0	29	8	25	75,047	1,340	19.1	28.6	52.3	131	91	
Barbados	0.3	654	73	0.4	12	9	52	4,842	16,140	6.0	16.0	78.0	5,287	1,283	2,55
Belarus	9.7	47	70	-0.4	10	14	72	40,897	10,740	8.4	41.5	50.1	3,777	3,279	
Belgium	10.4	341	79	0.1	10	10	97	432,540	34,790	1.0	24.2	74.8	36,077	35,856	9
Belize	0.3	13	68	2.2	28	6	48	1,157	6,200	29.0	16.9	54.1	2,393	1,653	4
Benin	8.5	76	59	3.0	40	10	40	5,120	1,310	33.2	14.5	52.3	159	91	
Bhutan	0.7	15	66	1.3	21	8	11	1,166	4,980	22.3	37.9	39.8	457	500	
Bolivia	9.2	8	67	1.4	22	7	64	11,964	4,140	11.3	36.9	51.8	520	694	
Bosnia-Herzegovina	4.6	90	78	0.7	9	9	45	14,302	7,700	10.2	23.8	66.0	2,596	1,107	1
Botswana	1.8	3	50	1.4	23	14	57	10,991	12,420	1.6	52.6	45.8	2,184	2,848	3
Brazil	196.3	23	72	1.2	19	6	84	1,133,030	9,370	5.5	28.5	66.0	897	1,019	
Brunei	0.4	66	76	1.8	18	3	73	10,287	49,900	0.7	75.0	24.3	5,000	16,918	
Bulgaria	7.3	66	73	-0.8	10	14	70	35,062	11,180	4.6	28.7	66.7	5,118	3,260	
Burkina Faso	15.3	56	53	3.1	45	14	18	6,384	1,120	29.1	19.9	51.0	109	53	
Burma (Myanmar)	47.8	70	63	0.8	17	9	30	10,516	220	40.9	19.7	39.4	75	129	
Burundi	8.7	312	52	3.4	42	13	10	923	330	32.9	21.3	45.8	35	5	
Cambodia	14.2	79	62	1.8	26	8	19	7,858	1,690	29.0	30.0	41.0	452	325	
Cameroon	18.5	39	53	2.2	35	12	54	19,447	2,120	43.5	16.0	40.5	236	284	
Canada	33.2	3	81	0.8	10	8	80	1,300,025	35,310	2.0	28.4	69.6	13,154	13,910	4
Cape Verde Is.	0.4	106	71	0.6	24	6	57	1,287	2,940	9.0	16.9	74.1	2,218	255	30
Central African Rep.	4.4	7	44	1.5	33	18	38	1,667	740	55.0	20.0	25.0	54	34	
Chad	10.1	8	47	2.2	42	16	25	5,760	1,280	20.5	48.0	31.5	146	545	
Chile	16.5	22	77	0.9	15	6	87	138,630	12,590	4.8	50.5	44.7	3,586	4,188	
China	1330.0	139	73	0.6	14	7	40	3,120,891	5,370	10.6	49.2	40.2	869	1,102	
Colombia	45.0	40	73	1.4	20	6	72	149,934	6,640	9.4	36.6	54.0	864	913	
Comoros	0.7	337	63	2.8	36	8	36	425	1,150	40.0	4.0	56.0	204	46	
Congo	3.9	11	54	2.7	42	12	60	5,797	2,750	5.6	57.1	37.3	698	2,310	
Congo (Dem. Rep.)	66.5	28	54	3.2	43	12	32	8,573	290	55.0	11.0	34.0	34	24	
Costa Rica	4.2	82	77	1.4	18	4	61	24,831	10,700	7.6	29.1	63.3	3,583	2,304	38
Croatia	4.5	79	75	-0.0	10	12	56	46,426	15,050	7.0	31.6	61.4	7,218	3,408	1,6
Cuba	11.4	103	77	0.3	11	7	76	13,338	1,170	4.4	22.8	72.8	1,030	307	1
Cyprus	0.8	86	78	0.5	13	8	69	19,617	26,370	2.6	19.1	78.3	10,861	1,913	2,9
Czech Republic	10.2	130	77	-0.1	9	11	74	149,378	22,020	2.6	38.7	58.7	14,225	14,755	45
Denmark	5.5	127	78	0.3	11	10	86	299,804	36,300	1.4	25.9	72.7	21,945	21,727	89
Djibouti	0.5	22	43	1.9	39	19	86	908	2,260	3.2	14.9	81.9	3,110	680	
Dominican Republic	9.5	195	73	1.5	23	5	73	34,611	6,340	11.3	23.5	65.2	1,686	755	38
East Timor	1.1	74	67	2.1	27	6	26	1,604	3,080	32.2	12.8	55.0	184	9	
Ecuador	13.9	49	77	0.9	22	4	62	41,148	7,040	6.6	33.9	59.5	1,194	1,396	3
Egypt	81.7	82	72	1.7	22	5	43	119,405	5,400	13.4	37.7	48.9	691	408	8
El Salvador	7.1	336	72	1.7	26	6	60	19,520	5,640	11.2	24.7	64.1	1,238	649	
Equatorial Guinea	0.6	22	61	2.7	37	10	39	6,527	21,230	2.7	92.6	4.7	5,352	26,367	
Eritrea	5.5	45	61	2.6	35	9	19	1,108	520	17.4	23.2	59.4	109	3	
Estonia	1.3	29	73	-0.6	10	13	69	17,706	19,810	2.9	32.3	64.8	12,485	10,123	7
Ethiopia	82.5	73	55	3.2	44	12	16	17,565	780	45.9	12.9	41.2	75	17	
Fiji	0.9	51	70	1.4	22	6	50	3,189	4,370	8.9	13.5	77.6	3,467	1,336	48
Finland	5.2	16	79	0.1	10	10	61	234,833	34,550	2.8	33.2	64.0	17,938	20,058	42
France	64.1	117	81	0.6	13	8	77	2,447,090	33,600	2.2	20.3	77.5	11,207	9,824	
Gabon	1.5	6	54	2.0	36	13	83	8,876	13,080	5.7	57.3	37.0	1,887	6,495	
Gambia, The	1.7	154	55	2.7	38	12	53	544	1,140	33.0	8.7	58.3	177	65	
Gaza Strip (OPT)*	1.5	4,167	73	3.4	38	4	72	4,452	2,968	8.0	13.0	79.0	1,893	225	
Georgia	4.6	66	77	-0.3	11	10	52	9,337	4,770	12.8	28.4	58.8	1,588	600	5
Germany	82.4	231	79	-0.0	8	11	75	3,197,029	33,530	0.9	30.1	69.0	14,587	18,568	35
Ghana	23.4	98	59	1.9	29	9	47	13,902	1,330	37.3	25.3	37.4	419	232	
Greece	10.7	81	80	0.1	10	10	59	331,658	32,330	3.5	23.4	73.1	7,690	2,561	1,28

	ENERGY			LAND & AGRICULTURE				SOCIAL INDICATORS							
	Energy produced (tonnes of oil equivalent per capita 2007)	Energy consumed (tonnes of oil equivalent per capita 2007)	CO_2 emissions (tonnes per capita 2006)	Land area (thousand km2)	Arable and Permanent crops (% of land area 2005)	Permanent pasture (% of land area 2005)	Forest (% of land area 2005)	Human development index (HDI value 2005)	Food intake (calories per capita per day 2003)	Doctors (per 100,000 people 2004)	Adults living with HIV/AIDS (percentage 2007)	Gender development index (GDI value 2005)	Adult illiteracy rate (percentage 2005)	Motor vehicles (per thousand people 2003)	Internet usage (per thousand people 2007)
Afghanistan	0.01	0.01	0.03	652	12	46	2	–	1,539	18.6	0.1	–	–	9	1.8
Albania	0.51	0.85	1.31	29	26	15	36	0.801	2,848	130.5	0.1	0.797	1	71	13.1
Algeria	5.87	1.17	2.83	2,382	3	13	1	0.733	3,022	113.1	0.1	0.720	30	88	10.5
Angola	6.39	0.34	1.77	1,247	3	43	56	0.446	2,083	7.7	2.1	0.439	33	18	0.8
Argentina	2.38	1.98	4.06	2,780	13	52	13	0.869	2,992	300.9	0.5	0.865	3	198	23.1
Armenia	0.39	1.68	3.48	30	20	30	12	0.775	2,268	358.8	0.1	0.772	1	–	5.8
Australia	14.04	6.91	20.58	7,741	6	51	21	0.962	3,054	247.4	0.2	0.960	1	624	55.0
Austria	1.53	4.68	9.32	84	18	22	47	0.948	3,673	337.8	0.2	0.934	1	501	52.2
Azerbaijan	5.18	2.19	4.94	87	25	33	13	0.746	2,575	354.7	0.2	0.743	1	45	12.8
Bahamas	0	5.59	16.48	14	1	0	84	0.845	2,755	105.4	3.0	0.841	–	342	39.3
Bahrain	18.26	17.35	38.44	0.7	8	6	0	0.866	–	108.7	0.1	0.857	14	322	35.3
Bangladesh	0.09	0.13	0.29	144	65	5	10	0.547	2,205	25.7	0.1	0.539	53	2	0.3
Barbados	0.27	1.76	5.34	0.4	40	5	5	0.892	3,091	120.6	1.2	0.887	–	338	57.0
Belarus	0.20	2.77	6.68	208	27	16	45	0.804	3,000	455.0	0.2	0.803	1	168	61.7
Belgium	1.19	6.61	14.22	31	26	16	22	0.946	3,584	449.4	0.2	0.940	1	470	50.2
Belize	0.54	1.35	3.44	23	4	2	59	0.778	2,869	104.6	2.1	–	25	161	10.9
Benin	0.01	0.12	0.34	113	25	5	24	0.437	2,548	4.5	0.1	0.422	65	2	1.9
Bhutan	0.30	0.26	0.49	47	4	9	64	0.579	–	5.1	0.1	–	53	–	1.7
Bolivia	1.72	0.60	1.38	1,099	3	31	49	0.695	2,235	121.8	0.2	0.691	13	56	11.0
Bosnia-Herzegovina	1.06	1.41	3.87	51	21	21	45	0.803	2,894	134.0	0.1	–	3	–	23.2
Botswana	0.37	0.92	2.39	582	1	45	22	0.654	2,151	39.8	23.9	0.639	19	38	4.4
Brazil	1.07	1.28	2.01	8,514	8	23	63	0.800	3,050	115.3	0.6	0.798	11	112	26.3
Brunei	60.87	11.08	26.89	6	4	1	84	0.894	2,855	100.6	–	0.886	7	397	42.5
Bulgaria	1.43	3.03	6.63	111	31	17	33	0.824	2,848	356.2	0.1	0.823	2	295	25.9
Burkina Faso	0	0.03	0.07	274	16	22	26	0.370	2,462	5.9	1.6	0.364	76	4	0.6
Burma (Myanmar)	0.27	0.23	0.27	677	16	1	52	0.583	2,937	35.5	0.7	–	10	6	0.1
Burundi	0	0.02	0.05	28	53	38	4	0.413	1,649	2.8	2.0	0.409	41	3	0.7
Cambodia	0	0.02	0.05	181	22	9	53	0.598	2,046	15.6	0.8	0.594	26	1	0.5
Cameroon	0.32	0.13	0.41	475	15	4	51	0.532	2,273	19.2	5.1	0.524	32	11	2.0
Canada	14.54	10.54	18.81	9,971	6	3	27	0.961	3,589	213.9	0.4	0.956	1	561	83.9
Cape Verde Is.	0	0.24	0.62	4	11	1	21	0.736	3,243	48.8	–	0.723	19	40	8.7
Central African Rep.	0.01	0.03	0.08	623	3	5	37	0.384	1,980	8.5	6.3	0.368	51	3	0.3
Chad	0.91	0.01	0.02	1,284	3	36	10	0.388	2,114	3.9	3.5	0.370	74	1	0.6
Chile	0.60	1.95	4.01	757	3	17	21	0.867	2,863	109.1	0.3	0.859	4	89	34.2
China	1.29	1.4	4.58	9,597	17	43	18	0.777	2,951	105.5	0.1	0.776	9	10	19.1
Colombia	2.03	0.75	1.42	1,139	3	37	48	0.791	2,585	135.0	0.6	0.789	7	28	27.3
Comoros	0	0.06	0.16	2	59	8	4	0.561	1,754	14.6	0.1	0.554	–	–	3.0
Congo	3.58	0.19	1.49	342	1	29	65	0.548	2,162	19.8	3.5	0.540	15	15	1.8
Congo (Dem. Rep.)	0.05	0.04	0.04	2,345	3	7	60	0.411	1,599	10.7	3.2	0.398	33	–	0.4
Costa Rica	0.56	1.08	1.41	51	10	46	39	0.846	2,876	132.5	0.4	0.842	5	103	36.3
Croatia	0.93	2.30	4.77	57	22	26	32	0.850	2,779	244.4	0.1	0.848	2	291	44.4
Cuba	0.31	0.87	2.52	111	34	26	21	0.838	3,152	590.6	0.1	0.839	–	1	11.5
Cyprus	0	3.79	11.37	9	15	0	13	0.903	3,255	234.2	0.1	0.899	3	393	48.2
Czech Republic	2.83	4.43	11.36	79	43	13	34	0.891	3,171	351.3	0.1	0.887	1	395	43.0
Denmark	5.52	4.00	10.85	43	53	8	11	0.949	3,439	292.5	0.1	0.944	1	431	64.0
Djibouti	0	1.34	4.12	23	0	57	0	0.516	2,220	18.1	3.1	0.507	–	3	2.2
Dominican Republic	0.04	0.73	1.89	49	33	44	28	0.779	2,347	187.6	1.1	0.773	13	100	17.9
East Timor	4.46	–	–	15	9	–	–	0.514	2,806	9.6	–	–	50	–	0.1
Ecuador	2.33	0.78	1.88	284	9	18	38	0.772	2,754	147.6	0.3	–	9	47	11.3
Egypt	1.03	0.81	1.92	1001	4	0	0	0.708	3,338	53.5	0.1	0.634	29	35	10.7
El Salvador	0.16	0.48	0.92	21	44	38	6	0.735	2,584	123.7	0.8	0.726	19	64	10.1
Equatorial Guinea	38.07	2.51	8.37	28	8	4	62	0.642	–	30.2	3.4	0.631	13	–	1.5
Eritrea	0	0.06	0.15	118	5	58	16	0.483	1,513	5.0	1.3	0.469	–	–	2.4
Estonia	2.30	4.46	14.06	45	14	5	49	0.860	3,002	447.5	1.3	0.858	0	321	59.3
Ethiopia	0.01	0.03	0.07	1,104	11	18	5	0.406	1,857	2.7	2.1	0.393	64	1	0.4
Fiji	0.19	0.71	1.47	18	16	10	45	0.762	2,894	33.7	0.1	0.757	–	126	8.7
Finland	2.11	6.36	11.15	338	7	0	72	0.952	3,100	316.5	0.1	0.947	1	434	68.7
France	2.11	4.70	6.60	552	36	18	28	0.952	3,654	336.7	0.4	0.950	1	495	51.4
Gabon	9.34	0.74	3.04	268	2	18	85	0.677	2,637	29.2	5.9	–	16	16	10.0
Gambia, The	–	0.07	0.19	11	26	46	48	0.502	2,273	10.9	0.9	0.670	–	6	5.9
Gaza Strip (OPT)*	–	–	–	0.4	–	–	–	0.731	2,180	–	–	0.496	8	–	24.0
Georgia	0.29	0.72	1.00	70	15	28	43	0.754	2,354	408.9	0.1	–	1	50	7.7
Germany	1.59	4.44	10.40	357	35	14	31	0.935	3,496	336.9	0.1	0.931	1	546	51.6
Ghana	0.08	0.18	0.32	239	28	37	28	0.553	2,667	15.2	1.9	0.549	42	11	2.8
Greece	0.95	3.47	10.02	132	29	36	28	0.926	3,721	438.0	0.2	0.922	4	414	23.7

| | POPULATION | | | | | | | WEALTH | | | | | TRADE | | |
	Total population (millions 2008)	Population density (persons per km2 2008)	Life expectancy (years 2008)	Population change (average annual percentage 2008)	Birth rate (births per thousand people 2008)	Death rate (deaths per thousand people 2008)	Urban population (percentage of total 2006)	Gross National Income (million US$ 2007)	Gross National Income per capita (PPP US$ 2007)	GDP from agriculture (percentage of GDP 2007)	GDP from industry (percentage of GDP 2007)	GDP from services (percentage of GDP 2007)	Imports (US$ per capita 2008)	Exports (US$ per capita 2008)	Tourism receipts (US$ per capita 2005)
Guatemala	13.0	119	70	2.1	29	5	47	32,585	4,520	13.2	25.8	61.0	1,186	628	
Guinea	9.8	40	57	2.5	38	11	33	3,722	1,120	22.4	40.9	36.7	142	123	
Guinea-Bissau	1.5	42	48	2.0	36	16	30	331	470	62.0	12.0	26.0	133	89	
Guyana	0.8	4	66	0.2	18	8	28	959	2,880	31.9	21.0	47.1	1,453	974	
Haiti	8.9	322	58	2.5	36	10	38	5,366	1,150	28.0	20.0	52.0	235	55	
Honduras	7.6	68	69	2.0	27	5	46	11,339	3,620	13.4	28.2	58.4	1,342	821	
Hungary	9.9	107	73	-0.3	10	13	66	116,303	17,210	3.2	31.8	65.0	10,859	11,040	4
Iceland	0.3	3	81	0.8	14	7	93	16,826	33,960	5.0	26.5	68.5	21,810	22,820	1,3
India	1148.0	349	69	1.6	22	6	29	1,069,427	2,740	17.2	29.1	53.7	250	153	
Indonesia	237.5	124	70	1.2	19	6	47	373,125	3,580	13.5	45.6	40.9	482	594	
Iran	65.9	40	71	0.8	17	6	66	246,544	10,800	10.8	44.3	44.9	1,029	1,615	
Iraq	28.2	65	70	2.6	31	5	68	–	–	5.0	68.0	27.0	1,324	2,350	
Ireland	4.2	59	78	1.1	14	8	60	210,168	37,090	5.0	46.0	49.0	21,731	30,476	1,1
Israel	7.1	342	81	1.7	20	5	92	157,065	25,930	2.7	31.7	65.6	8,806	7,628	4
Italy	58.1	193	80	-0.0	8	11	68	1,991,284	29,850	2.0	26.7	71.3	9,756	9,744	6
Ivory Coast	20.2	63	55	2.2	33	11	45	17,543	1,590	27.9	21.9	50.2	393	592	
Jamaica	2.8	255	74	0.8	20	6	53	9,923	6,210	5.2	32.9	61.9	2,568	918	5
Japan	127.3	337	82	-0.1	8	9	66	4,813,341	34,600	1.4	26.4	72.2	5,469	6,102	
Jordan	6.2	67	79	2.3	20	3	82	16,282	5,160	3.6	10.1	86.3	2,524	1,052	2
Kazakhstan	15.3	6	68	0.4	16	9	57	78,281	9,700	5.8	39.4	54.8	2,453	4,351	
Kenya	38.0	65	57	2.8	38	10	21	25,559	1,540	23.8	16.7	59.5	250	124	
Korea, North	23.5	195	72	0.7	15	7	60	–	–	23.2	43.1	33.7	123	62	
Korea, South	48.4	491	79	0.3	9	6	81	955,802	24,750	3.0	39.5	57.5	9,502	9,471	
Kuwait	2.6	146	78	3.6	22	2	98	80,221	49,970	0.3	52.2	47.5	10,208	36,715	
Kyrgyzstan	5.4	27	69	1.4	23	7	36	3,099	1,950	32.4	18.6	49.0	644	310	
Laos	6.7	28	56	2.3	34	11	20	3,413	1,940	39.2	34.3	26.5	191	154	
Latvia	2.2	35	72	-0.6	10	14	68	22,595	16,890	3.3	22.3	74.4	6,450	3,802	1
Lebanon	4.0	382	73	1.2	18	6	87	23,651	10,050	5.1	19.1	75.8	4,145	1,274	1,3
Lesotho	2.1	70	40	0.1	24	22	19	2,007	1,890	15.1	46.7	38.2	638	505	
Liberia	3.3	30	41	3.7	43	21	45	554	290	76.9	5.4	17.7	2,165	363	
Libya	6.2	4	77	2.2	26	3	85	55,473	14,710	1.5	61.7	36.8	3,329	10,666	
Lithuania	3.6	55	75	-0.3	9	11	67	33,472	17,180	4.3	32.8	62.9	8,403	6,522	2
Luxembourg	0.5	188	79	1.2	12	8	83	36,420	63,590	0.4	13.6	86.0	56,240	41,560	7,2
Macedonia (FYROM)	2.1	81	74	0.3	12	9	68	7,052	8,510	11.4	27.2	61.4	3,173	2,094	
Madagascar	20.0	34	63	3.0	38	8	27	6,331	920	26.0	15.9	58.1	127	66	
Malawi	13.9	118	43	2.4	42	18	17	3,506	750	38.1	17.7	44.2	74	49	
Malaysia	25.3	77	73	1.7	22	5	66	173,705	13,570	9.7	44.6	45.7	6,174	7,735	3
Mali	1.2	1	50	2.7	49	16	30	6,136	1,040	45.0	17.0	38.0	1,965	245	
Malta	0.4	1,277	79	0.4	10	8	95	6,216	20,990	1.4	18.0	80.6	12,408	8,728	1,9
Mauritania	3.4	3	54	2.9	40	12	40	2,636	2,010	12.5	46.7	40.8	434	410	
Mauritius	1.3	625	74	0.8	15	7	42	6,878	11,390	4.5	24.9	70.6	3,464	1,815	
Mexico	110.0	56	76	1.1	20	5	76	878,020	12,580	3.7	34.1	62.2	2,781	2,673	1
Micronesia, Fed. States	0.1	153	71	-0.2	24	5	22	274	3,270	28.9	15.2	55.9	1,330	140	1
Moldova	4.3	128	71	-0.1	11	11	47	4,323	2,930	17.3	21.5	61.2	1,163	416	
Mongolia	3.0	2	67	1.5	21	6	57	3,362	3,160	20.6	38.4	41.0	706	650	
Montenegro	0.7	48	75	-0.9	11	9	52	3,109	10,290	–	–	–	860	244	
Morocco	34.3	77	72	1.5	21	5	58	69,352	3,990	14.7	38.9	46.4	1,004	471	1
Mozambique	21.3	27	41	1.8	38	20	34	6,787	690	23.4	30.7	45.9	155	126	
Namibia	2.1	3	50	0.9	23	14	35	6,970	5,120	10.4	36.2	53.4	1,695	1,419	1
Nepal	29.5	210	61	2.1	30	9	15	9,660	1,040	38.0	20.0	42.0	81	28	
Netherlands	16.6	401	79	0.4	11	9	80	750,526	39,310	2.0	24.4	73.6	29,235	32,380	6
New Zealand	4.2	16	80	1.0	14	7	86	121,708	26,340	4.4	26.0	69.6	7,407	7,031	1,1
Nicaragua	5.8	45	71	1.8	24	4	59	5,519	2,520	17.0	26.1	56.9	910	549	
Niger	13.3	11	44	2.9	50	20	17	3,992	630	39.0	17.0	44.0	60	32	
Nigeria	146.3	158	47	2.0	37	17	47	137,091	1,770	18.0	50.9	31.1	317	568	
Norway	4.6	14	80	0.4	11	9	77	360,036	53,320	2.4	40.7	56.9	20,263	38,609	7
Oman	3.3	16	74	3.2	35	4	72	27,887	19,740	2.1	37.2	60.7	4,036	10,273	1
Pakistan	172.8	215	64	2.0	28	8	35	141,009	2,570	20.4	26.6	53.0	205	119	
Panama	3.3	42	77	1.5	21	5	70	18,423	10,610	6.2	16.1	77.7	4,600	3,142	2
Papua New Guinea	5.9	13	66	2.1	28	7	13	5,400	1,870	32.8	36.5	30.7	511	959	
Paraguay	6.8	17	76	2.4	28	4	58	10,225	4,380	23.1	17.2	59.7	1,081	1,015	
Peru	29.2	23	70	1.3	20	6	72	96,241	7,240	8.5	21.2	70.3	996	1,139	
Philippines	96.1	320	71	2.0	26	5	62	142,623	3,730	14.7	31.6	53.7	660	531	
Poland	38.5	123	75	-0.0	10	10	62	374,633	15,330	4.0	31.3	64.7	5,556	4,948	
Portugal	10.7	116	78	0.3	10	10	57	201,079	20,890	3.0	25.6	71.4	8,217	5,402	7

	ENERGY			LAND & AGRICULTURE				SOCIAL INDICATORS							
	Energy produced (tonnes of oil equivalent per capita 2007)	Energy consumed (tonnes of oil equivalent per capita 2007)	CO_2 emissions (tonnes per capita 2006)	Land area (thousand km²)	Arable and Permanent crops (% of land area 2005)	Permanent pasture (% of land area 2005)	Forest (% of land area 2005)	Human development index (HDI value 2005)	Food intake (calories per capita per day 2003)	Doctors (per 100,000 people 2004)	Adults living with HIV/AIDS (percentage 2007)	Gender development index (GDI value 2005)	Adult illiteracy rate (percentage 2005)	Motor vehicles (per thousand people 2003)	Internet usage (per thousand people 2007)
Guatemala	0.18	0.41	0.90	109	18	24	26	0.689	2,219	89.6	0.8	0.675	31	62	10.4
Guinea	0.01	0.06	0.14	246	6	43	28	0.456	2,409	11.5	1.6	0.446	71	2	0.5
Guinea-Bissau	0	0.10	0.28	36	19	39	78	0.374	2,024	12.2	1.8	0.355	–	–	2.5
Guyana	0	0.70	2.15	215	3	6	86	0.750	2,692	48.2	2.5	0.742	–	101	24.7
Haiti	0.01	0.08	0.21	28	40	18	3	0.529	2,086	25.0	2.2	–	–	19	11.5
Honduras	0.09	0.43	1.02	112	13	13	48	0.700	2,356	56.9	0.7	0.694	20	12	4.6
Hungary	0.99	2.86	5.88	93	52	11	20	0.874	3,483	332.9	0.1	0.872	1	274	42.2
Iceland	10.35	14.19	11.50	103	0	23	0	0.968	3,249	361.6	0.2	0.962	1	577	67.0
India	0.28	0.40	1.16	3,287	57	4	22	0.619	2,459	59.7	0.3	0.600	39	13	7.1
Indonesia	0.98	0.42	1.21	1,905	20	6	58	0.728	2,904	13.4	0.2	0.721	10	28	5.5
Iran	4.77	2.80	7.25	1,648	11	27	5	0.759	3,085	45.0	0.2	0.750	18	26	35.2
Iraq	4.05	1.16	3.69	438	14	9	2	–	2,197	65.8	0.1	–	–	47	0.2
Ireland	0.25	4.29	11.54	70	18	44	10	0.959	3,656	278.6	0.2	0.940	1	382	41.6
Israel	0.14	3.31	9.80	21	18	6	6	0.932	3,666	382.0	0.1	0.927	3	231	31.1
Italy	0.53	3.47	8.05	301	35	15	34	0.941	3,671	420.3	0.4	0.936	2	641	55.0
Ivory Coast	0.28	0.16	0.36	322	22	41	–	0.432	2,631	12.3	3.9	0.413	51	7	1.7
Jamaica	0.02	1.46	4.36	11	26	21	30	0.736	2,685	85.0	1.6	0.732	20	75	54.0
Japan	0.84	4.47	9.78	378	13	1	64	0.953	2,761	197.6	0.1	0.942	1	433	69.1
Jordan	0.05	1.31	3.37	89	3	8	1	0.773	2,674	203.0	0.1	0.760	9	67	18.6
Kazakhstan	9.39	4.89	14.02	2,725	8	69	5	0.794	2,677	353.9	0.1	0.792	1	77	12.4
Kenya	0.04	0.15	0.30	580	9	37	30	0.521	2,090	13.9	7.8	0.521	26	17	8.1
Korea, North	1.05	1.03	3.36	121	25	0	68	–	2,142	157.3	–	–	–	–	–
Korea, South	0.78	4.84	10.53	99	19	1	63	0.921	3,058	329.1	0.1	0.910	1	215	72.6
Kuwait	63.96	11.84	30.92	18	1	8	0	0.891	3,010	152.5	0.1	0.884	7	326	35.9
Kyrgyzstan	0.69	0.95	0.95	200	7	49	5	0.696	2,999	251.1	0.1	0.692	1	37	14.2
Laos	0.07	0.09	0.09	237	5	4	54	0.601	2,312	58.6	0.2	0.593	31	–	1.5
Latvia	0.30	1.98	3.84	65	18	10	47	0.855	2,938	300.8	0.8	0.853	1	280	52.1
Lebanon	0.04	1.32	3.69	10	31	2	4	0.772	3,196	325.3	0.1	0.759	–	417	24.2
Lesotho	0.02	0.07	0.11	30	11	67	0	0.549	2,638	4.9	23.2	0.541	18	–	3.3
Liberia	0	0.06	0.18	111	6	21	36	–	1,900	3.0	1.7	–	–	10	0
Libya	18.20	3.30	9.07	1,760	1	8	0	0.818	3,320	129.0	0.1	0.797	16	140	4.3
Lithuania	0.72	2.42	4.39	65	31	14	31	0.862	3,325	397.3	0.1	0.924	1	364	37.3
Luxembourg	0.13	10.06	26.28	3	2	2	–	0.944	3,701	266.2	0.2	–	1	641	71.8
Macedonia (FYROM)	0.69	1.35	3.50	26	24	25	36	0.801	2,655	219.1	0.1	0.795	4	167	33.3
Madagascar	0.01	0.06	0.14	587	6	41	20	0.533	2,005	29.1	0.1	0.530	29	5	0.6
Malawi	0.02	0.05	0.07	118	26	20	28	0.437	2,155	2.2	11.9	0.432	36	7	1.0
Malaysia	3.89	2.62	6.70	330	23	1	59	0.811	2,881	70.2	0.5	0.802	11	220	63.9
Mali	0.01	0.03	0.06	1,240	4	28	11	0.380	2,174	7.9	1.5	0.371	76	4	0.8
Malta	0	2.60	7.78	0.3	31	0	0	0.878	3,587	318.3	0.1	0.873	12	520	39.3
Mauritania	0.52	0.37	0.95	1,026	0	38	0	0.550	2,772	10.5	0.8	0.543	49	11	0.9
Mauritius	0.02	1.16	3.22	2	52	3	8	0.804	2,955	105.7	1.7	0.796	16	88	27.2
Mexico	2.41	1.71	4.05	1,958	14	42	29	0.829	3,145	198.0	0.3	0.820	8	133	21.0
Micronesia, Fed. States	0	–	–	0.7	51	16	0	–	–	59.8	–	–	–	–	13.9
Moldova	0.03	0.82	1.74	34	65	11	10	0.708	2,806	263.6	0.4	0.704	1	60	16.2
Mongolia	0.78	0.86	2.91	1,567	1	83	7	0.700	2,249	263.1	0.1	0.695	2	18	10.8
Montenegro	0	0	4.81	14	37	18	-	–	–	206.3	0.1	–	–	–	40.9
Morocco	0.02	0.38	1.04	447	21	47	7	0.646	3,052	51.5	0.1	0.621	48	57	21.6
Mozambique	0.26	0.28	0.24	802	6	56	39	0.384	2,079	2.7	12.5	0.373	61	9	1.0
Namibia	0.20	0.75	1.32	824	1	46	10	0.650	2,278	29.7	15.3	0.645	15	38	4.9
Nepal	0.02	0.06	0.11	147	17	12	27	0.534	2,453	20.9	0.5	0.520	51	6	1.2
Netherlands	4.02	6.27	15.79	42	28	29	11	0.953	3,362	314.9	0.2	0.951	1	439	90.5
New Zealand	4.03	5.27	9.38	271	13	52	30	0.943	3,219	236.6	0.1	0.935	1	632	81.6
Nicaragua	0.05	0.32	0.82	130	18	40	27	0.710	2,298	37.4	0.2	0.696	23	16	2.7
Niger	0.01	0.03	0.10	1,267	4	9	1	0.374	2,130	3.0	0.8	0.355	71	9	0.3
Nigeria	1.21	0.19	0.77	924	36	43	15	0.470	2,726	28.2	3.1	0.456	31	1	7.4
Norway	55.61	10.29	9.79	324	3	1	29	0.968	3,484	313.3	0.1	0.957	1	424	82.1
Oman	19.92	4.43	11.19	310	3	5	0	0.814	-	131.9	0.1	0.788	19	192	10.6
Pakistan	0.24	0.35	0.78	796	29	6	3	0.551	2,419	73.9	0.1	0.525	50	11	10.6
Panama	0.27	1.77	0.82	76	9	21	39	0.812	2,272	150.2	1.0	0.810	8	96	16.2
Papua New Guinea	0.46	0.32	0.58	463	2	0	68	0.530	2,175	5.2	1.5	0.529	43	21	1.9
Paraguay	2.03	1.64	1.05	407	8	55	59	0.755	2,565	110.7	0.6	0.744	7	66	4.2
Peru	0.43	0.54	0.81	1,285	3	21	51	0.773	2,571	116.7	0.5	0.769	12	30	26.6
Philippines	0.14	0.36	0.87	300	36	5	19	0.771	2,379	58.5	0.1	0.768	7	34	5.8
Poland	1.90	2.50	7.87	323	41	11	31	0.870	3,375	246.9	0.1	0.867	1	294	41.5
Portugal	0.37	2.56	5.82	89	25	16	40	0.897	3,741	342.3	0.5	0.895	6	734	33.3

	POPULATION							WEALTH					TRADE		
	Total population (millions 2008)	Population density (persons per km² 2008)	Life expectancy (years 2008)	Population change (average annual percentage 2008)	Birth rate (births per thousand people 2008)	Death rate (deaths per thousand people 2008)	Urban population (percentage of total 2006)	Gross National Income (million US$ 2007)	Gross National Income per capita (PPP US$ 2007)	GDP from agriculture (percentage of GDP 2007)	GDP from industry (percentage of GDP 2007)	GDP from services (percentage of GDP 2007)	Imports (US$ per capita 2008)	Exports (US$ per capita 2008)	Tourism receipts (US$ per capita 2005)
Qatar	0.8	72	75	1.1	16	2	95	—	—	0.1	79.4	20.5	31,200	78,050	8
Romania	22.2	94	72	-0.1	11	12	54	132,502	10,980	8.1	36.0	55.9	4,148	2,691	4
Russia	140.7	8	66	-0.5	11	16	73	1,070,999	14,400	4.1	41.1	54.8	2,146	3,383	3
Rwanda	10.2	387	50	2.8	40	14	19	3,072	860	35.0	22.1	42.9	74	21	
Saudi Arabia	28.1	14	76	2.0	29	2	81	373,490	22,910	3.1	61.6	35.3	3,822	11,733	22
Senegal	12.9	66	57	2.6	37	11	41	10,170	1,640	16.0	19.4	64.6	361	148	
Serbia†	10.2	115	75	0.0	12	10	52	34,969	10,220	12.3	24.2	63.5	1,799	865	
Sierra Leone	6.3	88	41	2.3	45	22	40	1,537	660	49.0	31.0	20.0	89	34	
Singapore	4.6	6,650	82	1.1	9	5	100	148,992	48,520	0.0	33.2	66.8	66,870	75,978	1,27
Slovak Republic	5.5	112	75	0.1	11	10	56	63,324	19,340	2.6	33.4	64.0	14,502	14,385	22
Slovenia	2.0	99	77	-0.1	9	11	51	42,306	26,640	2.2	34.2	63.6	19,060	17,135	90
Solomon Is.	0.6	20	73	2.5	28	4	17	363	1,680	42.0	11.0	47.0	512	474	
Somalia	9.6	15	49	2.8	44	16	33	1,248	130	65.0	10.0	25.0	83	31	
South Africa	48.8	40	49	0.8	20	17	59	274,009	9,560	3.4	31.3	65.3	1,789	1,669	16
Spain	40.5	80	80	0.1	10	10	77	1,321,756	30,820	3.6	28.9	67.5	10,985	7,230	1,18
Sri Lanka	21.1	322	75	0.9	17	6	15	30,785	4,210	15.5	27.0	57.5	596	433	2
Sudan	40.2	16	50	2.1	34	14	40	37,031	1,880	32.9	31.1	36.0	193	339	
Suriname	0.5	3	73	1.1	17	6	74	2,166	7,640	10.8	24.4	64.8	2,594	2,782	4
Swaziland	1.1	65	32	-0.4	27	31	24	2,951	4,930	11.9	45.1	43.0	1,798	1,664	8
Sweden	9.0	20	81	0.2	10	10	84	421,342	36,590	1.5	28.9	69.6	18,511	20,567	82
Switzerland	7.6	184	81	0.3	10	9	75	452,121	43,870	1.5	34.0	64.5	28,000	22,724	1,47
Syria	19.7	107	71	2.2	27	5	51	34,993	4,370	22.5	27.9	49.6	727	666	1
Taiwan	22.9	637	78	0.2	9	7	78	—	—	1.5	27.8	70.7	11,118	11,939	2
Tajikistan	7.2	50	65	1.9	27	7	25	3,103	1,710	23.0	29.4	47.6	528	233	
Tanzania	40.2	43	51	2.1	35	13	24	16,287	1,200	27.0	22.7	50.3	147	62	
Thailand	65.5	127	73	0.6	14	7	32	217,348	7,880	11.4	44.5	44.1	2,429	2,670	1
Togo	5.9	103	58	2.7	37	9	39	2,383	800	40.0	25.0	35.0	292	170	
Trinidad & Tobago	1.2	240	71	-0.1	14	8	76	18,795	22,490	0.5	47.9	51.6	8,550	13,942	4
Tunisia	10.4	64	76	1.0	16	5	65	32,820	7,130	10.8	28.2	61.0	2,212	1,894	20
Turkey	71.9	92	73	1.0	16	6	67	592,850	12,350	8.5	28.6	62.9	2,848	1,972	2
Turkmenistan	5.2	11	69	1.6	25	6	46	22,620	4,350	10.7	38.8	50.5	1,018	1,901	
Uganda	31.4	133	52	3.6	48	12	13	10,469	920	29.0	24.8	46.2	114	65	
Ukraine	46.0	76	68	-0.7	10	16	68	118,445	6,810	9.3	31.7	59.0	1,794	1,411	
United Arab Emirates	4.6	56	76	3.8	16	2	77	—	—	1.6	61.8	36.6	30,674	45,152	8
United Kingdom	60.9	249	79	0.3	11	10	90	2,608,513	33,800	0.9	22.8	76.3	10,603	7,696	50
USA	303.8	32	78	0.9	14	8	81	13,886,472	45,850	1.2	19.6	79.2	7,209	4,533	2
Uruguay	3.5	20	76	0.5	14	9	92	21,186	11,040	9.8	32.8	57.4	2,442	2,170	1
Uzbekistan	27.3	61	72	1.0	18	5	37	19,721	2,430	28.2	33.9	37.9	238	365	
Venezuela	26.4	29	73	1.5	20	5	93	201,146	11,920	3.6	35.3	61.1	2,024	3,920	1
Vietnam	86.1	261	71	1.0	16	6	26	67,236	2,550	19.0	42.7	38.3	922	740	
West Bank (OPT)*	2.4	411	74	2.2	26	4	72	4,452	1,855	8.0	13.0	79.0	542	141	
Western Sahara	0.4	2	54	2.9	40	12	94	—	—	—	—	—	—	—	
Yemen	23.0	44	62	3.5	42	8	27	19,421	2,200	9.4	52.4	38.2	401	401	
Zambia	11.7	16	39	1.7	41	21	35	9,479	1,220	16.7	26.0	57.3	378	481	
Zimbabwe	11.4	29	44	-0.8	32	17	35	4,466	392	18.1	22.6	59.3	205	158	

NOTES

SERBIA†
Kosovo separated from Serbia in February 2008.

OPT*
Occupied Palestinian Territory.

PER CAPITA
An amount divided by the total population of a country or the amount per person.

PPP
Purchasing Power Parity (PPP) is a method used to enable real comparisons to be made between countries when measuring wealth. The UN International Comparison Programme gives estimates of the PPP for each country, so it can be used as an indicator of real price levels for goods and services rather than using currency exchange rates (see GNI and GNI per capita).

POPULATION TOTAL
These are estimates of the mid-year total in 2008.

POPULATION DENSITY
The total population divided by the land area (both are recorded in the table above).

LIFE EXPECTANCY
The average age that a child born today is expected to live to, if mortality levels of today last throughout its lifetime.

BIRTH/DEATH RATES
These are 2008 estimates from the CIA World Factbook.

URBAN POPULATION
The urban population shows the percentage of the total population living in towns and cities (each country will differ with regard to the size or type of town that is defined as an urban area).

GNI
Gross National Income: this used to be referred to as GNP (Gross National Product) and is a good indication of a country's wealth. It is the income in US dollars from goods and services in a country for one year, including income from overseas.

GNI PER CAPITA
The GNI (see note) divided by the total population by using the PPP method (see note).

AGRICULTURE, INDUSTRY AND SERVICES
The percentage contributions that each of these three sectors makes to a country's GDP (see note).

IMPORTS AND EXPORTS
The total value of goods imported into a country and exported to other countries, given in US dollars ($) per capita.

TOURISM RECEIPTS
The amount of income generated from tourism in US dollars per capita.

	ENERGY		LAND & AGRICULTURE				SOCIAL INDICATORS							
Energy produced (tonnes of oil equivalent per capita 2007)	Energy consumed (tonnes of oil equivalent per capita 2007)	CO₂ emissions (tonnes per capita 2006)	Land area (thousand km²)	Arable and Permanent crops (% of land area 2005)	Permanent pasture (% of land area 2005)	Forest (% of land area 2005)	Human development index (HDI value 2005)	Food intake (calories per capita per day 2003)	Doctors (per 100,000 people 2004)	Adults living with HIV/AIDS (percentage 2007)	Gender development index (GDI value 2005)	Adult illiteracy rate (percentage 2005)	Motor vehicles (per thousand people 2003)	Internet usage (per thousand people 2007)
..tar	112.63	25.17	61.19	11	2	5	0	0.875	—	221.7	0.1	0.863	11	517	38.7
..mania	1.31	1.88	4.42	238	43	20	28	0.813	3,455	190.5	0.1	0.812	3	166	53.9
..ssia	9.33	5.32	12.00	17,075	7	5	50	0.802	3,072	425.2	1.1	0.801	1	185	21.2
..vanda	0	0.04	0.09	26	56	19	12	0.452	2,084	4.7	2.8	0.450	35	4	1.0
..udi Arabia	22.85	6.38	15.70	2,150	2	79	1	0.812	2,845	137.5	0.1	0.783	17	372	22.5
..negal	0.01	0.17	0.47	197	13	29	32	0.499	2,280	5.7	1.0	0.492	61	28	6.5
..bia†	0.06	0	4.81	88	37	18	3	—	2,678	206.3	0.1	—	—	172	18.7
..rra Leone	0	0.07	0.20	72	8	31	67	0.336	1,936	3.3	1.7	0.320	65	8	0.2
..gapore	0	11.90	31.41	0.7	1	0	3	0.922	—	140.0	0.2	—	8	101	68.2
..vak Republic	1.42	3.76	7.01	49	29	11	42	0.863	2,889	317.9	0.1	0.860	1	252	43.1
..venia	1.79	4.04	8.77	20	10	15	55	0.917	3,001	225.3	0.1	0.914	1	446	64.7
..lomon Is.	0	0.12	0.38	29	3	1	91	0.602	2,265	12.7	—	—	23	—	1.4
..malia	0	0.03	0.08	638	2	69	12	—	1,628	4.0	0.5	—	—	1	1.1
..uth Africa	3.40	2.93	10.04	1,221	13	69	7	0.674	2,956	77.0	18.1	0.667	18	145	11.6
..ain	0.86	4.03	9.22	498	37	21	29	0.949	3,371	329.5	0.5	0.944	1	455	48.7
..Lanka	0.04	0.27	0.61	66	30	7	30	0.743	2,385	54.5	0.1	0.735	9	34	3.7
..dan	0.43	0.11	0.32	2,506	7	49	26	0.526	2,228	22.0	1.4	0.502	39	3	3.8
..riname	2.58	2.61	4.31	163	0	0	90	0.774	2,652	44.9	2.4	0.767	10	204	9.3
..aziland	0.22	0.39	0.91	17	11	71	30	0.547	2,322	15.8	26.1	0.529	20	40	3.7
..eden	3.74	6.16	6.36	450	7	1	66	0.956	3,185	328.4	0.1	0.955	1	455	77.5
..itzerland	1.99	4.28	6.06	41	11	28	30	0.955	3,526	361.5	0.6	0.946	1	511	61.0
..ria	1.64	1.07	2.71	185	31	45	3	0.724	3,038	139.9	0.1	0.710	19	12	18.0
..wan	0.51	4.97	13.19	36	23	—	58	—	—	—	—	—	—	—	64.6
..jikistan	0.58	0.96	1.06	143	8	23	3	0.673	1,828	203.3	0.3	0.669	1	22	0.3
..nzania	0.01	0.05	0.12	945	6	40	44	0.467	1,975	2.3	6.2	0.464	31	4	1.0
..ailand	0.71	1.45	3.79	513	38	2	29	0.781	2,467	36.8	1.4	0.779	7	126	20.6
..go	0	0.17	0.45	57	48	19	9	0.512	2,345	4.5	3.3	0.494	47	16	5.6
..nidad & Tobago	39.45	18.65	44.32	5	24	2	50	0.814	2,732	78.8	1.5	0.808	2	220	40.8
..nisia	0.66	0.82	2.06	164	32	31	3	0.766	3,238	134.1	0.1	0.750	26	87	16.8
..rkey	0.42	1.39	3.35	775	35	19	13	0.775	3,357	134.6	0.1	0.763	13	67	18.5
..rkmenistan	13.53	4.36	10.03	488	4	65	8	0.713	2,742	417.9	0.1	—	1	—	1.4
..anda	0.01	0.03	0.06	241	37	26	21	0.505	2,410	8.3	5.4	0.501	33	6	6.6
..raine	1.78	3.14	7.05	604	58	14	17	0.788	3,054	295.1	1.6	0.785	1	114	21.6
..ited Arab Emirates	75.66	23.69	35.05	84	3	4	4	0.868	3,225	202.3	0.1	0.855	11	442	51.8
..ited Kingdom	3.25	4.04	9.66	242	24	46	11	0.946	3,412	230.0	0.2	0.944	1	439	66.1
..A	5.90	8.29	19.78	9,629	19	26	25	0.951	3,774	256.4	0.6	0.937	1	800	74.1
..uguay	0.26	0.98	1.85	175	8	77	7	0.852	2,828	365.2	0.6	0.849	3	217	28.0
..zbekistan	2.34	2.02	4.43	447	12	54	5	0.702	2,241	274.5	0.1	0.699	1	—	4.3
..nezuela	7.86	3.10	5.93	912	4	21	56	0.792	2,336	193.9	0.7	0.787	7	100	22.0
..etnam	0.64	0.42	1.09	332	28	2	30	0.733	2,566	53.4	0.5	0.732	10	1	21.0
..est Bank (OPT)*	0	0	—	6	—	—	—	0.731	2,180	—	—	—	—	—	14.0
..estern Sahara	0	0.35	0.84	266	0	19	0	—	—	—	—	—	—	—	—
..men	0.91	0.31	0.84	528	3	30	1	0.508	2,038	32.5	0.1	0.472	46	50	1.4
..mbia	0.21	0.27	0.23	753	7	40	42	0.434	1,927	11.6	15.2	0.425	32	1	4.4
..mbabwe	0.30	0.38	0.84	394	9	44	49	0.513	1,943	16.1	15.3	0.505	11	51	11.0

..RODUCTION AND CONSUMPTION ..F ENERGY

..he total amount of commercial energy ..oduced or consumed in a country per ..pita (see note). It is expressed in metric ..nnes of oil equivalent (an energy unit ..ving the heating value derived from one ..nne of oil).

..ARBON DIOXIDE EMISSIONS

..he amount of carbon dioxide that each ..untry produces per capita.

..ND AREA

..is is the total land area of a country, ..ss the area of major lakes and rivers, ..square kilometres.

..RABLE AND PERMANENT CROPS

..ese figures give a percentage of the ..tal land area that is used for crops and fruit (including temporary fallow land or meadows).

PERMANENT PASTURE

This is the percentage of land area that has permanent forage crops for cattle or horses, cultivated or wild. Some land may be classified both as permanent pasture or as forest (see Forest), especially areas of scrub or savanna.

FOREST

Natural/planted trees including cleared land that will be reforested in the near future as a percentage of the land area.

HUMAN DEVELOPMENT INDEX (HDI)

Produced by the UN Development Programme using indicators of life expectancy, knowledge and standards of living to give a value between 0 and 1 for each country. A high value shows a higher human development.

FOOD INTAKE

The amount of food (measured in calories) supplied, divided by the total population to show the amount each person consumes.

DOCTORS

The number of qualified doctors for every 100,000 people.

ADULTS LIVING WITH HIV/AIDS

The percentage of all adults (aged 15–49) who have the Human Immunodeficiency Virus or the Acquired Immunodeficiency Syndrome. The total number of adults and children with HIV/AIDS in 2007 was 32 million.

GENDER DEVELOPMENT INDEX (GDI)

Like the HDI (see note), the GDI uses the same UNDP indicators but gives a value between 0 and 1 to measure the social and economic differences between men and women. The higher the value, the more equality exists between men and women.

ILLITERACY

The percentage of all adult men and women (over 15 years) who cannot read or write simple sentences.

MOTOR VEHICLES AND INTERNET USAGE

These are good indicators of a country's development wealth. They are shown in total numbers per 1,000 people.

Each topic list is divided into continents and within a continent the items are listed in order of size. The bottom part of many of the lists is selective in order to give examples from as many different countries as possible. The figures are rounded as appropriate.

World, Continents, Oceans

	km²	miles²	%
The World	509,450,000	196,672,000	–
Land	149,450,000	57,688,000	29.3
Water	360,000,000	138,984,000	70.7
Asia	44,500,000	17,177,000	29.8
Africa	30,302,000	11,697,000	20.3
North America	24,241,000	9,357,000	16.2
South America	17,793,000	6,868,000	11.9
Antarctica	14,100,000	5,443,000	9.4
Europe	9,957,000	3,843,000	6.7
Australia & Oceania	8,557,000	3,303,000	5.7
Pacific Ocean	155,557,000	60,061,000	46.4
Atlantic Ocean	76,762,000	29,638,000	22.9
Indian Ocean	68,556,000	26,470,000	20.4
Southern Ocean	20,327,000	7,848,000	6.1
Arctic Ocean	14,056,000	5,427,000	4.2

Ocean Depths

Atlantic Ocean	m	ft
Puerto Rico (Milwaukee) Deep	8,605	28,232
Cayman Trench	7,680	25,197
Gulf of Mexico	5,203	17,070
Mediterranean Sea	5,121	16,801
Black Sea	2,211	7,254
North Sea	660	2,165

Indian Ocean	m	ft
Java Trench	7,450	24,442
Red Sea	2,635	8,454

Pacific Ocean	m	ft
Mariana Trench	11,022	36,161
Tonga Trench	10,882	35,702
Japan Trench	10,554	34,626
Kuril Trench	10,542	34,587

Arctic Ocean	m	ft
Molloy Deep	5,608	18,399

Mountains

Europe		m	ft
Elbrus	*Russia*	5,642	18,510
Dyka-Tau	*Russia*	5,205	17,076
Shkhara	*Russia/Georgia*	5,201	17,064
Koshtan-Tau	*Russia*	5,152	16,903
Kazbek	*Russia/Georgia*	5,047	16,558
Pushkin	*Russia/Georgia*	5,033	16,512
Katyn-Tau	*Russia/Georgia*	4,979	16,335
Shota Rustaveli	*Russia/Georgia*	4,860	15,945
Mont Blanc	*France/Italy*	4,808	15,774
Monte Rosa	*Italy/Switzerland*	4,634	15,203
Dom	*Switzerland*	4,545	14,911
Liskamm	*Switzerland*	4,527	14,852
Weisshorn	*Switzerland*	4,505	14,780
Taschorn	*Switzerland*	4,490	14,730
Matterhorn/Cervino	*Italy/Switzerland*	4,478	14,691
Grossglockner	*Austria*	3,797	12,457
Mulhacén	*Spain*	3,478	11,411
Zugspitze	*Germany*	2,962	9,718
Olympus	*Greece*	2,917	9,570
Galdhøpiggen	*Norway*	2,469	8,100
Kebnekaise	*Sweden*	2,117	6,946
Ben Nevis	*UK*	1,342	4,403

Asia		m	ft
Everest	*China/Nepal*	8,850	29,035
K2 (Godwin Austen)	*China/Kashmir*	8,611	28,251
Kanchenjunga	*India/Nepal*	8,598	28,208
Lhotse	*China/Nepal*	8,516	27,939
Makalu	*China/Nepal*	8,481	27,824
Cho Oyu	*China/Nepal*	8,201	26,906
Dhaulagiri	*Nepal*	8,167	26,795
Manaslu	*Nepal*	8,156	26,758
Nanga Parbat	*Kashmir*	8,126	26,660
Annapurna	*Nepal*	8,078	26,502
Gasherbrum	*China/Kashmir*	8,068	26,469
Xixabangma	*China*	8,012	26,286
Kangbachen	*India/Nepal*	7,902	25,925
Trivor	*Pakistan*	7,720	25,328
Pik Imeni Ismail Samani	*Tajikistan*	7,495	24,590
Demavend	*Iran*	5,604	18,386
Ararat	*Turkey*	5,165	16,945
Gunong Kinabalu	*Malaysia (Borneo)*	4,101	13,455
Fuji-San	*Japan*	3,776	12,388

Africa		m	ft
Kilimanjaro	*Tanzania*	5,895	19,340
Mt Kenya	*Kenya*	5,199	17,057
Ruwenzori	*Uganda/Congo (D.R.)*	5,109	16,762
Ras Dashen	*Ethiopia*	4,620	15,157
Meru	*Tanzania*	4,565	14,977
Karisimbi	*Rwanda/Congo (D.R.)*	4,507	14,787
Mt Elgon	*Kenya/Uganda*	4,321	14,176
Batu	*Ethiopia*	4,307	14,130
Toubkal	*Morocco*	4,165	13,665
Mt Cameroun	*Cameroon*	4,070	13,353

Oceania		m	ft
Puncak Jaya	*Indonesia*	5,029	16,499
Puncak Trikora	*Indonesia*	4,730	15,518
Puncak Mandala	*Indonesia*	4,702	15,427
Mt Wilhelm	*Papua New Guinea*	4,508	14,790
Mauna Kea	*USA (Hawaii)*	4,205	13,796
Mauna Loa	*USA (Hawaii)*	4,169	13,678
Aoraki Mt Cook	*New Zealand*	3,753	12,313
Mt Kosciuszko	*Australia*	2,228	7,310

North America		m	ft
Mt McKinley (Denali)	*USA (Alaska)*	6,194	20,321
Mt Logan	*Canada*	5,959	19,551
Pico de Orizaba	*Mexico*	5,610	18,405
Mt St Elias	*USA/Canada*	5,489	18,008
Popocatépetl	*Mexico*	5,452	17,887
Mt Foraker	*USA (Alaska)*	5,304	17,401
Iztaccihuatl	*Mexico*	5,286	17,342
Lucania	*Canada*	5,226	17,146
Mt Steele	*Canada*	5,073	16,644
Mt Bona	*USA (Alaska)*	5,005	16,420
Mt Whitney	*USA*	4,418	14,495
Tajumulco	*Guatemala*	4,220	13,845
Chirripó Grande	*Costa Rica*	3,837	12,589
Pico Duarte	*Dominican Rep.*	3,175	10,417

South America		m	ft
Aconcagua	*Argentina*	6,962	22,841
Bonete	*Argentina*	6,872	22,546
Ojos del Salado	*Argentina/Chile*	6,863	22,516
Pissis	*Argentina*	6,779	22,241
Mercedario	*Argentina/Chile*	6,770	22,211
Huascarán	*Peru*	6,768	22,204
Llullaillaco	*Argentina/Chile*	6,723	22,057
Nevado de Cachi	*Argentina*	6,720	22,047
Yerupaja	*Peru*	6,632	21,758
Sajama	*Bolivia*	6,520	21,391
Chimborazo	*Ecuador*	6,267	20,561
Pico Cristóbal Colón	*Colombia*	5,800	19,029
Pico Bolivar	*Venezuela*	5,007	16,427

Antarctica		m	ft
Vinson Massif		4,897	16,066
Mt Kirkpatrick		4,528	14,855

Rivers

Europe		km	miles
Volga	*Caspian Sea*	3,700	2,300
Danube	*Black Sea*	2,850	1,770
Ural	*Caspian Sea*	2,535	1,575
Dnieper	*Black Sea*	2,285	1,420
Kama	*Volga*	2,030	1,260
Don (Dnieper)	*Volga*	1,990	1,240
Petchora	*Arctic Ocean*	1,790	1,110
Oka	*Volga*	1,480	920
Dniester	*Black Sea*	1,400	870
Vyatka	*Kama*	1,370	850
Rhine	*North Sea*	1,320	820
North Dvina	*Arctic Ocean*	1,290	800
Elbe	*North Sea*	1,145	710

Asia		km	miles
Yangtse	*Pacific Ocean*	6,380	3,960
Yenisey–Angara	*Arctic Ocean*	5,550	3,445
Huang He	*Pacific Ocean*	5,464	3,395
Ob–Irtysh	*Arctic Ocean*	5,410	3,360
Mekong	*Pacific Ocean*	4,500	2,795
Amur	*Pacific Ocean*	4,442	2,760
Lena	*Arctic Ocean*	4,402	2,735
Irtysh	*Ob*	4,250	2,640
Yenisey	*Arctic Ocean*	4,090	2,540
Ob	*Arctic Ocean*	3,680	2,285
Indus	*Indian Ocean*	3,100	1,925
Brahmaputra	*Indian Ocean*	2,900	1,800
Syrdarya	*Aral Sea*	2,860	1,775
Salween	*Indian Ocean*	2,800	1,740
Euphrates	*Indian Ocean*	2,700	1,675
Amudarya	*Aral Sea*	2,540	1,575

Africa		km	miles
Nile	*Mediterranean*	6,670	4,140
Congo	*Atlantic Ocean*	4,670	2,900
Niger	*Atlantic Ocean*	4,180	2,595
Zambezi	*Indian Ocean*	3,540	2,200
Oubangi/Uele	*Congo (Dem. Rep.)*	2,250	1,400
Kasai	*Congo (Dem. Rep.)*	1,950	1,210
Shaballe	*Indian Ocean*	1,930	1,200
Orange	*Atlantic Ocean*	1,860	1,155
Cubango	*Okavango Delta*	1,800	1,120
Limpopo	*Indian Ocean*	1,770	1,100
Senegal	*Atlantic Ocean*	1,640	1,020

Australia		km	miles
Murray–Darling	*Southern Ocean*	3,750	2,330
Darling	*Murray*	3,070	1,905
Murray	*Southern Ocean*	2,575	1,600
Murrumbidgee	*Murray*	1,690	1,050

North America		km	miles
Mississippi–Missouri	*Gulf of Mexico*	5,971	3,710
Mackenzie	*Arctic Ocean*	4,240	2,630
Missouri	*Mississippi*	4,088	2,540
Mississippi	*Gulf of Mexico*	3,782	2,350
Yukon	*Pacific Ocean*	3,185	1,980
Rio Grande	*Gulf of Mexico*	3,030	1,880
Arkansas	*Mississippi*	2,340	1,450
Colorado	*Pacific Ocean*	2,330	1,445
Red	*Mississippi*	2,040	1,270
Columbia	*Pacific Ocean*	1,950	1,210
Saskatchewan	*Lake Winnipeg*	1,940	1,205

South America		km	miles
Amazon	*Atlantic Ocean*	6,450	4,010
Paraná–Plate	*Atlantic Ocean*	4,500	2,800
Purus	*Amazon*	3,350	2,080
Madeira	*Amazon*	3,200	1,990
São Francisco	*Atlantic Ocean*	2,900	1,800
Paraná	*Plate*	2,800	1,740
Tocantins	*Atlantic Ocean*	2,750	1,710
Orinoco	*Atlantic Ocean*	2,740	1,700
Paraguay	*Paraná*	2,550	1,580
Pilcomayo	*Paraná*	2,500	1,550
Araguaia	*Tocantins*	2,250	1,400

Lakes

Europe		km²	miles²
Lake Ladoga	*Russia*	17,700	6,800
Lake Onega	*Russia*	9,700	3,700
Saimaa system	*Finland*	8,000	3,100
Vänern	*Sweden*	5,500	2,100

Asia		km²	miles²
Caspian Sea	*Asia*	371,000	143,000
Lake Baikal	*Russia*	30,500	11,780
Tonlé Sap	*Cambodia*	20,000	7,700
Lake Balqash	*Kazakhstan*	18,500	7,100
Aral Sea	*Kazakhstan/Uzbekistan*	17,160	6,625

Africa		km²	miles²
Lake Victoria	*East Africa*	68,000	26,000
Lake Tanganyika	*Central Africa*	33,000	13,000
Lake Malawi/Nyasa	*East Africa*	29,600	11,430
Lake Chad	*Central Africa*	25,000	9,700
Lake Turkana	*Ethiopia/Kenya*	8,500	3,290
Lake Volta	*Ghana*	8,480	3,270

Australia		km²	miles²
Lake Eyre	*Australia*	8,900	3,400
Lake Torrens	*Australia*	5,800	2,200
Lake Gairdner	*Australia*	4,800	1,900

North America		km²	miles²
Lake Superior	*Canada/USA*	82,350	31,800
Lake Huron	*Canada/USA*	59,600	23,010
Lake Michigan	*USA*	58,000	22,400
Great Bear Lake	*Canada*	31,800	12,280
Great Slave Lake	*Canada*	28,500	11,000
Lake Erie	*Canada/USA*	25,700	9,900
Lake Winnipeg	*Canada*	24,400	9,400
Lake Ontario	*Canada/USA*	19,500	7,500
Lake Nicaragua	*Nicaragua*	8,200	3,200

South America		km²	miles²
Lake Titicaca	*Bolivia/Peru*	8,300	3,200
Lake Poopo	*Bolivia*	2,800	1,100

Islands

Europe		km²	miles²
Great Britain	*UK*	229,880	88,700
Iceland	*Atlantic Ocean*	103,000	39,800
Ireland	*Ireland/UK*	84,400	32,600
Novaya Zemlya (N.)	*Russia*	48,200	18,600
Sicily	*Italy*	25,500	9,800
Sardinia	*Italy*	23,950	9,250

Asia		km²	miles²
Borneo	*South-east Asia*	744,360	287,400
Sumatra	*Indonesia*	473,600	182,860
Honshu	*Japan*	230,500	88,980
Celebes	*Indonesia*	189,000	73,000
Java	*Indonesia*	126,700	48,900
Luzon	*Philippines*	104,700	40,400
Hokkaido	*Japan*	78,400	30,300

Africa		km²	miles²
Madagascar	*Indian Ocean*	587,040	226,660
Socotra	*Indian Ocean*	3,600	1,400
Réunion	*Indian Ocean*	2,500	965

Oceania		km²	miles²
New Guinea	*Indonesia/Papua NG*	821,030	317,000
New Zealand (S.)	*Pacific Ocean*	150,500	58,100
New Zealand (N.)	*Pacific Ocean*	114,700	44,300
Tasmania	*Australia*	67,800	26,200
New Caledonia	*Pacific Ocean*	16,650	6,470

North America		km²	miles²
Greenland	*Atlantic Ocean*	2,175,600	839,800
Baffin I.	*Canada*	508,000	196,100
Victoria I.	*Canada*	212,200	81,900
Ellesmere I.	*Canada*	212,000	81,800
Cuba	*Caribbean Sea*	110,860	42,800
Newfoundland	*Canada*	108,860	42,030
Banks I.	*Canada*	70,028	27,038
Hispaniola	*Dominican Rep./Haiti*	76,200	29,400

South America		km²	miles²
Tierra del Fuego	*Argentina/Chile*	47,000	18,100
Chiloé	*Chile*	8,480	3,275
Falkland I. (E.)	*Atlantic Ocean*	6,800	2,600

How to use the Index

The index contains the names of all the principal places and features shown on the maps. Each name is followed by an additional entry in italics giving the country or region within which it is located. The alphabetical order of names composed of two or more words is governed primarily by the first word and then by the second. This is an example of the rule:

Albert, L. *Africa* 1°30N 31°0E **96** D6
Albert Lea *U.S.A.* 43°39N 93°22W **111** B8
Albert Nile → *Uganda* 3°36N 32°2E **96** D6
Alberta *Canada* 54°40N 115°0W **108** D8
Albertville *France* 45°40N 6°22E **66** D7

Physical features composed of a proper name (Erie) and a description (Lake) are positioned alphabetically by the proper name. The description is positioned after the proper name and is usually abbreviated:

Erie, L. *N. Amer.* 42°15N 81°0W **112** D7

Where a description forms part of a settlement or administrative name, however, it is always written in full and put in its true alphabetical position:

Mount Isa *Australia* 20°42S 139°26E **98** E6

Names beginning with M' and Mc are indexed as if they were spelled Mac. Names beginning St. are alphabetized under Saint, but Santa and San are spelled in full and are alphabetized accordingly. If the same place name occurs two or more times in the index and all are in the same country, each is followed by the name of the administrative subdivision in which it is located.

The geographical co-ordinates that follow each name in the index give the latitude and longitude of each place. The first co-ordinate indicates latitude – the distance north or south of the Equator. The second co-ordinate indicates longitude – the distance east or west of the Greenwich Meridian. Both latitude and longitude are measured in degrees and minutes (there are 60 minutes in a degree).

The latitude is followed by N(orth) or S(outh) and the longitude by E(ast) or W(est).

The number in bold type that follows the geographical co-ordinates refers to the number of the map page where that feature or place will be found. This is usually the largest scale at which the place or feature appears.

The letter and figure that are immediately after the page number give the grid square on the map page, within which the feature is situated. The letter represents the latitude and the figure the longitude. A lower-case letter immediately after the page number refers to an inset map on that page.

In some cases the feature itself may fall within the specified square, while the name is outside. This is usually the case only with features that are larger than a grid square.

Rivers are indexed to their mouths or confluences, and carry the symbol → after their names. The following symbols are also used in the index: ■ country, ⧄ overseas territory or dependency, □ first-order administrative area, △ national park, ✈ (LHR) principal airport (and location identifier).

Abbreviations used in the Index

Afghan. – Afghanistan
Ala. – Alabama
Alta. – Alberta
Amer. – America(n)
Arch. – Archipelago
Ariz. – Arizona
Ark. – Arkansas
Atl. Oc. – Atlantic Ocean
B. – Baie, Bahía, Bay, Bucht, Bugt
B.C. – British Columbia
Bangla. – Bangladesh
C. – Cabo, Cap, Cape, Coast
C.A.R. – Central African Republic
Calif. – California
Cent. – Central
Chan. – Channel
Colo. – Colorado
Conn. – Connecticut
Cord. – Cordillera
Cr. – Creek
D.C. – District of Columbia
Del. – Delaware
Dom. Rep. – Dominican Republic
E. – East
El Salv. – El Salvador
Eq. Guin. – Equatorial Guinea
Fla. – Florida
Falk. Is. – Falkland Is.
G. – Golfe, Golfo, Gulf
Ga. – Georgia
Hd. – Head
Hts. – Heights
I.(s). – Île, Ilha, Insel, Isla, Island, Isle(s)
Ill. – Illinois
Ind. – Indiana
Ind. Oc. – Indian Ocean
Ivory C. – Ivory Coast
Kans. – Kansas
Ky. – Kentucky
L. – Lac, Lacul, Lago, Lagoa, Lake, Limni, Loch, Lough
La. – Louisiana
Lux. – Luxembourg
Madag. – Madagascar
Man. – Manitoba
Mass. – Massachusetts
Md. – Maryland
Me. – Maine
Mich. – Michigan
Minn. – Minnesota
Miss. – Mississippi
Mo. – Missouri
Mont. – Montana
Mozam. – Mozambique
Mt.(s) – Mont, Monte, Monti, Montaña, Mountain
N. – Nord, Norte, North, Northern,
N.B. – New Brunswick
N.C. – North Carolina
N. Cal. – New Caledonia
N. Dak. – North Dakota
N.H. – New Hampshire
N.J. – New Jersey
N. Mex. – New Mexico
N.S. – Nova Scotia
N.S.W. – New South Wales
N.W.T. – North West Territory
N.Y. – New York
N.Z. – New Zealand
Nat. Park – National Park
Nebr. – Nebraska
Neths. – Netherlands
Nev. – Nevada
Nfld. – Newfoundland and Labrador
Nic. – Nicaragua
Okla. – Oklahoma
Ont. – Ontario
Oreg. – Oregon
P.E.I. – Prince Edward Island
Pa. – Pennsylvania
Pac. Oc. – Pacific Ocean
Papua N.G. – Papua New Guinea
Pen. – Peninsula, Péninsule
Phil. – Philippines
Pk. – Peak
Plat. – Plateau
Prov. – Province, Provincial
Pt. – Point
Pta. – Ponta, Punta
Pte. – Pointe
Qué. – Québec
Queens. – Queensland
R. – Rio, River
R.I. – Rhode Island
Ra.(s) – Range(s)
Reg. – Region
Rep. – Republic
Res. – Reserve, Reservoir
S. – San, South
Si. Arabia – Saudi Arabia
S.C. – South Carolina
S. Dak. – South Dakota
Sa. – Serra, Sierra
Sask. – Saskatchewan
Scot. – Scotland
Sd. – Sound
Sib. – Siberia
St. – Saint, Sankt, Sint
Str. – Strait, Stretto
Switz. – Switzerland
Tas. – Tasmania
Tenn. – Tennessee
Tex. – Texas
Trin. & Tob.. – Trinidad & Tobago
U.A.E. – United Arab Emirates
U.K. – United Kingdom
U.S.A. – United States of America
Va. – Virginia
Vic. – Victoria
Vol. – Volcano
Vt. – Vermont
W. – West
W. Va. – West Virginia
Wash. – Washington
Wis. – Wisconsin

A

Aachen *Germany* 50°45N 6°6E **64** C4
Aalborg *Denmark* 57°2N 9°54E **63** F5
Aarau *Switz.* 47°23N 8°4E **64** E5
Aare → *Switz.* 47°33N 8°14E **64** E5
Aba *Nigeria* 5°10N 7°19E **94** G7
Abaco I. *Bahamas* 26°25N 77°10W **115** B9
Ābādān *Iran* 30°22N 48°20E **86** D7
Abaetetuba *Brazil* 1°40S 48°50W **120** C5
Abakan *Russia* 53°40N 91°10E **77** D10
Abancay *Peru* 13°35S 72°55W **120** D2
Abariringa *Kiribati* 2°50S 171°40W **99** A16
Abaya, L. *Ethiopia* 6°30N 37°50E **89** F2
Abbé, L. *Ethiopia* 11°8N 41°47E **89** E3
Abbeville *France* 50°6N 1°49E **66** A4
Abbey Town *U.K.* 54°51N 3°17W **22** C2
Abbot Ice Shelf *Antarctica* 73°0S 92°0W **55** D16
Abbots Bromley *U.K.* 52°50N 1°52W **23** G5
Abbotsbury *U.K.* 50°40N 2°37W **24** E3
Abéché *Chad* 13°50N 20°35E **95** F10
Abeokuta *Nigeria* 7°3N 3°19E **94** G6
Aberaeron *U.K.* 52°15N 4°15W **26** C5
Aberchirder *U.K.* 57°34N 2°37W **19** G12
Aberdare *U.K.* 51°43N 3°27W **26** D7
Aberdeen *U.K.* 57°9N 2°5W **19** H13
Aberdeen *S. Dak., U.S.A.* 45°28N 98°29W **110** A7
Aberdeen *Wash., U.S.A.* 46°59N 123°50W **110** A2
Aberdeenshire □ *U.K.* 57°17N 2°36W **19** H12
Aberdyfi *U.K.* 52°33N 4°3W **26** B5
Aberfeldy *U.K.* 56°37N 3°51W **21** A8
Aberfoyle *U.K.* 56°11N 4°23W **20** B7
Abergavenny *U.K.* 51°49N 3°1W **26** D7
Abergele *U.K.* 53°17N 3°35W **26** A6
Aberporth *U.K.* 52°8N 4°33W **26** C4
Abersoch *U.K.* 52°49N 4°30W **26** B5
Abersychan *U.K.* 51°44N 3°3W **26** D7
Abert, L. *U.S.A.* 42°38N 120°14W **110** B2
Abertillery *U.K.* 51°44N 3°8W **26** D7
Aberystwyth *U.K.* 52°25N 4°5W **26** C5
Abhā *Si. Arabia* 18°0N 42°34E **89** D3
Abidjan *Ivory C.* 5°26N 3°58W **94** G5
Abilene *U.S.A.* 32°28N 99°43W **110** D7
Abingdon *U.K.* 51°40N 1°17W **24** C6
Abitibi, L. *Canada* 48°40N 79°40W **109** E12
Abkhazia □ *Georgia* 43°12N 41°5E **71** F7
Abomey *Benin* 7°10N 2°5E **94** G6
Aboyne *U.K.* 57°4N 2°47W **19** H12
Abrolhos, Banco dos *Brazil* 18°0S 38°0W **122** C3
Absaroka Range *U.S.A.* 44°45N 109°50W **110** B5
Abu Dhabi *U.A.E.* 24°28N 54°22E **87** E8
Abu Hamed *Sudan* 19°32N 33°13E **95** E12
Abuja *Nigeria* 9°5N 7°32E **94** G7
Abunã *Brazil* 9°40S 65°20W **120** C3
Abunã → *Brazil* 9°41S 65°20W **120** C3
Acaponeta *Mexico* 22°30N 105°22W **114** C3
Acapulco *Mexico* 16°51N 99°55W **114** D5
Acaraí, Serra *Brazil* 1°50N 57°50W **120** B4
Acarigua *Venezuela* 9°33N 69°12W **120** B3
Accomac *U.S.A.* 37°43N 75°40W **113** G10
Accra *Ghana* 5°35N 0°6W **94** G5
Accrington *U.K.* 53°45N 2°22W **23** E4
Aceh □ *Indonesia* 4°15N 97°30E **82** D1
Acharnes *Greece* 38°5N 23°44E **69** E10
Acheloos → *Greece* 38°19N 21°7E **69** E9
Achill Hd. *Ireland* 53°58N 10°15W **28** D1
Achill I. *Ireland* 53°58N 10°1W **28** D1
Acklins I. *Bahamas* 22°30N 74°0W **115** C10
Acle *U.K.* 52°39N 1°33E **25** A12
Aconcagua, Cerro *Argentina* 32°39S 70°0W **121** F3
Acre □ *Brazil* 9°1S 71°0W **120** C2
Acre → *Brazil* 8°45S 67°22W **120** C3
Acton Burnell *U.K.* 52°37N 2°41W **23** G3
Ad Dammām *Si. Arabia* 26°20N 50°5E **86** E7
Ad Dīwānīyah *Iraq* 32°0N 45°0E **86** D6
Adair, C. *Canada* 71°30N 71°34W **109** B12
Adak I. *U.S.A.* 51°45N 176°45W **108** D2
Adamaoua, Massif de l' *Cameroon* 7°20N 12°20E **95** G8
Adam's Bridge *Sri Lanka* 9°15N 79°40E **84** Q11
Adana *Turkey* 37°0N 35°16E **71** G6
Adare, C. *Antarctica* 71°0S 171°0E **55** D11
Addis Ababa *Ethiopia* 9°2N 38°42E **89** F2
Adelaide *Australia* 34°52S 138°30E **98** G6
Adelaide I. *Antarctica* 67°15S 68°30W **55** C17
Adelaide Pen. *Canada* 68°15N 97°30W **108** C10
Adélie, Terre *Antarctica* 68°0S 140°0E **55** C10
Aden *Yemen* 12°45N 45°0E **89** E4
Aden, G. of *Ind. Oc.* 12°30N 47°30E **89** E4
Adige → *Italy* 45°9N 12°20E **68** B5
Adigrat *Ethiopia* 14°20N 39°26E **89** E2
Adirondack Mts. *U.S.A.* 44°0N 74°0W **113** D10
Adjuntas *Puerto Rico* 18°10N 66°43W **115** d
Admiralty Is. *Papua N. G.* 2°0S 147°0E **102** H6
Adour → *France* 43°32N 1°32W **66** E3
Adrar *Mauritania* 20°30N 7°30W **94** D3
Adrar des Iforas *Africa* 19°40N 1°40E **94** C5
Adrian *U.S.A.* 41°54N 84°2W **112** E5
Adriatic Sea *Medit. S.* 43°0N 16°0E **68** C6
Adwa *Ethiopia* 14°15N 38°52E **89** E2
Adwick le Street *U.K.* 53°34N 1°10W **23** E6
Adygea □ *Russia* 45°0N 40°0E **71** F7
Ægean Sea *Medit. S.* 38°30N 25°0E **69** E11
Afghanistan ■ *Asia* 33°0N 65°0E **87** C11
Africa 10°0N 20°0E **90** E6
Afyon *Turkey* 38°45N 30°33E **71** G5
Agadez *Niger* 16°58N 7°59E **94** E7
Agadir *Morocco* 30°28N 9°55W **94** B4
Agartala *India* 23°50N 91°23E **85** H17
Agen *France* 44°12N 0°38E **66** D4
Agra *India* 27°17N 77°58E **84** F10
Ağri *Turkey* 39°44N 43°3E **71** G7
Agrigento *Italy* 37°19N 13°34E **68** F5
Agua Prieta *Mexico* 31°18N 109°34W **114** A3
Aguadilla *Puerto Rico* 18°26N 67°10W **115** d
Aguascalientes *Mexico* 21°53N 102°18W **114** C4
Aguila, Punta *Puerto Rico* 17°57N 67°13W **115** d
Aguja, C. de la *Colombia* 11°18N 74°12W **117** B3
Agujereada, Pta. *Puerto Rico* 18°30N 67°8W **115** d
Agulhas, C. *S. Africa* 34°52S 20°0E **97** L4
Ahaggar *Algeria* 23°0N 6°30E **94** D76
Ahmadabad *India* 23°0N 72°40E **84** H8
Ahmadnagar *India* 19°7N 74°46E **84** K9
Ahmadpur East *Pakistan* 29°12N 71°10E **84** E7
Ahvāz *Iran* 31°20N 48°40E **86** D7
Ahvenanmaa *Finland* 60°15N 20°0E **63** E8
Aḩwar *Yemen* 13°30N 46°40E **89** E4
Ailsa Craig *U.K.* 55°15N 5°6W **20** D5
Aimorés *Brazil* 19°30S 41°4W **122** C2
Aïn Témouchent *Algeria* 35°16N 1°8W **94** A5
Ainsdale *U.K.* 53°37N 3°2W **23** E2
Aïr *Niger* 18°30N 8°0E **94** E7
Air Force I. *Canada* 67°58N 74°5W **109** C12
Aird, The *U.K.* 57°25N 4°33W **19** H8
Airdrie *Canada* 51°18N 114°2W **108** D8
Airdrie *U.K.* 55°52N 3°57W **21** C8
Aire → *U.K.* 53°43N 0°55W **23** E7
Aisgill *U.K.* 54°23N 2°21W **22** D4
Aisne → *France* 49°26N 2°50E **66** B5
Aix-en-Provence *France* 43°32N 5°27E **66** E6
Aix-les-Bains *France* 45°41N 5°53E **66** D6
Aizawl *India* 23°40N 92°44E **85** H18
Aizuwakamatsu *Japan* 37°30N 139°56E **81** E6
Ajaccio *France* 41°55N 8°40E **66** F8
Ajanta Ra. *India* 20°28N 75°50E **84** J9
Ajaria □ *Georgia* 41°30N 42°0E **71** F7
Ajdābiyā *Libya* 30°54N 20°4E **95** B10
'Ajmān *U.A.E.* 25°25N 55°30E **87** E8
Ajmer *India* 26°28N 74°37E **84** F9
Aketi *Dem. Rep. of the Congo* 2°38N 23°47E **96** D4
Akhisar *Turkey* 38°56N 27°48E **71** G4
Akimiski I. *Canada* 52°50N 81°30W **109** D11
Akita *Japan* 39°45N 140°7E **81** D7
'Akko *Israel* 32°55N 35°4E **86** C3
Aklavik *Canada* 68°12N 135°0W **108** C6
Akola *India* 20°42N 77°2E **84** J10
Akpatok I. *Canada* 60°25N 68°8W **109** C13
Akranes *Iceland* 64°19N 22°5W **63** B1
Akron *U.S.A.* 41°5N 81°31W **112** E7
Aksai Chin *China* 35°15N 79°55E **84** B11
Aksaray *Turkey* 38°25N 34°2E **71** G5
Akşehir Gölü *Turkey* 38°30N 31°25E **71** G5
Aksu *China* 41°5N 80°10E **78** C5
Aksum *Ethiopia* 14°5N 38°40E **89** E2
Akure *Nigeria* 7°15N 5°5E **94** G7
Akureyri *Iceland* 65°40N 18°6W **63** A2
Al 'Amārah *Iraq* 31°55N 47°15E **86** D6
Al 'Aqabah *Jordan* 29°31N 35°0E **86** D3
Al 'Aramah *Si. Arabia* 25°30N 46°0E **86** E6
Al 'Ayn *U.A.E.* 24°15N 55°45E **87** E8
Al Bayḑā *Libya* 32°50N 21°44E **95** B10
Al Fallūjah *Iraq* 33°20N 43°55E **86** C5
Al Fāw *Iraq* 30°0N 48°30E **86** D7
Al Ḩadīthah *Iraq* 34°0N 41°13E **86** C5
Al Ḩillah *Iraq* 32°30N 44°25E **86** C6
Al Hoceïma *Morocco* 35°8N 3°58W **94** A5
Al Ḩudaydah *Yemen* 14°50N 43°0E **89** E3
Al Hufūf *Si. Arabia* 25°25N 49°45E **86** E7
Al Jahrah *Kuwait* 29°25N 47°40E **86** D6
Al Jawf *Libya* 24°10N 23°24E **95** D10
Al Jawf *Si. Arabia* 29°55N 39°40E **86** D4
Al Jubayl *Si. Arabia* 27°0N 49°50E **86** E7
Al Khalīl *West Bank* 31°32N 35°6E **86** D3
Al Khums *Libya* 32°40N 14°17E **95** B8
Al Kufrah *Libya* 24°17N 23°15E **95** D10
Al Kūt *Iraq* 32°30N 46°0E **86** C6
Al Manāmah *Bahrain* 26°10N 50°30E **87** E7
Al Mubarraz *Si. Arabia* 25°30N 49°40E **86** E7
Al Mukallā *Yemen* 14°33N 49°2E **89** E4
Al Musayyib *Iraq* 32°49N 44°20E **86** C6
Al Qāmishlī *Syria* 37°2N 41°14E **86** B5
Al Qaţīf *Si. Arabia* 26°35N 50°0E **86** E7
Al Qunfudhah *Si. Arabia* 19°3N 41°4E **89** D3
Alabama □ *U.S.A.* 33°0N 87°0W **111** D9
Alabama → *U.S.A.* 31°8N 87°57W **111** D9
Alagoas □ *Brazil* 9°0S 36°0W **122** A3
Alagoinhas *Brazil* 12°7S 38°20W **122** B3
Alai Range *Asia* 39°45N 72°0E **87** B13
Alamogordo *U.S.A.* 32°54N 105°57W **110** D5
Alamosa *U.S.A.* 37°28N 105°52W **110** C5
Åland = Ahvenanmaa *Finland* 60°15N 20°0E **63** E8
Alanya *Turkey* 36°38N 32°0E **71** G5
Alaşehir *Turkey* 38°23N 28°30E **71** G4
Alaska □ *U.S.A.* 64°0N 154°0W **108** C5
Alaska, G. of *Pac. Oc.* 58°0N 145°0W **108** D5
Alaska Peninsula *U.S.A.* 56°0N 159°0W **108** D4
Alaska Range *U.S.A.* 62°50N 151°0W **108** C4
Alba-Iulia *Romania* 46°8N 23°39E **65** E12
Albacete *Spain* 39°0N 1°50W **67** C5
Albanel, L. *Canada* 50°55N 73°12W **109** D12
Albania ■ *Europe* 41°0N 20°0E **69** D9
Albany *Australia* 35°1S 117°58E **98** H2
Albany *Ga., U.S.A.* 31°35N 84°10W **111** D10
Albany *N.Y., U.S.A.* 42°39N 73°45W **113** D11
Albany *Oreg., U.S.A.* 44°38N 123°6W **110** B2
Albany → *Canada* 52°17N 81°31W **109** D11
Albemarle Sd. *U.S.A.* 36°5N 76°0W **111** C11
Albert, L. *Africa* 1°30N 31°0E **96** D6
Albert Lea *U.S.A.* 43°39N 93°22W **111** B8
Albert Nile → *Uganda* 3°36N 32°2E **96** D6
Alberta □ *Canada* 54°40N 115°0W **108** D8
Albertville *France* 45°40N 6°22E **66** D7
Albi *France* 43°56N 2°9E **66** E5
Albion *U.S.A.* 42°15N 84°45W **112** D5
Albrighton *U.K.* 52°38N 2°16W **23** G4
Albuquerque *U.S.A.* 35°5N 106°39W **110** C5
Albury *Australia* 36°3S 146°56E **98** H8
Alcalá de Henares *Spain* 40°28N 3°22W **67** B4
Alcester *U.K.* 52°14N 1°52W **24** B5
Alchevsk *Ukraine* 48°30N 38°45E **71** E6
Alcoy *Spain* 38°43N 0°30W **67** C5
Aldabra Is. *Seychelles* 9°22S 46°28E **91** G8
Aldan *Russia* 58°40N 125°30E **77** D13
Aldan → *Russia* 63°28N 129°35E **77** C13
Aldborough *U.K.* 54°5N 1°22W **22** D6
Aldbourne *U.K.* 51°29N 1°37W **24** D5
Aldbrough *U.K.* 53°49N 0°6W **23** E8
Aldeburgh *U.K.* 52°10N 1°37E **25** B12
Alderbury *U.K.* 51°3N 1°44W **24** D5

Alderley Edge   Babuyan Chan.

Alderley Edge *U.K.* 53°18N 2°13W 23 F4
Alderney *U.K.* 49°42N 2°11W 27 H9
Aldershot *U.K.* 51°15N 0°44W 25 D7
Aledo *U.S.A.* 41°12N 90°45W 112 E2
Alegrete *Brazil* 29°40S 56°0W 121 E4
Aleksandrovsk-Sakhalinskiy
Russia 50°50N 142°20E 79 A17
Além Paraíba *Brazil* 21°52S 42°41W 122 D2
Alençon *France* 48°27N 0°4E 66 B4
Alenquer *Brazil* 1°56S 54°46W 120 C4
'Alenuihāhā Channel
U.S.A. 20°30N 156°0W 110 H17
Aleppo *Syria* 36°10N 37°15E 86 B4
Alert *Canada* 83°2N 60°0W 109 A13
Alès *France* 44°9N 4°5E 66 D6
Alessándria *Italy* 44°54N 8°37E 68 B3
Ålesund *Norway* 62°28N 6°12E 63 E5
Aleutian Is. *Pac. Oc.* 52°0N 175°0W 102 D10
Aleutian Trench *Pac. Oc.* 48°0N 180°0E 102 C10
Alexander Arch. *U.S.A.* 56°0N 136°0W 108 D6
Alexander I. *Antarctica* 69°0S 70°0W 55 C17
Alexandria *Egypt* 31°13N 29°58E 95 B11
Alexandria *U.K.* 55°59N 4°35W 20 C6
Alexandria *La., U.S.A.* 31°18N 92°27W 111 D8
Alexandria *Va., U.S.A.* 38°49N 77°5W 112 F9
Alford *Aberds., U.K.* 57°14N 2°41W 19 H12
Alford *Lincs., U.K.* 53°15N 0°10E 23 F9
Alfreton *U.K.* 53°6N 1°24W 23 F6
Alfriston *U.K.* 50°48N 0°10E 25 E9
Algarve *Portugal* 36°58N 8°20W 67 D1
Algeciras *Spain* 36°9N 5°28W 67 D3
Algeria ■ *Africa* 28°30N 2°0E 94 C6
Algiers *Algeria* 36°42N 3°8E 94 A6
Algoa B. *S. Africa* 33°50S 25°45E 90 K6
Alicante *Spain* 38°23N 0°30W 67 C5
Alice Springs *Australia* 23°40S 133°50E 98 E5
Aligarh *India* 27°55N 78°10E 84 F11
Alipur Duar *India* 26°30N 89°35E 85 F16
Aliquippa *U.S.A.* 40°37N 80°15W 112 E7
Aliwal North *S. Africa* 30°45S 26°45E 97 L5
Alkmaar *Neths.* 52°37N 4°45E 64 B3
Allahabad *India* 25°25N 81°58E 85 G12
Allegan *U.S.A.* 42°32N 85°51W 112 D5
Allegheny → *U.S.A.* 40°27N 80°1W 112 E8
Allegheny Mts. *U.S.A.* 38°15N 80°10W 111 C11
Allègre, Pte. *Guadeloupe* 16°22N 61°46W 114 b
Allen → *U.K.* 54°58N 2°18W 22 C4
Allen, Bog of *Ireland* 53°15N 7°0W 31 B9
Allen, L. *Ireland* 54°8N 8°4W 28 C5
Allendale Town *U.K.* 54°53N 2°14W 22 C4
Allenheads *U.K.* 54°49N 2°12W 22 C4
Allentown *U.S.A.* 40°37N 75°29W 113 E10
Alleppey *India* 9°30N 76°28E 84 Q10
Alleynes B. *Barbados* 13°13N 59°39W 115 g
Alliance *U.S.A.* 42°6N 102°52W 110 B6
Allier → *France* 46°57N 3°4E 66 C5
Alligator Pond *Jamaica* 17°52N 77°34W 114 a
Alloa *U.K.* 56°7N 3°47W 21 B8
Allonby *U.K.* 54°46N 3°26W 22 C2
Alma *U.S.A.* 43°23N 84°39W 112 D5
Alma Ata *Kazakhstan* 43°15N 76°57E 78 C4
Almada *Portugal* 38°41N 9°8W 67 C1
Almelo *Neths.* 52°22N 6°42E 64 B4
Almería *Spain* 36°52N 2°27W 67 D4
Almondsbury *U.K.* 51°32N 2°34W 24 C3
Aln → *U.K.* 55°24N 1°37W 22 B5
Alness *U.K.* 57°41N 4°16W 19 G9
Alnmouth *U.K.* 55°24N 1°37W 22 B5
Alnwick *U.K.* 55°24N 1°42W 22 B5
Alor *Indonesia* 8°15S 124°30E 83 F6
Alor Setar *Malaysia* 6°7N 100°22E 82 C2
Alpena *U.S.A.* 45°4N 83°27W 112 C6
Alpes Maritimes *Europe* 44°10N 7°10E 66 D7
Alphington *U.K.* 50°42N 3°31W 27 F6
Alpine *U.S.A.* 30°22N 103°40W 110 D6
Alps *Europe* 46°30N 9°30E 64 E5
Alrewas *U.K.* 52°44N 1°44W 23 G5
Alsace □ *France* 48°15N 7°25E 66 B7
Alsager *U.K.* 53°6N 2°18W 23 F4
Alston *U.K.* 54°49N 2°25W 22 C4
Altai *Mongolia* 46°40N 92°45E 78 B7
Altamira *Brazil* 3°12S 52°10W 120 C4
Altamura *Italy* 40°49N 16°33E 68 D7
Altanbulag *Mongolia* 50°16N 106°30E 78 A10
Altarnun *U.K.* 50°35N 4°32W 27 F4
Altay *China* 47°48N 88°10E 78 B6
Altiplano *Bolivia* 17°0S 68°0W 120 D3
Alton *U.K.* 51°9N 0°59W 25 D7
Alton *U.S.A.* 38°53N 90°11W 112 F2
Alton Towers *U.K.* 52°59N 1°52W 23 G5
Altoona *U.S.A.* 40°31N 78°24W 112 E8
Altrincham *U.K.* 53°24N 2°21W 23 F4
Altun Shan *China* 38°30N 88°0E 78 D6
Altus *U.S.A.* 34°38N 99°20W 110 D7
Alucra *Turkey* 40°22N 38°47E 71 F6
Alvechurch *U.K.* 52°21N 1°57W 24 B5
Alwar *India* 27°38N 76°34E 84 F10
Alwinton *U.K.* 55°21N 2°7W 22 B4
Alxa Zuoqi *China* 38°50N 105°40E 78 D10
Alyth *U.K.* 56°38N 3°13W 19 J11
Amadjuak L. *Canada* 65°0N 71°8W 109 C12
Amagasaki *Japan* 34°42N 135°23E 81 F4
Amapá *Brazil* 2°5N 50°50W 120 B4
Amapá □ *Brazil* 1°40N 52°0W 120 B4
Amarillo *U.S.A.* 35°13N 101°50W 110 C6
Amasya *Turkey* 40°40N 35°50E 71 F6
Amazon = Amazonas →
S. Amer. 0°5S 50°0W 120 C4
Amazonas □ *Brazil* 5°0S 65°0W 120 C3
Amazonas → *S. Amer.* 0°5S 50°0W 120 C4
Ambala *India* 30°23N 76°56E 84 D10
Ambato *Ecuador* 1°5S 78°42W 120 C2
Ambergris Cay *Belize* 18°0N 87°55W 114 D7
Ambikapur *India* 23°15N 83°15E 85 H13
Ambilobé *Madag.* 13°10S 49°3E 97 G9
Amble *U.K.* 55°20N 1°36W 22 B5
Ambleside *U.K.* 54°26N 2°58W 22 C3
Ambon *Indonesia* 3°43S 128°12E 83 E7
Amchitka I. *U.S.A.* 51°32N 179°0E 108 D1
Amderma *Russia* 69°45N 61°30E 76 C7
Amdo *China* 32°20N 91°40E 78 E7

Ameca *Mexico* 20°33N 104°2W 114 C4
Ameland *Neths.* 53°27N 5°45E 64 B3
American Highland *Antarctica* 73°0S 75°0E 55 D6
Americana *Brazil* 22°45S 47°20W 122 D1
Amersham *U.K.* 51°40N 0°36W 25 C7
Ames *U.S.A.* 42°2N 93°37W 111 B8
Amesbury *U.K.* 51°10N 1°46W 24 D5
Amherst *Canada* 45°48N 64°8W 109 E13
Amiens *France* 49°54N 2°16E 66 B5
Amirante Is. *Seychelles* 6°0S 53°0E 72 J7
Amlia I. *U.S.A.* 52°4N 173°30W 108 D2
Amlwch *U.K.* 53°24N 4°20W 26 A5
'Ammān *Jordan* 31°57N 35°52E 86 D3
Ammanford *U.K.* 51°48N 3°59W 26 D6
Amos *Canada* 48°35N 78°5W 109 E12
Ampleforth *U.K.* 54°13N 1°6W 22 D6
Ampthill *U.K.* 52°2N 0°30W 25 B8
Amravati *India* 20°55N 77°45E 84 J10
Amreli *India* 21°35N 71°17E 84 J7
Amritsar *India* 31°35N 74°57E 84 D9
Amroha *India* 28°53N 78°30E 84 E11
Amsterdam *Neths.* 52°23N 4°54E 64 B3
Amsterdam *U.S.A.* 42°56N 74°11W 113 D10
Amsterdam I. *Ind. Oc.* 38°30S 77°30E 53 F13
Amudarya → *Uzbekistan* 43°58N 59°34E 87 A9
Amund Ringnes I. *Canada* 78°20N 96°25W 109 B10
Amundsen Gulf *Canada* 71°0N 124°0W 108 B7
Amundsen Sea *Antarctica* 72°0S 115°0W 55 D15
Amur → *Russia* 52°56N 141°10E 77 D15
An Najaf *Iraq* 32°3N 44°15E 86 C6
An Uaimh *Ireland* 53°39N 6°41W 29 D8
Anaconda *U.S.A.* 46°8N 112°57W 110 A4
Anadyr *Russia* 64°35N 177°20E 77 C18
Anadyr, G. of *Russia* 64°0N 180°0E 77 C19
Anaheim *U.S.A.* 33°50N 117°55W 110 D3
Anambas, Kepulauan
Indonesia 3°20N 106°30E 82 D3
Anamur *Turkey* 36°8N 32°58E 71 G5
Anantapur *India* 14°39N 77°42E 84 M10
Anápolis *Brazil* 16°15S 48°50W 122 C1
Anār *Iran* 30°55N 55°13E 87 D8
Anatolia *Turkey* 39°0N 30°0E 71 G5
Añatuya *Argentina* 28°20S 62°50W 121 E3
Ancaster *U.K.* 52°59N 0°32W 23 G7
Ancholme → *U.K.* 53°40N 0°32W 23 E7
Anchorage *U.S.A.* 61°13N 149°54W 108 C5
Anci *China* 39°20N 116°40E 79 D12
Ancohuma *Bolivia* 16°0S 68°50W 120 D3
Ancona *Italy* 43°38N 13°30E 68 C5
Ancrum *U.K.* 55°31N 2°35W 21 C10
Ancud *Chile* 42°0S 73°50W 121 G2
Ancud, G. de *Chile* 42°0S 73°0W 121 G2
Anda *China* 46°24N 125°19E 79 B14
Andalgalá *Argentina* 27°40S 66°30W 121 E3
Andalucía □ *Spain* 37°35N 5°0W 67 D3
Andalusia *U.S.A.* 31°18N 86°29W 111 D9
Andaman Is. *Ind. Oc.* 12°30N 92°45E 53 D14
Anderson *Alaska, U.S.A.* 64°25N 149°15W 108 C5
Anderson *Ind., U.S.A.* 40°10N 85°41W 112 E5
Anderson *S.C., U.S.A.* 34°31N 82°39W 111 D10
Andes, Cord. de los *S. Amer.* 20°0S 68°0W 121 E3
Andhra Pradesh □ *India* 18°0N 79°0E 84 L11
Andijon *Uzbekistan* 41°10N 72°15E 87 A13
Andorra ■ *Europe* 42°30N 1°30E 66 E4
Andorra La Vella *Andorra* 42°31N 1°32E 66 E4
Andover *U.K.* 51°12N 1°29W 24 D6
Andradina *Brazil* 20°54S 51°23W 120 E4
Andreanof Is. *U.S.A.* 51°30N 176°0W 108 D2
Ándria *Italy* 41°13N 16°17E 68 D7
Andros *Greece* 37°50N 24°57E 69 F11
Andros I. *Bahamas* 24°30N 78°0W 115 C9
Aneityum *Vanuatu* 20°12S 169°45E 99 E12
Angara → *Russia* 58°5N 94°20E 77 D10
Angarsk *Russia* 52°30N 104°0E 78 A9
Änge *Sweden* 62°31N 15°35E 63 E7
Angel Falls *Venezuela* 5°57N 62°30W 120 B3
Angeles *Phil.* 15°9N 120°33E 83 A6
Ångermanälven → *Sweden* 64°0N 17°20E 63 E7
Angers *France* 47°30N 0°35W 66 C3
Anglesey □ *U.K.* 53°16N 4°18W 26 A5
Angoche *Mozam.* 16°8S 39°55E 97 H7
Angola ■ *Africa* 12°0S 18°0E 97 G3
Angoulême *France* 45°39N 0°10E 66 D4
Angoumois *France* 45°50N 0°25E 66 D3
Angra dos Reis *Brazil* 23°0S 44°10W 122 D2
Angren *Uzbekistan* 41°1N 70°12E 87 A12
Anguilla ☑ *W. Indies* 18°14N 63°5W 115 D12
Angus *U.K.* 56°46N 2°56W 19 J11
Angus, Braes of *U.K.* 56°51N 3°10W 19 J11
Anhui □ *China* 32°0N 117°0E 79 C12
Anjou *France* 47°20N 0°15W 66 C3
Ankang *China* 32°40N 109°1E 79 C10
Ankara *Turkey* 39°57N 32°54E 71 G5
Ann, C. *U.S.A.* 42°38N 70°35W 113 D12
Ann Arbor *U.S.A.* 42°17N 83°45W 112 D6
Annaba *Algeria* 36°50N 7°46E 94 A7
Annalee → *Ireland* 54°2N 7°24W 28 D7
Annan *U.K.* 54°59N 3°16W 21 E9
Annan → *U.K.* 54°58N 3°16W 21 E9
Annandale *U.K.* 55°10N 3°25W 21 D9
Annapolis *U.S.A.* 38°59N 76°30W 112 F9
Annapurna *Nepal* 28°34N 83°50E 85 E14
Annecy *France* 45°55N 6°8E 66 D7
Annfield Plain *U.K.* 54°52N 1°44W 22 C5
Anning *China* 24°55N 102°26E 78 D9
Anniston *U.S.A.* 33°39N 85°50W 111 D9
Annobón *Atl. Oc.* 1°25S 5°36E 90 G4
Annotto B. *Jamaica* 18°17N 76°45W 114 a
Anqing *China* 30°30N 117°3E 79 C12
Anshan *China* 41°5N 122°58E 79 C13
Anshun *China* 26°18N 105°57E 78 F10
Anstey *U.K.* 52°41N 1°12W 23 G6
Anstruther *U.K.* 56°14N 2°41W 21 B10
Antalaha *Madag.* 14°57S 50°20E 97 G10
Antalya *Turkey* 36°52N 30°45E 71 G5
Antalya Körfezi *Turkey* 36°15N 31°30E 71 G5
Antananarivo *Madag.* 18°55S 47°31E 97 H9

Antarctic Pen. *Antarctica* 67°0S 60°0W 55 C18
Antarctica 90°0S 0°0 55 E3
Anti Atlas *Morocco* 30°0N 8°30W 94 C4
Antibes *France* 43°34N 7°6E 66 E7
Anticosti, Î. d' *Canada* 49°30N 63°0W 109 E13
Antigo *U.S.A.* 45°9N 89°9W 112 C3
Antigonish *Canada* 45°38N 61°58W 109 E13
Antigua & Barbuda ■
W. Indies 17°20N 61°48W 115 D12
Antilles *Cent. Amer.* 15°0N 65°0W 104 H13
Antioch = Hatay *Turkey* 36°14N 36°10E 71 G6
Antioquia *Colombia* 6°40N 75°55W 120 B2
Antipodes Is. *Pac. Oc.* 49°45S 178°40E 102 M9
Antofagasta *Chile* 23°50S 70°30W 121 E2
Antrim *U.K.* 54°43N 6°14W 29 B9
Antrim □ *U.K.* 54°56N 6°25W 29 B9
Antrim, Mts. of *U.K.* 55°3N 6°14W 29 A9
Antsirabe *Madag.* 19°55S 47°2E 97 H9
Antsiranana *Madag.* 12°25S 49°20E 97 G9
Antwerp *Belgium* 51°13N 4°25E 64 C3
Anuradhapura *Sri Lanka* 8°22N 80°28E 84 Q12
Anxi *China* 40°30N 95°43E 78 C8
Anyang *China* 36°5N 114°21E 79 D11
Anzhero-Sudzhensk *Russia* 56°10N 86°0E 76 D9
Anzio *Italy* 41°27N 12°37E 68 D5
Aomori *Japan* 40°45N 140°45E 81 C7
Aoraki Mount Cook *N.Z.* 43°36S 170°9E 99 J13
Aosta *Italy* 45°45N 7°20E 68 B2
Aozou, Couloir d' *Chad* 22°0N 19°0E 95 D9
Apalachee B. *U.S.A.* 30°0N 84°0W 111 E10
Apaporis → *Colombia* 1°23S 69°25W 120 C3
Aparecida de Goiânia *Brazil* 16°49S 49°14W 122 C1
Apatity *Russia* 67°34N 33°22E 70 A5
Apeldoorn *Neths.* 52°13N 5°57E 64 B3
Apia *Samoa* 13°50S 171°50W 99 C16
Apostle Is. *U.S.A.* 47°0N 90°40W 112 B2
Appalachian Mts. *U.S.A.* 38°0N 80°0W 112 G7
Appennini *Italy* 44°30N 10°0E 68 B4
Appleby-in-Westmorland
U.K. 54°35N 2°29W 22 C4
Applecross Forest *U.K.* 57°27N 5°40W 18 H6
Appledore *Devon, U.K.* 51°3N 4°13W 27 E5
Appledore *Kent, U.K.* 51°1N 0°47E 25 D10
Appleton *U.S.A.* 44°16N 88°25W 112 C3
Apure → *Venezuela* 7°37N 66°25W 120 B3
Apurimac → *Peru* 12°17S 73°56W 120 D2
Aqaba, G. of *Red Sea* 29°0N 34°40E 86 D3
Aqtaū *Kazakhstan* 43°39N 51°12E 71 F9
Aqtöbe *Kazakhstan* 50°17N 57°10E 71 D10
Aquitain, Bassin *France* 44°0N 0°30E 66 D3
Ar Ramādī *Iraq* 33°25N 43°20E 86 C5
Ara *India* 25°35N 84°32E 85 G14
'Arab, Bahr el → *Sudan* 9°0N 29°30E 95 G11
'Arab, Shatt al → *Asia* 29°57N 48°34E 86 D7
Arabia *Asia* 25°0N 45°0E 72 F6
Arabian Sea *Ind. Oc.* 16°0N 65°0E 72 G8
Aracaju *Brazil* 10°55S 37°4W 122 B3
Aracati *Brazil* 4°30S 37°44W 120 C6
Araçatuba *Brazil* 21°10S 50°30W 120 E4
Araçuaí *Brazil* 16°52S 42°4W 122 C2
Arad *Romania* 46°10N 21°20E 65 E11
Arafura Sea *E. Indies* 9°0S 135°0E 98 B5
Aragón □ *Spain* 41°25N 0°40W 67 B5
Araguacema *Brazil* 8°50S 49°20W 120 C5
Araguaia → *Brazil* 5°21S 48°41W 120 C5
Araguari *Brazil* 18°38S 48°11W 122 C1
Arāk *Iran* 34°0N 49°40E 86 C7
Arakan Coast *Burma* 19°0N 94°0E 85 K19
Arakan Yoma *Burma* 20°0N 94°40E 85 K19
Aral *Kazakhstan* 46°41N 61°45E 76 E7
Aral Sea *Asia* 44°30N 60°0E 76 E6
Aran I. *Ireland* 55°0N 8°30W 28 B4
Aran Is. *Ireland* 53°6N 9°38W 30 B3
Aransas Pass *U.S.A.* 27°55N 97°9W 111 E7
Arapiraca *Brazil* 9°45S 36°39W 122 A3
Araraquara *Brazil* 21°50S 48°0W 122 D1
Araras *Brazil* 22°22S 47°23W 122 D1
Ararat *Turkey* 39°50N 44°15E 71 G7
Araripe, Chapada do *Brazil* 7°20S 40°0W 120 C5
Aras, Rūd-e → *Asia* 40°5N 48°29E 86 A7
Arauca → *Venezuela* 7°24N 66°35W 120 B3
Araxá *Brazil* 19°35S 46°55W 122 C1
Arbil *Iraq* 36°15N 44°5E 86 B6
Arbroath *U.K.* 56°34N 2°35W 21 A10
Arcachon *France* 44°40N 1°10W 66 D3
Arctic Bay *Canada* 73°1N 85°7W 109 B11
Arctic Ocean *Arctic* 78°0N 160°0W 54 B18
Ardabīl *Iran* 38°15N 48°18E 86 B7
Ardee *Ireland* 53°52N 6°33W 29 D8
Ardennes *Belgium* 49°50N 5°5E 64 D3
Arderin *Ireland* 53°2N 7°39W 31 B7
Ardgour *U.K.* 56°45N 5°25W 18 J7
Ardingly *U.K.* 51°3N 0°4W 25 D8
Ardivachar Pt. *U.K.* 57°23N 7°26W 18 H3
Ardmore *U.S.A.* 34°10N 97°8W 111 D7
Ardnamurchan *U.K.* 56°43N 6°0W 18 J5
Ardnamurchan, Pt. of *U.K.* 56°43N 6°14W 18 J5
Ardnave Pt. *U.K.* 55°53N 6°20W 20 C3
Ardrossan *U.K.* 55°39N 4°49W 20 C6
Ards Pen. *U.K.* 54°33N 5°34W 29 B10
Arecibo *Puerto Rico* 18°29N 66°43W 115 d
Arena, Pt. *U.S.A.* 38°57N 123°44W 110 C2
Arendal *Norway* 58°28N 8°46E 63 F5
Arequipa *Peru* 16°20S 71°30W 120 D2
Arezzo *Italy* 43°25N 11°53E 68 C4
Argentan *France* 48°45N 0°1W 66 B3
Argentina ■ *S. Amer.* 35°0S 66°0W 121 F3
Argentino, L. *Argentina* 50°10S 73°0W 121 H2
Argostoli *Greece* 38°11N 20°29E 69 E9
Argun → *Russia* 53°20N 121°28E 79 A13
Argyle, L. *Australia* 16°20S 128°40E 98 D4
Argyll *U.K.* 56°13N 5°28W 20 B4
Argyll & Bute □ *U.K.* 56°13N 5°28W 20 B4
Århus *Denmark* 56°8N 10°11E 63 F6
Ariana *Tunisia* 36°52N 10°12E 95 A8
Arica *Chile* 18°32S 70°20W 120 D2
Arinos → *Brazil* 10°25S 58°20W 120 D4
Aripuanã → *Brazil* 5°7S 60°25W 120 C3
Arisaig *U.K.* 56°55N 5°51W 18 J6
Arizona □ *U.S.A.* 34°0N 112°0W 110 D4
Arkaig, L. *U.K.* 56°59N 5°10W 18 J7

Arkansas □ *U.S.A.* 35°0N 92°30W 111 D8
Arkansas → *U.S.A.* 33°47N 91°4W 111 D8
Arkansas City *U.S.A.* 37°4N 97°2W 111 C7
Arkhangelsk *Russia* 64°38N 40°36E 70 B7
Arkle → *U.K.* 54°24N 1°56W 22 D5
Arklow *Ireland* 52°48N 6°10W 31 C10
Arles *France* 43°41N 4°40E 66 E6
Arlington *U.S.A.* 38°53N 77°7W 112 F9
Arlon *Belgium* 49°42N 5°49E 64 D3
Armagh *U.K.* 54°21N 6°39W 29 C8
Armagh □ *U.K.* 54°18N 6°37W 29 C8
Armavir *Russia* 45°2N 41°7E 71 E7
Armenia *Colombia* 4°35N 75°45W 120 B2
Armenia ■ *Asia* 40°20N 45°0E 71 F7
Arnaud → *Canada* 59°59N 69°46W 109 D13
Arnhem *Neths.* 51°58N 5°55E 64 C3
Arnhem, C. *Australia* 12°20S 137°30E 98 C6
Arnhem Land *Australia* 13°10S 134°30E 98 C5
Arno → *Italy* 43°41N 10°17E 68 C4
Arnold *U.K.* 53°1N 1°7W 23 F6
Arnprior *Canada* 45°26N 76°21W 112 C9
Arnside *U.K.* 54°12N 2°49W 22 D3
Arra Mts. *Ireland* 52°50N 8°22W 30 C6
Arran *U.K.* 55°34N 5°12W 20 C5
Arras *France* 50°17N 2°46E 66 A5
Arrecife *Canary Is.* 28°57N 13°37W 94 C3
Arrow, L. *Ireland* 54°3N 8°19W 28 C5
Artemovsk *Ukraine* 48°35N 38°0E 71 E6
Artigas *Uruguay* 30°20S 56°30W 121 F4
Artois *France* 50°20N 2°30E 66 A5
Artvin *Turkey* 41°14N 41°44E 71 F7
Artux *China* 39°40N 76°10E 78 D4
Aru, Kepulauan *Indonesia* 6°0S 134°30E 83 F8
Arua *Uganda* 3°1N 30°58E 96 D6
Aruanã *Brazil* 14°54S 51°10W 120 D4
Aruba ☑ *W. Indies* 12°30N 70°0W 115 E11
Arun → *U.K.* 50°49N 0°33W 25 E7
Arunachal Pradesh □ *India* 28°0N 95°0E 85 F19
Arundel *U.K.* 50°51N 0°33W 25 E7
Arusha *Tanzania* 3°20S 36°40E 96 E7
Aruwimi →
Dem. Rep. of the Congo 1°13N 23°36E 96 D4
Arvayheer *Mongolia* 46°15N 102°48E 78 B9
Arviat *Canada* 61°6N 93°59W 108 C10
Arxan *China* 47°11N 119°57E 79 B12
Arzamas *Russia* 55°27N 43°55E 70 C7
As Sulaymānīyah *Iraq* 35°35N 45°29E 86 C6
As Sulaymānīyah *Si. Arabia* 24°9N 47°18E 86 E6
As Suwayq *Oman* 23°51N 57°26E 89 C6
Aş Şuwayrah *Iraq* 32°55N 45°0E 86 C6
Asahigawa *Japan* 43°46N 142°22E 81 B8
Asama-Yama *Japan* 36°24N 138°31E 81 E6
Asamankese *Ghana* 5°50N 0°40W 94 G5
Asansol *India* 23°40N 87°1E 85 H15
Asbestos *Canada* 45°47N 71°58W 113 C12
Asbury Park *U.S.A.* 40°13N 74°1W 113 E10
Ascension I. *Atl. Oc.* 7°57S 14°23W 52 E9
Áscoli Piceno *Italy* 42°51N 13°34E 68 C5
Ascot *U.K.* 51°25N 0°40W 25 D7
Aseb *Eritrea* 13°0N 42°40E 89 E3
Asenovgrad *Bulgaria* 42°1N 24°51E 69 C11
Asfordby *U.K.* 52°47N 0°57W 23 G7
Ash *Kent, U.K.* 51°16N 1°17E 25 D11
Ash *Surrey, U.K.* 51°15N 0°43W 25 D7
Ashbourne *U.K.* 53°2N 1°43W 23 F5
Ashburton *U.K.* 50°30N 3°46W 27 F6
Ashby de la Zouch *U.K.* 52°46N 1°29W 23 G6
Ashchurch *U.K.* 52°0N 2°5W 24 C4
Ashdown Forest *U.K.* 51°3N 0°5E 25 D9
Asheville *U.S.A.* 35°36N 82°33W 111 C10
Ashford *Derby, U.K.* 53°14N 1°42W 23 F5
Ashford *Kent, U.K.* 51°8N 0°53E 25 D10
Ashington *U.K.* 55°11N 1°33W 22 B5
Ashkhabad *Turkmenistan* 38°0N 57°50E 87 B9
Ashland *Ky., U.S.A.* 38°28N 82°38W 112 F6
Ashland *Ohio, U.S.A.* 40°52N 82°19W 112 E6
Ashland *Wis., U.S.A.* 46°35N 90°53W 111 B8
Ashqelon *Israel* 31°42N 34°35E 86 D3
Ashtabula *U.S.A.* 41°52N 80°47W 112 E7
Ashton-in-Makerfield *U.K.* 53°30N 2°40W 23 F3
Ashton under Lyne *U.K.* 53°29N 2°6E 23 F4
Ashuanipi, L. *Canada* 52°45N 66°15W 109 D13
Ashwater *U.K.* 50°43N 4°19W 27 F5
Ashwick *U.K.* 51°13N 2°31W 24 D3
Asia 45°0N 75°0E 72 E9
Asinara *Italy* 41°4N 8°16E 68 D3
'Asir *Si. Arabia* 18°40N 42°30E 89 D3
Askrigg *U.K.* 54°19N 2°6W 22 D4
Aslackby *U.K.* 52°53N 0°23W 23 G8
Asmera *Eritrea* 15°19N 38°55E 89 D2
Aspatria *U.K.* 54°47N 3°19W 22 C2
Aspen *U.S.A.* 39°11N 106°49W 110 C5
Assal, L. *Djibouti* 11°40N 42°26E 89 E3
Assam □ *India* 26°0N 93°0E 85 G18
Assen *Neths.* 53°0N 6°35E 64 B4
Assiniboia *Canada* 49°40N 105°59W 108 E9
Assiniboine → *Canada* 49°53N 97°8W 108 E10
Assisi *Italy* 43°4N 12°37E 68 C5
Assynt *U.K.* 58°12N 5°12W 18 F7
Assynt, L. *U.K.* 58°10N 5°3W 18 F7
Astana *Kazakhstan* 51°10N 71°30E 76 D8
Asti *Italy* 44°54N 8°12E 68 B3
Astipálea *Greece* 36°32N 26°22E 69 F12
Astrakhan *Russia* 46°25N 48°5E 71 E8
Asturias □ *Spain* 43°15N 6°0W 67 A3
Astwood Bank *U.K.* 52°15N 1°56W 24 B5
Asunción *Paraguay* 25°10S 57°30W 121 E4
Aswân *Egypt* 24°4N 32°57E 95 D12
Aswan High Dam *Egypt* 23°54N 32°54E 95 D12
Asyût *Egypt* 27°11N 31°4E 95 C12
At Tā'if *Si. Arabia* 21°5N 40°27E 89 C3
Atacama, Desierto de *Chile* 24°0S 69°20W 121 E3
Atar *Mauritania* 20°30N 13°5W 94 D3
Atatürk Baraji *Turkey* 37°28N 38°30E 71 G6
Atbara *Sudan* 17°42N 33°59E 95 E12
Atbara → *Sudan* 17°40N 33°56E 95 E12
Atchafalaya B. *U.S.A.* 29°25N 91°25W 111 E8
Athabasca *Canada* 54°45N 113°20W 108 D8
Athabasca → *Canada* 58°40N 110°50W 108 D8
Athabasca, L. *Canada* 59°15N 109°15W 108 D9

Athboy *Ireland* 53°37N 6°56W 29 D8
Athenry *Ireland* 53°18N 8°44W 30 B5
Athens *Ga., U.S.A.* 33°57N 83°23W 111 D10
Athens *Ohio, U.S.A.* 39°20N 82°6W 112 F6
Atherstone *U.K.* 52°35N 1°33W 23 G5
Atherton *U.K.* 53°32N 2°30W 23 E4
Athlone *Ireland* 53°25N 7°56W 30 B7
Atholl, Forest of *U.K.* 56°51N 3°50W 19 J10
Athos *Greece* 40°9N 24°22E 69 D11
Athy *Ireland* 53°0N 7°0W 31 B8
Atikokan *Canada* 48°45N 91°37W 112 A2
Atka I. *U.S.A.* 52°7N 174°30W 108 D2
Atlanta *U.S.A.* 33°45N 84°23W 111 D10
Atlantic City *U.S.A.* 39°21N 74°27W 113 F10
Atlantic Ocean 0°0 20°0W 50 F9
Atlas Saharien *Algeria* 33°30N 1°0E 94 B6
Atlin *Canada* 59°31N 133°41W 108 D6
Attawapiskat *Canada* 52°56N 82°24W 109 D11
Attawapiskat → *Canada* 52°57N 82°18W 109 D11
Attleborough *U.K.* 52°32N 1°1E 25 A11
Attu I. *U.S.A.* 52°55N 172°55E 108 D1
Atyraū *Kazakhstan* 47°5N 52°0E 71 E9
Au Sable → *U.S.A.* 44°25N 83°20W 112 C6
Aube → *France* 48°34N 3°43E 66 B5
Auburn *Ind., U.S.A.* 41°22N 85°4W 112 E5
Auburn *N.Y., U.S.A.* 42°56N 76°34W 112 D9
Aubusson *France* 45°57N 2°11E 66 D5
Auch *France* 43°39N 0°36E 66 E4
Auchterarder *U.K.* 56°18N 3°41W 21 B9
Auchtermuchty *U.K.* 56°18N 3°13W 21 B9
Auckland *N.Z.* 36°52S 174°46E 99 H13
Auckland Is. *Pac. Oc.* 50°40S 166°5E 102 N8
Aude → *France* 43°13N 3°14E 66 E5
Audlem *U.K.* 52°59N 2°30W 23 G4
Aughnacloy *U.K.* 54°25N 6°59W 29 C8
Augsburg *Germany* 48°25N 10°52E 64 D6
Augusta *Australia* 34°19S 115°9E 98 G2
Augusta *U.S.A.* 33°28N 81°58W 111 D10
Aunis *France* 46°5N 0°50W 66 C3
Aurangabad *Bihar, India* 24°45N 84°18E 85 G14
Aurangabad *Maharashtra,
India* 19°50N 75°23E 84 K9
Aurillac *France* 44°55N 2°26E 66 D5
Aurora *Colo., U.S.A.* 39°43N 104°49W 110 C6
Aurora *Ill., U.S.A.* 41°45N 88°19W 112 E3
Austin *U.S.A.* 30°17N 97°45W 110 D7
Australia ■ *Oceania* 23°0S 135°0E 98 E5
Australian Capital Territory □
Australia 35°30S 149°0E 98 H8
Austria ■ *Europe* 47°0N 14°0E 64 E8
Autun *France* 46°58N 4°17E 66 C6
Auvergne □ *France* 45°20N 3°15E 66 D5
Auvergne, Mts. d' *France* 45°20N 2°55E 66 D5
Auxerre *France* 47°48N 3°32E 66 C5
Avallon *France* 47°30N 3°53E 66 C5
Avaré *Brazil* 23°4S 48°58W 122 D1
Avebury *U.K.* 51°26N 1°50W 24 D5
Avellaneda *Argentina* 34°40S 58°22W 121 F4
Avellino *Italy* 40°54N 14°47E 68 D6
Aversa *Italy* 40°58N 14°12E 68 D6
Aveton Gifford *U.K.* 50°18N 3°50W 27 G6
Aviemore *U.K.* 57°12N 3°50W 19 H10
Avignon *France* 43°57N 4°50E 66 E6
Ávila *Spain* 40°39N 4°43E 67 B3
Avilés *Spain* 43°35N 5°57W 67 A3
Avoca → *Ireland* 52°48N 6°10W 31 C10
Avon → *Bristol, U.K.* 51°29N 2°41W 24 D3
Avon → *Dorset, U.K.* 50°44N 1°46W 24 E5
Avon → *Warks., U.K.* 52°0N 2°8W 24 B5
Avonmouth *U.K.* 51°30N 2°42W 24 D3
Avranches *France* 48°40N 1°20W 66 B3
Awasa *Ethiopia* 7°2N 38°28E 89 F2
Awash *Ethiopia* 9°1N 40°10E 89 F3
Awbārī, Idehan *Libya* 27°10N 11°30E 95 C8
Awe, L. *U.K.* 56°17N 5°16W 20 B5
Axbridge *U.K.* 51°17N 2°49W 24 D3
Axe → *U.K.* 50°42N 3°4W 27 E8
Axe Edge *U.K.* 53°14N 1°57W 23 F5
Axel Heiberg I. *Canada* 80°0N 90°0W 109 B11
Axholme, Isle of *U.K.* 53°32N 0°50W 23 E7
Axios → *Greece* 40°57N 22°35E 69 D10
Axminster *U.K.* 50°46N 3°0W 27 F8
Axmouth *U.K.* 50°42N 3°3W 27 F7
Ayacucho *Argentina* 37°5S 58°20W 121 F4
Ayacucho *Peru* 13°0S 74°0W 120 D2
Aydın *Turkey* 37°51N 27°51E 71 G4
Aydıngkol Hu *China* 42°40N 89°15E 78 C6
Ayers Rock = Uluru *Australia* 25°23S 131°5E 98 F5
Aylesbury *U.K.* 51°49N 0°49W 25 C7
Aylesford *U.K.* 51°18N 0°30E 25 D10
Aylmer, L. *Canada* 64°5N 108°30W 108 C8
Aylsham *U.K.* 52°48N 1°15E 25 A11
Aynho *U.K.* 52°0N 1°15W 24 C6
Ayr *U.K.* 55°28N 4°38W 20 D6
Ayr → *U.K.* 55°28N 4°38W 20 D6
Aysgarth *U.K.* 54°18N 2°1W 22 D4
Ayton *Borders, U.K.* 55°51N 2°6W 21 C11
Ayton *N. Yorks., U.K.* 54°15N 0°28W 22 D8
Ayvalık *Turkey* 39°20N 26°46E 71 G4
Az Zarqā *Jordan* 32°5N 36°4E 86 C4
Az Zāwiyah *Libya* 32°52N 12°56E 95 B8
Azad Kashmir □ *Pakistan* 33°50N 73°50E 84 B8
Azamgarh *India* 26°5N 83°13E 85 F13
Azare *Nigeria* 11°55N 10°10E 94 F8
Azerbaijan ■ *Asia* 40°20N 48°0E 71 F8
Azores *Atl. Oc.* 38°0N 27°0W 91 C1
Azov *Russia* 47°3N 39°25E 71 E6
Azov, Sea of *Europe* 46°0N 36°30E 71 E6
Azuero, Pen. de *Panama* 7°30N 80°30W 115 F8
Azul *Argentina* 36°42S 59°43W 121 F4

B

Bab el Mandeb *Red Sea* 12°35N 43°25E 89 E3
Bābā, Koh-i- *Afghan.* 34°30N 67°0E 84 B5
Babine L. *Canada* 54°48N 126°0W 108 D7
Bābol *Iran* 36°40N 52°50E 87 B8
Babruysk *Belarus* 53°10N 29°15E 65 B15
Babuyan Chan. *Phil.* 18°40N 121°30E 83 A6

Babylon

Big Belt Mts.

Babylon *Iraq* 32°34N 44°22E 86 C6
Bac Lieu *Vietnam* 9°17N 105°43E 82 C3
Bacabal *Brazil* 4°15S 44°45W 120 C5
Bacău *Romania* 46°35N 26°55E 65 E14
Back → *Canada* 65°10N 104°0W 108 C9
Bacolod *Phil.* 10°40N 122°57E 83 B6
Bacton *U.K.* 52°52N 1°27E 25 A11
Bacup *U.K.* 53°42N 2°11W 23 E4
Bad Axe *U.S.A.* 43°48N 83°0W 112 D6
Badagara *India* 11°35N 75°40E 84 P9
Badain Jaran Desert *China* 40°23N 102°0E 78 C9
Badajoz *Spain* 38°50N 6°59W 67 C2
Badakhshān □ *Afghan.* 36°30N 71°0E 87 B12
Badalona *Spain* 41°26N 2°15E 67 B7
Baden-Württemberg □ *Germany* 48°20N 8°40E 64 D5
Badenoch *U.K.* 56°59N 4°15W 19 J9
Bādghīs □ *Afghan.* 35°0N 63°0E 87 C10
Badlands *U.S.A.* 43°55N 102°30W 110 B6
Baffin B. *N. Amer.* 72°0N 64°0W 109 B13
Baffin I. *Canada* 68°0N 75°0W 109 C12
Bafoulabé *Mali* 13°50N 10°55W 94 F3
Bafoussam *Cameroon* 5°28N 10°25E 96 C2
Bafra *Turkey* 41°34N 35°54E 71 F6
Bafq *Iran* 31°40N 55°25E 87 D8
Bafwasende *Dem. Rep. of the Congo*
Bagamoyo *Tanzania* 6°28S 38°55E 96 F7
Bagé *Brazil* 31°20S 54°15W 121 F4
Baggy Pt. *U.K.* 51°8N 4°16W 27 E5
Baghdād *Iraq* 33°20N 44°23E 86 C6
Baghlān *Afghan.* 32°12N 68°46E 87 B12
Bagshot *U.K.* 51°22N 0°41W 25 D7
Baguio *Phil.* 16°26N 120°34E 83 A6
Bahamas ■ *N. Amer.* 24°0N 75°0W 115 C10
Baharampur *India* 24°2N 88°27E 85 G16
Bahawalpur *Pakistan* 29°24N 71°40E 84 E7
Bahia = Salvador *Brazil* 13°0S 38°30W 122 B3
Bahia □ *Brazil* 12°0S 42°0W 122 B2
Bahía, Is. de la *Honduras* 16°45N 86°15W 114 D7
Bahía Blanca *Argentina* 38°35S 62°13W 121 F3
Bahir Dar *Ethiopia* 11°37N 37°10E 89 E2
Bahraich *India* 27°38N 81°37E 85 F12
Bahrain ■ *Asia* 26°0N 50°35E 87 E7
Baia Mare *Romania* 47°40N 23°35E 65 E12
Baicheng *China* 45°38N 122°42E 79 B13
Baie-Comeau *Canada* 49°12N 68°10W 109 E13
Baie-St-Paul *Canada* 47°28N 70°32W 113 B12
Baie Verte *Canada* 49°55N 56°12W 109 E14
Ba'iji *Iraq* 35°0N 43°30E 86 C5
Baikal, L. *Russia* 53°0N 108°0E 77 D11
Baildon *U.K.* 53°51N 1°46W 23 E5
Bain → *U.K.* 53°6N 0°12W 23 F8
Bainbridge *U.K.* 54°18N 2°6W 22 D4
Baiyin *China* 36°45N 104°14E 78 D9
Baja, Pta. *Mexico* 29°58N 115°49W 114 B1
Baker, L. *Canada* 64°0N 90°0W 108 C10
Baker City *U.S.A.* 44°47N 117°50W 110 B3
Baker I. *Pac. Oc.* 0°10N 176°35W 99 A15
Baker Lake *Canada* 64°20N 96°3W 108 C10
Bakers Dozen Is. *Canada* 56°45N 78°45W 109 D12
Bakersfield *U.S.A.* 35°23N 119°1W 110 C3
Bakewell *U.K.* 53°13N 1°40W 23 F5
Baku *Azerbaijan* 40°29N 49°56E 71 F8
Bala *U.K.* 52°54N 3°36W 26 B6
Bala, L. *U.K.* 52°53N 3°37W 26 B6
Balabac Str. *E. Indies* 7°53N 117°5E 82 C5
Balaghat Ra. *India* 18°50N 76°30E 84 K10
Balaklava *Ukraine* 44°30N 33°30E 71 F5
Balakovo *Russia* 52°4N 47°55E 70 D8
Balashov *Russia* 51°30N 43°10E 71 D7
Balaton *Hungary* 46°50N 17°40E 65 E9
Balbi, Mt. *Papua N. G.* 5°55S 154°58E 99 B10
Balbina, Represa de *Brazil* 2°0S 59°30W 120 C4
Balbriggan *Ireland* 53°37N 6°11W 29 D9
Balcarce *Argentina* 38°0S 58°10W 121 F4
Balderton *U.K.* 53°3N 0°47W 23 F7
Baldock *U.K.* 52°0N 0°11W 25 C8
Baldoyle *Ireland* 53°24N 6°8W 31 B10
Baldwin *U.S.A.* 43°54N 85°51W 112 D5
Baldy Peak *U.S.A.* 33°54N 109°34W 110 D5
Balearic Is. *Spain* 39°30N 3°0E 67 C7
Baleine → *Canada* 58°15N 67°40W 109 D13
Baleshare *U.K.* 57°31N 7°22W 18 G3
Baleshwar *India* 21°35N 87°3E 85 J15
Bali *Indonesia* 8°20S 115°0E 82 F4
Balıkesir *Turkey* 39°39N 27°53E 71 G4
Balikpapan *Indonesia* 1°10S 116°55E 82 E5
Balkan Mts. *Bulgaria* 43°15N 23°0E 69 C10
Balkanabat *Turkmenistan* 39°30N 54°22E 87 B8
Balkhash, L. *Kazakhstan* 46°0N 74°50E 78 B3
Ballachulish *U.K.* 56°41N 5°8W 18 J7
Ballaghaderreen *Ireland* 53°55N 8°34W 28 D4
Ballantrae *U.K.* 55°6N 4°59W 20 D6
Ballarat *Australia* 37°33S 143°50E 98 H7
Ballater *U.K.* 57°3N 3°3W 19 H11
Balleny Is. *Antarctica* 66°30S 163°0E 55 C11
Ballina *Ireland* 54°7N 9°9W 28 C3
Ballinasloe *Ireland* 53°20N 8°13W 30 B6
Ballinrobe *Ireland* 53°38N 9°13W 28 D3
Ballinskelligs B. *Ireland* 51°48N 10°13W 30 E2
Ballybunion *Ireland* 52°31N 9°40W 30 C3
Ballycastle *U.K.* 55°12N 6°15W 29 A9
Ballyclare *U.K.* 54°46N 6°0W 29 B10
Ballyhaunis *Ireland* 53°46N 8°46W 28 D4
Ballyhoura Mts. *Ireland* 52°18N 8°33W 30 D5
Ballymena *U.K.* 54°52N 6°17W 29 B9
Ballymoney *U.K.* 55°5N 6°31W 29 A8
Ballymote *Ireland* 54°5N 8°31W 28 C4
Ballynahinch *U.K.* 54°24N 5°54W 29 C10
Ballyquintin Pt. *U.K.* 54°20N 5°30W 29 C11
Ballyshannon *Ireland* 54°30N 8°11W 28 B5
Balmoral Forest *U.K.* 52°13N 9°40W 30 C3
Balrampur *India* 27°30N 82°20E 85 F13
Balsas → *Mexico* 17°55N 102°10W 114 D4
Baltic Sea *Europe* 57°0N 19°0E 63 F7
Baltimore *Ireland* 51°29N 9°22W 30 F4
Baltimore *U.S.A.* 39°17N 76°36W 112 F9
Baluchistan □ *Pakistan* 27°30N 65°0E 84 F4
Bam *Iran* 29°7N 58°14E 87 D9
Bamako *Mali* 12°34N 7°55W 94 F4
Bambari *C.A.R.* 5°40N 20°35E 96 C4

Bamberg *Germany* 49°54N 10°54E 64 D6
Bamburgh *U.K.* 55°37N 1°43W 22 A5
Bamenda *Cameroon* 5°57N 10°11E 96 C2
Bamford *U.K.* 53°22N 1°41W 23 F5
Bāmīān □ *Afghan.* 35°0N 67°0E 87 C11
Bampton *Devon, U.K.* 50°59N 3°29W 27 F7
Bampton *Oxon., U.K.* 51°44N 1°32W 24 C5
Banaba *Kiribati* 0°45S 169°50E 102 H8
Bananal, I. do *Brazil* 11°30S 50°30W 120 D4
Banbridge *U.K.* 54°22N 6°16W 29 C9
Banbury *U.K.* 52°4N 1°20W 24 B6
Banchory *U.K.* 57°3N 2°29W 19 H13
Bancroft *Canada* 45°3N 77°51W 112 C9
Banda *India* 25°30N 80°26E 84 G12
Banda, Kepulauan *Indonesia* 4°37S 129°50E 83 E7
Banda Aceh *Indonesia* 5°35N 95°20E 82 C1
Banda Sea *Indonesia* 6°0S 130°0E 83 F7
Bandar-e Abbās *Iran* 27°15N 56°15E 87 E9
Bandar-e Anzalī *Iran* 37°30N 49°30E 86 B7
Bandar-e Ma'shur *Iran* 30°35N 49°10E 86 D7
Bandar-e Torkeman *Iran* 37°0N 54°10E 87 B8
Bandar Lampung *Indonesia* 5°20S 105°10E 82 F3
Bandar Seri Begawan *Brunei* 4°52N 115°0E 82 C4
Bandeira, Pico da *Brazil* 20°26S 41°47W 122 D2
Banderas, B. de *Mexico* 20°40N 105°25W 104 G9
Bandırma *Turkey* 40°20N 28°0E 71 F4
Bandon *Ireland* 51°44N 8°44W 30 E5
Bandon → *Ireland* 51°43N 8°37W 30 E5
Bandundu *Dem. Rep. of the Congo* 3°15S 17°22E 96 E3
Bandung *Indonesia* 6°54S 107°36E 82 F3
Banes *Cuba* 21°0N 75°42W 115 C9
Banff *Canada* 51°10N 115°34W 108 D8
Banff *U.K.* 57°40N 2°33W 19 G13
Bangalore *India* 12°59N 77°40E 84 N10
Bangassou *C.A.R.* 4°55N 23°7E 96 D4
Banggai, Kepulauan *Indonesia* 1°40S 123°30E 83 E6
Bangka *Indonesia* 2°0S 105°50E 82 E3
Bangkok *Thailand* 13°45N 100°35E 82 B2
Bangladesh ■ *Asia* 24°0N 90°0E 85 H17
Bangor *Down, U.K.* 54°40N 5°40W 29 B10
Bangor *Gwynedd, U.K.* 53°14N 4°8W 26 A5
Bangui *C.A.R.* 4°23N 18°35E 96 D3
Banham *U.K.* 52°27N 1°2E 25 B11
Bani *Dom. Rep.* 18°16N 70°22W 115 D10
Banja Luka *Bos.-H.* 44°49N 17°11E 68 B7
Banjarmasin *Indonesia* 3°20S 114°35E 82 E4
Banjul *Gambia* 13°28N 16°40W 94 F2
Bankend *U.K.* 55°1N 3°33W 21 D8
Banks I. *Canada* 73°15N 121°30W 108 B7
Banks Is. *Vanuatu* 13°50S 167°30E 99 C12
Bann → *U.K.* 55°8N 6°41W 29 A8
Bannockburn *U.K.* 56°5N 3°55W 21 B8
Bannu *Pakistan* 33°0N 70°18E 84 C7
Banská Bystrica *Slovak Rep.* 48°46N 19°14E 65 D10
Bantry *Ireland* 51°41N 9°27W 30 E4
Bantry B. *Ireland* 51°37N 9°44W 30 E3
Banwell *U.K.* 51°19N 2°52W 24 D3
Banyak, Kepulauan *Indonesia* 2°10N 97°10E 82 D1
Banyuwangi *Indonesia* 8°13S 114°21E 82 F4
Baoding *China* 38°50N 115°28E 79 D12
Baoji *China* 34°20N 107°5E 78 E10
Baoshan *China* 25°10N 99°5E 78 F8
Baotou *China* 40°32N 110°2E 79 C11
Ba'qūbah *Iraq* 33°45N 44°50E 86 C6
Bar Harbor *U.S.A.* 44°23N 68°13W 113 C13
Bar-le-Duc *France* 48°47N 5°10E 66 B6
Baraboo *U.S.A.* 43°28N 89°45W 112 D3
Baracoa *Cuba* 20°20N 74°30W 115 C10
Barahona *Dom. Rep.* 18°13N 71°7W 115 D10
Barail Range *India* 25°15N 93°20E 85 G18
Barakaldo *Spain* 43°18N 2°59W 67 A4
Baranavichy *Belarus* 53°10N 26°0E 65 B14
Baranof I. *U.S.A.* 57°0N 135°0W 108 D6
Barbacena *Brazil* 21°15S 43°56W 122 D2
Barbados ■ *W. Indies* 13°10N 59°30W 115 g
Barberton *U.S.A.* 41°1N 81°39W 112 E7
Barcelona *Spain* 41°22N 2°10E 67 B7
Barcelona *Venezuela* 10°10N 64°40W 120 A3
Barceloneta *Puerto Rico* 18°27N 66°32W 115 d
Barddhaman *India* 23°14N 87°39E 85 H15
Bardīyah *Libya* 31°45N 25°5E 95 B10
Bardney *U.K.* 53°13N 0°19W 23 F8
Bardsey I. *U.K.* 52°45N 4°47W 26 B4
Bardstown *U.S.A.* 37°49N 85°28W 112 G5
Bareilly *India* 28°22N 79°27E 84 E11
Barford *U.K.* 52°16N 1°35W 24 B5
Bargoed *U.K.* 51°42N 3°15W 26 D7
Barham *U.K.* 51°12N 1°11E 25 D11
Barhi *India* 24°15N 85°25E 85 G14
Bari *Italy* 41°8N 16°51E 68 D7
Bari Doab *Pakistan* 30°20N 73°0E 84 D8
Barīm *Yemen* 12°39N 43°25E 90 E8
Barinas *Venezuela* 8°36N 70°15W 120 B2
Baring, C. *Canada* 70°0N 117°30W 108 C8
Barisal *Bangla.* 22°45N 90°20E 85 H17
Barisal □ *Bangla.* 22°45N 90°20E 85 H17
Barking and Dagenham □ *U.K.* 51°32N 0°10E 25 C9
Barkly Tableland *Australia* 17°50S 136°40E 98 D6
Barlborough *U.K.* 53°17N 1°17W 23 F6
Barlby *U.K.* 53°48N 1°2W 23 E6
Barlee, L. *Australia* 29°15S 119°30E 98 F2
Barletta *Italy* 41°19N 16°17E 68 D7
Barmby Moor *U.K.* 53°56N 0°49W 23 E7
Barmer *India* 25°45N 71°20E 84 G7
Barmoor Castle *U.K.* 55°39N 1°59W 22 A5
Barmouth *U.K.* 52°44N 4°4W 26 B5
Barnard Castle *U.K.* 54°33N 1°55W 22 C5
Barnaul *Russia* 53°20N 83°40E 76 D9
Barnet □ *U.K.* 51°38N 0°9W 25 C8
Barnetby le Wold *U.K.* 53°34N 0°24W 23 E8
Barnoldswick *U.K.* 53°55N 2°11W 23 E4
Barnsley *U.K.* 53°34N 1°27W 23 E6
Barnstaple *U.K.* 51°5N 4°4W 27 E5
Barotseland *Zambia* 15°0S 24°0E 97 H4
Barques, Pt. Aux *U.S.A.* 44°4N 82°58W 112 C6
Barquisimeto *Venezuela* 10°4N 69°19W 120 A3

Barra *Brazil* 11°5S 43°10W 122 B2
Barra *U.K.* 57°0N 7°29W 18 J2
Barra, Sd. of *U.K.* 57°4N 7°25W 18 H3
Barra do Corda *Brazil* 5°30S 45°10W 120 C5
Barra do Piraí *Brazil* 22°30S 43°50W 122 D2
Barra Hd. *U.K.* 56°47N 7°40W 18 J2
Barra Mansa *Brazil* 22°35S 44°12W 122 D2
Barrancabermeja *Colombia* 7°0N 73°50W 120 B2
Barranquilla *Colombia* 11°0N 74°50W 120 A2
Barreiras *Brazil* 12°8S 45°0W 122 B2
Barreiro *Portugal* 38°39N 9°5W 67 C1
Barreiros *Brazil* 8°49S 35°12W 122 A3
Barretos *Brazil* 20°30S 48°35W 122 D1
Barrhead *U.K.* 55°48N 4°23W 20 C7
Barrie *Canada* 44°24N 79°40W 109 E12
Barrow → *Ireland* 52°25N 6°58W 31 D9
Barrow *U.S.A.* 71°18N 156°47W 108 B4
Barrow, Pt. *U.S.A.* 71°23N 156°29W 104 B4
Barrow-in-Furness *U.K.* 54°7N 3°14W 22 D2
Barrow upon Humber *U.K.* 53°41N 0°23W 23 E8
Barrowford *U.K.* 53°51N 2°14W 23 E4
Barry *U.K.* 51°24N 3°16W 27 F7
Barry I. *U.K.* 51°23N 3°16W 27 F7
Barry's Bay *Canada* 45°29N 77°41W 112 C9
Barstow *U.S.A.* 34°54N 117°1W 110 D3
Bartlesville *U.S.A.* 36°45N 95°59W 111 C7
Barton *U.K.* 54°29N 1°38W 22 D5
Barton upon Humber *U.K.* 53°41N 0°25W 23 E8
Barú, Volcan *Panama* 8°55N 82°35W 115 F8
Baruun-Urt *Mongolia* 46°46N 113°15E 79 B11
Barysaw *Belarus* 54°17N 28°28E 65 A15
Bashkortostan □ *Russia* 54°0N 57°0E 70 D10
Basilan *Phil.* 6°35N 122°0E 83 C6
Basildon *U.K.* 51°34N 0°28E 25 C9
Basingstoke *U.K.* 51°15N 1°5W 24 D6
Baskatong, Rés. *Canada* 46°46N 75°50W 113 B10
Basque Provinces = País Vasco □ *Spain* 42°50N 2°45W 67 A4
Basra *Iraq* 30°30N 47°50E 86 D6
Bass Rock *U.K.* 56°5N 2°38W 21 B10
Bass Str. *Australia* 39°15S 146°30E 98 H8
Bassas da India *Ind. Oc.* 22°0S 39°0E 97 J7
Basse-Pointe *Martinique* 14°52N 61°8W 114 c
Basse-Terre *Guadeloupe* 16°0N 61°44W 114 b
Bassein *Burma* 16°45N 94°30E 85 L19
Bassenthwaite L. *U.K.* 54°40N 3°14W 22 C2
Basses, Pte. des *Guadeloupe* 15°52N 61°17W 114 b
Basseterre *St. Kitts & Nevis* 17°17N 62°43W 115 D12
Basti *India* 26°52N 82°55E 85 F13
Bastia *France* 42°40N 9°30E 66 E8
Bastogne *Belgium* 50°1N 5°43E 64 C3
Bata *Eq. Guin.* 1°57N 9°50E 96 D1
Batabanó, G. de *Cuba* 22°30N 82°30W 115 C8
Batangas *Phil.* 13°35N 121°10E 83 B6
Batatais *Brazil* 20°54S 47°37W 122 D1
Batavia *U.S.A.* 43°0N 78°11W 112 D8
Batdambang *Cambodia* 13°7N 103°12E 82 B2
Bath *U.K.* 51°23N 2°22W 24 D4
Bath *Maine, U.S.A.* 43°55N 69°49W 113 D13
Bath *N.Y., U.S.A.* 42°20N 77°19W 112 D9
Bathford *U.K.* 51°24N 2°18W 24 D4
Bathgate *U.K.* 55°54N 3°39W 21 C8
Bathsheba *Barbados* 13°13N 59°32W 115 g
Bathurst *Australia* 33°25S 149°31E 98 G8
Bathurst *Canada* 47°37N 65°43W 109 C11
Bathurst, C. *Canada* 70°34N 128°0W 108 B7
Bathurst I. *Canada* 76°0N 100°30W 109 B9
Bathurst Inlet *Canada* 66°50N 108°1W 108 C9
Batley *U.K.* 53°43N 1°38W 23 E5
Batman *Turkey* 37°55N 41°5E 71 G7
Batna *Algeria* 35°34N 6°15E 94 A7
Baton Rouge *U.S.A.* 30°27N 91°11W 111 D8
Batticaloa *Sri Lanka* 7°43N 81°45E 84 R12
Battle *U.K.* 50°55N 0°30E 25 E9
Battle Creek *U.S.A.* 42°19N 85°11W 112 D5
Batu, Kepulauan *Indonesia* 0°30S 98°25E 82 E1
Batu Pahat *Malaysia* 1°50N 102°56E 82 D2
Batumi *Georgia* 41°39N 41°44E 71 F7
Bauld, C. *Canada* 51°38N 55°26W 109 D14
Bauru *Brazil* 22°10S 49°0W 122 D1
Bavaria = Bayern □ *Germany* 48°50N 12°0E 64 D6
Bawdsey *U.K.* 52°1N 1°27E 25 B11
Bawtry *U.K.* 53°26N 1°2W 23 F6
Bay City *U.S.A.* 43°36N 83°54W 112 D6
Bayamo *Cuba* 20°20N 76°40W 115 C9
Bayamón *Puerto Rico* 18°24N 66°9W 115 d
Bayan Har Shan *China* 34°0N 98°0E 78 E8
Bayanhongor *Mongolia* 46°8N 102°43E 78 B9
Baydhabo *Somali Rep.* 3°8N 43°30E 89 G3
Bayern □ *Germany* 48°50N 12°0E 64 D6
Bayeux *France* 49°17N 0°42W 66 B3
Bayonne *France* 43°30N 1°28W 66 E3
Beachley *U.K.* 51°37N 2°39W 24 C3
Beachy Hd. *U.K.* 50°44N 0°15E 25 E9
Beacon *U.S.A.* 41°30N 73°58W 113 E11
Beaconsfield *U.K.* 51°36N 0°38W 25 C7
Beadnell *U.K.* 55°33N 1°38W 22 A5
Beagle, Canal *S. Amer.* 55°0S 68°30W 121 H3
Beaminster *U.K.* 50°48N 2°44W 24 E3
Bear → *U.S.A.* 41°30N 112°8W 110 B4
Bear I. *Arctic* 74°30N 19°0E 54 B8
Bear I. *Ireland* 51°38N 9°50W 30 E3
Bear L. *U.S.A.* 41°59N 111°21W 110 B4
Beardmore Glacier *Antarctica* 84°30S 170°0E 55 E11
Beardstown *U.S.A.* 40°1N 90°26W 112 E2
Béarn *France* 43°20N 0°30W 66 E3
Bearsden *U.K.* 55°55N 4°21W 20 C7
Bearsted *U.K.* 51°16N 0°35E 25 D10
Beatrice *U.S.A.* 40°16N 96°45W 111 B7
Beattock *U.K.* 55°20N 3°28W 21 D9
Beauce, Plaine de la *France* 48°10N 1°45E 66 B4
Beaufort Sea *Arctic* 72°0N 140°0W 104 B5
Beaufort West *S. Africa* 32°18S 22°36E 97 L4
Beauharnois *Canada* 45°20N 73°52W 113 C11
Beaulieu *U.K.* 50°48N 1°27W 24 E6
Beauly *U.K.* 57°30N 4°28W 19 H9
Beauly → *U.K.* 57°29N 4°27W 19 H9

Beauly Firth *U.K.* 57°30N 4°20W 19 H9
Beaumaris *U.K.* 53°16N 4°6W 26 A5
Beaumont *U.S.A.* 30°5N 94°6W 111 D8
Beaune *France* 47°2N 4°50E 66 C6
Beauvais *France* 49°25N 2°8E 66 B5
Beaver → *Canada* 55°26N 107°45W 108 D9
Beaver Creek *Canada* 63°0N 141°0W 108 C5
Beaver Dam *U.S.A.* 43°28N 88°50W 112 D3
Beaver Falls *U.S.A.* 40°46N 80°20W 112 E7
Beaver I. *U.S.A.* 45°40N 85°33W 112 C5
Beawar *India* 26°3N 74°18E 84 F9
Bebedouro *Brazil* 21°0S 48°25W 122 D1
Bebington *U.K.* 53°22N 3°0W 23 F3
Beccles *U.K.* 52°27N 1°35E 25 B12
Béchar *Algeria* 31°38N 2°18W 94 B5
Beckermet *U.K.* 54°27N 3°30W 22 D1
Beckfoot *U.K.* 54°50N 3°24W 22 C2
Beckingham *U.K.* 53°24N 0°50W 23 F7
Beckley *U.S.A.* 37°47N 81°11W 112 G7
Bedale *U.K.* 54°18N 1°36W 22 D5
Beddgelert *U.K.* 53°1N 4°6W 26 A5
Bedford *U.K.* 52°8N 0°28W 25 B8
Bedford *Ind., U.S.A.* 38°52N 86°29W 112 F4
Bedford *Va., U.S.A.* 37°20N 79°31W 112 G8
Bedford □ *U.K.* 52°4N 0°28W 25 B8
Bedford Level *U.K.* 52°32N 0°7W 25 A8
Bedlington *U.K.* 55°8N 1°35W 22 B5
Bedworth *U.K.* 52°29N 1°28W 24 B6
Beef I. *Br. Virgin Is.* 18°26N 64°30W 115 e
Beeford *U.K.* 53°58N 0°17W 23 E8
Beer *U.K.* 50°41N 3°6W 27 F7
Be'er Sheva *Israel* 31°15N 34°48E 86 D3
Beeston *U.K.* 52°56N 1°14W 23 G6
Bei Jiang → *China* 23°2N 112°58E 79 G11
Bei Shan *China* 41°30N 96°0E 78 C8
Bei'an *China* 48°10N 126°20E 79 B14
Beighton *U.K.* 53°21N 1°20W 23 F6
Beihai *China* 21°28N 109°6E 79 G10
Beijing *China* 39°53N 116°21E 79 D12
Beira *Mozam.* 19°50S 34°52E 97 H6
Beirut *Lebanon* 33°53N 35°31E 86 C3
Beitbridge *Zimbabwe* 22°12S 30°0E 97 J6
Beith *U.K.* 55°45N 4°38W 20 C6
Béja *Tunisia* 36°43N 9°12E 95 A7
Bejaïa *Algeria* 36°42N 5°2E 94 A7
Békéscsaba *Hungary* 46°40N 21°5E 65 E11
Bela *Pakistan* 26°12N 66°20E 84 F5
Belarus ■ *Europe* 53°30N 27°0E 70 D4
Belau = Palau ■ *Palau* 7°30N 134°30E 102 G5
Belbroughton *U.K.* 52°24N 2°7W 24 B4
Belcher Chan. *Canada* 77°15N 95°0W 109 B10
Belcher Is. *Canada* 56°15N 78°45W 109 D12
Beledweyne *Somali Rep.* 4°30N 45°5E 89 G4
Belém *Brazil* 1°20S 48°30W 120 C5
Belep, Îs. *N. Cal.* 19°45S 163°40E 99 D11
Belet Uen = Beledweyne *Somali Rep.* 4°30N 45°5E 89 G4
Belfast *U.K.* 54°37N 5°56W 29 B10
Belfast *U.S.A.* 44°26N 69°1W 113 C13
Belfast L. *U.K.* 54°40N 5°50W 29 B10
Belford *U.K.* 55°36N 1°49W 22 A5
Belfort *France* 47°38N 6°50E 66 C7
Belgaum *India* 15°55N 74°35E 84 M9
Belgium ■ *Europe* 50°30N 5°0E 64 C3
Belgorod *Russia* 50°35N 36°35E 71 D6
Belgrade *Serbia* 44°50N 20°37E 69 B9
Belitung *Indonesia* 3°10S 107°50E 82 E3
Belize ■ *Cent. Amer.* 17°0N 88°30W 114 D7
Belize City *Belize* 17°25N 88°10W 114 D7
Bell Peninsula *Canada* 63°50N 82°0W 109 C11
Bell Ville *Argentina* 32°40S 62°40W 121 F3
Bella Coola *Canada* 52°25N 126°40W 108 D7
Bellaire *U.S.A.* 40°1N 80°45W 112 E7
Bellary *India* 15°10N 76°56E 84 M10
Belle Fourche → *U.S.A.* 44°26N 102°18W 110 B6
Belle-Île *France* 47°20N 3°10W 66 C2
Belle Isle *Canada* 51°57N 55°25W 109 D14
Belle Isle, Str. of *Canada* 51°30N 56°30W 109 D14
Bellefontaine *U.S.A.* 40°22N 83°46W 112 E6
Belleplaine *Barbados* 13°15N 59°34W 115 g
Belleville *Canada* 44°10N 77°23W 109 E12
Belleville *U.S.A.* 38°31N 89°59W 112 F3
Bellingham *U.K.* 55°9N 2°16W 22 B4
Bellingham *U.S.A.* 48°46N 122°29W 110 A2
Bellingshausen Sea *Antarctica* 66°0S 80°0W 55 C17
Bellinzona *Switz.* 46°11N 9°1E 64 E5
Belmonte *Brazil* 16°0S 39°0W 122 C3
Belmopan *Belize* 17°18N 88°30W 114 D7
Belmullet *Ireland* 54°14N 9°58W 28 C2
Belo Horizonte *Brazil* 19°55S 43°56W 122 C2
Belo Jardim *Brazil* 8°20S 36°26W 122 A3
Belogorsk *Russia* 51°0N 128°20E 77 D13
Beloit *U.S.A.* 42°31N 89°2W 112 D3
Belomorsk *Russia* 64°35N 34°54E 70 B5
Beloretsk *Russia* 53°58N 58°24E 70 D10
Beloye, L. *Russia* 60°10N 37°35E 70 B6
Belper *U.K.* 53°2N 1°29W 23 F6
Belsay *U.K.* 55°6N 1°51W 22 B5
Belton *N. Lincs., U.K.* 53°33N 0°48W 23 E7
Belton *Norfolk, U.K.* 52°35N 1°40E 25 A12
Beltsy *Moldova* 47°48N 27°58E 65 E14
Belturbet *Ireland* 54°6N 7°26W 28 C7
Belukha *Russia* 49°50N 86°50E 78 B6
Belvidere *U.S.A.* 42°15N 88°50W 112 D3
Bembridge *U.K.* 50°41N 1°5W 24 E6
Bemidji *U.S.A.* 47°28N 94°53W 111 A8
Ben Cruachan *U.K.* 56°26N 5°8W 20 B5
Ben Dearg *U.K.* 57°47N 4°56W 19 G8
Ben Hope *U.K.* 58°25N 4°36W 19 F8
Ben Lawers *U.K.* 56°32N 4°14W 20 B7
Ben Lomond *U.K.* 56°11N 4°38W 20 B6
Ben Macdhui *U.K.* 57°4N 3°40W 19 H11
Ben Mhor *U.K.* 57°15N 7°18W 18 H3
Ben More *Argyll & Bute, U.K.* 56°26N 6°1W 20 B4
Ben More *Stirling, U.K.* 56°23N 4°32W 20 B6
Ben More Assynt *U.K.* 58°8N 4°52W 19 F8
Ben Nevis *U.K.* 56°48N 5°1W 18 J7
Ben Vorlich *U.K.* 56°21N 4°14W 20 B7
Ben Wyvis *U.K.* 57°40N 4°35W 19 G8
Benares = Varanasi *India* 25°22N 83°0E 85 G13
Benbecula *U.K.* 57°26N 7°21W 18 H3
Bend *U.S.A.* 44°4N 121°19W 110 B2

Benderloch *U.K.* 56°30N 5°22W 20 A5
Bendigo *Australia* 36°40S 144°15E 98 H7
Benevento *Italy* 41°8N 14°45E 68 D6
Bengal, Bay of *Ind. Oc.* 15°0N 90°0E 85 M17
Bengbu *China* 32°58N 117°20E 79 E12
Benghazi *Libya* 32°11N 20°3E 95 B10
Bengkulu *Indonesia* 3°50S 102°12E 82 E2
Benguela *Angola* 12°37S 13°25E 97 G2
Beni → *Bolivia* 10°23S 65°24W 120 D3
Beni Mellal *Morocco* 32°21N 6°21W 94 B4
Beni Suef *Egypt* 29°5N 31°6E 95 C12
Benidorm *Spain* 38°33N 0°9W 67 C5
Benin ■ *Africa* 10°0N 2°0E 94 G6
Benin, Bight of *W. Afr.* 5°0N 3°0E 94 H6
Benin City *Nigeria* 6°20N 5°31E 94 G7
Benington *U.K.* 53°0N 0°5E 23 F9
Benjamin Constant *Brazil* 4°40S 70°15W 120 C2
Benoni *S. Africa* 26°11S 28°18E 97 K5
Benson *U.K.* 51°37N 1°6W 24 C6
Bentley *Hants., U.K.* 51°12N 0°52W 25 D7
Bentley *S. Yorks., U.K.* 53°33N 1°8W 23 E6
Bentley Subglacial Trench *Antarctica* 80°0S 115°0W 55 E14
Benton *U.S.A.* 38°0N 88°55W 112 G3
Benton Harbor *U.S.A.* 42°6N 86°27W 112 D4
Benue → *Nigeria* 7°48N 6°46E 94 G7
Benxi *China* 41°20N 123°48E 79 C13
Beppu *Japan* 33°15N 131°30E 81 G2
Berber *Sudan* 18°0N 34°0E 95 E12
Berbera *Somali Rep.* 10°30N 45°2E 89 E4
Berbérati *C.A.R.* 4°15N 15°40E 96 D3
Berbice → *Guyana* 6°20N 57°32W 120 B4
Berdyansk *Ukraine* 46°45N 36°50E 71 E6
Berdychiv *Ukraine* 49°57N 28°30E 71 E4
Bere Alston *U.K.* 50°29N 4°13W 27 G5
Bere Regis *U.K.* 50°45N 2°14W 24 E4
Berea *U.S.A.* 37°34N 84°17W 112 G5
Berens → *Canada* 52°25N 97°2W 108 D10
Berezina → *Belarus* 52°33N 30°14E 70 D5
Bereznik *Russia* 62°51N 42°40E 70 B7
Berezniki *Russia* 59°24N 56°46E 70 C10
Bérgamo *Italy* 45°41N 9°43E 68 B3
Bergen *Norway* 60°20N 5°20E 63 E5
Bergerac *France* 44°51N 0°30E 66 D4
Bering Sea *Pac. Oc.* 58°0N 171°0W 104 D2
Bering Strait *Pac. Oc.* 65°30N 169°0W 108 C3
Berkeley *U.S.A.* 51°41N 2°27W 24 C4
Berkhamsted *U.K.* 51°45N 0°33W 25 C7
Berkner I. *Antarctica* 79°30S 50°0W 55 D18
Berkshire Downs *U.K.* 51°33N 1°29W 24 C6
Berlin *Germany* 52°31N 13°23E 64 B7
Berlin *U.S.A.* 44°28N 71°11W 113 C12
Bermejo → *Argentina* 26°51S 58°23W 121 E4
Bermuda □ *Atl. Oc.* 32°18N 64°45W 52 C6
Bern *Switz.* 46°57N 7°28E 64 E4
Berneray *U.K.* 57°43N 7°11W 18 G3
Berry *France* 46°50N 2°0E 66 C5
Berry Hd. *U.K.* 50°24N 3°29W 27 G7
Bertraghboy B. *Ireland* 53°22N 9°54W 30 B3
Berwick *U.S.A.* 41°3N 76°14W 112 E9
Berwick-upon-Tweed *U.K.* 55°46N 2°0W 22 A5
Berwyn Mts. *U.K.* 52°54N 3°26W 26 B7
Besançon *France* 47°15N 6°2E 66 C7
Bessarabiya *Moldova* 47°0N 28°10E 65 E15
Bessemer *U.S.A.* 46°29N 90°3W 112 B2
Bethel *U.S.A.* 60°48N 161°45W 108 C3
Bethesda *U.K.* 53°10N 4°3W 26 A5
Bethlehem *S. Africa* 28°14S 28°18E 97 K5
Bethlehem *U.S.A.* 40°37N 75°23W 113 E10
Béthune *France* 50°30N 2°38E 66 A5
Betim *Brazil* 19°58S 44°7W 122 C2
Bettiah *India* 26°48N 84°33E 85 F14
Betul *India* 21°58N 77°59E 84 J10
Betws-y-Coed *U.K.* 53°5N 3°48W 26 A6
Beverley *U.K.* 53°51N 0°26W 23 E8
Bewdley *U.K.* 52°23N 2°19W 24 B4
Bexhill *U.K.* 50°51N 0°29E 25 E9
Bexley □ *U.K.* 51°27N 0°9E 25 D9
Beyneu *Kazakhstan* 45°18N 55°9E 71 E10
Beypazari *Turkey* 40°10N 31°56E 71 F5
Beyşehir Gölü *Turkey* 37°41N 31°33E 71 G5
Béziers *France* 43°20N 3°12E 66 E5
Bhagalpur *India* 25°10N 87°0E 85 G15
Bhaktapur *Nepal* 27°38N 85°24E 85 F14
Bhanrer Ra. *India* 23°40N 79°45E 84 H11
Bharatpur *India* 27°15N 77°30E 84 F10
Bharuch *India* 21°47N 73°0E 84 J8
Bhatpara *India* 22°50N 88°25E 85 H16
Bhavnagar *India* 21°45N 72°10E 84 J8
Bhilainagar-Durg *India* 21°13N 81°26E 85 J12
Bhilwara *India* 25°25N 74°38E 84 G9
Bhima → *India* 16°25N 77°17E 84 L10
Bhind *India* 26°30N 78°46E 84 F11
Bhiwandi *India* 19°20N 73°0E 84 K8
Bhiwani *India* 28°50N 76°9E 84 E10
Bhopal *India* 23°20N 77°30E 84 H10
Bhubaneshwar *India* 20°15N 85°50E 85 J14
Bhuj *India* 23°15N 69°49E 84 H6
Bhusawal *India* 21°3N 75°46E 84 J9
Bhutan ■ *Asia* 27°25N 90°30E 85 F17
Biała Podlaska *Poland* 52°4N 23°6E 65 B12
Białystok *Poland* 53°10N 23°10E 65 B12
Biarritz *France* 43°29N 1°33W 66 E3
Bibury *U.K.* 51°45N 1°49W 24 C5
Bicester *U.K.* 51°54N 1°9W 24 C6
Bicton *U.K.* 52°44N 2°48W 23 G3
Bida *Nigeria* 9°3N 5°58E 94 G7
Biddeford *U.S.A.* 43°30N 70°28W 113 D12
Biddenden *U.K.* 51°7N 0°40E 25 D10
Biddulph *U.K.* 53°7N 2°10W 23 F4
Bideford *U.K.* 51°1N 4°13W 27 E5
Bideford Bay *U.K.* 51°5N 4°20W 27 E5
Bidford-on-Avon *U.K.* 52°11N 1°50W 24 B5
Bié Plateau *Angola* 12°0S 16°0E 97 G3
Biel *Switz.* 47°8N 7°14E 64 E4
Bielefeld *Germany* 52°1N 8°33E 64 B5
Biella *Italy* 45°34N 8°3E 68 B3
Bielsko-Biała *Poland* 49°50N 19°2E 65 D10
Bien Hoa *Vietnam* 10°57N 106°49E 82 B3
Bienville, L. *Canada* 55°5N 72°40W 109 D12
Big Belt Mts. *U.S.A.* 46°30N 111°25W 110 A4

Big Rapids — Burton upon Stather

Big Rapids U.S.A. 43°42N 85°29W 112 D5
Big Sioux → U.S.A. 42°29N 96°27W 111 B7
Big Spring U.S.A. 32°15N 101°28W 110 D6
Big Trout L. Canada 53°40N 90°0W 109 D11
Bigbury U.K. 50°18N 3°53W 27 G6
Bigbury B. U.K. 50°16N 3°54W 27 G6
Biggar Canada 52°4N 108°0W 108 D9
Biggar U.K. 55°38N 3°32W 21 C8
Biggleswade U.K. 52°5N 0°14W 25 B8
Bighorn → U.S.A. 46°10N 107°28W 110 A5
Bighorn Mts. U.S.A. 44°25N 107°0W 110 B5
Bihar □ India 25°5N 85°40E 85 G14
Bihar India 25°0N 86°0E 85 G15
Bijagós, Arquipélago dos
  Guinea-Biss. 11°15N 16°10W 94 F2
Bijapur India 16°50N 75°55E 84 L9
Bikaner India 28°2N 73°18E 84 E8
Bikin Russia 46°50N 134°20E 79 B15
Bikini Atoll Marshall Is. 12°0N 167°30E 102 F8
Bila Tserkva Ukraine 49°45N 30°10E 65 D16
Bilaspur India 22°2N 82°15E 85 H13
Bilbao Spain 43°16N 2°56W 67 A4
Bilecik Turkey 40°5N 30°5E 71 F5
Bilhorod-Dnistrovskyy
  Ukraine 46°11N 30°23E 71 E5
Billericay U.K. 51°38N 0°26E 25 C9
Billesdon U.K. 52°38N 0°54W 23 G7
Billingham U.K. 54°36N 1°17W 22 C6
Billinghay U.K. 53°5N 0°15W 23 F8
Billings U.S.A. 45°47N 108°30W 110 A5
Billingshurst U.K. 51°2N 0°27W 25 D8
Bilma Niger 18°50N 13°30E 95 E8
Biloxi U.S.A. 30°24N 88°53W 111 D9
Bilston U.K. 52°34N 2°4W 23 G4
Bimini Is. Bahamas 25°42N 79°25W 115 B9
Binbrook U.K. 53°26N 0°10W 23 F8
Bingham U.K. 52°57N 0°58W 23 G7
Binghamton U.S.A. 42°6N 75°55W 113 D10
Bingley U.K. 53°51N 1°50W 23 E5
Bioko Eq. Guin. 3°30N 8°40E 96 D1
Biratnagar Nepal 26°27N 87°17E 85 F15
Birchington U.K. 51°22N 1°19E 25 D11
Birdlip U.K. 51°50N 2°5W 24 C4
Birkdale U.K. 53°38N 3°1W 23 E2
Birkenhead U.K. 53°23N 3°2W 23 F2
Birmingham U.K. 52°29N 1°52W 23 G5
Birmingham U.S.A. 33°31N 86°48W 111 D9
Birmingham Int. ✈ (BHX)
  U.K. 52°26N 1°45W 23 H5
Birnin Kebbi Nigeria 12°32N 4°12E 94 F6
Birobidzhan Russia 48°50N 132°50E 79 B15
Birr Ireland 53°6N 7°54W 30 B7
Birtley Northumberland, U.K. 55°6N 2°12W 22 B4
Birtley Tyne & W., U.K. 54°54N 1°34W 22 C5
Biscay, B. of Atl. Oc. 45°0N 2°0W 66 D1
Bishkek Kyrgyzstan 42°54N 74°46E 78 C3
Bishop Auckland U.K. 54°39N 1°40W 22 C5
Bishop's Castle U.K. 52°30N 2°59W 23 H3
Bishop's Cleeve U.K. 51°57N 2°3W 24 C4
Bishop's Frome U.K. 52°8N 2°29W 24 B4
Bishop's Nympton U.K. 51°0N 3°47W 27 F6
Bishop's Stortford U.K. 51°52N 0°10E 25 C9
Bishop's Waltham U.K. 50°57N 1°11W 24 E6
Bishopsteignton U.K. 50°33N 3°33W 27 F6
Bishopstoke U.K. 50°58N 1°19W 24 E6
Biskra Algeria 34°50N 5°44E 94 B7
Bismarck U.S.A. 46°48N 100°47W 110 A6
Bismarck Arch. Papua N. G. 2°30S 150°0E 98 A9
Bissau Guinea-Biss. 11°45N 15°45W 94 F2
Bitola Macedonia 41°1N 21°20E 69 D9
Bitterfontein S. Africa 31°1S 18°32E 97 L3
Bitterroot Range U.S.A. 46°0N 114°20W 110 A4
Bitton U.K. 51°25N 2°27W 24 D4
Biu Nigeria 10°40N 12°3E 95 F8
Biwa-Ko Japan 35°15N 136°10E 81 F5
Biysk Russia 52°40N 85°0E 76 D9
Bizerte Tunisia 37°15N 9°50E 95 A7
Blaby U.K. 52°35N 1°10W 23 G6
Black Combe U.K. 54°16N 3°20W 22 D2
Black Esk → U.K. 55°12N 3°11W 21 D9
Black Forest = Schwarzwald
  Germany 48°30N 8°20E 64 D5
Black Hd. Ireland 53°9N 9°16W 30 B4
Black Hd. U.K. 50°0N 5°7W 27 H3
Black Hills U.S.A. 44°0N 103°45W 110 B6
Black Isle U.K. 57°35N 4°16W 19 G9
Black Mts. U.K. 51°55N 3°7W 26 D7
Black Range U.S.A. 33°15N 107°50W 110 D5
Black River Jamaica 18°0N 77°50W 114 a
Black River Falls U.S.A. 44°18N 90°51W 112 C2
Black Rock Barbados 13°7N 59°37W 115 g
Black Sea Eurasia 43°30N 35°0E 71 F6
Blackburn U.K. 53°45N 2°29W 23 E4
Blackdown Hills U.K. 50°57N 3°15W 24 E2
Blackmoor Vale U.K. 50°54N 2°28W 24 E4
Blackpool U.K. 53°49N 3°3W 23 E2
Blackrock Ireland 53°18N 6°11W 31 B10
Blacksburg U.S.A. 37°14N 80°25W 112 G7
Blacksod B. Ireland 54°6N 10°0W 28 C1
Blackwater → Meath, Ireland 53°39N 6°41W 29 D8
Blackwater → Waterford,
  Ireland 52°4N 7°52W 30 D7
Blackwater → Armagh, U.K. 54°31N 6°35W 29 B8
Blackwater → Essex, U.K. 51°44N 0°53E 25 C10
Blaenau Ffestiniog U.K. 53°0N 3°56W 26 B6
Blaenavon U.K. 51°46N 3°5W 26 D7
Blagdon U.K. 51°20N 2°43W 24 D3
Blagoevgrad Bulgaria 42°2N 23°5E 69 C10
Blagoveshchensk Russia 50°20N 127°30E 79 A14
Blair Atholl U.K. 56°46N 3°50E 19 J10
Blairgowrie U.K. 56°35N 3°21W 21 A9
Blakeney Glouce., U.K. 51°46N 2°28W 24 C4
Blakeney Norfolk, U.K. 52°58N 1°1E 25 A11
Blanc, Mont Europe 45°48N 6°50E 66 D7
Blanca, B. Argentina 39°10S 61°30W 121 F3
Blanca Peak U.S.A. 37°35N 105°29W 110 C5
Blanco, C. Costa Rica 9°34N 85°8W 104 J11
Blanco, C. U.S.A. 42°51N 124°34W 110 B2
Blandford Forum U.K. 50°51N 2°9W 24 E4
Blanquilla Venezuela 11°51N 64°37W 115 E12

Blantyre Malawi 15°45S 35°0E 97 H6
Blarney Ireland 51°56N 8°33W 30 E5
Blaydon U.K. 54°58N 1°42W 22 C5
Blean U.K. 51°18N 1°3E 25 D11
Bleasdale Moors U.K. 53°55N 2°35W 23 E3
Blenheim N.Z. 41°38S 173°57E 99 J13
Bletchingdon U.K. 51°51N 1°15W 24 C6
Bletchley U.K. 51°59N 0°44W 25 C7
Blida Algeria 36°30N 2°49E 94 A6
Blisworth U.K. 52°10N 0°56W 25 B7
Blitar Indonesia 8°5S 112°11E 82 F4
Blockley U.K. 52°1N 1°44W 24 B5
Bloemfontein S. Africa 29°6S 26°7E 97 K5
Blofield U.K. 52°38N 1°26E 25 A11
Blois France 47°35N 1°20E 66 C4
Bloody Foreland Ireland 55°10N 8°17W 28 A5
Bloomington Ill., U.S.A. 40°28N 89°0W 112 E3
Bloomington Ind., U.S.A. 39°10N 86°32W 112 F4
Bloomsburg U.S.A. 41°0N 76°27W 112 E9
Bloxham U.K. 52°1N 1°21W 24 B6
Blue Mountain Pk. Jamaica 18°3N 76°36W 114 a
Blue Mt. U.S.A. 40°30N 76°30W 112 E9
Blue Mts. Jamaica 18°3N 76°36W 114 a
Blue Mts. U.S.A. 45°0N 118°20W 110 A3
Blue Nile → Sudan 15°38N 32°31E 95 E12
Blue Ridge U.S.A. 36°40N 80°50W 111 C10
Blue Stack Mts. Ireland 54°42N 8°12W 28 B5
Bluefield U.S.A. 37°15N 81°17W 112 G7
Bluefields Nic. 12°20N 83°50W 115 E8
Blumenau Brazil 27°0S 49°0W 121 E5
Blundeston U.K. 52°31N 1°42E 25 A12
Blyth Northumberland, U.K. 55°8N 1°31W 22 B5
Blyth Notts., U.K. 53°22N 1°3W 23 F6
Blyth → U.K. 55°8N 1°33W 22 B5
Blyth Bridge U.K. 55°42N 3°22W 21 C9
Blyton U.K. 53°27N 0°42W 23 F7
Bo S. Leone 7°55N 11°50W 94 G3
Bo Hai China 39°0N 119°0E 79 D12
Boa Vista Brazil 2°48N 60°30W 120 B3
Bobcaygeon Canada 44°33N 78°33W 112 C8
Bobo-Dioulasso Burkina Faso 11°8N 4°13W 94 F5
Bóbr → Poland 52°4N 15°4E 64 B8
Bochum Germany 51°28N 7°13E 64 C4
Boddam U.K. 59°56N 1°17W 18 C15
Bodiam U.K. 51°0N 0°34E 25 D10
Bodinnick U.K. 50°20N 4°38W 27 G4
Bodmin U.K. 50°28N 4°43W 27 G4
Bodmin Moor U.K. 50°33N 4°36W 27 F4
Bodø Norway 67°17N 14°24E 63 D6
Bodrog → Hungary 48°11N 21°22E 65 D11
Bodrum Turkey 37°3N 27°30E 71 G4
Bogalusa U.S.A. 30°47N 89°52W 111 D9
Bogda Shan China 43°35N 89°40E 78 C6
Boggeragh Mts. Ireland 52°2N 8°55W 30 D5
Bognor Regis U.K. 50°47N 0°40W 25 E7
Bogor Indonesia 6°36S 106°48E 82 F3
Bogotá Colombia 4°34N 74°0W 120 B2
Bogra Bangla. 24°51N 89°22E 85 G16
Böhmerwald Germany 49°8N 13°14E 64 D7
Bohol Sea Phil. 9°0N 124°0E 83 C6
Boise U.S.A. 43°37N 116°13W 110 B3
Bole China 44°55N 81°37E 78 B5
Bolívar, Pico Venezuela 8°32N 71°2W 115 F10
Bolivia ■ S. Amer. 17°6S 64°0W 120 D3
Bollington U.K. 53°18N 2°6W 23 F4
Bolney U.K. 50°59N 0°12W 25 E8
Bologna Italy 44°29N 11°20E 68 B4
Bologoye Russia 57°55N 34°5E 70 C5
Bolsena, L. di Italy 42°36N 11°56E 68 C4
Bolsover U.K. 53°14N 1°16W 23 F6
Bolt Head U.K. 50°12N 3°48W 27 G6
Bolt Tail U.K. 50°14N 3°52W 27 G6
Bolton U.K. 53°35N 2°26W 23 E4
Bolton Abbey U.K. 53°59N 1°53W 23 E5
Bolton by Bowland U.K. 53°56N 2°20W 23 E4
Bolton le Sands U.K. 54°6N 2°48W 22 D3
Bolu Turkey 40°45N 31°35E 71 F5
Bolvadin Turkey 38°45N 31°4E 71 G5
Bolzano Italy 46°31N 11°22E 68 A4
Bom Despacho Brazil 19°43S 45°15W 122 C1
Bom Jesus da Lapa Brazil 13°15S 43°25W 122 B2
Boma Dem. Rep. of the Congo 5°50S 13°4E 96 F2
Bombala Australia 36°56S 149°15E 98 H8
Bombay = Mumbai India 18°56N 72°50E 84 K8
Bomu → C.A.R. 4°40N 22°30E 96 D4
Bon, C. Tunisia 37°1N 11°2E 90 C5
Bonaire Neth. Ant. 12°10N 68°15W 115 E11
Bonar Bridge U.K. 57°54N 4°20W 19 G9
Bonavista Canada 48°40N 53°5W 109 E14
Bonchester Bridge U.K. 55°24N 2°39W 21 D10
Bonchurch U.K. 50°37N 1°11W 24 E6
Bo'ness U.K. 56°1N 3°37W 21 B8
Bongor Chad 10°35N 15°20E 95 F9
Bongos, Massif des C.A.R. 8°40N 22°25E 96 C4
Bonifacio France 41°24N 9°10E 66 F8
Bonn Germany 50°46N 7°6E 64 C4
Bonny, Bight of Africa 3°30N 9°20E 96 D1
Bonnyrigg U.K. 55°53N 3°6W 21 C9
Boonville U.S.A. 38°3N 87°16W 112 F4
Boosaaso Somali Rep. 11°12N 49°18E 89 E4
Boot U.K. 54°24N 3°13W 22 D2
Boothia, Gulf of Canada 71°0N 90°0W 109 B11
Boothia Pen. Canada 71°0N 94°0W 108 B10
Bootle Cumb., U.K. 54°18N 3°22W 22 D2
Bootle Mersey., U.K. 53°28N 3°1W 23 F2
Borås Sweden 57°43N 12°56E 63 F6
Bordeaux France 44°50N 0°36W 66 D3
Borden I. Canada 78°30N 111°30W 109 B8
Borden Pen. Canada 73°0N 83°0W 109 B11
Bordon U.K. 51°8N 0°52W 25 D7
Borehamwood U.K. 51°40N 0°15W 25 D8
Boreland U.K. 55°13N 3°17W 21 D9
Borger U.S.A. 35°39N 101°24W 110 C6
Borhoyn Tal Mongolia 43°50N 111°58E 79 C11
Borisoglebsk Russia 51°27N 42°5E 71 D7
Borkou Chad 18°15N 18°50E 95 E9
Borneo E. Indies 1°0N 115°0E 82 D5
Bornholm Denmark 55°10N 15°0E 63 F7

Borohoro Shan China 44°6N 83°10E 78 C5
Boroughbridge U.K. 54°6N 1°24W 22 D6
Borovichi Russia 58°25N 33°55E 70 C5
Borrowdale U.K. 54°31N 3°10W 22 C2
Borth U.K. 52°29N 4°2W 26 C5
Borüjerd Iran 33°55N 48°50E 86 C7
Borzya Russia 50°24N 116°31E 79 A12
Bosbury U.K. 52°5N 2°26W 24 B4
Boscastle U.K. 50°41N 4°42W 27 F4
Boscobelle Barbados 13°17N 59°35W 115 g
Bose China 23°53N 106°35E 78 G10
Bosham U.K. 50°49N 0°51W 25 E7
Bosnia-Herzegovina ■ Europe 44°0N 18°0E 69 B7
Bosporus Turkey 41°5N 29°3E 71 F4
Bossangoa C.A.R. 6°35N 17°30E 96 C3
Bosten Hu China 41°55N 87°40E 78 C6
Boston U.K. 52°59N 0°2W 23 G8
Boston U.S.A. 42°22N 71°3W 113 D12
Bothel U.K. 54°45N 3°15W 22 C2
Bothnia, G. of Europe 62°0N 20°0E 63 E8
Botlete → Botswana 20°10S 23°15E 97 J4
Botoşani Romania 47°42N 26°41E 65 E14
Botswana ■ Africa 22°0S 24°0E 97 J4
Bottesford U.K. 52°57N 0°47W 23 G7
Botucatu Brazil 22°55S 48°30W 122 D1
Bou Saâda Algeria 35°11N 4°9E 94 A6
Bouaké Ivory C. 7°40N 5°2W 94 G4
Bouar C.A.R. 6°0N 15°40E 96 C3
Bouârfa Morocco 32°32N 1°58W 94 B5
Bougainville I. Papua N. G. 6°0S 155°0E 99 B10
Bouillante Guadeloupe 16°8N 61°46W 114 b
Boulder U.S.A. 40°1N 105°17W 110 B5
Boulogne-sur-Mer France 50°42N 1°36E 66 A4
Bounty Is. Pac. Oc. 48°0S 178°30E 102 M9
Bourbonnais France 46°28N 3°0E 66 C5
Bourg-en-Bresse France 46°13N 5°12E 66 C6
Bourges France 47°9N 2°25E 66 C5
Bourgogne □ France 47°0N 4°50E 66 C6
Bourke Australia 30°8S 145°55E 98 G8
Bourne U.K. 52°47N 0°22W 23 G8
Bournemouth U.K. 50°43N 1°52W 24 E5
Bourton-on-the-Water U.K. 51°52N 1°45W 24 C5
Bouvet I. Antarctica 54°26S 3°24E 52 G10
Bovey Tracey U.K. 50°36N 3°41W 27 F6
Bow → Canada 49°57N 111°41W 108 D8
Bowes U.K. 54°32N 1°59W 22 C5
Bowland, Forest of U.K. 54°0N 2°30W 23 E3
Bowling Green Ky., U.S.A. 36°59N 86°27W 112 G4
Bowling Green Ohio, U.S.A. 41°23N 83°39W 112 E6
Bowmore U.K. 55°45N 6°17W 20 C3
Bowness-on-Solway U.K. 54°57N 3°12W 22 C2
Bowness-on-Windermere
  U.K. 54°22N 2°55W 22 D3
Box U.K. 51°25N 2°15W 24 D4
Box Hill U.K. 51°15N 0°16W 25 D8
Boyle Ireland 53°59N 8°18W 28 D5
Boyne → Ireland 53°43N 6°15W 29 D9
Boyoma, Chutes
  Dem. Rep. of the Congo 0°35N 25°23E 90 F6
Bozeat U.K. 52°14N 0°40W 25 B7
Bozeman U.S.A. 45°41N 111°2W 110 A4
Bozoum C.A.R. 6°25N 16°35E 96 C3
Brač Croatia 43°20N 16°40E 68 C7
Bracadale, L. U.K. 57°20N 6°30W 18 H4
Bracebridge Canada 45°2N 79°19W 112 C8
Bracebridge Heath U.K. 53°12N 0°32W 23 F7
Bräcke Sweden 62°45N 15°26E 63 E7
Brackley U.K. 52°2N 1°8W 24 B6
Bracknell U.K. 51°25N 0°43W 25 D7
Bradford U.K. 53°47N 1°45W 23 E5
Bradford U.S.A. 41°58N 78°38W 112 E8
Bradford on Avon U.K. 51°21N 2°14W 24 D4
Brading U.K. 50°41N 1°8W 24 E6
Bradwell-on-Sea U.K. 51°43N 0°56E 25 C10
Bradworthy U.K. 50°53N 4°24W 27 F5
Braemar U.K. 57°2N 3°26W 19 H11
Braga Portugal 41°35N 8°25W 67 B1
Bragança Brazil 1°0S 47°2W 120 C5
Bragança Paulista Brazil 22°55S 46°32W 122 D1
Brahmanbaria Bangla. 23°58N 91°15E 85 H17
Brahmani → India 20°39N 86°46E 85 J15
Brahmapur India 19°15N 84°54E 85 K14
Brahmaputra → Asia 23°40N 90°35E 85 H17
Braich-y-pwll U.K. 52°47N 4°46W 26 B4
Brăila Romania 45°19N 27°59E 65 F14
Brailsford U.K. 52°58N 1°35W 23 G5
Brainerd U.S.A. 46°22N 94°12W 111 A8
Braintree U.K. 51°53N 0°34E 25 C10
Bramford U.K. 52°4N 1°7E 25 B11
Brampton Canada 43°45N 79°45W 112 D8
Brampton Cambs., U.K. 52°20N 0°14W 25 B8
Brampton Cumb., U.K. 54°57N 2°44W 22 C3
Brancaster U.K. 52°58N 0°38E 25 A10
Branco → Brazil 1°20S 61°50W 120 C3
Brandenburg Germany 52°25N 12°33E 64 B7
Brandenburg □ Germany 52°50N 13°0E 64 B6
Branderburgh U.K. 57°43N 3°17W 19 G11
Brandon Canada 49°50N 99°57W 108 E10
Brandon Durham, U.K. 54°46N 1°37W 22 C5
Brandon Suffolk, U.K. 52°27N 0°38E 25 B10
Brandon B. Ireland 52°17N 10°8W 30 D2
Brandon Mt. Ireland 52°15N 10°15W 30 D2
Branston U.K. 53°12N 0°27W 23 F8
Bras d'Or L. Canada 45°50N 60°50W 113 C17
Brasília Brazil 15°47S 47°55W 122 C1
Braşov Romania 45°38N 25°35E 65 F13
Bratislava Slovak Rep. 48°10N 17°7E 65 D9
Bratsk Russia 56°10N 101°30E 77 D11
Bratsk Res. Russia 56°15N 101°45E 77 D11
Brattleboro U.S.A. 42°51N 72°34W 113 D11
Braunschweig Germany 52°15N 10°31E 64 B6
Braunton U.K. 51°7N 4°10W 27 E5
Bray Ireland 53°13N 6°7W 31 B10
Bray → U.K. 51°30N 0°14W 25 D8
Brazil U.S.A. 39°32N 87°8W 112 F4
Brazil ■ S. Amer. 12°0S 50°0W 120 D4
Brazilian Highlands Brazil 18°0S 46°30W 117 E6
Brazos → U.S.A. 28°53N 95°23W 111 E7
Brazzaville Congo 4°9S 15°12E 96 E3

Breadalbane U.K. 56°30N 4°15W 20 A7
Breage U.K. 50°6N 5°20W 27 G3
Breamish → U.K. 55°35N 2°2W 22 A4
Brechin U.K. 56°44N 2°39W 19 J12
Breckland U.K. 52°30N 0°40E 25 B10
Brecon U.K. 51°57N 3°23W 26 D7
Brecon Beacons U.K. 51°53N 3°26W 26 D7
Brecon Beacons △ U.K. 51°50N 3°30W 26 D6
Breda Neths. 51°35N 4°45E 64 C3
Brede U.K. 50°56N 0°36E 25 E10
Bredon Hill U.K. 52°3N 2°2W 24 B4
Bregenz Austria 47°30N 9°45E 64 E5
Breiðafjörður Iceland 65°15N 23°15W 63 A1
Bremen Germany 53°4N 8°47E 64 B5
Bremerhaven Germany 53°33N 8°36E 64 B5
Bremerton U.S.A. 47°34N 122°37W 110 A2
Brendon Hills U.K. 51°6N 3°25W 24 D2
Brennerpass Austria 47°2N 11°30E 64 E6
Brent □ U.K. 51°33N 0°16W 25 C8
Brentwood U.K. 51°37N 0°19E 25 C9
Bréscia Italy 45°33N 10°15E 68 B4
Bressay U.K. 60°9N 1°6W 18 B15
Brest Belarus 52°10N 23°40E 65 B12
Brest France 48°24N 4°31W 66 B1
Bretagne □ France 48°10N 3°0W 66 B2
Breton Sd. U.S.A. 29°35N 89°15W 111 E9
Brewer U.S.A. 44°48N 68°46W 113 C13
Brewood U.K. 52°41N 2°9W 23 G4
Briançon France 44°54N 6°39E 66 D7
Bridestowe U.K. 50°41N 4°7W 27 F5
Bridge U.K. 51°15N 1°8E 25 D11
Bridgefield Barbados 13°9N 59°36W 115 g
Bridgend U.K. 51°30N 3°34W 27 D6
Bridgeport U.S.A. 41°11N 73°12W 113 E11
Bridgeton U.S.A. 39°26N 75°14W 113 F10
Bridgetown Barbados 13°6N 59°37W 115 g
Bridgewater Canada 44°25N 64°31W 109 E13
Bridgnorth U.K. 52°32N 2°25W 23 G4
Bridgwater U.K. 51°8N 2°59W 24 D3
Bridgwater B. U.K. 51°15N 3°15W 24 D2
Bridlington U.K. 54°5N 0°12W 22 D8
Bridlington B. U.K. 54°4N 0°10W 23 D8
Bridport U.K. 50°44N 2°45W 24 E3
Brierfield U.K. 53°49N 2°14W 23 E4
Brierley Hill U.K. 52°29N 2°6W 23 H4
Brigg U.K. 53°34N 0°28W 23 E8
Brigham City U.S.A. 41°31N 112°1W 110 B4
Brighouse U.K. 53°42N 1°46W 23 E5
Brighstone U.K. 50°38N 1°24W 24 E6
Brightlingsea U.K. 51°49N 1°2E 25 C11
Brighton U.K. 50°49N 0°7W 25 E8
Brigstock U.K. 52°27N 0°36W 25 B7
Brill U.K. 51°49N 1°1W 24 C6
Brimfield U.K. 52°18N 2°41W 24 B3
Brindisi Italy 40°39N 17°55E 69 D7
Brinklow U.K. 52°25N 1°22W 24 B6
Brinkworth U.K. 51°33N 1°59W 24 C5
Brisbane Australia 27°25S 153°2E 98 F9
Bristol U.K. 51°26N 2°35W 24 D3
Bristol B. U.S.A. 58°0N 160°0W 108 D4
Bristol Channel U.K. 51°18N 4°30W 27 E5
Briston U.S. 52°51N 1°4E 25 A11
British Columbia □ Canada 55°0N 125°15W 108 D7
British Isles Europe 54°0N 4°0W 56 E5
British Virgin Is. ☑ W. Indies 18°30N 64°30W 115 e
Brittany = Bretagne □ France 48°10N 3°0W 66 B2
Brive-la-Gaillarde France 45°10N 1°32E 66 D4
Brixham U.K. 50°23N 3°31W 27 G6
Brixworth U.K. 52°20N 0°54W 25 B7
Brize Norton U.K. 51°46N 1°34W 24 C5
Brno Czech Rep. 49°10N 16°35E 65 D9
Broad B. U.K. 58°14N 6°18W 18 F5
Broad Chalke U.K. 51°2N 1°56W 24 D5
Broad Haven Ireland 54°20N 9°55W 28 C2
Broad Law U.K. 55°30N 3°21W 21 C9
Broad Sd. U.K. 49°55N 6°21W 27 H1
Broadclyst U.K. 50°46N 3°27W 27 F7
Broadhembury U.K. 50°49N 3°18W 27 F7
Broadstairs U.K. 51°21N 1°27E 25 D11
Broadway U.K. 52°2N 1°50W 24 B5
Broadwindsor U.K. 50°48N 2°47W 24 E3
Brochet Canada 57°53N 101°40W 108 D9
Brock I. Canada 77°52N 114°19W 109 B8
Brocken Germany 51°47N 10°37E 64 C6
Brockenhurst U.K. 50°49N 1°34W 24 E5
Brockville Canada 44°35N 75°41W 113 C10
Brockworth U.K. 51°51N 2°9W 24 C4
Brodeur Pen. Canada 72°30N 88°10W 109 B11
Brodick U.K. 55°35N 5°9W 20 C5
Broken Hill Australia 31°58S 141°29E 98 G7
Bromfield U.K. 52°24N 2°45W 23 H3
Bromham U.K. 51°23N 2°1W 24 D4
Bromley □ U.K. 51°24N 0°2E 25 D9
Brompton U.K. 54°21N 1°25W 22 D6
Bromsgrove U.K. 52°21N 2°2W 24 B4
Bromyard U.K. 52°11N 2°30W 24 B4
Brookings U.S.A. 44°19N 96°48W 111 B7
Brooks Canada 50°35N 111°55W 108 D8
Brooks Range U.S.A. 68°0N 152°0W 108 C5
Broom, L. U.K. 57°55N 5°15W 18 G7
Broome Australia 18°0S 122°15E 98 D3
Broomhill U.K. 55°18N 1°36W 22 B5
Brora U.K. 58°0N 3°51W 19 F10
Brora → U.K. 58°0N 3°51W 19 F10
Broseley U.K. 52°37N 2°29W 23 G4
Brosna → Ireland 53°14N 7°58W 30 B7
Brothertoft U.K. 53°0N 0°7W 23 F8
Brotton U.K. 54°35N 0°56W 22 C7
Brough Cumb., U.K. 54°32N 2°18W 22 C4
Brough E. Riding, U.K. 53°44N 0°36W 23 E7
Brough Hd. U.K. 59°8N 3°20W 19 D11
Broughton Borders, U.K. 55°37N 3°24W 21 C9
Broughton N. Lincs., U.K. 53°34N 0°34W 23 E7
Broughton Northants., U.K. 52°22N 0°46W 25 B7
Broughton-in-Furness U.K. 54°17N 3°12W 22 D2
Broughty Ferry U.K. 56°29N 2°51W 21 B10
Brown Willy U.K. 50°35N 4°37W 27 F4
Brownhills U.K. 52°39N 1°54W 23 G5
Brownsville U.S.A. 25°54N 97°30W 111 E7
Brownwood U.S.A. 31°43N 98°59W 110 D7

Broxburn U.K. 55°56N 3°28W 21 C9
Bruay-la-Buissière France 50°29N 2°33E 66 A5
Bruce, Mt. Australia 22°37S 118°8E 98 E2
Bruce → U.K. 51°13N 2°59W 24 D3
Brugge Belgium 51°13N 3°13E 64 C2
Brumado Brazil 14°14S 41°40W 122 B2
Brunei ■ Asia 4°50N 115°0E 82 D4
Brunswick Ga., U.S.A. 31°10N 81°30W 111 D10
Brunswick Maine, U.S.A. 43°55N 69°58W 113 D13
Brunton U.K. 55°2N 2°6W 22 A4
Brussels Belgium 50°51N 4°21E 64 C3
Bruton U.K. 51°7N 2°27W 24 D4
Bryan Ohio, U.S.A. 41°28N 84°33W 112 E5
Bryan Tex., U.S.A. 30°40N 96°22W 111 D7
Bryansk Russia 53°13N 34°25E 70 D5
Bryher U.K. 49°57N 6°22W 27 H1
Brynamman U.K. 51°49N 3°51W 26 D6
Brynmawr U.K. 51°48N 3°10W 26 D7
Bucaramanga Colombia 7°0N 73°0W 120 B2
Buchan U.K. 57°32N 2°21W 19 G13
Buchan Ness U.K. 57°29N 1°46W 19 H14
Buchanan Liberia 5°57N 10°2W 94 G3
Bucharest Romania 44°27N 26°10E 65 F14
Buckden U.K. 52°18N 0°14W 25 B8
Buckfastleigh U.K. 50°28N 3°48W 27 G6
Buckhannon U.S.A. 39°0N 80°8W 112 F7
Buckhaven U.K. 56°11N 3°3W 21 B9
Buckie U.K. 57°41N 2°58W 19 G12
Buckingham Canada 45°37N 75°24W 113 C10
Buckingham U.K. 51°59N 0°57W 25 C7
Buckinghamshire □ U.K. 51°53N 0°55W 25 C7
Buckland Brewer U.K. 50°58N 4°15W 27 F5
Buckland Newton U.K. 50°50N 2°26W 24 E4
Buckley U.K. 53°10N 3°5W 26 A7
Budapest Hungary 47°29N 19°3E 65 E10
Bude U.K. 50°49N 4°34W 27 F4
Bude B. U.K. 50°49N 4°35W 27 F4
Budle B. U.K. 55°37N 1°45W 22 A5
Budleigh Salterton U.K. 50°37N 3°19W 27 F7
Buena Vista U.S.A. 37°44N 79°21W 112 G8
Buenaventura Colombia 3°53N 77°4W 120 B2
Buenos Aires Argentina 34°36S 58°22W 121 F4
Buenos Aires, L. Argentina 46°35S 72°30W 121 G2
Buffalo N.Y., U.S.A. 42°53N 78°53W 112 D8
Buffalo Wyo., U.S.A. 44°21N 106°42W 110 B5
Bug → Poland 52°31N 21°5E 65 B11
Bug → Ukraine 46°59N 31°58E 71 E5
Bugle U.K. 50°24N 4°47W 27 G4
Bugulma Russia 54°33N 52°48E 70 D9
Buguruslan Russia 53°39N 52°26E 70 D9
Builth Wells U.K. 52°9N 3°25W 26 C7
Buir Nur Mongolia 47°50N 117°42E 79 B12
Bujumbura Burundi 3°16S 29°18E 96 E5
Bukavu Dem. Rep. of the Congo 2°20S 28°52E 96 E5
Bukhara Uzbekistan 39°48N 64°25E 87 B11
Bukittinggi Indonesia 0°20S 100°20E 82 E2
Bulawayo Zimbabwe 20°7S 28°32E 97 J5
Bulford U.K. 51°11N 1°45W 24 D5
Bulgan Mongolia 48°45N 103°34E 78 B9
Bulgaria ■ Europe 42°35N 25°30E 69 C11
Bullhead City U.S.A. 35°8N 114°32W 110 C4
Bunbury Australia 33°20S 115°35E 98 G2
Bunclody Ireland 52°39N 6°40W 31 C9
Buncrana Ireland 55°8N 7°27W 28 A7
Bundaberg Australia 24°54S 152°22E 98 E9
Bundi India 25°30N 75°35E 84 G9
Bundoran Ireland 54°28N 8°16W 28 C5
Bungay U.K. 52°27N 1°28E 25 B11
Buntingford U.K. 51°56N 0°0 25 C8
Bunwell U.K. 52°30N 1°9E 25 A11
Buon Ma Thuot Vietnam 12°40N 108°3E 82 B3
Bûr Safâga Egypt 26°43N 33°57E 95 C12
Buraydah Si. Arabia 26°20N 43°59E 86 E5
Burbage Derby., U.K. 53°15N 1°55W 23 F5
Burbage Leics., U.K. 52°32N 1°21W 23 G6
Burbage Wilts., U.K. 51°21N 1°39W 24 D5
Burco Somali Rep. 9°32N 45°32E 89 F4
Burdur Turkey 37°45N 30°17E 71 G5
Bure → U.K. 52°38N 1°43E 25 A12
Burford U.K. 51°49N 1°38W 24 C5
Burgas Bulgaria 42°33N 27°29E 69 C12
Burgess Hill U.K. 50°58N 0°6W 25 E8
Burgh le Marsh U.K. 53°9N 0°15E 23 F9
Burghead U.K. 57°43N 3°30W 19 G11
Burgos Spain 42°21N 3°41W 67 A4
Burgundy = Bourgogne □
  France 47°0N 4°50E 66 C6
Burhanpur India 21°18N 76°14E 84 J10
Burica, Pta. Costa Rica 8°3N 82°51W 104 J11
Burkina Faso ■ Africa 12°0N 1°0W 94 F5
Burley Hants., U.K. 50°49N 1°43W 24 E5
Burley W. Yorks., U.K. 53°54N 1°45W 23 E5
Burley U.S.A. 42°32N 113°48W 110 B4
Burlington Colo., U.S.A. 39°18N 102°16W 110 C6
Burlington Iowa, U.S.A. 40°49N 91°14W 111 B8
Burlington Vt., U.S.A. 44°29N 73°12W 113 C11
Burlington Wis., U.S.A. 42°41N 88°17W 112 D3
Burma ■ Asia 21°0N 96°30E 85 J20
Burnham Market U.K. 52°57N 0°44E 25 A10
Burnham-on-Crouch U.K. 51°38N 0°49E 25 C10
Burnham-on-Sea U.K. 51°14N 3°0W 24 D2
Burnie Australia 41°4S 145°56E 98 J8
Burnley U.K. 53°47N 2°14W 23 E4
Burnmouth U.K. 55°50N 2°4W 21 C11
Burns U.S.A. 43°35N 119°3W 110 B3
Burnside → Canada 66°51N 108°4W 108 C9
Burntisland U.K. 56°4N 3°13W 21 B9
Burqin China 47°43N 87°0E 78 B6
Burray U.K. 58°51N 2°54W 19 E12
Burren △ Ireland 53°1N 8°58W 30 B4
Burrow Hd. U.K. 54°41N 4°24W 20 E7
Burry Port U.K. 51°41N 4°15W 26 D5
Bursa Turkey 40°15N 29°5E 71 F4
Burstwick U.K. 53°44N 0°8W 23 E8
Burton U.K. 54°11N 2°43W 22 D3
Burton Agnes U.K. 54°4N 0°18W 22 D8
Burton Bradstock U.K. 50°42N 2°43W 24 E3
Burton Fleming U.K. 54°8N 0°20W 22 D8
Burton Latimer U.K. 52°22N 0°41W 25 B7
Burton upon Stather U.K. 53°39N 0°41W 23 E7

Burton upon Trent   Chesterfield Inlet

Burton upon Trent *U.K.* 52°48N 1°38W 23 G5
Buru *Indonesia* 3°30S 126°30E 83 E7
Burundi ■ *Africa* 3°15S 30°0E 96 E5
Burwash *U.K.* 50°59N 0°23E 25 E9
Burwell *U.K.* 52°17N 0°20E 25 B9
Burwick *U.K.* 58°45N 2°58W 19 E12
Bury *U.K.* 53°35N 2°17W 23 E4
Bury St. Edmunds *U.K.* 52°15N 0°43E 25 B10
Buryatia □ *Russia* 53°0N 110°0E 77 D11
Busan *S. Korea* 35°5N 129°0E 79 D14
Büshehr *Iran* 28°55N 50°55E 87 D7
Bushey *U.K.* 51°38N 0°22W 25 C8
Busto Arsízio *Italy* 45°37N 8°51E 68 B3
Buta *Dem. Rep. of the Congo* 2°50N 24°53E 96 D4
Butare *Rwanda* 2°31S 29°52E 96 E5
Butaritari *Kiribati* 3°30N 174°0E 102 G9
Bute *U.K.* 55°48N 5°2W 20 C5
Butembo *Dem. Rep. of the Congo* 0°9N 29°18E 96 D5
Butha Qi *China* 48°0N 122°32E 79 B13
Butler *U.S.A.* 40°52N 79°54W 112 E8
Buton *Indonesia* 5°0S 122°45E 83 E6
Butte *U.S.A.* 46°0N 112°32W 110 A4
Buttermere *U.K.* 54°32N 3°16W 22 C2
Butterworth *Malaysia* 5°24N 100°23E 82 C2
Buttevant *Ireland* 52°14N 8°40W 30 D5
Butuan *Phil.* 8°57N 125°33E 83 C7
Buurhakaba *Somali Rep.* 3°12N 44°20E 89 G3
Buxton *U.K.* 53°16N 1°54W 23 F5
Buyant-Uhaa *Mongolia* 44°55N 110°11E 79 C11
Buzău *Romania* 45°10N 26°50E 65 F14
Buzuluk *Russia* 52°48N 52°12E 70 D9
Bydgoszcz *Poland* 53°10N 18°0E 65 B9
Byfield *U.K.* 52°10N 1°14W 24 B6
Bylot I. *Canada* 73°13N 78°34W 109 B12
Byrranga Ra. *Russia* 75°0N 100°0E 77 B11
Bytom *Poland* 50°25N 18°54E 65 C10

C

Ca Mau *Vietnam* 9°7N 105°8E 82 C3
Cabanatuan *Phil.* 15°30N 120°58E 83 A6
Cabedelo *Brazil* 7°0S 34°50W 120 C6
Cabimas *Venezuela* 10°23N 71°25W 120 A2
Cabinda *Angola* 5°33S 12°11E 96 F2
Cabinda □ *Angola* 5°0S 12°30E 96 F2
Cabo Frio *Brazil* 22°51S 42°3W 122 D2
Cabo San Lucas *Mexico* 22°53N 109°54W 114 C3
Cabonga, Réservoir *Canada* 47°20N 76°40W 109 E12
Cabora Bassa Dam *Mozam.* 15°20S 32°50E 97 H6
Cabot Str. *Canada* 47°15N 59°40W 109 E14
Čačak *Serbia* 43°54N 20°20E 69 C9
Cáceres *Brazil* 16°5S 57°40W 120 D4
Cáceres *Spain* 39°26N 6°23W 67 C2
Cachimbo, Serra do *Brazil* 9°30S 55°30W 120 C4
Cachoeira *Brazil* 12°30S 39°0W 122 B3
Cachoeira do Sul *Brazil* 30°3S 52°53W 121 F4
Cachoeiro de Itapemirim
  Brazil 20°51S 41°7W 122 D2
Cader Idris *U.K.* 52°42N 3°53W 26 B6
Cadillac *U.S.A.* 44°15N 85°24W 112 C5
Cádiz *Spain* 36°30N 6°20W 67 D2
Cádiz, G. de *Spain* 36°40N 7°0W 67 D2
Caen *France* 49°10N 0°22W 66 B3
Caenby Corner *U.K.* 53°24N 0°33W 23 F7
Caernarfon *U.K.* 53°8N 4°16W 26 A5
Caernarfon B. *U.K.* 53°4N 4°40W 26 A4
Caerphilly *U.K.* 51°35N 3°13W 27 D7
Caersws *U.K.* 52°31N 3°26W 26 B7
Caeté *Brazil* 19°55S 43°40W 122 C2
Caetité *Brazil* 13°50S 42°32W 122 B2
Cagayan de Oro *Phil.* 8°30N 124°40E 83 C6
Cágliari *Italy* 39°13N 9°7E 68 E3
Caguas *Puerto Rico* 18°14N 66°2W 115 d
Caha Mts. *Ireland* 51°45N 9°40W 30 E3
Caher *Ireland* 52°22N 7°56W 30 D7
Cahersiveen *Ireland* 51°56N 10°14W 30 E2
Cahore Pt. *Ireland* 52°33N 6°12W 31 C10
Cahors *France* 44°27N 1°27E 66 D4
Cairn Gorm *U.K.* 57°7N 3°39W 19 H10
Cairngorm Mts. *U.K.* 57°6N 3°42W 19 H10
Cairngorms △ *U.K.* 57°10N 3°50W 19 H10
Cairnryan *U.K.* 54°59N 5°1W 20 E5
Cairns *Australia* 16°57S 145°45E 98 D8
Cairnsmore of Fleet *U.K.* 54°59N 4°20W 20 E7
Cairo *Egypt* 30°2N 31°13E 95 B12
Cairo *U.S.A.* 37°0N 89°11W 112 G3
Caister-on-Sea *U.K.* 52°40N 1°43E 25 A12
Caistor *U.K.* 53°30N 0°18W 23 F8
Caithness *U.K.* 58°25N 3°35W 19 F10
Caithness, Ord of *U.K.* 58°8N 3°36W 19 F11
Caja de Muertos, I.
  Puerto Rico 17°54N 66°32W 115 d
Cajamarca *Peru* 7°5S 78°28W 120 C2
Calabar *Nigeria* 4°57N 8°20E 94 H7
Calábria □ *Italy* 39°0N 16°30E 68 E7
Calais *France* 50°57N 1°56E 66 A4
Calais *U.S.A.* 45°11N 67°17W 113 C14
Calama *Chile* 22°30S 68°55W 121 E3
Calamian Group *Phil.* 11°50N 119°55E 83 B5
Calanscio, Sarir *Libya* 27°30N 21°30E 95 C10
Calapan *Phil.* 13°25N 121°7E 83 B6
Calbayog *Phil.* 12°4N 124°38E 83 B6
Calcutta = Kolkata *India* 22°34N 88°21E 85 H16
Caldbeck *U.K.* 54°45N 3°3W 22 C2
Calder → *U.K.* 53°44N 1°22W 23 E6
Calder Bridge *U.K.* 54°27N 3°29W 22 D2
Caldera *Chile* 27°5S 70°55W 121 E2
Caldew → *U.K.* 54°54N 2°56W 22 C3
Caldwell *U.S.A.* 43°40N 116°41W 110 B3
Caledonian Canal *U.K.* 57°29N 4°15W 19 H9
Calgary *Canada* 51°0N 114°10W 108 D8
Cali *Colombia* 3°25N 76°35W 120 B2
Calicut *India* 11°15N 75°43E 84 P9
California □ *U.S.A.* 37°30N 119°30W 110 C2
California, G. de *Mexico* 27°0N 111°0W 114 B2
Callan *Ireland* 52°32N 7°24W 31 C8
Callander *U.K.* 56°15N 4°13W 20 B7
Callao *Peru* 12°3S 77°8W 120 D2
Calne *U.K.* 51°26N 2°0W 24 D5

Calshot *U.K.* 50°48N 1°19W 24 E6
Calstock *U.K.* 50°30N 4°13W 27 F5
Caltanissetta *Italy* 37°29N 14°4E 68 F6
Calvi *France* 42°34N 8°45E 66 E8
Calvinia *S. Africa* 31°28S 19°45E 97 L3
Cam → *U.K.* 52°21N 0°16E 25 B9
Cam Ranh *Vietnam* 11°54N 109°12E 82 B3
Camagüey *Cuba* 21°20N 77°55W 115 C9
Camargue *France* 43°34N 4°34E 66 E6
Camberley *U.K.* 51°20N 0°44W 25 D7
Cambo *U.K.* 55°10N 1°57W 22 B5
Cambodia ■ *Asia* 12°15N 105°0E 82 B3
Camborne *U.K.* 50°12N 5°19W 27 G3
Cambrai *France* 50°11N 3°14E 66 A5
Cambrian Mts. *U.K.* 52°3N 3°57W 26 C6
Cambridge *Jamaica* 18°18N 77°54W 114 a
Cambridge *U.K.* 52°12N 0°8E 25 B9
Cambridge *Mass., U.S.A.* 42°23N 71°7W 113 D12
Cambridge *Md., U.S.A.* 38°34N 76°5W 113 F9
Cambridge *Ohio, U.S.A.* 40°2N 81°35W 112 E7
Cambridge Bay *Canada* 69°10N 105°0W 108 C9
Cambridgeshire □ *U.K.* 52°25N 0°7W 25 B8
Camden *Ark., U.S.A.* 33°35N 92°50W 111 D8
Camden *N.J., U.S.A.* 39°55N 75°7W 113 F10
Camden □ *U.K.* 51°32N 0°8W 25 C8
Camel → *U.K.* 50°31N 4°51W 27 F4
Camelford *U.K.* 50°37N 4°42W 27 F4
Cameroon ■ *Africa* 6°0N 12°30E 96 C2
Cameroun, Mt. *Cameroon* 4°13N 9°10E 96 D1
Cametá *Brazil* 2°12S 49°30W 120 C5
Camocim *Brazil* 2°55S 40°50W 120 C5
Campana, I. *Chile* 48°20S 75°20W 121 G2
Campánia □ *Italy* 41°0N 14°30E 68 D6
Campbell I. *Pac. Oc.* 52°30S 169°0E 102 N8
Campbell River *Canada* 50°5N 125°20W 108 D7
Campbellsville *U.S.A.* 37°21N 85°20W 112 G5
Campbellton *Canada* 47°57N 66°43W 109 E13
Campbeltown *U.K.* 55°26N 5°36W 20 D4
Campeche *Mexico* 19°51N 90°32W 114 D6
Campeche, Golfo de *Mexico* 19°30N 93°0W 114 D6
Campina Grande *Brazil* 7°20S 35°47W 120 C6
Campinas *Brazil* 22°50S 47°0W 122 D1
Campo Belo *Brazil* 20°52S 45°16W 122 D1
Campo Grande *Brazil* 20°25S 54°40W 120 E4
Campos *Brazil* 21°50S 41°20W 122 D2
Campos Belos *Brazil* 13°10S 47°3W 122 B1
Camrose *Canada* 53°0N 112°50W 108 D8
Can Tho *Vietnam* 10°2N 105°46E 82 B3
Canada ■ *N. Amer.* 60°0N 100°0W 108 D10
Canadian → *U.S.A.* 35°28N 95°3W 111 C7
Canadian Shield *Canada* 53°0N 75°0W 104 D12
Çanakkale *Turkey* 40°8N 26°24E 71 F4
Canandaigua *U.S.A.* 42°54N 77°17W 112 D9
Cananea *Mexico* 31°0N 110°18W 114 A2
Canaries *St. Lucia* 13°55N 61°4W 115 f
Canary Is. *Atl. Oc.* 28°30N 16°0W 94 C2
Canaveral, C. *U.S.A.* 28°27N 80°32W 111 E10
Canavieiras *Brazil* 15°39S 39°0W 122 B3
Canberra *Australia* 35°15S 149°8E 98 H8
Cancún *Mexico* 21°8N 86°44W 114 C7
Cangzhou *China* 38°19N 116°52E 79 D12
Caniapiscau → *Canada* 56°40N 69°30W 109 D13
Caniapiscau, L. *Canada* 54°10N 69°55W 109 D13
Çankırı *Turkey* 40°40N 33°37E 71 F5
Canna *U.K.* 57°3N 6°33W 18 H4
Canna, Sd. of *U.K.* 57°1N 6°30W 18 H5
Cannanore *India* 11°53N 75°27E 84 P9
Cannes *France* 43°32N 7°1E 66 E7
Cannington *U.K.* 51°9N 3°4W 24 D2
Cannock *U.K.* 52°41N 2°1W 23 G4
Cannock Chase *U.K.* 52°44N 2°4W 23 G4
Canoas *Brazil* 29°56S 51°11W 121 E5
Cañon City *U.S.A.* 38°27N 105°14W 110 C5
Canonbie *U.K.* 55°5N 2°58W 21 D10
Canora *Canada* 51°40N 102°30W 108 D9
Canso *Canada* 45°20N 61°0W 113 C17
Cantabria □ *Spain* 43°10N 4°0W 67 A4
Cantábrica, Cordillera *Spain* 43°0N 5°10W 67 A3
Canterbury *U.K.* 51°16N 1°6E 25 D11
Canton = Guangzhou *China* 23°6N 113°13E 79 G11
Canton *Ill., U.S.A.* 40°33N 90°2W 112 E2
Canton *N.Y., U.S.A.* 44°36N 75°10W 113 C10
Canton *Ohio, U.S.A.* 40°48N 81°23W 112 E7
Canvey *U.K.* 51°31N 0°37E 25 C10
Cap-de-la-Madeleine
  Canada 46°22N 72°31W 113 B11
Cap-Haïtien *Haiti* 19°40N 72°20W 115 D10
Cap Pt. *St. Lucia* 14°7N 60°57W 115 f
Cape Breton I. *Canada* 46°0N 60°30W 113 C17
Cape Charles *U.S.A.* 37°16N 76°1W 113 G10
Cape Coast *Ghana* 5°5N 1°15W 94 G5
Cape Coral *U.S.A.* 26°33N 81°57W 111 E10
Cape Fear → *U.S.A.* 33°53N 78°1W 111 D11
Cape Girardeau *U.S.A.* 37°19N 89°32W 112 G3
Cape May *U.S.A.* 38°56N 74°56W 113 F10
Cape Town *S. Africa* 33°55S 18°22E 97 L3
Cape Verde Is. ■ *Atl. Oc.* 16°0N 24°0W 91 E1
Cape York Peninsula
  Australia 12°0S 142°30E 98 C7
Capela *Brazil* 10°30S 37°0W 122 B3
Capesterre-Belle-Eau
  Guadeloupe 16°4N 61°36W 114 b
Capesterre-de-Marie-Galante
  Guadeloupe 15°53N 61°14W 114 b
Capreol *Canada* 46°43N 80°56W 112 B7
Capri *Italy* 40°33N 14°14E 68 D6
Caprivi Strip *Namibia* 18°0S 23°0E 97 H4
Caquetá → *Colombia* 1°15S 69°15W 120 C3
Caracas *Venezuela* 10°30N 66°55W 120 A3
Caracol *Brazil* 9°15S 43°22W 122 A2
Carangola *Brazil* 20°44S 42°5W 122 D2
Caratasca, L. de *Honduras* 15°20N 83°40W 115 D8
Caratinga *Brazil* 19°50S 42°10W 122 C2
Caravelas *Brazil* 17°45S 39°15W 122 C3
Caravelle, Presqu'île de la
  Martinique 14°46N 60°48W 114 c
Carbón, L. del *Argentina* 49°35S 68°21W 121 G3
Carbondale *Ill., U.S.A.* 37°44N 89°13W 112 G3
Carbondale *Pa., U.S.A.* 41°35N 75°30W 113 E10

Carbonear *Canada* 47°42N 53°13W 109 E14
Carcassonne *France* 43°13N 2°20E 66 E5
Carcross *Canada* 60°13N 134°45W 108 C6
Cardamon Hills *India* 9°30N 77°15E 84 Q10
Cárdenas *Cuba* 23°0N 81°30W 115 C8
Cardiff *U.K.* 51°29N 3°10W 27 E7
Cardigan *U.K.* 52°5N 4°40W 26 C4
Cardigan B. *U.K.* 52°30N 4°30W 26 B4
Cardington *U.K.* 52°6N 0°25W 25 B8
Cardston *Canada* 49°15N 113°20W 108 E8
Cariacica *Brazil* 20°16S 40°25W 122 D2
Caribbean Sea *W. Indies* 15°0N 75°0W 115 E10
Cariboo Mts. *Canada* 53°0N 121°0W 108 D7
Caribou *U.S.A.* 46°52N 68°1W 113 B13
Caribou Mts. *Canada* 59°12N 115°40W 108 D8
Carinhanha *Brazil* 14°15S 44°46W 122 B2
Carinhanha → *Brazil* 14°20S 43°47W 122 B2
Carinthia = Kärnten □
  Austria 46°52N 13°30E 64 E8
Carisbrooke *U.K.* 50°41N 1°19W 24 E6
Cark *U.K.* 54°11N 2°58W 22 D3
Carleton Place *Canada* 45°8N 76°9W 113 C9
Carleton Rode *U.K.* 52°30N 1°7E 25 A11
Carlingford L. *U.K.* 54°3N 6°9W 29 C9
Carlinville *U.S.A.* 39°17N 89°53W 112 F3
Carlisle *U.K.* 54°54N 2°56W 22 C3
Carlisle *U.S.A.* 40°12N 77°12W 112 E9
Carlisle B. *Barbados* 13°5N 59°37W 115 g
Carlops *U.K.* 55°47N 3°20W 21 C9
Carlow *Ireland* 52°50N 6°56W 31 C9
Carlow □ *Ireland* 52°43N 6°50W 31 C9
Carlsbad *U.S.A.* 32°25N 104°14W 110 D6
Carlton *U.K.* 52°59N 1°5W 23 G6
Carlton Colville *U.K.* 52°27N 1°43E 25 B12
Carlton Miniott *U.K.* 54°12N 1°22W 22 D6
Carluke *U.K.* 55°45N 3°50W 21 C8
Carmacks *Canada* 62°5N 136°16W 108 C6
Carmarthen *U.K.* 51°52N 4°19W 26 D5
Carmarthen B. *U.K.* 51°40N 4°30W 26 D4
Carmarthenshire □ *U.K.* 51°55N 4°13W 26 D5
Carmaux *France* 44°3N 2°10E 66 D5
Carmi *U.S.A.* 38°5N 88°10W 112 F3
Carn Ban *U.K.* 57°7N 4°15W 19 H9
Carn Eige *U.K.* 57°17N 5°8W 18 H7
Carnarvon *Australia* 24°51S 113°42E 98 E1
Carnarvon *S. Africa* 30°56S 22°8E 97 L4
Carndonagh *Ireland* 55°16N 7°15W 29 A7
Carnegie, L. *Australia* 26°5S 122°30E 98 F3
Carnforth *U.K.* 54°7N 2°45W 22 D3
Carno *U.K.* 52°34N 3°30W 26 B6
Carnoustie *U.K.* 56°30N 2°42W 21 A10
Carnsore Pt. *Ireland* 52°10N 6°22W 31 D10
Caro *U.S.A.* 43°29N 83°24W 112 D6
Carolina *Puerto Rico* 18°23N 65°58W 115 d
Caroline I. *Kiribati* 9°58S 150°13W 103 H12
Caroline Is. *Micronesia* 8°0N 150°0E 102 G6
Carondelet Reef *Kiribati* 5°33S 173°50W 99 B16
Caroní → *Venezuela* 8°21N 62°43W 120 B3
Carpathians *Europe* 49°30N 21°0E 65 D11
Carpentaria, G. of *Australia* 14°0S 139°0E 98 C6
Carpentras *France* 44°3N 5°2E 66 D6
Carpi *Italy* 44°47N 10°53E 68 B4
Carrara *Italy* 44°5N 10°6E 68 B4
Carrauntoohill *Ireland* 52°0N 9°45W 30 E3
Carrick-on-Shannon *Ireland* 53°57N 8°5W 28 D5
Carrick-on-Suir *Ireland* 52°21N 7°24W 31 D8
Carrickfergus *Ireland* 54°43N 5°49W 29 B10
Carrickmacross *Ireland* 53°59N 6°43W 29 D8
Carrollton *U.S.A.* 39°18N 90°24W 112 F2
Carron → *U.K.* 57°53N 4°22W 19 G9
Carron, L. *U.K.* 57°22N 5°35W 18 H6
Carson City *U.S.A.* 39°10N 119°46W 110 C3
Carson Sink *U.S.A.* 39°50N 118°25W 110 C3
Cartagena *Colombia* 10°25N 75°33W 120 A2
Cartagena *Spain* 37°38N 0°59W 67 D5
Cartago *Colombia* 4°45N 75°55W 120 B2
Carthage *Tunisia* 36°52N 10°20E 95 A8
Cartmel *U.K.* 54°12N 2°57W 22 D3
Cartwright *Canada* 53°41N 56°58W 109 D14
Caruaru *Brazil* 8°15S 35°55W 122 A3
Carúpano *Venezuela* 10°39N 63°15W 120 A3
Casa Grande *U.S.A.* 32°53N 111°45W 110 D4
Casa Nova *Brazil* 9°25S 41°5W 122 A2
Casablanca *Morocco* 33°36N 7°36W 94 B4
Cascade Ra. *U.S.A.* 47°0N 121°30W 110 A2
Cascavel *Ceará, Brazil* 4°7S 38°14W 120 C6
Cascavel *Paraná, Brazil* 24°57S 53°28W 121 E4
Caserta *Italy* 41°4N 14°20E 68 D6
Cashel *Ireland* 52°30N 7°53W 30 C7
Casiquiare → *Venezuela* 2°1N 67°7W 120 B3
Casper *U.S.A.* 42°51N 106°19W 110 B5
Caspian Depression *Eurasia* 47°0N 48°0E 71 E8
Caspian Sea *Eurasia* 43°0N 50°0E 71 F9
Cassiar Mts. *Canada* 59°30N 130°30W 108 D6
Castellammare di Stábia *Italy* 40°42N 14°29E 68 D6
Castelló de la Plana *Spain* 39°58N 0°3W 67 C5
Castelsarrasin *France* 44°2N 1°7E 66 E4
Castilla-La Mancha □ *Spain* 39°30N 3°30W 67 C4
Castilla y León □ *Spain* 42°0N 5°0W 67 B3
Castle Acre *U.K.* 52°42N 0°42E 25 A10
Castle Cary *U.K.* 51°6N 2°31W 24 D3
Castle Donington *U.K.* 52°51N 1°20W 23 G6
Castle Douglas *U.K.* 54°56N 3°56W 21 E8
Castlebar *Ireland* 53°52N 9°18W 28 D3
Castlebay *U.K.* 56°57N 7°31W 18 J2
Castleblaney *Ireland* 54°7N 6°44W 29 C8
Castlederg *U.K.* 54°42N 7°35W 28 C6
Castleford *U.K.* 53°43N 1°21W 23 E6
Castlemaine Harbour *Ireland* 52°8N 9°50W 30 D3
Castlepollard *Ireland* 53°41N 7°19W 28 D7
Castlerea *Ireland* 53°46N 8°29W 28 D5
Castleside *U.K.* 54°50N 1°52W 22 C5
Castleton *Derby, U.K.* 53°22N 1°46W 23 F5
Castleton *N. Yorks., U.K.* 54°28N 0°57W 22 D7
Castletown *I. of Man* 54°5N 4°38W 29 C13
Castletown Bearhaven *Ireland* 51°39N 9°55W 30 E3
Castres *France* 43°37N 2°13E 66 E5
Castries *St. Lucia* 14°2N 60°58W 115 f
Castro *Chile* 42°30S 73°50W 121 G2
Castro Alves *Brazil* 12°46S 39°33W 122 B3

Cat I. *Bahamas* 24°30N 75°30W 115 C9
Cataguases *Brazil* 21°23S 42°39W 122 D2
Catalão *Brazil* 18°10S 47°57W 122 C1
Cataluña □ *Spain* 41°40N 1°15E 67 B6
Catamarca *Argentina* 28°30S 65°50W 121 E3
Catanduanes *Phil.* 13°50N 124°20E 83 B6
Catanduva *Brazil* 21°5S 48°58W 122 D1
Catánia *Italy* 37°30N 15°6E 68 F6
Catanzaro *Italy* 38°54N 16°35E 68 E7
Catcleugh *U.K.* 55°20N 2°24W 22 B4
Caterham *U.K.* 51°15N 0°4W 25 D8
Catoche, C. *Mexico* 21°35N 87°5W 114 C7
Caton *U.K.* 54°5N 2°42W 22 D3
Catsfield *U.K.* 50°54N 0°28E 25 E9
Catskill *U.S.A.* 42°14N 73°52W 113 D11
Catskill Mts. *U.S.A.* 42°10N 74°25W 113 D10
Catterick *U.K.* 54°23N 1°37W 22 D5
Catterick Camp *U.K.* 54°22N 1°42W 22 D5
Catton *U.K.* 54°55N 2°15W 22 C4
Cauca → *Colombia* 8°54N 74°28W 120 B2
Caucaia *Brazil* 3°40S 38°35W 120 C6
Caucasus Mountains *Eurasia* 42°50N 44°0E 71 F7
Caulkerbush *U.K.* 54°54N 3°41W 21 E9
Caura → *Venezuela* 7°38N 64°53W 120 B3
Cauvery → *India* 11°9N 78°52E 84 P11
Cavan *Ireland* 54°0N 7°22W 28 D7
Cavan □ *Ireland* 54°1N 7°16W 29 C7
Caviana, I. *Brazil* 0°10N 50°10W 120 B4
Cawood *U.K.* 53°50N 1°8W 23 E6
Cawston *U.K.* 52°47N 1°9E 25 A11
Caxias *Brazil* 4°55S 43°20W 120 C5
Caxias do Sul *Brazil* 29°10S 51°10W 121 E4
Cayenne *Fr. Guiana* 5°5N 52°18W 120 B4
Cayey *Puerto Rico* 18°7N 66°10W 115 d
Cayman Is. ☒ *W. Indies* 19°40N 80°30W 115 D8
Cayman Trench *Caribbean* 17°0N 83°0W 115 D8
Cayuga L. *U.S.A.* 42°41N 76°41W 112 D9
Ceanannus Mor *Ireland* 53°44N 6°53W 29 D8
Ceará □ *Brazil* 5°0S 40°0W 120 C6
Cebu *Phil.* 10°18N 123°54E 83 B6
Cedar City *U.S.A.* 37°41N 113°4W 110 C4
Cedar L. *Canada* 53°10N 100°0W 108 D10
Cedar Rapids *U.S.A.* 41°59N 91°40W 111 B81
Cefalù *Italy* 38°2N 14°1E 68 E6
Ceglėd *Hungary* 47°11N 19°47E 65 E10
Celaya *Mexico* 20°31N 100°37W 114 C4
Celebes Sea *Indonesia* 3°0N 123°0E 83 D6
Celina *U.S.A.* 40°33N 84°35W 112 E5
Cellar Hd. *U.K.* 58°25N 6°11W 18 F5
Celtic Sea *Atl. Oc.* 50°9N 9°34W 62 F2
Cemaes *U.K.* 53°24N 4°27W 26 A5
Central, Cordillera *Colombia* 5°0N 75°0W 117 C3
Central, Cordillera *Puerto Rico* 18°8N 66°35W 115 d
Central African Rep. ■ *Africa* 7°0N 20°0E 96 C4
Central America *America* 12°0N 85°0W 104 H11
Central Bedfordshire □ *U.K.* 52°5N 0°20W 25 B8
Central Makran Range
  Pakistan 26°30N 64°15E 84 F4
Central Russian Uplands
  Europe 54°0N 36°0E 56 E13
Central Siberian Plateau
  Russia 65°0N 105°0E 72 B12
Centralia *Ill., U.S.A.* 38°32N 89°8W 112 F3
Centralia *Wash., U.S.A.* 46°43N 122°58W 110 A2
Cephalonia = Kefalonia
  Greece 38°15N 20°30E 69 E9
Ceredigion □ *U.K.* 52°16N 4°15W 26 C5
Cerignola *Italy* 41°17N 15°53E 68 D6
Cerne Abbas *U.K.* 50°49N 2°29W 24 E4
Cerrigydrudion *U.K.* 53°1N 3°36W 26 A6
Cerro de Pasco *Peru* 10°45S 76°10W 120 D2
Cesena *Italy* 44°8N 12°15E 68 B5
České Budějovice *Czech Rep.* 48°55N 14°25E 64 D8
Çeşme *Turkey* 38°20N 26°23E 71 G4
Ceuta *N. Afr.* 35°52N 5°18W 67 E3
Cévennes *France* 44°10N 3°50E 66 D5
Chacewater *U.K.* 50°15N 5°11W 27 G3
Chachapoyas *Peru* 6°15S 77°50W 120 C2
Chaco Austral *S. Amer.* 27°0S 61°30W 121 E3
Chaco Boreal *S. Amer.* 22°0S 60°0W 121 E4
Chaco Central *S. Amer.* 24°0S 61°0W 121 E3
Chad ■ *Africa* 15°0N 17°15E 95 F8
Chad, L. *Chad* 13°30N 14°30E 95 F8
Chadron *U.S.A.* 42°50N 103°0W 110 B6
Chagford *U.K.* 50°40N 3°50W 27 F6
Chaghcharān *Afghan.* 34°31N 65°15E 87 C11
Chagos Arch. ☒ *Ind. Oc.* 6°0S 72°0E 73 J9
Chāh Gay Hills *Afghan.* 29°30N 64°0E 87 D10
Chakradharpur *India* 22°45N 85°40E 85 H14
Chaleur B. *Canada* 47°55N 65°30W 113 B15
Chalisgaon *India* 20°30N 75°10E 84 J9
Challenger Deep *Pac. Oc.* 11°30N 142°0E 102 F6
Chalon-sur-Saône *France* 46°48N 4°50E 66 C6
Châlons-en-Champagne
  France 48°58N 4°20E 66 B6
Chambal → *India* 26°29N 79°15E 84 F11
Chambersburg *U.S.A.* 39°56N 77°40W 112 F9
Chambéry *France* 45°34N 5°55E 66 D6
Chamonix-Mont Blanc *France* 45°55N 6°51E 66 D7
Champagne *France* 48°40N 4°20E 66 B6
Champaign *U.S.A.* 40°7N 88°15W 112 E3
Champlain, L. *U.S.A.* 44°40N 73°20W 113 C11
Chañaral *Chile* 26°23S 70°40W 121 E2
Chancery Lane *Barbados* 13°3N 59°30W 115 g
Chandigarh *India* 30°43N 76°47E 84 D10
Chandler's Ford *U.K.* 50°59N 1°22W 24 E6
Chandpur *Bangla.* 23°8N 90°45E 85 H17
Chandrapur *India* 19°57N 79°25E 84 K11
Changbai Shan *China* 42°20N 129°0E 79 C14
Changchun *China* 43°57N 125°17E 79 C14
Changde *China* 29°4N 111°35E 79 F11
Changhua *Taiwan* 24°2N 120°30E 79 G13
Changji *China* 44°1N 87°19E 78 C6
Changsha *China* 28°12N 113°0E 79 F11
Changzhi *China* 36°10N 113°6E 79 D11
Changzhou *China* 31°47N 119°58E 79 E12

Channel-Port aux Basques
  Canada 47°30N 59°9W 109 E14
Chantrey Inlet *Canada* 67°48N 96°20W 108 C10
Chaoyang *China* 41°35N 120°22E 79 C13
Chaozhou *China* 23°42N 116°32E 79 G12
Chapala, L. de *Mexico* 20°15N 103°0W 114 C4
Chapayevsk *Russia* 53°0N 49°40E 70 D8
Chapel en le Frith *U.K.* 53°20N 1°54W 23 F5
Chapel St. Leonards *U.K.* 53°13N 0°20E 23 F9
Chapleau *Canada* 47°50N 83°24W 109 E11
Charaña *Bolivia* 17°30S 69°25W 120 D3
Chard *U.K.* 50°52N 2°58W 24 E3
Chari → *Chad* 12°58N 14°31E 95 F8
Chārīkār *Afghan.* 35°0N 69°10E 87 C12
Charing *U.K.* 51°12N 0°49E 25 D10
Charlbury *U.K.* 51°53N 1°28W 24 C6
Charleroi *Belgium* 50°24N 4°27E 64 C3
Charles, C. *U.S.A.* 37°7N 75°58W 113 G10
Charles City *U.S.A.* 43°4N 92°41W 111 B81
Charleston *Ill., U.S.A.* 39°30N 88°10W 112 F3
Charleston *Mo., U.S.A.* 36°55N 89°21W 112 G3
Charleston *S.C., U.S.A.* 32°46N 79°56W 111 D11
Charleston *W. Va., U.S.A.* 38°21N 81°38W 112 F7
Charlestown *Ireland* 53°58N 8°48W 28 D4
Charlestown of Aberlour
  U.K. 57°28N 3°14W 19 H11
Charleville *Australia* 26°24S 146°15E 98 F8
Charleville-Mézières *France* 49°44N 4°40E 66 B6
Charlevoix *U.S.A.* 45°19N 85°16W 112 C5
Charlotte *Mich., U.S.A.* 42°34N 84°50W 112 D5
Charlotte *N.C., U.S.A.* 35°13N 80°50W 111 C10
Charlotte Amalie
  U.S. Virgin Is. 18°21N 64°56W 115 e
Charlotte Harbor *U.S.A.* 26°57N 82°4W 111 E10
Charlottesville *U.S.A.* 38°2N 78°30W 112 F8
Charlottetown *Canada* 46°14N 63°8W 113 B16
Charlton I. *Canada* 52°0N 79°20W 109 D12
Charlton Kings *U.K.* 51°53N 2°3W 24 C4
Charlwood *U.K.* 51°9N 0°13W 25 D8
Charminster *U.K.* 50°44N 2°28W 24 E4
Charmouth *U.K.* 50°44N 2°54W 24 E3
Charnwood Forest *U.K.* 52°44N 1°17W 23 G6
Charolles *France* 46°27N 4°16E 66 C6
Charters Towers *Australia* 20°5S 146°13E 98 E8
Chartham *U.K.* 51°14N 1°1E 25 D11
Chartres *France* 48°29N 1°30E 66 B4
Chascomús *Argentina* 35°30S 58°0W 121 F4
Châteaubriant *France* 47°43N 1°23W 66 C3
Châteaulin *France* 48°11N 4°8W 66 B1
Châteauroux *France* 46°50N 1°40E 66 C4
Châteaux, Pte. des *Guadeloupe* 16°15N 61°10W 114 b
Châtellerault *France* 46°50N 0°30E 66 C4
Chatham *N.B., Canada* 47°2N 65°28W 109 E13
Chatham *Ont., Canada* 42°24N 82°11W 112 D6
Chatham *U.K.* 51°22N 0°32E 25 D10
Chatham Is. *Pac. Oc.* 44°0S 176°40W 99 J15
Chatsworth *U.K.* 53°13N 1°36W 23 F5
Chattahoochee → *U.S.A.* 30°54N 84°57W 104 F11
Chattanooga *U.S.A.* 35°3N 85°19W 111 C9
Chatteris *U.K.* 52°28N 0°2E 25 B9
Chatton *U.K.* 55°35N 2°0W 22 A5
Chaumont *France* 48°7N 5°8E 66 B6
Chaykovskiy *Russia* 56°47N 54°9E 70 C9
Cheadle *Gt. Man., U.K.* 53°23N 2°12W 23 F4
Cheadle *Staffs., U.K.* 52°59N 1°58W 23 G5
Cheb *Czech Rep.* 50°9N 12°28E 64 C7
Cheboksary *Russia* 56°8N 47°12E 70 C8
Cheboygan *U.S.A.* 45°39N 84°29W 112 C5
Chech, Erg *Africa* 25°0N 2°15W 94 D5
Chechnia □ *Russia* 43°30N 45°29E 71 F8
Chedabucto B. *Canada* 45°25N 61°8W 113 C17
Cheddar *U.K.* 51°17N 2°46W 24 D3
Cheddleton *U.K.* 53°4N 2°2W 23 F4
Cheduba I. *Burma* 18°45N 93°40E 85 K18
Chegutu *Zimbabwe* 18°10S 30°14E 97 H6
Chelm *Poland* 51°8N 23°30E 65 C12
Chelmer → *U.K.* 51°44N 0°30E 25 C10
Chelmsford *U.K.* 51°44N 0°29E 25 C9
Cheltenham *U.K.* 51°54N 2°4W 24 C4
Chelyabinsk *Russia* 55°10N 61°24E 76 D7
Chelyuskin, C. *Russia* 77°30N 103°0E 77 B11
Chemnitz *Germany* 50°51N 12°54E 64 C7
Chenab → *Pakistan* 30°23N 71°2E 84 D7
Chengde *China* 40°59N 117°58E 79 C12
Chengdu *China* 30°38N 104°2E 78 E9
Chengjiang *China* 24°39N 103°0E 78 G9
Chennai *India* 13°8N 80°19E 84 N12
Chepstow *U.K.* 51°38N 2°41W 26 D8
Cher → *France* 47°21N 0°29E 66 C4
Cherbourg *France* 49°39N 1°40W 66 B3
Cheremkhovo *Russia* 53°8N 103°1E 78 A9
Cherepovets *Russia* 59°5N 37°55E 70 C6
Chergui, Chott ech *Algeria* 34°21N 0°25E 94 B6
Cheriton *U.K.* 51°3N 1°8W 24 D6
Cheriton Fitzpaine *U.K.* 50°51N 3°35W 27 F6
Cherkasy *Ukraine* 49°27N 32°4E 71 E5
Cherkessk *Russia* 44°15N 42°5E 71 F7
Chernihiv *Ukraine* 51°28N 31°20E 70 D5
Chernivtsi *Ukraine* 48°15N 25°52E 65 D13
Chernobyl *Ukraine* 51°20N 30°15E 65 C16
Cherokee *U.S.A.* 42°45N 95°33W 111 B7
Cherrapunji *India* 25°17N 91°47E 85 G17
Cherski Ra. *Russia* 65°0N 143°0E 77 C15
Chertsey *U.K.* 51°23N 0°30W 25 D7
Chervonohrad *Ukraine* 50°25N 24°10E 71 D3
Cherwell → *U.K.* 51°44N 1°14W 24 C6
Chesapeake B. *U.S.A.* 38°0N 76°10W 112 F9
Chesha B. *Russia* 67°20N 47°0E 70 A8
Chesham *U.K.* 51°43N 0°36W 25 C7
Cheshire East □ *U.K.* 53°15N 2°15W 23 F4
Cheshire West and Chester □
  U.K. 53°15N 2°40W 23 F3
Cheshunt *U.K.* 51°43N 0°1W 25 C8
Chesil Beach *U.K.* 50°37N 2°33W 24 E3
Chester *U.K.* 53°12N 2°53W 23 F3
Chester *U.S.A.* 39°51N 75°22W 113 F10
Chester-le-Street *U.K.* 54°51N 1°34W 22 C5
Chesterfield *U.K.* 53°15N 1°25W 23 F6
Chesterfield, Îs. *N. Cal.* 19°52S 158°15E 99 D10
Chesterfield Inlet *Canada* 63°30N 90°45W 108 C10

Chesuncook L.   Culebra

Chesuncook L. U.S.A. 46°0N 69°21W 113 B13
Chetumal Mexico 18°30N 88°20W 114 D7
Chetwynd Canada 55°45N 121°36W 108 D7
Cheviot, The U.K. 55°29N 2°9W 22 B4
Cheviot Hills U.K. 55°20N 2°30W 22 B3
Chew Bahir Ethiopia 4°40N 36°50E 89 G2
Chew Magna U.K. 51°22N 2°37W 24 D3
Cheyenne U.S.A. 41°8N 104°49W 110 B6
Cheyenne → U.S.A. 44°41N 101°18W 110 B6
Chhapra India 25°48N 84°44E 85 G14
Chhattisgarh □ India 22°0N 82°0E 85 J12
Chi → Thailand 15°11N 104°43E 82 A3
Chiai Taiwan 23°29N 120°25E 79 G13
Chiávari Italy 44°19N 9°19E 68 B3
Chiba Japan 35°30N 140°7E 81 F7
Chibougamau Canada 49°56N 74°24W 109 E12
Chibougamau, L. Canada 49°50N 74°20W 113 A10
Chic-Chocs, Mts. Canada 48°55N 66°0W 113 A14
Chicago U.S.A. 41°52N 87°38W 112 E4
Chichagof I. U.S.A. 57°30N 135°30W 108 D6
Chichester U.K. 50°50N 0°47W 25 E7
Chickasha U.S.A. 35°3N 97°58W 110 C7
Chiclayo Peru 6°42S 79°50W 120 C2
Chico U.S.A. 39°44N 121°50W 110 C2
Chico → Chubut, Argentina 44°0S 67°0W 121 G3
Chico → Santa Cruz, Argentina 50°0S 68°30W 121 G3
Chicopee U.S.A. 42°9N 72°37W 113 D11
Chicoutimi Canada 48°28N 71°5W 113 A12
Chiddingfold U.K. 51°7N 0°37W 25 D7
Chidley, C. Canada 60°23N 64°26W 109 C13
Chieti Italy 42°21N 14°10E 68 C6
Chifeng China 42°18N 118°58E 79 C12
Chihuahua Mexico 28°38N 106°5W 114 B3
Chilapa Mexico 17°36N 99°10W 114 D5
Chilaw Sri Lanka 7°30N 79°50E 84 R11
Childress U.S.A. 34°25N 100°13W 110 D6
Chile ■ S. Amer. 35°0S 72°0W 121 F2
Chilham U.K. 51°15N 0°59E 25 D10
Chililabombwe Zambia 12°18S 27°43E 97 G5
Chilka L. India 19°40N 85°25E 85 K14
Chillán Chile 36°40S 72°10W 121 F2
Chillicothe Ill., U.S.A. 40°55N 89°29W 112 E3
Chillicothe Ohio, U.S.A. 39°20N 82°59W 112 F6
Chilliwack Canada 49°10N 121°54W 108 D7
Chiloé, I. de Chile 42°30S 73°50W 121 G2
Chilpancingo Mexico 17°33N 99°30W 114 D5
Chiltern Hills U.K. 51°40N 0°53W 25 C7
Chilton U.S.A. 44°2N 88°10W 112 D3
Chilung Taiwan 25°3N 121°45E 79 F13
Chilwa, L. Malawi 15°15S 35°40E 97 H7
Chimborazo Ecuador 1°29S 78°55W 120 C2
Chimbote Peru 9°0S 78°35W 120 C2
Chin □ Burma 22°0N 93°0E 85 J18
Chin Hills Burma 22°30N 93°30E 85 H18
China ■ Asia 30°0N 110°0E 79 E11
China, Great Plain of Asia 35°0N 115°0E 72 E13
Chinandega Nic. 12°35N 87°12W 114 E7
Chincha Alta Peru 13°25S 76°7W 120 D2
Chindwin → Burma 21°26N 95°15E 85 J19
Chingola Zambia 12°31S 27°53E 97 G5
Chinhoyi Zimbabwe 17°20S 30°8E 97 H6
Chiniot Pakistan 31°45N 73°0E 84 D8
Chinon France 47°10N 0°15E 66 C4
Chióggia Italy 45°13N 12°17E 68 B5
Chipata Zambia 13°38S 32°28E 97 G6
Chipman Canada 46°6N 65°53W 113 B15
Chippenham U.K. 51°27N 2°6W 24 D4
Chippewa Falls U.S.A. 44°56N 91°24W 112 C2
Chipping Campden U.K. 52°3N 1°45W 24 B5
Chipping Norton U.K. 51°56N 1°32W 24 C5
Chipping Ongar U.K. 51°42N 0°15E 25 C9
Chipping Sodbury U.K. 51°33N 2°23W 24 C4
Chiquinquira Colombia 5°37N 73°50W 120 B2
Chirbury U.K. 52°35N 3°4W 23 G2
Chirchiq Uzbekistan 41°29N 69°35E 87 A12
Chiredzi Zimbabwe 21°0S 31°38E 97 J6
Chirnside U.K. 55°48N 2°12W 21 C11
Chisasibi Canada 53°50N 79°0W 109 D12
Chiseldon U.K. 51°31N 1°44W 24 C5
Chistopol Russia 55°25N 50°38E 70 C9
Chita Russia 52°0N 113°35E 79 A11
Chitral Pakistan 35°50N 71°56E 84 B7
Chittagong Bangla. 22°19N 91°48E 85 H17
Chittagong □ Bangla. 24°5N 91°0E 85 G17
Chitungwiza Zimbabwe 18°0S 31°6E 97 H6
Choiseul St. Lucia 13°47N 61°3W 115 f
Choiseul Solomon Is. 7°0S 156°40E 99 B10
Chōkai-San Japan 39°6N 140°3E 81 D7
Cholet France 47°4N 0°52W 66 C3
Chollerton U.K. 55°4N 2°7W 22 B4
Cholsey U.K. 51°35N 1°8W 24 C6
Choluteca Honduras 13°20N 87°14W 114 E7
Chon Buri Thailand 13°21N 101°1E 82 B2
Ch'ŏngjin N. Korea 41°47N 129°50E 79 C14
Chongqing China 29°35N 106°25E 78 F10
Chongqing Shi □ China 30°0N 108°0E 78 F10
Chonos, Arch. de los Chile 45°0S 75°0W 121 G2
Chorley U.K. 53°39N 2°38W 23 E3
Chorzów Poland 50°18N 18°57E 65 C10
Choybalsan Mongolia 48°4N 114°30E 79 B11
Christchurch N.Z. 43°33S 172°47E 99 J13
Christchurch U.K. 50°44N 1°47W 24 E5
Christmas I. Ind. Oc. 10°30S 105°40E 102 J2
Chubut → Argentina 43°20S 65°5W 121 G3
Chudleigh U.K. 50°36N 3°36W 27 F6
Chudskoye, L. Russia 58°13N 27°30E 70 C4
Chukchi Sea Russia 68°0N 175°0W 77 C19
Chukot Ra. Russia 68°0N 175°0E 77 C18
Chulmleigh U.K. 50°54N 3°51W 27 F6
Chuncheon S. Korea 37°58N 127°44E 79 D14
Chuquicamata Chile 22°15S 69°0W 121 E3
Chur Switz. 46°52N 9°32E 64 E5
Church Stretton U.K. 52°32N 2°48W 23 G3
Churchdown U.K. 51°52N 2°10W 24 C4
Churchill Canada 58°47N 94°11W 108 D10
Churchill → Man., Canada 58°47N 94°12W 108 D10
Churchill → Nfld. & L., Canada 53°19N 60°10W 109 D13
Churchill, C. Canada 58°46N 93°12W 108 D10
Churchill Falls Canada 53°36N 64°19W 109 D13

Churchill L. Canada 55°55N 108°20W 108 D9
Churchill Pk. Canada 58°10N 125°10W 108 D7
Churu India 28°20N 74°50E 84 E9
Chuska Mts. U.S.A. 36°15N 108°50W 110 C5
Chusovoy Russia 58°22N 57°50E 70 C10
Chuvashia □ Russia 55°30N 47°0E 70 C8
Cicero U.S.A. 41°51N 87°44W 112 E4
Ciechanów Poland 52°52N 20°38E 65 B11
Ciego de Ávila Cuba 21°50N 78°50W 115 C9
Cienfuegos Cuba 22°10N 80°30W 115 C8
Cilo Daği Turkey 37°28N 43°55E 71 G7
Cimarron → U.S.A. 36°10N 96°16W 111 C7
Cincinnati U.S.A. 39°9N 84°27W 112 F5
Cinderford U.K. 51°49N 2°30W 24 C3
Cinto, Mte. France 42°24N 8°54E 66 E8
Circle U.S.A. 65°50N 144°4W 108 C5
Circleville U.S.A. 39°36N 82°57W 112 F6
Cirebon Indonesia 6°45S 108°32E 82 F3
Cirencester U.K. 51°43N 1°57W 24 C5
Ciudad Acuña Mexico 29°18N 100°55W 114 B4
Ciudad Bolívar Venezuela 8°5N 63°36W 120 B3
Ciudad del Carmen Mexico 18°38N 91°50W 114 D6
Ciudad Guayana Venezuela 8°0N 62°30W 120 B3
Ciudad Guzmán Mexico 19°41N 103°29W 114 D4
Ciudad Juárez Mexico 31°44N 106°29W 114 A3
Ciudad Madero Mexico 22°19N 97°50W 114 C5
Ciudad Mante Mexico 22°44N 98°59W 114 C5
Ciudad Obregón Mexico 27°29N 109°56W 114 B3
Ciudad Real Spain 38°59N 3°55W 67 C4
Ciudad Valles Mexico 21°59N 99°1W 114 C5
Ciudad Victoria Mexico 23°44N 99°8W 114 C5
Civitavécchia Italy 42°6N 11°48E 68 C4
Cizre Turkey 37°19N 42°10E 71 G7
Clackmannan U.K. 56°7N 3°45W 21 B8
Clacton-on-Sea U.K. 51°47N 1°11E 25 C11
Claire, L. Canada 58°35N 112°5W 108 D8
Clara Ireland 53°21N 7°37W 28 E6
Clare U.K. 52°4N 0°34E 25 B10
Clare □ Ireland 52°45N 9°0W 30 C4
Clare → Ireland 53°20N 9°2W 28 E3
Clare I. Ireland 53°49N 10°0W 28 D1
Claremont U.S.A. 43°23N 72°20W 113 D11
Clarion Fracture Zone Pac. Oc. 20°0N 120°0W 104 H7
Clark Fork → U.S.A. 48°9N 116°15W 110 A3
Clarksburg U.S.A. 39°17N 80°30W 112 F7
Clarksdale U.S.A. 34°12N 90°35W 111 D8
Clarksville U.S.A. 36°32N 87°21W 111 C9
Claverley U.K. 52°32N 2°18W 23 G4
Clay Cross U.K. 53°10N 1°25W 23 F5
Claydon U.K. 52°7N 1°8E 25 B11
Clear, C. Ireland 51°25N 9°32W 30 F3
Clear I. Ireland 51°26N 9°30W 30 F3
Clearfield U.S.A. 41°2N 78°27W 112 E8
Clearwater U.S.A. 27°59N 82°48W 111 E10
Cleator Moor U.K. 54°31N 3°30W 22 C2
Clee Hills U.K. 52°26N 2°35W 23 H3
Cleethorpes U.K. 53°33N 0°3W 23 E8
Cleeve Cloud U.K. 51°56N 2°0W 24 C5
Cleft Hills U.K. 52°25N 2°4W 24 B4
Cleobury Mortimer U.K. 52°22N 2°28W 23 H4
Clermont-Ferrand France 45°46N 3°4E 66 D5
Clevedon U.K. 51°26N 2°52W 24 D3
Cleveland Miss., U.S.A. 33°45N 90°43W 111 D8
Cleveland Ohio, U.S.A. 41°29N 81°41W 112 E7
Cleveland Hills U.K. 54°25N 1°11W 22 D6
Clew B. Ireland 53°50N 9°49W 28 D2
Cley U.K. 52°57N 1°2E 25 A11
Clifden Ireland 53°29N 10°1W 28 E1
Cliffe U.K. 51°28N 0°31E 25 D10
Clifford U.K. 52°7N 3°6W 24 B2
Clinton Iowa, U.S.A. 41°51N 90°12W 112 E2
Clinton Okla., U.S.A. 35°31N 98°58W 110 C7
Clinton Colden L. Canada 63°58N 107°27W 108 C9
Clipperton, I. Pac. Oc. 10°18N 109°13W 103 F17
Clipston U.K. 52°27N 0°58W 25 B7
Clitheroe U.K. 53°53N 2°22W 23 E4
Clogher Hd. Ireland 53°48N 6°14W 29 D9
Cloghran Ireland 53°27N 6°14W 31 B10
Clonakilty Ireland 51°37N 8°53W 30 E5
Clonakilty B. Ireland 51°35N 8°51W 30 E5
Cloncurry → Australia 18°37S 140°40E 98 E7
Clondalkin Ireland 53°19N 6°25W 31 B10
Clones Ireland 54°11N 7°15W 29 C7
Clonmel Ireland 52°21N 7°42W 31 D7
Clontarf Ireland 53°22N 6°11W 31 B10
Cloughton U.K. 54°20N 0°26W 22 D8
Clovelly U.K. 51°0N 4°25W 27 E5
Clovis U.S.A. 34°24N 103°12W 110 D6
Clowne U.K. 53°16N 1°17W 23 F6
Cluj-Napoca Romania 46°47N 23°38E 65 E12
Clun Forest U.K. 52°27N 3°7W 23 H2
Clunbury U.K. 52°25N 2°55W 23 H3
Clwyd → U.K. 53°19N 3°31W 26 A6
Clyde → U.K. 55°55N 4°30W 20 C6
Clyde River Canada 70°30N 68°30W 109 B13
Clyde, Firth of U.K. 55°22N 5°1W 20 D5
Clydebank U.K. 55°54N 4°23W 20 C7
Clydesdale U.K. 55°43N 3°51W 21 C8
Coalbrookdale U.K. 52°39N 2°30W 23 G3
Coalisland U.K. 54°33N 6°42W 29 B8
Coalville U.K. 52°44N 1°23W 23 G6
Coamo Puerto Rico 18°5N 66°22W 115 d
Coast Mts. Canada 55°0N 129°20W 108 D7
Coast Ranges U.S.A. 39°0N 123°0W 110 B2
Coatbridge U.K. 55°52N 4°6W 21 C7
Coaticook Canada 45°10N 71°46W 113 C12
Coats I. Canada 62°30N 83°0W 109 C11
Coats Land Antarctica 77°0S 25°0W 55 D1
Coatzacoalcos Mexico 18°7N 94°25W 114 D6
Cobán Guatemala 15°30N 90°21W 114 D6
Cobar Australia 31°27S 145°48E 98 G8
Cóbh Ireland 51°51N 8°17W 30 E6
Cobija Bolivia 11°0S 68°50W 120 D3
Cobourg Canada 43°58N 78°10W 112 D8
Cochabamba Bolivia 17°26S 66°10W 120 D3
Cochin India 9°58N 76°20E 84 Q10
Cochrane Canada 49°0N 81°0W 109 E11
Cockburn, Canal Chile 54°30S 72°0W 121 H2
Cockburn I. Canada 45°55N 83°22W 112 C6

Cockburn Town Bahamas 24°2N 74°31W 115 C10
Cockerham U.K. 53°58N 2°49W 23 E3
Cockermouth U.K. 54°40N 3°22W 22 C2
Cockfield U.K. 52°10N 0°48E 25 B10
Cockpit Country, The Jamaica 18°15N 77°45W 114 a
Coco → Cent. Amer. 15°0N 83°8W 115 E8
Coco, I. del Pac. Oc. 5°25N 87°55W 114 F7
Cocos Is. Ind. Oc. 12°10S 96°55E 102 J1
Cod, C. U.S.A. 42°5N 70°10W 113 D12
Coddenham U.K. 52°9N 1°8E 25 B11
Codó Brazil 4°30S 43°55W 120 C5
Cody U.S.A. 44°32N 109°3W 110 B5
Coeur d'Alene U.S.A. 47°41N 116°46W 110 A3
Coggeshall U.K. 51°52N 0°42E 25 C10
Cognac France 45°41N 0°20W 66 D3
Coigach U.K. 57°59N 5°14W 18 G7
Coigeach, Rubha U.K. 58°6N 5°26W 18 F7
Coimbatore India 11°2N 76°59E 84 P10
Coimbra Portugal 40°15N 8°27W 67 B1
Colatina Brazil 19°32S 40°37W 122 C2
Colchester U.K. 51°54N 0°55E 25 C10
Cold Fell U.K. 54°53N 2°36W 22 C3
Coldstream U.K. 55°39N 2°15W 21 C11
Colebrook U.S.A. 44°54N 71°30W 113 C12
Colebrooke U.K. 50°47N 3°44W 27 F6
Coleford U.K. 51°47N 2°36W 24 C3
Coleraine U.K. 55°8N 6°41W 29 A8
Coleshill U.K. 52°30N 1°41W 23 G5
Colgrave Sd. U.K. 60°36N 0°58W 18 A16
Colima Mexico 19°14N 103°43W 114 D4
Colima, Nevado de Mexico 19°33N 103°38W 114 D4
Coll U.K. 56°39N 6°34W 20 J4
Collier Law U.K. 54°47N 1°59W 22 C5
Collin U.K. 55°4N 3°31W 21 D8
Collingbourne Kingston U.K. 51°18N 1°40W 24 D5
Collingham U.K. 53°8N 0°46W 23 F7
Collingwood Canada 44°29N 80°13W 112 C7
Collooney Ireland 54°11N 8°29W 28 C5
Colmar France 48°5N 7°20E 66 B7
Colne U.K. 53°51N 2°9W 23 E4
Colne → Bucks., U.K. 51°27N 0°32W 25 D7
Colne → Essex, U.K. 51°51N 0°58E 25 C10
Cologne Germany 50°56N 6°57E 64 C4
Colombia ■ S. Amer. 3°45N 73°0W 120 B2
Colombian Basin Caribbean 14°0N 76°0W 104 H12
Colombo Sri Lanka 6°56N 79°58E 84 R11
Colonsay U.K. 56°5N 6°12W 20 B3
Colorado □ U.S.A. 39°30N 105°30W 110 C5
Colorado → Argentina 39°50S 62°8W 121 F3
Colorado → N. Amer. 31°45N 114°40W 110 D4
Colorado → U.S.A. 28°36N 95°59W 111 E7
Colorado Plateau U.S.A. 37°0N 111°0W 110 C4
Colorado Springs U.S.A. 38°50N 104°49W 110 C6
Colsterworth U.K. 52°49N 0°37W 23 G7
Coltishall U.K. 52°44N 1°21E 25 A11
Columbia Mo., U.S.A. 38°57N 92°20W 111 C81
Columbia S.C., U.S.A. 34°0N 81°2W 111 D10
Columbia Tenn., U.S.A. 35°37N 87°2W 111 C9
Columbia → N. Amer. 46°15N 124°5W 110 A2
Columbia, C. Canada 83°6N 69°57W 104 A13
Columbia, District of □ U.S.A. 38°55N 77°0W 112 F9
Columbia Plateau U.S.A. 44°0N 117°30W 110 B3
Columbus Ga., U.S.A. 32°28N 84°59W 111 D10
Columbus Ind., U.S.A. 39°13N 85°55W 112 F5
Columbus Miss., U.S.A. 33°30N 88°25W 111 D9
Columbus Nebr., U.S.A. 41°26N 97°22W 111 E7
Columbus Ohio, U.S.A. 39°58N 83°0W 112 F6
Colville → U.S.A. 70°25N 150°30W 108 B4
Colwell U.K. 55°5N 2°4W 22 B4
Colwich U.K. 52°48N 1°58W 23 G5
Colwyn Bay U.K. 53°18N 3°44W 26 A6
Colyton U.K. 50°44N 3°5W 27 F1
Comayagua Honduras 14°25N 87°37W 114 E7
Combe Martin U.K. 51°12N 4°3W 27 E5
Comber U.K. 54°33N 5°45W 29 B10
Comeragh Mts. Ireland 52°18N 7°34W 31 D7
Comilla Bangla. 23°28N 91°10E 85 H17
Comitán Mexico 16°15N 92°8W 114 D6
Committee B. Canada 68°30N 86°30W 109 C11
Como Italy 45°47N 9°5E 68 B3
Como, Lago di Italy 46°0N 9°11E 68 B3
Comodoro Rivadavia Argentina 45°50S 67°40W 121 G3
Comoros ■ Ind. Oc. 12°10S 44°15W 91 H8
Compass Mt. S. Africa 31°45S 24°32E 90 K6
Compiègne France 49°24N 2°50E 66 B5
Conakry Guinea 9°29N 13°49W 94 G3
Conceição da Barra Brazil 18°35S 39°45W 122 C3
Concepción Chile 36°50S 73°0W 121 F2
Concepción Paraguay 23°22S 57°26W 121 E4
Concepción, Est. de Chile 50°30S 74°55W 121 H2
Concepción del Oro Mexico 24°38N 101°25W 114 C4
Concepción del Uruguay Argentina 32°35S 58°20W 121 F4
Conception, Pt. U.S.A. 34°27N 120°28W 110 D2
Conchos → Mexico 29°35N 104°25W 114 B4
Concord Calif., U.S.A. 37°59N 122°2W 110 C2
Concord N.H., U.S.A. 43°12N 71°32W 113 D12
Concordia Argentina 31°20S 58°2W 121 F4
Concordia U.S.A. 39°34N 97°40W 110 C7
Condeúba Brazil 14°52S 42°0W 122 B2
Condover U.K. 52°39N 2°44W 23 G3
Congleton U.K. 53°10N 2°13W 23 F4
Congo ■ Africa 1°0S 16°0E 96 E3
Congo → Africa 6°4S 12°24E 96 F2
Congo, Dem. Rep. of the ■ Africa 3°0S 23°0E 96 E4
Congo Basin Africa 0°10S 24°30E 96 E4
Congresbury U.K. 51°23N 2°48W 24 D3
Coningsby U.K. 53°7N 0°10W 23 F8
Conisbrough U.K. 53°29N 1°14W 23 F6
Coniston Canada 46°29N 80°51W 112 B7
Coniston U.K. 54°22N 3°5W 22 D2
Coniston Water U.K. 54°20N 3°5W 22 D2
Conn, L. Ireland 54°3N 9°15W 28 C3
Connacht □ Ireland 53°43N 9°12W 28 D3
Connah's Quay U.K. 53°13N 3°4W 26 A7
Conneaut U.S.A. 41°57N 80°34W 112 E7
Connecticut □ U.S.A. 41°30N 72°45W 113 E11
Connecticut → U.S.A. 41°16N 72°20W 113 E11

Connellsville U.S.A. 40°1N 79°35W 112 E8
Connemara Ireland 53°29N 9°45W 28 E2
Connemara △ Ireland 53°32N 9°52W 28 D2
Connersville U.S.A. 39°39N 85°8W 112 F5
Consett U.K. 54°51N 1°50W 22 C5
Conselheiro Lafaiete Brazil 20°40S 43°48W 122 D2
Constance, L. Europe 47°35N 9°25E 64 E5
Constanța Romania 44°14N 28°38E 65 F15
Constantine Algeria 36°25N 6°42E 94 A7
Constitución Chile 35°20S 72°30W 121 F2
Contagem Brazil 19°56S 44°3W 122 C2
Contas → Brazil 14°17S 39°1W 122 B3
Contwoyto L. Canada 65°42N 110°50W 108 C8
Conway Ark., U.S.A. 35°5N 92°26W 111 C8
Conway N.H., U.S.A. 43°59N 71°7W 113 D12
Conwy U.K. 53°17N 3°50W 26 A6
Conwy □ U.K. 53°10N 3°44W 26 A6
Conwy → U.K. 53°17N 3°50W 26 A6
Coober Pedy Australia 29°1S 134°43E 98 F6
Cook Inlet U.S.A. 60°0N 152°0W 108 D4
Cook Is. Pac. Oc. 17°0S 160°0W 103 J12
Cook Strait N.Z. 41°15S 174°29E 99 J13
Cookstown U.K. 54°39N 6°45W 29 B8
Cooktown Australia 15°30S 145°16E 98 D8
Coondapoor India 13°42N 74°40E 84 N9
Coos Bay U.S.A. 43°22N 124°13W 110 B2
Cootehill Ireland 54°4N 7°5W 29 C7
Copenhagen Denmark 55°40N 12°26E 63 F6
Copiapó Chile 27°30S 70°20W 121 E2
Copper Harbor U.S.A. 47°28N 87°53W 112 B4
Coppermine → Canada 67°49N 116°4W 108 C8
Coquet → U.K. 55°20N 1°32W 22 B5
Coquet I. U.K. 55°20N 1°36W 22 B5
Coquimbo Chile 30°0S 71°20W 121 E2
Coracora Peru 15°5S 73°45W 120 D2
Coral Harbour Canada 64°8N 83°10W 109 C11
Coral Sea Pac. Oc. 15°0S 150°0E 98 C9
Corbin U.S.A. 36°57N 84°6W 112 G5
Corbridge U.K. 54°58N 2°0W 22 C5
Corby U.K. 52°30N 0°41W 25 A7
Corby Glen U.K. 52°49N 0°30W 23 G7
Cordele U.S.A. 31°58N 83°47W 111 D10
Córdoba Argentina 31°20S 64°10W 121 F3
Córdoba Mexico 18°53N 96°56W 114 D5
Córdoba Spain 37°50N 4°50W 67 D3
Córdoba, Sierra de Argentina 31°10S 64°25W 121 F3
Cordova U.S.A. 60°33N 145°45W 108 C5
Corfe Castle U.K. 50°38N 2°3W 24 E4
Corfe Mullen U.K. 50°46N 2°1W 24 E4
Corfu Greece 39°38N 19°50E 69 E8
Corinth U.S.A. 37°56N 22°55E 69 F10
Corinth Greece 34°56N 88°31W 111 D9
Corinth, G. of Greece 38°16N 22°30E 69 E10
Corinto Brazil 18°20S 44°30W 122 C2
Cork Ireland 51°54N 8°29W 30 E6
Cork □ Ireland 51°57N 8°40W 30 E5
Cork Harbour Ireland 51°47N 8°16W 30 E6
Corner Brook Canada 48°57N 57°58W 109 E14
Corning U.S.A. 42°9N 77°3W 112 D9
Cornwall Canada 45°2N 74°44W 113 C10
Cornwall □ U.K. 50°26N 4°40W 27 G4
Cornwall, C. U.K. 50°8N 5°43W 27 G2
Cornwall I. Canada 77°37N 94°38W 109 B10
Cornwallis I. Canada 75°8N 95°0W 109 B10
Coro Venezuela 11°25N 69°41W 120 A3
Corocoro Bolivia 17°15S 68°28W 120 D3
Coromandel Coast India 12°30N 81°0E 84 N12
Coronation Gulf Canada 68°25N 110°0W 108 B8
Coronel Chile 37°0S 73°10W 121 F2
Coronel Fabriciano Brazil 19°31S 42°38W 122 C2
Coronel Pringles Argentina 38°0S 61°30W 121 F3
Coronel Suárez Argentina 37°30S 61°52W 121 F3
Coropuna, Nevado Peru 15°30S 72°41W 120 D2
Corpus Christi U.S.A. 27°47N 97°24W 110 E7
Corraun Pen. Ireland 53°54N 9°54W 28 D2
Corrib, L. Ireland 53°27N 9°16W 30 B4
Corrientes Argentina 27°30S 58°45W 121 E4
Corrientes, C. Colombia 5°30N 77°34W 120 B2
Corrientes, C. Mexico 20°25N 105°42W 114 C3
Corringham U.K. 53°25N 0°41W 23 F7
Corry U.S.A. 41°55N 79°39W 112 E8
Corse, C. France 43°1N 9°25E 66 E8
Corsham U.K. 51°27N 2°10W 24 D4
Corsica □ France 42°0N 9°0E 66 F8
Corsicana U.S.A. 32°6N 96°28W 111 D7
Corsley U.K. 51°13N 2°14W 24 D4
Corte France 42°19N 9°11E 66 E8
Cortez U.S.A. 37°21N 108°35W 110 C5
Cortland U.S.A. 42°36N 76°11W 113 D9
Çorum Turkey 40°30N 34°57E 71 F5
Corumbá Brazil 19°0S 57°30W 120 D4
Corunna = La Coruña Spain 43°20N 8°25W 67 A1
Corvallis U.S.A. 44°34N 123°16W 110 B2
Corve → U.K. 52°22N 2°43W 23 H3
Coseley U.K. 52°33N 2°9W 23 G4
Cosenza Italy 39°18N 16°15E 68 E7
Cosham U.K. 50°51N 1°2W 24 E6
Coshocton U.S.A. 40°16N 81°51W 112 E7
Costa Blanca Spain 38°25N 0°10W 67 C5
Costa Brava Spain 41°30N 3°0E 67 B7
Costa Cálida Spain 37°30N 1°30W 67 D5
Costa Daurada Spain 41°12N 1°15E 67 B6
Costa de la Luz Spain 36°15N 5°58W 67 D2
Costa del Azahar Spain 40°30N 0°30E 67 B6
Costa del Sol Spain 36°30N 4°30W 67 D3
Costa Rica ■ Cent. Amer. 10°0N 84°0W 115 F8
Costa Verde Spain 43°0N 4°14W 67 A3
Cotabato Phil. 7°14N 124°15E 83 C6
Côte d'Azur France 43°25N 7°10E 66 E7
Côte-d'Ivoire = Ivory Coast ■ Africa 7°30N 5°0W 94 G4
Coteau du Missouri U.S.A. 47°0N 100°0W 110 A6
Cotentin France 49°15N 1°30W 66 B3
Cotherstone U.K. 54°35N 1°59W 22 C5
Cotonou Benin 6°20N 2°25E 94 G6
Cotopaxi Ecuador 0°40S 78°30W 120 C2

Cotswold Hills U.K. 51°42N 2°10W 24 C4
Cottbus Germany 51°45N 14°20E 64 C8
Cottenham U.K. 52°18N 0°9E 25 B9
Coudersport U.S.A. 41°46N 78°1W 112 E8
Courantyne → S. Amer. 5°55N 57°5W 120 B4
Courtenay Canada 49°45N 125°0W 108 D7
Cove U.K. 56°0N 4°51W 20 B6
Coventry U.K. 52°25N 1°28W 24 B6
Cover → U.K. 54°17N 1°47W 22 D5
Coverack U.K. 50°1N 5°7W 27 G3
Covington U.S.A. 39°5N 84°30W 112 F5
Cowal U.K. 56°5N 5°8W 20 B5
Cowbridge U.K. 51°27N 3°27W 27 E7
Cowdenbeath U.K. 56°7N 3°21W 21 B9
Cowes U.K. 50°45N 1°18W 24 E6
Cowfold U.K. 50°59N 0°16W 25 E8
Cowpen U.K. 55°8N 1°32W 22 B5
Cox's Bazar Bangla. 21°26N 91°59E 85 J17
Cozumel, Isla Mexico 20°30N 86°40W 114 C7
Crab Hill Barbados 13°19N 59°38W 115 g
Cradock S. Africa 32°8S 25°36E 97 L5
Craig U.S.A. 40°31N 107°33W 110 B5
Craigavon U.K. 54°27N 6°23W 29 C9
Crail U.K. 56°16N 2°37W 21 B10
Craiova Romania 44°21N 23°48E 65 F12
Cramlington U.K. 55°6N 1°34W 22 B5
Cranborne U.K. 50°55N 1°54W 24 E5
Cranborne Chase U.K. 50°56N 2°6W 24 E4
Cranbrook Canada 49°30N 115°46W 108 E8
Cranbrook U.K. 51°6N 0°34E 25 D10
Crandon U.S.A. 45°34N 88°54W 112 C3
Crane, The Barbados 13°6N 59°27W 115 g
Cranleigh U.K. 51°8N 0°28W 25 D8
Crateús Brazil 5°10S 40°39W 120 C5
Crato Brazil 7°10S 39°25W 120 C6
Craven Arms U.K. 52°26N 2°50W 23 H3
Crawfordsville U.S.A. 40°2N 86°54W 112 E4
Crawley U.K. 51°7N 0°11W 25 D8
Credenhill U.K. 52°5N 2°48W 24 B3
Crediton U.K. 50°47N 3°40W 27 F6
Cree → Canada 58°57N 105°47W 108 D9
Cree → U.K. 54°55N 4°25W 20 E7
Cree L. Canada 57°30N 106°30W 108 D9
Cremona Italy 45°7N 10°2E 68 B4
Cres Croatia 44°58N 14°25E 68 B6
Crete Greece 35°15N 25°0E 69 G11
Créteil France 48°47N 2°27E 66 B5
Creuse → France 47°0N 0°34E 66 C4
Crewe U.K. 53°6N 2°26W 23 F4
Crewkerne U.K. 50°53N 2°48W 24 E3
Crianlarich U.K. 56°24N 4°37W 20 B6
Criccieth U.K. 52°55N 4°13W 26 B5
Crick U.K. 52°22N 1°8W 24 B6
Crickhowell U.K. 51°52N 3°8W 26 D7
Cricklade U.K. 51°38N 1°50W 24 C5
Crieff U.K. 56°22N 3°50W 21 B8
Criffell U.K. 54°56N 3°39W 21 E9
Crimea □ Ukraine 45°30N 33°10E 71 E5
Crimean Pen. Ukraine 45°0N 34°0E 71 F5
Crişul Alb → Romania 46°42N 21°17E 65 E11
Crişul Negru → Romania 46°42N 21°16E 65 E11
Croagh Patrick Ireland 53°46N 9°40W 28 D2
Croatia ■ Europe 45°20N 16°0E 68 B7
Croglin U.K. 54°50N 2°39W 22 C3
Crohy Hd. Ireland 54°55N 8°26W 28 B5
Croker, C. Australia 10°58S 132°35E 98 C5
Cromarty U.K. 57°40N 4°2W 19 G9
Cromarty Firth U.K. 57°40N 4°15W 19 G9
Cromdale, Hills of U.K. 57°20N 3°28W 19 H11
Cromer U.K. 52°56N 1°17E 25 A11
Crondall U.K. 51°14N 0°51W 25 D7
Crook U.K. 54°43N 1°45W 22 C5
Crooked I. Bahamas 22°50N 74°10W 115 C10
Crooklands U.K. 54°16N 2°42W 22 D3
Crosby Cumb., U.K. 54°45N 3°25W 22 C2
Crosby Mersey., U.K. 53°30N 3°3W 23 F2
Crosby Ravensworth U.K. 54°33N 2°35W 22 C3
Cross Fell U.K. 54°43N 2°28W 22 C4
Cross Sound U.S.A. 58°0N 135°0W 108 D6
Crosshaven Ireland 51°47N 8°17W 30 E6
Crossmaglen U.K. 54°5N 6°36W 29 C8
Crotone Italy 39°5N 17°8E 68 E7
Crouch → U.K. 51°37N 0°53E 25 C10
Crow Hd. Ireland 51°35N 10°9W 32 E2
Crow Sound U.K. 49°56N 6°16W 27 H1
Crowborough U.K. 51°3N 0°11E 25 D9
Crowland U.K. 52°41N 0°10W 23 G8
Crowle U.K. 53°36N 0°49W 23 E7
Crowsnest Pass Canada 49°40N 114°40W 108 E8
Croyde U.K. 51°7N 4°14W 27 E5
Croydon □ U.K. 51°22N 0°5W 25 D8
Crozet, Is. Ind. Oc. 46°27S 52°0E 53 G12
Cruden Bay U.K. 57°25N 1°52W 19 H14
Crudgington U.K. 52°46N 2°32W 23 G3
Crummock Water U.K. 54°33N 3°18W 22 C2
Cruz Bay U.S. Virgin Is. 18°20N 64°48W 115 e
Cruz das Almas Brazil 12°0S 39°6W 122 B3
Cruzeiro Brazil 22°33S 45°0W 122 D2
Cruzeiro do Sul Brazil 7°35S 72°35W 120 C2
Crystal Falls U.S.A. 46°5N 88°20W 112 B3
Cuando → Angola 17°30S 23°15E 97 H4
Cuango = Kwango → Dem. Rep. of the Congo 3°14S 17°22E 96 E3
Cuanza → Angola 9°21S 13°9E 96 F2
Cuauhtémoc Mexico 28°25N 106°52W 114 B3
Cuba ■ W. Indies 22°0N 79°0W 115 C9
Cubango → Africa 18°50S 22°25E 97 H4
Cuckfield U.K. 51°1N 0°8W 25 D8
Cúcuta Colombia 7°54N 72°31W 120 B2
Cuddalore India 11°46N 79°45E 84 P11
Cuenca Ecuador 2°50S 79°9W 120 C2
Cuenca Spain 40°5N 2°10W 67 B4
Cuernavaca Mexico 18°55N 99°15W 114 D5
Cuiabá Brazil 15°30S 56°0W 120 D4
Cuillin Hills U.K. 57°13N 6°15W 18 H5
Cuillin Sd. U.K. 57°4N 6°20W 18 H5
Cuito → Angola 18°1S 20°48E 97 H4
Culebra Puerto Rico 18°19N 65°18W 115 d

Culiacán

Eastern Group

Culiacán Mexico 24°50N 107°23W 114 C3
Cullen U.K. 57°42N 2°49W 19 G12
Cullompton U.K. 50°51N 3°24W 27 F7
Culm → U.K. 50°46N 3°31W 27 F6
Culpeper U.S.A. 38°30N 78°0W 112 F9
Cumaná Venezuela 10°30N 64°5W 120 A3
Cumberland U.S.A. 39°39N 78°46W 112 F8
Cumberland → U.S.A. 37°9N 88°25W 111 G9
Cumberland Pen. Canada 67°0N 64°0W 109 C13
Cumberland Plateau U.S.A. 36°0N 85°0W 111 C10
Cumberland Sd. Canada 65°30N 66°0W 109 C13
Cumbernauld U.K. 55°57N 3°58W 21 C8
Cumbrae Is. U.K. 55°46N 4°54W 20 C6
Cumbria □ U.K. 54°42N 2°52W 22 C3
Cumbrian Mts. U.K. 54°30N 3°0W 22 D2
Cummertrees U.K. 54°59N 3°20W 21 E9
Cumnock U.K. 55°28N 4°17W 20 D7
Cumnor U.K. 51°44N 1°19W 24 C6
Cumwhinton U.K. 54°52N 2°50W 22 C3
Cunene → Angola 17°20S 11°50E 97 H2
Cúneo Italy 44°23N 7°32E 68 B2
Cunnamulla Australia 28°2S 145°38E 98 F8
Cunninghame U.K. 55°38N 4°35W 20 C6
Cupar U.K. 56°19N 3°1W 21 B9
Curaçao Neth. Ant. 12°10N 69°0W 115 E11
Curicó Chile 34°55S 71°20W 121 F2
Curitiba Brazil 25°20S 49°10W 122 E1
Curlew Mts. Ireland 54°0N 8°20W 28 D5
Curry Rivel U.K. 51°1N 2°52W 24 D3
Curvelo Brazil 18°45S 44°27W 122 C2
Cuttack India 20°25N 85°57E 85 J14
Cuxhaven Germany 53°51N 8°41E 64 B5
Cuyahoga Falls U.S.A. 41°8N 81°29W 112 E7
Cuyuni → Guyana 6°23N 58°41W 120 B4
Cuzco Peru 13°32S 72°0W 120 D2
Cwmbran U.K. 51°39N 3°2W 26 D7
Cyclades Greece 37°0N 24°30E 69 F11
Cynthiana U.S.A. 38°23N 84°18W 112 F5
Cyprus ■ Asia 35°0N 33°0E 86 C3
Cyrenaica Libya 27°0N 23°0E 95 C10
Czech Rep. ■ Europe 50°0N 15°0E 64 D8
Częstochowa Poland 50°49N 19°7E 65 C10

D
Da Lat Vietnam 11°56N 108°25E 82 B3
Da Nang Vietnam 16°4N 108°13E 82 A3
Da Qaidam China 37°50N 95°15E 78 D8
Da Yunhe → China 34°25N 120°5E 79 E12
Daba Shan China 32°0N 109°0E 79 E10
Dabie Shan China 31°20N 115°20E 79 E11
Dadra & Nagar Haveli □ India 20°5N 73°0E 84 J8
Dadu Pakistan 26°45N 67°45E 84 F5
Daegu S. Korea 35°50N 128°37E 79 D14
Daejeon S. Korea 36°20N 127°28E 79 D14
Dagestan □ Russia 42°30N 47°0E 71 F8
Dagupan Phil. 16°3N 120°20E 83 A6
Dahod India 22°50N 74°15E 84 H9
Dahongliutan China 35°45N 79°20E 78 D4
Daingean Ireland 53°18N 7°17W 31 B8
Dajarra Australia 21°42S 139°30E 98 E6
Dakar Senegal 14°34N 17°29W 94 F2
Dakhla W. Sahara 23°50N 15°53W 94 D2
Dakhla, El Wâhât el Egypt 25°30N 28°50E 95 C11
Dalandzadgad Mongolia 43°27N 104°30E 78 C9
Dalbeattie U.K. 54°56N 3°50W 21 E8
Dalhart U.S.A. 36°4N 102°31W 110 C6
Dalhousie Canada 48°5N 66°26W 113 A14
Dali China 25°40N 100°10E 78 F9
Dalian China 38°50N 121°40E 79 D13
Daliang Shan China 28°0N 102°45E 78 F9
Dalkeith U.K. 55°54N 3°4W 21 C9
Dalkey Ireland 53°16N 6°6W 31 B10
Dallas U.S.A. 32°47N 96°48W 111 D7
Dalles, The U.S.A. 45°36N 121°10W 110 A2
Dalmatia Croatia 43°20N 17°0E 68 C7
Dalmellington U.K. 55°19N 4°23W 20 D7
Daloa Ivory C. 7°0N 6°30W 94 G4
Dalry U.K. 55°42N 4°43W 20 C6
Dalrymple, L. Australia 20°45S 147°0E 98 E8
Dalton Dumf. & Gall., U.K. 55°4N 3°24W 21 D9
Dalton N. Yorks., U.K. 54°28N 1°32W 22 D5
Dalton-in-Furness U.K. 54°10N 3°11W 22 D2
Daly Waters Australia 16°15S 133°24E 98 D5
Daman India 20°25N 72°57E 84 J8
Damanhûr Egypt 31°0N 30°30E 95 B12
Damaraland Namibia 20°0S 15°0E 97 H2
Damascus Syria 33°30N 36°18E 86 C4
Damerham U.K. 50°56N 1°51W 24 E5
Dampier Australia 20°41S 116°42E 98 E2
Danakil Desert Ethiopia 12°45N 41°0E 89 E3
Danbury U.K. 51°24N 73°28W 113 E11
Dandong China 40°10N 124°20E 79 C13
Danube → Europe 45°20N 29°40E 65 F15
Danville Ill., U.S.A. 40°8N 87°37W 112 E4
Danville Ky., U.S.A. 37°39N 84°46W 112 G5
Danville Va., U.S.A. 36°36N 79°23W 111 C11
Daqing China 46°35N 125°0E 79 B13
Dar Banda Africa 8°0N 23°0E 90 F6
Dar es Salaam Tanzania 6°50S 39°12E 96 F7
Darbhanga India 26°15N 85°55E 85 F14
Dardanelles Turkey 40°17N 26°32E 86 D12
Darent → U.K. 51°28N 0°14E 25 D9
Dârfûr Sudan 13°40N 24°0E 95 F10
Darhan Mongolia 49°37N 106°21E 78 B10
Darién, G. del Colombia 9°0N 77°0W 120 B2
Darjiling India 27°3N 88°18E 85 F16
Darling → Australia 34°4S 141°54E 98 G7
Darling Ra. Australia 32°30S 116°20E 98 G2
Darlington U.K. 54°32N 1°33W 22 C5
Darmstadt Germany 49°51N 8°39E 64 D5
Darnah Libya 32°45N 22°45E 95 B10
Darnley, C. Antarctica 68°0S 69°0E 54 C6
Darnley B. Canada 69°30N 123°30W 108 C7
Dart → U.K. 50°24N 3°39W 27 G6
Dartford U.K. 51°26N 0°13E 25 D9
Dartington U.K. 50°27N 3°43W 27 G6
Dartmoor U.K. 50°38N 3°57W 27 F6
Dartmoor △ U.K. 50°37N 3°59W 27 F6
Dartmouth Canada 44°40N 63°30W 113 C16

Dartmouth U.K. 50°21N 3°36W 27 G6
Darton U.K. 53°35N 1°31W 23 E5
Darwen U.K. 53°42N 2°29W 23 E4
Darwin Australia 12°25S 130°51E 98 C5
Dashen, Ras Ethiopia 13°8N 38°26E 89 E2
Dashoguz Turkmenistan 41°49N 59°58E 87 A9
Dasht → Pakistan 25°10N 61°40E 84 G2
Datong China 40°6N 113°18E 79 C11
Dauphin Canada 51°9N 100°5W 108 D9
Dauphiné France 45°15N 5°25E 66 D6
Davangere India 14°25N 75°55E 84 M9
Davao Phil. 7°0N 125°40E 83 C7
Davenport U.S.A. 41°32N 90°35W 112 E2
Daventry U.K. 52°16N 1°10W 24 B6
David Panama 8°30N 82°30W 115 F8
Davis Str. N. Amer. 65°0N 58°0W 104 C14
Dawlish U.K. 50°35N 3°28W 27 F7
Dawna Ra. Burma 16°30N 98°30E 85 L21
Dawros Hd. Ireland 54°50N 8°33W 28 B4
Dawson City Canada 64°10N 139°30W 108 C6
Dawson Creek Canada 55°45N 120°15W 108 D7
Dax France 43°44N 1°3W 66 E3
Daxian China 31°15N 107°23E 78 E10
Daxue Shan China 30°30N 101°30E 78 E9
Dayr az Zawr Syria 35°20N 40°5E 86 C5
Dayton U.S.A. 39°45N 84°12W 112 F5
Daytona Beach U.S.A. 29°13N 81°1W 111 E10
De Aar S. Africa 30°39S 24°0E 97 L4
De Pere U.S.A. 44°27N 88°4W 112 C3
Dead Sea Asia 31°30N 35°30E 86 D3
Deal U.K. 51°13N 1°25E 25 D11
Dean, Forest of U.K. 51°45N 2°33W 24 C3
Dearham U.K. 54°44N 3°25W 22 C2
Dease → Canada 59°56N 128°32W 108 D7
Dease Lake Canada 58°25N 130°6W 108 D6
Death Valley U.S.A. 36°15N 116°50W 110 C3
Deben → U.K. 52°1N 1°25E 25 B11
Debenham U.K. 52°14N 1°12E 25 B11
Debre Markos Ethiopia 10°20N 37°40E 89 E2
Debre Tabor Ethiopia 11°50N 38°26E 89 E2
Debrecen Hungary 47°33N 21°42E 65 E11
Decatur Ala., U.S.A. 34°36N 86°59W 111 D9
Decatur Ill., U.S.A. 39°51N 88°57W 112 F3
Decatur Ind., U.S.A. 40°50N 84°56W 112 E5
Deccan India 18°0N 79°0E 84 L11
Deddington U.K. 51°59N 1°18W 24 C6
Dee → Aberds., U.K. 57°9N 2°5W 19 H13
Dee → Dumf. & Gall., U.K. 54°51N 4°3W 20 E7
Dee → Wales, U.K. 53°22N 3°17W 26 A7
Deeping Fen U.K. 52°45N 0°15W 23 G8
Deeping St. Nicholas U.K. 52°45N 0°11W 23 G8
Deer Lake Canada 49°11N 57°27W 109 E14
Defiance U.S.A. 41°17N 84°22W 112 E5
Dehra Dun India 30°20N 78°4E 84 D11
DeKalb U.S.A. 41°56N 88°46W 112 E3
Del Rio U.S.A. 29°22N 100°54W 110 E6
Delabole U.K. 50°37N 4°46W 27 F4
Delaware U.S.A. 40°18N 83°4W 112 E6
Delaware □ U.S.A. 39°0N 75°20W 113 F10
Delaware → U.S.A. 39°15N 75°20W 113 F10
Delaware B. U.S.A. 39°0N 75°10W 111 C12
Delgado, C. Mozam. 10°45S 40°40E 96 G8
Delhi India 28°39N 77°13E 84 E10
Delice Turkey 39°54N 34°2E 71 G5
Delicias Mexico 28°13N 105°28W 114 B3
Déline Canada 65°11N 123°25W 108 C7
Delphos U.S.A. 40°51N 84°21W 112 E5
Delta Junction U.S.A. 64°2N 145°44W 108 C5
Demanda, Sierra de la Spain 42°15N 3°0W 67 A4
Demavend Iran 35°56N 52°10E 87 C8
Deming U.S.A. 32°16N 107°46W 110 D5
Demopolis U.S.A. 32°31N 87°50W 111 D9
Den Helder Neths. 52°57N 4°45E 64 B3
Denbigh U.K. 53°12N 3°25W 26 A7
Denbighshire □ U.K. 53°8N 3°22W 26 A7
Denby Dale U.K. 53°34N 1°40W 23 E5
Denham, Mt. Jamaica 18°13N 77°32W 114 a
Denia Spain 38°49N 0°8E 67 C6
Denizli Turkey 37°42N 29°2E 71 G4
Denmark ■ Europe 55°45N 10°0E 63 F6
Denmark Str. Atl. Oc. 66°0N 30°0W 104 C17
Dennery St. Lucia 13°55N 60°54W 115 f
Denny U.K. 56°1N 3°55W 21 B8
Denpasar Indonesia 8°39S 115°13E 82 F5
Dent U.K. 54°17N 2°27W 22 D4
Denton Gt. Man., U.K. 53°27N 2°9W 23 F4
Denton Lincs., U.K. 52°53N 0°43W 23 G7
Denton U.S.A. 33°13N 97°8W 111 D7
D'Entrecasteaux Is. Papua N. G. 9°0S 151°0E 98 B9
Denver U.S.A. 39°42N 104°59W 110 C5
Deoghar India 24°30N 86°42E 85 G15
Deolali India 19°58N 73°50E 84 K8
Deosai Mts. Pakistan 35°40N 75°0E 84 B9
Dera Ghazi Khan Pakistan 30°5N 70°43E 84 D7
Dera Ismail Khan Pakistan 31°50N 70°50E 84 D7
Derbent Russia 42°5N 48°15E 71 F8
Derby Australia 17°18S 123°38E 98 D3
Derby U.K. 52°56N 1°28W 23 G6
Derbyshire □ U.K. 53°11N 1°38W 23 F5
Dereham U.K. 52°41N 0°57E 25 A10
Derg → U.K. 54°44N 7°26W 28 B7
Derg, L. Ireland 53°0N 8°20W 30 B6
Deridder U.S.A. 30°51N 93°17W 111 D8
Derry = Londonderry U.K. 55°0N 7°20W 28 A7
Derrynasaggart Mts. Ireland 51°58N 9°15W 30 E4
Derwent → Derby, U.K. 52°57N 1°28W 23 G6
Derwent → N. Yorks., U.K. 53°45N 0°58W 23 E7
Derwent → Tyne & W., U.K. 54°58N 1°35W 22 C5
Derwent Water U.K. 54°35N 3°9W 22 C2
Des Moines U.S.A. 41°35N 93°37W 111 B8
Des Moines → U.S.A. 40°23N 91°25W 111 B8
Desborough U.K. 52°27N 0°49W 23 G7
Deschutes → U.S.A. 45°38N 120°55W 110 A2
Dese Ethiopia 11°5N 39°40E 89 E2
Deseado → Argentina 47°45S 65°54W 121 G3
Desford U.K. 52°37N 1°17W 23 G6
Desolación, I. Chile 53°0S 74°0W 121 H2

Dessau Germany 51°51N 12°14E 64 C7
Detour, Pt. U.S.A. 45°40N 86°40W 112 C4
Detroit U.S.A. 42°19N 83°12W 112 D6
Deutsche Bucht Germany 54°15N 8°0E 64 A5
Deventer Neths. 52°15N 6°10E 64 B4
Deveron → U.K. 57°41N 2°32W 19 G12
Devils Lake U.S.A. 48°7N 98°52W 110 A7
Devizes U.K. 51°22N 1°58W 24 D5
Devon □ U.K. 50°50N 3°40W 27 F6
Devon I. Canada 75°10N 85°0W 109 B11
Devonport U.K. 50°22N 4°11W 27 G5
Dewey Puerto Rico 18°18N 65°18W 115 d
Dewsbury U.K. 53°42N 1°37W 23 E5
Dexter U.S.A. 36°48N 89°57W 112 G3
Deyang China 31°3N 104°27E 78 E9
Dezfūl Iran 32°20N 48°30E 86 C7
Dezhneva, C. Russia 66°5N 169°40W 77 C20
Dezhou China 37°26N 116°18E 79 D12
Dhahran Si. Arabia 26°10N 50°7E 86 E7
Dhaka Bangla. 23°43N 90°26E 85 H17
Dhaka □ Bangla. 24°25N 90°25E 85 G17
Dhamār Yemen 14°30N 44°20E 89 E3
Dhamtari India 20°42N 81°35E 85 J12
Dhanbad India 23°50N 86°30E 85 H15
Dharwad India 15°30N 75°4E 84 M9
Dhaulagiri Nepal 28°39N 83°28E 85 E13
Dhenkanal India 20°45N 85°35E 85 J14
Dhuburi India 26°2N 89°59E 85 F16
Dhule India 20°58N 74°50E 84 J9
Diamantina Brazil 18°17S 43°40W 122 C2
Diamantina → Australia 26°45S 139°10E 98 F6
Diamantino Brazil 14°30S 56°30W 120 D4
Dibrugarh India 27°29N 94°55E 85 F19
Dickinson U.S.A. 46°53N 102°47W 110 A6
Didcot U.K. 51°36N 1°14W 24 C6
Diefenbaker, L. Canada 51°0N 106°55W 108 D9
Dieppe France 49°54N 1°4E 66 B4
Digby Canada 44°38N 65°50W 109 E13
Digne-les-Bains France 44°5N 6°12E 66 D7
Dijon France 47°20N 5°3E 66 C6
Dikson Russia 73°40N 80°5E 76 B9
Dili E. Timor 8°39S 125°34E 83 F7
Dillingham U.S.A. 59°3N 158°28W 108 D4
Dimitrovgrad Bulgaria 42°5N 25°35E 69 C11
Dimitrovgrad Russia 54°14N 49°39E 70 D8
Dinajpur Bangla. 25°33N 88°43E 85 G16
Dinan France 48°28N 2°2W 66 B2
Dinant Belgium 50°16N 4°55E 64 C3
Dinaric Alps Croatia 44°0N 16°30E 68 C7
Dingle Ireland 52°9N 10°17W 30 D2
Dingle B. Ireland 52°3N 10°20W 30 D2
Dingwall U.K. 57°36N 4°26W 19 G9
Dipolog Phil. 8°36N 123°20E 83 C6
Dire Dawa Ethiopia 9°35N 41°45E 89 F3
Dirranbandi Australia 28°33S 148°17E 98 F8
Disappointment, C. U.S.A. 46°18N 124°5W 110 A2
Disappointment, L. Australia 23°20S 122°40E 98 E3
Diss U.K. 52°23N 1°7E 25 B11
Distington U.K. 54°36N 3°32W 22 C1
District of Columbia □ U.S.A. 38°55N 77°0W 112 F9
Distrito Federal □ Brazil 15°45S 47°45W 122 C1
Ditchingham U.K. 52°28N 1°28E 25 B11
Ditchling Beacon U.K. 50°54N 0°6W 25 E8
Dittisham U.K. 50°22N 3°37W 27 G6
Ditton Priors U.K. 52°30N 2°34W 23 H3
Diu India 20°45N 70°58E 84 J7
Divinópolis Brazil 20°10S 44°54W 122 D2
Dixon U.S.A. 41°50N 89°29W 112 E3
Dixon Entrance U.S.A. 54°30N 132°0W 108 D6
Diyarbakır Turkey 37°55N 40°18E 71 G7
Dizzard Pt. U.K. 50°44N 4°40W 27 F4
Djerba, Î. de Tunisia 33°50N 10°48E 95 B8
Djelfa Algeria 34°40N 3°15E 94 B6
Djerid, Chott Tunisia 33°42N 8°30E 94 B7
Djibouti Djibouti 11°30N 43°5E 89 E3
Djibouti ■ Africa 12°0N 43°0E 89 E3
Djourab, Erg du Chad 16°40N 18°50E 95 E9
Dmitri Laptev Str. Russia 73°0N 140°0E 77 B15
Dnepropetrovsk Ukraine 48°30N 35°0E 71 E6
Dnieper → Ukraine 46°30N 32°18E 71 E5
Dniester → Europe 46°18N 30°17E 65 E16
Dniprodzerzhynsk Ukraine 48°32N 34°37E 71 E5
Doba Chad 8°40N 16°50E 95 G9
Doberai, Jazirah Indonesia 1°25S 133°0E 83 E8
Dobrich Bulgaria 43°37N 27°49E 69 C12
Dobruja Europe 44°30N 28°15E 65 F15
Docking U.K. 52°54N 0°38E 25 A10
Doddington Cambs., U.K. 52°30N 0°3E 25 B9
Doddington Northumberland, U.K. 55°33N 1°54W 22 A5
Dodecanese Greece 36°35N 27°0E 69 F12
Dodge City U.S.A. 37°45N 100°1W 110 C6
Dodman Pt. U.K. 50°13N 4°48W 27 G4
Dodoma Tanzania 6°8S 35°45E 96 F7
Doha Qatar 25°15N 51°35E 87 E7
Dolbeau-Mistassini Canada 48°53N 72°14W 109 E12
Dole France 47°7N 5°31E 66 C6
Dolgarrog U.K. 53°11N 3°50W 26 A6
Dolgellau U.K. 52°45N 3°53W 26 B6
Dolo Ethiopia 4°11N 42°3E 89 G3
Dolomites Italy 46°23N 11°51E 68 A4
Dolores Argentina 36°20S 57°40W 121 F4
Dolphin and Union Str. Canada 69°5N 114°45W 108 C8
Dolphinton U.K. 55°42N 3°28W 21 D8
Dolton U.K. 50°53N 4°2W 27 F5
Dominica ■ W. Indies 15°20N 61°20W 115 D12
Dominican Rep. ■ W. Indies 19°0N 70°30W 115 D10
Don → Russia 47°4N 39°18E 71 E6
Don → Aberds., U.K. 57°11N 2°5W 19 H13
Don → S. Yorks., U.K. 53°41N 0°52W 23 E7
Don Figueroa Mts. Jamaica 18°5N 77°36W 114 a
Donaghadee U.K. 54°39N 5°33W 29 B10
Doncaster U.K. 53°32N 1°6W 23 E6
Dondra Head Sri Lanka 5°55N 80°40E 84 S12
Donegal Ireland 54°39N 8°5W 28 B5
Donegal □ Ireland 54°53N 8°0W 28 B5
Donegal B. Ireland 54°31N 8°49W 28 B4
Donets → Russia 47°33N 40°55E 71 E7
Donetsk Ukraine 48°0N 37°45E 71 E6
Dong Hoi Vietnam 17°29N 106°36E 82 A3

Dongguan China 22°58N 113°44E 79 G11
Dongola Sudan 19°9N 30°22E 95 E12
Dongting Hu China 29°18N 112°45E 79 F11
Donhead U.K. 51°1N 2°7W 24 D4
Donington U.K. 52°54N 0°12W 23 G8
Donna Nook U.K. 53°29N 0°8E 23 F9
Donostia-San Sebastián Spain 43°17N 1°58W 67 A5
Doon → U.K. 55°27N 4°39W 20 D6
Dorchester Dorset, U.K. 50°42N 2°27W 24 E4
Dorchester Oxon., U.K. 51°39N 1°10W 24 C6
Dorchester, C. Canada 65°27N 77°27W 109 C12
Dordogne → France 45°2N 0°36W 66 D3
Dordrecht Neths. 51°48N 4°39E 64 C3
Dores do Indaiá Brazil 19°27S 45°36W 122 C1
Dorking U.K. 51°14N 0°19W 25 D8
Dornie U.K. 57°17N 5°31W 18 H6
Dornoch U.K. 57°53N 4°2W 19 G9
Dornoch Firth U.K. 57°51N 4°4W 19 G9
Dörööö Nuur Mongolia 48°0N 93°0E 78 B7
Dorset □ U.K. 50°45N 2°26W 24 E4
Dorstone U.K. 52°3N 2°59W 24 B3
Dortmund Germany 51°30N 7°28E 64 C4
Dos Bahias, C. Argentina 44°58S 65°32W 121 G3
Dos Hermanas Spain 37°16N 5°55W 67 D3
Dothan U.S.A. 31°13N 85°24W 111 D9
Douai France 50°21N 3°4E 66 A5
Douala Cameroon 4°0N 9°45E 96 D1
Doubs → France 46°53N 5°1E 66 C6
Douglas I. of Man 54°10N 4°28W 29 C13
Douglas U.S.A. 31°21N 109°33W 110 D5
Dounreay U.K. 58°35N 3°44W 19 E10
Dourados Brazil 22°9S 54°50W 120 E4
Douro → Europe 41°8N 8°40W 67 B1
Dove → Derby, U.K. 52°51N 1°36W 23 G5
Dove → N. Yorks., U.K. 54°15N 0°55W 22 D7
Dove Dale U.K. 53°7N 1°46W 23 F5
Dover U.K. 51°7N 1°19E 25 D11
Dover Del., U.S.A. 39°10N 75°32W 113 F10
Dover N.H., U.S.A. 43°12N 70°56W 113 D12
Dover, Str. of Europe 51°0N 1°30E 62 F7
Dover-Foxcroft U.S.A. 45°11N 69°13W 113 C13
Doveridge U.K. 52°54N 1°49W 23 G5
Dovrefjell Norway 62°15N 9°33E 63 E5
Down □ U.K. 54°23N 6°2W 29 C9
Downham U.K. 52°26N 0°14E 25 B9
Downham Market U.K. 52°37N 0°23E 25 B9
Downpatrick U.K. 54°20N 5°43W 29 C10
Downpatrick Hd. Ireland 54°20N 9°21W 28 B3
Downton U.K. 50°59N 1°44W 24 E5
Drâa, Oued → Morocco 28°40N 11°0W 94 C3
Draguignan France 43°32N 6°27E 66 E7
Drake Passage S. Ocean 58°0S 68°0W 55 B17
Drakensberg S. Africa 31°0S 28°0E 97 L5
Drammen Norway 59°42N 10°12E 63 F6
Drava → Croatia 45°33N 18°55E 69 B8
Dresden Germany 51°3N 13°44E 64 C7
Dreux France 48°44N 1°23E 66 B4
Driffield U.K. 54°0N 0°26W 23 D8
Drina → Bos.-H. 44°53N 19°21E 69 B8
Drobeta-Turnu Severin Romania 44°39N 22°41E 65 F12
Drogheda Ireland 53°43N 6°22W 29 D9
Drohobych Ukraine 49°20N 23°30E 71 E3
Droichead Nua Ireland 53°11N 6°48W 31 B9
Droitwich U.K. 52°16N 2°8W 24 B4
Dromore U.K. 54°31N 7°28W 28 B7
Dromore West Ireland 54°15N 8°52W 28 C4
Dronfield U.K. 53°19N 1°27W 23 F6
Dronning Maud Land Antarctica 72°30S 12°0E 55 D3
Drumheller Canada 51°25N 112°40W 108 D8
Drummond I. U.S.A. 46°1N 83°39W 112 B5
Drummondville Canada 45°55N 72°25W 113 C11
Druridge B. U.K. 55°17N 1°32W 22 B5
Dry Harbour Mts. Jamaica 18°19N 77°24W 114 a
Dryden Canada 49°47N 92°50W 108 E10
Drygalski I. Antarctica 66°0S 92°0E 55 C7
Du Quoin U.S.A. 38°1N 89°14W 112 F3
Duarte, Pico Dom. Rep. 19°2N 70°59W 115 D10
Dubai U.A.E. 25°18N 55°20E 87 E8
Dubawnt → Canada 64°33N 100°6W 108 C9
Dubawnt L. Canada 63°8N 101°28W 108 C9
Dubbo Australia 32°11S 148°35E 98 G8
Dublin Ireland 53°21N 6°15W 31 B10
Dublin U.S.A. 32°32N 82°54W 111 D10
Dublin □ Ireland 53°24N 6°20W 31 B10
Dublin ✈ (DUB) Ireland 53°26N 6°15W 31 B10
DuBois U.S.A. 41°7N 78°46W 112 E8
Dubrovnik Croatia 42°39N 18°6E 69 C8
Dubuque U.S.A. 42°30N 90°41W 112 D2
Duddington U.K. 52°36N 0°32E 25 A7
Duddon → U.K. 54°12N 3°15W 22 D2
Dudinka Russia 69°30N 86°13E 77 C9
Dudley U.K. 52°31N 2°5W 23 G4
Duffield U.K. 52°59N 1°29W 23 G6
Dufftown U.K. 57°27N 3°8W 19 H11
Dugi Otok Croatia 44°0N 15°3E 68 C6
Duisburg Germany 51°26N 6°45E 64 C4
Dukinfield U.K. 53°28N 2°4W 23 F4
Dulce → Argentina 30°32S 62°33W 121 F3
Duluth U.S.A. 46°47N 92°6W 112 B1
Dulverton U.K. 51°2N 3°33W 27 E6
Dumaguete Phil. 9°17N 123°15E 83 C6
Dumbarton U.K. 55°57N 4°33W 20 C6
Dumfries U.K. 55°4N 3°37W 21 D8
Dumfries & Galloway □ U.K. 55°9N 3°58W 21 D8
Dumyât Egypt 31°24N 31°48E 95 B12
Dún Laoghaire Ireland 53°17N 6°8W 31 B10
Duncan U.S.A. 34°30N 97°57W 110 D7
Duncansby Head U.K. 58°38N 3°1W 19 E11
Dunchurch U.K. 52°21N 1°17W 24 B6
Dundalk Ireland 54°1N 6°24W 29 C9
Dundalk Bay Ireland 53°55N 6°15W 29 D9
Dundee U.K. 56°28N 2°59W 21 B10
Dundrum Ireland 53°17N 6°14W 31 B10
Dundrum U.K. 54°16N 5°52W 29 C10
Dundrum B. U.K. 54°13N 5°47W 29 C10
Dunedin N.Z. 45°50S 170°33E 99 K13

Dunfermline U.K. 56°5N 3°27W 21 B9
Dungannon U.K. 54°31N 6°46W 29 B8
Dungarvan Ireland 52°5N 7°37W 31 D7
Dungarvan Harbour Ireland 52°4N 7°35W 31 D7
Dungeness U.K. 50°54N 0°59E 25 E10
Dunhua China 43°20N 128°14E 79 C14
Dunhuang China 40°8N 94°36E 78 C7
Dunkeld U.K. 56°34N 3°35W 21 A8
Dunkerque France 51°2N 2°20E 66 A5
Dunkery Beacon U.K. 51°9N 3°36W 27 E6
Dunkirk U.S.A. 42°29N 79°20W 112 D8
Dunleer Ireland 53°50N 6°24W 29 D9
Dunmanway Ireland 51°43N 9°6W 30 E4
Dunmore U.S.A. 41°25N 75°38W 113 E10
Dunnet Hd. U.K. 58°40N 3°21W 19 E11
Dunoon U.K. 55°57N 4°56W 20 C6
Duns U.K. 55°47N 2°20W 21 C11
Dunsford U.K. 50°41N 3°42W 27 F6
Dunstable U.K. 51°53N 0°32W 25 C7
Dunster U.K. 51°11N 3°27W 24 D2
Dunston U.K. 52°46N 2°7W 23 G4
Dunvegan U.K. 57°27N 6°35W 18 H4
Duque de Caxias Brazil 22°46S 43°18W 122 D2
Durance → France 43°55N 4°45E 66 E6
Durango Mexico 24°3N 104°39W 114 C4
Durango U.S.A. 37°16N 107°53W 110 C5
Durant U.S.A. 33°59N 96°25W 111 D7
Durazno Uruguay 33°25S 56°31W 121 F4
Durban S. Africa 29°49S 31°1E 97 K6
Düren Germany 50°48N 6°29E 64 C4
Durgapur India 23°30N 87°20E 85 H15
Durham U.K. 54°47N 1°34W 22 C5
Durham U.S.A. 35°59N 78°54W 111 C11
Durham □ U.K. 54°42N 1°45W 22 C5
Durlston Hd. U.K. 50°36N 1°57W 24 E5
Durness U.K. 58°34N 4°45W 19 E8
Durrës Albania 41°19N 19°28E 69 D8
Durrington U.K. 51°12N 1°47W 24 D5
Durrow Ireland 52°51N 7°24W 31 D8
Dursey I. Ireland 51°36N 10°12W 30 E2
Dursley U.K. 51°40N 2°21W 24 C4
Dushanbe Tajikistan 38°33N 68°48E 87 B12
Düsseldorf Germany 51°14N 6°47E 64 C4
Dutch Harbor U.S.A. 53°53N 166°32W 108 D3
Duyun China 26°18N 107°29E 78 F10
Dvina, N. → Russia 64°32N 40°30E 70 B7
Dvina B. Russia 65°0N 39°0E 70 B6
Dwarka India 22°18N 69°8E 84 H6
Dyce U.K. 57°13N 2°12W 19 H13
Dyer, C. Canada 66°37N 61°16W 109 C13
Dyersburg U.S.A. 36°3N 89°23W 111 C9
Dyfi → U.K. 52°32N 4°3W 26 B5
Dymchurch U.K. 51°1N 1°0E 25 D11
Dymock U.K. 51°59N 2°26W 24 C4
Dzerzhinsk Russia 56°14N 43°30E 70 C7
Dzhankoy Ukraine 45°40N 34°20E 71 E5
Dzhugdzhur Ra. Russia 57°30N 138°0E 77 D14
Dzungarian Basin China 44°30N 86°0E 78 C6
Dzüünmod Mongolia 47°45N 106°58E 78 B10

E
Eagle U.S.A. 64°47N 141°12W 108 C5
Eagle L. U.S.A. 46°20N 69°22W 113 B13
Eagle Pass U.S.A. 28°43N 100°30W 110 E6
Eagle River U.S.A. 47°25N 88°18W 112 B3
Eaglesfield U.K. 55°4N 3°12W 21 D9
Eakring U.K. 53°9N 0°58W 23 F7
Ealing □ U.K. 51°31N 0°20W 25 C8
Earby U.K. 53°55N 2°7W 23 E4
Eardisley U.K. 52°8N 3°1W 24 B2
Earith U.K. 52°22N 0°2E 25 B9
Earl Shilton U.K. 52°35N 1°18W 23 G6
Earl Soham U.K. 52°14N 1°18E 25 B11
Earls Barton U.K. 52°16N 0°45W 25 B7
Earl's Colne U.K. 51°56N 0°43E 25 C10
Earlston U.K. 55°39N 2°40W 21 C10
Earn → U.K. 56°21N 3°18W 21 B9
Earn, L. U.K. 56°23N 4°13W 20 B7
Earsdon U.K. 55°3N 1°29W 22 B6
Easebourne U.K. 51°0N 0°43W 25 D7
Easington Durham, U.K. 54°47N 1°21W 22 C6
Easington E. Riding, U.K. 53°39N 0°6E 23 E9
Easington Colliery U.K. 54°48N 1°19W 22 C6
Easingwold U.K. 54°8N 1°11W 22 D6
East Ayrshire □ U.K. 55°26N 4°11W 20 C7
East Bengal Bangla. 24°0N 90°0E 85 H17
East Bergholt U.K. 51°59N 1°3E 25 C11
East Beskids Europe 49°20N 22°0E 65 D11
East Brent U.K. 51°15N 2°56W 24 D3
East C. = Dezhneva, C. Russia 66°5N 169°40W 77 C20
East China Sea Asia 30°0N 126°0E 79 F14
East Cowes U.K. 50°45N 1°16W 24 E6
East Falkland Falk. Is. 51°30S 58°30W 121 H4
East Fen U.K. 53°4N 0°5E 23 F9
East Grinstead U.K. 51°7N 0°0 25 D8
East Harling U.K. 52°26N 0°56E 25 B10
East Ilsley U.K. 51°33N 1°15W 24 D6
East Indies Asia 0°0 120°0E 72 J14
East Kilbride U.K. 55°47N 4°11W 20 C7
East Lansing U.S.A. 42°44N 84°29W 112 D5
East London S. Africa 33°0S 27°55E 97 L5
East Lothian □ U.K. 55°58N 2°44W 21 C10
East Markham U.K. 53°15N 0°53W 23 F7
East Moor U.K. 53°16N 1°34W 23 F5
East Pt. Br. Virgin Is. 18°40N 64°18W 115 e
East Pt. Canada 46°27N 61°58W 113 B17
East St. Louis U.S.A. 38°37N 90°9W 112 F2
East Sea = Japan, Sea of Asia 40°0N 135°0E 81 D4
East Siberian Sea Russia 73°0N 160°0E 77 B17
East Sussex □ U.K. 50°56N 0°19E 25 E9
East Timor ■ Asia 8°50S 126°0E 83 F7
East Wittering U.K. 50°46N 0°52W 25 E7
East Woodhay U.K. 51°21N 1°25W 24 D6
Eastbourne U.K. 50°46N 0°18E 25 E9
Eastern Desert Egypt 27°30N 32°30E 95 C12
Eastern Ghats India 14°0N 78°50E 84 N11
Eastern Group Fiji 17°0S 178°30W 99 D15

Eastleigh *U.K.* 50°58N 1°21W **24** E6
Eastmain *Canada* 52°10N 78°30W **109** D12
Eastmain → *Canada* 52°27N 78°26W **109** D12
Eastnor *U.K.* 52°2N 2°23W **24** B4
Easton *Dorset, U.K.* 50°33N 2°26W **24** E4
Easton *Northants., U.K.* 52°37N 0°31W **25** A7
Easton *Md., U.S.A.* 38°47N 76°5W **113** F9
Easton *Pa., U.S.A.* 40°41N 75°13W **113** E10
Easton-in-Gordano *U.K.* 51°28N 2°42W **24** D3
Eastport *U.S.A.* 44°56N 67°0W **113** C14
Eastry *U.K.* 51°14N 1°19E **25** D11
Eastwood *U.K.* 53°1N 1°18W **23** F6
Eaton *U.K.* 52°51N 0°49W **23** G7
Eaton Socon *U.K.* 52°14N 0°17W **25** B8
Eau Claire *U.S.A.* 44°49N 91°30W **112** C2
Eau Claire, L. à l' *Canada* 56°10N 74°25W **109** D12
Ebberston *U.K.* 54°14N 0°37W **22** D7
Ebbw Vale *U.K.* 51°46N 3°12W **26** D7
Eberswalde-Finow *Germany* 52°50N 13°49E **64** B7
Ebetsu *Japan* 43°7N 141°34E **81** B7
Ebinur Hu *China* 44°55N 82°55E **78** C5
Ebolowa *Cameroon* 2°55N 11°10E **96** D2
Ebro → *Spain* 40°43N 0°54E **67** B6
Ecclefechan *U.K.* 55°4N 3°16W **21** D9
Eccleshall *U.K.* 52°52N 2°15W **23** G4
Ech Chéliff *Algeria* 36°10N 1°20E **94** A6
Echo Bay *Canada* 66°5N 117°55W **108** C8
Eckington *U.K.* 53°18N 1°22W **23** F6
Eclipse Sd. *Canada* 72°38N 79°0W **109** B12
Ecuador ■ *S. Amer.* 2°0S 78°0W **120** C2
Ed Damazin *Sudan* 11°46N 34°21E **95** F12
Eday *U.K.* 59°11N 2°47W **19** D12
Eddrachillis B. *U.K.* 58°17N 5°14W **18** F7
Eddystone *U.K.* 50°11N 4°16W **27** G5
Eden → *U.K.* 54°57N 3°1W **22** C2
Edenbridge *U.K.* 51°12N 0°5E **25** D9
Edenderry *Ireland* 53°21N 7°4W **31** B8
Edfu *Egypt* 24°55N 32°49E **95** D12
Edge Hill *U.K.* 52°8N 1°26W **24** B6
Edinburgh *U.K.* 55°57N 3°13W **21** C9
Edinburgh ✕ (EDI) *U.K.* 55°54N 3°22W **21** C9
Edington *U.K.* 51°17N 2°5W **24** D4
Edirne *Turkey* 41°40N 26°34E **71** F4
Edmonton *Canada* 53°30N 113°30W **108** D8
Edmundbyers *U.K.* 54°50N 1°58W **22** C5
Edmundston *Canada* 47°23N 68°20W **109** E13
Edremit *Turkey* 39°34N 27°0E **86** B1
Edson *Canada* 53°35N 116°28W **108** D8
Edward, L. *Africa* 0°25S 29°40E **96** E5
Edward VII Land *Antarctica* 80°0S 150°0W **55** E13
Edwards Plateau *U.S.A.* 30°45N 101°20W **110** D6
Effingham *U.S.A.* 39°7N 88°33W **112** F3
Égadi, Ísole *Italy* 37°55N 12°16E **68** F5
Eganville *Canada* 45°32N 77°5W **112** C9
Eger *Hungary* 47°53N 20°27E **65** E11
Egham *U.K.* 51°25N 0°32W **25** D7
Eglinton I. *Canada* 75°48N 118°30W **109** B8
Egremont *U.K.* 54°29N 3°32W **22** D1
Eğridir *Turkey* 37°52N 30°51E **71** G5
Eğridir Gölü *Turkey* 37°53N 30°50E **71** G5
Egton *U.K.* 54°28N 0°44W **22** D7
Egypt ■ *Africa* 28°0N 31°0E **95** C12
Eifel *Germany* 50°15N 6°50E **64** C4
Eigg *U.K.* 56°54N 6°10W **18** J5
Eil, L. *U.K.* 56°51N 5°16W **18** J7
Eindhoven *Neths.* 51°26N 5°28E **64** C3
Eire = Ireland ■ *Europe* 53°50N 7°52W **62** E2
Eivissa *Spain* 38°54N 1°26E **67** C6
Ekaterinburg *Russia* 56°50N 60°30E **76** D7
Ekibastuz *Kazakhstan* 51°50N 75°10E **76** D8
El Aaiún *W. Sahara* 27°9N 13°12W **94** C3
El Alamein *Egypt* 30°48N 28°58E **95** B11
El Centro *U.S.A.* 32°48N 115°34W **110** D3
El Djouf *Mauritania* 20°0N 9°0W **94** D4
El Dorado *U.S.A.* 33°12N 92°40W **111** D8
El Faiyûm *Egypt* 29°19N 30°50E **95** C12
El Fâsher *Sudan* 13°33N 25°26E **95** F11
El Fuerte *Mexico* 26°25N 108°39W **114** B3
El Geneina *Sudan* 13°27N 22°45E **95** F10
El Gezira □ *Sudan* 15°0N 33°0E **95** F12
El Gîza *Egypt* 30°0N 31°12E **95** C12
El Istiwa'iya *Sudan* 5°0N 28°0E **95** G11
El Jadida *Morocco* 33°11N 8°17W **94** B4
El Khârga *Egypt* 25°30N 30°33E **95** C12
El Mahalla el Kubra *Egypt* 31°0N 31°0E **95** B12
El Mansûra *Egypt* 31°0N 31°19E **95** B12
El Minyâ *Egypt* 28°7N 30°33E **95** C12
El Obeid *Sudan* 13°8N 30°10E **95** F12
El Oued *Algeria* 33°20N 6°58E **94** B7
El Paso *U.S.A.* 31°45N 106°29W **110** D5
El Puerto de Santa María *Spain* 36°36N 6°13W **67** D2
El Reno *U.S.A.* 35°32N 97°57W **110** C7
El Salvador ■ *Cent. Amer.* 13°50N 89°0W **114** E7
El Tigre *Venezuela* 8°44N 64°15W **120** B3
El Uqsur *Egypt* 25°41N 32°38E **95** C12
Elat *Israel* 29°30N 34°56E **86** D3
Elâzığ *Turkey* 38°37N 39°14E **71** G6
Elba *Italy* 42°46N 10°17E **68** C4
Elbasan *Albania* 41°9N 20°9E **69** D9
Elbe → *Europe* 53°50N 9°0E **64** B5
Elbert, Mt. *U.S.A.* 39°7N 106°27W **110** C5
Elbeuf *France* 49°17N 1°2E **66** B4
Elbląg *Poland* 54°10N 19°25E **65** A10
Elbrus *Russia* 43°21N 42°30E **71** F7
Elburz Mts. *Iran* 36°0N 52°0E **87** B8
Elche *Spain* 38°15N 0°42W **67** C5
Elda *Spain* 38°29N 0°47W **67** C5
Eldoret *Kenya* 0°30N 35°17E **96** D7
Elektrostal *Russia* 55°41N 38°32E **70** C6
Elemi Triangle *Africa* 5°0N 35°20E **96** D7
Elephant Butte Res. *U.S.A.* 33°9N 107°11W **110** D5
Elephant I. *Antarctica* 61°0S 55°0W **55** C18
Eleuthera *Bahamas* 25°0N 76°20W **115** C9
Elgin *U.K.* 57°39N 3°19W **19** G11
Elgin *U.S.A.* 42°2N 88°17W **112** D3
Elgon, Mt. *Africa* 1°10N 34°30E **96** D6
Elham *U.K.* 51°9N 1°8E **25** D11
Elishaw *U.K.* 55°15N 2°14W **22** B4
Elista *Russia* 46°16N 44°14E **71** E7
Elizabeth *U.S.A.* 40°39N 74°12W **113** E10
Elizabeth City *U.S.A.* 36°18N 76°14W **111** C11
Elizabethtown *U.S.A.* 37°42N 85°52W **112** G5
Elkhart *U.S.A.* 41°41N 85°58W **112** E5
Elkins *U.S.A.* 38°55N 79°51W **112** F8
Elko *U.S.A.* 40°50N 115°46W **110** B3
Elland *U.K.* 53°41N 1°50W **23** E5
Ellef Ringnes I. *Canada* 78°30N 102°2W **109** B9
Ellen → *U.K.* 54°44N 3°30W **22** C2
Ellensburg *U.S.A.* 46°59N 120°34W **110** A2
Ellerton *Barbados* 13°7N 59°33W **115** g
Ellesmere *U.K.* 52°55N 2°53W **23** G3
Ellesmere I. *Canada* 79°30N 80°0W **109** B12
Ellesmere Port *U.K.* 53°17N 2°54W **23** F3
Ellington *U.K.* 55°14N 1°33W **22** B5
Elliot Lake *Canada* 46°25N 82°35W **109** E11
Ellon *U.K.* 57°22N 2°4W **19** H13
Ellsworth Land *Antarctica* 76°0S 89°0W **55** D16
Elmalı *Turkey* 36°44N 29°56E **71** G4
Elmira *U.S.A.* 42°6N 76°48W **112** D9
Elmswell *U.K.* 52°15N 0°55E **25** B10
Eluru *India* 16°48N 81°8E **85** L12
Ely *U.K.* 52°24N 0°16E **25** B9
Ely *U.S.A.* 39°15N 114°54W **110** C4
Elyria *U.S.A.* 41°22N 82°7W **112** E6
eMalahleni *S. Africa* 25°51S 29°14E **97** K5
Emāmrūd *Iran* 36°30N 55°0E **87** B8
Embarcación *Argentina* 23°10S 64°0W **121** E3
Embleton *U.K.* 55°29N 1°38W **22** B5
Emden *Germany* 53°21N 7°12E **64** B4
Emerald *Australia* 37°56S 145°29E **98** E8
Emmen *Neths.* 52°48N 6°57E **64** B4
Emmonak *U.S.A.* 62°47N 164°31W **108** C3
Empalme *Mexico* 27°58N 110°51W **114** B2
Empangeni *S. Africa* 28°50S 31°52E **97** K6
Empedrado *Argentina* 28°0S 58°46W **121** E4
Emporia *U.S.A.* 38°25N 96°11W **111** C7
Emporium *U.S.A.* 41°31N 78°14W **112** E8
Empty Quarter = Rub' al Khālī *Si. Arabia* 19°0N 48°0E **89** D4
Ems → *Germany* 53°20N 7°12E **64** B4
En Nahud *Sudan* 12°45N 28°25E **95** F11
Enard B. *U.K.* 58°5N 5°20W **18** F7
Encarnación *Paraguay* 27°15S 55°50W **121** E4
Encounter B. *Australia* 35°45S 138°45E **98** H6
Ende *Indonesia* 8°45S 121°40E **83** F6
Enderbury *Kiribati* 3°8S 171°5W **102** H10
Enderby *U.K.* 52°36N 1°13W **23** G6
Enderby Land *Antarctica* 66°0S 53°0E **55** C5
Endicott *U.S.A.* 42°6N 76°4W **113** D9
Enewetak Atoll *Marshall Is.* 11°30N 162°15E **102** F8
Enez *Turkey* 40°45N 26°5E **71** F4
Enfer, Pte. d' *Martinique* 14°22N 60°54W **114** c
Enfield □ *U.K.* 51°38N 0°5W **25** C8
Engadin *Switz.* 46°45N 10°10E **64** E6
Engels *Russia* 51°28N 46°6E **71** D8
Enggano *Indonesia* 5°20S 102°40E **82** F2
England □ *U.K.* 53°0N 2°0W **62** E6
English → *Canada* 49°12N 91°5W **108** D10
English Channel *Europe* 50°0N 2°0W **62** F6
Enid *U.S.A.* 36°24N 97°53W **110** C7
Ennadai L. *Canada* 60°58N 101°20W **108** C9
Ennedi *Chad* 17°15N 22°0E **95** E10
Ennerdale Water *U.K.* 54°32N 3°24W **22** C2
Ennis *Ireland* 52°51N 8°59W **30** C5
Enniscorthy *Ireland* 52°30N 6°34W **31** D9
Enniskillen *U.K.* 54°21N 7°39W **28** C6
Ennistimon *Ireland* 52°57N 9°17W **30** C4
Enns → *Austria* 48°14N 14°32E **64** D8
Enschede *Neths.* 52°13N 6°53E **64** B4
Ensenada *Mexico* 31°52N 116°37W **114** A1
Enshi *China* 30°18N 109°29E **79** E10
Enstone *U.K.* 51°55N 1°27W **24** C6
Entebbe *Uganda* 0°4N 32°28E **96** D6
Entre Rios □ *Argentina* 30°30S 58°30W **121** F4
Enugu *Nigeria* 6°30N 7°30E **94** G7
Eólie, Ís. *Italy* 38°30N 14°57E **68** E6
Épernay *France* 49°3N 3°56E **66** B5
Épinal *France* 48°10N 6°27E **66** B7
Epping *U.K.* 51°41N 0°7E **25** C9
Epping Forest *U.K.* 51°40N 0°5E **25** C9
Epsom *U.K.* 51°19N 0°16W **25** D8
Epworth *U.K.* 53°32N 0°48W **23** E7
Equatorial Guinea ■ *Africa* 2°0N 8°0E **96** D1
Er Rachidia *Morocco* 31°58N 4°20W **94** B5
Erciyaş Dağı *Turkey* 38°30N 35°30E **86** B3
Erdenet *Mongolia* 49°2N 104°5E **78** B9
Erebus, Mt. *Antarctica* 77°35S 167°0E **55** D11
Ereğli *Konya, Turkey* 37°31N 34°4E **71** G5
Ereğli *Zonguldak, Turkey* 41°15N 31°24E **71** F5
Erfurt *Germany* 50°58N 11°2E **64** C6
Ergeni Lowlands *Russia* 47°0N 44°0E **71** E7
Eriboll, L. *U.K.* 58°30N 4°42W **19** E8
Erie *U.S.A.* 42°8N 80°5W **112** D7
Erie, L. *N. Amer.* 42°15N 81°0W **112** D7
Eriskay *U.K.* 57°4N 7°18W **18** H3
Eritrea ■ *Africa* 14°0N 38°30E **89** D2
Erlangen *Germany* 49°36N 11°0E **64** D6
Ermoupoli *Greece* 37°28N 24°57E **69** F11
Ernakulam *India* 9°59N 76°22E **84** Q10
Erne → *Ireland* 54°30N 8°16W **28** C5
Erne, Lower L. *U.K.* 54°28N 7°47W **28** C6
Erne, Upper L. *U.K.* 54°14N 7°32W **28** C6
Erode *India* 11°24N 77°45E **84** P10
Erramala Hills *India* 15°30N 78°15E **84** M11
Errigal *Ireland* 55°2N 8°6W **28** A5
Erris Hd. *Ireland* 54°19N 10°0W **28** C1
Erromango *Vanuatu* 18°45S 169°5E **99** D12
Erzgebirge *Germany* 50°27N 12°55E **64** C7
Erzincan *Turkey* 39°46N 39°30E **71** G6
Erzurum *Turkey* 39°57N 41°15E **71** G7
Esbjerg *Denmark* 55°29N 8°29E **63** F5
Escada *Brazil* 8°22S 35°8W **122** A3
Escanaba *U.S.A.* 45°45N 87°4W **112** C4
Esch-sur-Alzette *Lux.* 49°32N 6°0E **64** D3
Escrick *U.K.* 53°53N 1°2W **23** E6
Escuinapa de Hidalgo *Mexico* 22°50N 105°50W **114** C3
Escuintla *Guatemala* 14°20N 90°48W **114** E6
Eşfahān *Iran* 32°39N 51°43E **87** C7
Esha Ness *U.K.* 60°29N 1°38W **18** B14
Esk → *Cumb., U.K.* 54°20N 3°24W **22** D2
Esk → *Dumf. & Gall., U.K.* 54°58N 3°2W **21** E9
Esk → *N. Yorks., U.K.* 54°30N 0°37W **22** D7
Eskdale *U.K.* 55°12N 3°4W **21** D9
Esker Siding *Canada* 53°53N 66°25W **109** D13
Eskilstuna *Sweden* 59°22N 16°32E **63** F7
Eskişehir *Turkey* 39°50N 30°30E **71** G5
Eslāmābād-e Gharb *Iran* 34°10N 46°30E **86** C6
Esna *Egypt* 25°17N 32°30E **95** C12
Esperance *Australia* 33°45S 121°55E **98** G3
Esperanza *Puerto Rico* 18°6N 65°28W **115** d
Espinhaço, Serra do *Brazil* 17°30S 43°30W **122** C2
Espírito Santo □ *Brazil* 20°0S 40°45W **122** C2
Espíritu Santo *Vanuatu* 15°15S 166°50E **99** D12
Espoo *Finland* 60°12N 24°40E **63** E8
Essaouira *Morocco* 31°32N 9°42W **94** B4
Essen *Germany* 51°28N 7°2E **64** C4
Essequibo → *Guyana* 6°50N 58°30W **120** B4
Essex □ *U.K.* 51°54N 0°27E **25** C9
Esslingen *Germany* 48°44N 9°18E **64** D5
Estados, I. de Los *Argentina* 54°40S 64°30W **121** H3
Estância *Brazil* 11°16S 37°26W **122** B3
Estevan *Canada* 49°10N 102°59W **108** E9
Eston *U.K.* 54°34N 1°8W **22** C6
Estonia ■ *Europe* 58°30N 25°30E **63** F8
Estrela, Serra da *Portugal* 40°10N 7°45W **67** B2
Estrondo, Serra do *Brazil* 7°20S 48°0W **120** C5
Etawah *India* 26°48N 79°6E **84** F11
Etchingham *U.K.* 51°0N 0°26E **25** D9
Ethiopia ■ *Africa* 8°0N 40°0E **89** F3
Ethiopian Highlands *Ethiopia* 10°0N 37°0E **89** F2
Etive, L. *U.K.* 56°29N 5°10W **20** B5
Etna *Italy* 37°50N 14°55E **68** F6
Eton *U.K.* 51°30N 0°36W **25** C7
Etosha Pan *Namibia* 18°40S 16°30E **97** H3
Ettington *U.K.* 52°8N 1°35W **24** B5
Ettrick Forest *U.K.* 55°30N 3°0W **21** C9
Ettrick Water → *U.K.* 55°31N 2°55W **21** C10
Euclid *U.S.A.* 41°34N 81°32W **112** E7
Eugene *U.S.A.* 44°5N 123°4W **110** B2
Euphrates → *Asia* 31°0N 47°25E **86** D6
Eureka *Canada* 80°0N 85°56W **109** B11
Eureka *U.S.A.* 40°47N 124°9W **110** B2
Europa, Île *Ind. Oc.* 22°20S 40°22E **97** J8
Europa, Picos de *Spain* 43°10N 4°49W **67** A3
Europe 50°0N 20°0E **56** E10
Eurotunnel Terminal *U.K.* 51°6N 1°10E **25** D11
Euxton *U.K.* 53°41N 2°41W **23** E3
Evanston *Ill., U.S.A.* 42°3N 87°40W **112** D4
Evanston *Wyo., U.S.A.* 41°16N 110°58W **110** B4
Evansville *U.S.A.* 37°58N 87°35W **112** G4
Evercreech *U.K.* 51°9N 2°30W **24** D4
Everest, Mt. *Nepal* 28°5N 86°58E **85** E15
Everett *U.S.A.* 47°59N 122°12W **110** A2
Everglades, The *U.S.A.* 25°50N 81°0W **111** E10
Evesham *U.K.* 52°6N 1°56W **24** B5
Évia *Greece* 38°30N 24°0E **69** E11
Évora *Portugal* 38°33N 7°57W **67** C2
Évreux *France* 49°3N 1°8E **66** B4
Evros → *Greece* 41°40N 26°34E **69** D12
Ewe, L. *U.K.* 57°49N 5°38W **18** G6
Ewell *U.K.* 51°20N 0°14W **25** D8
Ewhurst *U.K.* 51°9N 0°25W **25** D8
Exe → *U.K.* 50°41N 3°29W **27** F7
Exeter *U.K.* 50°43N 3°31W **27** F6
Exminster *U.K.* 50°40N 3°29W **27** F7
Exmoor *U.K.* 51°12N 3°45W **27** E6
Exmoor △ *U.K.* 51°8N 3°42W **27** E6
Exmouth *U.K.* 50°37N 3°25W **27** F7
Exton *U.K.* 52°42N 0°38W **23** G7
Extremadura □ *Spain* 39°30N 6°5W **67** C2
Eyam *U.K.* 53°17N 1°40W **23** F5
Eyasi, L. *Tanzania* 3°30S 35°0E **96** E6
Eye *Cambs., U.K.* 52°37N 0°11W **25** A8
Eye *Suffolk, U.K.* 52°19N 1°9E **25** B11
Eye Pen. *U.K.* 58°13N 6°10W **18** F5
Eyemouth *U.K.* 55°52N 2°5W **21** C11
Eynsham *U.K.* 51°47N 1°22W **24** C6
Eyre, L. *Australia* 29°30S 137°26E **98** F6
Eyre Pen. *Australia* 33°30S 136°17E **98** G6

F

F.Y.R.O.M. = Macedonia ■ *Europe* 41°53N 21°40E **69** D9
Faenza *Italy* 44°17N 11°53E **68** B4
Fair Hd. *U.K.* 55°14N 6°9W **29** A9
Fair Isle *U.K.* 59°32N 1°38W **18** C14
Fairbanks *U.S.A.* 64°51N 147°43W **108** C5
Fairfield *U.S.A.* 38°23N 88°22W **112** F3
Fairford *U.K.* 51°43N 1°46W **24** C5
Fairlight *U.K.* 50°52N 0°40E **25** E10
Fairmont *U.S.A.* 39°29N 80°9W **112** F7
Fairweather, Mt. *U.S.A.* 58°55N 137°32W **108** D6
Faisalabad *Pakistan* 31°30N 73°5E **84** D8
Faizabad *India* 26°45N 82°10E **85** F13
Fajardo *Puerto Rico* 18°20N 65°39W **115** d
Fakenham *U.K.* 52°51N 0°51E **25** A10
Falcon Res. *U.S.A.* 26°34N 99°10W **110** E7
Faldingworth *U.K.* 53°21N 0°24W **23** F8
Falkirk *U.K.* 56°0N 3°47W **21** C8
Falkland *U.K.* 56°16N 3°12W **21** B9
Falkland Is. ☑ *Atl. Oc.* 51°30S 59°0W **121** H4
Fall River *U.S.A.* 41°43N 71°10W **113** E12
Falmouth *Jamaica* 18°30N 77°40W **114** a
Falmouth *U.K.* 50°9N 5°5W **27** G3
Falmouth B. *U.K.* 50°6N 5°5W **27** G3
Falsa, Pta. *Mexico* 27°51N 115°3W **104** G8
Falstone *U.K.* 55°11N 2°26W **22** B4
Falun *Sweden* 60°37N 15°37E **63** E7
Famagusta *Cyprus* 35°8N 33°55E **86** C3
Fanad Hd. *Ireland* 55°17N 7°38W **28** A6
Fannich, L. *U.K.* 57°38N 4°59W **19** G8
Fano *Italy* 43°50N 13°1E **68** C5
Far East *Asia* 40°0N 130°0E **72** E14
Farāh *Afghan.* 32°20N 62°7E **87** C10
Farasān *Si. Arabia* 16°45N 41°55E **89** D3
Fareham *U.K.* 50°51N 1°11W **24** E6
Farewell C. *Greenland* 59°48N 43°55W **104** D15
Farghona *Uzbekistan* 40°23N 71°19E **76** E7
Fargo *U.S.A.* 46°53N 96°48W **111** A7
Faridabad *India* 28°26N 77°19E **84** E10
Faringdon *U.K.* 51°39N 1°34W **24** C5
Farmington *U.S.A.* 36°44N 108°12W **110** C5
Farmville *U.S.A.* 37°18N 78°24W **112** G8
Farnborough *U.K.* 51°16N 0°45W **25** D7
Farne Is. *U.K.* 55°38N 1°37W **22** A5
Farnham *U.K.* 51°13N 0°47W **25** D7
Farnworth *U.K.* 53°34N 2°25W **23** E4
Faro *Canada* 62°11N 133°22W **108** C6
Faro *Portugal* 37°2N 7°55W **67** D2
Faroe Is. ☑ *Atl. Oc.* 62°0N 7°0W **57** C4
Fārs □ *Iran* 29°30N 55°0E **87** D8
Fāryāb □ *Afghan.* 36°0N 65°0E **87** B11
Faslane *U.K.* 56°5N 4°49W **20** B6
Fataka *Solomon Is.* 11°55S 170°12E **99** C12
Fatehgarh *India* 27°25N 79°35E **84** F11
Fatehpur *Raj., India* 28°0N 74°40E **84** F9
Fatehpur *Ut. P., India* 25°56N 81°13E **85** G12
Fauldhouse *U.K.* 55°50N 3°43W **21** C8
Faversham *U.K.* 51°19N 0°56E **25** D10
Fawley *U.K.* 50°50N 1°20W **24** E6
Fayetteville *Ark., U.S.A.* 36°4N 94°10W **111** C8
Fayetteville *N.C., U.S.A.* 35°3N 78°53W **111** D11
Fazeley *U.K.* 52°37N 1°40W **23** G5
Fazilka *India* 30°27N 74°2E **84** D9
Fdérik *Mauritania* 22°40N 12°45W **94** D3
Feale → *Ireland* 52°27N 9°37W **30** D3
Fear, C. *U.S.A.* 33°50N 77°58W **111** D11
Fécamp *France* 49°45N 0°22E **66** B4
Fehmarn *Germany* 54°27N 11°7E **64** A6
Feira de Santana *Brazil* 12°15S 38°57W **122** B3
Felipe Carrillo Puerto *Mexico* 19°38N 88°3W **114** D7
Felixstowe *U.K.* 51°58N 1°23E **25** C11
Felton *U.K.* 55°18N 1°42W **22** B5
Feltwell *U.K.* 52°30N 0°32E **25** B10
Fenny Bentley *U.K.* 53°3N 1°45W **23** F5
Fenny Compton *U.K.* 52°10N 1°23W **24** B6
Fenny Stratford *U.K.* 52°0N 0°44W **25** C7
Fens, The *U.K.* 52°38N 0°2W **25** A8
Fenyang *China* 37°18N 111°48E **79** D11
Feodosiya *Ukraine* 45°2N 35°16E **71** E6
Fergus Falls *U.S.A.* 46°17N 96°4W **111** A7
Ferkéssédougou *Ivory C.* 9°35N 5°6W **94** G4
Fermanagh □ *U.K.* 54°21N 7°40W **28** C6
Fermont *Canada* 52°47N 67°5W **109** D13
Fermoy *Ireland* 52°9N 8°16W **30** D6
Fernhurst *U.K.* 51°3N 0°43W **25** D7
Ferrara *Italy* 44°50N 11°35E **68** B4
Ferret, C. *France* 44°38N 1°15W **66** D3
Ferrol *Spain* 43°29N 8°15W **67** A1
Ferryhill *U.K.* 54°41N 1°33W **22** C5
Fès *Morocco* 34°0N 5°0W **94** B5
Fethiye *Turkey* 36°36N 29°6E **71** G4
Fetlar *U.K.* 60°36N 0°52W **18** A16
Feuilles → *Canada* 58°47N 70°4W **109** D12
Feyzābād *Afghan.* 37°7N 70°33E **87** B12
Fezzan *Libya* 27°0N 13°0E **95** C8
Ffestiniog *U.K.* 52°57N 3°55W **26** B6
Fianarantsoa *Madag.* 21°26S 47°5E **97** J9
Fife □ *U.K.* 56°16N 3°1W **21** B9
Fife Ness *U.K.* 56°17N 2°35W **21** B10
Figeac *France* 44°37N 2°2E **66** D5
Figueres *Spain* 42°18N 2°58E **67** A7
Fiji ■ *Pac. Oc.* 17°20S 179°0E **99** D14
Filby *U.K.* 52°40N 1°39E **25** A12
Filey *U.K.* 54°12N 0°18W **22** D8
Filey B. *U.K.* 54°12N 0°15W **22** D8
Filton *U.K.* 51°30N 2°34W **24** C3
Fincham *U.K.* 52°38N 0°30E **25** A9
Findhorn → *U.K.* 57°38N 3°38W **19** G10
Findlay *U.S.A.* 41°2N 83°39W **112** E6
Finedon *U.K.* 52°21N 0°39W **25** B7
Fingal's Cave *U.K.* 56°27N 6°21W **20** B3
Fingals *Ireland* 53°23N 6°19W **31** B10
Finike *Turkey* 36°21N 30°10E **86** B2
Finland ■ *Europe* 63°0N 27°0E **63** E9
Finland, G. of *Europe* 60°0N 26°0E **63** F9
Finlay → *Canada* 57°0N 125°10W **108** D7
Finn → *Ireland* 54°51N 7°28W **28** B7
Firozabad *India* 27°10N 78°25E **84** F11
Firozpur *India* 30°55N 74°40E **84** D9
Fish → *Namibia* 28°7S 17°10E **97** K3
Fishguard *U.K.* 52°0N 4°58W **26** D4
Fishtoft *U.K.* 52°58N 0°1E **23** G9
Fisterra, C. *Spain* 42°50N 9°19W **67** A1
Fitchburg *U.S.A.* 42°35N 71°48W **113** D12
Flagstaff *U.S.A.* 35°12N 111°39W **110** C4
Flamborough *U.K.* 54°7N 0°7W **22** D8
Flamborough Hd. *U.K.* 54°7N 0°5W **22** D8
Flandre *Europe* 50°50N 2°30E **64** C2
Flathead L. *U.S.A.* 47°51N 114°8W **110** A4
Flattery, C. *U.S.A.* 48°23N 124°29W **110** A2
Fleet *U.K.* 51°17N 0°50W **25** D7
Fleetwood *U.K.* 53°55N 3°1W **23** E2
Flensburg *Germany* 54°47N 9°27E **64** A5
Flers *France* 48°47N 0°33W **66** B3
Flimby *U.K.* 54°42N 3°30W **22** C2
Flin Flon *Canada* 54°46N 101°53W **108** D9
Flinders → *Australia* 17°36S 140°36E **98** D7
Flinders I. *Australia* 40°0S 148°0E **98** H8
Flinders Ranges *Australia* 31°30S 138°30E **98** G6
Flint *U.K.* 53°15N 3°8W **26** A7
Flint *U.S.A.* 43°1N 83°41W **112** D6
Flint → *U.S.A.* 30°57N 84°34W **111** D10
Flint I. *Kiribati* 11°26S 151°48W **103** J12
Flintshire □ *U.K.* 53°17N 3°17W **26** A7
Flitwick *U.K.* 52°0N 0°30W **25** C8
Flodden *U.K.* 55°37N 2°8W **22** A4
Flora *U.S.A.* 38°40N 88°29W **112** F3
Florence *Italy* 43°46N 11°15E **68** C4
Florence *U.S.A.* 34°12N 79°46W **111** D11
Florencia *Colombia* 1°36N 75°36W **120** B2
Flores *Indonesia* 8°35S 121°0E **83** F6
Flores Sea *Indonesia* 6°30S 120°0E **83** F6
Florianópolis *Brazil* 27°30S 48°30W **121** E5
Florida *Uruguay* 34°7S 56°10W **121** F4
Florida □ *U.S.A.* 28°0N 82°0W **111** E10
Florida, Straits of *U.S.A.* 25°0N 80°0W **115** C9
Florida Keys *U.S.A.* 24°40N 81°0W **111** F10
Florø *Norway* 61°35N 5°1E **63** E5
Fly → *Papua N. G.* 8°25S 143°0E **98** B7
Fochabers *U.K.* 57°37N 3°6W **19** G11
Focşani *Romania* 45°41N 27°15E **65** F14
Fóggia *Italy* 41°27N 15°34E **68** D6
Foix *France* 42°58N 1°38E **66** E4
Foligno *Italy* 42°57N 12°42E **68** C5
Folkestone *U.K.* 51°5N 1°12E **25** D11
Fond-du-Lac *Canada* 59°19N 107°12W **108** D9
Fond du Lac *U.S.A.* 43°47N 88°27W **112** D3
Fongafale *Tuvalu* 8°31S 179°13E **99** B14
Fonseca, G. de *Cent. Amer.* 13°10N 87°40W **104** H11
Fontainebleau *France* 48°24N 2°40E **66** B5
Fontenay-le-Comte *France* 46°28N 0°48W **66** C3
Fordham *U.K.* 52°19N 0°23E **25** B9
Fordingbridge *U.K.* 50°56N 1°47W **24** E5
Forel, Mt. *Greenland* 66°52N 36°55W **54** C6
Forest Row *U.K.* 51°5N 0°3E **25** D9
Forfar *U.K.* 56°39N 2°53W **19** J12
Forlì *Italy* 44°13N 12°3E **68** B5
Formartine *U.K.* 57°20N 2°15W **19** H13
Formby *U.K.* 53°34N 3°4W **23** E2
Formby Pt. *U.K.* 53°33N 3°6W **23** E2
Formentera *Spain* 38°43N 1°27E **67** C6
Formiga *Brazil* 20°27S 45°25W **122** D1
Formosa *Argentina* 26°15S 58°10W **121** E4
Formosa *Brazil* 15°32S 47°20W **122** C1
Forres *U.K.* 57°37N 3°37W **19** G10
Forsayth *Australia* 18°33S 143°34E **98** D7
Fort Albany *Canada* 52°15N 81°35W **109** D11
Fort Augustus *U.K.* 57°9N 4°42W **19** H8
Fort Chipewyan *Canada* 58°42N 111°8W **108** D8
Fort Collins *U.S.A.* 40°35N 105°5W **110** B5
Fort-Coulonge *Canada* 45°50N 76°45W **112** C9
Fort-de-France *Martinique* 14°36N 61°2W **114** c
Fort Dodge *U.S.A.* 42°30N 94°11W **111** B8
Fort Good Hope *Canada* 66°14N 128°40W **108** C7
Fort Kent *U.S.A.* 47°15N 68°36W **113** B13
Fort Lauderdale *U.S.A.* 26°7N 80°8W **111** E10
Fort Liard *Canada* 60°14N 123°30W **108** C7
Fort MacKay *Canada* 57°12N 111°41W **108** D8
Fort Macleod *Canada* 49°45N 113°30W **108** E8
Fort McMurray *Canada* 56°44N 111°7W **108** D8
Fort McPherson *Canada* 67°30N 134°55W **108** C6
Fort Morgan *U.S.A.* 40°15N 103°48W **110** B6
Fort Myers *U.S.A.* 26°39N 81°52W **111** E10
Fort Nelson *Canada* 58°50N 122°44W **108** D7
Fort Nelson → *Canada* 59°32N 124°0W **108** D7
Fort Peck L. *U.S.A.* 48°0N 106°26W **110** A5
Fort Providence *Canada* 61°3N 117°40W **108** C8
Fort Resolution *Canada* 61°10N 113°40W **108** C8
Fort St. John *Canada* 56°15N 120°50W **108** D7
Fort Scott *U.S.A.* 37°50N 94°42W **111** C8
Fort Shevchenko *Kazakhstan* 44°35N 50°23E **71** F9
Fort Simpson *Canada* 61°45N 121°15W **108** C7
Fort Smith *Canada* 60°0N 111°51W **108** B8
Fort Smith *U.S.A.* 35°23N 94°25W **111** C8
Fort Stockton *U.S.A.* 30°53N 102°53W **110** D6
Fort Wayne *U.S.A.* 41°4N 85°9W **112** E5
Fort William *U.K.* 56°49N 5°7W **18** J7
Fort Worth *U.S.A.* 32°43N 97°19W **111** D7
Fort Yukon *U.S.A.* 66°34N 145°16W **108** C5
Fortaleza *Brazil* 3°45S 38°35W **120** C6
Forth → *U.K.* 56°9N 3°50W **21** B8
Forth, Firth of *U.K.* 56°5N 2°55W **21** B10
Fortrose *U.K.* 57°35N 4°9W **19** G9
Foshan *China* 23°6N 113°9E **79** G11
Fostoria *U.S.A.* 41°10N 83°25W **112** E6
Fothergill *U.K.* 54°43N 3°29W **22** C2
Fotheringhay *U.K.* 52°32N 0°27W **25** A8
Fougères *France* 48°21N 1°14W **66** B3
Foula *U.K.* 60°10N 2°5W **62** A5
Foulness I. *U.K.* 51°36N 0°55E **25** C10
Foulness Pt. *U.K.* 51°37N 0°58E **25** C10
Foulsham *U.K.* 52°48N 0°59E **25** A10
Fountainhall *U.K.* 55°44N 2°53W **21** C10
Fouta Djallon *Guinea* 11°20N 12°10W **94** F3
Fovant *U.K.* 51°4N 2°0W **24** D5
Fowey *U.K.* 50°20N 4°39W **27** G4
Fownhope *U.K.* 52°0N 2°36W **24** B3
Foxe Basin *Canada* 66°0N 77°0W **109** C12
Foxe Chan. *Canada* 65°0N 80°0W **109** C12
Foxe Pen. *Canada* 65°0N 76°0W **109** C12
Foyle → *U.K.* 55°3N 7°15W **29** A7
Foyle, Lough *U.K.* 55°7N 7°4W **29** A7
Foynes *Ireland* 52°37N 9°7W **30** C4
Foz do Iguaçu *Brazil* 25°30S 54°30W **121** E4
Fraddon *U.K.* 50°23N 4°58W **27** G4
Framlingham *U.K.* 52°14N 1°21E **25** B11
Franca *Brazil* 20°33S 47°30W **122** D1
France ■ *Europe* 47°0N 3°0E **66** C5
Franceville *Gabon* 1°40S 13°32E **96** E2
Franche-Comté □ *France* 46°50N 5°55E **66** C6
Francis Case, L. *U.S.A.* 43°4N 98°34W **110** B7
Francistown *Botswana* 21°7S 27°33E **97** J5
François L. *Canada* 54°0N 125°30W **108** D7
Frankfort *Ind., U.S.A.* 40°17N 86°31W **112** E4
Frankfort *Ky., U.S.A.* 38°12N 84°52W **112** F5
Frankfurt *Brandenburg, Germany* 52°20N 14°32E **64** B8
Frankfurt *Hessen, Germany* 50°7N 8°41E **64** C5
Fränkische Alb *Germany* 49°10N 11°23E **64** D6
Franklin *N.H., U.S.A.* 43°27N 71°39W **113** D12
Franklin *Pa., U.S.A.* 41°24N 79°50W **112** E8
Franklin B. *Canada* 69°45N 126°0W **108** C7
Franklin D. Roosevelt L. *U.S.A.* 48°18N 118°9W **110** A3
Franklin L. *U.S.A.* 40°25N 115°22W **110** B3
Franklin Mts. *Canada* 65°0N 125°0W **108** C7
Franklin Str. *Canada* 72°0N 96°0W **108** B10
Frant *U.K.* 51°5N 0°16E **25** D9
Franz Josef Land *Russia* 82°0N 55°0E **54** A10
Fraser → *Canada* 49°7N 123°11W **108** E7
Fraserburgh *U.K.* 57°42N 2°1W **19** G13
Frederick *U.S.A.* 39°25N 77°25W **112** F9
Fredericksburg *U.S.A.* 38°18N 77°28W **112** F9
Fredericktown *U.S.A.* 37°34N 90°18W **112** G2
Fredericton *Canada* 45°57N 66°40W **113** C14
Frederikshavn *Denmark* 57°28N 10°31E **63** F6

Fredonia

Guadix

Fredonia *U.S.A.* 42°26N 79°20W **112** D8
Fredrikstad *Norway* 59°13N 10°57E **63** F6
Free State □ *S. Africa* 28°30S 27°0E **97** K5
Freeport *Bahamas* 26°30N 78°47W **115** B9
Freeport *Ill., U.S.A.* 42°17N 89°36W **112** D3
Freeport *Tex., U.S.A.* 28°57N 95°21W **111** E7
Freetown *S. Leone* 8°30N 13°17W **94** G3
Freiburg *Germany* 47°59N 7°51E **64** E4
Fréjus *France* 43°25N 6°44E **66** E7
Fremont *U.S.A.* 41°21N 83°7W **112** E6
French Creek → *U.S.A.* 41°24N 79°50W **112** E8
French Guiana ☑ *S. Amer.* 4°0N 53°0W **120** B4
French Polynesia ☑ *Pac. Oc.* 20°0S 145°0W **103** J13
Frenchman Cr. →
 N. Amer. 48°31N 107°10W **110** A5
Freshwater *U.K.* 50°41N 1°31W **24** E5
Fresnillo *Mexico* 23°10N 102°53W **114** C4
Fresno *U.S.A.* 36°44N 119°47W **110** C3
Fria, C. *Namibia* 18°0S 12°0E **90** H5
Fridaythorpe *U.K.* 54°2N 0°39W **23** D7
Friedrichshafen *Germany* 47°39N 9°30E **64** E5
Frimley *U.K.* 51°19N 0°44W **25** D7
Frinton-on-Sea *U.K.* 51°49N 1°15E **25** C11
Frio, C. *Brazil* 22°50S 41°50W **117** F6
Frizington *U.K.* 54°33N 3°28W **22** C2
Frobisher B. *Canada* 62°30N 66°0W **109** C13
Frobisher L. *Canada* 56°20N 108°15W **108** D9
Frodsham *U.K.* 53°18N 2°43W **23** F3
Frome *U.K.* 51°14N 2°19W **24** D4
Frome → *U.K.* 50°41N 2°6W **24** E4
Front Range *U.S.A.* 40°25N 105°45W **110** B5
Front Royal *U.S.A.* 38°55N 78°12W **112** F8
Frutal *Brazil* 20°0S 49°0W **122** C1
Frýdek-Místek *Czech Rep.* 49°40N 18°20E **65** D10
Fuchū *Japan* 34°34N 133°14E **81** F3
Fuengirola *Spain* 36°32N 4°41W **67** D3
Fuerte → *Mexico* 25°54N 109°22W **114** B3
Fuerteventura *Canary Is.* 28°30N 14°0W **94** C3
Fuhai *China* 47°2N 87°25E **78** B6
Fuji *Japan* 35°9N 138°39E **81** F6
Fuji-San *Japan* 35°22N 138°44E **81** F6
Fujian □ *China* 26°0N 118°0E **79** F12
Fujin *China* 47°16N 132°1E **79** B15
Fukui *Japan* 36°5N 136°10E **81** E5
Fukuoka *Japan* 33°39N 130°21E **81** G2
Fukushima *Japan* 37°44N 140°28E **81** E7
Fukuyama *Japan* 34°35N 133°20E **81** F3
Fulda *Germany* 50°32N 9°40E **64** C5
Fulda → *Germany* 51°25N 9°39E **64** C5
Fulton *U.S.A.* 43°19N 76°25W **112** D9
Fulwood *U.K.* 53°47N 2°40W **23** E3
Funabashi *Japan* 35°45N 140°0E **81** F7
Funchal *Madeira* 32°38N 16°54W **94** B2
Fundy, B. of *Canada* 45°0N 66°0W **113** C15
Furnas, Represa de *Brazil* 20°50S 45°30W **122** D1
Furneaux Group *Australia* 40°10S 147°50E **98** J8
Fürth *Germany* 49°28N 10°59E **64** D6
Fury and Hecla Str. *Canada* 69°56N 84°0W **109** C11
Fushun *China* 41°50N 123°56E **79** C13
Fustic *Barbados* 13°16N 59°38W **115** g
Fuxin *China* 42°5N 121°48E **79** C13
Fuyang *China* 33°0N 115°48E **79** E12
Fuyu *Heilongjiang, China* 47°49N 124°27E **79** B13
Fuyu *Jilin, China* 45°12N 124°43E **79** B13
Fuyun *China* 47°0N 89°28E **78** B6
Fuzhou *China* 26°5N 119°16E **79** F12
Fylingdales Moor *U.K.* 54°25N 0°41W **22** D7
Fyn *Denmark* 55°20N 10°30E **63** F6
Fyne, L. *U.K.* 55°59N 5°23W **20** C5

G

Gaalkacyo *Somali Rep.* 6°30N 47°30E **89** F4
Gabès *Tunisia* 33°53N 10°2E **95** B8
Gabès, G. de *Tunisia* 34°0N 10°30E **95** B8
Gabon ■ *Africa* 0°10S 10°0E **96** E2
Gaborone *Botswana* 24°45S 25°57E **97** J5
Gabrovo *Bulgaria* 42°52N 25°19E **69** C11
Gachsārān *Iran* 30°15N 50°45E **87** D7
Gadarwara *India* 22°50N 78°50E **84** H11
Gadsden *U.S.A.* 34°1N 86°1W **111** D9
Gafsa *Tunisia* 34°24N 8°43E **95** B7
Gagnoa *Ivory C.* 6°56N 5°16W **94** G4
Gagnon *Canada* 51°50N 68°5W **109** D13
Gainesville *Fla., U.S.A.* 29°40N 82°20W **111** E10
Gainesville *Ga., U.S.A.* 34°18N 83°50W **111** D10
Gainford *U.K.* 54°34N 1°43W **22** C5
Gainsborough *U.K.* 53°24N 0°46W **23** F7
Gairdner, L. *Australia* 31°30S 136°0E **98** G6
Gairloch *U.K.* 57°43N 5°41W **18** G6
Gairloch, L. *U.K.* 57°43N 5°45W **18** G6
Galapagos *Ecuador* 0°0 91°0W **117** D1
Galashiels *U.K.* 55°37N 2°49W **21** C10
Galați *Romania* 45°27N 28°2E **65** F15
Galdhøpiggen *Norway* 61°38N 8°18E **63** E5
Galena *U.S.A.* 64°44N 156°56W **108** C4
Galesburg *U.S.A.* 40°57N 90°22W **112** E2
Galgate *U.K.* 53°59N 2°46W **23** E3
Galicia □ *Spain* 42°43N 7°45W **67** A2
Galilee, Sea of *Israel* 32°45N 35°35E **86** C3
Galina Pt. *Jamaica* 18°24N 76°58W **114** a
Gallan Hd. *U.K.* 58°15N 7°2W **18** F3
Galle *Sri Lanka* 6°5N 80°10E **84** R12
Galley Hd. *Ireland* 51°32N 8°55W **30** E5
Gallinas, Pta. *Colombia* 12°28N 71°40W **120** A2
Gallipolis *U.S.A.* 38°49N 82°12W **112** F6
Gällivare *Sweden* 67°9N 20°40E **63** D8
Galloway *U.K.* 55°1N 4°29W **20** D7
Galloway, Mull of *U.K.* 54°39N 4°52W **20** D6
Gallup *U.S.A.* 35°32N 108°45W **110** C5
Galmpton *U.K.* 50°23N 3°35W **27** G6
Galston *U.K.* 55°36N 4°24W **20** D7
Galty Mts. *Ireland* 52°22N 8°10W **30** D6
Galtymore *Ireland* 52°21N 8°11W **30** D6
Galveston *U.S.A.* 29°18N 94°48W **111** E8
Galway *Ireland* 53°17N 9°3W **30** B4
Galway □ *Ireland* 53°22N 9°1W **30** B4
Galway B. *Ireland* 53°13N 9°10W **30** B4
Gambia ■ *W. Afr.* 13°25N 16°0W **94** F2
Gambia → *W. Afr.* 13°28N 16°34W **94** F2

Gamlingay *U.K.* 52°10N 0°11W **25** B8
Gan Jiang → *China* 29°15N 116°0E **79** F12
Gananoque *Canada* 44°20N 76°10W **113** C9
Gäncä *Azerbaijan* 40°45N 46°20E **71** F8
Gand = Gent *Belgium* 51°2N 3°42E **64** C2
Gandak → *India* 25°39N 85°13E **85** G14
Gander *Canada* 48°58N 54°35W **109** E14
Gandhi Sagar *India* 24°40N 75°40E **84** G9
Gandia *Spain* 38°58N 0°9W **67** C5
Ganganagar *India* 29°56N 73°56E **84** E8
Gangdisê Shan *China* 31°20N 81°0E **78** E5
Ganges → *India* 23°20N 90°30E **85** H17
Gangneung *S. Korea* 37°45N 128°54E **79** D14
Gangtok *India* 27°20N 88°37E **85** F16
Gannett Peak *U.S.A.* 43°11N 109°39W **110** B5
Gansu □ *China* 36°0N 104°0E **78** D9
Ganzhou *China* 25°51N 114°56E **79** F11
Gao *Mali* 16°15N 0°5W **94** E5
Gap *France* 44°33N 6°5E **66** D7
Gar *China* 32°10N 79°58E **78** E4
Garanhuns *Brazil* 8°50S 36°30W **122** A3
Garboldisham *U.K.* 52°23N 0°57E **25** B10
Garda, L. di *Italy* 45°40N 10°41E **68** B4
Garden City *U.S.A.* 37°58N 100°53W **110** C6
Gardēz *Afghan.* 33°37N 69°9E **87** C12
Gare L. *U.K.* 56°1N 4°50W **20** B6
Garforth *U.K.* 53°47N 1°24W **23** E6
Gargrave *U.K.* 53°59N 2°7W **23** E4
Garioch *U.K.* 57°18N 2°40W **19** H12
Garissa *Kenya* 0°25S 39°40E **96** E7
Garonne → *France* 45°2N 0°36W **66** D3
Garoowe *Somali Rep.* 8°25N 48°33E **89** F4
Garoua *Cameroon* 9°19N 13°21E **95** G8
Garron Pt. *U.K.* 55°3N 5°59W **29** A10
Garry → *U.K.* 56°44N 3°47W **19** J10
Garsdale Head *U.K.* 54°20N 2°20W **22** C4
Garstang *U.K.* 53°55N 2°46W **23** E3
Gary *U.S.A.* 41°36N 87°20W **112** E4
Garzê *China* 31°38N 100°1E **78** E9
Gascogne *France* 43°45N 0°20E **66** E4
Gascogne, G. de *Europe* 44°0N 2°0W **66** D2
Gashua *Nigeria* 12°54N 11°0E **95** F8
Gaspé *Canada* 48°52N 64°30W **113** A15
Gaspé, C. de *Canada* 48°48N 64°7W **113** A15
Gaspésie, Pén. de la *Canada* 48°45N 65°40W **113** A15
Gata, Sierra de *Spain* 40°20N 6°45W **67** B2
Gatehouse of Fleet *U.K.* 54°53N 4°12W **20** E7
Gateshead *U.K.* 54°57N 1°35W **22** C5
Gatineau *Canada* 45°29N 75°39W **113** C10
Gatineau → *Canada* 45°27N 75°42W **113** C10
Gatley *U.K.* 53°24N 2°15W **23** F4
Gatwick, London ✈ (LGW)
 U.K. 51°10N 0°11W **25** D8
Gävle *Sweden* 60°40N 17°9E **63** E7
Gawilgarh Hills *India* 21°15N 76°45E **84** J10
Gawthwaite *U.K.* 54°16N 3°8W **22** D2
Gaxun Nur *China* 42°22N 100°30E **78** C9
Gaya *India* 24°47N 85°4E **85** G14
Gaylord *U.S.A.* 45°2N 84°41W **112** C5
Gayton *U.K.* 52°45N 0°36E **25** A10
Gaywood *U.K.* 52°46N 0°26E **25** A9
Gaza *Gaza Strip* 31°30N 34°28E **86** D3
Gaza Strip ■ *Asia* 31°29N 34°25E **86** D3
Gaziantep *Turkey* 37°6N 37°23E **71** G6
Gdańsk *Poland* 54°22N 18°40E **65** A10
Gdynia *Poland* 54°35N 18°33E **65** A10
Gebze *Turkey* 40°47N 29°25E **71** F4
Gedaref *Sudan* 14°2N 35°28E **95** F13
Gedney *U.K.* 52°48N 0°4E **23** G9
Gedser *Denmark* 54°35N 11°55E **63** G6
Geelong *Australia* 38°10S 144°22E **98** H7
Gejiu *China* 23°20N 103°10E **78** G9
Gela *Italy* 37°4N 14°15E **68** F6
Gelibolu *Turkey* 40°28N 26°43E **71** F4
Gelsenkirchen *Germany* 51°32N 7°6E **64** C4
General Acha *Argentina* 37°20S 64°38W **121** F3
General Alvear *Argentina* 35°0S 67°40W **121** F3
General Pico *Argentina* 35°45S 63°50W **121** F3
General Santos *Phil.* 6°5N 125°14E **83** C7
Geneva *U.S.A.* 42°52N 76°59W **112** D9
Gennargentu, Mti. del *Italy* 40°1N 9°19E **68** D3
Genoa *Italy* 44°25N 8°57E **68** B3
Génova, G. di *Italy* 44°0N 9°0E **68** C3
Gent *Belgium* 51°2N 3°42E **64** C2
George *S. Africa* 33°58S 22°29E **97** L4
George → *Canada* 58°49N 66°10W **109** D13
George, L. *U.S.A.* 29°17N 81°36W **111** E10
George Town *Cayman Is.* 19°20N 81°24W **115** D8
George Town *Malaysia* 5°25N 100°20E **82** C2
George V Land *Antarctica* 69°0S 148°0E **55** C10
Georgetown *Guyana* 6°50N 58°12W **120** B4
Georgetown *Ky., U.S.A.* 38°13N 84°33W **112** F5
Georgetown *U.S.A.* 33°23N 79°17W **111** D11
Georgia □ *U.S.A.* 32°50N 83°15W **111** D10
Georgia ■ *Asia* 42°0N 43°0E **71** F7
Georgia, Str. of *N. Amer.* 49°25N 124°0W **104** E7
Georgian B. *Canada* 45°15N 81°0W **112** C7
Georgiyevsk *Russia* 44°12N 43°28E **71** F7
Gera *Germany* 50°53N 12°4E **64** C7
Geraldton *Australia* 28°48S 114°32E **98** F1
Germany ■ *Europe* 51°0N 10°0E **64** C6
Germiston *S. Africa* 26°13S 28°10E **97** K5
Gerrans B. *U.K.* 50°12N 4°57W **27** G4
Gerrards Cross *U.K.* 51°35N 0°33W **25** C7
Getafe *Spain* 40°18N 3°43W **67** B4
Ghaghara → *India* 25°45N 84°40E **85** G14
Ghana ■ *W. Afr.* 8°0N 1°0W **94** G5
Ghardaïa *Algeria* 32°20N 3°37E **94** B6
Gharyān *Libya* 32°10N 13°0E **95** B8
Ghats, Eastern *India* 14°0N 78°50E **84** N11
Ghats, Western *India* 14°0N 75°0E **84** N9
Ghazal, Bahr el → *Chad* 13°0N 15°47E **95** F9
Ghazāl, Bahr el → *Sudan* 9°31N 30°25E **95** G12
Ghaziabad *India* 28°42N 77°26E **84** E10
Ghazipur *India* 25°38N 83°35E **85** G13
Ghaznī *Afghan.* 33°30N 68°28E **87** C12

Ghent = Gent *Belgium* 51°2N 3°42E **64** C2
Ghowr □ *Afghan.* 34°0N 64°20E **87** C11
Ghugri → *India* 55°16N 6°29W **29** A9
Giant's Causeway *U.K.* 55°16N 6°29W **29** A9
Gibraltar ☑ *Europe* 36°7N 5°22W **67** D3
Gibraltar, Str. of *Medit. S.* 35°55N 5°40W **67** E3
Gibraltar Pt. *U.K.* 53°6N 0°19E **23** F9
Gibson Desert *Australia* 24°0S 126°0E **98** E4
Gifu *Japan* 35°30N 136°45E **81** F5
Giggleswick *U.K.* 54°5N 2°17W **22** D4
Gigha *U.K.* 55°42N 5°44W **20** C4
Gijón *Spain* 43°32N 5°42W **67** A3
Gila → *U.S.A.* 32°43N 114°33W **110** D4
Gīlān □ *Iran* 37°0N 50°0E **86** B7
Gilbert Is. *Kiribati* 1°0N 172°0E **102** G9
Gilgit *India* 35°50N 74°15E **84** B9
Gillam *Canada* 56°20N 94°40W **108** D10
Gillette *U.S.A.* 44°18N 105°30W **110** B5
Gillingham *Dorset, U.K.* 51°2N 2°18W **24** D4
Gillingham *Medway, U.K.* 51°23N 0°33E **25** D10
Gilsland *U.K.* 55°0N 2°34W **22** C3
Gimie, Mt. *St. Lucia* 13°54N 61°0W **115** f
Girdle Ness *U.K.* 57°9N 2°3W **19** H13
Giresun *Turkey* 40°55N 38°30E **71** F6
Girga *Egypt* 26°17N 31°55E **95** C12
Girona *Spain* 41°58N 2°46E **67** B7
Gironde → *France* 45°32N 1°7W **66** D3
Girvan *U.K.* 55°14N 4°51W **20** D6
Gisborne *N.Z.* 38°39S 178°5E **99** H14
Gisburn *U.K.* 53°56N 2°16W **23** E4
Gitega *Burundi* 3°26S 29°56E **96** E5
Gizhiga *Russia* 62°3N 160°30E **77** C17
Gjoa Haven *Canada* 68°38N 95°53W **108** C10
Glace Bay *Canada* 46°11N 59°58W **113** B18
Glacier Nat. Park △ *U.S.A.* 48°42N 113°48W **110** A4
Gladstone *Australia* 23°52S 151°16E **98** E9
Gladstone *U.S.A.* 45°51N 87°1W **112** C4
Gladwin *U.S.A.* 43°59N 84°29W **112** D5
Glamorgan, Vale of □ *U.K.* 51°28N 3°25W **27** F7
Glanaruddery Mts. *Ireland* 52°20N 9°27W **30** D4
Glanton *U.K.* 55°26N 1°54W **22** B5
Glasgow *U.K.* 55°51N 4°15W **20** C7
Glasgow *Ky., U.S.A.* 37°0N 85°55W **112** G5
Glasgow *Mont., U.S.A.* 48°12N 106°38W **110** A5
Glasgow Int. ✈ (GLA) *U.K.* 55°51N 4°21W **20** C7
Glasnevin *Ireland* 53°22N 6°15W **31** B10
Glastonbury *U.K.* 51°9N 2°43W **24** D4
Glazov *Russia* 58°9N 52°40E **70** C9
Glemsford *U.K.* 52°6N 0°40E **25** B9
Glen → *U.K.* 52°51N 0°7W **23** G8
Glen Affric *U.K.* 57°17N 5°1W **18** H7
Glen Almond *U.K.* 56°28N 3°50W **21** B8
Glen Coe *U.K.* 56°40N 5°0W **18** J7
Glen Etive *U.K.* 56°37N 5°0W **18** J7
Glen Garry *Highl., U.K.* 57°3N 5°7W **18** H7
Glen Garry *Perth & Kinr., U.K.* 56°47N 4°5W **19** J9
Glen Mor *U.K.* 57°11N 4°52W **19** H8
Glen Moriston *U.K.* 57°11N 4°52W **19** H8
Glen Orchy *U.K.* 56°27N 4°52W **20** B6
Glen Orrin *U.K.* 57°31N 4°45W **19** H8
Glen Oykel *U.K.* 58°5N 4°50W **19** F8
Glen Roy *U.K.* 56°56N 4°50W **19** J8
Glen Shee *U.K.* 56°50N 3°28W **19** J11
Glen Shiel *U.K.* 57°9N 5°18W **18** H7
Glen Spean *U.K.* 56°53N 4°40W **19** J8
Glendale *Ariz., U.S.A.* 33°32N 112°11W **110** D4
Glendale *Calif., U.S.A.* 34°9N 118°15W **110** D3
Glendive *U.S.A.* 47°7N 104°43W **110** A6
Gleneagles *U.K.* 56°17N 3°43W **21** B8
Glenfinnan *U.K.* 56°53N 5°27W **18** J7
Glengarriff *Ireland* 51°45N 9°34W **30** E3
Glenkens, The *U.K.* 55°12N 4°12W **20** D7
Glenluce *U.K.* 54°52N 4°48W **20** E6
Glennallen *U.S.A.* 62°7N 145°33W **108** C5
Glennamaddy *Ireland* 53°37N 8°33W **28** D4
Glenrothes *U.K.* 56°12N 3°10W **21** B9
Glens Falls *U.S.A.* 43°19N 73°39W **113** D11
Glenties *Ireland* 54°49N 8°16W **28** B5
Glenveagh △ *Ireland* 55°3N 8°1W **28** A5
Gliwice *Poland* 50°22N 18°41E **65** C10
Globe *U.S.A.* 33°24N 110°47W **110** D4
Głogów *Poland* 51°37N 16°5E **64** C9
Glomma → *Norway* 59°12N 10°57E **63** F6
Glossop *U.K.* 53°27N 1°56W **23** F5
Gloucester *U.K.* 51°53N 2°15W **24** C4
Gloucestershire □ *U.K.* 51°46N 2°15W **24** C4
Gloversville *U.S.A.* 43°3N 74°21W **113** D10
Gniezno *Poland* 52°30N 17°35E **65** B9
Gnosall *U.K.* 52°48N 2°14W **23** G4
Goa *India* 15°33N 73°59E **84** M8
Goa □ *India* 15°33N 73°59E **84** M8
Goat Fell *U.K.* 55°38N 5°11W **20** D5
Gobi *Asia* 44°0N 110°0E **79** C11
Godalming *U.K.* 51°11N 0°36W **25** D7
Godavari → *India* 16°25N 82°18E **85** L13
Goderich *Canada* 43°45N 81°41W **112** D7
Godhra *India* 22°49N 73°40E **84** H8
Godmanchester *U.K.* 52°20N 0°11W **25** B8
Godoy Cruz *Argentina* 32°56S 68°52W **121** F3
Gods → *Canada* 56°22N 92°51W **108** D10
Gods L. *Canada* 54°40N 94°15W **108** D10
Godshill *U.K.* 50°38N 1°15W **24** E6
Godstone *U.K.* 51°14N 0°3W **25** D8
Gogama *Canada* 47°35N 81°43W **112** B7
Goiânia *Brazil* 16°43S 49°20W **122** C1
Goiás *Brazil* 15°55S 50°10W **120** D4
Goiás □ *Brazil* 12°10S 48°0W **122** B1
Goio-Erê *Brazil* 24°12S 53°1W **121** E4
Gold Coast *Australia* 28°0S 153°25E **98** F9
Gold Coast *W. Afr.* 4°0N 1°40W **94** H5
Golden Vale *Ireland* 52°33N 8°17W **30** D6
Goldsboro *U.S.A.* 35°23N 77°59W **111** C11
Golmud *China* 36°25N 94°53E **78** D7
Golspie *U.K.* 57°58N 3°59W **19** H10
Goma *Dem. Rep. of the Congo* 1°37S 29°10E **96** E5
Gomel = Homyel *Belarus* 52°28N 31°0E **65** B16
Gomera *Canary Is.* 28°7N 17°14W **94** C2
Gómez Palacio *Mexico* 25°34N 103°30W **114** B4
Gonābād *Iran* 34°15N 58°45E **87** C9
Gonaïves *Haiti* 19°20N 72°42W **115** D10

Gonda *India* 27°9N 81°58E **85** F12
Gonder *Ethiopia* 12°39N 37°30E **89** E2
Gongga Shan *China* 29°40N 101°55E **78** F9
Gonghe *China* 36°18N 100°32E **78** D9
Good Hope, C. of *S. Africa* 34°24S 18°30E **97** L3
Goodrich *U.K.* 51°52N 2°37W **24** C4
Goodwood *U.K.* 50°53N 0°44W **25** E7
Goole *U.K.* 53°42N 0°53W **23** E7
Goose L. *U.S.A.* 41°56N 120°26W **110** B2
Gorakhpur *India* 26°47N 83°23E **85** F13
Gordon *U.K.* 55°41N 2°34W **21** C10
Gore *Ethiopia* 8°12N 35°32E **89** F2
Goré *Ethiopia* 8°12N 35°32E **89** F2
Gorebridge *U.K.* 55°50N 3°2W **21** C9
Gorey *Ireland* 52°41N 6°18W **31** C10
Gorgān *Iran* 36°55N 54°30E **87** B8
Goring *U.K.* 51°31N 1°7W **24** C6
Goring-by-Sea *U.K.* 50°49N 0°24W **25** E8
Gorleston *U.K.* 52°35N 1°44E **25** A12
Görlitz *Germany* 51°9N 14°58E **64** C8
Gorno-Altay □ *Russia* 51°0N 86°0E **76** D9
Gorontalo *Indonesia* 0°35N 123°5E **83** D6
Gort *Ireland* 53°3N 8°49W **30** B5
Gorzów Wielkopolski *Poland* 52°43N 15°15E **64** B8
Gosberton *U.K.* 52°53N 0°9W **23** G8
Gosforth *U.K.* 54°26N 3°27W **22** D2
Gosport *U.K.* 50°48N 1°9W **24** E6
Göta kanal *Sweden* 58°30N 15°58E **63** F7
Götaland *Sweden* 57°30N 14°30E **63** F6
Göteborg *Sweden* 57°43N 11°59E **63** F6
Gotha *Germany* 50°56N 10°42E **64** C6
Gothenburg = Göteborg *Sweden* 57°43N 11°59E **63** F6
Gotland *Sweden* 57°30N 18°33E **63** F7
Gotō-Rettō *Japan* 32°55N 129°5E **81** G1
Göttingen *Germany* 51°31N 9°55E **64** C5
Gouda *Neths.* 52°1N 4°42E **64** B3
Goudhurst *U.K.* 51°6N 0°29E **25** D9
Gouin, Rés. *Canada* 48°35N 74°40W **113** A10
Goulburn *Australia* 34°44S 149°44E **98** G8
Goulimine *Morocco* 28°56N 10°0W **94** C3
Goundam *Mali* 16°27N 3°40W **94** E5
Gourock *U.K.* 55°57N 4°49W **20** C6
Governador Valadares *Brazil* 18°15S 41°57W **122** C2
Gower *U.K.* 51°35N 4°10W **27** D5
Gowna, L. *Ireland* 53°51N 7°34W **28** D6
Goya *Argentina* 29°10S 59°10W **121** E4
Gozo *Malta* 36°3N 14°15E **68** a
Graaff-Reinet *S. Africa* 32°13S 24°32E **97** L4
Gracias a Dios, C. *Honduras* 15°0N 83°10W **115** E8
Grafham Water *U.K.* 52°19N 0°18E **25** B8
Grafton *Australia* 29°38S 152°58E **98** F9
Grafton *U.S.A.* 48°25N 97°25W **111** A7
Graham Land *Antarctica* 65°0S 64°0W **55** C17
Grahamstown *S. Africa* 33°19S 26°31E **97** L5
Grain Coast *W. Afr.* 4°20N 10°0W **94** H3
Grainthorpe *U.K.* 53°27N 0°5E **23** F9
Grampian Mts. *U.K.* 56°50N 4°0W **19** J9
Gran Canaria *Canary Is.* 27°55N 15°35W **94** C2
Gran Chaco *S. Amer.* 25°0S 61°0W **121** E3
Gran Sasso d'Itália *Italy* 42°27N 13°42E **68** C5
Granada *Nic.* 11°58N 86°0W **114** E7
Granada *Spain* 37°10N 3°35W **67** D4
Granard *Ireland* 53°47N 7°30W **28** D6
Granby *Canada* 45°25N 72°45W **113** C11
Grand → *U.S.A.* 45°40N 100°45W **110** A6
Grand Bahama I. *Bahamas* 26°40N 78°30W **115** B9
Grand-Bourg *Guadeloupe* 15°53N 61°19W **114** b
Grand Canyon *U.S.A.* 36°3N 112°9W **110** C4
Grand Canyon Nat. Park △ *U.S.A.* 36°15N 112°30W **110** C4
Grand Cayman *Cayman Is.* 19°20N 81°20W **115** D8
Grand Erg de Bilma *Niger* 18°30N 14°0E **95** E8
Grand Falls *Canada* 47°3N 67°44W **109** E13
Grand Falls-Windsor *Canada* 48°56N 55°40W **109** E14
Grand Forks *U.S.A.* 47°55N 97°3W **111** A7
Grand Haven *U.S.A.* 43°4N 86°13W **112** D4
Grand Island *U.S.A.* 40°55N 98°21W **110** B7
Grand Junction *U.S.A.* 39°4N 108°33W **110** C5
Grand L. *Canada* 45°57N 66°7W **113** C14
Grand Manan I. *Canada* 44°45N 66°52W **113** C14
Grand-Mère *Canada* 46°36N 72°40W **113** B11
Grand Rapids *Canada* 53°12N 99°19W **108** D10
Grand Rapids *U.S.A.* 42°58N 85°40W **112** D4
Grand St-Bernard, Col du *Europe* 45°50N 7°10E **64** F4
Grand Teton *U.S.A.* 43°54N 110°50W **110** B4
Grande → *Bolivia* 15°51S 64°39W **120** D3
Grande → *Brazil* 11°30S 44°30W **122** B2
Grande, Rio → *N. Amer.* 25°58N 97°9W **111** E7
Grande Baleine → *Canada* 55°16N 77°47W **109** D12
Grande Prairie *Canada* 55°10N 118°50W **108** D8
Grande-Terre *Guadeloupe* 16°20N 61°25W **114** b
Grande Vigie, Pte. de la *Guadeloupe* 16°32N 61°27W **114** b
Grange-over-Sands *U.K.* 54°12N 2°54W **22** D3
Grangemouth *U.K.* 56°1N 3°42W **21** B8
Grangeville *U.S.A.* 45°56N 116°7W **110** A3
Grantham *U.K.* 52°55N 0°38W **23** G7
Grantown-on-Spey *U.K.* 57°20N 3°36W **19** H10
Grants Pass *U.S.A.* 42°26N 123°19W **110** B2
Granville *U.S.A.* 43°24N 73°16W **113** D11
Grasmere *U.K.* 54°28N 3°1W **22** D2
Grasse *France* 43°38N 6°56E **66** E7
Grassington *U.K.* 54°5N 1°59W **22** D5
Graulhet *France* 43°45N 1°59E **66** E4
Gravesend *U.K.* 51°26N 0°22E **25** D9
Grayling *U.S.A.* 44°40N 84°43W **112** C5
Grays *U.K.* 51°28N 0°21E **25** D9
Graz *Austria* 47°4N 15°27E **64** E8
Great Australian Bight *Australia* 33°30S 130°0E **98** G5
Great Ayton *U.K.* 54°30N 1°8W **22** D6
Great Baddow *U.K.* 51°43N 0°31E **25** C10
Great Barrier Reef *Australia* 18°0S 146°50E **98** D8
Great Basin *U.S.A.* 40°0N 117°0W **110** B3
Great Bear → *Canada* 65°0N 126°0W **108** C7

Great Bear L. *Canada* 65°30N 120°0W **108** B7
Great Bend *U.S.A.* 38°22N 98°46W **110** C7
Great Bentley *U.K.* 51°51N 1°4E **25** C11
Great Bernera *U.K.* 58°14N 6°50W **18** F4
Great Blasket I. *Ireland* 52°6N 10°32W **30** D1
Great Britain *Europe* 54°0N 2°15W **16** D5
Great Broughton *U.K.* 54°26N 1°9W **22** D6
Great Camanoe *Br. Virgin Is.* 18°30N 64°35W **115** e
Great Chesterford *U.K.* 52°4N 0°13E **25** B9
Great Clifton *U.K.* 54°39N 3°29W **22** C2
Great Dividing Ra. *Australia* 23°0S 146°0E **98** E8
Great Dunmow *U.K.* 51°52N 0°23E **25** C9
Great Exuma I. *Bahamas* 23°30N 75°50W **115** C9
Great Falls *U.S.A.* 47°30N 111°17W **110** A4
Great Harwood *U.K.* 53°47N 2°24W **23** E4
Great Inagua I. *Bahamas* 21°0N 73°20W **115** C10
Great Karoo *S. Africa* 31°55S 21°0E **97** L4
Great Khingan Mts. *China* 48°0N 121°0E **79** B13
Great Lakes *N. Amer.* 46°0N 84°0W **104** E11
Great Malvern *U.K.* 52°7N 2°18W **24** B4
Great Massingham *U.K.* 52°47N 0°40E **25** A10
Great Missenden *U.K.* 51°42N 0°41W **25** C7
Great Ormes Head *U.K.* 53°20N 3°52W **26** A6
Great Ouse → *U.K.* 52°48N 0°21E **25** A9
Great Pedro Bluff *Jamaica* 17°51N 77°44W **114** a
Great Plains *N. Amer.* 47°0N 105°0W **104** E9
Great Salt Desert *Iran* 34°30N 55°0E **87** C8
Great Salt L. *U.S.A.* 41°15N 112°40W **110** B4
Great Salt Lake Desert *U.S.A.* 40°50N 113°30W **110** B4
Great Sandy Desert *Australia* 21°0S 124°0E **98** E3
Great Sandy Desert *U.S.A.* 43°35N 120°15W **110** B2
Great Shefford *U.K.* 51°28N 1°28W **24** D6
Great Shelford *U.K.* 52°9N 0°8E **25** B9
Great Shunner Fell *U.K.* 54°22N 2°14W **22** D4
Great Skellig *Ireland* 51°47N 10°33W **30** E1
Great Slave L. *Canada* 61°23N 115°38W **108** C8
Great Snow Mt. *Canada* 57°26N 124°0W **108** D7
Great Torrington *U.K.* 50°57N 4°9W **27** F5
Great Victoria Desert *Australia* 29°30S 126°30E **98** F4
Great Wall of China *China* 38°30N 109°30E **79** D10
Great Waltham *U.K.* 51°47N 0°28E **25** C9
Great Whernside *U.K.* 54°10N 1°58E **22** D5
Great Yarmouth *U.K.* 52°37N 1°44E **25** A12
Greater Antilles *W. Indies* 17°40N 74°0W **115** D10
Greater London □ *U.K.* 51°31N 0°6W **25** C8
Greater Manchester □ *U.K.* 53°30N 2°15W **23** E4
Greater Sunda Is. *Indonesia* 7°0S 112°0E **82** F4
Greatham *U.K.* 54°39N 1°14W **22** C6
Greece ■ *Europe* 40°0N 23°0E **69** E9
Greeley *U.S.A.* 40°25N 104°42W **110** B6
Greely Fd. *Canada* 80°30N 85°0W **109** A11
Green → *Ky., U.S.A.* 37°54N 87°30W **112** G4
Green → *Utah, U.S.A.* 38°11N 109°53W **110** C5
Green B. *U.S.A.* 45°0N 87°30W **112** C4
Green Bay *U.S.A.* 44°31N 88°0W **112** C3
Green Hammerton *U.K.* 54°1N 1°18W **23** D6
Green River *U.S.A.* 41°32N 109°28W **110** B5
Greencastle *U.S.A.* 39°38N 86°52W **112** F4
Greenfield *Ind., U.S.A.* 39°47N 85°46W **112** F5
Greenfield *Mass., U.S.A.* 42°35N 72°36W **113** D11
Greenhead *U.K.* 54°59N 2°30W **22** C3
Greenland ☑ *N. Amer.* 66°0N 45°0W **54** C5
Greenland Sea *Arctic* 73°0N 10°0W **54** B7
Greenlaw *U.K.* 55°43N 2°27W **21** C11
Greenock *U.K.* 55°57N 4°46W **20** C6
Greenodd *U.K.* 54°14N 3°4W **22** D2
Greenore *Ireland* 54°2N 6°8W **29** C9
Greenore Pt. *Ireland* 52°14N 6°19W **31** D10
Greensboro *U.S.A.* 36°4N 79°48W **111** C11
Greensburg *Ind., U.S.A.* 39°20N 85°29W **112** F5
Greensburg *Pa., U.S.A.* 40°18N 79°33W **112** E8
Greenstone Pt. *U.K.* 57°55N 5°37W **18** G6
Greenville *Ala., U.S.A.* 31°50N 86°38W **111** D9
Greenville *Maine, U.S.A.* 45°28N 69°35W **113** C13
Greenville *Mich., U.S.A.* 43°11N 85°15W **112** D5
Greenville *Miss., U.S.A.* 33°24N 91°4W **111** D8
Greenville *Ohio, U.S.A.* 40°6N 84°38W **112** E5
Greenville *S.C., U.S.A.* 34°51N 82°24W **111** D10
Greenwich □ *U.K.* 51°29N 0°1E **25** D9
Greenwood *U.S.A.* 33°31N 90°11W **111** D8
Gremikha *Russia* 67°59N 39°47E **70** A6
Grenada ■ *W. Indies* 12°10N 61°40W **115** E12
Grenen *Denmark* 57°44N 10°40E **63** F6
Grenoble *France* 45°12N 5°42E **66** D6
Greta → *U.K.* 54°9N 2°37W **22** D3
Gretna *U.K.* 55°0N 3°3W **21** E9
Gretna Green *U.K.* 55°1N 3°3W **21** D9
Gretton *U.K.* 52°33N 0°40W **25** A7
Grey Ra. *Australia* 27°0S 143°30E **98** F7
Greymouth *N.Z.* 42°29S 171°13E **99** J13
Greystoke *U.K.* 54°41N 2°51W **22** C3
Greystones *Ireland* 53°9N 6°5W **31** B10
Griffith *Australia* 34°18S 146°2E **98** G8
Grimsay *U.K.* 57°29N 7°14W **18** H3
Grimsby *U.K.* 53°34N 0°5W **23** E8
Gris-Nez, C. *France* 50°52N 1°35E **66** A4
Grise Fiord *Canada* 76°25N 82°57W **109** B11
Grizebeck *U.K.* 54°16N 3°10W **22** D2
Groningen *Neths.* 53°15N 6°35E **64** B4
Groote Eylandt *Australia* 14°0S 136°40E **98** C6
Gros Islet *St. Lucia* 14°5N 60°58W **115** f
Gros Piton *St. Lucia* 13°49N 61°5W **115** f
Gros Piton Pt. *St. Lucia* 13°49N 61°5W **115** f
Grosseto *Italy* 42°46N 11°8E **68** C4
Grossglockner → *Austria* 47°5N 12°40E **64** E7
Groundhog → *Canada* 48°45N 82°58W **112** A6
Groznyy *Russia* 43°20N 45°45E **71** F8
Grudziądz *Poland* 53°30N 18°47E **65** B10
Gruinard B. *U.K.* 57°56N 5°35W **18** G6
Guadalajara *Mexico* 20°40N 103°20W **114** C4
Guadalajara *Spain* 40°37N 3°12W **67** B4
Guadalcanal *Solomon Is.* 9°32S 160°12E **99** B11
Guadalete → *Spain* 36°35N 6°13W **67** D2
Guadalquivir → *Spain* 36°47N 6°22W **67** D2
Guadalupe I. *Pac. Oc.* 29°0N 118°50W **104** G8
Guadarrama, Sierra de *Spain* 41°0N 4°0W **67** B4
Guadeloupe ☑ *W. Indies* 16°20N 61°40W **114** b
Guadiana → *Portugal* 37°14N 7°22W **67** D2
Guadix *Spain* 37°18N 3°11W **67** D4

Guafo, Boca del · Huelva

Guafo, Boca del Chile 43°35S 74°0W 121 G2
Guajará-Mirim Brazil 10°50S 65°20W 120 D3
Guajira, Pen. de la Colombia 12°0N 72°0W 120 A2
Gualeguaychú Argentina 33°3S 59°31W 121 F4
Guam ☑ Pac. Oc. 13°27N 144°45E 102 F6
Guamúchil Mexico 25°28N 108°6W 114 B3
Guana I. Br. Virgin Is. 18°30N 64°30W 115 e
Guanajuato Mexico 21°1N 101°15W 114 C4
Guane Cuba 22°10N 84°7W 115 C8
Guangdong ☐ China 23°0N 113°0E 79 G11
Guangxi Zhuang ☐ China 24°0N 109°0E 79 G10
Guangyuan China 32°26N 105°51E 78 E10
Guangzhou China 23°6N 113°13E 79 G11
Guanica Puerto Rico 17°58N 66°55W 115 d
Guantánamo Cuba 20°10N 75°14W 115 C9
Guantánamo B. Cuba 19°59N 75°10W 115 D9
Guaporé → Brazil 11°55S 65°4W 120 D3
Guaqui Bolivia 16°41S 68°54W 120 D3
Guarapuava Brazil 25°20S 51°30W 121 E4
Guaratinguetá Brazil 22°49S 45°9W 122 D1
Guarulhos Brazil 23°29S 46°33W 122 D1
Guatemala Guatemala 14°40N 90°22W 114 E6
Guatemala ■ Cent. Amer. 15°40N 90°30W 114 D6
Guatemala Trench Pac. Oc. 14°0N 95°0W 104 H10
Guaviare → Colombia 4°3N 67°44W 120 B3
Guaxupé Brazil 21°10S 47°5W 122 D1
Guayama Puerto Rico 17°59N 66°7W 115 d
Guayaquil Ecuador 2°15S 79°52W 120 C2
Guayaquil, G. de Ecuador 3°10S 81°0W 120 C1
Guaymas Mexico 27°56N 110°54W 114 B2
Gubkin Russia 51°17N 37°32E 71 D6
Guelph Canada 43°35N 80°20W 112 D7
Guéret France 46°11N 1°51E 66 C4
Guernsey U.K. 49°26N 2°35W 27 J8
Guestling Green U.K. 50°53N 0°39E 25 E10
Guiana Highlands S. Amer. 5°10N 60°40W 117 C4
Guidónia-Montecélio Italy 42°1N 12°45E 68 C5
Guildford U.K. 51°14N 0°34W 25 D7
Guilin China 25°18N 110°15E 79 F11
Guinea ■ W. Afr. 10°20N 11°30W 94 F3
Guinea, Gulf of Atl. Oc. 3°0N 2°30E 90 F4
Guinea-Bissau ■ Africa 12°0N 15°0W 94 F3
Güines Cuba 22°50N 82°0W 115 C8
Guingamp France 48°34N 3°10W 66 B2
Guisborough U.K. 54°33N 1°4W 22 C6
Guiyang China 26°32N 106°40E 78 F10
Guizhou ☐ China 27°0N 107°0E 78 F10
Gujarat ☐ India 23°20N 71°0E 84 H7
Gujranwala Pakistan 32°10N 74°12E 84 C9
Gujrat Pakistan 32°40N 74°2E 84 C9
Gulbarga India 17°20N 76°50E 84 L10
Gulf, The = Persian Gulf Asia 27°0N 50°0E 87 E7
Gulfport U.S.A. 30°22N 89°6W 111 D9
Gulu Uganda 2°48N 32°17E 96 D6
Guna India 24°40N 77°19E 84 G10
Gunnison → U.S.A. 39°4N 108°35W 110 C5
Gunsan S. Korea 35°59N 126°45E 79 D14
Guntur India 16°23N 80°30E 85 L12
Gurbantüngüt Desert China 45°8N 87°20E 78 B6
Gurgueia → Brazil 6°50S 43°24W 120 C5
Guri, Embalse de Venezuela 7°50N 62°52W 120 B3
Gurkha Nepal 28°5N 84°40E 85 E14
Gurnard's Hd. U.K. 50°11N 5°37W 27 G2
Gürün Turkey 38°43N 37°15E 71 G6
Gurupi Brazil 11°43S 49°4W 122 B1
Gurupi → Brazil 1°13S 46°6W 120 C5
Gurvan Sayhan Uul Mongolia 43°50N 104°0E 78 C9
Gusau Nigeria 12°12N 6°40E 94 F7
Guwahati India 26°10N 91°45E 85 F17
Guyana ■ S. Amer. 5°0N 59°0W 120 B4
Guyenne France 44°30N 0°40E 66 D4
Gwädar Pakistan 25°10N 62°18E 84 G3
Gwalchmai U.K. 53°16N 4°25W 26 A3
Gwalior India 26°12N 78°10E 84 F11
Gwanda Zimbabwe 20°55S 29°0E 97 J5
Gwangju S. Korea 35°9N 126°54E 79 D14
Gweebarra B. Ireland 54°51N 8°23W 28 B5
Gweedore Ireland 55°3N 8°13W 28 A5
Gweek U.K. 50°5N 5°13W 27 G3
Gwennap U.K. 50°12N 5°11W 27 G3
Gweru Zimbabwe 19°28S 29°45E 97 H5
Gwynedd ☐ U.K. 52°52N 4°10W 26 B6
Gyaring Hu China 34°50N 97°40E 78 E8
Gydan Peninsula Russia 70°0N 78°0E 76 B8
Gympie Australia 26°11S 152°38E 98 F9
Győr Hungary 47°41N 17°40E 65 E9
Gyumri Armenia 40°47N 43°50E 71 F7

H

Ha'apai Group Tonga 19°47S 174°27W 99 D16
Haarlem Neths. 52°23N 4°39E 64 B3
Habahe China 48°3N 86°23E 78 B6
Hachinohe Japan 40°30N 141°29E 81 C7
Hackney ☐ U.K. 51°33N 0°3W 25 C8
Hackthorpe U.K. 54°34N 2°42W 22 C3
Hadd, Ra's al Oman 22°35N 59°50E 87 F9
Haddenham U.K. 51°46N 0°55W 25 C7
Haddington U.K. 55°57N 2°47W 21 C10
Hadejia Nigeria 12°30N 10°5E 94 F7
Hadleigh U.K. 52°3N 0°58E 25 B10
Hadlow U.K. 51°13N 0°22E 25 D9
Hadramawt Yemen 15°30N 49°30E 89 D4
Hadrian's Wall U.K. 55°0N 2°30W 22 B4
Haeju N. Korea 38°3N 125°45E 79 D14
Hafizabad Pakistan 32°5N 73°40E 84 C8
Hagen Germany 51°21N 7°27E 64 C4
Hagerstown U.S.A. 39°39N 77°43W 112 F9
Hags Hd. Ireland 52°57N 9°28W 30 C4
Hague, C. de la France 49°44N 1°56W 66 B3
Hague, The Neths. 52°7N 4°17E 64 B3
Haguenau France 48°49N 7°47E 66 B7
Haifa Israel 32°46N 35°0E 86 C3
Haikou China 20°1N 110°16E 79 G11
Hā'il Si. Arabia 27°28N 41°45E 86 E5
Hailar China 49°10N 119°38E 79 B12
Hailey U.S.A. 43°31N 114°19W 110 B4
Haileybury Canada 47°30N 79°38W 112 B8
Hailsham U.K. 50°52N 0°16E 25 E9
Hailun China 47°28N 126°50E 79 B14

Hainan ☐ China 19°0N 109°30E 79 H10
Haines Junction Canada 60°45N 137°30W 108 C6
Hainton U.K. 53°21N 0°14W 23 F8
Haiphong Vietnam 20°47N 106°41E 78 G10
Haiti ■ W. Indies 19°0N 72°30W 115 D10
Haji Ibrahim Iraq 36°40N 44°30E 86 B6
Hajjah Yemen 15°42N 43°36E 89 D3
Hakkoda-San Japan 40°39N 140°53E 81 C7
Hakodate Japan 41°45N 140°44E 81 C7
Haku-San Japan 36°9N 136°46E 81 E5
Halaib Triangle Africa 22°30N 35°20E 95 D13
Halberstadt Germany 51°54N 11°3E 64 C6
Halberton U.K. 50°54N 3°25W 27 F7
Halden Norway 59°9N 11°23E 63 F6
Haldia India 22°5N 88°3E 85 H16
Haldwani India 29°31N 79°30E 84 E11
Halesowen U.K. 52°27N 2°3W 23 H4
Halesworth U.K. 52°20N 1°31E 25 B12
Halifax Canada 44°38N 63°35W 113 C16
Halifax U.K. 53°43N 1°52W 23 E5
Halkirk U.K. 58°30N 3°29W 19 E11
Hall Beach Canada 68°46N 81°12W 109 C11
Hall Pen. Canada 63°30N 66°0W 109 C13
Halle Germany 51°30N 11°56E 64 C6
Hallow U.K. 52°14N 2°15W 24 B4
Halls Creek Australia 18°16S 127°38E 98 D4
Hallworthy U.K. 50°39N 4°35W 27 F4
Halmahera Indonesia 0°40N 128°0E 83 D7
Halmstad Sweden 56°41N 12°52E 63 F6
Halstead U.K. 51°57N 0°40E 25 C10
Haltwhistle U.K. 54°58N 2°26W 22 C4
Hamadān Iran 34°52N 48°32E 86 C7
Ḥamāh Syria 35°5N 36°40E 86 C4
Hamamatsu Japan 34°45N 137°45E 81 F5
Hamar Norway 60°48N 11°7E 63 E6
Hambantota Sri Lanka 6°10N 81°10E 84 R12
Hambledon U.K. 50°55N 1°5W 24 E6
Hambleton Hills U.K. 54°17N 1°12W 22 D6
Hamburg Germany 53°33N 9°59E 64 B5
Hämeenlinna Finland 61°0N 24°28E 63 E8
Hameln Germany 52°6N 9°21E 64 B5
Hamersley Ra. Australia 22°0S 117°45E 98 E2
Hami China 42°55N 93°25E 78 C7
Hamilton Canada 43°15N 79°50W 109 E12
Hamilton N.Z. 37°47S 175°19E 99 H14
Hamilton U.K. 55°46N 4°2W 20 C7
Hamilton U.S.A. 39°24N 84°34W 112 F5
Hamilton Inlet Canada 54°0N 57°30W 104 D14
Hamm Germany 51°40N 7°50E 64 C4
Hammerfest Norway 70°39N 23°41E 63 C8
Hammersmith and Fulham ☐
 U.K. 51°30N 0°14W 25 D8
Hammond U.S.A. 41°38N 87°30W 112 E4
Hammonton U.S.A. 39°39N 74°48W 113 F10
Hampshire ☐ U.K. 51°7N 1°23W 24 D6
Hampshire Downs U.K. 51°15N 1°10W 24 D6
Hampton in Arden U.K. 52°26N 1°41W 23 H5
Han Shui → China 30°34N 114°17E 79 E11
Hancock U.S.A. 47°8N 88°35W 112 B3
Handan China 36°35N 114°28E 79 D11
Hanford U.S.A. 36°20N 119°39W 110 C3
Hangayn Nuruu Mongolia 47°30N 99°0E 78 B8
Hangzhou China 30°18N 120°11E 79 E13
Hangzhou Wan China 30°15N 120°45E 79 E13
Hankö Finland 59°50N 22°57E 63 F8
Hanna Canada 51°40N 111°54W 108 D8
Hannibal U.S.A. 39°42N 91°22W 111 C8
Hanningfield Res. U.K. 51°40N 0°31E 25 C10
Hannover Germany 52°22N 9°46E 64 B5
Hanoi Vietnam 21°5N 105°55E 78 G10
Hanover U.S.A. 39°48N 76°59W 112 F9
Hanover, I. Chile 51°0S 74°50W 121 H2
Hanzhong China 33°10N 107°1E 78 E10
Haora India 22°34N 88°18E 85 H16
Haparanda Sweden 65°52N 24°8E 63 D8
Happy Valley-Goose Bay
 Canada 53°15N 60°20W 109 D13
Har Hu China 38°20N 97°38E 78 D8
Har Us Nuur Mongolia 48°0N 92°0E 78 B7
Ḥaraḍ Si. Arabia 24°22N 49°0E 86 E7
Harare Zimbabwe 17°43S 31°2E 97 H6
Harbin China 45°48N 126°40E 79 B14
Harbor Beach U.S.A. 43°51N 82°39W 112 D6
Hardangerfjorden Norway 60°5N 6°0E 63 E5
Hardy, Pte. St. Lucia 14°6N 60°56W 115 f
Harer Ethiopia 9°20N 42°8E 89 F3
Harewood U.K. 53°54N 1°30W 23 E6
Hargeisa Somali Rep. 9°30N 44°2E 89 F3
Haridwar India 29°58N 78°9E 84 E11
Haringey ☐ U.K. 51°34N 0°5W 25 C8
Haringhata → Bangla. 22°0N 89°58E 85 J16
Harīrūd → Asia 37°24N 60°38E 87 B10
Harlech U.K. 52°52N 4°6W 26 B5
Harleston U.K. 52°24N 1°18E 25 B11
Harlingen U.S.A. 26°12N 97°42W 110 E7
Harlow U.K. 51°46N 0°8E 25 C9
Harney L. U.S.A. 43°14N 119°8W 110 B3
Härnösand Sweden 62°38N 17°55E 63 E7
Haroldswick U.K. 60°48N 0°50W 18 A16
Harpenden U.K. 51°49N 0°21W 25 C8
Harricana → Canada 50°56N 79°32W 109 D12
Harrietsham U.K. 51°14N 0°41E 25 D10
Harrington U.K. 54°37N 3°33W 22 C1
Harris U.K. 57°50N 6°55W 18 G4
Harris, Sd. of U.K. 57°44N 7°6W 18 G3
Harrisburg U.S.A. 40°16N 76°53W 112 E9
Harrison, C. Canada 54°55N 57°55W 109 D14
Harrisonburg U.S.A. 38°27N 78°52W 112 F8
Harrisville U.S.A. 44°39N 83°17W 112 C6
Harrogate U.K. 54°0N 1°33W 23 D5
Harrow ☐ U.K. 51°35N 0°21W 25 C8
Hart U.S.A. 43°42N 86°22W 112 D4
Hartest U.K. 52°6N 0°41E 25 B10
Hartford Conn., U.S.A. 41°46N 72°41W 113 E11
Hartford Ky., U.S.A. 37°27N 86°55W 112 G4
Hartford Wis., U.S.A. 43°19N 88°22W 112 D3
Hartland U.K. 51°1N 4°29W 27 F5
Hartland Pt. U.K. 51°1N 4°32W 27 E4

Hartlebury U.K. 52°20N 2°14W 24 B4
Hartlepool U.K. 54°42N 1°13W 22 C6
Hartley U.K. 55°5N 1°28W 22 B6
Hartpury U.K. 51°55N 2°17W 24 C4
Harvey U.S.A. 41°36N 87°50W 112 E4
Harwell U.K. 51°36N 1°17W 24 C6
Harwich U.K. 51°56N 1°17E 25 C11
Haryana ☐ India 29°0N 76°10E 84 E10
Harz Germany 51°38N 10°44E 64 C6
Hasa Si. Arabia 25°50N 49°0E 86 E7
Haslemere U.K. 51°5N 0°43W 25 D7
Haslingden U.K. 53°42N 2°19W 23 E4
Hastings U.K. 50°51N 0°35E 25 E10
Hastings U.S.A. 40°35N 98°23W 110 B7
Hat Yai Thailand 7°1N 100°27E 82 C2
Hatay Turkey 36°14N 36°10E 71 G6
Hatfield U.K. 51°46N 0°13W 25 C8
Hatgal Mongolia 50°26N 100°9E 78 A9
Hatherleigh U.K. 50°49N 4°5W 27 F5
Hathersage U.K. 53°20N 1°39W 23 F5
Hathras India 27°36N 78°6E 84 F11
Hatia Bangla. 22°30N 91°5E 85 H17
Hatteras, C. U.S.A. 35°14N 75°32W 111 C11
Hattiesburg U.S.A. 31°20N 89°17W 111 D9
Haugesund Norway 59°23N 5°13E 63 F5
Haughley U.K. 52°14N 0°57E 25 B10
Haut Atlas Morocco 32°30N 5°0W 94 B4
Hauts Plateaux Algeria 35°0N 1°0E 94 B6
Havana = La Habana Cuba 23°8N 82°22W 115 C8
Havant U.K. 50°51N 0°58W 25 E7
Havasu, L. U.S.A. 34°18N 114°28W 110 D4
Havel → Germany 52°50N 12°3E 64 B7
Haverfordwest U.K. 51°48N 4°58W 26 D4
Haverhill U.K. 52°5N 0°28E 25 B9
Haverhill U.S.A. 42°47N 71°5W 113 D12
Haverigg U.K. 54°13N 3°17W 22 D2
Havering U.K. 51°34N 0°13E 25 C9
Havre U.S.A. 48°33N 109°41W 110 A5
Havre-St.-Pierre Canada 50°18N 63°33W 109 D13
Hawai'i U.S.A. 19°30N 155°30W 110 J17
Hawai'i ☐ U.S.A. 19°30N 156°30W 110 H16
Hawaiian Is. Pac. Oc. 20°30N 156°0W 103 E12
Hawes U.K. 54°19N 2°12W 22 D4
Haweswater U.K. 54°31N 2°47W 22 C3
Hawick U.K. 55°26N 2°47W 21 D10
Hawkchurch U.K. 50°48N 2°56W 24 E3
Hawkesbury Canada 45°37N 74°37W 113 C10
Hawkesbury Upton U.K. 51°34N 2°18W 24 C4
Hawkhurst U.K. 51°2N 0°32E 25 D10
Hawkshead U.K. 54°23N 2°59W 22 D3
Haworth U.K. 53°50N 1°58W 23 E5
Hawsker U.K. 54°27N 0°34W 22 D7
Haxby U.K. 54°1N 1°4W 23 D6
Hay Australia 34°30S 144°51E 98 G8
Hay → Canada 60°50N 116°26W 108 C8
Hay-on-Wye U.K. 52°5N 3°8W 26 C7
Hay River Canada 60°51N 115°44W 108 C8
Hayes → Canada 57°3N 92°12W 108 D10
Hayle U.K. 50°11N 5°26W 27 G3
Hays U.S.A. 38°53N 99°20W 110 C7
Hayton U.K. 54°55N 2°45W 22 C3
Hayward U.S.A. 46°1N 91°29W 112 B2
Haywards Heath U.K. 51°0N 0°5W 25 E8
Hazar Turkmenistan 39°34N 53°16E 71 G9
Hazard U.S.A. 37°15N 83°12W 112 G6
Hazaribag India 23°58N 85°26E 85 H14
Heacham U.K. 52°54N 0°29E 25 A9
Headcorn U.K. 51°10N 0°38E 25 D10
Heanor U.K. 53°1N 1°21W 23 F6
Heard I. Ind. Oc. 53°6S 72°36E 53 G13
Hearst Canada 49°40N 83°41W 109 E11
Heathfield U.K. 50°58N 0°16E 25 E9
Heathrow, London ✈ (LHR)
 U.K. 51°28N 0°27W 25 D8
Hebburn U.K. 54°59N 1°32W 22 C5
Hebden Bridge U.K. 53°45N 2°0W 23 E5
Hebei ☐ China 39°0N 116°0E 79 D12
Hebrides U.K. 57°30N 7°0W 56 D4
Hebrides, Sea of the U.K. 57°5N 7°0W 18 H4
Hebron Canada 58°5N 62°30W 109 D13
Hecate Str. Canada 53°10N 130°30W 108 D6
Hechi China 24°40N 108°2E 78 G10
Hechuan China 30°2N 106°12E 78 E10
Heckington U.K. 52°59N 0°17W 23 G8
Hednesford U.K. 52°43N 1°59W 23 G5
Hedon U.K. 53°44N 0°12W 23 E8
Heerlen Neths. 50°55N 5°58E 64 C3
Hefei China 31°52N 117°18E 79 E12
Hegang China 47°20N 130°19E 79 B15
Heidelberg Germany 49°24N 8°42E 64 D5
Heihe China 50°10N 127°30E 79 A14
Heilbronn Germany 49°9N 9°13E 64 D5
Heilongjiang ☐ China 48°0N 126°0E 79 B14
Heimaey Iceland 63°26N 20°17W 63 B1
Hekou China 22°30N 103°59E 78 G9
Helena U.S.A. 46°36N 112°2W 110 A4
Helensburgh U.K. 56°1N 4°43W 20 B6
Helgoland Germany 54°10N 7°53E 64 A4
Hellifield U.K. 54°1N 2°12W 23 D4
Helmand → Afghan. 31°12N 61°34E 87 D10
Helmsdale U.K. 58°7N 3°39W 19 F10
Helmsdale → U.K. 58°8N 3°43W 19 F10
Helmsley U.K. 54°15N 1°3W 22 D6
Helperby U.K. 54°8N 1°19W 22 D6
Helsby U.K. 53°17N 2°46W 23 F3
Helsingborg Sweden 56°3N 12°42E 63 F6
Helsinki Finland 60°10N 24°55E 63 E9
Helston U.K. 50°6N 5°17W 27 G3
Helvellyn U.K. 54°32N 3°1W 22 C2
Helwân Egypt 29°50N 31°20E 95 C12
Hemel Hempstead U.K. 51°44N 0°28W 25 C8
Hempton U.K. 52°50N 0°50E 25 A10
Hemsby U.K. 52°41N 1°41E 25 A12
Hemsworth U.K. 53°37N 1°21W 23 E6
Hemyock U.K. 50°54N 3°15W 27 F7
Henan ☐ China 34°0N 114°0E 79 E11
Henares → Spain 40°24N 3°30W 67 B4
Henderson Ky., U.S.A. 37°50N 87°35W 112 G4
Henderson Nev., U.S.A. 36°2N 114°58W 110 C3
Henfield U.K. 50°56N 0°16W 25 E8
Hengduan Shan China 27°30N 99°0E 78 F8
Hengyang China 26°59N 112°22E 79 F11

Henley-in-Arden U.K. 52°18N 1°46W 24 B5
Henley-on-Thames U.K. 51°32N 0°54W 25 C7
Henlopen, C. U.S.A. 38°48N 75°6W 113 F10
Henlow U.K. 52°2N 0°17W 25 B8
Henrietta Maria, C. Canada 55°9N 82°20W 109 D11
Henstridge U.K. 50°58N 2°24W 24 E4
Hentiyn Nuruu Mongolia 48°30N 108°30E 79 B10
Herāt Afghan. 34°20N 62°7E 87 C10
Hereford U.K. 52°4N 2°43W 24 B3
Herefordshire ☐ U.K. 52°8N 2°40W 24 B3
Herlen → Asia 48°48N 117°0E 79 B12
Herm U.K. 49°30N 2°28W 27 J9
Herma Ness U.K. 60°50N 0°54W 18 A16
Hermosillo Mexico 29°10N 111°0W 114 B2
Hernád → Hungary 47°56N 21°8E 65 D11
Herne Bay U.K. 51°21N 1°8E 25 D11
Herstmonceux U.K. 50°53N 0°20E 25 E9
Hertford U.K. 51°48N 0°4W 25 C8
Hertfordshire ☐ U.K. 51°51N 0°5W 25 C8
's-Hertogenbosch Neths. 51°42N 5°17E 64 C3
Hessen ☐ Germany 50°30N 9°0E 64 C5
Hessle U.K. 53°44N 0°24W 23 E8
Hethersett U.K. 52°36N 1°10E 25 A11
Hetton-le-Hole U.K. 54°50N 1°26W 22 C6
Hexham U.K. 54°58N 2°4W 22 C4
Heybridge U.K. 51°45N 0°42E 25 C10
Heysham U.K. 54°3N 2°53W 22 D3
Heytesbury U.K. 51°11N 2°6W 24 D4
Heywood U.K. 53°35N 2°12W 23 E4
Heze China 35°14N 115°20E 79 D12
Hibbing U.S.A. 47°25N 92°56W 111 A8
Hickman U.S.A. 36°34N 89°11W 112 G3
Hidalgo del Parral Mexico 26°56N 105°40W 114 B3
Hierro Canary Is. 27°44N 18°0W 94 C2
Higashiōsaka Japan 34°39N 135°37E 81 F4
High Bentham U.K. 54°7N 2°28W 22 D4
High Ercall U.K. 52°45N 2°35W 23 G3
High Hesket U.K. 54°48N 2°49W 22 C3
High Level Canada 58°31N 117°8W 108 D8
High Pike U.K. 54°42N 3°4W 22 C2
High Prairie Canada 55°30N 116°30W 108 D8
High River Canada 50°30N 113°50W 108 D8
High Veld Africa 27°0S 27°0E 90 J6
High Willhays U.K. 50°40N 4°0W 27 F5
High Wycombe U.K. 51°37N 0°45W 25 C7
Higham Ferrers U.K. 52°19N 0°35W 25 B7
Highbridge U.K. 51°13N 2°58W 24 D3
Highclere U.K. 51°20N 1°21W 24 D6
Highland ☐ U.K. 57°17N 4°21W 18 H7
Highley U.K. 52°27N 2°23W 23 H4
Hightae U.K. 55°6N 3°26W 21 D9
Highworth U.K. 51°37N 1°43W 24 C5
Hiiumaa Estonia 58°50N 22°45E 63 F8
Ḥijāz Si. Arabia 24°0N 40°0E 86 E4
Hildesheim Germany 52°9N 9°56E 64 B5
Hilgay U.K. 52°34N 0°24E 25 A9
Hillaby, Mt. Barbados 13°12N 59°35W 115 g
Hillcrest Barbados 13°13N 59°31W 115 g
Hillingdon ☐ U.K. 51°32N 0°27W 25 C8
Hillsborough U.K. 54°28N 6°5W 29 C9
Hillsdale U.S.A. 41°56N 84°38W 112 E5
Hilo U.S.A. 19°44N 155°5W 110 J17
Hilpsford Pt. U.K. 54°3N 3°12W 22 D2
Himachal Pradesh ☐ India 31°30N 77°0E 84 D10
Himalaya Asia 29°0N 84°0E 85 E14
Himeji Japan 34°50N 134°40E 81 F4
Hinckley U.K. 52°33N 1°22W 23 G6
Hinderwell U.K. 54°32N 0°45W 22 C7
Hindhead U.K. 51°7N 0°43W 25 D7
Hindley U.K. 53°32N 2°35W 23 E3
Hindu Kush Asia 36°0N 71°0E 87 C12
Hingham U.K. 52°35N 0°59E 25 A10
Hingoli India 19°41N 77°15E 84 K10
Hinckley Pt. U.K. 51°13N 3°8W 24 D2
Hinstock U.K. 52°50N 2°27W 23 G4
Hinton U.S.A. 37°40N 80°54W 112 G7
Hios Greece 38°27N 26°9E 69 E12
Hirosaki Japan 40°34N 140°28E 81 C7
Hiroshima Japan 34°24N 132°30E 81 F3
Hisar India 29°12N 75°45E 84 E9
Hispaniola W. Indies 19°0N 71°0W 115 D10
Histon U.K. 52°16N 0°7E 25 B9
Hitachi Japan 36°36N 140°39E 81 E7
Hitchin U.K. 51°58N 0°16W 25 C8
Hjälmaren Sweden 59°18N 15°40E 63 F7
Hkakabo Razi Burma 28°25N 97°23E 85 E20
Ho Chi Minh City Vietnam 10°58N 106°40E 82 B3
Hoare B. Canada 65°17N 62°30W 109 C13
Hobart Australia 42°50S 147°21E 98 J8
Hobbs U.S.A. 32°42N 103°8W 110 D6
Hodder → U.K. 53°57N 2°27W 23 E4
Hoddesdon U.K. 51°45N 0°1W 25 C8
Hodge → U.K. 54°16N 0°56W 22 D7
Hodgson Canada 51°13N 97°36W 108 D10
Hódmezővásárhely Hungary 46°28N 20°22E 65 E11
Hodna, Chott el Algeria 35°26N 4°43E 94 A6
Hoek van Holland Neths. 52°0N 4°7E 64 B3
Hoff U.K. 54°34N 2°31W 22 C3
Hōfu Japan 34°3N 131°34E 81 F2
Hog's Back U.K. 51°13N 0°38W 25 D7
Hoh Xil Shan China 36°30N 89°0E 78 D6
Hoher Rhön Germany 50°24N 9°58E 64 C5
Hokkaidō ☐ Japan 43°30N 143°0E 81 B8
Holbeach U.K. 52°48N 0°1E 23 G9
Holbeach Marsh U.K. 52°52N 0°5E 23 G9
Holderness U.K. 53°45N 0°5W 23 E8
Holguín Cuba 20°50N 76°20W 115 C9
Holkham U.K. 52°57N 0°49E 23 F7
Holland Fen U.K. 53°0N 0°8W 23 F8
Holland on Sea U.K. 51°48N 1°13E 25 C11
Holman Canada 70°44N 117°44W 108 B8
Holme U.K. 53°50N 0°46W 23 E7
Holmes Chapel U.K. 53°12N 2°21W 23 F4
Holmfirth U.K. 53°35N 1°46W 23 E5

Holstebro Denmark 56°22N 8°37E 63 F5
Holsworthy U.K. 50°48N 4°22W 27 F5
Holt U.K. 52°55N 1°6E 25 A11
Holy I. Anglesey, U.K. 53°17N 4°37W 26 A4
Holy I. Northumberland, U.K. 55°40N 1°47W 22 A5
Holyhead U.K. 53°18N 4°38W 26 A4
Holywell U.K. 53°16N 3°14W 26 A7
Home B. Canada 68°40N 67°10W 109 C13
Homer U.S.A. 59°39N 151°33W 108 D4
Homs Syria 34°40N 36°45E 86 C4
Honduras ■ Cent. Amer. 14°40N 86°30W 114 E7
Honduras, G. of Caribbean 16°50N 87°0W 114 D7
Honefoss Norway 60°10N 10°18E 63 E6
Honey L. U.S.A. 40°15N 120°19W 110 B2
Hong Kong ☐ China 22°11N 114°14E 79 a
Hongjiang China 27°7N 109°59E 79 F10
Hongshui He → China 23°48N 109°30E 79 G10
Hongze Hu China 33°15N 118°35E 79 E12
Honiara Solomon Is. 9°27S 159°57E 99 B10
Honington U.K. 52°59N 0°35W 23 G7
Honiton U.K. 50°47N 3°11W 27 F7
Honolulu U.S.A. 21°19N 157°52W 103 E12
Honshū Japan 36°0N 138°0E 81 F6
Hoo U.K. 51°25N 0°35E 25 D10
Hood, Mt. U.S.A. 45°23N 121°42W 110 A2
Hook U.K. 51°17N 0°57W 25 D7
Hook Hd. Ireland 52°7N 6°56W 31 D9
Hooper Bay U.S.A. 61°32N 166°6W 108 C3
Hoopeston U.S.A. 40°28N 87°40W 112 E4
Hoorn Neths. 52°38N 5°4E 64 B3
Hoover Dam U.S.A. 36°1N 114°44W 110 C4
Hope U.S.A. 33°40N 93°36W 111 D8
Hope, Pt. U.S.A. 68°21N 166°47W 108 C3
Hopedale Canada 55°28N 60°13W 109 D13
Horden U.K. 54°46N 1°19W 22 C6
Horley U.K. 51°10N 0°10W 25 D8
Horlivka Ukraine 48°19N 38°5E 71 E6
Hormozgān ☐ Iran 27°30N 56°0E 87 E9
Hormuz, Str. of The Gulf 26°30N 56°30E 87 E9
Horn, C. = Hornos, C. de
 Chile 55°50S 67°30W 121 H3
Horn, Is. Wall. & F. Is. 14°16S 178°6W 99 C15
Horn Head Ireland 55°14N 8°0W 28 A6
Hornavan Sweden 66°15N 17°30E 63 D7
Horncastle U.K. 53°13N 0°7W 23 F8
Horndean U.K. 50°55N 1°1W 24 E6
Hornell U.S.A. 42°20N 77°40W 112 D9
Hornepayne Canada 49°14N 84°48W 112 A5
Horningsham U.K. 51°10N 2°15W 24 D4
Hornos, C. de Chile 55°50S 67°30W 121 H3
Hornsea U.K. 53°55N 0°11W 23 E8
Horqin Youyi Qianqi China 46°5N 122°3E 79 B13
Horsforth U.K. 53°50N 1°39W 23 E5
Horsham Australia 36°44S 142°13E 98 H7
Horsham U.K. 51°4N 0°20W 25 D8
Horsham St. Faith U.K. 52°43N 1°14E 25 A11
Horsted Keynes U.K. 51°2N 0°1W 25 D8
Horton → Canada 69°56N 126°52W 108 C7
Horton in Ribblesdale U.K. 54°9N 2°17W 22 D4
Horwich U.K. 53°36N 2°33W 23 E4
Hoste, I. Chile 55°0S 69°0W 121 H3
Hot Springs Ark., U.S.A. 34°31N 93°3W 111 D8
Hot Springs S. Dak., U.S.A. 43°26N 103°29W 110 B6
Hotan China 37°25N 79°55E 78 D4
Houghton U.S.A. 47°7N 88°34W 112 B3
Houghton L. U.S.A. 44°21N 84°44W 112 C5
Houghton-le-Spring U.K. 54°51N 1°28W 22 C6
Houghton Regis U.K. 51°54N 0°32W 25 C7
Houlton U.S.A. 46°8N 67°51W 113 B14
Houma U.S.A. 29°36N 90°43W 111 E8
Hounslow ☐ U.K. 51°28N 0°21W 25 D8
Hourn, L. U.K. 57°7N 5°35W 18 H6
Houston U.S.A. 29°45N 95°21W 111 E7
Hove U.K. 50°50N 0°10W 25 E8
Hoveton U.K. 52°43N 1°25E 25 A11
Hovingham U.K. 54°11N 0°58W 22 D7
Hövsgöl Nuur Mongolia 51°0N 100°30E 78 A9
Howden U.K. 53°45N 0°52W 23 E7
Howe, C. Australia 37°30S 150°0E 98 H9
Howell U.S.A. 42°36N 83°56W 112 D6
Howland I. Pac. Oc. 0°48N 176°38W 102 G10
Howth Ireland 53°23N 6°4W 31 B10
Howth Hd. Ireland 53°22N 6°4W 31 B10
Hoxne U.K. 52°21N 1°12E 25 B11
Hoy U.K. 58°50N 3°15W 19 E11
Høyanger Norway 61°13N 6°4E 63 E5
Hoylake U.K. 53°24N 3°10W 23 F2
Hradec Králové Czech Rep. 50°15N 15°50E 64 C8
Hrodna Belarus 53°42N 23°52E 65 B12
Hron → Slovak Rep. 47°49N 18°45E 65 E10
Hsinchu Taiwan 24°48N 120°58E 79 G13
Huacho Peru 11°10S 77°35W 120 D2
Huai He → China 33°0N 118°30E 79 E12
Huaibei China 34°0N 116°48E 79 E12
Huaihua China 27°32N 109°57E 79 F10
Huainan China 32°38N 116°58E 79 E12
Huallaga → Peru 5°15S 75°30W 120 C2
Huambo Angola 12°42S 15°54E 97 G3
Huancavelica Peru 12°50S 75°5W 120 D2
Huancayo Peru 12°5S 75°12W 120 D2
Huang He → China 37°55N 118°50E 79 D12
Huangshan China 30°10N 118°3E 79 F12
Huangshi China 30°10N 115°3E 79 E12
Huánuco Peru 9°55S 76°15W 120 C2
Huaraz Peru 9°30S 77°32W 120 C2
Huascarán, Nevado Peru 9°7S 77°37W 120 C2
Huasco Chile 28°30S 71°15W 121 E2
Huatabampo Mexico 26°50N 109°38W 114 B3
Hubei ☐ China 31°0N 112°0E 79 E11
Hubli India 15°22N 75°15E 84 M9
Hucknall U.K. 53°3N 1°13W 23 F6
Huddersfield U.K. 53°39N 1°47W 23 E5
Hudiksvall Sweden 61°43N 17°10E 63 E7
Hudson → U.S.A. 40°42N 74°2W 113 E10
Hudson Bay Canada 60°0N 86°0W 109 C11
Hudson Falls U.S.A. 43°18N 73°35W 113 D11
Hudson Str. Canada 62°0N 70°0W 109 C13
Hue Vietnam 16°30N 107°35E 82 A3
Huelva Spain 37°18N 6°57W 67 D2

Huesca   **Karamay**

Huesca Spain 42°8N 0°25W 67 A5
Hugh Town U.K. 49°55N 6°19W 27 H1
Hughenden Australia 20°52S 144°10E 98 E7
Hugli ➤ India 21°56N 88°4E 85 J16
Huila, Nevado del Colombia 3°0N 76°0W 120 B2
Huize China 26°24N 103°15E 78 F9
Hull = Kingston upon Hull U.K. 53°45N 0°21W 23 E8
Hull Canada 45°26N 75°43W 113 C10
Hull ➤ U.K. 53°44N 0°20W 23 E8
Hullavington U.K. 51°32N 2°8W 24 C4
Hulme End U.K. 53°8N 1°50W 23 F5
Hulun Nur China 49°0N 117°30E 79 B12
Humacao Puerto Rico 18°9N 65°50W 115 d
Humaitá Brazil 7°35S 63°1W 120 C3
Humber ➤ U.K. 53°42N 0°27W 23 E8
Humber, Mouth of the U.K. 53°32N 0°8E 23 E9
Humboldt Canada 52°15N 105°9W 108 D9
Humboldt ➤ U.S.A. 39°59N 118°36W 110 B3
Humphreys Peak U.S.A. 35°21N 111°41W 110 C4
Humshaugh U.K. 55°3N 2°8W 22 B4
Húnaflói Iceland 65°50N 20°50W 63 A1
Hunan □ China 27°30N 112°0E 79 F11
Hungary ■ Europe 47°20N 19°20E 65 E10
Hungary, Plain of Europe 47°0N 20°0E 56 F10
Hungerford U.K. 51°25N 1°31W 24 D5
Hŭngnam N. Korea 39°49N 127°45E 79 D14
Hunmanby U.K. 54°10N 0°20W 22 D8
Hunsrück Germany 49°56N 7°27E 64 D4
Hunstanton U.K. 52°56N 0°29E 25 A9
Huntingdon U.K. 52°20N 0°11W 25 B8
Huntington Ind., U.S.A. 40°53N 85°30W 112 E5
Huntington W. Va., U.S.A. 38°25N 82°27W 112 F6
Huntly U.K. 57°27N 2°47W 19 H12
Huntsville Canada 45°20N 79°14W 109 E12
Huntsville Ala., U.S.A. 34°44N 86°35W 111 D9
Huntsville Tex., U.S.A. 30°43N 95°33W 111 E7
Hurghada Egypt 27°15N 33°50E 95 C12
Hurley U.S.A. 46°27N 90°11W 112 B2
Huron U.S.A. 44°22N 98°13W 110 B7
Huron, L. U.S.A. 44°30N 82°40W 112 C6
Hursley U.K. 51°2N 1°23W 24 D6
Hurstbourne Tarrant U.K. 51°17N 1°26W 24 D6
Hurstpierpoint U.K. 50°56N 0°11W 25 E8
Húsavík Iceland 66°3N 17°21W 63 A2
Husband's Bosworth U.K. 52°28N 1°4W 23 H6
Hutchinson U.S.A. 38°5N 97°56W 110 C7
Huyton U.K. 53°25N 2°51W 23 F3
Huzhou China 30°51N 120°8E 79 E13
Hvar Croatia 43°11N 16°28E 68 C7
Hwang Ho = Huang He ➤ China 37°55N 118°50E 79 D12
Hwange Zimbabwe 18°18S 26°30E 97 H5
Hyargas Nuur Mongolia 49°0N 93°0E 78 B7
Hyde U.K. 53°27N 2°4W 23 F4
Hyderabad India 17°22N 78°29E 84 L11
Hyderabad Pakistan 25°23N 68°24E 84 G6
Hyères France 43°8N 6°9E 66 E7
Hyères, Îs. d' France 43°0N 6°20E 66 E7
Hyndman Peak U.S.A. 43°45N 114°8W 110 B4
Hythe U.K. 51°4N 1°5E 25 D11

I
Ialomiţa ➤ Romania 44°42N 27°51E 65 F14
Iaşi Romania 47°10N 27°40E 65 E14
Ibadan Nigeria 7°22N 3°58E 94 G6
Ibagué Colombia 4°20N 75°20W 120 B2
Ibarra Ecuador 0°21N 78°7W 120 B2
Ibb Yemen 14°2N 44°10E 89 E3
Iberian Peninsula Europe 40°0N 5°0W 56 H5
Ibiá Brazil 19°30S 46°30W 122 C1
Ibiapaba, Sa. da Brazil 4°0S 41°30W 120 C5
Ibicaraí Brazil 14°51S 39°36W 122 B3
Ibiza = Eivissa Spain 38°54N 1°26E 67 C6
Ibotirama Brazil 12°13S 43°12W 122 B2
Ibstock U.K. 52°42N 1°24W 23 G6
Ica Peru 14°0S 75°48W 120 D2
Iça ➤ Brazil 2°55S 67°58W 120 C3
İçel Turkey 36°51N 34°36E 71 G5
Iceland ■ Europe 64°45N 19°0W 63 B2
Ichihara Japan 35°28N 140°5E 81 F7
Ichinomiya Japan 35°18N 136°48E 81 F5
Icy C. U.S.A. 70°20N 161°52W 104 B3
Idaho □ U.S.A. 45°0N 115°0W 110 B4
Idaho Falls U.S.A. 43°30N 112°2W 110 B4
Idar-Oberstein Germany 49°43N 7°16E 64 D4
Idle ➤ U.K. 53°27N 0°49W 23 F7
Idlib Syria 35°55N 36°36E 86 C4
Idmiston U.K. 51°9N 1°42W 24 D6
Ife Nigeria 7°30N 4°31E 94 G6
Iforas, Adrar des Africa 19°40N 1°40E 94 E6
Igarapava Brazil 20°3S 47°47W 122 D1
Igarka Russia 67°30N 86°33E 76 C9
Iglésias Italy 39°19N 8°32E 68 E3
Iglulik Canada 69°20N 81°49W 109 C11
Ignace Canada 49°30N 91°40W 112 A2
Igoumenitsa Greece 39°32N 20°18E 69 E9
Iguaçu ➤ Brazil 25°36S 54°36W 121 B5
Iguaçu, Cat. del Brazil 25°41S 54°26W 121 E4
Iguala Mexico 18°21N 99°32W 114 D5
Iguatu Brazil 6°20S 39°18W 120 C6
Iguidi, Erg Africa 27°0N 7°0W 94 C4
Iisalmi Finland 63°32N 27°10E 63 E9
IJsselmeer Neths. 52°45N 5°20E 64 B3
Ikare Nigeria 7°32N 5°40E 94 G7
Ikaria Greece 37°35N 26°10E 69 F8
Ikeda Japan 34°1N 133°48E 81 F3
Ilagan Phil. 17°7N 121°53E 83 A6
Îlâm Iran 33°36N 46°36E 86 C6
Ilchester U.K. 51°0N 2°41W 24 D3
Île-de-France □ France 49°0N 2°20E 66 B5
Ilebo Dem. Rep. of the Congo 4°17S 20°55E 96 E4
Ilesha Nigeria 7°37N 4°40E 94 G6
Ilfracombe U.K. 51°12N 4°8W 27 E5
Ilhéus Brazil 14°49S 39°2W 122 B3
Ili ➤ Kazakhstan 45°53N 77°10E 76 E8
Iliamna L. U.S.A. 59°30N 155°0W 108 D4

Iligan Phil. 8°12N 124°13E 83 C6
Ilkeston U.K. 52°58N 1°19W 23 G6
Ilkley U.K. 53°56N 1°48W 23 E5
Illapel Chile 32°0S 71°10W 121 F2
Iller ➤ Germany 48°23N 9°58E 64 D6
Illimani Bolivia 16°30S 67°50W 120 D3
Illinois □ U.S.A. 40°15N 89°30W 111 B9
Illinois ➤ U.S.A. 38°58N 90°28W 111 C8
Ilmen, L. Russia 58°15N 31°10E 70 C5
Ilminster U.K. 50°55N 2°55W 24 E3
Iloilo Phil. 10°45N 122°33E 83 B6
Ilorin Nigeria 8°30N 4°35E 94 G6
Imabari Japan 34°4N 133°0E 81 F3
Imandra, L. Russia 67°30N 33°0E 70 A5
Imatra Finland 61°12N 28°48E 63 E9
imeni Ismail Samani, Pik Tajikistan 39°0N 72°2E 87 B13
Immingham U.K. 53°37N 0°13W 23 E8
Ímola Italy 44°20N 11°42E 68 B4
Imperatriz Brazil 5°30S 47°29W 120 C5
Impéria Italy 43°53N 8°3E 68 C3
Imphal India 24°48N 93°56E 85 G18
In Salah Algeria 27°10N 2°32E 94 C6
Inari Finland 68°54N 27°1E 63 D9
Inarijärvi Finland 69°0N 28°0E 63 D9
İnce Burun Turkey 42°7N 34°56E 71 F5
Incheon S. Korea 37°27N 126°40E 79 D14
Incomáti ➤ Mozam. 25°46S 32°43E 97 K6
Indalsälven ➤ Sweden 62°36N 17°30E 63 E7
India ■ Asia 20°0N 78°0E 84 K11
Indian Ocean 5°0S 75°0E 53 E13
Indiana U.S.A. 40°37N 79°9W 112 E8
Indiana □ U.S.A. 40°0N 86°0W 112 E4
Indianapolis U.S.A. 39°46N 86°9W 112 F4
Indigirka ➤ Russia 70°48N 148°54E 77 B15
Indira Gandhi Canal India 28°0N 72°0E 84 F8
Indo-China Asia 15°0N 102°0E 72 G12
Indonesia ■ Asia 5°0S 115°0E 82 F5
Indore India 22°42N 75°53E 84 H9
Indre ➤ France 47°16N 0°11E 66 C4
Indus ➤ Pakistan 24°20N 67°47E 84 G5
İnebolu Turkey 41°55N 33°40E 71 F5
Ingatestone U.K. 51°40N 0°24E 25 C9
Ingleborough U.K. 54°10N 2°22W 22 D4
Ingleton U.K. 54°10N 2°27W 22 D4
Ingolstadt Germany 48°46N 11°26E 64 D6
Ingraj Bazar India 24°58N 88°10E 85 G16
Ingushetia □ Russia 43°20N 44°50E 71 F8
Inishbofin Ireland 53°37N 10°13W 28 D1
Inisheer Ireland 53°3N 9°32W 30 B3
Inishfree B. Ireland 55°4N 8°23W 28 A5
Inishkea North Ireland 54°9N 10°11W 28 C1
Inishkea South Ireland 54°7N 10°12W 28 C1
Inishmaan Ireland 53°5N 9°35W 30 B3
Inishmore Ireland 53°8N 9°45W 30 B3
Inishowen Pen. Ireland 55°14N 7°15W 29 A7
Inishshark Ireland 53°37N 10°16W 28 D1
Inishtrahull Ireland 55°26N 7°13W 29 A7
Inishturk Ireland 53°42N 10°7W 28 D1
Inishvickillane Ireland 52°3N 10°37W 30 D1
Inkberrow U.K. 52°13N 1°58W 24 B5
Inland Sea Japan 34°20N 133°30E 81 F3
Inn ➤ Austria 48°35N 13°28E 64 D7
Inner Hebrides U.K. 57°0N 6°30W 18 J4
Inner Mongolia □ China 42°0N 112°0E 79 C11
Inner Sound U.K. 57°30N 5°55W 18 H6
Innerleithen U.K. 55°37N 3°4W 21 C9
Innsbruck Austria 47°16N 11°23E 64 E6
Inowrocław Poland 52°50N 18°12E 65 B10
Insein Burma 16°50N 96°5E 85 L20
Inta Russia 66°5N 60°8E 70 A11
Interlaken Switz. 46°41N 7°50E 64 E4
Inukjuak Canada 58°25N 78°15W 109 D12
Inuvik Canada 68°16N 133°40W 108 C6
Inveraray U.K. 56°14N 5°5W 20 B5
Inverbervie U.K. 56°51N 2°17W 19 J13
Invercargill N.Z. 46°24S 168°24E 99 K12
Invergordon U.K. 57°41N 4°10W 19 G9
Inverkeithing U.K. 56°2N 3°24W 21 B9
Inverness U.K. 57°29N 4°13W 19 H9
Inverurie U.K. 57°17N 2°23W 19 H13
Ioannina Greece 39°42N 20°47E 69 E9
Iona U.K. 56°20N 6°25W 20 B3
Ionia U.S.A. 42°59N 85°4W 112 D5
Ionian Is. Greece 38°40N 20°0E 69 E9
Ionian Sea Medit. S. 37°30N 17°30E 69 E7
Ios Greece 36°41N 25°20E 69 F11
Iowa □ U.S.A. 42°18N 93°30W 111 B8
Iowa City U.S.A. 41°40N 91°32W 111 B8
Ipameri Brazil 17°44S 48°9W 122 C1
Ipatinga Brazil 19°32S 42°30W 122 C2
Ipiales Colombia 0°50N 77°37W 120 B2
Ipoh Malaysia 4°35N 101°5E 82 D2
Ipswich Australia 27°35S 152°40E 98 F9
Ipswich U.K. 52°4N 1°10E 25 B11
Iqaluit Canada 63°44N 68°31W 109 C13
Iquique Chile 20°19S 70°5W 120 E2
Iquitos Peru 3°45S 73°10W 120 C2
Iraklio Greece 35°20N 25°12E 69 G11
Iran ■ Asia 33°0N 53°0E 87 C8
Irapuato Mexico 20°41N 101°28W 114 C4
Iraq ■ Asia 33°0N 44°0E 86 C5
Irazú, Vol. Costa Rica 10°10N 84°20W 115 E8
Irchester U.K. 52°18N 0°39W 25 B7
Ireland ■ Europe 53°50N 7°52W 62 E2
Ireland's Eye Ireland 53°24N 6°4W 31 B10
Iringa Tanzania 7°48S 35°43E 96 F7
Irish Sea Europe 53°38N 4°48W 62 E4
Irkutsk Russia 52°18N 104°20E 78 A4
Irlam U.K. 53°26N 2°26W 23 F4
Iron Gate Europe 44°44N 22°30E 65 F12
Iron Mountain U.S.A. 45°49N 88°4W 112 C3
Ironbridge U.K. 52°38N 2°30W 23 G3
Ironton U.S.A. 38°32N 82°41W 112 F6
Ironwood U.S.A. 46°27N 90°9W 112 B2
Irrawaddy ➤ Burma 15°50N 95°6E 85 M19
Irt ➤ U.K. 54°23N 3°26W 22 D2
Irthlingborough U.K. 52°20N 0°37W 25 B7
Irtysh ➤ Russia 61°4N 68°52E 76 C7
Irún Spain 43°20N 1°52W 67 A5

Irvine U.K. 55°37N 4°41W 20 C4
Irvinestown U.K. 54°28N 7°39W 28 C6
Isabela Puerto Rico 18°30N 67°2W 115 d
Ísafjörður Iceland 66°5N 23°9W 63 A1
Isar ➤ Germany 48°48N 12°57E 64 D7
Isère ➤ France 44°59N 4°51E 66 D6
Ishim ➤ Russia 57°45N 71°10E 76 D8
Ishinomaki Japan 38°32N 141°20E 81 D7
Ishpeming U.S.A. 46°29N 87°40W 112 B4
Isiro Dem. Rep. of the Congo 2°53N 27°40E 96 D5
İskenderun Turkey 36°32N 36°10E 71 G6
Isla ➤ U.K. 56°32N 3°20W 21 A9
Islamabad Pakistan 33°40N 73°10E 84 C8
Island L. Canada 53°47N 94°25W 108 D10
Island Pond U.S.A. 44°49N 71°53W 113 C12
Islay U.K. 55°46N 6°10W 20 C3
Isleham U.K. 52°21N 0°25E 25 B9
Islington □ U.K. 51°33N 0°9W 25 C8
Islip U.K. 51°50N 1°12W 24 C6
İsmâ'ilîya Egypt 30°37N 32°18E 95 B12
Ísparta Turkey 37°47N 30°30E 71 G5
Israel ■ Asia 32°0N 34°50E 86 C3
Issoire France 45°32N 3°15E 66 D5
Issyk Kul Kyrgyzstan 42°25N 77°15E 72 D9
İstanbul Turkey 41°0N 28°58E 71 F4
Istres France 43°31N 4°59E 66 E6
Istria Croatia 45°10N 14°0E 68 B5
Itaberaba Brazil 12°32S 40°18W 122 B2
Itabira Brazil 19°37S 43°13W 122 C2
Itabuna Brazil 14°48S 39°16W 122 B3
Itacoatiara Brazil 3°8S 58°25W 120 C4
Itaipú, Represa de Brazil 25°30S 54°30W 117 F5
Itajaí Brazil 27°50S 48°39W 121 E5
Itajubá Brazil 22°24S 45°30W 122 D1
Italy ■ Europe 42°0N 13°0E 68 C5
Itaperuna Brazil 21°10S 41°54W 122 D2
Itapetinga Brazil 15°15S 40°15W 122 C2
Itapetininga Brazil 23°36S 48°7W 122 D1
Itapicuru ➤ Brazil 11°47S 37°32W 122 B3
Itararé Brazil 24°6S 49°23W 122 D1
Itaúna Brazil 20°4S 44°34W 122 D2
Itchen ➤ U.K. 50°55N 1°22W 24 E6
Ithaca U.S.A. 42°27N 76°30W 112 D9
Ittoqqortoormiit Greenland 70°20N 23°0W 54 B6
Itu Brazil 23°17S 47°15W 122 D1
Ivanava Belarus 52°7N 25°29E 65 B13
Ivano-Frankivsk Ukraine 48°40N 24°40E 65 D13
Ivanovo Russia 57°5N 41°0E 70 C7
Ivinghoe U.K. 51°50N 0°37W 25 C7
Ivory Coast ■ Africa 7°30N 5°0W 94 G4
Ivujivik Canada 62°24N 77°55W 109 C12
Ivybridge U.K. 50°23N 3°56W 27 G6
Iwaki Japan 37°3N 140°55E 81 E7
Iwakuni Japan 34°15N 132°8E 81 F3
Iwo Nigeria 7°39N 4°9E 94 G6
Ixworth U.K. 52°18N 0°51E 25 B10
Izhevsk Russia 56°51N 53°14E 70 C9
Izmayil Ukraine 45°22N 28°46E 71 E4
İzmir Turkey 38°25N 27°8E 71 G4
İznik Gölü Turkey 40°27N 29°30E 71 F4
Izumi-Sano Japan 34°23N 135°18E 81 F4

J
Jabalpur India 23°9N 79°58E 84 H11
Jaboatão Brazil 8°7S 35°1W 120 C6
Jaboticabal Brazil 21°15S 48°17W 122 D1
Jacareí Brazil 23°20S 46°0W 122 D1
Jackson Barbados 13°7N 59°36W 115 g
Jackson Ky., U.S.A. 37°33N 83°23W 112 G6
Jackson Mich., U.S.A. 42°15N 84°24W 112 D5
Jackson Miss., U.S.A. 32°18N 90°12W 111 D8
Jackson Mo., U.S.A. 37°23N 89°40W 112 G3
Jackson Tenn., U.S.A. 35°37N 88°49W 111 C9
Jacksonville Fla., U.S.A. 30°20N 81°39W 111 D10
Jacksonville Ill., U.S.A. 39°44N 90°14W 112 F2
Jacmel Haiti 18°14N 72°32W 115 D10
Jacobabad Pakistan 28°20N 68°29E 84 E6
Jacobina Brazil 11°11S 40°30W 122 B2
Jade Mt. Taiwan 23°25N 120°52E 79 G13
Jaén Spain 37°44N 3°43W 67 D4
Jaffna Sri Lanka 9°45N 80°2E 84 Q12
Jahrom Iran 28°30N 53°31E 87 D8
Jaipur India 27°0N 75°50E 84 F9
Jakarta Indonesia 6°9S 106°52E 82 F3
Jalālābād Afghan. 34°30N 70°29E 87 C12
Jalgaon India 21°0N 75°42E 84 J9
Jalna India 19°48N 75°38E 84 K9
Jalpaiguri India 26°32N 88°46E 85 F16
Jaluit I. Marshall Is. 6°0N 169°30E 102 G8
Jamaica ■ W. Indies 18°10N 77°30W 114 a
Jamalpur Bangla. 24°52N 89°56E 85 G16
Jamalpur India 25°18N 86°28E 85 G15
Jambi Indonesia 1°38S 103°30E 82 E2
James ➤ U.S.A. 42°52N 97°18W 111 B7
James B. Canada 54°0N 80°0W 109 D12
Jamestown N. Dak., U.S.A. 46°54N 98°42W 110 A7
Jamestown N.Y., U.S.A. 42°6N 79°14W 112 D8
Jammu India 32°43N 74°54E 84 C9
Jammu & Kashmir □ India 34°25N 77°0E 84 B10
Jamnagar India 22°30N 70°6E 84 H7
Jamshedpur India 22°44N 86°12E 85 H15
Jan Mayen Arctic 71°0N 9°0W 54 B7
Janaúba Brazil 15°48S 43°19W 122 C2
Janesville U.S.A. 42°41N 89°1W 112 D3
Januária Brazil 15°25S 44°25W 122 C2
Jaora India 23°40N 75°10E 84 H9
Japan ■ Asia 36°0N 136°0E 81 F5
Japan, Sea of Asia 40°0N 135°0E 81 D4
Japan Trench Pac. Oc. 32°0N 142°0E 102 D6
Japurá ➤ Brazil 3°8S 65°46W 120 C3
Jari ➤ Brazil 1°9S 51°54W 120 C4
Jarrow U.K. 54°59N 1°28W 22 C6
Jarvis I. Pac. Oc. 0°15S 160°5W 103 H12
Jāsk Iran 25°38N 57°45E 87 E9
Jasper Canada 52°55N 118°5W 108 D8
Jaú Brazil 22°10S 48°30W 122 D1
Jauja Peru 11°45S 75°15W 120 D2

Jaunpur India 25°46N 82°44E 85 G13
Java Indonesia 7°0S 110°0E 82 F3
Java Sea Indonesia 4°35S 107°15E 82 E3
Java Trench Ind. Oc. 9°0S 105°0E 82 F3
Jawhar Somali Rep. 2°48N 45°30E 89 G4
Jaya, Puncak Indonesia 3°57S 137°17E 83 E9
Jebel, Bahr el ➤ Sudan 9°30N 30°25E 95 G12
Jedburgh U.K. 55°29N 2°33W 21 D10
Jedda Si. Arabia 21°29N 39°10E 86 F4
Jeffersonville U.S.A. 38°17N 85°44W 112 F5
Jeju-do S. Korea 33°29N 126°34E 79 E14
Jelenia Góra Poland 50°50N 15°45E 64 C8
Jelgava Latvia 56°41N 23°49E 63 F8
Jena Germany 50°54N 11°35E 64 C6
Jeonju S. Korea 35°50N 127°4E 79 D14
Jequié Brazil 13°51S 40°5W 122 B2
Jequitinhonha Brazil 16°30S 41°0W 122 C2
Jequitinhonha ➤ Brazil 15°51S 38°53W 122 C3
Jérémie Haiti 18°40N 74°10W 115 D10
Jerez de la Frontera Spain 36°41N 6°7W 67 D2
Jersey U.K. 49°11N 2°7W 27 J9
Jersey City U.S.A. 40°42N 74°4W 113 E11
Jerseyville U.S.A. 39°7N 90°20W 112 F2
Jerusalem Israel/West Bank 31°47N 35°10E 86 D3
Jervaulx U.K. 54°16N 1°43W 22 D5
Jessore Bangla. 23°10N 89°10E 85 H16
Jhang Maghiana Pakistan 31°15N 72°22E 84 D8
Jhansi India 25°30N 78°36E 84 G11
Jharkhand □ India 24°0N 85°50E 85 H14
Jhelum Pakistan 33°0N 73°45E 84 C8
Jhelum ➤ Pakistan 31°20N 72°10E 84 D8
Jiamusi China 46°40N 130°26E 79 B15
Ji'an China 27°6N 114°59E 79 F11
Jiangsu □ China 33°0N 120°0E 79 E12
Jiangxi □ China 27°30N 116°0E 79 F12
Jiaxing China 30°49N 120°45E 79 E13
Jihlava ➤ Czech Rep. 48°55N 16°36E 65 D9
Jijiga Ethiopia 9°20N 42°50E 89 F3
Jilib Somali Rep. 0°29N 42°46E 89 G3
Jilin China 43°44N 126°30E 79 C14
Jilin □ China 44°0N 127°0E 79 C14
Jima Ethiopia 7°40N 36°47E 89 F2
Jiménez Mexico 27°8N 104°54W 114 B4
Jinan China 36°38N 117°1E 79 D12
Jinchang China 38°30N 102°10E 78 D9
Jincheng China 35°29N 112°50E 79 D11
Jingdezhen China 29°20N 117°11E 79 F12
Jinggu China 23°35N 100°41E 78 G9
Jingmen China 31°0N 112°10E 79 E11
Jinhua China 29°8N 119°38E 79 F12
Jining Nei Monggol Zizhiqu, China 41°5N 113°0E 79 C11
Jining Shandong, China 35°22N 116°34E 79 D12
Jinja Uganda 0°25N 33°12E 96 D6
Jinxi China 40°52N 120°50E 79 C13
Jinzhong China 37°42N 112°46E 79 D11
Jinzhou China 41°5N 121°3E 79 C13
Jipijapa Ecuador 1°0S 80°40W 120 C1
Jishou China 28°21N 109°43E 79 F10
Jiujiang China 29°42N 115°58E 79 F12
Jiwani Pakistan 25°1N 61°44E 87 E10
Jixi China 45°20N 130°50E 79 B15
Jīzān Si. Arabia 17°0N 42°20E 89 D3
Jizzax Uzbekistan 40°6N 67°50E 87 A11
João Pessoa Brazil 7°10S 34°52W 120 C6
Jodhpur India 26°23N 73°8E 84 F8
Joensuu Finland 62°37N 29°49E 63 E9
Johannesburg S. Africa 26°11S 28°2E 97 K5
John Crow Mts. Jamaica 18°5N 76°25W 114 a
John Day ➤ U.S.A. 45°44N 120°39W 110 A2
John o' Groats U.K. 58°38N 3°4W 19 E11
Johnson City U.S.A. 36°19N 82°21W 111 C10
Johnstone U.K. 55°49N 4°31W 20 C6
Johnstown U.S.A. 40°20N 78°55W 112 E8
Johor Bahru Malaysia 1°28N 103°46E 82 D2
Joinville Brazil 26°15S 48°55W 121 E5
Joliet U.S.A. 41°32N 88°5W 112 E3
Joliette Canada 46°3N 73°24W 109 E12
Jolo Phil. 6°0N 121°0E 83 C6
Jones Sound Canada 76°0N 85°0W 109 B11
Jonesboro U.S.A. 35°50N 90°42W 111 C8
Jönköping Sweden 57°45N 14°8E 63 F6
Jonquière Canada 48°27N 71°14W 113 A12
Joplin U.S.A. 37°6N 94°31W 111 C8
Jordan ■ Asia 31°0N 36°0E 86 D4
Jordan ➤ Asia 31°48N 35°32E 86 D3
Jos Nigeria 9°53N 8°51E 94 G7
Joseph Bonaparte G. Australia 14°35S 128°50E 98 C4
Jost Van Dyke I. Br. Virgin Is. 18°29N 64°47W 115 e
Jotunheimen Norway 61°35N 8°25E 63 E5
Jowzjān □ Afghan. 36°10N 66°0E 87 B11
Juan de Fuca, Str. of N. Amer. 48°15N 124°0W 110 A2
Juan Fernández, Arch. de Pac. Oc. 33°50S 80°0W 103 L20
Juàzeiro Brazil 9°30S 40°30W 122 B2
Juàzeiro do Norte Brazil 7°10S 39°18W 120 C6
Jûbâ Sudan 4°50N 31°35E 95 H12
Juba ➤ Somali Rep. 1°30N 42°35E 89 G3
Juchitán de Zaragoza Mexico 16°26N 95°1W 114 D5
Juiz de Fora Brazil 21°43S 43°19W 122 D2
Juliaca Peru 15°25S 70°10W 120 D2
Jullundur India 31°20N 75°40E 84 D9
Junagadh India 21°30N 70°30E 84 J7
Jundiaí Brazil 24°30S 47°0W 122 D1
Juneau U.S.A. 58°18N 134°25W 108 D6
Junín Argentina 34°33S 60°57W 121 F3
Jur, Nahr el ➤ Sudan 8°45N 29°15E 95 G11
Jura Europe 46°40N 6°5E 66 C6
Jura U.K. 56°0N 5°50W 20 C4
Jura, Sd. of U.K. 55°57N 5°45W 20 C4
Juruá ➤ Brazil 2°37S 65°44W 120 C3
Juruena ➤ Brazil 7°20S 58°3W 120 C4
Juticalpa Honduras 14°40N 86°12W 114 E7
Jutland Denmark 56°25N 9°30E 63 F5
Juventud, I. de la Cuba 21°40N 82°40W 115 C8
Jyväskylä Finland 62°14N 25°50E 63 E9

K
K2 Pakistan 35°58N 76°32E 84 B10
Kabardino-Balkaria □ Russia 43°30N 43°30E 71 F7
Kābul Afghan. 34°28N 69°11E 87 C12
Kabwe Zambia 14°30S 28°29E 97 G5
Kachchh, Gulf of India 22°50N 69°15E 84 H6
Kachchh, Rann of India 24°0N 70°0E 84 H7
Kachin □ Burma 26°0N 97°30E 85 G20
Kaçkar Turkey 40°45N 41°10E 71 F7
Kadavu Fiji 19°0S 178°15E 99 E14
Kade Ghana 6°7N 0°56W 94 G5
Kadoma Zimbabwe 18°20S 29°52E 97 H5
Kaduna Nigeria 10°30N 7°21E 94 F7
Kaesŏng N. Korea 37°58N 126°35E 79 D14
Kafue ➤ Zambia 15°30S 29°0E 97 H5
Kaga Bandoro C.A.R. 7°0N 19°10E 96 C3
Kagera ➤ Uganda 0°57S 31°47E 96 E6
Kagoshima Japan 31°35N 130°33E 81 H2
Kaho'olawe U.S.A. 20°33N 156°37W 110 H16
Kahramanmaraş Turkey 37°37N 36°53E 71 G6
Kai, Kepulauan Indonesia 5°55S 132°45E 83 F8
Kaieteur Falls Guyana 5°1N 59°10W 120 B4
Kaifeng China 34°48N 114°21E 79 E11
Kailua Kona U.S.A. 19°39N 155°59W 110 J17
Kainji Res. Nigeria 10°1N 4°40E 94 F6
Kairouan Tunisia 35°45N 10°5E 95 A8
Kaiserslautern Germany 49°26N 7°45E 64 D4
Kaitaia N.Z. 35°8S 173°17E 99 H13
Kaiyuan China 23°40N 103°12E 78 G9
Kajaani Finland 64°17N 27°46E 63 E9
Kajabbi Australia 20°0S 140°1E 98 E7
Kakamega Kenya 0°20N 34°46E 96 D6
Kakhovka Res. Ukraine 47°5N 34°0E 71 E5
Kakinada India 16°57N 82°11E 85 L13
Kalaallit Nunaat = Greenland ☑ N. Amer. 66°0N 45°0W 54 C5
Kalahari Africa 24°0S 21°30E 97 J4
Kalamata Greece 37°3N 22°10E 69 F10
Kalamazoo U.S.A. 42°17N 85°35W 112 D5
Kalamazoo ➤ U.S.A. 42°40N 86°10W 112 D4
Kalemie Dem. Rep. of the Congo 5°55S 29°9E 96 F5
Kalgoorlie-Boulder Australia 30°40S 121°22E 98 G3
Kalimantan Indonesia 0°0 114°0E 82 E4
Kálimnos Greece 37°0N 27°0E 69 F12
Kaliningrad Russia 54°42N 20°32E 63 G8
Kalispell U.S.A. 48°12N 114°19W 110 A4
Kalisz Poland 51°45N 18°8E 65 C10
Kalkaska U.S.A. 44°44N 85°11W 112 C5
Kallsjön Sweden 63°38N 13°0E 63 E6
Kalmar Sweden 56°40N 16°20E 63 F7
Kalmykia □ Russia 46°5N 46°1E 71 E8
Kaluga Russia 54°35N 36°10E 70 D6
Kalutara Sri Lanka 6°35N 80°0E 84 R12
Kalyan India 19°15N 73°9E 84 K8
Kama ➤ Russia 55°45N 52°0E 70 C9
Kamchatka Pen. Russia 57°0N 160°0E 77 D16
Kamensk Uralskiy Russia 56°25N 62°2E 76 D7
Kamina Dem. Rep. of the Congo 8°45S 25°0E 96 F5
Kamloops Canada 50°40N 120°20W 108 D7
Kampala Uganda 0°20N 32°30E 96 D6
Kampong Saom Cambodia 10°38N 103°30E 82 B2
Kamyanets-Podilskyy Ukraine 48°45N 26°40E 65 D14
Kamyshin Russia 50°10N 45°24E 71 D8
Kananga Dem. Rep. of the Congo 5°55S 22°18E 96 F4
Kanash Russia 55°30N 47°32E 70 C8
Kanawha ➤ U.S.A. 38°50N 82°9W 112 F6
Kanazawa Japan 36°30N 136°38E 81 E5
Kanchenjunga Nepal 27°50N 88°10E 85 F16
Kanchipuram India 12°52N 79°45E 84 N11
Kandahār Afghan. 31°32N 65°43E 87 D11
Kandalaksha Russia 67°9N 32°30E 70 A5
Kandalaksha, G. of Russia 66°0N 35°0E 70 A6
Kandi Benin 11°7N 2°55E 94 F6
Kandla India 23°0N 70°10E 84 H7
Kandy Sri Lanka 7°18N 80°43E 84 R12
Kane U.S.A. 41°40N 78°49W 112 E8
Kane Basin Greenland 79°1N 70°0W 104 B12
Kāne'ohe U.S.A. 21°25N 157°48W 110 H16
Kangaroo I. Australia 35°45S 137°0E 98 H6
Kangiqsualujjuaq Canada 58°30N 65°59W 109 D13
Kangiqsujuaq Canada 61°30N 72°0W 109 C12
Kangirsuk Canada 60°0N 70°0W 109 D13
Kanin Pen. Russia 68°0N 45°0E 70 A8
Kankakee U.S.A. 41°7N 87°52W 112 E4
Kankakee ➤ U.S.A. 41°23N 88°15W 112 E3
Kankan Guinea 10°23N 9°15W 94 F4
Kannyakumari India 8°3N 77°40E 84 Q10
Kano Nigeria 12°2N 8°30E 94 F7
Kanpur India 26°28N 80°20E 84 F12
Kansas □ U.S.A. 38°30N 99°0W 110 C7
Kansas ➤ U.S.A. 39°7N 94°37W 111 C8
Kansas City U.S.A. 39°6N 94°35W 111 C8
Kansk Russia 56°20N 95°37E 77 D10
Kanturk Ireland 52°11N 8°54W 30 D5
Kanye Botswana 24°55S 25°28E 97 J5
Kaohsiung Taiwan 22°35N 120°16E 79 G13
Kaolack Senegal 14°5N 16°8W 94 F2
Kapa'a U.S.A. 22°5N 159°19W 110 G15
Kapiri Mposhi Zambia 13°59S 28°43E 97 G5
Kāpīsā □ Afghan. 35°0N 69°20E 87 C12
Kaposvár Hungary 46°25N 17°47E 65 E9
Kaptai L. Bangla. 22°40N 92°20E 85 H18
Kapuas ➤ Indonesia 0°25S 109°20E 82 E3
Kapuskasing Canada 49°25N 82°30W 112 A6
Kara Bogaz Gol Turkmenistan 41°0N 53°30E 87 A8
Kara Kum Turkmenistan 39°30N 60°0E 87 B9
Kara Sea Russia 75°0N 70°0E 76 B7
Karabük Turkey 41°12N 32°37E 71 F5
Karachey-Cherkessia □ Russia 43°40N 41°30E 71 F7
Karachi Pakistan 24°50N 67°0E 84 G5
Karaganda Kazakhstan 49°50N 73°10E 78 B3
Karagiye Depression Kazakhstan 43°27N 51°45E 71 F9
Karakalpakstan □ Uzbekistan 43°0N 58°0E 87 A9
Karakoram Pakistan 35°30N 77°0E 84 B10
Karaman Turkey 37°14N 33°13E 71 G5
Karamay China 45°30N 84°58E 78 B5

Karatax Shan Ladock

Karatax Shan China 35°57N 81°0E 78 D5
Karayazı Turkey 39°41N 42°9E 71 G7
Karbalā' Iraq 32°36N 44°3E 86 C6
Karelia □ Russia 65°30N 32°30E 70 A5
Kariba, L. Zimbabwe 16°40S 28°25E 97 H5
Kariba Dam Zimbabwe 16°30S 28°35E 97 H5
Karimata, Str. of Indonesia 2°0S 108°40E 82 E3
Karlovac Croatia 45°31N 15°36E 68 B6
Karlskrona Sweden 56°10N 15°35E 63 F7
Karlsruhe Germany 49°0N 8°23E 64 D5
Karlstad Sweden 59°23N 13°30E 63 F6
Karnak Egypt 25°43N 32°39E 95 C12
Karnal India 29°42N 77°2E 84 E10
Karnataka □ India 13°15N 77°0E 84 N10
Kärnten □ Austria 46°52N 13°30E 64 E8
Karpathos Greece 35°37N 27°10E 69 G12
Kars Turkey 40°40N 43°5E 71 F7
Karwar India 14°55N 74°13E 84 M9
Kasai → Dem. Rep. of the Congo 3°30S 16°10E 96 E3
Kasaragod India 12°30N 74°58E 84 N9
Kasba L. Canada 60°20N 102°10W 108 C9
Kāshān Iran 34°5N 51°30E 87 C7
Kashi China 39°30N 76°2E 78 D4
Kasongo Dem. Rep. of the Congo 4°30S 26°33E 96 E5
Kassalâ Sudan 15°30N 36°0E 95 E13
Kassel Germany 51°18N 9°26E 64 C5
Kastamonu Turkey 41°25N 33°43E 71 F5
Kasur Pakistan 31°5N 74°25E 84 D9
Katanga □ Dem. Rep. of the Congo 8°0S 25°0E 96 F4
Kathiawar India 22°20N 71°0E 84 H7
Kathmandu Nepal 27°45N 85°20E 85 F14
Katihar India 25°34N 87°36E 85 G15
Katima Mulilo Namibia 17°28S 24°13E 97 H4
Katiola Ivory C. 8°10N 5°10W 94 G4
Katowice Poland 50°17N 19°5E 65 C10
Katrine, L. U.K. 56°15N 4°30W 20 B7
Katsina Nigeria 13°0N 7°32E 94 F7
Kattegat Denmark 56°40N 11°20E 63 F6
Kaua'i U.S.A. 22°3N 159°30W 110 H15
Kauai Channel U.S.A. 21°45N 158°50W 110 H16
Kaukauna U.S.A. 44°17N 88°17W 112 C3
Kaunakakai U.S.A. 21°6N 157°1W 110 H16
Kaunas Lithuania 54°54N 23°54E 63 G8
Kavala Greece 40°57N 24°28E 69 D11
Kavieng Papua N. G. 2°36S 150°51E 98 A9
Kawagoe Japan 35°55N 139°29E 81 F6
Kawaguchi Japan 35°52N 139°45E 81 F6
Kawardha India 22°0N 81°17E 85 J12
Kawasaki Japan 35°31N 139°43E 81 F6
Kawawachikamach Canada 54°48N 66°50W 109 D13
Kayah □ Burma 19°15N 97°15E 85 K20
Kayes Mali 14°25N 11°30W 94 F3
Kayin □ Burma 18°0N 97°30E 85 L20
Kayseri Turkey 38°45N 35°30E 71 G6
Kazan Russia 55°50N 49°10E 70 C8
Kazan-Rettō Pac. Oc. 25°0N 141°0E 102 E6
Kazanlŭk Bulgaria 42°38N 25°20E 69 C11
Kea Greece 37°35N 24°22E 69 F11
Kea U.K. 50°14N 5°6W 27 G3
Keady U.K. 54°15N 6°42W 29 C8
Kearney U.S.A. 40°42N 99°5W 110 B7
Keban Turkey 38°50N 38°50E 71 G6
Keban Baraji Turkey 38°41N 38°33E 71 G6
Kebnekaise Sweden 67°53N 18°33E 63 D7
Kebri Dehar Ethiopia 6°45N 44°17E 89 F3
Kebumen Indonesia 7°42S 109°40E 82 F3
Kecskemét Hungary 46°57N 19°42E 65 E10
Kediri Indonesia 7°51S 112°1E 82 F4
Keelby U.K. 53°35N 0°16W 23 E8
Keele U.K. 53°0N 2°17W 23 F4
Keene U.S.A. 42°56N 72°17W 113 D11
Keeper Hill Ireland 52°45N 8°16W 30 C6
Keetmanshoop Namibia 26°35S 18°8E 97 K3
Kefalonia Greece 38°15N 20°30E 69 E9
Keflavík Iceland 64°2N 22°35W 63 B1
Kegworth U.K. 52°50N 1°17W 23 G6
Keighley U.K. 53°52N 1°54W 23 E5
Keith U.K. 57°32N 2°57W 19 G12
Keld U.K. 54°24N 2°10W 22 D4
Kelkit → Turkey 40°45N 36°32E 71 F6
Kellett, C. Canada 72°0N 126°0W 109 B7
Kellogg U.S.A. 47°32N 116°7W 110 A3
Kelowna Canada 49°50N 119°25W 108 E8
Kelsale U.K. 52°14N 1°31E 25 B12
Kelsall U.K. 53°13N 2°43W 23 F3
Kelso U.K. 55°36N 2°26W 21 C11
Kelvedon U.K. 51°50N 0°43E 25 C10
Kem Russia 65°0N 34°38E 70 B5
Kemble U.K. 51°40N 1°59W 24 C5
Kemerovo Russia 55°20N 86°5E 76 D9
Kemi Finland 65°44N 24°34E 63 D8
Kemijoki → Finland 65°47N 24°32E 63 D8
Kemp Land Antarctica 69°0S 55°0E 55 C5
Kempsey U.K. 52°8N 2°12W 24 B4
Kempston U.K. 52°7N 0°30W 25 B7
Kempten Germany 47°45N 10°17E 64 E6
Kenai U.S.A. 60°33N 151°16W 108 C4
Kendal U.K. 54°20N 2°44W 22 C3
Kendari Indonesia 3°50S 122°30E 83 E6
Kenema S. Leone 7°50N 11°14W 94 G3
Kenilworth U.K. 52°21N 1°34W 24 B5
Kenitra Morocco 34°15N 6°40W 94 B4
Kenmare Ireland 51°53N 9°36W 30 E3
Kenmare River Ireland 51°48N 9°51W 30 E3
Kennet → U.K. 51°27N 0°57W 25 D7
Kennewick U.S.A. 46°12N 119°7W 110 A3
Kenninghall U.K. 52°26N 1°0E 25 B11
Kenogami → Canada 51°6N 84°28W 109 D11
Kenora Canada 49°47N 94°29W 108 E10
Kenosha U.S.A. 42°35N 87°49W 112 D4
Kent U.S.A. 41°9N 81°22W 112 E7
Kent □ U.K. 51°12N 0°40E 25 D10
Kent Pen. Canada 68°30N 107°0W 108 C9
Kentisbeare U.K. 50°51N 3°29W 27 F7
Kenton U.S.A. 40°39N 83°37W 112 E6
Kentucky □ U.S.A. 37°0N 84°0W 112 G5
Kentucky → U.S.A. 38°41N 85°11W 112 F5
Kentville Canada 45°6N 64°29W 109 E13
Kenya ■ Africa 1°0N 38°0E 96 D7

Kenya, Mt. Kenya 0°10S 37°18E 96 E7
Kerala □ India 11°0N 76°15E 84 P10
Kerch Ukraine 45°20N 36°20E 71 E6
Kerguelen Ind. Oc. 49°15S 69°10E 53 G13
Kericho Kenya 0°22S 35°15E 96 E7
Kerinci Indonesia 1°40S 101°15E 82 E2
Kermadec Is. Pac. Oc. 30°0S 178°15W 99 G15
Kermadec Trench Pac. Oc. 30°30S 176°0W 99 G15
Kermān Iran 30°15N 57°1E 87 D9
Kermānshāh Iran 34°23N 47°0E 86 C6
Kerrera U.K. 56°24N 5°33W 20 B4
Kerrobert Canada 51°56N 109°8W 108 D9
Kerry □ Ireland 52°7N 9°35W 30 D3
Kerry Hd. Ireland 52°25N 9°56W 30 D3
Kessingland U.K. 52°26N 1°43E 25 B12
Keswick U.K. 54°36N 3°8W 22 C2
Ketchikan U.S.A. 55°21N 131°39W 108 D6
Kettering U.K. 52°24N 0°43W 25 B7
Kettle Ness U.K. 54°33N 0°42W 22 C7
Kettlewell U.K. 54°9N 2°3W 22 C4
Kewaunee U.S.A. 44°27N 87°31W 112 C4
Keweenaw B. U.S.A. 47°0N 88°15W 112 B3
Keweenaw Pen. U.S.A. 47°15N 88°15W 112 B3
Keweenaw Pt. U.S.A. 47°25N 87°43W 112 B4
Kexby U.K. 53°22N 0°42W 23 F7
Key West U.S.A. 24°33N 81°48W 111 F10
Keyingham U.K. 53°43N 0°7W 23 E8
Keymer U.K. 50°55N 0°7W 25 E8
Keynsham U.K. 51°24N 2°29W 24 D4
Keyser U.S.A. 39°26N 78°59W 112 F8
Keyworth U.K. 52°52N 1°5W 23 G6
Khabarovsk Russia 48°30N 135°5E 79 B16
Khairpur Pakistan 27°32N 68°49E 84 F6
Khambhat India 22°23N 72°33E 84 H8
Khambhat, G. of India 20°45N 72°30E 84 J8
Khamis Mushayt Si. Arabia 18°18N 42°44E 89 D3
Khandyga Russia 62°42N 135°35E 77 C14
Khanewal Pakistan 30°20N 71°55E 84 D7
Khanka, L. Asia 45°0N 132°24E 79 C15
Kharagpur India 22°20N 87°25E 85 H15
Kharg Iran 29°15N 50°28E 86 D7
Khârga, El Wâhât el Egypt 25°10N 30°35E 95 C12
Kharkov Ukraine 49°58N 36°20E 71 E6
Khartoum Sudan 15°31N 32°35E 95 E12
Khaskovo Bulgaria 41°56N 25°30E 69 D11
Khatanga Russia 72°0N 102°20E 77 B11
Khemisset Morocco 33°50N 6°1W 94 B4
Khenchela Algeria 35°28N 7°11E 94 A7
Kherson Ukraine 46°35N 32°35E 71 E5
Khmelnytskyy Ukraine 49°23N 27°0E 65 D14
Khojak Pass Afghan. 30°51N 66°34E 87 B11
Kholm Afghan. 36°45N 67°40E 87 B11
Khon Kaen Thailand 16°30N 102°47E 82 A2
Khorramābād Iran 33°30N 48°25E 86 C7
Khorrāmshahr Iran 30°29N 48°15E 86 D7
Khouribga Morocco 32°58N 6°57W 94 B4
Khūjand Tajikistan 40°17N 69°37E 87 B12
Khulna Bangla. 22°45N 89°34E 85 H16
Khulna □ Bangla. 22°25N 89°35E 85 H16
Khunjerab Pass Asia 36°40N 75°25E 84 A9
Khushab Pakistan 32°20N 72°20E 84 C8
Khuzdar Pakistan 27°52N 66°30E 84 F5
Khvoy Iran 38°35N 45°0E 86 B6
Khyber Pass Afghan. 34°10N 71°8E 84 B7
Kibworth Beauchamp U.K. 52°33N 0°59W 23 G7
Kicking Horse Pass Canada 51°28N 116°16W 108 D8
Kidderminster U.K. 52°24N 2°15W 24 B4
Kidlington U.K. 51°50N 1°15W 24 C6
Kidsgrove U.K. 53°5N 2°14W 23 F4
Kidstones U.K. 54°13N 2°2W 22 C4
Kidwelly U.K. 51°44N 4°18W 26 D5
Kiel Germany 54°19N 10°8E 64 A6
Kiel Canal = Nord-Ostsee-Kanal Germany 54°12N 9°32E 64 A5
Kielce Poland 50°52N 20°42E 65 C11
Kielder U.K. 55°14N 2°35W 22 B3
Kieler Bucht Germany 54°35N 10°25E 64 A6
Kiev Ukraine 50°30N 30°28E 65 C16
Kigali Rwanda 1°59S 30°4E 96 E6
Kigoma-Ujiji Tanzania 4°55S 29°36E 96 E5
Kikwit Dem. Rep. of the Congo 5°0S 18°45E 96 E3
Kīlauea U.S.A. 19°25N 155°17W 110 J17
Kilbirnie U.K. 55°46N 4°41W 20 C6
Kilbrannan Sd. U.K. 55°37N 5°26W 20 C5
Kildare Ireland 53°9N 6°55W 31 B9
Kildare □ Ireland 53°10N 6°50W 31 B9
Kilfinnane Ireland 52°21N 8°28W 30 D6
Kilham U.K. 54°4N 0°23W 22 D8
Kilifi Kenya 3°40S 39°48E 96 E7
Kilimanjaro Tanzania 3°7S 37°20E 96 E7
Kilindini Kenya 4°4S 39°40E 96 E7
Kilkee Ireland 52°41N 9°39W 30 C3
Kilkeel U.K. 54°4N 6°0W 29 C10
Kilkenny Ireland 52°39N 7°15W 31 C8
Kilkenny □ Ireland 52°35N 7°15W 31 C8
Kilkhampton U.K. 50°52N 4°31W 27 F4
Kilkieran B. Ireland 53°20N 9°41W 30 B3
Killala Ireland 54°13N 9°12W 28 C3
Killala B. Ireland 54°16N 9°8W 28 C3
Killaloe Ireland 52°48N 8°28W 30 C6
Killarney Ireland 52°4N 9°30W 30 D4
Killarney △ Ireland 52°0N 9°33W 30 E3
Killary Harbour Ireland 53°38N 9°52W 28 D2
Killeen U.S.A. 31°7N 97°44W 110 D7
Killin U.K. 56°28N 4°19W 20 B6
Killiney Ireland 53°15N 6°7W 31 B10
Killinghall U.K. 54°2N 1°33W 23 D5
Killorglin Ireland 52°6N 9°47W 30 D3
Killybegs Ireland 54°38N 8°26W 28 B5
Kilmarnock U.K. 55°37N 4°29W 20 C7
Kilrush Ireland 52°38N 9°29W 30 C4
Kilsby U.K. 52°20N 1°10W 24 B6
Kilsyth U.K. 55°59N 4°3W 20 C7
Kilwa Kivinje Tanzania 8°45S 39°25E 96 F7
Kilwinning U.K. 55°39N 4°43W 20 C6
Kimberley Australia 16°20S 127°0E 98 D4
Kimberley S. Africa 28°43S 24°46E 97 K4
Kimbolton U.K. 52°18N 0°24W 25 B8
Kimch'aek N. Korea 40°40N 129°10E 79 C14
Kimmirut Canada 62°50N 69°50W 109 C13

Kimry Russia 56°55N 37°15E 70 C6
Kinabalu, Gunung Malaysia 6°3N 116°14E 82 C5
Kincardine Canada 44°10N 81°40W 112 C7
Kincardine Aberds., U.K. 56°57N 2°25W 19 J13
Kincardine Fife, U.K. 56°4N 3°43W 21 B8
Kinder Scout U.K. 53°24N 1°52W 23 F5
Kindersley Canada 51°30N 109°10W 108 D9
Kindia Guinea 10°0N 12°52W 94 F3
Kindu Dem. Rep. of the Congo 2°55S 25°50E 96 E5
Kineshma Russia 57°30N 42°5E 70 C7
Kineton U.K. 52°10N 1°31W 24 B5
King George I. Antarctica 60°0S 60°0W 55 C18
King George Is. Canada 57°20N 80°30W 109 D11
King I. Australia 39°50S 144°0E 98 H7
King William I. Canada 69°10N 97°25W 108 C10
Kingman U.S.A. 35°12N 114°4W 110 C4
King's Lynn U.K. 52°45N 0°24E 25 A9
King's Sutton U.K. 52°2N 1°15W 24 B6
King's Worthy U.K. 51°6N 1°17W 24 D6
Kingsbridge U.K. 50°17N 3°47W 27 G6
Kingsbury U.K. 52°34N 1°40W 23 G5
Kingscourt Ireland 53°55N 6°48W 29 D8
Kingskerswell U.K. 50°29N 3°35W 27 G6
Kingsland U.K. 52°15N 2°48W 24 B3
Kingsteignton U.K. 50°33N 3°36W 27 F6
Kingston Canada 44°14N 76°30W 109 E12
Kingston Jamaica 18°0N 76°50W 114 a
Kingston N.Y., U.S.A. 41°56N 73°59W 113 E10
Kingston Pa., U.S.A. 41°16N 75°54W 113 E10
Kingston upon Hull U.K. 53°45N 0°21W 23 E8
Kingston-upon-Thames □ U.K. 51°24N 0°17W 25 D8
Kingstown St. Vincent 13°10N 61°10W 115 E12
Kingstown U.K. 54°56N 2°53W 22 C3
Kingsville U.S.A. 27°31N 97°52W 110 E7
Kingswear U.K. 50°21N 3°35W 27 G6
Kingswood U.K. 51°27N 2°31W 24 D3
Kington U.K. 52°13N 3°1W 24 B2
Kingussie U.K. 57°6N 4°2W 19 H8
Kinlochleven U.K. 56°43N 5°0W 18 J7
Kinnairds Hd. U.K. 57°43N 2°1W 19 G13
Kinngait Canada 64°14N 76°32W 109 C12
Kinross U.K. 56°13N 3°25W 21 B9
Kinsale Ireland 51°42N 8°31W 30 E5
Kinsale, Old Hd. of Ireland 51°37N 8°33W 30 E5
Kinshasa Dem. Rep. of the Congo 4°20S 15°15E 96 E3
Kintore U.K. 57°14N 2°20W 19 H13
Kintyre U.K. 55°30N 5°35W 20 D4
Kintyre, Mull of U.K. 55°17N 5°47W 20 D4
Kippure Ireland 53°11N 6°21W 31 B10
Kirensk Russia 57°50N 107°55E 77 D11
Kirgiz Steppe Eurasia 50°0N 55°0E 71 E11
Kiribati ■ Pac. Oc. 3°0S 180°0E 102 H10
Kırıkkale Turkey 39°51N 33°32E 71 G5
Kiritimati Kiribati 1°58N 157°27W 103 G12
Kirkbean U.K. 54°55N 3°36W 21 E9
Kirkbride U.K. 54°54N 3°12W 22 C2
Kirkburton U.K. 53°37N 1°42W 23 E5
Kirkby U.K. 53°30N 2°54W 23 F3
Kirkby-in-Ashfield U.K. 53°6N 1°14W 23 F6
Kirkby Lonsdale U.K. 54°12N 2°36W 22 C3
Kirkby Malzeard U.K. 54°10N 1°37W 22 C5
Kirkby Stephen U.K. 54°29N 2°21W 22 C4
Kirkby Thore U.K. 54°37N 2°32W 22 C3
Kirkbymoorside U.K. 54°17N 0°56W 22 D7
Kirkcaldy U.K. 56°7N 3°9W 21 B9
Kirkcudbright U.K. 54°50N 4°2W 20 E7
Kirkham U.K. 53°47N 2°53W 23 E3
Kirkintilloch U.K. 55°56N 4°8W 20 C7
Kirkland Lake Canada 48°9N 80°2W 109 E11
Kırklareli Turkey 41°44N 27°15E 86 A1
Kirkoswald U.K. 54°46N 2°41W 22 C3
Kirksville U.S.A. 40°12N 92°35W 111 B81
Kirkūk Iraq 35°30N 44°21E 86 C6
Kirkwall U.K. 58°59N 2°58W 19 E12
Kirkwhelpington U.K. 55°9N 1°59W 22 B5
Kirov Russia 58°35N 49°40E 70 C8
Kirovohrad Ukraine 48°35N 32°20E 71 E5
Kirriemuir U.K. 56°41N 3°1W 19 J11
Kırşehir Turkey 39°14N 34°5E 71 G5
Kirthar Range Pakistan 27°0N 67°0E 84 F5
Kirtling U.K. 52°12N 0°28E 25 B9
Kirtlington U.K. 51°53N 1°15W 24 C6
Kirton U.K. 52°56N 0°3W 23 G8
Kirton in Lindsey U.K. 53°29N 0°34W 23 F7
Kiruna Sweden 67°52N 20°15E 63 D8
Kiryū Japan 36°24N 139°20E 81 E6
Kisangani Dem. Rep. of the Congo 0°35N 25°15E 96 D5
Kiselevsk Russia 54°5N 86°39E 76 D9
Kishanganj India 26°3N 88°14E 85 F16
Kishinev Moldova 47°0N 28°50E 65 E15
Kisii Kenya 0°40S 34°45E 96 E6
Kislovodsk Russia 43°50N 42°45E 71 F7
Kismaayo Somali Rep. 0°22S 42°32E 89 H3
Kisumu Kenya 0°3S 34°45E 96 E6
Kitakyūshū Japan 33°50N 130°50E 81 G2
Kitale Kenya 1°0N 35°0E 96 D7
Kitami Japan 43°48N 143°54E 81 B8
Kitchener Canada 43°27N 80°29W 112 D7
Kithnos Greece 37°26N 24°27E 69 F11
Kitimat Canada 54°3N 128°38W 108 D7
Kittanning U.S.A. 40°49N 79°31W 112 E8
Kitwe Zambia 12°54S 28°13E 97 G5
Kivu, L. Dem. Rep. of the Congo 1°48S 29°0E 96 E5
Kızıl Irmak → Turkey 41°44N 35°58E 71 F6
Kizlyar Russia 43°51N 46°40E 71 F8
Kladno Czech Rep. 50°10N 14°7E 64 C8
Klagenfurt Austria 46°38N 14°20E 64 E8
Klaipėda Lithuania 55°43N 21°10E 63 F8
Klamath → U.S.A. 41°33N 124°5W 110 B2
Klamath Falls U.S.A. 42°13N 121°46W 110 B2
Klang Malaysia 3°2N 101°26E 82 D2
Klarälven → Sweden 59°23N 13°32E 63 F6
Klerksdorp S. Africa 26°53S 26°38E 97 K5
Kluane L. Canada 61°15N 138°40W 108 C6
Klyuchevskaya, Gora Russia 55°50N 160°30E 77 D17
Knaresborough U.K. 54°1N 1°28W 23 D6
Knebworth U.K. 51°52N 0°11W 25 C8

Knighton U.K. 52°21N 3°3W 26 C7
Knock Ireland 53°48N 8°55W 28 D4
Knockmealdown Mts. Ireland 52°14N 7°56W 30 D7
Knossos Greece 35°16N 25°10E 69 G11
Knottingley U.K. 53°43N 1°16W 23 E6
Knowle U.K. 52°24N 1°44W 23 H5
Knoxville U.S.A. 35°58N 83°55W 111 C10
Knoydart U.K. 57°3N 5°33W 18 H6
Knutsford U.K. 53°18N 2°21W 23 F4
Kōbe Japan 34°41N 135°13E 81 F4
Koblenz Germany 50°21N 7°36E 64 C4
Kocaeli Turkey 40°45N 29°50E 71 F4
Koch Bihar India 26°22N 89°29E 85 F16
Kōchi Japan 33°30N 133°35E 81 G3
Kodiak U.S.A. 57°47N 152°24W 108 D4
Kodiak I. U.S.A. 57°30N 152°45W 108 D4
Koforidua Ghana 6°3N 0°17W 94 G5
Kōfu Japan 35°40N 138°30E 81 F6
Kogalym Russia 62°16N 74°29E 76 C8
Kohat Pakistan 33°40N 71°29E 84 C7
Kohima India 25°35N 94°10E 85 G19
Kohtla-Järve Estonia 59°20N 27°20E 63 F9
Kokkola Finland 63°50N 23°8E 63 E8
Koko Kyunzu Burma 14°7N 93°22E 85 M18
Kokomo U.S.A. 40°29N 86°8W 112 E4
Kökshetaū Kazakhstan 53°20N 69°25E 76 D7
Koksoak → Canada 58°30N 68°10W 109 D13
Kola Pen. Russia 67°30N 38°0E 70 A6
Kolar Gold Fields India 12°58N 78°16E 84 N11
Kolguyev Russia 69°20N 48°30E 70 A8
Kolhapur India 16°43N 74°15E 84 L9
Kolkata India 22°34N 88°21E 85 H16
Kolomna Russia 55°8N 38°45E 70 C6
Kolomyya Ukraine 48°31N 25°2E 71 E4
Kolpino Russia 59°44N 30°39E 70 C5
Kolwezi Dem. Rep. of the Congo 10°40S 25°25E 96 G5
Kolyma → Russia 69°30N 161°0E 77 C17
Kolyma Ra. Russia 63°0N 157°0E 77 C16
Komatsu Japan 36°25N 136°30E 81 E5
Komi □ Russia 64°0N 55°0E 70 B10
Kompong Cham Cambodia 12°0N 105°30E 82 B3
Komsomolsk-na-Amur Russia 50°30N 137°0E 77 D14
Konar □ Afghan. 34°30N 71°3E 87 C12
Kondūz Afghan. 36°50N 68°50E 87 B12
Kongur Shan China 38°34N 75°18E 78 D4
Konin Poland 52°12N 18°15E 65 B10
Konosha Russia 61°0N 40°5E 70 B7
Konotop Ukraine 51°12N 33°7E 71 D5
Konqi He → China 41°0N 86°0E 78 C6
Konya Turkey 37°52N 32°35E 71 G5
Kootenay L. Canada 49°45N 116°50W 108 E8
Kopet Dagh Asia 38°0N 58°0E 87 B9
Korça Albania 40°37N 20°50E 69 D9
Korčula Croatia 42°56N 16°57E 68 C7
Kordestān □ Iran 36°0N 47°0E 86 C6
Kordofân Sudan 13°0N 29°0E 95 F11
Korea, North ■ Asia 40°0N 127°0E 79 D14
Korea, South ■ Asia 36°0N 128°0E 79 D14
Korea Bay Korea 39°0N 124°0E 79 D13
Korea Strait Asia 34°0N 129°30E 79 E14
Korhogo Ivory C. 9°29N 5°28W 94 G4
Kōriyama Japan 37°24N 140°23E 81 E7
Korla China 41°45N 86°4E 78 C6
Koror Palau 7°20N 134°28E 102 G5
Körös → Hungary 46°43N 20°12E 65 E11
Korosten Ukraine 50°54N 28°36E 71 D4
Kortrijk Belgium 50°50N 3°17E 64 C2
Koryak Ra. Russia 61°0N 171°0E 77 C18
Kos Greece 36°50N 27°15E 69 F12
Kosciuszko, Mt. Australia 36°27S 148°16E 98 H8
Košice Slovak Rep. 48°42N 21°15E 65 D11
Kosovo ■ Europe 42°30N 21°0E 69 C9
Košti Sudan 13°8N 32°43E 95 F12
Kostroma Russia 57°50N 40°58E 70 C7
Koszalin Poland 54°11N 16°8E 64 A9
Kota India 25°14N 75°49E 84 G9
Kota Bharu Malaysia 6°7N 102°14E 82 C2
Kota Kinabalu Malaysia 6°0N 116°4E 82 C5
Kotabumi Indonesia 4°49S 104°54E 82 E2
Kotelnich Russia 58°22N 48°24E 70 C8
Kotka Finland 60°28N 26°58E 63 E9
Kotlas Russia 61°17N 46°43E 70 B8
Kotor Montenegro 42°25N 18°47E 69 C8
Kotri Pakistan 25°22N 68°22E 84 G6
Kotuy → Russia 71°54N 102°6E 77 B11
Kotzebue U.S.A. 66°53N 162°39W 108 C3
Kotzebue Sound U.S.A. 66°20N 163°0W 104 C3
Koudougou Burkina Faso 12°10N 2°20W 94 F5
Koumra Chad 8°50N 17°35E 95 G9
Kovel Ukraine 51°11N 24°38E 65 C13
Kovrov Russia 56°25N 41°25E 70 C7
Kowloon China 22°19N 114°11E 79 a
Koyukuk → U.S.A. 64°55N 157°32W 104 C4
Kpalimé Togo 6°57N 0°44E 94 G6
Kra, Isthmus of Thailand 10°15N 99°30E 82 B1
Kragujevac Serbia 44°2N 20°56E 69 B9
Krakatoa Indonesia 6°10S 105°20E 82 F3
Kraków Poland 50°4N 19°57E 65 C10
Kraljevo Serbia 43°44N 20°41E 69 C9
Kramatorsk Ukraine 48°50N 37°30E 71 E6
Krasnodar Russia 45°5N 39°0E 71 E6
Krasnokamsk Russia 58°4N 55°48E 70 C10
Krasnoturinsk Russia 59°46N 60°12E 70 C11
Krasnoyarsk Russia 56°8N 93°0E 77 D10
Krasnyy Luch Ukraine 48°13N 39°0E 71 E6
Krefeld Germany 51°20N 6°33E 64 C4
Kremenchuk Ukraine 49°5N 33°25E 71 E5
Kribi Cameroon 2°57N 9°56E 96 D1
Krishna → India 15°57N 80°59E 85 M12
Kristiansand Norway 58°8N 8°1E 63 F5
Kristiansund Norway 63°7N 7°45E 63 E5
Krivoy Rog Ukraine 47°51N 33°20E 71 E5
Krk Croatia 45°8N 14°40E 68 B6
Kronshtadt Russia 59°57N 29°51E 70 B4
Kroonstad S. Africa 27°43S 27°19E 97 K5
Kropotkin Russia 45°28N 40°28E 71 E7
Krosno Poland 49°42N 21°46E 65 D11

Kruševac Serbia 43°35N 21°28E 69 C9
Ksar el Kebir Morocco 35°0N 6°0W 94 B4
Kuala Belait Malaysia 4°35N 114°11E 82 D4
Kuala Lumpur Malaysia 3°9N 101°41E 82 D2
Kuala Terengganu Malaysia 5°20N 103°8E 82 C2
Kuantan Malaysia 3°49N 103°20E 82 D2
Kuching Malaysia 1°33N 110°25E 82 D4
Kudymkar Russia 59°1N 54°39E 70 C9
Kuujjuk Canada 67°50N 115°5W 108 C8
Kuito Angola 12°22S 16°55E 97 G3
Kūlob Tajikistan 37°55N 69°50E 87 B12
Kuma → Russia 44°55N 47°0E 71 F8
Kumagaya Japan 36°9N 139°22E 81 E6
Kumamoto Japan 32°45N 130°45E 81 G2
Kumanovo Macedonia 42°9N 21°42E 69 C9
Kumasi Ghana 6°41N 1°38W 94 G5
Kumba Cameroon 4°36N 9°24E 96 D1
Kumbakonam India 10°58N 79°25E 84 P11
Kumertau Russia 52°45N 55°57E 70 D10
Kumtag Desert China 39°40N 92°0E 78 C7
Kungur Russia 57°25N 56°57E 70 C10
Kunlun Shan Asia 36°0N 86°30E 78 D6
Kunming China 25°1N 102°41E 78 F9
Kuopio Finland 62°53N 27°35E 63 E9
Kupang Indonesia 10°19S 123°39E 83 F6
Kuqa China 41°35N 82°30E 78 C5
Kür → Azerbaijan 39°29N 49°15E 71 G8
Kurdistan Asia 37°20N 43°30E 86 B5
Kure Japan 34°14N 132°32E 81 F3
Kurgan Russia 55°26N 65°18E 76 D7
Kuril Is. Russia 45°0N 150°0E 77 E16
Kuril-Kamchatka Trench Pac. Oc. 44°0N 153°0E 102 C7
Kurnool India 15°45N 78°0E 84 M11
Kursk Russia 51°42N 36°11E 70 D6
Kuruktag China 41°0N 89°0E 78 C6
Kurume Japan 33°15N 130°30E 81 G2
Kushiro Japan 43°0N 144°25E 81 B9
Kushtia Bangla. 23°55N 89°5E 85 H16
Kuskokwim → U.S.A. 60°5N 162°25W 104 C3
Kuskokwim B. U.S.A. 59°45N 162°25W 108 D3
Kütahya Turkey 39°30N 30°2E 71 G4
Kutaisi Georgia 42°19N 42°40E 71 F7
Kuujjuaq Canada 58°6N 68°15W 109 D13
Kuujjuarapik Canada 55°20N 77°35W 109 D12
Kuwait Kuwait 29°30N 48°0E 86 D7
Kuwait ■ Asia 29°30N 47°30E 86 D6
Kuybyshev Res. Russia 55°2N 49°30E 70 C8
Kuznetsk Russia 53°12N 46°40E 70 D8
Kuzomen Russia 66°22N 36°50E 70 A6
KwaMashu S. Africa 29°45S 30°58E 97 K6
KwaZulu Natal □ S. Africa 29°0S 30°0E 97 K6
Kwekwe Zimbabwe 18°58S 29°48E 97 H5
Kyle of Lochalsh U.K. 57°17N 5°44W 18 H6
Kyoga, L. Uganda 1°35N 33°0E 96 D6
Kyōto Japan 35°0N 135°45E 81 F4
Kyrenia Cyprus 35°20N 33°20E 86 C3
Kyrgyzstan ■ Asia 42°0N 75°0E 76 E8
Kythira Greece 36°8N 23°0E 69 F10
Kyūshū Japan 33°0N 131°0E 81 G2
Kyustendil Bulgaria 42°16N 22°41E 69 C10
Kyzyl Kum Uzbekistan 42°30N 65°0E 87 A10
Kyzyl-Orda Kazakhstan 44°48N 65°28E 76 E7

L

La Alcarria Spain 40°31N 2°45W 67 B4
La Barra Nic. 12°54N 83°33W 115 E8
La Ceiba Honduras 15°40N 86°50W 114 D7
La Coruña Spain 43°20N 8°25W 67 A1
La Crosse U.S.A. 43°48N 91°15W 112 D2
La Désirade Guadeloupe 16°18N 61°3W 114 b
La Grande → U.S.A. 45°20N 118°5W 110 A3
La Grande → Canada 53°50N 79°0W 109 D12
La Grange U.S.A. 33°2N 85°2W 111 D10
La Habana Cuba 23°8N 82°22W 115 C8
La Junta U.S.A. 37°59N 103°33W 110 C6
La Línea de la Concepción Spain 36°15N 5°23W 67 D3
La Loche Canada 56°29N 109°26W 108 D9
La Mancha Spain 39°10N 2°54W 67 C4
La Oroya Peru 11°32S 75°54W 120 D2
La Palma Canary Is. 28°40N 17°50W 94 C2
La Paz Bolivia 16°20S 68°10W 120 D3
La Paz Mexico 24°10N 110°18W 114 C2
La Perouse Str. Asia 45°40N 142°0E 102 C6
La Plata Argentina 35°0S 57°55W 121 F4
La Quiaca Argentina 22°5S 65°35W 121 E3
La Rioja Argentina 29°20S 67°0W 121 E3
La Rioja □ Spain 42°20N 2°20W 67 A4
La Roche-sur-Yon France 46°40N 1°25W 66 C3
La Rochelle France 46°10N 1°9W 66 C3
La Romana Dom. Rep. 18°27N 68°57W 115 D11
La Ronge Canada 55°5N 105°20W 108 D9
La Sarre Canada 48°45N 79°15W 112 A8
La Serena Chile 29°55S 71°10W 121 E2
La Seyne-sur-Mer France 43°7N 5°52E 66 E6
La Spézia Italy 44°7N 9°50E 68 B3
La Tortuga Venezuela 11°0N 65°22W 120 A3
La Trinité Martinique 14°45N 60°58W 114 c
La Tuque Canada 47°30N 72°50W 109 E12
La Vega Dom. Rep. 19°20N 70°30W 115 D10
Labé Guinea 11°24N 12°16W 94 F3
Labinsk Russia 44°40N 40°48E 71 F7
Laborie St. Lucia 13°45N 61°2W 115 f
Labrador Canada 53°20N 61°0W 109 D13
Labrador City Canada 52°57N 66°55W 109 D13
Labrador Sea Atl. Oc. 57°0N 54°0W 109 D14
Labuan Malaysia 5°21N 115°13E 82 C5
Lac La Biche Canada 54°45N 111°58W 108 D8
Lac-Mégantic Canada 45°35N 70°53W 113 C12
Laccadive Is. = Lakshadweep Is. India 10°0N 72°30E 72 G9
Lacock U.K. 51°24N 2°7W 24 D4
Lacombe Canada 52°30N 113°44W 108 D8
Laconia U.S.A. 43°32N 71°28W 113 D12
Ladakh Ra. India 34°0N 78°0E 84 B11
Ladder Hills U.K. 57°13N 3°16W 19 H11
Ladock U.K. 50°19N 4°58W 27 G4

Ladoga, L. *Russia* 61°15N 30°30E **70** B5
Ladysmith *S. Africa* 28°32S 29°46E **97** K5
Ladysmith *U.S.A.* 45°28N 91°12W **112** C2
Lae *Papua N. G.* 6°40S 147°2E **98** B8
Lafayette *Ind., U.S.A.* 40°25N 86°54W **112** E4
Lafayette *La., U.S.A.* 30°14N 92°1W **111** D8
Lafia *Nigeria* 8°30N 8°34E **94** G7
Lagan → *U.K.* 54°36N 5°55W **29** B10
Lagarto *Brazil* 10°54S 37°41W **122** B3
Lagdo, L. de *Cameroon* 8°40N 14°0E **95** G8
Laghouat *Algeria* 33°50N 2°59E **94** B6
Lagos *Nigeria* 6°25N 3°27E **94** G6
Lagos *Portugal* 37°5N 8°41W **67** D1
Lahn → *Germany* 50°19N 7°37E **64** C4
Lahore *Pakistan* 31°32N 74°22E **84** D9
Lahti *Finland* 60°58N 25°40E **63** E9
Lairg *U.K.* 58°2N 4°24W **19** F9
Laizhou *China* 37°8N 119°57E **79** D12
Lake Charles *U.S.A.* 30°14N 93°13W **111** D8
Lake City *U.S.A.* 30°11N 82°38W **111** D10
Lake District △ *U.K.* 54°30N 3°21W **22** C2
Lake Havasu City *U.S.A.* 34°27N 114°22W **110** D4
Lakeland *U.S.A.* 28°3N 81°57W **111** E10
Lakenheath *U.K.* 52°25N 0°32E **25** B10
Lakewood *U.S.A.* 41°28N 81°47W **112** E7
Lakshadweep Is. *India* 10°0N 72°30E **72** G9
Lamar *U.S.A.* 38°5N 102°37W **110** C6
Lambaréné *Gabon* 0°41S 10°12E **96** E2
Lambay I. *Ireland* 53°29N 6°1W **31** B10
Lamberhurst *U.K.* 51°5N 0°24E **25** D9
Lambeth □ *U.K.* 51°28N 0°6W **25** D8
Lambley *U.K.* 54°56N 2°30W **22** C4
Lambourn *U.K.* 51°30N 1°32W **24** C5
Lamesa *U.S.A.* 32°44N 101°58W **110** D6
Lammermuir *U.K.* 55°50N 2°25W **21** C11
Lammermuir Hills *U.K.* 55°50N 2°40W **21** C10
Lamon B. *Phil.* 14°30N 122°20E **83** B6
Lampedusa *Medit. S.* 35°36N 12°40E **68** G5
Lampeter *U.K.* 52°7N 4°4W **26** C5
Lamu *Kenya* 2°16S 40°55E **96** E8
Lanark *U.K.* 55°40N 3°47W **21** C8
Lancashire □ *U.K.* 53°50N 2°48W **23** E3
Lancaster *U.K.* 54°3N 2°48W **22** D3
Lancaster *N.H., U.S.A.* 44°29N 71°34W **113** C12
Lancaster *Pa., U.S.A.* 40°2N 76°19W **112** E9
Lancaster *Wis., U.S.A.* 42°51N 90°43W **112** D2
Lancaster Sd. *Canada* 74°13N 84°0W **109** B11
Lanchester *U.K.* 54°50N 1°44W **22** C5
Lancing *U.K.* 50°49N 0°19W **25** E8
Landes *France* 44°0N 1°0W **66** D3
Landkey *U.K.* 51°3N 4°0W **27** E6
Land's End *U.K.* 50°4N 5°44W **27** G2
Langholm *U.K.* 55°9N 3°0W **21** D10
Langport *U.K.* 51°2N 2°50W **24** D3
Langreo *Spain* 43°18N 5°40W **67** A3
Langres *France* 47°52N 5°20E **66** C6
Langres, Plateau de *France* 47°45N 5°3E **66** C6
Langsa *Indonesia* 4°30N 97°57E **82** D1
Langstrothdale Chase *U.K.* 54°14N 2°13W **22** D4
Langtoft *U.K.* 52°42N 0°20W **23** G8
Langtree *U.K.* 50°55N 4°13W **27** F5
Languedoc *France* 43°58N 3°55E **66** E5
Lannion *France* 48°46N 3°29W **66** B2
L'Annonciation *Canada* 46°25N 74°55W **113** B10
L'Anse *U.S.A.* 46°45N 88°27W **112** B31
L'Anse la Raye *St. Lucia* 13°55N 61°3W **115** f
Lansing *U.S.A.* 42°44N 84°33W **112** D5
Lanzarote *Canary Is.* 29°0N 13°40W **94** C3
Lanzhou *China* 36°1N 103°52E **78** D9
Laoag *Phil.* 18°7N 120°34E **83** A6
Laois □ *Ireland* 52°57N 7°36W **31** C7
Laon *France* 49°33N 3°35E **66** B5
Laos ■ *Asia* 17°45N 105°0E **82** A3
Lapeer *U.S.A.* 43°3N 83°19W **112** D6
Lapford *U.K.* 50°51N 3°48W **27** F6
Lapland *Europe* 68°7N 24°0E **63** D8
LaPorte *U.S.A.* 41°36N 86°43W **112** E4
Laptev Sea *Russia* 76°0N 125°0E **77** B13
L'Aquila *Italy* 42°22N 13°22E **68** C5
Laramie *U.S.A.* 41°19N 105°35W **110** B5
Laramie Mts. *U.S.A.* 42°0N 105°30W **110** B5
Laredo *U.S.A.* 27°30N 99°30W **110** E7
Largs *U.K.* 55°47N 4°52W **20** C6
Larisa *Greece* 39°36N 22°27E **69** E10
Larnaca *Cyprus* 34°55N 33°38E **86** C3
Larne *U.K.* 54°51N 5°51W **29** B10
Larne L. *U.K.* 54°50N 5°48W **29** B10
Larrimah *Australia* 15°35S 133°12E **98** D5
Larsen Ice Shelf *Antarctica* 67°0S 62°0W **55** C17
Larvik *Norway* 59°4N 10°2E **63** F6
Las Cruces *U.S.A.* 32°19N 106°47W **110** D5
Las Palmas *Canary Is.* 28°7N 15°26W **94** C2
Las Tunas *Cuba* 20°58N 76°59W **115** C9
Las Vegas *N. Mex., U.S.A.* 35°36N 105°13W **110** C5
Las Vegas *Nev., U.S.A.* 36°10N 115°8W **110** C3
Lashio *Burma* 22°56N 97°45E **85** H20
Lassen Pk. *U.S.A.* 40°29N 121°30W **110** B2
Lastoursville *Gabon* 0°55S 12°38E **96** E2
Latacunga *Ecuador* 0°50S 78°35W **120** C2
Latakia *Syria* 35°30N 35°45E **86** C3
Latina *Italy* 41°28N 12°52E **68** D5
Latvia ■ *Europe* 56°50N 24°0E **63** F8
Lauder *U.K.* 55°43N 2°43W **21** C10
Lauderdale *U.K.* 55°44N 2°41W **21** C10
Launceston *Australia* 41°24S 147°8E **98** J8
Launceston *U.K.* 50°38N 4°22W **27** F5
Laune → *Ireland* 52°7N 9°47W **30** D3
Laurel *U.S.A.* 31°41N 89°8W **111** D9
Laurencekirk *U.K.* 56°50N 2°28W **19** J13
Laurentian Plateau *Canada* 52°0N 70°0W **104** E12
Lausanne *Switz.* 46°32N 6°38E **64** E4
Lavagh More *Ireland* 54°46N 8°6W **28** B5
Laval *Canada* 45°33N 73°42W **113** C11
Laval *France* 48°4N 0°48W **66** B3
Lavendon *U.K.* 52°11N 0°39W **25** B7
Lavenham *U.K.* 52°6N 0°48E **25** B10
Lavras *Brazil* 21°20S 45°0W **122** D2
Lawrence *Kans., U.S.A.* 38°58N 95°14W **111** C7
Lawrence *Mass., U.S.A.* 42°43N 71°10W **113** D12
Lawton *U.S.A.* 34°37N 98°25W **110** D7
Laxey *U.K.* 54°14N 4°23W **29** C13
Laxfield *U.K.* 52°18N 1°22E **25** B11
Laxford, L. *U.K.* 58°24N 5°6W **18** F7
Lazio □ *Italy* 42°10N 12°30E **68** C5
Lazonby *U.K.* 54°46N 2°42W **22** C3
Le Creusot *France* 46°48N 4°24E **66** C6
Le François *Martinique* 14°38N 60°57W **114** c
Le Gosier *Guadeloupe* 16°14N 61°29W **114** b
Le Havre *France* 49°30N 0°5E **66** B4
Le Lamentin *Martinique* 14°35N 61°2W **114** c
Le Mans *France* 48°0N 0°10E **66** C4
Le Marin *Martinique* 14°27N 60°55W **114** c
Le Moule *Guadeloupe* 16°20N 61°22W **114** b
Le Prêcheur *Martinique* 14°50N 61°12W **114** c
Le Puy-en-Velay *France* 45°3N 3°52E **66** D5
Le Robert *Martinique* 14°40N 60°56W **114** c
Le St-Esprit *Martinique* 14°34N 60°56W **114** c
Lea *U.K.* 53°22N 0°45W **23** F7
Lea → *U.K.* 51°31N 0°1E **25** C9
Leadenham *U.K.* 53°3N 0°35W **23** F7
Leamington *Canada* 42°3N 82°36W **112** D6
Leane, L. *Ireland* 52°2N 9°32W **30** D3
Leatherhead *U.K.* 51°18N 0°20W **25** D8
Leavenworth *U.S.A.* 39°19N 94°55W **111** C8
Lebanon *Ind., U.S.A.* 40°3N 86°28W **112** E4
Lebanon *Ky., U.S.A.* 37°34N 85°15W **112** G5
Lebanon *Mo., U.S.A.* 37°41N 92°40W **111** C81
Lebanon *Pa., U.S.A.* 40°20N 76°26W **112** E9
Lebanon ■ *Asia* 34°0N 36°0E **86** C3
Lebu *Chile* 37°40S 73°47W **121** F2
Lecce *Italy* 40°23N 18°11E **69** D8
Lechlade *U.K.* 51°42N 1°41W **24** C5
Ledbury *U.K.* 52°2N 2°25W **24** B4
Lee → *Ireland* 51°53N 8°56W **30** E5
Lee-on-the-Solent *U.K.* 50°48N 1°12W **24** E6
Leech L. *U.S.A.* 47°10N 94°24W **111** A8
Leeds *U.K.* 53°48N 1°33W **23** E5
Leek *U.K.* 53°7N 2°1W **23** F4
Leeuwarden *Neths.* 53°15N 5°48E **64** B3
Leeuwin, C. *Australia* 34°20S 115°9E **98** G2
Leeward Is. *Atl. Oc.* 16°30N 63°30W **115** D12
Lefkada *Greece* 38°40N 20°43E **69** E9
Leganés *Spain* 40°19N 3°45W **67** B4
Legazpi *Phil.* 13°10N 123°45E **83** B6
Legionowo *Poland* 52°25N 20°50E **65** B11
Legnica *Poland* 51°12N 16°10E **64** C9
Leicester *U.K.* 52°38N 1°8W **23** G6
Leicestershire □ *U.K.* 52°41N 1°17W **23** G6
Leiden *Neths.* 52°9N 4°30E **64** B3
Leigh *Gt. Man., U.K.* 53°30N 2°32W **23** E3
Leigh *Hereford, U.K.* 52°11N 2°20W **24** B4
Leighton Buzzard *U.K.* 51°54N 0°38W **25** C7
Leine → *Germany* 52°43N 9°36E **64** B5
Leinster □ *Ireland* 53°3N 7°8W **31** B8
Leinster, Mt. *Ireland* 52°37N 6°46W **31** C9
Leintwardine *U.K.* 52°22N 2°51W **24** B3
Leipzig *Germany* 51°18N 12°22E **64** C7
Leiston *U.K.* 52°12N 1°36E **25** B12
Leith *U.K.* 55°59N 3°11W **21** C9
Leith Hill *U.K.* 51°11N 0°22W **25** D8
Leitholm *U.K.* 55°41N 2°20W **21** C11
Leitrim *Ireland* 54°0N 8°5W **28** C5
Leitrim □ *Ireland* 54°8N 8°0W **28** C5
Leixlip *Ireland* 53°22N 6°30W **31** B9
Leizhou Pen. *China* 21°0N 110°0E **79** G11
Lelant *U.K.* 50°11N 5°28W **27** G3
Léman, L. *Europe* 46°26N 6°30E **64** E4
Lena → *Russia* 72°52N 126°40E **77** B13
Lenham *U.K.* 51°14N 0°44E **25** D10
Leninsk-Kuznetskiy *Russia* 54°44N 86°10E **76** D9
Lennox Hills *U.K.* 56°3N 4°12W **20** B7
Lens *France* 50°26N 2°50E **66** A5
Leominster *U.K.* 52°14N 2°43W **24** B3
Leominster *U.S.A.* 42°32N 71°46W **113** D12
León *Mexico* 21°6N 101°41W **114** C4
León *Nic.* 12°20N 86°51W **114** E7
León *Spain* 42°38N 5°34W **67** A3
Leonora *Australia* 28°49S 121°19E **98** F3
Leopoldina *Brazil* 21°28S 42°40W **122** D2
Lerwick *U.K.* 60°9N 1°9W **18** B15
Les Cayes *Haiti* 18°15N 73°46W **115** D10
Les Sables-d'Olonne *France* 46°30N 1°45W **66** C3
Lesbos *Greece* 39°10N 26°20E **69** E12
Lesbury *U.K.* 55°25N 1°36W **22** B5
Leshan *China* 29°33N 103°41E **78** F9
Leskovac *Serbia* 43°0N 21°58E **69** C9
Lesosibirsk *Russia* 58°14N 92°29E **77** D10
Lesotho ■ *Africa* 29°40S 28°0E **97** K5
Lesser Antilles *W. Indies* 15°0N 61°0W **115** E12
Lesser Slave L. *Canada* 55°30N 115°25W **108** D8
Lesser Sunda Is. *Indonesia* 8°0S 120°0E **83** F6
Leszno *Poland* 51°50N 16°30E **65** C9
Letchworth *U.K.* 51°59N 0°13W **25** C8
Lethbridge *Canada* 49°45N 112°45W **108** E8
Leti, Kepulauan *Indonesia* 8°10S 128°0E **83** F7
Leticia *Colombia* 4°9S 70°0W **120** C2
Letterkenny *Ireland* 54°57N 7°45W **28** B6
Leuchars *U.K.* 56°24N 2°53W **21** B10
Leuven *Belgium* 50°52N 4°42E **64** C3
Leven *E. Riding, U.K.* 53°53N 0°18W **23** E8
Leven *Fife, U.K.* 56°12N 3°0W **21** B10
Leven → *U.K.* 54°31N 1°19W **22** C6
Leven, L. *Highl., U.K.* 56°42N 5°6W **18** J7
Leven, L. *Perth & Kinr., U.K.* 56°12N 3°22W **21** B9
Lévis *Canada* 46°48N 71°9W **113** B12
Lewes *U.K.* 50°52N 0°1E **25** E9
Lewis *U.K.* 58°9N 6°40W **18** F4
Lewis, Butt of *U.K.* 58°31N 6°16W **18** E5
Lewisham □ *U.K.* 51°27N 0°1W **25** D8
Lewisporte *Canada* 49°15N 55°3W **109** E14
Lewiston *Idaho, U.S.A.* 46°25N 117°1W **110** A3
Lewiston *Maine, U.S.A.* 44°6N 70°13W **113** C12
Lewistown *Mont., U.S.A.* 47°4N 109°26W **110** A5
Lewistown *Pa., U.S.A.* 40°36N 77°34W **112** E9
Lexington *U.S.A.* 38°3N 84°30W **112** F5
Lexington Park *U.S.A.* 38°16N 76°27W **112** F9
Leyburn *U.K.* 54°19N 1°48W **22** D5
Leyland *U.K.* 53°42N 2°43W **23** E3
Leysdown on Sea *U.K.* 51°24N 0°56E **25** D10
Leyte *Phil.* 11°0N 125°0E **83** B6
Lhasa *China* 29°25N 90°58E **78** F7
Lhazê *China* 29°5N 87°38E **78** F6
L'Hospitalet de Llobregat *Spain* 41°21N 2°6E **67** B7
Lianyungang *China* 34°40N 119°11E **79** E12
Liaodong Pen. *China* 40°0N 122°30E **79** D13
Liaoning □ *China* 41°40N 122°30E **79** C13
Liaoyang *China* 41°15N 122°58E **79** C13
Liaoyuan *China* 42°58N 125°2E **79** C14
Liard → *Canada* 61°51N 121°18W **108** C7
Liberal *U.S.A.* 37°3N 100°55W **110** C6
Liberec *Czech Rep.* 50°47N 15°7E **64** C8
Liberia ■ *W. Afr.* 6°30N 9°30W **94** G4
Libourne *France* 44°55N 0°14W **66** D3
Libreville *Gabon* 0°25N 9°26E **96** D1
Libya ■ *N. Afr.* 27°0N 17°0E **95** C9
Libyan Desert *Africa* 25°0N 25°0E **95** C10
Libyan Plateau *Egypt* 30°40N 26°30E **95** B11
Lichfield *U.K.* 52°41N 1°49W **23** G5
Liddesdale *U.K.* 55°14N 2°50W **21** D10
Liechtenstein ■ *Europe* 47°8N 9°35E **64** E5
Liège *Belgium* 50°38N 5°35E **64** C3
Liepāja *Latvia* 56°30N 21°0E **63** F8
Liffey → *Ireland* 53°21N 6°13W **31** B10
Lifford *Ireland* 54°51N 7°29W **28** B7
Liguria □ *Italy* 44°30N 8°50E **68** B3
Ligurian Sea *Medit. S.* 43°20N 9°0E **68** C3
Lihu'e *U.S.A.* 21°59N 159°23W **110** H15
Lijiang *China* 26°55N 100°20E **78** F9
Likasi *Dem. Rep. of the Congo* 10°55S 26°48E **96** G5
Lille *France* 50°38N 3°3E **66** A5
Lillehammer *Norway* 61°8N 10°30E **63** E6
Lilleshall *U.K.* 52°44N 2°23W **23** G4
Lilongwe *Malawi* 14°0S 33°48E **97** G6
Lima *Peru* 12°3S 77°2W **120** D2
Lima *U.S.A.* 40°44N 84°6W **112** E5
Limassol *Cyprus* 34°42N 33°1E **86** C3
Limavady *U.K.* 55°3N 6°56W **29** A8
Limay → *Argentina* 39°0S 68°0W **121** F3
Limbe *Cameroon* 4°1N 9°10E **96** D1
Limeira *Brazil* 22°35S 47°28W **122** D1
Limerick *Ireland* 52°40N 8°37W **30** C5
Limerick □ *Ireland* 52°30N 8°50W **30** C5
Limfjorden *Denmark* 56°55N 9°0E **63** F5
Limnos *Greece* 39°50N 25°5E **69** E11
Limoges *France* 45°50N 1°15E **66** D4
Limón *Costa Rica* 10°0N 83°2W **115** F8
Limousin □ *France* 45°30N 1°30E **66** D4
Limoux *France* 43°4N 2°12E **66** E5
Limpopo → *Africa* 25°5S 33°30E **97** K6
Linares *Chile* 35°50S 71°40W **121** F2
Linares *Mexico* 24°52N 99°34W **114** C5
Linares *Spain* 38°10N 3°40W **67** C4
Linchuan *China* 27°57N 116°15E **79** F12
Lincoln *U.K.* 53°14N 0°32W **23** F7
Lincoln *Ill., U.S.A.* 40°9N 89°22W **112** E3
Lincoln *Maine, U.S.A.* 45°22N 68°30W **113** C13
Lincoln *Nebr., U.S.A.* 40°49N 96°41W **111** B7
Lincoln Sea *Arctic* 84°0N 55°0W **54** A5
Lincolnshire □ *U.K.* 53°14N 0°32W **23** F7
Lincolnshire Wolds *U.K.* 53°26N 0°13W **23** F8
Lindale *U.K.* 54°14N 2°53W **22** D3
Lindesnes *Norway* 57°58N 7°3E **63** F5
Lindsay *Canada* 44°22N 78°43W **112** C8
Linfen *China* 36°3N 111°30E **79** D11
Lingfield *U.K.* 51°11N 0°0 **25** D8
Lingga, Kepulauan *Indonesia* 0°10S 104°30E **82** E2
Linhai *China* 28°50N 121°8E **79** F13
Linhares *Brazil* 19°25S 40°4W **122** C2
Linhe *China* 40°48N 107°20E **78** C10
Linkinhorne *U.K.* 50°32N 4°24W **27** F5
Linköping *Sweden* 58°28N 15°36E **63** F7
Linnhe, L. *U.K.* 56°36N 5°25W **20** A5
Linqing *China* 36°50N 115°42E **79** D12
Linslade *U.K.* 51°54N 0°41W **25** C7
Linstead *Jamaica* 18°8N 77°2W **114** a
Linton *U.K.* 52°6N 0°17E **25** B9
Linton *U.S.A.* 39°2N 87°10W **112** F4
Linxia *China* 35°36N 103°10E **78** D9
Linyi *China* 35°5N 118°21E **79** D12
Linz *Austria* 48°18N 14°18E **64** D8
Lion, G. du *France* 43°10N 4°0E **66** E6
Lipa *Phil.* 13°57N 121°10E **83** B6
Lipari *Italy* 38°26N 14°58E **68** E6
Lipetsk *Russia* 52°37N 39°35E **70** D6
Lippe → *Germany* 51°39N 6°36E **64** C4
Lisbon *Portugal* 38°42N 9°8W **67** C1
Lisburn *U.K.* 54°31N 6°3W **29** B9
Liscannor B. *Ireland* 52°55N 9°24W **30** C4
Lisianski I. *U.S.A.* 26°2N 174°0W **102** E10
Lisieux *France* 49°10N 0°12E **66** B4
Liskeard *U.K.* 50°27N 4°29W **27** G5
Liski *Russia* 51°3N 39°30E **71** D6
Lismore *Australia* 28°44S 153°21E **98** F9
Lismore *Ireland* 52°8N 7°55W **30** D7
Liss *U.K.* 51°3N 0°54W **25** D7
Listowel *Canada* 43°44N 80°58W **112** D7
Listowel *Ireland* 52°27N 9°29W **30** D4
Litani → *Lebanon* 33°20N 35°15E **86** C3
Litcham *U.K.* 52°44N 0°47E **25** A10
Litchfield *U.S.A.* 39°11N 89°39W **112** F3
Litherland *U.K.* 53°29N 2°59W **23** F3
Lithuania ■ *Europe* 55°30N 24°0E **63** F8
Little Current *Canada* 45°55N 82°0W **112** C7
Little Khingan Mts. *China* 49°0N 127°0E **79** B14
Little Minch *U.K.* 57°35N 6°45W **18** G4
Little Missouri → *U.S.A.* 47°36N 102°25W **110** A6
Little Ouse → *U.K.* 52°22N 1°12E **25** B11
Little Rock *U.S.A.* 34°45N 92°17W **111** D8
Little Walsingham *U.K.* 52°54N 0°52E **25** A10
Littlehampton *U.K.* 50°49N 0°32W **25** E7
Littleport *U.K.* 52°27N 0°18E **25** B9
Littlestone-on-Sea *U.K.* 50°58N 0°58E **25** E10
Liupanshui *China* 26°38N 104°48E **78** F9
Liuwa Plain *Zambia* 14°20S 22°30E **97** G4
Liuzhou *China* 24°22N 109°22E **79** G10
Liverpool *Canada* 44°5N 64°41W **109** E13
Liverpool *U.K.* 53°25N 3°0W **23** F3
Livingston *U.K.* 55°54N 3°30W **21** C9
Livingston *U.S.A.* 45°40N 110°34W **110** A4
Livingstone *Zambia* 17°46S 25°52E **97** H5
Livonia *U.S.A.* 42°23N 83°23W **112** D6
Livorno *Italy* 43°33N 10°19E **68** C4
Lizard *U.K.* 49°58N 5°13W **27** H3
Lizard Pt. *U.K.* 49°57N 5°13W **27** H3
Ljubljana *Slovenia* 46°4N 14°33E **64** E8
Llandeilo *U.K.* 51°53N 3°59W **26** D6
Llandovery *U.K.* 51°59N 3°48W **26** D6
Llandrindod Wells *U.K.* 52°14N 3°22W **26** C7
Llandudno *U.K.* 53°19N 3°50W **26** A6
Llanelli *U.K.* 51°41N 4°10W **26** D5
Llanerchymedd *U.K.* 53°20N 4°23W **26** A5
Llanfair Caereinion *U.K.* 52°39N 3°20W **26** B7
Llanfair Talhaiarn *U.K.* 53°13N 3°37W **26** A6
Llanfairfechan *U.K.* 53°15N 3°58W **26** A6
Llangefni *U.K.* 53°15N 4°18W **26** A5
Llangollen *U.K.* 52°58N 3°11W **26** B7
Llanidloes *U.K.* 52°27N 3°31W **26** C6
Llanllyfni *U.K.* 53°2N 4°17W **26** A5
Llano Estacado *U.S.A.* 33°30N 103°0W **110** D6
Llanos *S. Amer.* 5°0N 71°35W **120** B2
Llanquihue, L. *Chile* 41°10S 72°50W **121** G2
Llanrhystyd *U.K.* 52°19N 4°7W **26** C5
Llantrisant *U.K.* 51°32N 3°22W **27** D7
Llantwit-Major *U.K.* 51°24N 3°29W **27** E7
Llanwrtyd Wells *U.K.* 52°7N 3°38W **26** C6
Llanyblodwel *U.K.* 52°48N 3°8W **26** B7
Llanymynech *U.K.* 52°47N 3°5W **26** B7
Lleida *Spain* 41°37N 0°39E **67** B6
Lleyn Peninsula *U.K.* 52°51N 4°36W **26** B4
Llobregat → *Spain* 41°19N 2°5E **67** B7
Lloret de Mar *Spain* 41°41N 2°53E **67** B7
Lloydminster *Canada* 53°17N 110°0W **108** D9
Llullaillaco, Volcán *S. Amer.* 24°43S 68°30W **121** E3
Lobatse *Botswana* 25°12S 25°40E **97** K5
Lobito *Angola* 12°18S 13°35E **97** G2
Loch Lomond and the Trossachs △ *U.K.* 56°10N 4°40W **20** B6
Lochaber *U.K.* 56°59N 5°1W **18** J7
Locharbriggs *U.K.* 55°7N 3°35W **21** D8
Lochboisdale *U.K.* 57°9N 7°20W **18** H3
Loches *France* 47°7N 1°0E **66** C4
Lochgelly *U.K.* 56°7N 3°19W **21** B9
Lochgilphead *U.K.* 56°2N 5°26W **20** B5
Lochinver *U.K.* 58°9N 5°14W **18** F7
Lochmaben *U.K.* 55°8N 3°26W **21** D9
Lochmaddy *U.K.* 57°36N 7°10W **18** G3
Lochnagar *U.K.* 56°57N 3°15W **19** J11
Lochy, L. *U.K.* 57°0N 4°53W **19** J8
Lock Haven *U.S.A.* 41°8N 77°28W **112** E9
Lockerbie *U.K.* 55°7N 3°21W **21** D9
Loddon *U.K.* 52°32N 1°31E **25** A12
Lodwar *Kenya* 3°7N 35°36E **96** D7
Łódź *Poland* 51°45N 19°27E **65** C10
Lofoten *Norway* 68°30N 13°59E **63** D6
Loftus *U.K.* 54°34N 0°53W **22** C7
Logan *Ohio, U.S.A.* 39°32N 82°25W **112** F6
Logan *Utah, U.S.A.* 41°44N 111°50W **110** B4
Logan *W. Va., U.S.A.* 37°51N 81°59W **112** G7
Logan, Mt. *Canada* 60°34N 140°23W **108** C5
Logansport *U.S.A.* 40°45N 86°22W **112** E4
Logroño *Spain* 42°28N 2°27W **67** A4
Lohardaga *India* 23°27N 84°45E **85** H14
Loir → *France* 47°33N 0°32W **66** C3
Loire → *France* 47°16N 2°10W **66** C2
Loja *Ecuador* 3°59S 79°16W **120** C2
Lomami → *Dem. Rep. of the Congo* 0°46N 24°16E **96** D4
Lombárdia □ *Italy* 45°40N 9°30E **68** B3
Lomblen *Indonesia* 8°30S 123°32E **83** F6
Lombok *Indonesia* 8°45S 116°30E **82** F5
Lomé *Togo* 6°9N 1°20E **94** G6
Lomela → *Dem. Rep. of the Congo* 0°15S 20°40E **96** E4
Lomond, L. *U.K.* 56°8N 4°38W **20** B6
Łomża *Poland* 53°10N 22°2E **65** B12
London *Canada* 42°59N 81°15W **112** D7
London *U.K.* 51°30N 0°3W **25** D8
London Gatwick ✕ **(LGW)** *U.K.* 51°10N 0°11W **25** D8
London Heathrow ✕ **(LHR)** *U.K.* 51°28N 0°27W **25** D8
London Stansted ✕ **(STN)** *U.K.* 51°54N 0°14E **25** C9
Londonderry *U.K.* 55°0N 7°20W **28** A7
Londonderry □ *U.K.* 55°0N 7°20W **29** B7
Londonderry, C. *Australia* 13°45S 126°55E **98** C4
Londrina *Brazil* 23°18S 51°10W **121** E4
Long, L. *U.K.* 56°4N 4°50W **20** B6
Long Beach *U.S.A.* 33°46N 118°11W **110** D3
Long Bennington *U.K.* 52°59N 0°44W **23** G7
Long Branch *U.S.A.* 40°18N 74°0W **113** E11
Long Clawson *U.K.* 52°51N 0°55W **23** G7
Long Crendon *U.K.* 51°46N 0°59W **25** C7
Long Eaton *U.K.* 52°53N 1°15W **23** G6
Long I. *Bahamas* 23°20N 75°10W **115** C9
Long I. *Ireland* 51°30N 9°34W **30** F3
Long I. *U.S.A.* 40°45N 73°30W **113** E11
Long Itchington *U.K.* 52°16N 1°22W **24** B6
Long Melford *U.K.* 52°4N 0°45E **25** B10
Long Mynd, The *U.K.* 52°35N 2°50W **23** G3
Long Preston *U.K.* 54°2N 2°14W **23** D4
Long Sutton *U.K.* 52°48N 0°7E **23** G9
Long Xuyen *Vietnam* 10°19N 105°28E **82** B3
Longford *Ireland* 53°43N 7°49W **28** D6
Longford *U.K.* 51°54N 2°14W **24** C4
Longford □ *Ireland* 53°42N 7°45W **28** D6
Longframlington *U.K.* 55°18N 1°47W **22** B5
Longhoughton *U.K.* 55°26N 1°37W **22** B5
Longlac *Canada* 49°45N 86°25W **112** A4
Longreach *Australia* 23°28S 144°14E **98** E7
Longridge *U.K.* 53°50N 2°35W **23** E3
Longton *U.K.* 53°44N 2°48W **23** E3
Longtown *Cumb., U.K.* 55°1N 2°58W **22** B3
Longtown *Hereford, U.K.* 51°58N 2°59W **24** C3
Longueuil *Canada* 45°31N 73°29W **113** C11
Longview *Tex., U.S.A.* 32°30N 94°44W **111** D8
Longview *Wash., U.S.A.* 46°8N 122°57W **110** A2
Longyan *China* 25°10N 117°0E **79** F12
Lons-le-Saunier *France* 46°40N 5°31E **66** C6
Looe *U.K.* 50°22N 4°28W **27** G5
Loop Hd. *Ireland* 52°34N 9°56W **30** C3
Lop *China* 37°3N 80°11E **78** D5
Lop Nur *China* 40°20N 90°10E **78** C7
Lopez, C. *Gabon* 0°47S 8°40E **90** G4
Lorain *U.S.A.* 41°28N 82°11W **112** E6
Loralai *Pakistan* 30°20N 68°41E **84** D6
Lorca *Spain* 37°41N 1°42W **67** D5
Lord Howe I. *Pac. Oc.* 31°33S 159°6E **99** G10
Lord Howe Rise *Pac. Oc.* 30°0S 162°30E **99** H12
Lordsburg *U.S.A.* 32°21N 108°43W **110** D5
Lorestān □ *Iran* 33°30N 48°40E **86** C7
Lorient *France* 47°45N 3°23W **66** C2
Lorn *U.K.* 56°26N 5°10W **20** B5
Lorn, Firth of *U.K.* 56°20N 5°40W **20** B4
Lorraine □ *France* 48°53N 6°0E **66** B7
Los Alamos *U.S.A.* 35°53N 106°19W **110** C5
Los Andes *Chile* 32°50S 70°40W **121** F2
Los Angeles *Chile* 37°28S 72°23W **121** F2
Los Angeles *U.S.A.* 34°4N 118°15W **110** D3
Los Mochis *Mexico* 25°45N 108°57W **114** B3
Los Roques Is. *Venezuela* 11°50N 66°45W **120** A3
Lošinj *Croatia* 44°30N 14°30E **68** B6
Lossiemouth *U.K.* 57°42N 3°17W **19** G11
Lostwithiel *U.K.* 50°24N 4°41W **27** G4
Lot → *France* 44°18N 0°20E **66** D4
Lota *Chile* 37°5S 73°10W **121** F2
Loubomo *Congo* 4°9S 12°47E **96** E2
Loughborough *U.K.* 52°47N 1°11W **23** G6
Lougheed I. *Canada* 77°26N 105°6W **109** B9
Loughrea *Ireland* 53°12N 8°33W **30** B5
Loughros More B. *Ireland* 54°48N 8°32W **28** B4
Louis XIV, Pte. *Canada* 54°37N 79°45W **109** D12
Louisa *U.S.A.* 38°7N 82°36W **112** F6
Louisiade Arch. *Papua N. G.* 11°10S 153°0E **98** C9
Louisiana □ *U.S.A.* 30°50N 92°0W **111** D8
Louisville *U.S.A.* 38°15N 85°46W **112** F5
Lourdes *France* 43°6N 0°3W **66** E3
Louth *Ireland* 53°58N 6°32W **29** D8
Louth *U.K.* 53°22N 0°1W **23** F8
Louth □ *Ireland* 53°56N 6°34W **29** D8
Lovech *Bulgaria* 43°8N 24°42E **69** C11
Lowell *U.S.A.* 42°38N 71°19W **113** D12
Lower Beeding *U.K.* 51°2N 0°15W **25** D8
Lower Saxony = Niedersachsen □ *Germany* 52°50N 9°0E **64** B5
Lower Tunguska → *Russia* 65°48N 88°4E **77** C9
Lowestoft *U.K.* 52°29N 1°45E **25** B12
Lowick *U.K.* 55°39N 1°57W **22** A5
Lowther Hills *U.K.* 55°20N 3°40W **21** D8
Lowville *U.S.A.* 43°47N 75°29W **113** D10
Loyauté, Îs. *N. Cal.* 20°50S 166°30E **99** E12
Lualaba → *Dem. Rep. of the Congo* 0°26N 25°20E **96** D5
Luanda *Angola* 8°50S 13°15E **96** F2
Luangwa → *Zambia* 14°25S 30°25E **97** G6
Luanshya *Zambia* 13°3S 28°28E **97** G5
Luapula → *Africa* 9°26S 28°33E **96** F5
Lubango *Angola* 14°55S 13°30E **97** G2
Lubbock *U.S.A.* 33°35N 101°51W **110** D6
Lübeck *Germany* 53°52N 10°40E **64** B6
Lublin *Poland* 51°12N 22°38E **65** C12
Lubumbashi *Dem. Rep. of the Congo* 11°40S 27°28E **97** G5
Lucan *Ireland* 53°22N 6°28W **31** B10
Lucania, Mt. *Canada* 61°1N 140°27W **108** C5
Lucca *Italy* 43°50N 10°29E **68** C4
Luce Bay *U.K.* 54°45N 4°48W **20** E6
Lucea *Jamaica* 18°27N 78°10W **114** a
Lucena *Phil.* 13°56N 121°37E **83** B6
Lucknow *India* 26°50N 81°0E **85** F12
Lüda = Dalian *China* 38°50N 121°40E **79** D13
Lüderitz *Namibia* 26°41S 15°8E **97** K3
Ludgershall *U.K.* 51°15N 1°37W **24** D5
Ludgvan *U.K.* 50°9N 5°30W **27** G2
Ludhiana *India* 30°57N 75°56E **84** D9
Ludington *U.S.A.* 43°57N 86°27W **112** D4
Ludlow *U.K.* 52°22N 2°42W **23** H3
Ludwigsburg *Germany* 48°53N 9°11E **64** D5
Ludwigshafen *Germany* 49°29N 8°26E **64** D5
Lufkin *U.S.A.* 31°21N 94°44W **111** D8
Luga *Russia* 58°40N 29°55E **70** C4
Lugano *Switz.* 46°1N 8°57E **64** E5
Lugansk *Ukraine* 48°38N 39°15E **71** E6
Lugnaquillia *Ireland* 52°58N 6°28W **31** C10
Lugo *Spain* 43°2N 7°35W **67** A2
Lugwardine *U.K.* 52°4N 2°39W **24** B3
Luing *U.K.* 56°14N 5°39W **20** B4
Luleå *Sweden* 65°35N 22°10E **63** D8
Luleälven → *Sweden* 65°35N 22°10E **63** D8
Lundy *U.K.* 51°10N 4°41W **27** E4
Lune → *U.K.* 54°0N 2°51W **23** D3
Lüneburger Heide *Germany* 53°10N 10°12E **64** B6
Lunéville *France* 48°36N 6°29E **66** B7
Luni → *India* 24°41N 71°14E **84** G7
Luofu *Dem. Rep. of the Congo* 0°10S 29°15E **96** E5
Luoyang *China* 34°40N 112°26E **79** E11
Luquillo, Sierra de *Puerto Rico* 18°20N 65°47W **115** d
Luray *U.S.A.* 38°40N 78°28W **112** F8
Lurgan *U.K.* 54°28N 6°19W **29** C9
Lusaka *Zambia* 15°28S 28°16E **97** H5
Lūt, Dasht-e *Iran* 31°30N 58°0E **87** D9
Lutherstadt Wittenberg *Germany* 51°53N 12°39E **64** C7
Luton *U.K.* 51°53N 0°24W **25** C8
Lutsel K'e *Canada* 62°24N 110°44W **108** C8
Lutsk *Ukraine* 50°50N 25°15E **65** C13
Lutterworth *U.K.* 52°28N 1°12W **23** H6
Luvua → *Dem. Rep. of the Congo* 6°50S 27°30E **96** F5
Luxembourg *Lux.* 49°37N 6°9E **64** D4
Luxembourg ■ *Europe* 49°45N 6°0E **64** D4
Luxor = El Uqsur *Egypt* 25°41N 32°38E **95** C12
Luzern *Switz.* 47°3N 8°18E **64** E5
Luzhou *China* 28°52N 105°20E **78** F10
Luziânia *Brazil* 16°20S 48°0W **122** C1
Luzon *Phil.* 16°0N 121°0E **83** A6
Lvov *Ukraine* 49°50N 24°0E **65** D13
Lyakhov Is. *Russia* 73°40N 141°0E **77** B15
Lybster *U.K.* 58°18N 3°15W **19** F11
Lydd *U.K.* 50°57N 0°55E **25** E10
Lydford *U.K.* 50°38N 4°8W **27** F5
Lydham *U.K.* 52°31N 2°58W **23** G3

Lyme B.   Meru

Lyme B. U.K. 50°42N 2°53W 24 E3
Lyme Regis U.K. 50°43N 2°57W 24 E3
Lyminge U.K. 51°7N 1°6E 25 D11
Lymington U.K. 50°45N 1°32W 24 E5
Lymm U.K. 53°23N 2°29W 23 F4
Lympne U.K. 51°4N 1°2E 25 D11
Lynchburg U.S.A. 37°25N 79°9W 112 G8
Lyndhurst U.K. 50°52N 1°35W 24 E5
Lyneham U.K. 51°30N 1°58W 24 C5
Lynmouth U.K. 51°13N 3°49W 27 E6
Lynn Lake Canada 56°51N 101°3W 108 D9
Lynton U.K. 51°13N 3°50W 27 E6
Lyonnais France 45°45N 4°15E 66 D6
Lyons France 45°46N 4°50E 66 D6
Lysva Russia 58°7N 57°49E 70 C10
Lysychansk Ukraine 48°55N 38°30E 71 E6
Lytchett Minster U.K. 50°44N 2°4W 24 E4
Lytham St. Anne's U.K. 53°45N 3°0W 23 E2
Lythe U.K. 54°31N 0°41W 22 C7
Lyubertsy Russia 55°40N 37°51E 70 C6

M

Ma-ubin Burma 16°44N 95°39E 85 L19
Ma'ān Jordan 30°12N 35°44E 86 D3
Maas → Neths. 51°45N 4°32E 64 C3
Maastricht Neths. 50°50N 5°40E 64 C3
Mablethorpe U.K. 53°20N 0°15E 23 F9
Macaé Brazil 22°20S 41°43W 122 D2
McAlester U.S.A. 34°56N 95°46W 111 D7
McAllen U.S.A. 26°12N 98°14W 110 E7
MacAlpine L. Canada 66°32N 102°45W 108 C9
Macapá Brazil 0°5N 51°4W 120 B4
Macau Brazil 5°15S 36°40W 120 C6
Macau China 22°12N 113°33E 79 a
Macclesfield U.K. 53°15N 2°8W 23 F4
Macdonnell Ranges Australia 23°40S 133°0E 98 E5
Macduff U.K. 57°40N 2°31W 19 G12
Macedonia □ Greece 40°39N 22°0E 69 D10
Macedonia ■ Europe 41°53N 21°40E 69 D9
Maceió Brazil 9°40S 35°41W 122 A3
Macgillycuddy's Reeks Ireland 51°58N 9°45W 30 E3
Mach Pakistan 29°50N 67°20E 84 E5
Machakos Kenya 1°30S 37°15E 96 E7
Machala Ecuador 3°20S 79°57W 120 C2
Machars, The U.K. 54°46N 4°30W 20 G4
Machias U.S.A. 44°43N 67°28W 113 C14
Machilipatnam India 16°12N 81°8E 85 L12
Machrihanish U.K. 55°25N 5°43W 20 D4
Machu Picchu Peru 13°8S 72°30W 120 D2
Machynlleth U.K. 52°35N 3°50W 26 B6
Mackay Australia 21°8S 149°11E 98 E8
Mackay, L. Australia 22°30S 129°0E 98 E4
McKeesport U.S.A. 40°20N 79°51W 112 E8
Mackenzie Canada 55°20N 123°5W 108 D7
Mackenzie → Canada 69°10N 134°20W 108 C6
Mackenzie Bay Canada 69°0N 137°30W 104 C6
Mackenzie King I. Canada 77°45N 111°0W 109 B8
Mackenzie Mts. Canada 64°0N 130°0W 108 C6
Mackinaw City U.S.A. 45°47N 84°44W 112 C5
McKinley, Mt. U.S.A. 63°4N 151°0W 108 C4
McKinley Sea Arctic 82°0N 0°0 54 A7
McMinnville U.S.A. 45°13N 123°12W 110 A2
McMurdo Sd. Antarctica 77°0S 170°0E 55 D11
Macomb U.S.A. 40°27N 90°40W 112 E2
Mâcon France 46°19N 4°50E 66 C6
Macon U.S.A. 32°51N 83°38W 111 D10
McPherson U.S.A. 38°22N 97°40W 110 C7
Macquarie Is. Pac. Oc. 54°36S 158°55E 102 N7
Macroom Ireland 51°54N 8°57W 30 E5
Madagascar ■ Africa 20°0S 47°0E 97 J9
Madang Papua N. G. 5°12S 145°49E 98 B8
Madeira Atl. Oc. 32°50N 17°0W 94 B2
Madeira → Brazil 3°22S 58°45W 120 C4
Madeleine, Îs. de la Canada 47°30N 61°40W 113 B17
Madeley U.K. 53°0N 2°20W 23 F4
Madhya Pradesh □ India 22°50N 78°0E 84 H11
Madison S. Dak., U.S.A. 44°0N 97°7W 111 B7
Madison Wis., U.S.A. 43°4N 89°24W 112 D3
Madisonville U.S.A. 37°20N 87°30W 112 G4
Madiun Indonesia 7°38S 111°32E 82 F4
Madley U.K. 52°2N 2°51W 24 B3
Madras = Chennai India 13°8N 80°19E 84 N12
Madre, L. U.S.A. 25°15N 97°30W 104 G10
Madre de Dios → Bolivia 10°59S 66°8W 120 D3
Madre de Dios, I. Chile 50°20S 75°10W 121 H2
Madre del Sur, Sierra Mexico 17°30N 100°0W 104 H10
Madre Occidental, Sierra Mexico 27°0N 107°0W 104 B3
Madre Oriental, Sierra Mexico 25°0N 100°0W 114 C5
Madrid Spain 40°24N 3°42W 67 B4
Madura Indonesia 7°30S 114°0E 82 F4
Madurai India 9°55N 78°10E 84 Q11
Maebashi Japan 36°24N 139°4E 81 E6
Maesteg U.K. 51°36N 3°40W 27 D6
Mafeking S. Africa 25°50S 25°38E 97 K5
Mafia I. Tanzania 7°45S 39°50E 96 F7
Magadan Russia 59°38N 150°50E 77 D16
Magallanes, Estrecho de Chile 52°30S 75°0W 121 H2
Magangué Colombia 9°14N 74°45W 120 B2
Magdalena → Colombia 11°6N 74°51W 120 A2
Magdeburg Germany 52°7N 11°38E 64 B6
Magee, I. U.K. 54°48N 5°43W 29 B10
Magelang Indonesia 7°29S 110°13E 82 F4
Magellan's Str. = Magallanes, Estrecho de Chile 52°30S 75°0W 121 H2
Maggiore, Lago Italy 45°57N 8°39E 68 B3
Maggotty Jamaica 18°9N 77°46W 114 a
Maghāgha Egypt 28°38N 30°50E 95 C12
Magherafelt U.K. 54°45N 6°37W 29 B8
Maghreb N. Afr. 32°0N 4°0W 90 C3

Maghull U.K. 53°31N 2°57W 23 E3
Magnetic Pole (North) Arctic 82°42N 114°24W 54 A2
Magnetic Pole (South) Antarctica 64°8S 138°8E 55 C9
Magnitogorsk Russia 53°27N 59°4E 70 D10
Magog Canada 45°18N 72°9W 113 C11
Magwe Burma 20°10N 95°0E 85 J19
Mahābād Iran 36°50N 45°45E 86 B6
Mahajanga Madag. 15°40S 46°25E 97 H9
Mahakam → Indonesia 0°35S 117°17E 82 E5
Mahalapye Botswana 23°1S 26°51E 97 J5
Maḥallāt Iran 33°55N 50°30E 87 C7
Mahanadi → India 20°20N 86°25E 85 J15
Maharashtra □ India 20°30N 75°30E 84 J9
Mahdia Tunisia 35°28N 11°0E 95 A8
Mahesana India 23°39N 72°26E 84 H8
Mahilyow Belarus 53°55N 30°18E 65 B16
Mai-Ndombe, L. Dem. Rep. of the Congo 2°0S 18°20E 96 E3
Maiden Bradley U.K. 51°9N 2°17W 24 D4
Maiden Newton U.K. 50°46N 2°34W 24 E3
Maidenhead U.K. 51°31N 0°42W 25 C7
Maidstone U.K. 51°16N 0°32E 25 D10
Maiduguri Nigeria 12°0N 13°20E 95 F8
Main → Germany 50°0N 8°18E 64 C5
Main → U.K. 54°48N 6°18W 29 B9
Maine France 48°20N 0°15W 66 C3
Maine □ U.S.A. 45°20N 69°0W 113 C13
Maine → Ireland 52°9N 9°45W 30 D3
Mainland Orkney, U.K. 58°59N 3°8W 19 E11
Mainland Shet., U.K. 60°15N 1°22W 18 B15
Mainz Germany 50°1N 8°14E 64 C5
Maiquetía Venezuela 10°36N 66°57W 120 A3
Majorca = Mallorca Spain 39°30N 3°0E 67 C7
Majuro Marshall Is. 7°9N 171°12E 102 G9
Makale Indonesia 3°6S 119°51E 83 E5
Makasar, Str. of Indonesia 1°0S 118°20E 83 E5
Makgadikgadi Salt Pans Botswana 20°40S 25°45E 97 J5
Makhachkala Russia 43°0N 47°30E 71 F8
Makhado S. Africa 23°1S 29°43E 97 J5
Makran Coast Range Pakistan 25°40N 64°0E 84 G4
Makurdi Nigeria 7°43N 8°35E 94 G7
Mal B. Ireland 52°50N 9°30W 30 C4
Malabar Coast India 11°0N 75°0E 84 P9
Malacca, Straits of Indonesia 3°0N 101°0E 82 D2
Málaga Spain 36°43N 4°23W 67 D3
Malahide Ireland 53°26N 6°9W 31 B10
Malaita Solomon Is. 9°0S 161°0E 99 B11
Malakal Sudan 9°33N 31°40E 95 G12
Malakula Vanuatu 16°15S 167°30E 99 C12
Malang Indonesia 7°59S 112°45E 82 F4
Malanje Angola 9°36S 16°17E 96 F3
Mälaren Sweden 59°30N 17°10E 63 F7
Malatya Turkey 38°25N 38°20E 71 G6
Malawi ■ Africa 11°55S 34°0E 97 G6
Malawi, L. Africa 12°30S 34°30E 97 G6
Malay Pen. Asia 7°25N 100°0E 72 H12
Malāyer Iran 34°19N 48°51E 86 C7
Malaysia ■ Asia 5°0N 110°0E 82 D4
Malden U.S.A. 36°34N 89°57W 112 G3
Malden I. Kiribati 4°3S 155°1W 103 H12
Maldives ■ Ind. Oc. 5°0N 73°0E 73 H9
Maldon U.K. 51°44N 0°42E 25 C10
Maldonado Uruguay 34°59S 55°0W 121 F4
Malegaon India 20°30N 74°38E 84 J9
Malham Tarn U.K. 54°6N 2°10W 22 D4
Malheur L. U.S.A. 43°20N 118°48W 110 B3
Mali ■ Africa 17°0N 3°0W 94 E5
Malin Hd. Ireland 55°23N 7°23W 28 A7
Malin Pen. Ireland 55°20N 7°17W 29 A7
Malindi Kenya 3°12S 40°5E 96 E8
Mallaig U.K. 57°0N 5°50W 18 H6
Mallawi Egypt 27°44N 30°44E 95 C12
Mallorca Spain 39°30N 3°0E 67 C7
Mallow Ireland 52°8N 8°39W 30 D5
Malmesbury U.K. 51°35N 2°5W 24 C4
Malmö Sweden 55°36N 12°59E 63 F6
Malone U.S.A. 44°51N 74°18W 113 C10
Malpas U.K. 53°1N 2°45W 23 F3
Malpelo, I. de Colombia 4°3N 81°35W 115 d
Malta ■ Europe 35°55N 14°26E 68 a
Maltby U.K. 53°25N 1°12W 23 F5
Malton U.K. 54°8N 0°49W 22 D7
Malvinas, Is. = Falkland Is. ☑ Atl. Oc. 51°30S 59°0W 121 H4
Mamoré → Bolivia 10°23S 65°53W 120 D3
Mamoudzou Mayotte 12°48S 45°14E 91 H8
Man Ivory C. 7°30N 7°40W 94 G4
Man, I. of U.K. 54°15N 4°30W 29 C12
Manacles, The U.K. 50°2N 5°4W 27 G3
Manado Indonesia 1°29N 124°51E 83 D6
Managua Nic. 12°6N 86°20W 114 E7
Manas China 44°17N 86°10E 78 B6
Manatí Puerto Rico 18°26N 66°29W 115 d
Manaus Brazil 3°0S 60°0W 120 C3
Manby U.K. 53°21N 0°6E 23 F9
Manchester U.K. 53°29N 2°12W 23 F4
Manchester U.S.A. 42°59N 71°28W 113 D12
Manchester Int. ✈ (MAN) U.K. 53°21N 2°17W 23 F4
Manchuria China 45°0N 125°0E 79 C14
Manchurian Plain China 47°0N 124°0E 72 D14
Mandal Norway 58°2N 7°25E 63 F5
Mandalay Burma 22°0N 96°4E 85 J20
Mandalgovi Mongolia 45°45N 106°10E 78 B10
Mandan U.S.A. 46°50N 100°54W 110 A6
Mandaue Phil. 10°20N 123°56E 83 B6
Mandeville Jamaica 18°2N 77°31W 114 a
Mandla India 22°39N 80°30E 85 H12
Mandsaur India 24°3N 75°8E 84 G9
Mandvi India 22°51N 69°22E 84 H6
Manea U.K. 52°29N 0°10E 25 B9
Manfalūt Egypt 27°20N 30°52E 95 C12
Manfredónia Italy 41°38N 15°55E 68 D6
Mangabeiras, Chapada das Brazil 10°0S 46°30W 122 B1
Mangalore India 12°55N 74°47E 84 N9
Mangnai China 37°52N 91°43E 78 D7

Mangole Indonesia 1°50S 125°55E 83 E6
Mangotsfield U.K. 51°29N 2°30W 24 D4
Manhattan U.S.A. 39°11N 96°35W 111 C7
Manhuaçu Brazil 20°15S 42°2W 122 D2
Manica Mozam. 18°58S 32°59E 97 H6
Manicoré Brazil 5°48S 61°16W 120 C3
Manicouagan → Canada 49°30N 68°30W 109 E13
Manicouagan, Rés. Canada 51°5N 68°40W 109 D13
Manihiki Cook Is. 10°24S 161°1W 103 J11
Manila Phil. 14°35N 120°58E 83 B6
Manipur □ India 25°0N 94°0E 85 G19
Manisa Turkey 38°38N 27°30E 71 G4
Manistee U.S.A. 44°15N 86°19W 112 C4
Manistee → U.S.A. 44°15N 86°21W 112 C4
Manistique U.S.A. 45°57N 86°15W 112 C4
Manitoba □ Canada 53°30N 97°0W 108 D10
Manitoba, L. Canada 51°0N 98°45W 108 D10
Manitou Is. U.S.A. 45°8N 86°0W 112 C4
Manitoulin I. Canada 45°40N 82°30W 112 C6
Manitowoc U.S.A. 44°5N 87°40W 112 C4
Manizales Colombia 5°5N 75°32W 120 B2
Mankato U.S.A. 44°10N 94°0W 111 B8
Mannar Sri Lanka 9°1N 79°54E 84 Q11
Mannar, G. of Asia 8°30N 79°0E 84 Q11
Mannheim Germany 49°29N 8°29E 64 D5
Manning Canada 56°53N 117°39W 108 D8
Manningtree U.K. 51°56N 1°5E 25 C11
Manokwari Indonesia 0°54S 134°0E 83 E8
Manosque France 43°49N 5°47E 66 E6
Manresa Spain 41°48N 1°50E 67 B6
Mansel I. Canada 62°0N 80°0W 109 C12
Mansfield U.K. 53°9N 1°11W 23 F6
Mansfield U.S.A. 40°45N 82°31W 112 E6
Mansfield Woodhouse U.K. 53°11N 1°12W 23 F6
Manta Ecuador 1°0S 80°40W 120 C1
Mantes-la-Jolie France 48°58N 1°41E 66 B4
Mantiqueira, Serra da Brazil 22°0S 44°0W 117 F6
Manton U.K. 52°38N 0°41W 23 G7
Manton U.S.A. 44°25N 85°24W 112 C5
Mántova Italy 45°9N 10°48E 68 B4
Manuel Alves → Brazil 11°19S 48°28W 122 B1
Manzai Pakistan 32°12N 70°15E 84 C7
Manzanillo Cuba 20°20N 77°31W 115 C9
Manzanillo Mexico 19°3N 104°20W 114 D4
Manzhouli China 49°35N 117°25E 79 B12
Maoming China 21°50N 110°54E 79 G11
Mapam Yumco China 30°45N 81°28E 78 E5
Maputo Mozam. 25°58S 32°32E 97 K6
Maputo B. Mozam. 25°50S 32°45E 90 J7
Maquinchao Argentina 41°15S 68°50W 121 G3
Maquoketa U.S.A. 42°4N 90°40W 112 D2
Mar U.K. 57°11N 2°53W 19 H12
Mar, Serra do Brazil 25°30S 49°0W 117 F6
Mar Chiquita, L. Argentina 30°40S 62°50W 121 F3
Mar del Plata Argentina 38°0S 57°30W 121 F4
Mara Rosa Brazil 14°1S 49°11W 122 B1
Marabá Brazil 5°20S 49°5W 120 C5
Maracá, I. de Brazil 2°10N 50°30W 120 B4
Maracaibo Venezuela 10°40N 71°37W 120 A2
Maracaibo, L. de Venezuela 9°40N 71°30W 120 B2
Maracay Venezuela 10°15N 67°28W 120 A3
Maradi Niger 13°29N 7°20E 94 F7
Marágogipe Brazil 12°46S 38°55W 122 B3
Marajó, I. de Brazil 1°0S 49°30W 120 C5
Maranguape Brazil 3°55S 38°50W 120 C6
Maranhão □ Brazil 5°0S 46°0W 120 C5
Marañón → Peru 4°30S 73°35W 120 C2
Marazion U.K. 50°7N 5°29W 27 G3
Marbella Spain 36°30N 4°57W 67 D3
March U.K. 52°33N 0°5E 25 B9
Marche France 46°5N 1°20E 66 C4
Marcus I. Pac. Oc. 24°20N 153°58E 102 E7
Mardan Pakistan 34°20N 72°0E 84 B8
Marden U.K. 52°7N 2°42W 24 B3
Mardin Turkey 37°20N 40°43E 71 G7
Maree, L. U.K. 57°40N 5°26W 18 G7
Mareham le Fen U.K. 53°8N 0°4W 23 F8
Marfleet U.K. 53°45N 0°17W 23 E8
Margarita, I. de Venezuela 11°0N 64°0W 120 A3
Margate U.K. 51°23N 1°23E 25 D11
Marghilon Uzbekistan 40°27N 71°42E 87 A12
Mārgow, Dasht-e Afghan. 30°40N 62°30E 87 D10
Mari El □ Russia 56°30N 48°0E 70 C8
Mariana Trench Pac. Oc. 13°0N 145°0E 102 F6
Marías, Is. Mexico 21°25N 106°28W 114 C3
Maribor Slovenia 46°36N 15°40E 64 E8
Marie Byrd Land Antarctica 79°30S 125°0W 55 D14
Marie-Galante Guadeloupe 15°56N 61°16W 114 b
Mariental Namibia 24°36S 18°0E 97 J3
Marietta U.S.A. 39°25N 81°27W 112 F7
Marília Brazil 22°13S 50°0W 120 E4
Marinette U.S.A. 45°6N 87°38W 112 C4
Marion Ill., U.S.A. 37°44N 88°56W 112 G3
Marion Ind., U.S.A. 40°32N 85°40W 112 E5
Marion Ohio, U.S.A. 40°35N 83°8W 112 E6
Mariupol Ukraine 47°5N 37°31E 71 E6
Marka Somali Rep. 1°48N 44°50E 88 G3
Markam China 29°42N 98°38E 78 F8
Market Bosworth U.K. 52°38N 1°24E 23 G6
Market Deeping U.K. 52°41N 0°19W 23 G8
Market Drayton U.K. 52°54N 2°29W 23 G4
Market Harborough U.K. 52°29N 0°55W 23 H7
Market Lavington U.K. 51°17N 1°58W 24 D5
Market Rasen U.K. 53°24N 0°20W 23 F8
Market Weighton U.K. 53°52N 0°40W 23 E7
Markfield U.K. 52°42N 1°17W 23 G6
Markham, Mt. Antarctica 83°0S 164°0E 55 E11
Marks Tey U.K. 51°52N 0°49E 25 C10
Marlborough U.K. 51°25N 1°43W 24 D5
Marlborough Downs U.K. 51°27N 1°53W 24 D5
Marlow U.K. 51°34N 0°46W 25 C7
Marmara, Sea of Turkey 40°45N 28°15E 71 F4
Marmora Canada 44°28N 77°41W 112 C9
Marne → France 48°47N 2°29E 66 B5
Marnhull U.K. 50°57N 2°19W 24 E4
Maroua Cameroon 10°40N 14°20E 95 F8
Marple U.K. 53°24N 2°4W 23 F4
Marquette U.S.A. 46°33N 87°24W 112 B4

Marquis St. Lucia 14°2N 60°54W 115 f
Marquises, Îs. French Polynesia 9°30S 140°0W 103 H14
Marrakesh Morocco 31°9N 8°0W 94 B4
Marree Australia 29°39S 138°1E 98 F6
Marsá Matrûh Egypt 31°19N 27°9E 95 B11
Marsabit Kenya 2°18N 38°0E 96 D7
Marsala Italy 37°48N 12°26E 68 F5
Marseilles France 43°18N 5°23E 66 E6
Marsh I. U.S.A. 29°34N 91°53W 111 E8
Marshall U.S.A. 32°33N 94°23W 111 D8
Marshall Is. ■ Pac. Oc. 9°0N 171°0E 102 G9
Marshfield U.K. 51°28N 2°19W 24 C4
Marshfield U.S.A. 44°40N 90°10W 112 C2
Marske by the Sea U.K. 54°36N 1°0W 22 C6
Marston Moor U.K. 53°58N 1°17W 23 E6
Martaban Burma 16°30N 97°35E 85 L20
Martaban, G. of Burma 16°5N 96°30E 85 L20
Martapura Indonesia 3°22S 114°47E 82 E4
Martham U.K. 52°42N 1°37E 25 A12
Martha's Vineyard U.S.A. 41°25N 70°38W 113 E12
Martigues France 43°24N 5°4E 66 E6
Martinique ☑ W. Indies 14°40N 61°0W 114 c
Martin's Bay Barbados 13°12N 59°29W 115 g
Martinsburg U.S.A. 39°27N 77°58W 112 F9
Martinsville U.S.A. 39°26N 86°25W 112 F4
Martley U.K. 52°15N 2°21W 24 B4
Martock U.K. 50°58N 2°46W 24 E3
Marwar India 25°43N 73°45E 84 G8
Mary Turkmenistan 37°40N 61°50E 87 B9
Maryborough Australia 25°31S 152°37E 98 F9
Maryland □ U.S.A. 39°0N 76°30W 112 F9
Maryport U.K. 54°44N 3°28W 22 C2
Marystown Canada 47°10N 55°10W 109 E14
Marytavy U.K. 50°36N 4°7W 27 F5
Marzūq Libya 25°53N 13°57E 95 C8
Masai Steppe Tanzania 4°30S 36°30E 96 E7
Masan S. Korea 35°11N 128°32E 79 D14
Masandam, Ra's Oman 26°30N 56°30E 89 B6
Masaya Nic. 12°0N 86°7W 114 E7
Masbate Phil. 12°21N 123°36E 83 B6
Mascara Algeria 35°26N 0°6E 94 A6
Maseru Lesotho 29°18S 27°30E 97 K5
Masham U.K. 54°14N 1°39W 22 D5
Mashhad Iran 36°20N 59°35E 87 B9
Mashonaland Zimbabwe 16°30S 31°0E 97 H6
Maşîrah, Jazîrat Oman 21°0N 58°50E 89 C6
Masjed Soleyman Iran 31°55N 49°18E 86 D7
Mask, L. Ireland 53°36N 9°22W 28 D3
Mason City U.S.A. 43°9N 93°12W 111 B8
Massa Italy 44°1N 10°9E 68 B4
Massachusetts □ U.S.A. 42°30N 72°0W 113 D11
Massawa Eritrea 15°35N 39°25E 89 D2
Massena U.S.A. 44°56N 74°54W 113 C10
Massiah Street Barbados 13°9N 59°29W 115 g
Massif Central France 44°55N 3°0E 66 D5
Massillon U.S.A. 40°48N 81°32W 112 E7
Masurian Lakes Poland 53°50N 21°0E 65 B11
Masvingo Zimbabwe 20°8S 30°49E 97 J6
Mata-Utu Wall. & F. Is. 13°17S 176°8W 99 C15
Matabeleland Zimbabwe 18°0S 27°0E 97 H5
Matadi Dem. Rep. of the Congo 5°52S 13°31E 96 F2
Matagalpa Nic. 13°0N 85°58W 114 E7
Matagami Canada 49°45N 77°34W 109 E12
Matagami, L. Canada 49°50N 77°40W 109 E12
Matagorda B. U.S.A. 28°15N 96°30N 111 E7
Matamoros Mexico 25°32N 103°15W 114 B5
Matane Canada 48°50N 67°33W 109 E13
Matanzas Cuba 23°0N 81°40W 115 C8
Matara Sri Lanka 5°58N 80°30E 84 S12
Mataró Spain 41°32N 2°29E 67 B7
Matehuala Mexico 23°39N 100°39W 114 C4
Mateke Hills Zimbabwe 21°48S 31°0E 97 J6
Matera Italy 40°40N 16°36E 68 D7
Mathura India 27°30N 77°40E 84 F10
Mati Phil. 6°55N 126°15E 83 C7
Matlock U.K. 53°9N 1°33W 23 F5
Mato Grosso □ Brazil 14°0S 55°0W 120 D4
Mato Grosso, Planalto do Brazil 15°0S 55°0W 120 D4
Mato Grosso do Sul □ Brazil 18°0S 55°0W 120 D4
Matopo Hills Zimbabwe 20°36S 28°20E 97 J5
Maţruḥ Oman 23°37N 58°30E 87 F9
Matsue Japan 35°25N 133°10E 81 F3
Matsumoto Japan 36°15N 138°0E 81 E6
Matsusaka Japan 34°34N 136°32E 81 F5
Matsuyama Japan 33°45N 132°45E 81 G3
Mattancheri India 9°50N 76°15E 84 Q10
Mattawa Canada 46°20N 78°45W 112 B8
Matterhorn Switz. 45°58N 7°39E 64 F4
Matthew, Î. N. Cal. 22°29S 171°15E 99 E13
Mattoon U.S.A. 39°29N 88°23W 112 F3
Maturín Venezuela 9°45N 63°11W 120 B3
Maubeuge France 50°17N 3°57E 66 A6
Maudin Sun Burma 16°0N 94°30E 85 M19
Maui U.S.A. 20°48N 156°20W 110 H16
Maumee → U.S.A. 41°42N 83°28W 112 E6
Maumturk Mts. Ireland 53°32N 9°42W 28 D2
Maun Botswana 20°0S 23°26E 97 H4
Mauna Kea U.S.A. 19°50N 155°28W 110 J17
Mauna Loa U.S.A. 19°30N 155°35W 110 J17
Mauritania ■ Africa 20°50N 10°0W 94 E3
Mauritius ■ Ind. Oc. 20°0S 57°0E 91 J9
Mawgan U.K. 50°4N 5°13W 27 G3
Mawlamyine Burma 16°30N 97°40E 85 L20
Maxwellheugh U.K. 55°35N 2°26W 21 C11
May, I. of U.K. 56°11N 2°32W 21 B10
May Pen Jamaica 17°58N 77°15W 114 a
Mayaguana Bahamas 22°30N 72°44W 115 C10
Mayagüez Puerto Rico 18°12N 67°9W 115 d
Maybole U.K. 55°21N 4°42W 20 D6
Mayfield E. Sussex, U.K. 51°1N 0°17E 25 D9
Mayfield Staffs., U.K. 53°1N 1°47W 23 F5
Maykop Russia 44°35N 40°10E 71 F7
Maynooth Ireland 53°23N 6°34W 31 B9
Mayo Canada 63°38N 135°57W 108 C6
Mayo □ Ireland 53°53N 9°3W 28 D3
Mayon Volcano Phil. 13°15N 123°41E 83 B6
Mayotte ☑ Ind. Oc. 12°50S 45°10E 97 G9

Maysville U.S.A. 38°39N 83°46W 112 F6
Māzandarān □ Iran 36°30N 52°0E 87 B8
Mazar China 36°32N 77°1E 78 D4
Mazār-e Sharīf Afghan. 36°41N 67°0E 87 B11
Mazaruni → Guyana 6°25N 58°35W 120 B4
Mazatlán Mexico 23°13N 106°25W 114 C3
Mazyr Belarus 51°59N 29°15E 70 D4
Mbabane Swaziland 26°18S 31°6E 97 K6
Mbaïki C.A.R. 3°53N 18°1E 96 D3
Mbala Zambia 8°46S 31°24E 96 F6
Mbale Uganda 1°8N 34°12E 96 D6
Mbandaka Dem. Rep. of the Congo 0°1N 18°18E 96 D3
Mbanza Ngungu Dem. Rep. of the Congo 5°12S 14°53E 96 F2
Mbeya Tanzania 8°54S 33°29E 96 F6
Mbour Senegal 14°22N 16°54W 94 F2
Mbuji-Mayi Dem. Rep. of the Congo 6°9S 23°40E 96 F4
Mdantsane S. Africa 32°56S 27°46E 97 L5
Mead, L. U.S.A. 36°0N 114°44W 110 C4
Meadow Lake Canada 54°10N 108°26W 108 D9
Meadville U.S.A. 41°39N 80°9W 112 E7
Meaford Canada 44°36N 80°35W 112 C7
Mealsgate U.K. 54°47N 3°13W 22 C2
Mearns, Howe of the U.K. 56°52N 2°26W 19 J13
Measham U.K. 52°43N 1°31W 23 G5
Meath □ Ireland 53°40N 6°57W 29 D8
Meaux France 48°58N 2°50E 66 B5
Mecca Si. Arabia 21°30N 39°54E 86 F4
Mechelen Belgium 51°2N 4°29E 64 C3
Mecklenburg Germany 53°33N 11°40E 64 B6
Mecklenburger Bucht Germany 54°20N 11°40E 64 A6
Medan Indonesia 3°40N 98°38E 82 D1
Médéa Algeria 36°12N 2°50E 94 A6
Medellín Colombia 6°15N 75°35W 120 B2
Medford Oreg., U.S.A. 42°19N 122°52W 110 B2
Medford Wis., U.S.A. 45°9N 90°20W 112 C2
Medicine Hat Canada 50°0N 110°45W 108 E8
Medina Si. Arabia 24°35N 39°52E 86 E4
Mediterranean Sea Europe 35°0N 15°0E 90 C5
Médoc France 45°10N 0°50W 66 D3
Medstead U.K. 51°8N 1°3W 24 D6
Medvezhyegorsk Russia 63°0N 34°25E 70 B5
Medway □ U.K. 51°27N 0°46E 25 D10
Meekatharra Australia 26°32S 118°29E 98 F2
Meerut India 29°1N 77°42E 84 E10
Meghalaya □ India 25°50N 91°0E 85 G17
Meghna → Bangla. 22°50N 90°50E 85 H17
Megisti Greece 36°8N 29°34E 86 B2
Meighen I. Canada 80°0N 99°30W 109 B9
Meiktila Burma 20°53N 95°54E 85 J19
Meizhou China 24°16N 116°6E 79 G12
Mejillones Chile 23°10S 70°30W 121 E2
Mekele Ethiopia 13°33N 39°30E 89 E2
Mekhtar Pakistan 30°30N 69°15E 84 D6
Meknès Morocco 33°57N 5°33W 94 B4
Mekong → Asia 9°30N 106°15E 82 C3
Melaka Malaysia 2°15N 102°15E 82 D2
Melanesia Pac. Oc. 4°0S 155°0E 102 H7
Melbourn U.K. 52°4N 0°1E 25 B9
Melbourne Australia 37°48S 144°58E 98 H8
Melbourne U.K. 52°50N 1°25W 23 G6
Melekeok Palau 7°27N 134°38E 102 G5
Mélèzes → Canada 57°40N 69°29W 109 D13
Melfort Canada 52°50N 104°37W 108 D9
Melilla N. Afr. 35°21N 2°57W 67 E4
Melitopol Ukraine 46°50N 35°22E 71 E6
Melksham U.K. 51°23N 2°8W 24 D4
Melmerby U.K. 54°45N 2°35W 22 C3
Melrhir, Chott Algeria 34°13N 6°30E 94 B7
Melrose U.K. 55°36N 2°43W 21 C10
Melsonby U.K. 54°29N 1°42W 22 D5
Melton Constable U.K. 52°52N 1°2E 25 A11
Melton Mowbray U.K. 52°47N 0°54W 23 G7
Melun France 48°32N 2°39E 66 B5
Melville Canada 50°55N 102°50W 108 D9
Melville I. Australia 11°30S 131°0E 98 C5
Melville I. Canada 75°30N 112°0W 109 B8
Melville Pen. Canada 68°0N 84°0W 109 C11
Memphis U.S.A. 35°8N 90°2W 111 C9
Menai Bridge U.K. 53°14N 4°10W 26 A5
Menai Strait U.K. 53°11N 4°13W 26 A5
Mende France 44°31N 3°30E 66 D5
Mendip Hills U.K. 51°17N 2°40W 24 D3
Mendlesham U.K. 52°16N 1°6E 25 B11
Mendocino, C. U.S.A. 40°26N 124°25W 110 B2
Mendota U.S.A. 41°33N 89°7W 112 E3
Mendoza Argentina 32°50S 68°52W 121 F3
Mengzi China 23°20N 103°22E 78 G9
Menominee U.S.A. 45°6N 87°37W 112 C4
Menominee → U.S.A. 45°6N 87°35W 112 C4
Menomonie U.S.A. 44°53N 91°55W 112 C2
Menorca Spain 40°0N 4°0E 67 C8
Mentawai, Kepulauan Indonesia 2°0S 99°0E 82 E1
Merced U.S.A. 37°18N 120°29W 110 C2
Mercedes Corrientes, Argentina 29°10S 58°5W 121 E4
Mercedes San Luis, Argentina 33°40S 65°21W 121 F3
Mercedes Uruguay 33°12S 58°0W 121 F4
Mercy, C. Canada 65°0N 63°30W 109 C13
Mere U.K. 51°6N 2°16W 24 D4
Mergui Burma 12°26N 98°34E 82 B1
Mérida Mexico 20°58N 89°37W 114 C7
Mérida Spain 38°55N 6°25W 67 C2
Mérida Venezuela 8°24N 71°8W 120 B2
Mérida, Cord. de Venezuela 9°0N 71°0W 117 C3
Meriden U.K. 52°26N 1°38W 23 H5
Meriden U.S.A. 41°32N 72°48W 113 E11
Meridian U.S.A. 32°22N 88°42W 111 D9
Merowe Dam Sudan 18°47N 32°3E 95 E12
Merrick U.K. 55°8N 4°28W 20 D7
Merrill U.S.A. 45°11N 89°41W 112 C3
Merritt Canada 50°10N 120°45W 108 D7
Mersea I. U.K. 51°47N 0°58E 25 C10
Mersey → U.K. 53°25N 3°1W 23 F2
Merseyside □ U.K. 53°31N 3°2W 23 E2
Merthyr Tydfil U.K. 51°45N 3°22W 26 D6
Merton □ U.K. 51°25N 0°11W 25 D8
Meru Kenya 0°3N 37°40E 96 D7

Meru Tanzania 3°15S 36°46E 96 E7
Mesa U.S.A. 33°25N 111°50W 110 D4
Mesopotamia Iraq 33°30N 44°0E 86 C5
Messina Italy 38°11N 15°34E 68 E6
Messina, Str. di Italy 38°15N 15°35E 68 F6
Mestre, Espigão Brazil 12°30S 46°10W 122 B1
Meta → S. Amer. 6°12N 67°28W 120 B3
Meta Incognita Pen. Canada 62°45N 68°30W 109 C13
Metheringham U.K. 53°9N 0°23W 23 F8
Methwold U.K. 52°32N 0°33E 25 A10
Metlakatla U.S.A. 55°8N 131°35W 108 D6
Metropolis U.S.A. 37°9N 88°44W 112 G3
Metz France 49°8N 6°10E 66 B7
Meuse → Europe 50°45N 5°41E 64 C3
Mevagissey U.K. 50°16N 4°48W 27 G4
Mevagissey B. U.K. 50°17N 4°47W 27 G4
Mexborough U.K. 53°30N 1°15W 23 E6
Mexiana, I. Brazil 0°0 49°30W 120 B5
Mexicali Mexico 32°40N 115°30W 114 A1
Mexican Plateau Mexico 25°0N 104°0W 104 G9
México Mexico 19°24N 99°9W 114 D5
Mexico ■ Cent. Amer. 25°0N 105°0W 114 C4
Mexico, G. of Cent. Amer. 25°0N 90°0W 114 C7
Meymaneh Afghan. 35°53N 64°38E 87 C11
Mezen → Russia 65°44N 44°22E 70 A7
Mezhdurechensk Russia 53°41N 88°3E 76 D9
Miami U.S.A. 25°46N 80°11W 111 E10
Miändowäb Iran 37°0N 46°5E 86 B6
Miäneh Iran 37°30N 47°40E 86 B6
Mianwali Pakistan 32°38N 71°28E 84 C7
Mianyang China 31°22N 104°47E 78 E9
Miass Russia 54°59N 60°6E 70 D11
Micheldever U.K. 51°9N 1°14W 24 D6
Michigan □ U.S.A. 44°0N 85°0W 112 B4
Michigan, L. U.S.A. 44°0N 87°0W 112 D4
Michipicoten I. Canada 47°40N 85°40W 112 B5
Michurinsk Russia 52°58N 40°27E 70 D7
Mickle Fell U.K. 54°37N 2°18W 22 C4
Mickleover U.K. 52°55N 1°33W 23 G5
Mickleton U.K. 54°36N 2°2W 22 C4
Micoud St. Lucia 13°49N 60°54W 115 f
Micronesia Pac. Oc. 11°0N 160°0E 102 G7
Micronesia, Federated States of ■ Pac. Oc. 9°0N 150°0E 102 G7
Middelburg S. Africa 31°30S 25°0E 97 L5
Middle East Asia 35°0N 40°0E 72 E5
Middleham U.K. 54°17N 1°48W 22 D5
Middlemarsh U.K. 50°51N 2°28W 24 E4
Middlesbrough U.K. 54°35N 1°13W 22 C6
Middleton Gt. Man., U.K. 53°33N 2°12W 23 E4
Middleton Norfolk, U.K. 52°43N 0°29E 25 A9
Middleton Cheney U.K. 52°5N 1°16W 24 B6
Middleton in Teesdale U.K. 54°38N 2°4W 22 C4
Middleton on the Wolds U.K. 53°56N 0°35W 23 E7
Middletown U.K. 54°17N 6°51W 29 C8
Middletown N.Y., U.S.A. 41°27N 74°25W 113 E10
Middletown Ohio, U.S.A. 39°31N 84°24W 112 F5
Middlewich U.K. 53°12N 2°28W 23 F4
Middlezoy U.K. 51°5N 2°54W 24 D3
Midhurst U.K. 50°59N 0°44W 25 E7
Midi, Canal du → France 43°45N 1°21E 66 E4
Midland Canada 44°45N 79°50W 112 C8
Midland Mich., U.S.A. 43°37N 84°14W 112 D5
Midland Tex., U.S.A. 32°0N 102°3W 110 D6
Midleton Ireland 51°55N 8°10W 30 E6
Midsomer Norton U.K. 51°17N 2°28W 24 D4
Midway Is. Pac. Oc. 28°13N 177°22W 102 E10
Midwest U.S.A. 42°0N 90°0W 111 C9
Mieres Spain 43°18N 5°48W 67 A3
Mikhaylovka Russia 50°3N 43°5E 71 D7
Milan Italy 45°28N 9°10E 68 B3
Milborne Port U.K. 50°58N 2°28W 24 E4
Mildenhall U.K. 52°21N 0°32E 25 B10
Mildura Australia 34°13S 142°9E 98 G7
Miles City U.S.A. 46°25N 105°51W 110 A5
Milford U.S.A. 38°55N 75°26W 113 F10
Milford Haven U.K. 51°42N 5°7W 26 D3
Milford on Sea U.K. 50°43N 1°35W 24 E5
Milh, Bahr al Iraq 32°40N 43°35E 86 C5
Milk → U.S.A. 48°4N 106°19W 110 A5
Millau France 44°8N 3°4E 66 D5
Millbrook U.K. 50°20N 4°14W 27 G5
Millet St. Lucia 13°55N 60°59W 115 f
Millinocket U.S.A. 45°39N 68°43W 113 C13
Millom U.K. 54°13N 3°16W 22 D2
Milltown Malbay Ireland 52°52N 9°24W 30 C4
Millville U.S.A. 39°24N 75°2W 113 F10
Milngavie U.K. 55°56N 4°19W 20 C7
Milnthorpe U.K. 54°14N 2°45W 22 D3
Milos Greece 36°44N 24°25E 69 F11
Milton Abbot U.K. 50°35N 4°16W 27 F5
Milton Keynes U.K. 52°1N 0°44W 25 B7
Milverton U.K. 51°1N 3°16W 24 D2
Milwaukee U.S.A. 43°2N 87°54W 112 D4
Min Jiang → Fujian, China 26°0N 119°35E 79 F12
Min Jiang → Sichuan, China 28°45N 104°40E 78 F9
Minas Uruguay 34°20S 55°10W 121 F4
Minas Gerais □ Brazil 18°50S 46°0W 122 C1
Minatitlán Mexico 17°59N 94°31W 114 D6
Minchinhampton U.K. 51°42N 2°11W 24 C4
Mindanao Phil. 8°0N 125°0E 83 C6
Mindoro Phil. 13°0N 121°0E 83 B6
Mindoro Str. Phil. 12°30N 120°30E 83 B6
Minehead U.K. 51°12N 3°29W 24 D2
Mineral Wells U.S.A. 32°48N 98°7W 110 D7
Minfeng China 37°4N 82°46E 78 D5
Minginish U.K. 57°14N 6°15W 18 H4
Mingulay U.K. 56°49N 7°39W 18 J2
Minna Nigeria 9°37N 6°30E 94 G7
Minneapolis U.S.A. 44°57N 93°16W 111 B8
Minnesota □ U.S.A. 46°0N 94°15W 111 A8
Minorca = Menorca Spain 40°0N 4°0E 67 C8
Minot U.S.A. 48°14N 101°18W 110 A6
Minsk Belarus 53°52N 27°30E 65 B14
Minster Kent, U.K. 51°20N 1°20E 25 D11
Minster Kent, U.K. 51°25N 0°50E 25 D10
Minsterley U.K. 52°39N 2°54W 23 G3
Minto, L. Canada 57°13N 75°0W 109 D12
Miramichi B. Canada 47°15N 65°0W 113 B15

Mirim, L. S. Amer. 32°45S 52°50W 121 F4
Mirnyy Russia 62°33N 113°53E 77 C12
Mirpur Khas Pakistan 25°30N 69°0E 84 G6
Mirtoo Sea Greece 37°0N 23°20E 69 F10
Mirzapur India 25°10N 82°34E 85 G13
Mishan China 45°37N 131°48E 79 B15
Mishawaka U.S.A. 41°40N 86°11W 112 E4
Miskolc Hungary 48°7N 20°50E 65 D11
Misool Indonesia 1°52S 130°10E 83 E8
Mişrātah Libya 32°24N 15°3E 95 B9
Missinaibi → Canada 50°43N 81°29W 109 D11
Mississippi □ U.S.A. 33°0N 90°0W 111 D9
Mississippi → U.S.A. 29°9N 89°15W 111 E9
Mississippi River Delta U.S.A. 29°10N 89°15W 111 E9
Missoula U.S.A. 46°52N 114°1W 110 A4
Missouri □ U.S.A. 38°25N 92°30W 111 C81
Missouri → U.S.A. 38°49N 90°7W 111 C81
Mistassini, L. Canada 51°0N 73°30W 109 D12
Misterton Notts., U.K. 53°27N 0°50W 23 F7
Misterton Somst., U.K. 50°52N 2°47W 24 E3
Mitcheldean U.K. 51°51N 2°28W 24 C4
Mitchell U.S.A. 43°43N 98°2W 110 B7
Mitchell → Australia 15°12S 141°35E 98 D7
Mitchell, Mt. U.S.A. 35°46N 82°16W 104 F11
Mitchelstown Ireland 52°15N 8°16W 30 D6
Mito Japan 36°20N 140°30E 81 E7
Mitrovica Kosovo 42°54N 20°52E 69 C9
Mitú Colombia 1°15N 70°13W 120 B2
Mitumba, Mts. Dem. Rep. of the Congo 7°0S 27°30E 96 F5
Miyakonojō Japan 31°40N 131°5E 81 H2
Miyazaki Japan 31°56N 131°30E 81 H2
Mizen Hd. Cork, Ireland 51°27N 9°50W 30 F3
Mizen Hd. Wicklow, Ireland 52°51N 6°4W 31 C10
Mizoram □ India 23°30N 92°40E 85 H18
Mjøsa Norway 60°40N 11°0E 63 E6
Mljet Croatia 42°43N 17°30E 68 C7
Mo i Rana Norway 66°20N 14°7E 63 D6
Moab U.S.A. 38°35N 109°33W 110 C5
Moate Ireland 53°24N 7°44W 28 E6
Mobaye C.A.R. 4°25N 21°5E 96 D4
Moberly U.S.A. 39°25N 92°26W 111 C81
Mobile U.S.A. 30°41N 88°3W 111 D9
Mobridge U.S.A. 45°32N 100°26W 110 A6
Moçâmbique Mozam. 15°3S 40°42E 97 H8
Mochudi Botswana 24°27S 26°7E 97 J5
Mocoa Colombia 1°7N 76°35W 120 B2
Mococa Brazil 21°28S 47°0W 122 D1
Mocuba Mozam. 16°54S 36°57E 97 H7
Modbury U.K. 50°21N 3°55W 27 G6
Módena Italy 44°40N 10°55E 68 B4
Modesto U.S.A. 37°39N 121°0W 110 C2
Moffat U.K. 55°21N 3°27W 21 D9
Mogadishu Somali Rep. 2°2N 45°25E 89 G4
Mogi-Mirim Brazil 22°29S 47°0W 122 D1
Mohammedia Morocco 33°44N 7°21W 94 B4
Moher, Cliffs of Ireland 52°58N 9°27W 30 C4
Moidart U.K. 56°49N 5°41W 18 J6
Moidart, L. U.K. 56°47N 5°52W 18 J6
Moisie → Canada 50°14N 66°5W 109 D13
Mojave Desert U.S.A. 35°0N 116°30W 110 D3
Moji das Cruzes Brazil 23°31S 46°11W 122 D1
Mokpo S. Korea 34°50N 126°25E 79 E14
Mold U.K. 53°9N 3°8W 26 A7
Molde Norway 62°45N 7°9E 63 E5
Moldova ■ Europe 47°0N 28°0E 65 E15
Mole → U.K. 51°24N 0°21W 25 D8
Molepolole Botswana 24°28S 25°28E 97 J5
Mollendo Peru 17°0S 72°0W 120 D2
Moloka'i U.S.A. 21°8N 157°0W 110 H16
Molopo → Africa 28°30S 20°12E 97 K4
Molucca Sea Indonesia 0°0 125°0E 83 E6
Moluccas Indonesia 1°0S 127°0E 83 E7
Mombasa Kenya 4°3S 39°40E 96 E7
Mompós Colombia 9°14N 74°26W 120 B2
Mon □ Burma 16°0N 97°30E 85 L20
Mona Passage W. Indies 18°30N 67°45W 115 D11
Monach Is. U.K. 57°32N 7°40W 18 G2
Monaco ■ Europe 43°46N 7°23E 66 E7
Monadhliath Mts. U.K. 57°10N 4°4W 19 H9
Monaghan Ireland 54°15N 6°57W 29 C8
Monaghan □ Ireland 54°11N 6°56W 29 C8
Monar, L. U.K. 57°26N 5°8W 18 H7
Monar Forest U.K. 57°27N 5°10W 18 H7
Monasterevin Ireland 53°8N 7°4W 31 B8
Monavullagh Mts. Ireland 52°14N 7°35W 31 D7
Mönchengladbach Germany 51°11N 6°27E 64 C4
Monclova Mexico 26°54N 101°25W 114 B4
Moncton Canada 46°7N 64°51W 113 B15
Moneague Jamaica 18°16N 77°7W 114 a
Moneymore U.K. 54°41N 6°40W 29 B8
Mongolia ■ Asia 47°0N 103°0E 78 B9
Mongolia, Plateau of Asia 45°0N 105°0E 72 D12
Mongu Zambia 15°16S 23°12E 97 H4
Monifieth U.K. 56°30N 2°48W 21 B10
Monmouth U.K. 51°48N 2°42W 26 D8
Monmouth U.S.A. 40°55N 90°39W 112 E2
Monmouthshire □ U.K. 51°48N 2°54W 26 D8
Monnow → U.K. 51°49N 2°43W 24 C3
Monroe La., U.S.A. 32°30N 92°7W 111 D8
Monroe Mich., U.S.A. 41°55N 83°24W 112 D6
Monroe Wis., U.S.A. 42°36N 89°38W 112 D3
Monrovia Liberia 6°18N 10°47W 94 G3
Mons Belgium 50°27N 3°58E 64 C3
Mont-de-Marsan France 43°54N 0°31W 66 E3
Mont-Laurier Canada 46°35N 75°30W 109 E12
Montana Bulgaria 43°27N 23°16E 69 C10
Montaña Peru 6°0S 73°0W 120 C2
Montana □ U.S.A. 47°0N 110°0W 110 A5
Montargis France 48°0N 2°43E 66 C5
Montauban France 44°2N 1°21E 66 D4
Montbéliard France 47°31N 6°48E 66 C7
Montceau-les-Mines France 46°40N 4°23E 66 C6
Monte Azul Brazil 15°9S 42°53W 122 C2
Monte-Carlo Monaco 43°44N 7°25E 66 E7
Monte Caseros Argentina 30°10S 57°50W 121 F4
Monte Cristi Dom. Rep. 19°52N 71°39W 115 D10
Montego Bay Jamaica 18°28N 77°55W 114 a
Montélimar France 44°33N 4°45E 66 D6

Montello U.S.A. 43°48N 89°20W 112 D3
Montemorelos Mexico 25°12N 99°49W 114 B5
Montenegro ■ Europe 42°40N 19°20E 69 C8
Monterey U.S.A. 36°37N 121°55W 110 C2
Montería Colombia 8°46N 75°53W 120 B2
Monterrey Mexico 25°40N 100°19W 114 B4
Montes Claros Brazil 16°30S 43°50W 122 C2
Montevideo Uruguay 34°50S 56°11W 121 F4
Montgomery U.K. 52°34N 3°8W 26 B7
Montgomery U.S.A. 32°23N 86°19W 111 D9
Monticello U.S.A. 40°45N 86°46W 112 E4
Montluçon France 46°22N 2°36E 66 C5
Montmagny Canada 46°58N 70°34W 113 B12
Montpelier Idaho, U.S.A. 42°19N 111°18W 110 B4
Montpelier Vt., U.S.A. 44°16N 72°35W 113 C11
Montpellier France 43°37N 3°52E 66 E5
Montreux Switz. 46°26N 6°55E 64 E4
Montrose U.K. 56°44N 2°27W 19 J13
Montrose U.S.A. 38°29N 107°53W 110 C5
Montserrat ☑ W. Indies 16°40N 62°10W 115 D12
Monywa Burma 22°7N 95°11E 85 H19
Monza Italy 45°35N 9°16E 68 B3
Monze, C. Pakistan 24°47N 66°37E 84 G5
Moorfoot Hills U.K. 55°44N 3°8W 21 C9
Moorhead U.S.A. 46°53N 96°45W 111 A7
Moose Jaw Canada 50°24N 105°30W 108 D9
Moosehead L. U.S.A. 45°38N 69°40W 113 C13
Moosomin Canada 50°9N 101°40W 108 D9
Moosonee Canada 51°17N 80°39W 109 D11
Mopti Mali 14°30N 4°0W 94 F5
Mora Sweden 61°2N 14°38E 63 E6
Moradabad India 28°50N 78°50E 84 E11
Morant Bay Jamaica 17°53N 76°25W 114 a
Morant Pt. Jamaica 17°55N 76°12W 114 a
Morar, L. U.K. 56°57N 5°40W 18 J6
Moratuwa Sri Lanka 6°45N 79°55E 84 R11
Morava → Serbia 44°36N 21°4E 69 B9
Morava → Slovak Rep. 48°10N 16°59E 65 D9
Moravian Hts. Czech Rep. 49°30N 15°40E 56 F9
Moray □ U.K. 57°31N 3°18W 19 H11
Moray Firth U.K. 57°40N 3°52W 19 G10
Morden Canada 49°15N 98°10W 108 E10
Mordvinia □ Russia 54°20N 44°30E 70 D7
Moreau → U.S.A. 45°18N 100°43W 110 A6
Morebattle U.K. 55°31N 2°22W 21 C11
Morecambe U.K. 54°5N 2°52W 22 D3
Morecambe B. U.K. 54°7N 3°0W 22 D3
Moree Australia 29°28S 149°54E 98 F9
Morehead U.S.A. 38°11N 83°26W 112 F6
Morelia Mexico 19°42N 101°7W 114 D4
Morena, Sierra Spain 38°20N 4°0W 67 C3
Moresby I. Canada 52°30N 131°40W 108 D6
Moreton-in-Marsh U.K. 51°59N 1°41W 24 C5
Moretonhampstead U.K. 50°39N 3°46W 27 F6
Morgan City U.S.A. 29°42N 91°12W 111 E8
Morgantown U.S.A. 39°38N 79°57W 112 F8
Morioka Japan 39°45N 141°8E 81 D7
Morlaix France 48°36N 3°52W 66 B2
Morley U.K. 53°45N 1°36W 23 E5
Morocco ■ N. Afr. 32°0N 5°50W 94 B4
Morogoro Tanzania 6°50S 37°40E 96 F7
Morón Cuba 22°8N 78°39W 115 C9
Mörön Mongolia 49°38N 100°9E 78 B9
Morondava Madag. 20°17S 44°17E 97 J8
Moroni Comoros Is. 11°40S 43°16E 91 H8
Morotai Indonesia 2°10N 128°30E 83 D7
Morpeth U.K. 55°10N 1°41W 22 B5
Morphou Cyprus 35°12N 32°59E 86 C3
Morrinhos Brazil 17°45S 49°10W 122 C1
Morris U.S.A. 41°22N 88°26W 112 E31
Morris Jesup, Kap Greenland 83°40N 34°0W 104 A16
Morte Bay U.K. 51°9N 4°14W 27 E5
Morte Pt. U.K. 51°11N 4°14W 27 E5
Mortehoe U.K. 51°11N 4°12W 27 E5
Mortimer's Cross U.K. 52°16N 2°50W 24 B3
Morton Fen U.K. 52°49N 0°20W 23 G8
Morvan France 47°5N 4°3E 66 C6
Morwenstow U.K. 50°54N 4°33W 27 F4
Moscos Is. Burma 14°0N 97°30E 85 N20
Moscow Russia 55°45N 37°37E 70 C6
Moscow U.S.A. 46°44N 117°0W 110 A3
Mosel → Europe 50°22N 7°36E 64 C4
Moses Lake U.S.A. 47°8N 119°17W 110 A3
Moshi Tanzania 3°22S 37°18E 96 E7
Mosjøen Norway 65°51N 13°12E 63 D6
Mossebaai S. Africa 34°11S 22°8E 97 L4
Mossley U.K. 53°33N 2°1W 23 E4
Mossoró Brazil 5°10S 37°15W 120 C6
Most Czech Rep. 50°31N 13°38E 64 C7
Mostaganem Algeria 35°54N 0°5E 94 A6
Mostar Bos.-H. 43°22N 17°50E 69 C7
Mosul Iraq 36°15N 43°5E 86 B5
Motcombe U.K. 51°1N 2°13W 24 D4
Motherwell U.K. 55°47N 3°58W 21 C8
Motihari India 26°30N 84°55E 85 F14
Motril Spain 36°31N 3°37W 67 D4
Mottisfont U.K. 51°2N 1°32W 24 D5
Mouila Gabon 1°50S 11°0E 96 E2
Moule à Chique, C. St. Lucia 13°43N 60°57W 115 f
Moulins France 46°35N 3°19E 66 C5
Moulmein Burma 16°30N 97°40E 85 L20
Moulouya, O. → Morocco 35°5N 2°25W 94 B5
Moulton U.K. 52°17N 0°52W 25 B7
Moundou Chad 8°40N 16°10E 95 G9
Moundsville U.S.A. 39°55N 80°44W 112 F7
Mount Carmel U.S.A. 38°25N 87°46W 112 F4
Mount Desert I. U.S.A. 44°21N 68°20W 113 C13
Mount Gambier Australia 37°50S 140°46E 98 H7
Mount Hagen Papua N. G. 5°52S 144°16E 98 B7
Mount Isa Australia 20°42S 139°26E 98 E6
Mount Magnet Australia 28°2S 117°47E 98 F2
Mount Pleasant U.S.A. 43°36N 84°46W 112 D5
Mount Sterling U.S.A. 38°4N 83°56W 112 F6
Mount Vernon Ind., U.S.A. 37°56N 87°54W 112 G4
Mount Vernon Ohio, U.S.A. 40°23N 82°29W 112 E6
Mountain Ash U.K. 51°40N 3°23W 26 D7
Mountain Home U.S.A. 43°8N 115°41W 110 B3
Mountain View U.S.A. 19°33N 155°7W 110 J17
Mountmellick Ireland 53°7N 7°20W 31 B8

Mountrath Ireland 53°0N 7°28W 31 C8
Mount's Bay U.K. 50°5N 5°31W 27 G2
Mountsorrel U.K. 52°44N 1°8W 23 G6
Mourne → U.K. 54°52N 7°26W 28 B7
Mourne Mts. U.K. 54°10N 6°0W 29 C9
Moville Ireland 55°11N 7°3W 29 A7
Moy → Ireland 54°8N 9°8W 28 C3
Mozambique ■ Africa 19°0S 35°0E 97 H7
Mozambique Chan. Africa 17°30S 42°30E 90 H8
Mozdok Russia 43°45N 44°48E 71 F7
Mpanda Tanzania 6°23S 31°1E 96 F6
Mpumalanga S. Africa 29°50S 30°33E 97 K6
Msaken Tunisia 35°49N 10°33E 95 A8
Mthatha S. Africa 31°36S 28°49E 97 L5
Mtwara-Mikindani Tanzania 10°20S 40°20E 96 G8
Muar Malaysia 2°3N 102°34E 82 D2
Mubi Nigeria 10°18N 13°16E 95 F8
Much Dewchurch U.K. 51°58N 2°45W 24 C3
Much Marcle U.K. 51°59N 2°29W 24 C4
Much Wenlock U.K. 52°35N 2°33W 23 G3
Muchinga Mts. Zambia 11°30S 31°30E 97 G6
Muck U.K. 56°50N 6°15W 18 J5
Muckle Flugga U.K. 60°51N 0°54W 18 A16
Muckle Roe U.K. 60°23N 1°27W 18 B15
Mucuri Brazil 18°0S 39°36W 122 C3
Mudanjiang China 44°38N 129°30E 79 C14
Mufulira Zambia 12°32S 28°15E 97 G5
Mugla Turkey 37°15N 28°22E 71 G4
Muine Bheag Ireland 52°42N 6°58W 31 C9
Muir of Ord U.K. 57°32N 4°28W 19 G9
Muktsar India 30°30N 74°30E 84 D9
Mulanje, Mt. Malawi 16°2S 35°33E 97 H7
Mulde → Germany 51°53N 12°15E 64 C7
Mulhacén Spain 37°4N 3°20W 67 D4
Mulhouse France 47°40N 7°20E 66 C7
Mull U.K. 56°25N 5°56W 20 B4
Mull, Sound of U.K. 56°30N 5°50W 20 A4
Mullaghareirk Mts. Ireland 52°20N 9°10W 30 D4
Mullet Pen. Ireland 54°13N 10°2W 28 C1
Mullingar Ireland 53°31N 7°21W 28 D7
Mullion U.K. 50°1N 5°16W 27 G3
Mulroy B. Ireland 55°15N 7°46W 28 A6
Multan Pakistan 30°15N 71°36E 84 D7
Mumbai India 18°56N 72°50E 84 K8
Mumbles Hd. U.K. 51°34N 3°59W 27 D6
Muna Indonesia 5°0S 122°30E 83 F6
Muncie U.S.A. 40°12N 85°23W 112 E5
Mundesley U.K. 52°53N 1°25E 25 A11
Mundo Novo Brazil 11°50S 40°29W 122 B2
Munger India 25°23N 86°30E 85 G15
Munich Germany 48°8N 11°34E 64 D6
Munising U.S.A. 46°25N 86°40W 112 B4
Münster Germany 51°58N 7°37E 64 C4
Münster □ Ireland 52°18N 8°44W 30 D5
Murashi Russia 59°30N 49°0E 70 C8
Murat → Turkey 38°46N 40°0E 71 G7
Murchison → Australia 27°45S 114°0E 98 F1
Murcia Spain 38°5N 1°10W 67 D5
Murcia □ Spain 37°50N 1°30W 67 D5
Mureş → Romania 46°15N 20°13E 65 E11
Murfreesboro U.S.A. 35°51N 86°24W 111 C9
Muriaé Brazil 21°8S 42°23W 122 D2
Müritz Germany 53°25N 12°42E 64 B7
Murmansk Russia 68°57N 33°10E 70 A5
Murom Russia 55°35N 42°3E 70 C7
Muroran Japan 42°25N 141°0E 81 B7
Murray → U.S.A. 36°37N 88°19W 112 G3
Murray → Australia 35°20S 139°22E 98 H6
Mururoa French Polynesia 21°52S 138°55W 103 K14
Murwara India 23°46N 80°28E 85 H12
Mus Turkey 38°45N 41°30E 71 G7
Mûsa, Gebel Egypt 28°33N 33°59E 86 D3
Muscat Oman 23°37N 58°36E 87 F9
Musgrave Ranges Australia 26°0S 132°0E 98 F5
Musina S. Africa 22°20S 30°5E 97 J6
Muskegon U.S.A. 43°14N 86°16W 112 D4
Muskegon → U.S.A. 43°14N 86°21W 112 D4
Muskogee U.S.A. 35°45N 95°22W 111 C7
Musselburgh U.K. 55°57N 3°2W 21 C9
Musselshell → U.S.A. 47°21N 107°57W 110 A5
Mutare Zimbabwe 18°58S 32°38E 97 H6
Mutton I. Ireland 52°49N 9°32W 30 C3
Muynak Uzbekistan 43°44N 59°10E 87 A9
Muz Tag China 36°25N 87°25E 78 D6
Muzaffarabad Pakistan 34°25N 73°30E 84 B8
Muzaffarnagar India 29°26N 77°40E 84 E10
Muztagh-Ata China 38°17N 75°7E 78 D4
Mwanza Tanzania 2°30S 32°58E 96 E6
Mweelrea Ireland 53°39N 9°49W 28 D2
Mwene-Ditu Dem. Rep. of the Congo 6°35S 22°27E 96 F4
Mweru, L. Zambia 9°0S 28°40E 96 F5
My Tho Vietnam 10°29N 106°23E 82 B3
Myanmar = Burma ■ Asia 21°0N 96°30E 85 J20
Mycenae Greece 37°43N 22°46E 69 F10
Myddle U.K. 52°49N 2°47W 23 G3
Myingyan Burma 21°30N 95°20E 85 J19
Myitkyina Burma 25°24N 97°26E 85 G20
Mymensingh Bangla. 24°45N 90°24E 85 G17
Mynydd Du U.K. 51°52N 3°50W 26 D6
Mynydd Preseli U.K. 51°57N 4°48W 26 D4
Mysore India 12°17N 76°41E 84 N10
Mytishchi Russia 55°50N 37°50E 70 C6

N

Naab → Germany 49°1N 12°2E 64 D6
Naas Ireland 53°12N 6°40W 31 B9
Naberezhnyye Chelny Russia 55°42N 52°19E 70 C9
Nabeul Tunisia 36°30N 10°44E 95 A8
Nābulus West Bank 32°14N 35°15E 86 C3
Nacala Mozam. 14°32S 40°34E 97 G8
Nacogdoches U.S.A. 31°36N 94°39W 111 D8
Nacozari de García Mexico 30°25N 109°38W 114 A3
Nadiad India 22°41N 72°56E 84 H8
Nador Morocco 35°14N 2°58W 94 B5
Nafferton U.K. 54°1N 0°23W 23 D8
Nafud Desert Si. Arabia 28°15N 41°0E 86 D5

Naga Phil. 13°38N 123°15E 83 B6
Nagaland □ India 26°0N 94°30E 85 G19
Nagano Japan 36°40N 138°10E 81 E6
Nagaoka Japan 37°27N 138°51E 81 E6
Nagappattinam India 10°46N 79°51E 84 P11
Nagasaki Japan 32°47N 129°50E 81 G1
Nagaur India 27°15N 73°45E 84 F8
Nagercoil India 8°12N 77°26E 84 Q10
Nagles Mts. Ireland 52°8N 8°30W 30 D6
Nagorno-Karabakh □ Azerbaijan 39°55N 46°45E 71 F8
Nagoya Japan 35°10N 136°50E 81 F5
Nagpur India 21°8N 79°10E 84 J11
Nagqu China 31°29N 92°3E 78 E7
Naguabo Puerto Rico 18°13N 65°44W 115 d
Naha Japan 26°13N 127°42E 79 F14
Nailsea U.K. 51°26N 2°44W 24 D3
Nailsworth U.K. 51°41N 2°14W 24 C4
Nain Canada 56°34N 61°40W 109 D13
Nairn U.K. 57°35N 3°53W 19 G10
Nairobi Kenya 1°17S 36°48E 96 E7
Naivasha Kenya 0°40S 36°30E 96 E7
Najafābād Iran 32°40N 51°15E 87 C7
Najd Si. Arabia 26°30N 42°0E 86 E5
Najibabad India 29°40N 78°20E 84 E11
Najrān Si. Arabia 17°34N 44°18E 89 D3
Nakhodka Russia 42°53N 132°54E 79 C15
Nakhon Ratchasima Thailand 14°59N 102°12E 82 B2
Nakhon Sawan Thailand 15°35N 100°10E 82 A2
Nakhon Si Thammarat Thailand 8°29N 100°0E 82 C2
Nakina Canada 50°10N 86°40W 109 D11
Nakuru Kenya 0°15S 36°4E 96 E7
Nalchik Russia 43°30N 43°33E 71 F7
Nallamalai Hills India 15°30N 78°50E 84 M11
Nam Co China 30°30N 90°45E 78 E7
Namak, Daryācheh-ye Iran 34°30N 52°0E 87 C8
Namaland Namibia 26°0S 17°0E 97 K3
Namangan Uzbekistan 41°0N 71°40E 87 A12
Namcha Barwa China 29°40N 95°10E 78 F8
Namib Desert Namibia 22°30S 15°0E 97 J3
Namibe Angola 15°7S 12°11E 97 H2
Namibia ■ Africa 22°0S 18°9E 97 J3
Nampa U.S.A. 43°34N 116°34W 110 B3
Namp'o N. Korea 38°52N 125°10E 79 D14
Nampula Mozam. 15°6S 39°15E 97 H7
Namumea Tuvalu 5°41S 176°9E 99 B14
Namur Belgium 50°27N 4°52E 64 C3
Nan-ch'ang China 28°42N 115°55E 79 F12
Nan Ling China 25°0N 112°30E 79 F11
Nanaimo Canada 49°10N 124°0W 108 E7
Nanchang China 30°43N 106°2E 78 E10
Nancy France 48°42N 6°12E 66 B7
Nanda Devi India 30°23N 79°59E 84 D11
Nanded India 19°10N 77°20E 84 K10
Nandurbar India 21°20N 74°15E 84 J9
Nanga Parbat Pakistan 35°10N 74°35E 84 B9
Nangarhār □ Afghan. 34°20N 70°0E 87 C12
Nanjing China 32°2N 118°47E 79 E12
Nanning China 22°48N 108°20E 78 G10
Nanping China 26°38N 118°10E 79 F12
Nansen Sd. Canada 81°0N 91°0W 109 A10
Nantes France 47°12N 1°33W 66 C3
Nantong China 32°1N 120°52E 79 E13
Nantucket I. U.S.A. 41°16N 70°5W 113 E12
Nantwich U.K. 53°4N 2°31W 23 F3
Nanuque Brazil 17°50S 40°21W 122 C2
Nanyang China 33°11N 112°30E 79 E11
Nanyuki Kenya 0°2N 37°4E 96 D7
Napa U.S.A. 38°18N 122°17W 110 C2
Napier N.Z. 39°30S 176°56E 99 H14
Naples Italy 40°50N 14°15E 68 D6
Napo → Peru 3°20S 72°40W 120 C2
Nappa U.K. 53°58N 2°13W 23 E4
Narayanganj Bangla. 23°40N 90°33E 85 H17
Narberth U.K. 51°47N 4°44W 26 D4
Narbonne France 43°11N 3°0E 66 E5
Narborough U.K. 52°34N 1°13W 23 G6
Nares Str. Arctic 80°0N 70°0W 109 A13
Narmada → India 21°38N 72°36E 84 J8
Narodnaya Russia 65°5N 59°58E 70 A10
Narva Estonia 59°23N 28°12E 63 F9
Narvik Norway 68°28N 17°26E 63 D7
Naryan-Mar Russia 67°42N 53°12E 70 A9
Naryn Kyrgyzstan 41°26N 75°58E 74 B
Naseby U.K. 52°24N 0°59W 25 B7
Nashua U.S.A. 42°45N 71°28W 113 D12
Nashville U.S.A. 36°10N 86°47W 111 C9
Nasik India 19°58N 73°50E 84 K8
Nasirabad India 26°15N 74°45E 84 F9
Nasiriyah Iraq 31°0N 46°15E 86 D6
Nassau Bahamas 25°5N 77°20W 115 B9
Nasser, L. Egypt 23°0N 32°30E 95 D12
Natal Brazil 5°47S 35°13W 120 C6
Natashquan Canada 50°14N 61°46W 109 D13
Natashquan → Canada 50°7N 61°50W 109 D13
Natchez U.S.A. 31°34N 91°24W 111 D8
Natchitoches U.S.A. 31°46N 93°5W 111 D8
Nathdwara India 24°55N 73°50E 84 G8
Natitingou Benin 10°20N 1°26E 94 F6
Natron, L. Tanzania 2°20S 36°0E 96 E7
Natuna Besar, Kepulauan Indonesia 4°0N 108°15E 82 D3
Nauru ■ Pac. Oc. 1°0S 166°0E 102 H8
Navarino, I. Chile 55°0S 67°40W 121 H3
Navarra □ Spain 42°40N 1°40W 67 A5
Navenby U.K. 53°6N 0°31W 23 F7
Naver → U.K. 58°32N 4°14W 19 E9
Navoiy Uzbekistan 40°9N 65°22E 76 E7
Navojoa Mexico 27°6N 109°26W 114 B3
Navsari India 20°57N 72°59E 84 J8
Nawabshah Pakistan 26°15N 68°25E 84 F6
Naxçıvan □ Azerbaijan 39°25N 45°26E 71 G8
Naxos Greece 37°8N 25°25E 69 F11
Naypyidaw Burma 19°44N 96°12E 85 K20
Nazaré Brazil 13°2S 39°0W 122 B3
Nazas → Mexico 25°12N 104°12W 114 B4
Nazca Peru 14°50S 74°57W 120 D2
Naze, The U.K. 51°53N 1°18E 25 C11

Nazret

Orléans

Nazret *Ethiopia* 8°32N 39°22E **89** F2
Ndjamena *Chad* 12°10N 15°0E **95** F8
Ndola *Zambia* 13°0S 28°34E **97** G5
Neagh, Lough *U.K.* 54°37N 6°25W **29** B9
Near Is. *U.S.A.* 52°30N 174°0E **108** D1
Neath *U.K.* 51°39N 3°48W **26** D6
Neath → *U.K.* 51°39N 3°48W **26** D6
Nebraska □ *U.S.A.* 41°30N 99°30W **110** B7
Nébrodi, Monti *Italy* 37°54N 14°35E **68** F6
Neckar → *Germany* 49°27N 8°29E **64** D5
Necochea *Argentina* 38°30S 58°50W **121** F4
Needham Market *U.K.* 52°9N 1°4E **25** B11
Needles, The *U.K.* 50°39N 1°35W **24** E5
Neenah *U.S.A.* 44°11N 88°28W **112** C3
Neepawa *Canada* 50°15N 99°30W **108** D10
Neftekumsk *Russia* 44°46N 44°50E **71** F7
Nefteyugansk *Russia* 61°5N 72°42E **76** C8
Negaunee *U.S.A.* 46°30N 87°36W **112** B4
Negele *Ethiopia* 5°20N 39°36E **89** F2
Negombo *Sri Lanka* 7°12N 79°50E **84** R11
Negra, Pta. *Peru* 6°6S 81°10W **117** D2
Negril *Jamaica* 18°22N 78°20W **114** a
Negro → *Argentina* 41°2S 62°47W **121** G3
Negro → *Brazil* 3°0S 60°0W **120** C3
Negros *Phil.* 9°30N 122°40E **83** C6
Neijiang *China* 29°35N 104°55E **78** F9
Neisse → *Europe* 52°4N 14°46E **64** B8
Neiva *Colombia* 2°56N 75°18W **120** C2
Nellore *India* 14°27N 79°59E **84** M11
Nelson *Canada* 49°30N 117°20W **108** E8
Nelson *N.Z.* 41°18S 173°16E **99** J13
Nelson *U.K.* 53°50N 2°13W **23** E4
Nelson → *Canada* 54°33N 98°2W **108** D10
Neman → *Lithuania* 55°25N 21°10E **63** F8
Nenagh *Ireland* 52°52N 8°11W **30** C6
Nene → *U.K.* 52°49N 0°11E **25** A9
Nenjiang *China* 49°10N 125°10E **79** B14
Neosho → *U.S.A.* 36°48N 95°18W **111** C7
Nepal ■ *Asia* 28°0N 84°30E **85** F14
Nephi *U.S.A.* 39°43N 111°50W **110** C4
Nephin *Ireland* 54°1N 9°22W **28** C3
Nephin Beg Range *Ireland* 54°0N 9°40W **28** C2
Nerastro, Sarīr *Libya* 24°20N 20°37E **95** D10
Neryungri *Russia* 57°38N 124°28E **77** D13
Ness, L. *U.K.* 57°15N 4°32W **19** H8
Neston *U.K.* 53°17N 3°4W **23** F2
Netherbury *U.K.* 50°46N 2°45W **24** E3
Netherlands ■ *Europe* 52°0N 5°30E **64** B3
Netherlands Antilles ☑
  W. Indies 12°15N 69°0W **115** E11
Netley *U.K.* 50°52N 1°20W **24** E6
Nettilling L. *Canada* 66°30N 71°0W **109** C12
Nettlebed *U.K.* 51°34N 0°59W **25** C7
Nettleham *U.K.* 53°16N 0°29W **23** F7
Neuchâtel *Switz.* 47°0N 6°55E **64** E4
Neuchâtel, Lac de *Switz.* 46°53N 6°50E **64** E4
Neuquén *Argentina* 38°55S 68°0W **121** F3
Neusiedler See *Austria* 47°50N 16°47E **65** E9
Neva → *Russia* 59°56N 30°20E **70** C5
Nevada □ *U.S.A.* 39°0N 117°0W **110** C3
Nevers *France* 47°0N 3°9E **66** C5
Nevinnomyssk *Russia* 44°40N 42°0E **71** F7
New Abbey *U.K.* 54°59N 3°37W **21** E8
New Alresford *U.K.* 51°5N 1°8W **24** D6
New Amsterdam *Guyana* 6°15N 57°36W **120** B4
New Bedford *U.S.A.* 41°38N 70°56W **113** E12
New Britain *Papua N. G.* 5°50S 150°20E **98** B9
New Britain *U.S.A.* 41°40N 72°47W **113** E11
New Brunswick *U.S.A.* 40°30N 74°27W **113** E10
New Brunswick □ *Canada* 46°50N 66°30W **113** C14
New Caledonia ☑ *Pac. Oc.* 21°0S 165°0E **99** E12
New Castle *Ind., U.S.A.* 39°55N 85°22W **112** F5
New Castle *Pa., U.S.A.* 41°0N 80°21W **112** E7
New Delhi *India* 28°36N 77°11E **84** E10
New England *U.S.A.* 43°0N 71°0W **111** B12
New Forest △ *U.K.* 50°53N 1°34W **24** E5
New Galloway *U.K.* 55°5N 4°9W **20** D7
New Georgia Is. *Solomon Is.* 8°15S 157°30E **99** B10
New Glasgow *Canada* 45°35N 62°36W **113** C16
New Guinea *Oceania* 4°0S 136°0E **98** B7
New Hampshire □ *U.S.A.* 44°0N 71°30W **113** D12
New Haven *U.S.A.* 41°18N 72°55W **113** E11
New Hebrides = Vanuatu ■
  Pac. Oc. 15°0S 168°0E **99** D12
New Holland *U.K.* 53°42N 0°21W **23** E8
New Iberia *U.S.A.* 30°1N 91°49W **111** D8
New Ireland *Papua N. G.* 3°20S 151°50E **98** A9
New Jersey □ *U.S.A.* 40°0N 74°30W **113** E10
New Lexington *U.S.A.* 39°43N 82°13W **112** F6
New Liskeard *Canada* 47°31N 79°41W **109** E12
New London *U.S.A.* 41°22N 72°6W **113** E11
New Madrid *U.S.A.* 36°36N 89°32W **112** G3
New Mexico □ *U.S.A.* 34°30N 106°0W **110** D5
New Mills *U.K.* 53°23N 2°0W **23** F5
New Milton *U.K.* 50°45N 1°40W **24** E5
New Orleans *U.S.A.* 29°57N 90°4W **111** E8
New Philadelphia *U.S.A.* 40°30N 81°27W **112** E7
New Plymouth *N.Z.* 39°4S 174°5E **99** H13
New Providence *Bahamas* 25°25N 78°35W **115** B9
New Quay *U.K.* 52°13N 4°21W **26** C5
New Radnor *U.K.* 52°15N 3°9W **26** C7
New Romney *U.K.* 50°59N 0°57E **25** E10
New Ross *Ireland* 52°23N 6°57W **31** D9
New Rossington *U.K.* 53°29N 1°4W **23** F6
New Siberian Is. *Russia* 75°0N 142°0E **77** B15
New South Wales □ *Australia* 33°0S 146°0E **98** G8
New York *U.S.A.* 40°43N 74°0W **113** E11
New York □ *U.S.A.* 43°0N 75°0W **113** D9
New Zealand ■ *Oceania* 40°0S 176°0E **99** J14
Newark *Del., U.S.A.* 39°41N 75°46W **113** F10
Newark *N.J., U.S.A.* 40°44N 74°10W **113** E10
Newark *N.Y., U.S.A.* 43°3N 77°6W **112** D9
Newark *Ohio, U.S.A.* 40°3N 82°24W **112** E6
Newark-on-Trent *U.K.* 53°5N 0°48W **23** F7
Newberry *U.S.A.* 46°21N 85°30W **112** B5
Newbiggin-by-the-Sea *U.K.* 55°11N 1°31W **22** B5
Newbigging *U.K.* 55°42N 3°34W **21** C8
Newburgh *U.S.A.* 41°30N 74°1W **113** E10
Newburn *U.K.* 54°59N 1°43W **22** C5
Newbury *U.K.* 51°24N 1°20W **24** D6

Newburyport *U.S.A.* 42°49N 70°53W **113** D12
Newby Bridge *U.K.* 54°17N 2°57W **22** D3
Newcastle *Australia* 33°0S 151°46E **98** G9
Newcastle *Canada* 47°1N 65°38W **113** B15
Newcastle *S. Africa* 27°45S 29°58E **97** K5
Newcastle *U.K.* 54°13N 5°54W **29** C10
Newcastle Emlyn *U.K.* 52°2N 4°28W **26** C5
Newcastle-under-Lyme *U.K.* 53°1N 2°14W **23** F4
Newcastle-upon-Tyne *U.K.* 54°58N 1°36W **22** C5
Newcastle West *Ireland* 52°27N 9°3W **30** D4
Newcastleton *U.K.* 55°11N 2°49W **21** D10
Newent *U.K.* 51°56N 2°24W **24** C4
Newfoundland *Canada* 49°0N 55°0W **104** E14
Newfoundland & Labrador □
  Canada 53°0N 58°0W **109** D14
Newham □ *U.K.* 51°31N 0°3E **25** C9
Newhaven *U.K.* 50°47N 0°3E **25** E9
Newington *Kent, U.K.* 51°6N 1°7E **25** D11
Newington *Kent, U.K.* 51°21N 0°41E **25** D10
Newlyn *U.K.* 50°6N 5°34W **27** G2
Newlyn East *U.K.* 50°22N 5°5W **27** G3
Newman *Australia* 23°18S 119°45E **98** E2
Newmarket *Ireland* 52°13N 9°0W **30** D5
Newmarket *U.K.* 52°15N 0°25E **25** B9
Newnham *U.K.* 51°48N 2°27W **24** C4
Newport *Ireland* 53°53N 9°33W **28** D2
Newport *Essex, U.K.* 51°59N 0°14E **25** C9
Newport *I. of W., U.K.* 50°42N 1°17W **24** E6
Newport *Newport, U.K.* 51°35N 3°0W **27** D8
Newport *Pembs., U.K.* 52°1N 4°51W **26** C4
Newport *Telford & Wrekin, U.K.* 52°46N 2°22W **23** G4
Newport *Ark., U.S.A.* 35°37N 91°16W **111** C8
Newport *Ky., U.S.A.* 39°5N 84°29W **112** F5
Newport *R.I., U.S.A.* 41°29N 71°19W **113** E12
Newport *Vt., U.S.A.* 44°56N 72°13W **113** C11
Newport News *U.S.A.* 36°58N 76°25W **111** C11
Newport Pagnell *U.K.* 52°5N 0°43W **25** B7
Newquay *U.K.* 50°25N 5°6W **27** G3
Newry *U.K.* 54°11N 6°21W **29** C9
Newton Abbot *U.K.* 50°32N 3°37W **27** F6
Newton Arlosh *U.K.* 54°53N 3°14W **22** C2
Newton Aycliffe *U.K.* 54°37N 1°34W **22** C5
Newton Ferrers *U.K.* 50°19N 4°3W **27** G5
Newton le Willows *U.K.* 53°28N 2°38W **23** F3
Newton St. Cyres *U.K.* 50°46N 3°36W **27** F6
Newton Stewart *U.K.* 54°57N 4°30W **20** E6
Newtonmore *U.K.* 57°4N 4°8W **19** H9
Newtown *U.K.* 52°31N 3°19W **26** B7
Newtown St. Boswells *U.K.* 55°34N 2°39W **21** C10
Newtownabbey *U.K.* 54°40N 5°56W **29** B10
Newtownards *U.K.* 54°36N 5°42W **29** B10
Newtownstewart *U.K.* 54°43N 7°23W **28** B7
Neyshābūr *Iran* 36°10N 58°50E **87** B9
Nganglong Kangri *China* 33°0N 81°0E **78** E5
Ngaoundéré *Cameroon* 7°15N 13°35E **96** C2
Ngoring Hu *China* 34°55N 97°5E **78** E8
Ngorongoro *Tanzania* 3°11S 35°32E **96** E7
Nguru *Nigeria* 12°56N 10°29E **95** F8
Nha Trang *Vietnam* 12°16N 109°10E **82** B3
Nhamundá → *Brazil* 2°12S 56°41W **120** C4
Niagara Falls *Canada* 43°7N 79°5W **109** E12
Niagara Falls *U.S.A.* 43°5N 79°4W **112** D8
Niamey *Niger* 13°27N 2°6E **94** F6
Nias *Indonesia* 1°0N 97°30E **82** D1
Nicaragua ■ *Cent. Amer.* 11°40N 85°30W **114** E7
Nicaragua, L. de *Nic.* 12°0N 85°30W **114** E7
Nice *France* 43°42N 7°14E **66** E7
Nicholasville *U.S.A.* 37°53N 84°34W **112** G5
Nicobar Is. *Ind. Oc.* 8°0N 93°30E **53** D14
Nicosia *Cyprus* 35°10N 33°25E **86** C3
Nicoya, Pen. de *Costa Rica* 9°45N 85°40W **114** F7
Nidd → *U.K.* 53°59N 1°23W **23** E6
Nidderdale *U.K.* 54°5N 1°46W **22** D5
Niedersachsen □ *Germany* 52°50N 9°0E **64** B5
Nieuw Nickerie *Suriname* 6°0N 56°59W **120** B4
Niğde *Turkey* 37°58N 34°40E **86** C3
Niger ■ *W. Afr.* 17°30N 10°0E **94** E7
Niger → *W. Afr.* 5°33N 6°33E **94** G7
Nigeria ■ *W. Afr.* 8°30N 8°0E **94** G7
Niigata *Japan* 37°58N 139°0E **81** E6
Ni'ihau *U.S.A.* 21°54N 160°9W **110** H14
Nijmegen *Neths.* 51°50N 5°52E **64** C3
Nikolayev *Ukraine* 46°58N 32°0E **71** E5
Nikolayevsk-na-Amur
  Russia 53°8N 140°44E **77** D15
Nikopol *Ukraine* 47°35N 34°25E **71** E5
Nikšić *Montenegro* 42°50N 18°57E **69** C8
Nile → *Africa* 30°10N 31°6E **95** B12
Nimach *India* 24°30N 74°56E **84** G9
Nîmes *France* 43°50N 4°23E **66** E6
Nimrūz □ *Afghan.* 30°0N 62°0E **87** D9
Nineveh *Iraq* 36°25N 43°10E **86** B5
Ninfield *U.K.* 50°53N 0°26E **25** E9
Ningbo *China* 29°51N 121°28E **79** F13
Ningjing Shan *China* 30°0N 98°20E **78** F8
Ningxia Hui □ *China* 38°0N 106°0E **78** D10
Niobrara → *U.S.A.* 42°46N 98°3W **110** B7
Niort *France* 46°19N 0°29W **66** C3
Nipawin *Canada* 53°20N 104°0W **108** D9
Nipigon *Canada* 49°0N 88°17W **112** A3
Nipigon, L. *Canada* 49°50N 88°30W **109** E11
Nipissing, L. *Canada* 46°20N 80°0W **109** E12
Niquelândia *Brazil* 14°33S 48°23W **122** B1
Niš *Serbia* 43°19N 21°58E **69** C9
Niterói *Brazil* 22°53S 43°7W **122** D2
Nith → *U.K.* 55°14N 3°33W **21** D8
Niton *U.K.* 50°35N 1°17W **24** E6
Nitra *Slovak Rep.* 48°19N 18°4E **65** D10
Nitra → *Slovak Rep.* 47°46N 18°10E **65** E10
Niuafo'ou *Tonga* 15°30S 175°58W **99** D15
Niue *Pac. Oc.* 19°2S 169°54W **99** D17
Nivernais *France* 47°15N 3°30E **66** C5
Nizamabad *India* 18°45N 78°7E **84** K11
Nizhnekamsk *Russia* 55°38N 51°49E **70** C9
Nizhnevartovsk *Russia* 60°56N 76°38E **76** C8
Nizhniy Novgorod *Russia* 56°20N 44°0E **70** C7
Nizhniy Tagil *Russia* 57°55N 59°57E **70** C10
Nizhyn *Ukraine* 51°5N 31°55E **71** D5
Nizwá *Oman* 22°56N 57°32E **89** C6
Nkawkaw *Ghana* 6°36N 0°49W **94** G5

Nkongsamba *Cameroon* 4°55N 9°55E **96** D1
Noakhali *Bangla.* 22°48N 91°10E **85** H17
Nobeoka *Japan* 32°36N 131°41E **81** G2
Noblesville *U.S.A.* 40°3N 86°1W **112** E5
Nogales *Mexico* 31°19N 110°56W **114** A2
Nogales *U.S.A.* 31°21N 110°56W **110** D4
Noirmoutier, Î. de *France* 46°58N 2°10W **66** C2
Nola *C.A.R.* 3°35N 16°4E **96** D3
Nome *U.S.A.* 64°30N 165°25W **108** C3
Nord-Ostsee-Kanal *Germany* 54°12N 9°32E **64** A5
Nordelph *U.K.* 52°35N 0°17E **25** A9
Norderstedt *Germany* 53°42N 10°1E **64** B5
Nordfriesische Inseln *Germany* 54°40N 8°20E **64** A5
Nordkapp *Norway* 71°10N 25°50E **63** C9
Nordrhein-Westfalen □
  Germany 51°45N 7°30E **64** C4
Nordvik *Russia* 74°2N 111°32E **77** B12
Nore → *Ireland* 52°25N 6°58W **31** D9
Norfolk *Nebr., U.S.A.* 42°2N 97°25W **111** B7
Norfolk *Va., U.S.A.* 36°50N 76°17W **111** C11
Norfolk □ *U.K.* 52°39N 0°54E **25** A10
Norfolk I. *Pac. Oc.* 28°58S 168°3E **99** F12
Norfolk Broads △ *U.K.* 52°45N 1°30E **25** A11
Norham *U.K.* 55°43N 2°9W **22** A4
Norilsk *Russia* 69°20N 88°6E **77** C9
Normal *U.S.A.* 40°31N 88°59W **112** E3
Norman *U.S.A.* 35°13N 97°26W **110** C7
Norman Wells *Canada* 65°17N 126°51W **108** C7
Normandie *France* 48°45N 0°10E **66** B4
Normanton *Australia* 17°40S 141°10E **98** D7
Normanton *U.K.* 53°42N 1°24W **23** E6
Norristown *U.S.A.* 40°7N 75°21W **113** E10
Norrköping *Sweden* 58°37N 16°11E **63** F7
Norrland *Sweden* 62°15N 15°45E **63** E7
Norseman *Australia* 32°8S 121°43E **98** G3
Norte, Serra do *Brazil* 11°20S 59°0W **120** D4
North, C. *Canada* 47°2N 60°20W **113** B17
North America 40°0N 100°0W **104** F10
North Ayrshire □ *U.K.* 55°45N 4°44W **20** C6
North Battleford *Canada* 52°50N 108°17W **108** D9
North Bay *Canada* 46°20N 79°30W **109** E12
North Berwick *U.K.* 56°4N 2°42W **21** B10
North C. *Canada* 47°5N 64°0W **113** B15
North C. *N.Z.* 34°23S 173°4E **99** G13
North Canadian → *U.S.A.* 35°22N 95°37W **110** C7
North Carolina □ *U.S.A.* 35°30N 80°0W **111** C11
North Cerney *U.K.* 51°45N 1°57W **24** C5
North Channel *Canada* 46°0N 83°0W **112** B6
North Channel *U.K.* 55°13N 5°52W **20** D4
North Dakota □ *U.S.A.* 47°30N 100°15W **110** A7
North Dorset Downs *U.K.* 50°51N 2°30W **24** E4
North Downs *U.K.* 51°19N 0°21E **25** D9
North Esk → *U.K.* 56°46N 2°24W **19** J13
North European Plain *Europe* 55°0N 25°0E **56** E10
North Foreland *U.K.* 51°22N 1°28E **25** D11
North Harris *U.K.* 58°0N 6°55W **18** F4
North Hill *U.K.* 50°33N 4°27W **27** F5
North Hykeham *U.K.* 53°11N 0°35W **23** F7
North I. *N.Z.* 38°0S 175°0E **99** H14
North Korea ■ *Asia* 40°0N 127°0E **79** D14
North Magnetic Pole *Arctic* 82°42N 114°24W **54** A2
North Minch *U.K.* 58°5N 5°55W **18** F6
North Molton *U.K.* 51°3N 3°49W **27** E6
North Ossetia □ *Russia* 43°30N 44°30E **71** F7
North Petherton *U.K.* 51°5N 3°1W **24** D2
North Platte *U.S.A.* 41°8N 100°46W **110** B6
North Platte → *U.S.A.* 41°7N 100°42W **110** B6
North Pole *Arctic* 90°0N 0°0 **54** A
North Pt. *Barbados* 13°20N 59°37W **115** g
North Ronaldsay *U.K.* 59°22N 2°26W **19** D13
North Saskatchewan →
  Canada 53°15N 105°5W **108** D9
North Sea *Europe* 56°0N 4°0E **56** D6
North Sea Canal = Nord-Ostsee-Kanal
  Germany 54°12N 9°32E **64** A5
North Somercotes *U.K.* 53°27N 0°8E **23** F9
North Sunderland *U.K.* 55°34N 1°40W **22** A5
North Tawton *U.K.* 50°48N 3°54W **27** F6
North Thompson →
  Canada 50°40N 120°20W **108** D7
North Thoresby *U.K.* 53°28N 0°4W **23** F8
North Tidworth *U.K.* 51°15N 1°40W **24** D5
North Tyne → *U.K.* 55°0N 2°8W **22** C4
North Uist *U.K.* 57°40N 7°15W **18** G3
North Vernon *U.S.A.* 39°0N 85°38W **112** F5
North Walsham *U.K.* 52°50N 1°22E **25** A11
North West C. *Australia* 21°45S 114°9E **98** E1
North West Frontier □ *Pakistan* 34°0N 72°0E **84** B8
North West Highlands *U.K.* 57°33N 4°58W **18** H8
North West River *Canada* 53°30N 60°10W **109** D13
North York Moors *U.K.* 54°23N 0°53W **22** D7
North York Moors △ *U.K.* 54°27N 0°51W **22** D7
North Yorkshire □ *U.K.* 54°15N 1°25W **22** D6
Northallerton *U.K.* 54°20N 1°26W **22** D6
Northam *Australia* 31°35S 116°42E **98** G2
Northam *U.K.* 51°2N 4°13W **27** E5
Northampton *U.K.* 52°15N 0°53W **25** B7
Northampton *U.S.A.* 42°19N 72°38W **113** D11
Northamptonshire □ *U.K.* 52°16N 0°55W **25** B7
Northern Areas □ *Pakistan* 36°30N 73°0E **84** B9
Northern Circars *India* 17°30N 82°30E **85** L13
Northern Ireland □ *U.K.* 54°45N 7°0W **29** B8
Northern Marianas ☑ *Pac. Oc.* 17°0N 145°0E **102** F6
Northern Sporades *Greece* 39°15N 23°30E **69** E10
Northern Territory □ *Australia* 20°0S 133°0E **98** E5
Northfleet *U.K.* 51°26N 0°20E **25** D9
Northiam *U.K.* 50°59N 0°36E **25** E10
Northleach *U.K.* 51°49N 1°50W **24** C5
Northrepps *U.K.* 52°54N 1°21E **25** A11
Northumberland □ *U.K.* 55°12N 2°0W **22** B4
Northumberland △ *Northumberland.,*
  U.K. 55°15N 2°20W **22** B4
Northumberland Str.
  Canada 46°20N 64°0W **109** E13
Northwest Territories □
  Canada 63°0N 118°0W **108** C8
Northwich *U.K.* 53°15N 2°31W **23** F3
Northwold *U.K.* 52°33N 0°36E **25** A9
Norton *N. Yorks., U.K.* 54°8N 0°47W **22** D7
Norton *Suffolk, U.K.* 52°16N 0°52E **25** B10

Norton Fitzwarren *U.K.* 51°1N 3°8W **24** D2
Norton Sd. *U.S.A.* 63°50N 164°0W **108** C3
Norwalk *U.S.A.* 41°15N 82°37W **112** E6
Norway ■ *Europe* 63°0N 11°0E **63** E6
Norway House *Canada* 53°59N 97°50W **108** D10
Norwegian B. *Canada* 77°30N 90°0W **109** B11
Norwegian Sea *Atl. Oc.* 66°0N 1°0E **56** B6
Norwich *U.K.* 52°38N 1°18E **25** A11
Norwich *U.S.A.* 42°32N 75°32W **113** D10
Noss Hd. *U.K.* 58°28N 3°3W **19** F11
Nossa Senhora do Socorro
  Brazil 10°52S 37°7W **122** B3
Nossob → *S. Africa* 26°55S 20°45E **97** K4
Notre Dame B. *Canada* 49°45N 55°30W **109** E14
Nottaway → *Canada* 51°22N 78°55W **109** D12
Nottingham *U.K.* 52°58N 1°10W **23** G6
Nottingham I. *Canada* 63°20N 77°55W **109** C12
Nottinghamshire □ *U.K.* 53°10N 1°3W **23** F6
Nouâdhibou *Mauritania* 20°54N 17°0W **94** D2
Nouâdhibou, Râs *Mauritania* 20°50N 17°0W **94** D2
Nouakchott *Mauritania* 18°9N 15°58W **94** E2
Nouméa *N. Cal.* 22°17S 166°30E **99** E12
Nova Friburgo *Brazil* 22°16S 42°30W **122** D2
Nova Iguaçu *Brazil* 22°45S 43°28W **122** D2
Nova Scotia □ *Canada* 45°10N 63°0W **113** C16
Nova Venécia *Brazil* 18°45S 40°24W **122** C2
Novara *Italy* 45°28N 8°38E **68** B3
Novaya Zemlya *Russia* 75°0N 56°0E **76** B6
Novi Pazar *Serbia* 43°12N 20°28E **69** C9
Novi Sad *Serbia* 45°18N 19°52E **69** B8
Novocherkassk *Russia* 47°27N 40°15E **71** E7
Novokuybyshevsk *Russia* 53°7N 49°58E **70** D8
Novokuznetsk *Russia* 53°45N 87°10E **76** D9
Novomoskovsk *Russia* 54°5N 38°15E **70** D6
Novorossiysk *Russia* 44°43N 37°46E **71** F6
Novoshakhtinsk *Russia* 47°46N 39°58E **71** E6
Novosibirsk *Russia* 55°0N 83°5E **76** D9
Novotroitsk *Russia* 51°10N 58°15E **70** D10
Novyy Urengoy *Russia* 65°48N 76°52E **76** C8
Nowy Sącz *Poland* 49°40N 20°41E **65** D11
Noyabrsk *Russia* 64°34N 76°21E **76** C8
Nubia *Africa* 21°0N 32°0E **90** D7
Nubian Desert *Sudan* 21°30N 33°30E **95** D12
Nueces → *U.S.A.* 27°51N 97°30W **110** E7
Nueltin L. *Canada* 60°30N 99°30W **108** C10
Nueva Rosita *Mexico* 27°57N 101°13W **114** B4
Nuevitas *Cuba* 21°30N 77°20W **115** C9
Nuevo Laredo *Mexico* 27°30N 99°31W **114** B5
Nuku'alofa *Tonga* 21°10S 175°12W **99** E16
Nukulaelae *Tuvalu* 9°23S 179°52E **99** B14
Nukus *Uzbekistan* 42°27N 59°41E **87** A9
Nullarbor Plain *Australia* 31°10S 129°0E **98** G4
Numan *Nigeria* 9°29N 12°3E **95** G8
Numazu *Japan* 35°7N 138°51E **81** F6
Nunavut □ *Canada* 66°0N 85°0W **109** C11
Nuneaton *U.K.* 52°32N 1°27W **23** G6
Nunivak I. *U.S.A.* 60°10N 166°30W **108** B3
Nunney *U.K.* 51°12N 2°22W **24** D4
Núoro *Italy* 40°20N 9°20E **68** D3
Nuremberg *Germany* 49°27N 11°3E **64** D6
Nusaybin *Turkey* 37°3N 41°10E **71** G7
Nuuk *Greenland* 64°10N 51°35W **54** C5
Nuweveldberge *S. Africa* 32°10S 21°45E **97** L4
Nyagan *Russia* 62°30N 65°38E **76** C7
Nyahururu *Kenya* 0°2N 36°27E **96** D7
Nyainqêntanglha Shan *China* 30°0N 90°0E **78** F7
Nyâlâ *Sudan* 12°2N 24°58E **95** F10
Nyíregyháza *Hungary* 47°58N 21°47E **65** E11
Nysa *Poland* 50°30N 17°22E **65** C9
Nzérékoré *Guinea* 7°49N 8°48W **94** G4**

O

Oa, Mull of *U.K.* 55°35N 6°20W **20** C3
Oadby *U.K.* 52°36N 1°5W **23** G6
Oahe, L. *U.S.A.* 44°27N 100°24W **110** A6
O'ahu *U.S.A.* 21°28N 157°58W **110** H16
Oak Hill *U.S.A.* 37°59N 81°9W **112** G7
Oak Ridge *U.S.A.* 36°1N 84°16W **111** C10
Oakengates *U.K.* 52°41N 2°26W **23** G4
Oakham *U.K.* 52°40N 0°43W **23** G7
Oakland *U.S.A.* 37°48N 122°18W **110** C2
Oates Land *Antarctica* 69°0S 160°0E **55** C11
Oaxaca *Mexico* 17°3N 96°43W **114** D5
Ob → *Russia* 66°45N 69°30E **76** C7
Ob, G. of *Russia* 69°0N 73°0E **76** C8
Oba *Canada* 49°4N 84°7W **109** E11
Oban *U.K.* 56°25N 5°29W **20** B5
Oberhausen *Germany* 51°28N 6°51E **64** C4
Obi, Kepulauan *Indonesia* 1°23S 127°45E **83** E7
Óbidos *Brazil* 1°50S 55°30W **120** C4
Obihiro *Japan* 42°56N 143°12E **81** B8
Obozerskiy *Russia* 63°34N 40°21E **70** B7
Obshchi Syrt *Russia* 52°0N 53°0E **56** E16
Ocala *U.S.A.* 29°11N 82°8W **111** E10
Occidental, Cordillera *Colombia* 5°0N 76°0W **117** C3
Occidental, Grand Erg *Algeria* 30°20N 1°0E **94** B6
Ocean City *U.S.A.* 39°17N 74°35W **113** F10
Oceanside *U.S.A.* 33°12N 117°23W **110** D3
Ochil Hills *U.K.* 56°14N 3°40W **21** B8
Ocho Rios *Jamaica* 18°24N 77°6W **114** a
Oconto *U.S.A.* 44°53N 87°52W **112** C4
Odawara *Japan* 35°20N 139°6E **81** F6
Odense *Denmark* 55°22N 10°23E **63** F6
Oder → *Europe* 53°33N 14°38E **64** B8
Odesa *Ukraine* 46°30N 30°45E **71** E5
Odessa *U.S.A.* 31°52N 102°23W **110** D6
Odiham *U.K.* 51°15N 0°55W **25** D7
Odzi *Zimbabwe* 19°0S 32°20E **97** H6
Offa *Nigeria* 8°13N 4°42E **94** G6
Offaly □ *Ireland* 53°15N 7°30W **31** B8
Offenbach *Germany* 50°6N 8°44E **64** C5
Ogaden *Ethiopia* 7°30N 45°30E **89** F3
Ōgaki *Japan* 35°21N 136°37E **81** F5
Ogbomosho *Nigeria* 8°1N 4°11E **94** G6
Ogden *U.S.A.* 41°13N 111°58W **110** B4
Ogdensburg *U.S.A.* 44°42N 75°30W **113** C10

Ogooué → *Gabon* 1°0S 9°0E **96** E1
Ohio □ *U.S.A.* 40°15N 82°45W **112** E5
Ohio → *U.S.A.* 36°59N 89°8W **111** C8
Ohře → *Czech Rep.* 50°30N 14°10E **64** C8
Oil City *U.S.A.* 41°26N 79°42W **112** E8
Oise → *France* 49°0N 2°4E **66** B5
Oistins *Barbados* 13°4N 59°33W **115** g
Oistins B. *Barbados* 13°4N 59°33W **115** g
Ōita *Japan* 33°14N 131°36E **81** G2
Ojos del Salado, Cerro
  Argentina 27°0S 68°40W **121** E3
Oka → *Russia* 56°20N 43°59E **70** C7
Okara *Pakistan* 30°50N 73°31E **84** D8
Okavango Delta *Botswana* 18°45S 22°45E **97** H4
Okayama *Japan* 34°40N 133°54E **81** F3
Okazaki *Japan* 34°57N 137°10E **81** F5
Okeechobee, L. *U.S.A.* 27°0N 80°50W **111** E10
Okehampton *U.K.* 50°44N 4°0W **27** F5
Okhotsk *Russia* 59°20N 143°10E **77** D15
Okhotsk, Sea of *Asia* 55°0N 145°0E **77** D15
Oki-Shotō *Japan* 36°5N 133°15E **81** E3
Okinawa-Jima *Japan* 26°32N 128°0E **79** F14
Oklahoma □ *U.S.A.* 35°20N 97°30W **110** C7
Oklahoma City *U.S.A.* 35°30N 97°30W **110** C7
Oktyabrskiy *Russia* 54°28N 53°28E **70** D9
Öland *Sweden* 56°45N 16°38E **63** F7
Olavarria *Argentina* 36°55S 60°20W **121** F3
Ólbia *Italy* 40°55N 9°31E **68** D3
Old Basing *U.K.* 51°16N 1°3W **24** D6
Old Crow *Canada* 67°30N 139°55W **108** C6
Old Fletton *U.K.* 52°33N 0°14W **25** A8
Old Leake *U.K.* 53°2N 0°5E **23** F9
Old Town *U.S.A.* 44°56N 68°39W **113** C13
Oldbury *U.K.* 51°38N 2°33W **24** C4
Oldcastle *Ireland* 53°46N 7°10W **29** D7
Oldenburg *Germany* 53°9N 8°13E **64** B5
Oldham *U.K.* 53°33N 2°7W **23** E4
Oldmeldrum *U.K.* 57°20N 2°19W **19** H13
Olean *U.S.A.* 42°5N 78°26W **112** D8
Olekminsk *Russia* 60°25N 120°30E **77** C13
Olenek → *Russia* 73°0N 120°10E **77** B13
Oléron, Î. d' *France* 45°55N 1°15W **66** D3
Ólgiy *Mongolia* 48°56N 89°57E **78** B6
Olimpia *Brazil* 20°44S 48°54W **122** D1
Oliveira *Brazil* 20°39S 44°50W **122** D2
Ollagüe *Chile* 21°15S 68°10W **120** E3
Ollerton *U.K.* 53°12N 1°1W **23** F6
Olmaliq *Uzbekistan* 40°50N 69°35E **76** E7
Olney *U.K.* 52°10N 0°41W **25** B7
Olney *U.S.A.* 38°44N 88°5W **112** F3
Olomouc *Czech Rep.* 49°38N 17°12E **65** D9
Olsztyn *Poland* 53°48N 20°29E **65** B11
Olt → *Romania* 43°43N 24°51E **65** G13
Olympia *Greece* 37°39N 21°39E **69** F9
Olympia *U.S.A.* 47°3N 122°53W **110** A2
Olympus, Mt. *Greece* 40°6N 22°23E **69** D10
Olympus, Mt. *U.S.A.* 47°48N 123°43W **110** A2
Omagh *U.K.* 54°36N 7°19W **28** B7
Omaha *U.S.A.* 41°17N 95°58W **111** B7
Oman ■ *Asia* 23°0N 58°0E **89** C6
Oman, G. of *Asia* 24°30N 58°30E **87** E9
Ombersley *U.K.* 52°16N 2°13W **24** B4
Omdurmân *Sudan* 15°40N 32°28E **95** E12
Ometepec *Mexico* 16°41N 98°25W **114** D5
Omsk *Russia* 55°0N 73°12E **76** D8
Ōmuta *Japan* 33°5N 130°26E **81** G2
Ondangwa *Namibia* 17°57S 16°4E **97** H3
Öndörhaan *Mongolia* 47°19N 110°39E **79** B11
Onega → *Russia* 63°58N 38°2E **70** B6
Onega, L. *Russia* 61°44N 35°22E **70** B6
Onega B. *Russia* 64°24N 36°38E **70** B6
O'Neill *U.S.A.* 42°27N 98°39W **110** B7
Oneonta *U.S.A.* 42°27N 75°4W **113** D10
Onitsha *Nigeria* 6°6N 6°42E **94** G7
Onny → *U.K.* 52°24N 2°47W **23** G3
Onslow B. *U.S.A.* 34°20N 77°15W **111** D11
Ontario *Canada* 44°2N 116°58W **110** B3
Ontario □ *Canada* 48°0N 83°0W **109** E11
Ontario, L. *N. Amer.* 43°20N 78°0W **112** D8
Ontonagon *U.S.A.* 46°52N 89°19W **112** B31
Oostende *Belgium* 51°15N 2°54E **64** C2
Opava *Czech Rep.* 49°57N 17°58E **65** D9
Opole *Poland* 50°42N 17°58E **65** C9
Oradea *Romania* 47°2N 21°58E **65** E11
Öræfajökull *Iceland* 64°2N 16°39W **63** B2
Oral *Kazakhstan* 51°20N 51°20E **71** D9
Oran *Algeria* 35°45N 0°39W **94** A5
Orange *Australia* 33°15S 149°7E **98** G8
Orange *France* 44°8N 4°47E **66** D6
Orange *U.S.A.* 38°15N 78°7W **112** F8
Orange → *S. Africa* 28°41S 16°28E **97** K3
Orange, C. *Brazil* 4°20N 51°30W **120** B4
Orangeburg *U.S.A.* 33°30N 80°52W **111** D10
Orangeville *Canada* 43°55N 80°5W **112** D7
Ordos Desert *China* 39°0N 109°0E **79** D10
Ordu *Turkey* 40°55N 37°53E **71** F6
Örebro *Sweden* 59°20N 15°18E **63** F7
Oregon □ *U.S.A.* 44°0N 121°0W **110** B2
Orekhovo-Zuyevo *Russia* 55°50N 38°55E **70** C6
Orel *Russia* 52°57N 36°3E **70** D6
Orem *U.S.A.* 40°19N 111°42W **110** B4
Orenburg *Russia* 51°45N 55°6E **70** D10
Orford *U.K.* 52°5N 1°35E **25** B12
Orford Ness *U.K.* 52°5N 1°35E **25** B12
Orhon Gol → *Mongolia* 50°21N 106°0E **78** A10
Oriental, Cordillera *Colombia* 6°0N 73°0W **117** C3
Oriental, Grand Erg *Algeria* 30°0N 6°30E **94** B7
Orihuela *Spain* 38°7N 0°55W **67** C5
Orinoco → *Venezuela* 9°15N 61°30W **120** B3
Orissa □ *India* 20°0N 84°0E **85** K14
Oristano *Italy* 39°54N 8°36E **68** E3
Orizaba *Mexico* 18°51N 97°6W **114** D5
Orizaba, Pico de *Mexico* 18°58N 97°15W **114** D5
Orkney □ *U.K.* 59°2N 3°13W **19** D11
Orkney Is. *U.K.* 59°0N 3°0W **19** E12
Orlando *U.S.A.* 28°32N 81°22W **111** E10
Orléanais *France* 48°0N 2°0E **66** C5
Orléans *France* 47°54N 1°52E **66** C4

Orléans, Î. d'   Poole

Orléans, Î. d' *Canada*	46°54N 70°58W **113** B12
Ormara *Pakistan*	25°16N 64°33E **84** G4
Ormesby St. Margaret *U.K.*	52°41N 1°41E **25** A12
Ormoc *Phil.*	11°0N 124°37E **83** B6
Ormskirk *U.K.*	53°35N 2°54W **23** E3
Örnsköldsvik *Sweden*	63°17N 18°40E **63** E7
Oronsay *U.K.*	56°1N 6°15W **20** B3
Orsha *Belarus*	54°30N 30°25E **70** D5
Ortegal, C. *Spain*	43°43N 7°52W **67** A2
Oruro *Bolivia*	18°0S 67°9W **120** D3
Oruzgän □ *Afghan.*	33°0N 66°0E **87** C11
Orwell → *U.K.*	51°59N 1°18E **25** C11
Ōsaka *Japan*	34°42N 135°30E **81** F4
Osh *Kyrgyzstan*	40°37N 72°49E **76** E8
Oshakati *Namibia*	17°45S 15°40E **97** H3
Oshawa *Canada*	43°50N 78°50W **109** E12
Oshkosh *U.S.A.*	44°1N 88°33W **112** C3
Oshogbo *Nigeria*	7°48N 4°37E **94** G6
Osijek *Croatia*	45°34N 18°41E **69** B8
Osizweni *S. Africa*	27°49S 30°7E **97** K6
Oskaloosa *U.S.A.*	41°18N 92°39W **111** B81
Oskarshamn *Sweden*	57°15N 16°27E **63** F7
Öskemen *Kazakhstan*	50°0N 82°36E **76** E9
Oslo *Norway*	59°54N 10°43E **63** F6
Oslofjorden *Norway*	59°20N 10°35E **63** F6
Osmaniye *Turkey*	37°5N 36°10E **71** G6
Osmotherley *U.K.*	54°22N 1°18W **22** D6
Osnabrück *Germany*	52°17N 8°3E **64** B5
Osorno *Chile*	40°25S 73°0W **121** G2
Ossa, Mt. *Australia*	41°52S 146°3E **98** J8
Ossett *U.K.*	53°41N 1°34W **23** E5
Ostend = Oostende *Belgium*	51°15N 2°54E **64** C2
Österdalälven → *Sweden*	60°30N 15°7E **63** E6
Östersund *Sweden*	63°10N 14°38E **63** E6
Ostfriesische Inseln *Germany*	53°42N 7°0E **64** B4
Ostrava *Czech Rep.*	49°51N 18°18E **65** D10
Ostrołęka *Poland*	53°4N 21°32E **65** B11
Ostrów Wielkopolski *Poland*	51°36N 17°44E **65** C9
Ostrowiec-Świętokrzyski *Poland*	50°55N 21°22E **65** C11
Oswaldtwistle *U.K.*	53°43N 2°26W **23** E4
Oswego *U.S.A.*	43°27N 76°31W **112** D9
Oswestry *U.K.*	52°52N 3°3W **23** G2
Otaru *Japan*	43°10N 141°0E **81** B7
Otjiwarongo *Namibia*	20°30S 16°33E **97** J3
Otley *U.K.*	53°54N 1°41W **23** E5
Otranto *Italy*	40°9N 18°28E **69** D8
Otranto, Str. of *Italy*	40°15N 18°40E **69** D8
Ōtsu *Japan*	35°0N 135°50E **81** F4
Ottawa *Canada*	45°26N 75°42W **113** C10
Ottawa *U.S.A.*	41°21N 88°51W **112** E13
Ottawa Is. *Canada*	59°35N 80°10W **109** D11
Otter → *U.K.*	50°38N 3°19W **27** F7
Otterburn *U.K.*	55°14N 2°11W **22** B4
Ottery St. Mary *U.K.*	50°44N 3°17W **27** F7
Ottumwa *U.S.A.*	41°1N 92°25W **111** B81
Ouachita → *U.S.A.*	31°38N 91°49W **111** D8
Ouachita Mts. *U.S.A.*	34°30N 94°30W **111** D8
Ouagadougou *Burkina Faso*	12°25N 1°30W **94** F5
Oubangi → *Dem. Rep. of the Congo*	0°30S 17°50E **96** E3
Oudtshoorn *S. Africa*	33°35S 22°14E **97** L4
Ouezzane *Morocco*	34°51N 5°35W **94** B4
Oughterard *Ireland*	53°26N 9°18W **30** B4
Oujda *Morocco*	34°41N 1°55W **94** B5
Oulton *U.K.*	52°30N 1°43E **25** B12
Oulton Broad *U.K.*	52°28N 1°42E **25** B12
Oulu *Finland*	65°1N 25°29E **63** D9
Oulujärvi *Finland*	64°25N 27°15E **63** E9
Oulujoki → *Finland*	65°1N 25°30E **63** D9
Oundle *U.K.*	52°29N 0°28W **25** B8
Ourense *Spain*	42°19N 7°55W **67** A2
Ouro Fino *Brazil*	22°16S 46°25W **122** D1
Ouro Prêto *Brazil*	20°20S 43°30W **122** D2
Ouse → *E. Sussex, U.K.*	50°47N 0°4E **25** E9
Ouse → *N. Yorks., U.K.*	53°44N 0°55W **23** E7
Outaouais → *Canada*	45°27N 74°8W **109** E12
Outer Hebrides *U.K.*	57°30N 7°40W **18** H2
Outjo *Namibia*	20°5S 16°7E **97** J3
Outwell *U.K.*	52°37N 0°14E **25** A9
Ovalle *Chile*	30°33S 71°18W **121** F2
Ovamboland *Namibia*	18°30S 16°0E **97** H3
Over Wallop *U.K.*	51°9N 1°36W **24** D5
Overton *U.K.*	51°15N 1°15W **24** D6
Oviedo *Spain*	43°25N 5°50W **67** A3
Owatonna *U.S.A.*	44°5N 93°14W **111** B8
Owen Sound *Canada*	44°35N 80°55W **109** E11
Owen Stanley Ra. *Papua N. G.*	8°30S 147°0E **98** B8
Owens → *U.S.A.*	36°26N 117°57W **110** C3
Owensboro *U.S.A.*	37°46N 87°7W **112** G4
Owo *Nigeria*	7°10N 5°39E **94** G7
Owosso *U.S.A.*	43°0N 84°10W **112** D5
Owston Ferry *U.K.*	53°29N 0°47W **23** F7
Owyhee → *U.S.A.*	43°49N 117°2W **110** B3
Oxford *U.K.*	51°46N 1°15W **24** C6
Oxfordshire □ *U.K.*	51°48N 1°16W **24** C6
Oxnard *U.S.A.*	34°12N 119°11W **110** D3
Oyama *Japan*	36°18N 139°48E **81** E6
Oyem *Gabon*	1°34N 11°31E **96** D2
Oykel → *U.K.*	57°56N 4°26W **19** G9
Oyo *Nigeria*	7°46N 3°56E **94** G6
Ozark Plateau *U.S.A.*	37°20N 91°40W **111** C81
Ozarks, L. of the *U.S.A.*	38°12N 92°38W **111** C81

P

Paarl *S. Africa*	33°45S 18°56E **97** L3
Pab Hills *Pakistan*	26°30N 66°45E **84** F5
Pabbay *U.K.*	57°46N 7°14W **18** G3
Pabna *Bangla.*	24°1N 89°18E **85** G16
Pacaraima, Sa. *S. Amer.*	4°0N 62°30W **120** B3
Pacasmayo *Peru*	7°20S 79°35W **120** C2
Pachuca *Mexico*	20°7N 98°44W **114** C5
Pacific Ocean	10°0N 140°0W **103** G14
Padang *Indonesia*	1°0S 100°20E **82** E2
Padangsidempuan *Indonesia*	1°30N 99°15E **82** D1
Paddock Wood *U.K.*	51°11N 0°24E **25** D9
Paderborn *Germany*	51°42N 8°45E **64** C5
Padiham *U.K.*	53°48N 2°18W **23** E4
Padre I. *U.S.A.*	27°10N 97°25W **111** E7

Padstow *U.K.*	50°33N 4°58W **27** F4
Padstow B. *U.K.*	50°34N 4°57W **27** F4
Padua *Italy*	45°25N 11°53E **68** B4
Pag *Croatia*	44°25N 15°3E **68** B6
Pagadian *Phil.*	7°55N 123°30E **83** C6
Page *U.S.A.*	36°57N 111°27W **110** C4
Pähala *U.S.A.*	19°12N 155°29W **110** J17
Paignton *U.K.*	50°26N 3°35W **27** G6
Paine Grande, Cerro *Chile*	50°59S 73°4W **121** H2
Painesville *U.S.A.*	41°43N 81°15W **112** E7
Painswick *U.K.*	51°47N 2°10W **24** C4
Painted Desert *U.S.A.*	36°0N 111°0W **110** C4
Paintsville *U.S.A.*	37°49N 82°48W **112** G6
País Vasco □ *Spain*	42°50N 2°45W **67** A4
Paisley *U.K.*	55°50N 4°25W **20** C7
Paita *Peru*	5°11S 81°9W **120** C1
Pakistan ■ *Asia*	30°0N 70°0E **84** E7
Paktiā □ *Afghan.*	33°30N 69°15E **87** C12
Pakxe *Laos*	15°5N 105°52E **82** A3
Palagruža *Croatia*	42°24N 16°15E **68** C7
Palani Hills *India*	10°14N 77°33E **84** P10
Palanpur *India*	24°10N 72°25E **84** G8
Palapye *Botswana*	22°30S 27°7E **97** J5
Palau ■ *Palau*	7°30N 134°30E **102** G5
Palawan *Phil.*	9°30N 118°30E **82** C5
Palembang *Indonesia*	3°0S 104°50E **82** E2
Palencia *Spain*	42°1N 4°34W **67** A3
Palermo *Italy*	38°7N 13°22E **68** E5
Palestine *U.S.A.*	31°46N 95°38W **111** D7
Palghat *India*	10°46N 76°42E **84** P10
Palgrave *U.K.*	52°22N 1°6E **25** B11
Pali *India*	25°50N 73°20E **84** G8
Palikir *Micronesia*	6°55N 158°9E **102** G7
Palk Strait *Asia*	10°0N 79°45E **84** Q11
Palm Springs *U.S.A.*	33°50N 116°33W **110** D3
Palma de Mallorca *Spain*	39°35N 2°39E **67** C7
Palmares *Brazil*	8°41S 35°28W **122** A3
Palmas *Brazil*	10°12S 48°21W **122** B1
Palmas, C. *Liberia*	4°27N 7°46W **94** H4
Palmeira dos Índios *Brazil*	9°25S 36°37W **122** A3
Palmer *U.S.A.*	61°36N 149°7W **108** C5
Palmer Land *Antarctica*	73°0S 63°0W **55** D18
Palmerston North *N.Z.*	40°21S 175°39E **99** J14
Palmira *Colombia*	3°32N 76°16W **120** B2
Palmyra *Syria*	34°36N 38°15E **86** C4
Palmyra Is. *Pac. Oc.*	5°52N 162°5W **103** G11
Palopo *Indonesia*	3°0S 120°16E **83** E6
Palu *Indonesia*	1°0S 119°52E **83** E5
Palu *Turkey*	38°45N 40°0E **71** G7
Pamiers *France*	43°7N 1°39E **66** E4
Pamir *Tajikistan*	37°40N 73°0E **87** B13
Pamlico Sd. *U.S.A.*	35°20N 76°0W **111** C11
Pampa *U.S.A.*	35°32N 100°58W **110** C6
Pampas *Argentina*	35°0S 63°0W **121** F3
Pamplona-Iruña *Spain*	42°48N 1°38W **67** A5
Panaji *India*	39°23N 89°5W **112** F3
Panaji *India*	15°25N 73°50E **84** M8
Panama ■ *Cent. Amer.*	8°48N 79°55W **115** F9
Panamá, G. de *Panama*	8°4N 79°20W **115** F9
Panama, Isthmus of *Cent. Amer.*	9°0N 79°0W **115** F9
Panama Canal *Panama*	9°10N 79°37W **115** F9
Panama City *U.S.A.*	30°10N 85°40W **111** D9
Panay *Phil.*	11°10N 122°30E **83** B6
Pančevo *Serbia*	44°52N 20°41E **69** B9
Panevėžys *Lithuania*	55°42N 24°25E **63** F8
Pangani *Tanzania*	5°25S 38°58E **96** F7
Pangbourne *U.K.*	51°29N 1°6W **24** D6
Pangkalpinang *Indonesia*	2°0S 106°0E **82** E3
Pangnirtung *Canada*	66°8N 65°43W **109** C13
Pantar *Indonesia*	8°28S 124°10E **83** F6
Pante Macassar *E. Timor*	9°30S 123°58E **83** F6
Pantelleria *Italy*	36°50N 11°57E **68** F4
Panzhihua *China*	26°33N 101°44E **78** F9
Papa Stour *U.K.*	60°20N 1°42W **18** B14
Papa Westray *U.K.*	59°20N 2°55W **19** D12
Papeete *Tahiti*	17°32S 149°34W **103** J13
Paphos *Cyprus*	34°46N 32°25E **86** C3
Papua □ *Indonesia*	4°0S 137°0E **83** E9
Papua, G. of *Papua N. G.*	9°0S 144°50E **98** B7
Papua New Guinea ■ *Oceania*	8°0S 145°0E **98** B8
Pará □ *Brazil*	3°20S 52°0W **120** C4
Paracatu *Brazil*	17°10S 46°50W **122** C1
Paracel Is. *S. China Sea*	15°50N 112°0E **82** A4
Paragould *U.S.A.*	36°3N 90°29W **111** C81
Paraguaçú → *Brazil*	12°45S 38°54W **122** B3
Paraguaná, Pen. de *Venezuela*	12°0N 70°0W **120** A3
Paraguarí *Paraguay*	25°36S 57°0W **121** E4
Paraguay ■ *S. Amer.*	23°0S 57°0W **121** E4
Paraguay → *Paraguay*	27°18S 58°38W **121** E4
Paraíba □ *Brazil*	7°0S 36°0W **120** C6
Parakou *Benin*	9°25N 2°40E **94** G6
Paramaribo *Suriname*	5°50N 55°10W **120** B4
Paraná *Argentina*	31°45S 60°30W **121** F3
Paraná □ *Brazil*	12°30S 47°48W **122** B1
Paraná □ *Brazil*	24°30S 51°0W **121** E4
Paraná → *Argentina*	33°43S 59°15W **121** F4
Paranaguá *Brazil*	25°30S 48°30W **122** E1
Paranaíba → *Brazil*	20°6S 51°4W **120** E4
Paranapanema → *Brazil*	22°40S 53°9W **121** E4
Parbhani *India*	19°8N 76°52E **84** K10
Pardo → *Brazil*	15°40S 39°0W **122** C3
Pardubice *Czech Rep.*	50°3N 15°45E **64** C8
Parecis, Serra dos *Brazil*	13°0S 60°0W **120** D4
Parepare *Indonesia*	4°0S 119°40E **83** E5
Parima, Serra *Brazil*	2°30N 64°0W **120** B3
Pariñas, Pta. *Peru*	4°30S 82°0W **117** D2
Parintins *Brazil*	2°40S 56°50W **120** C4
Paripiri Kyun *Burma*	14°52N 93°41E **85** M18
Paris *France*	48°53N 2°20E **66** B5
Paris *U.S.A.*	33°40N 95°33W **111** D7
Park Falls *U.S.A.*	45°56N 90°27W **112** C2
Parkersburg *U.S.A.*	39°16N 81°34W **112** F7
Parla *Spain*	40°14N 3°46W **67** B4
Parma *Italy*	44°48N 10°20E **68** B4
Parnaguá *Brazil*	10°10S 44°38W **122** B2
Parnaíba *Brazil*	2°54S 41°47W **120** C5
Parnaíba → *Brazil*	3°0S 41°50W **120** C5

Pärnu *Estonia*	58°28N 24°33E **63** F8
Paros *Greece*	37°5N 25°12E **69** F11
Parracombe *U.K.*	51°11N 3°56W **27** E6
Parrett → *U.K.*	51°12N 3°1W **24** D2
Parry Is. *Canada*	77°0N 110°0W **109** B9
Parry Sound *Canada*	45°20N 80°0W **109** E12
Parsons *U.S.A.*	37°20N 95°16W **111** C7
Partney *U.K.*	53°12N 0°7E **23** F9
Parton *U.K.*	54°35N 3°33W **22** C1
Partry Mts. *Ireland*	53°40N 9°28W **28** D3
Paru → *Brazil*	1°33S 52°38W **120** C4
Parván □ *Afghan.*	35°0N 69°0E **87** C12
Pas, The *Canada*	53°45N 101°15W **108** D9
Pasadena *Calif., U.S.A.*	34°9N 118°8W **110** D3
Pasadena *Tex., U.S.A.*	29°43N 95°13W **111** E7
Pascua, I. de *Chile*	27°7S 109°23W **103** K17
Paso Robles *U.S.A.*	35°38N 120°41W **110** C2
Passage West *Ireland*	51°52N 8°21W **30** E6
Passau *Germany*	48°34N 13°28E **64** D7
Passo Fundo *Brazil*	28°10S 52°20W **121** E4
Passos *Brazil*	20°45S 46°37W **122** D1
Pastaza → *Peru*	4°50S 76°52W **120** C2
Pasto *Colombia*	1°13N 77°17W **120** B2
Patagonia *Argentina*	45°0S 69°0W **121** G3
Patan *India*	23°54N 72°14E **84** H8
Pateley Bridge *U.K.*	54°5N 1°44W **22** D5
Paterson *U.S.A.*	40°54N 74°9W **113** E10
Pathankot *India*	32°18N 75°45E **84** C9
Pathfinder Res. *U.S.A.*	42°28N 106°51W **110** B5
Patiala *India*	30°23N 76°26E **84** D10
Patkai Bum *India*	27°0N 95°30E **85** F19
Patmos *Greece*	37°21N 26°36E **69** F12
Patna *India*	25°35N 85°12E **85** G14
Patos *Brazil*	6°55S 37°16W **120** C6
Patos, L. dos *Brazil*	31°20S 51°0W **121** F4
Patos de Minas *Brazil*	18°35S 46°32W **122** C1
Patra *Greece*	38°14N 21°47E **69** E9
Patrington *U.K.*	53°41N 0°1W **23** E8
Patrocínio *Brazil*	18°57S 47°0W **122** C1
Patten *U.S.A.*	46°0N 68°38W **113** C13
Patterdale *U.K.*	54°32N 2°56W **22** C3
Pau *France*	43°19N 0°25W **66** E3
Paulatuk *Canada*	69°25N 124°0W **108** C7
Paulistana *Brazil*	8°9S 41°9W **122** A2
Paull *U.K.*	53°44N 0°14W **23** E8
Paulo Afonso *Brazil*	9°21S 38°15W **122** A3
Pavia *Italy*	45°7N 9°8E **68** B3
Pavlodar *Kazakhstan*	52°33N 77°0E **76** D8
Pavlohrad *Ukraine*	48°30N 35°52E **71** E6
Pavlovo *Russia*	55°58N 43°5E **70** C7
Pawtucket *U.S.A.*	41°53N 71°23W **113** E12
Paxton *U.S.A.*	40°27N 88°6W **112** E3
Payakumbuh *Indonesia*	0°20S 100°35E **82** E2
Payette *U.S.A.*	44°5N 116°56W **110** B3
Payne L. *Canada*	59°30N 74°30W **109** D12
Paysandú *Uruguay*	32°19S 58°8W **121** F4
Payson *U.S.A.*	34°14N 111°20W **110** D4
Paz, B. de la *Mexico*	24°9N 110°25W **114** C2
Pazardzhik *Bulgaria*	42°12N 24°20E **69** C11
Peace → *Canada*	59°0N 111°25W **108** D8
Peace River *Canada*	56°15N 117°18W **108** D8
Peacehaven *U.K.*	50°48N 0°0 **25** E8
Peak District *U.K.*	53°24N 1°46W **23** F5
Pearl City *U.S.A.*	21°24N 157°59W **110** H16
Pearl Harbor *U.S.A.*	21°21N 157°57W **110** H16
Peasenhall *U.K.*	52°16N 1°27E **25** B11
Peawanuck *Canada*	55°15N 85°12W **109** D11
Pechora *Russia*	65°10N 57°11E **70** A10
Pechora → *Russia*	68°13N 54°15E **70** A9
Pechora B. *Russia*	68°40N 54°0E **70** A9
Pecos *U.S.A.*	31°26N 103°30W **110** D6
Pecos → *U.S.A.*	29°42N 101°22W **110** E6
Pécs *Hungary*	46°5N 18°15E **65** E10
Pedra Azul *Brazil*	16°2S 41°17W **122** C2
Pedro Afonso *Brazil*	9°0S 48°10W **122** A1
Peebles *U.K.*	55°40N 3°11W **21** C9
Peel I. of Man	54°13N 4°40W **29** C12
Peel → *Canada*	67°0N 135°0W **108** C6
Peel Fell *U.K.*	55°18N 2°34W **22** B5
Peel Sd. *Canada*	73°0N 96°0W **108** B10
Pegswood *U.K.*	55°11N 1°39W **22** B5
Pegu *Burma*	17°20N 96°29E **85** L20
Pegu Yoma *Burma*	19°0N 96°0E **85** K20
Pegwell Bay *U.K.*	51°18N 1°24E **25** D11
Peixe *Brazil*	12°0S 48°40W **122** B1
Peje *Kosovo*	42°40N 20°17E **69** C9
Pekalongan *Indonesia*	6°53S 109°40E **82** F3
Pekanbaru *Indonesia*	0°30N 101°15E **82** D2
Pekin *U.S.A.*	40°35N 89°40W **112** E3
Peking = Beijing *China*	39°53N 116°21E **79** D10
Pelagie, Is. *Italy*	35°39N 12°33E **68** G5
Pelée, Mt. *Martinique*	14°48N 61°10W **114** c
Peleng *Indonesia*	1°20S 123°30E **83** E6
Peljeŝac *Croatia*	42°55N 17°25E **68** C7
Pelly → *Canada*	62°47N 137°19W **108** C6
Pelly Bay *Canada*	68°38N 89°50W **109** C11
Peloponnesos □ *Greece*	37°10N 22°0E **69** F10
Pelotas *Brazil*	31°42S 52°23W **121** F4
Pelvoux, Massif du *France*	44°52N 6°20E **66** D7
Pematangsiantar *Indonesia*	2°57N 99°5E **82** D1
Pemba *Mozam.*	12°58S 40°30E **97** G8
Pemba I. *Tanzania*	5°0S 39°45E **96** F7
Pembridge *U.K.*	52°13N 2°52W **24** B3
Pembroke *Canada*	45°50N 77°7W **109** E12
Pembroke *U.K.*	51°41N 4°55W **26** D4
Pembrokeshire □ *U.K.*	51°52N 4°56W **26** D3
Pembrokeshire Coast △ *U.K.*	51°50N 5°2W **26** D3
Pembury *U.K.*	51°8N 0°20E **25** D9
Pen-y-Ghent *U.K.*	54°10N 2°14W **22** D4
Penarth *U.K.*	51°26N 3°11W **27** F7
Peñas, G. de *Chile*	47°0S 75°0W **121** G2
Pend Oreille, L. *U.S.A.*	48°10N 116°21W **110** A3
Pendeen *U.K.*	50°9N 5°41W **27** G2
Pendle Hill *U.K.*	53°52N 2°19W **23** E4
Pendleton *U.S.A.*	45°40N 118°47W **110** A3
Penedo *Brazil*	10°15S 36°36W **122** B3
Penetanguishene *Canada*	44°50N 79°55W **112** C8
Penicuik *U.K.*	55°50N 3°13W **21** C9

Penistone *U.K.*	53°31N 1°37W **23** E5
Penkridge *U.K.*	52°44N 2°6W **23** G4
Penmarch, Pte. de *France*	47°48N 4°22W **66** C1
Penn Yan *U.S.A.*	42°40N 77°3W **112** D9
Pennines *U.K.*	54°45N 2°27W **22** C4
Pennsylvania □ *U.S.A.*	40°45N 77°30W **112** E8
Penong *Australia*	31°56S 133°1E **98** G5
Penrith *U.K.*	54°40N 2°45W **22** C3
Penryn *U.K.*	50°9N 5°7W **27** G3
Pensacola *U.S.A.*	30°25N 87°13W **111** D9
Pensacola Mts. *Antarctica*	84°0S 40°0W **55** E1
Penshurst *U.K.*	51°10N 0°12E **25** D9
Penticton *Canada*	49°30N 119°38W **108** E8
Pentire Pt. *U.K.*	50°35N 4°56W **27** F4
Pentland Firth *U.K.*	58°43N 3°10W **19** E11
Pentland Hills *U.K.*	55°48N 3°25W **21** C9
Penwortham *U.K.*	53°45N 2°46W **23** E3
Penygroes *U.K.*	53°3N 4°17W **26** A5
Penza *Russia*	53°15N 45°5E **70** D8
Penzance *U.K.*	50°7N 5°33W **27** G2
Peoria *U.S.A.*	40°42N 89°36W **112** E3
Perabumilih *Indonesia*	3°27S 104°15E **82** E2
Perdido, Mte. *Spain*	42°40N 0°5E **67** A6
Pereira *Colombia*	4°49N 75°43W **120** B2
Pergamino *Argentina*	33°52S 60°30W **121** F3
Péribonka → *Canada*	48°45N 72°5W **109** E12
Périgueux *France*	45°10N 0°42E **66** D4
Perlas, Punta de *Nic.*	12°30N 83°30W **104** H11
Perm *Russia*	58°0N 56°10E **70** C10
Pernambuco □ *Brazil*	8°0S 37°0W **120** C6
Pernik *Bulgaria*	42°35N 23°2E **69** C10
Perpignan *France*	42°42N 2°53E **66** E5
Perranporth *U.K.*	50°20N 5°11W **27** G3
Perranzabuloe *U.K.*	50°18N 5°9W **27** G3
Perryton *U.S.A.*	36°24N 100°48W **110** C6
Perryville *U.S.A.*	37°43N 89°52W **112** G3
Persepolis *Iran*	29°55N 52°50E **87** D8
Persian Gulf *Asia*	27°0N 50°0E **87** E7
Perth *Australia*	31°57S 115°52E **98** G2
Perth *Canada*	44°55N 76°15W **112** C9
Perth *U.K.*	56°24N 3°26W **21** B9
Perth & Kinross □ *U.K.*	56°45N 3°55W **19** J9
Peru ■ *S. Amer.*	4°0S 75°0W **120** C2
Peru *U.S.A.*	40°45N 86°4W **112** E4
Peru-Chile Trench *Pac. Oc.*	20°0S 72°0W **103** K20
Perúgia *Italy*	43°7N 12°23E **68** C5
Pervomaysk *Ukraine*	48°10N 30°46E **71** E5
Pervouralsk *Russia*	56°59N 59°59E **70** C10
Pésaro *Italy*	43°54N 12°55E **68** C5
Pescara *Italy*	42°28N 14°13E **68** C6
Peshawar *Pakistan*	34°2N 71°37E **84** B7
Pesqueira *Brazil*	8°20S 36°42W **122** A3
Petah Tiqwa *Israel*	32°6N 34°53E **86** C3
Peter I. *Br. Virgin Is.*	18°22N 64°35W **115** e
Peterborough *Canada*	44°20N 78°20W **109** E12
Peterborough *U.K.*	52°35N 0°15W **25** A8
Peterchurch *U.K.*	52°2N 2°56W **24** B3
Peterculter *U.K.*	57°6N 2°16W **19** H13
Peterhead *U.K.*	57°31N 1°48W **19** H14
Peterlee *U.K.*	54°47N 1°20W **22** C6
Petersburg *Alaska, U.S.A.*	56°48N 132°58W **108** D6
Petersburg *Va., U.S.A.*	37°14N 77°24W **112** G9
Petersfield *U.K.*	51°1N 0°56W **25** D7
Petit-Canal *Guadeloupe*	16°25N 61°31W **114** b
Petit Piton *St. Lucia*	13°51N 61°5W **114** f
Petite Terre, Îles de la *Guadeloupe*	16°13N 61°9W **114** b
Petitot → *Canada*	60°14N 123°29W **108** C7
Petitsikapau L. *Canada*	54°37N 66°25W **109** D13
Peto *Mexico*	20°8N 88°55W **114** C7
Petoskey *U.S.A.*	45°22N 84°57W **112** C5
Petra *Jordan*	30°20N 35°22E **86** D3
Petrolândia *Brazil*	9°5S 38°20W **122** A3
Petrolina *Brazil*	9°24S 40°30W **122** A2
Petropavl *Kazakhstan*	54°53N 69°13E **76** D7
Petropavlovsk-Kamchatskiy *Russia*	53°3N 158°43E **77** D16
Petrópolis *Brazil*	22°33S 43°9W **122** D2
Petrozavodsk *Russia*	61°41N 34°20E **70** B5
Petworth *U.K.*	51°0N 0°36E **25** E7
Pevensey *U.K.*	50°49N 0°23E **25** E9
Pevensey Levels *U.K.*	50°50N 0°20E **25** E9
Pewsey *U.K.*	51°20N 1°45W **24** D5
Pewsey, Vale of *U.K.*	51°22N 1°40W **24** D5
Pforzheim *Germany*	48°52N 8°41E **64** D5
Phalodi *India*	27°12N 72°24E **84** F8
Phan Rang *Vietnam*	11°34N 109°0E **82** B3
Phan Thiet *Vietnam*	11°1N 108°9E **82** B3
Philadelphia *U.S.A.*	39°57N 75°9W **113** E10
Philippine Sea *Pac. Oc.*	18°0N 125°0E **72** G14
Philippine Trench *Pac. Oc.*	12°0N 126°6E **83** B7
Philippines ■ *Asia*	12°0N 123°0E **83** B6
Phillips *U.S.A.*	45°42N 90°24W **112** C2
Phitsanulok *Thailand*	16°50N 100°12E **82** A2
Phnom Penh *Cambodia*	11°33N 104°55E **82** B2
Phoenix *U.S.A.*	33°26N 112°4W **110** D4
Phoenix Is. *Kiribati*	3°30S 172°0W **99** A16
Phra Nakhon Si Ayutthaya *Thailand*	14°25N 100°30E **82** B2
Phuket *Thailand*	7°53N 98°24E **82** C1
Piacenza *Italy*	45°1N 9°40E **68** B3
Piatra Neamţ *Romania*	46°56N 26°21E **65** E14
Piauí □ *Brazil*	7°0S 43°0W **120** C5
Piauí → *Brazil*	6°38S 42°42W **120** C5
Piave → *Italy*	45°32N 12°44E **68** B5
Picardie □ *France*	49°50N 3°0E **66** B5
Pichilemu *Chile*	34°22S 72°0W **121** F2
Pickering *U.K.*	54°15N 0°46W **22** D7
Pickering, Vale of *U.K.*	54°14N 0°45W **22** D7
Picos *Brazil*	7°5S 41°28W **120** C5
Picton *Canada*	44°1N 77°9W **112** C9
Pidley *U.K.*	52°23N 0°2W **25** B8
Pidurutalagala *Sri Lanka*	7°10N 80°50E **84** R12
Piedmont *U.S.A.*	34°42N 82°28W **111** D10
Piedras Negras *Mexico*	28°42N 100°31W **114** B4
Piemonte □ *Italy*	45°0N 8°0E **68** B2
Pierre *U.S.A.*	44°22N 100°21W **110** B6
Pietermaritzburg *S. Africa*	29°35S 30°25E **97** K6
Pikes Peak *U.S.A.*	38°50N 105°3W **110** C5

Pikeville *U.S.A.*	37°29N 82°31W **112** G6
Pilar *Paraguay*	26°50S 58°20W **121** E4
Pilcomayo → *Paraguay*	25°21S 57°42W **121** E4
Pilibhit *India*	28°40N 79°50E **84** E11
Pilica → *Poland*	51°52N 21°17E **65** C11
Pilling *U.K.*	53°56N 2°54W **23** E3
Pilton *U.K.*	51°10N 2°36W **24** D3
Pimentel *Peru*	6°45S 79°55W **120** C2
Pinar del Río *Cuba*	22°26N 83°40W **115** C8
Pinatubo, Mt. *Phil.*	15°8N 120°21E **83** A6
Pinchbeck *U.K.*	52°50N 0°9W **23** G8
Pinckneyville *U.S.A.*	38°5N 89°23W **112** F3
Pindus Mts. *Greece*	40°0N 21°0E **69** E9
Pine Bluff *U.S.A.*	34°13N 92°1W **111** D8
Pine Point *Canada*	60°50N 114°28W **108** C8
Pinega → *Russia*	64°30N 44°19E **70** B8
Pingdingshan *China*	33°43N 113°27E **79** E11
Pingliang *China*	35°35N 106°31E **78** D10
P'ingtung *Taiwan*	22°38N 120°30E **79** G13
Pingxiang *Guangxi Zhuangzu, China*	22°6N 106°46E **78** G10
Pingxiang *Jiangxi, China*	27°43N 113°48E **79** F11
Pinheiro *Brazil*	2°31S 45°5W **120** C5
Pinhoe *U.K.*	50°44N 3°28W **27** F7
Pinsk *Belarus*	52°10N 26°1E **70** D4
Piombino *Italy*	42°55N 10°32E **68** C4
Piotrków Trybunalski *Poland*	51°23N 19°43E **65** C10
Pipmuacan, Rés. *Canada*	49°45N 70°30W **113** A12
Piracicaba *Brazil*	22°45S 47°40W **122** D1
Pirapora *Brazil*	17°20S 44°56W **122** C2
Pireas *Greece*	37°57N 23°42E **69** F10
Pirmasens *Germany*	49°12N 7°36E **64** D4
Pisa *Italy*	43°43N 10°23E **68** C4
Pisagua *Chile*	19°40S 70°15W **120** D2
Pishan *China*	37°30N 78°33E **78** D4
Pistóia *Italy*	43°55N 10°54E **68** C4
Pit → *U.S.A.*	40°47N 122°6W **110** B2
Pitcairn I. *Pac. Oc.*	25°5S 130°5W **103** K14
Piteå *Sweden*	65°20N 21°25E **63** D8
Piteşti *Romania*	44°52N 24°54E **65** F13
Pitlochry *U.K.*	56°42N 3°44W **19** J10
Pittsburg *U.S.A.*	37°25N 94°42W **111** C8
Pittsburgh *U.S.A.*	40°26N 79°58W **112** E8
Pittsfield *U.S.A.*	42°27N 73°15W **113** D11
Piura *Peru*	5°15S 80°38W **120** C1
Placentia *Canada*	47°20N 54°0W **109** E14
Placentia B. *Canada*	47°0N 54°40W **109** E14
Placetas *Cuba*	22°15N 79°44W **115** C9
Plainview *U.S.A.*	34°11N 101°43W **110** D6
Plata, Río de la → *S. Amer.*	34°45S 57°30W **121** F4
Platte → *Mo., U.S.A.*	39°16N 94°50W **111** C8
Platte → *Nebr., U.S.A.*	41°4N 95°53W **104** E10
Plattsburgh *U.S.A.*	44°42N 73°28W **113** C11
Plauen *Germany*	50°30N 12°8E **64** C7
Plenty, B. of *N.Z.*	37°45S 177°0E **99** H14
Plessisville *Canada*	46°14N 71°47W **113** B12
Pleven *Bulgaria*	43°26N 24°37E **69** C11
Płock *Poland*	52°32N 19°40E **65** B10
Ploieşti *Romania*	44°57N 26°5E **65** F14
Plovdiv *Bulgaria*	42°8N 24°44E **69** C11
Plymouth *U.K.*	50°22N 4°10W **27** G5
Plymouth *Ind., U.S.A.*	41°21N 86°19W **112** E4
Plymouth *Wis., U.S.A.*	43°45N 87°59W **112** D4
Plympton *U.K.*	50°23N 4°5W **27** G5
Plymstock *U.K.*	50°21N 4°7W **27** G5
Plzeň *Czech Rep.*	49°45N 13°22E **64** D7
Po → *Italy*	44°57N 12°4E **68** B5
Pobedy, Pik *Kyrgyzstan*	42°0N 79°58E **78** C4
Pocatello *U.S.A.*	42°52N 112°27W **110** B4
Pocklington *U.K.*	53°56N 0°46W **23** E7
Poços de Caldas *Brazil*	21°50S 46°33W **122** D1
Podgorica *Montenegro*	42°30N 19°19E **69** C8
Podolsk *Russia*	55°25N 37°30E **70** C6
Pohang *S. Korea*	36°1N 129°23E **79** D14
Pohnpei *Micronesia*	6°55N 158°10E **102** G7
Point Hope *U.S.A.*	68°21N 166°47W **108** C3
Point L. *Canada*	65°15N 113°4W **108** C8
Point Pleasant *U.S.A.*	38°51N 82°8W **112** F6
Pointe-à-Pitre *Guadeloupe*	16°10N 61°32W **114** b
Pointe-Noire *Congo*	4°48S 11°53E **96** E2
Pointe-Noire *Guadeloupe*	16°14N 61°47W **114** b
Poitiers *France*	46°35N 0°20E **66** C4
Poitou *France*	46°40N 0°10W **66** C3
Pokhara *Nepal*	28°14N 83°58E **85** E13
Poland ■ *Europe*	52°0N 20°0E **65** C10
Polatsk *Belarus*	55°30N 28°50E **70** C4
Polden Hills *U.K.*	51°7N 2°50W **24** D3
Polegate *U.K.*	50°49N 0°16E **25** E9
Polesworth *U.K.*	52°37N 1°36W **23** G5
Polevskoy *Russia*	56°26N 60°11E **70** C11
Polokwane *S. Africa*	23°54S 29°25E **97** J5
Polperro *U.K.*	50°20N 4°32W **27** G4
Polruan *U.K.*	50°19N 4°38W **27** G4
Poltava *Ukraine*	49°35N 34°35E **71** E5
Polynesia *Pac. Oc.*	10°0S 162°0W **103** F11
Pomeranian Lakes *Poland*	53°40N 16°37E **65** B9
Pomona *U.S.A.*	34°4N 117°45W **110** D3
Ponca City *U.S.A.*	36°42N 97°5W **111** C7
Ponce *Puerto Rico*	18°1N 66°37W **115** d
Pond Inlet *Canada*	72°40N 77°0W **109** B12
Ponferrada *Spain*	42°32N 6°35W **67** A2
Ponta Grossa *Brazil*	25°7S 50°10W **121** E4
Pontardawe *U.K.*	51°43N 3°51W **26** D6
Pontardulais *U.K.*	51°43N 4°3W **26** D5
Pontarlier *France*	46°54N 6°20E **66** C7
Pontchartrain, L. *U.S.A.*	30°5N 90°5W **111** D9
Ponte Nova *Brazil*	20°25S 42°54W **122** D2
Pontefract *U.K.*	53°42N 1°18W **23** E6
Ponteland *U.K.*	55°3N 1°45W **22** B5
Pontevedra *Spain*	42°26N 8°40W **67** A1
Pontiac *Ill., U.S.A.*	40°53N 88°38W **112** E3
Pontiac *Mich., U.S.A.*	42°38N 83°18W **112** D6
Pontianak *Indonesia*	0°3S 109°15E **82** E3
Pontine Mts. *Turkey*	41°0N 36°45E **71** F6
Pontivy *France*	48°5N 2°58W **66** B2
Pontrilas *U.K.*	51°56N 2°52W **24** C3
Pontypool *U.K.*	51°42N 3°2W **27** D7
Pontypridd *U.K.*	51°36N 3°20W **27** D7
Ponziane, Ísole *Italy*	40°55N 12°57E **68** D5
Poole *U.K.*	50°43N 1°59W **24** E5

Poole Harbour

Rivière-Pilote

Poole Harbour *U.K.* 50°41N 2°0W **24** E5
Pooley Bridge *U.K.* 54°37N 2°48W **22** C3
Poopó, L. de *Bolivia* 18°30S 67°35W **120** D3
Popayán *Colombia* 2°27N 76°36W **120** B2
Poplar Bluff *U.S.A.* 36°46N 90°24W **111** C8
Popocatépetl, Volcán *Mexico* 19°2N 98°38W **114** D5
Porbandar *India* 21°44N 69°43E **84** J6
Porcupine → *U.S.A.* 66°34N 145°19W **108** C5
Pori *Finland* 61°29N 21°48E **63** E8
Porlock *U.K.* 51°13N 3°35W **27** E6
Poronaysk *Russia* 49°13N 143°0E **79** B17
Port Alberni *Canada* 49°14N 124°50W **108** E7
Port Antonio *Jamaica* 18°10N 76°26W **114** a
Port Arthur *U.S.A.* 29°54N 93°56W **111** E8
Port-au-Prince *Haiti* 18°40N 72°20W **115** D10
Port Augusta *Australia* 32°30S 137°50E **98** G6
Port Carlisle *U.K.* 54°57N 3°11W **22** C2
Port-Cartier *Canada* 50°2N 66°50W **109** D13
Port-de-Paix *Haiti* 19°50N 72°50W **115** D10
Port Elgin *Canada* 44°25N 81°25W **112** C7
Port Elizabeth *S. Africa* 33°58S 25°40E **97** L5
Port Ellen *U.K.* 55°38N 6°11W **20** C3
Port Erin *I. of Man* 54°5N 4°45W **29** C12
Port-Gentil *Gabon* 0°40S 8°50E **96** E1
Port Glasgow *U.K.* 55°56N 4°41W **20** C6
Port Harcourt *Nigeria* 4°40N 7°10E **94** H7
Port Hawkesbury *Canada* 45°36N 61°22W **109** E13
Port Hedland *Australia* 20°25S 118°35E **98** E2
Port Hope Simpson *Canada* 52°33N 56°18W **109** D14
Port Huron *U.S.A.* 42°58N 82°26W **112** D6
Port Isaac *U.K.* 50°35N 4°50W **27** F4
Port Isaac B. *U.K.* 50°36N 4°50W **27** F4
Port Laoise *Ireland* 53°2N 7°18W **31** B8
Port Lincoln *Australia* 34°42S 135°52E **98** G6
Port-Louis *Guadeloupe* 16°28N 61°32W **114** b
Port Louis *Mauritius* 20°10S 57°30E **91** H9
Port McNeill *Canada* 50°35N 127°6W **108** D7
Port Macquarie *Australia* 31°25S 152°25E **98** G9
Port Maria *Jamaica* 18°22N 76°54W **114** a
Port Morant *Jamaica* 17°54N 76°19W **114** a
Port Moresby *Papua N. G.* 9°24S 147°8E **98** B8
Port Nolloth *S. Africa* 29°17S 16°52E **97** K3
Port of Spain *Trin. & Tob.* 10°40N 61°31W **120** A3
Port Pirie *Australia* 33°10S 138°1E **98** G6
Port Said *Egypt* 31°16N 32°18E **95** B12
Port St. Lucie *U.S.A.* 27°18N 80°21W **111** E10
Port St. Mary *U.K.* 54°5N 4°44W **29** C12
Port Shepstone *S. Africa* 30°44S 30°28E **97** L6
Port Sudan *Sudan* 19°32N 37°9E **95** E13
Port Talbot *U.K.* 51°35N 3°47W **27** D6
Port Vila *Vanuatu* 17°45S 168°18E **99** D12
Port Washington *U.S.A.* 43°23N 87°53W **112** D4
Port William *U.K.* 54°46N 4°35W **20** D6
Portadown *U.K.* 54°25N 6°27W **29** C9
Portaferry *U.K.* 54°23N 5°33W **29** C10
Portage *U.S.A.* 43°33N 89°28W **112** D10
Portage la Prairie *Canada* 49°58N 98°18W **108** E10
Portarlington *Ireland* 53°9N 7°14W **31** B8
Porthcawl *U.K.* 51°29N 3°42W **27** E6
Porthleven *U.K.* 50°4N 5°19W **27** G3
Porthmadog *U.K.* 52°55N 4°8W **26** B5
Portishead *U.K.* 51°29N 2°46W **24** D3
Portknockie *U.K.* 57°42N 2°51W **19** G12
Portland *Maine, U.S.A.* 43°39N 70°16W **113** D12
Portland *Oreg., U.S.A.* 45°32N 122°37W **110** A2
Portland, I. of *U.K.* 50°33N 2°26W **24** E4
Portland Bight *Jamaica* 17°52N 77°5W **114** a
Portland Bill *U.K.* 50°31N 2°28W **27** F9
Portland Pt. *Jamaica* 17°42N 77°11W **114** a
Portmarnock *Ireland* 53°26N 6°8W **31** B10
Portmore *Jamaica* 17°53N 76°53W **114** a
Porto *Portugal* 41°8N 8°40W **67** B1
Pôrto Alegre *Brazil* 30°5S 51°10W **121** F4
Pôrto Esperança *Brazil* 19°37S 57°29W **120** D4
Porto Nacional *Brazil* 10°40S 48°30W **122** B1
Porto-Novo *Benin* 6°23N 2°42E **94** G6
Porto Seguro *Brazil* 16°26S 39°5W **122** C3
Porto Tórres *Italy* 40°50N 8°24E **68** D3
Porto-Vecchio *France* 41°35N 9°16E **66** F8
Pôrto Velho *Brazil* 8°46S 63°54W **120** C3
Porton *U.K.* 51°8N 1°43W **24** D5
Portpatrick *U.K.* 54°51N 5°7W **20** D5
Portree *U.K.* 57°25N 6°12W **18** H5
Portrush *U.K.* 55°12N 6°40W **29** A8
Portslade *U.K.* 50°50N 0°12W **25** E8
Portsmouth *U.K.* 50°48N 1°6W **24** E6
Portsmouth *N.H., U.S.A.* 43°5N 70°45W **113** D12
Portsmouth *Ohio, U.S.A.* 38°44N 82°57W **112** F6
Portsmouth *Va., U.S.A.* 36°58N 76°23W **111** C11
Portsoy *U.K.* 57°41N 2°41W **19** G12
Portstewart *U.K.* 55°11N 6°43W **29** A8
Porttipahdan tekojärvi *Finland* 68°5N 26°40E **63** D9
Portugal ■ *Europe* 40°0N 8°0W **67** C1
Portumna *Ireland* 53°6N 8°14W **30** B6
Posadas *Argentina* 27°30S 55°50W **121** E4
Posse *Brazil* 14°4S 46°18W **122** B1
Postmasburg *S. Africa* 28°18S 23°5E **97** K4
Potchefstroom *S. Africa* 26°41S 27°7E **97** K5
Potenza *Italy* 40°38N 15°48E **68** D6
Poti *Georgia* 42°10N 41°38E **71** F7
Potiskum *Nigeria* 11°39N 11°2E **95** F8
Potomac → *U.S.A.* 38°0N 76°23W **112** F9
Potosí *Bolivia* 19°38S 65°50W **120** D3
Potsdam *Germany* 52°23N 13°3E **64** B7
Potsdam *U.S.A.* 44°40N 74°59W **113** C10
Potter Heigham *U.K.* 52°42N 1°34E **25** A12
Potterne *U.K.* 51°20N 2°0W **24** D4
Potters Bar *U.K.* 51°42N 0°11W **25** D8
Potterspury *U.K.* 52°5N 0°52W **25** B7
Pottstown *U.S.A.* 40°15N 75°39W **113** E10
Pottsville *U.S.A.* 40°41N 76°12W **113** E10
Pottuvil *Sri Lanka* 6°55N 81°50E **84** R12
Poughkeepsie *U.S.A.* 41°42N 73°56W **113** E11
Poulaphouca Res. *Ireland* 53°8N 6°30W **31** B10
Poulton-le-Fylde *U.K.* 53°51N 2°58W **23** D3
Poundstock *U.K.* 50°44N 4°36W **27** F4
Pouso Alegre *Brazil* 22°14S 45°57W **122** D1
Powder → *U.S.A.* 46°45N 105°26W **110** A5
Powell, L. *U.S.A.* 36°57N 111°29W **110** C4
Powell River *Canada* 49°50N 124°35W **108** E7

Powers *U.S.A.* 45°41N 87°32W **112** C4
Powick *U.K.* 52°10N 2°14W **24** B4
Powys □ *U.K.* 52°20N 3°20W **26** C7
Poyang Hu *China* 29°5N 116°20E **79** F12
Poza Rica *Mexico* 20°33N 97°27W **114** C5
Poznań *Poland* 52°25N 16°55E **65** B9
Pozzuoli *Italy* 40°49N 14°7E **68** D6
Prado *Brazil* 17°20S 39°13W **122** C3
Praia *C. Verde Is.* 15°2N 23°34W **91** E1
Praia Grande *Brazil* 24°0S 46°24W **122** D1
Prairie du Chien *U.S.A.* 43°3N 91°9W **112** D2
Prata *Brazil* 19°25S 48°54W **122** C1
Prato *Italy* 43°53N 11°6E **68** C4
Pratt *U.S.A.* 37°39N 98°44W **110** C7
Prawle Pt. *U.K.* 50°12N 3°44W **27** G6
Praya *Indonesia* 8°39S 116°17E **82** F5
Prees *U.K.* 52°54N 2°40W **23** G3
Preesall *U.K.* 53°55N 2°57W **23** E3
Preseigne *U.K.* 52°17N 3°0W **26** C7
Prescot *U.K.* 53°26N 2°48W **23** F3
Prescott *Canada* 44°45N 75°30W **113** C10
Prescott *U.S.A.* 34°33N 112°28W **110** D4
Presidencia Roque Saenz Peña *Argentina* 26°45S 60°30W **121** E3
Presidente Prudente *Brazil* 22°5S 51°25W **120** E4
Presidio *U.S.A.* 29°34N 104°22W **110** E6
Prespa, L. *Macedonia* 40°55N 21°0E **69** D9
Presque Isle *U.S.A.* 46°41N 68°1W **113** B13
Prestatyn *U.K.* 53°20N 3°24W **26** A7
Prestbury *U.K.* 51°54N 2°2W **24** C4
Presteigne *U.K.* 52°17N 3°0W **26** C7
Preston *Borders, U.K.* 55°49N 2°19W **21** C11
Preston *Dorset, U.K.* 50°38N 2°26W **24** E4
Preston *Lancs., U.K.* 53°46N 2°42W **23** E3
Preston *U.S.A.* 42°6N 111°53W **110** B4
Prestonpans *U.K.* 55°58N 2°58W **21** C10
Prestwich *U.K.* 53°32N 2°17W **23** E4
Prestwick *U.K.* 55°29N 4°37W **20** D6
Pretoria *S. Africa* 25°44S 28°12E **97** K5
Pribilof Is. *U.S.A.* 57°0N 170°0W **108** D2
Price *U.S.A.* 39°36N 110°49W **110** C4
Prieska *S. Africa* 29°40S 22°42E **97** K4
Prilep *Macedonia* 41°21N 21°32E **69** D9
Prince Albert *Canada* 53°15N 105°50W **108** D9
Prince Albert Pen. *Canada* 72°30N 116°0W **108** B8
Prince Albert Sd. *Canada* 70°25N 115°0W **108** B8
Prince Alfred, C. *Canada* 74°20N 124°40W **109** B7
Prince Charles I. *Canada* 67°47N 76°12W **109** C12
Prince Charles Mts. *Antarctica* 72°0S 67°0E **55** D6
Prince Edward I. □ *Canada* 46°20N 63°20W **113** B16
Prince Edward Is. *Ind. Oc.* 46°35S 38°0E **53** G11
Prince George *Canada* 53°55N 122°50W **108** D7
Prince Gustaf Adolf Sea *Canada* 78°30N 107°0W **109** B9
Prince of Wales, C. *U.S.A.* 65°36N 168°5W **104** C3
Prince of Wales I. *Canada* 73°0N 99°0W **108** B10
Prince of Wales I. *U.S.A.* 55°47N 132°50W **108** D6
Prince Patrick I. *Canada* 77°0N 120°0W **109** B8
Prince Rupert *Canada* 54°20N 130°20W **108** D6
Princes Risborough *U.K.* 51°43N 0°49W **25** C7
Princeton *Ill., U.S.A.* 41°23N 89°28W **112** E3
Princeton *Ind., U.S.A.* 38°21N 87°34W **112** F4
Princeton *Ky., U.S.A.* 37°7N 87°53W **112** G4
Princeton *W. Va., U.S.A.* 37°22N 81°6W **112** G7
Princetown *U.K.* 50°33N 4°0W **27** F5
Príncipe *São Tomé & Príncipe* 1°37N 7°25E **90** F4
Pripet → *Europe* 51°20N 30°15E **65** C16
Pripet Marshes *Europe* 52°10N 27°10E **65** C15
Priština *Kosovo* 42°40N 21°13E **69** C9
Privas *France* 44°45N 4°37E **66** D6
Prizren *Kosovo* 42°13N 20°45E **69** C9
Probolinggo *Indonesia* 7°46S 113°13E **82** F4
Probus *U.K.* 50°17N 4°58W **27** G4
Progreso *Mexico* 21°20N 89°40W **114** C7
Prome *Burma* 18°49N 95°13E **85** K19
Propriá *Brazil* 10°13S 36°51W **122** B3
Provence *France* 43°40N 5°46E **66** E6
Providence *U.S.A.* 41°49N 71°24W **113** E12
Providencia, I. de *Colombia* 13°25N 81°26W **115** E8
Provins *France* 48°33N 3°15E **66** B5
Provo *U.S.A.* 40°14N 111°39W **110** B4
Prudhoe *U.K.* 54°57N 1°52W **22** C5
Prudhoe Bay *U.S.A.* 70°18N 148°22W **108** B5
Pruszków *Poland* 52°9N 20°49E **65** B11
Prut → *Romania* 45°28N 28°10E **65** F15
Pryluky *Ukraine* 50°30N 32°24E **71** D5
Przemyśl *Poland* 49°50N 22°45E **65** D12
Pskov *Russia* 57°50N 28°25E **70** C4
Puddletown *U.K.* 50°44N 2°20W **24** E4
Pudsey *U.K.* 53°47N 1°40W **23** E5
Puducherry *India* 11°59N 79°50E **84** P11
Puebla *Mexico* 19°3N 98°12W **114** D5
Pueblo *U.S.A.* 38°16N 104°37W **110** C6
Puerca, Pta. *Puerto Rico* 18°13N 65°36W **115** d
Puerto Aisén *Chile* 45°27S 73°0W **121** G2
Puerto Barrios *Guatemala* 15°40N 88°32W **114** D7
Puerto Cabello *Venezuela* 10°28N 68°1W **120** A3
Puerto Cabezas *Nic.* 14°0N 83°30W **115** E8
Puerto Carreño *Colombia* 6°12N 67°22W **120** B3
Puerto Cortés *Honduras* 15°51N 88°0W **114** D7
Puerto Deseado *Argentina* 47°55S 66°0W **121** G3
Puerto La Cruz *Venezuela* 10°13N 64°38W **120** A3
Puerto Madryn *Argentina* 42°48S 65°4W **121** G3
Puerto Maldonado *Peru* 12°30S 69°10W **120** C3
Puerto Montt *Chile* 41°28S 73°0W **121** G2
Puerto Plata *Dom. Rep.* 19°48N 70°45W **115** D10
Puerto Princesa *Phil.* 9°46N 118°45E **83** C5
Puerto Rico ☑ *W. Indies* 18°15N 66°45W **115** d
Puerto San Julián *Argentina* 49°18S 67°43W **121** G3
Puerto Suárez *Bolivia* 18°58S 57°52W **120** D4
Puerto Wilches *Colombia* 7°21N 73°54W **120** B2
Puertollano *Spain* 38°43N 4°7W **67** C3
Puffin I. *Ireland* 51°50N 10°24W **30** E2
Puget Sound *U.S.A.* 47°50N 122°30W **110** A2
Pukapuka *Cook Is.* 10°53S 165°49W **103** J11
Pula *Croatia* 44°54N 13°57E **68** B5
Pulacayo *Bolivia* 20°25S 66°41W **120** E3
Pulaski *U.S.A.* 37°3N 80°47W **112** G7
Pulborough *U.K.* 50°58N 0°30W **25** E8
Pulham Market *U.K.* 52°26N 1°13E **25** B11
Pulham St. Mary *U.K.* 52°26N 1°16E **25** B11

Pullman *U.S.A.* 46°44N 117°10W **110** A3
Pumlumon Fawr *U.K.* 52°28N 3°46W **26** C6
Pune *India* 18°29N 73°57E **84** K8
Punjab □ *India* 31°0N 76°0E **84** D10
Punjab □ *Pakistan* 32°0N 72°30E **84** E9
Puno *Peru* 15°55S 70°3W **120** D2
Punta, Cerro de *Puerto Rico* 18°10N 66°37W **115** d
Punta Arenas *Chile* 53°10S 71°0W **121** H2
Puntland *Somali Rep.* 8°0N 49°0E **89** F4
Punxsutawney *U.S.A.* 40°57N 78°59W **112** E8
Purbeck, Isle of *U.K.* 50°39N 1°59W **24** E5
Purfleet *U.K.* 51°29N 0°16E **25** D9
Puri *India* 19°50N 85°58E **85** K14
Purley on Thames *U.K.* 51°29N 1°3W **24** D6
Purnia *India* 25°45N 87°31E **85** G15
Puruliya *India* 23°17N 86°24E **85** H15
Purus → *Brazil* 3°42S 61°28W **120** C3
Putian *China* 25°23N 119°0E **79** F12
Putorana, Gory *Russia* 69°0N 95°0E **77** C10
Puttalam *Sri Lanka* 8°1N 79°55E **84** Q11
Putumayo → *S. Amer.* 3°7S 67°58W **120** C3
Puvirnituq *Canada* 60°2N 77°10W **109** C12
Puy-de-Dôme *France* 45°46N 2°57E **66** D5
Pwllheli *U.K.* 52°53N 4°25W **26** B5
Pyatigorsk *Russia* 44°2N 43°6E **71** F7
Pyinmana *Burma* 19°45N 96°12E **85** K20
P'yŏngyang *N. Korea* 39°0N 125°30E **79** D14
Pyramid L. *U.S.A.* 40°1N 119°35W **110** C3
Pyrénées *Europe* 42°45N 0°18E **66** E4

Q

Qaanaaq *Greenland* 77°30N 69°10W **54** B4
Qā'emshahr *Iran* 36°30N 52°53E **87** B8
Qaidam Basin *China* 37°0N 95°0E **78** C8
Qandyaghash *Kazakhstan* 49°28N 57°25E **71** E10
Qaqortoq *Greenland* 60°43N 46°0W **54** C5
Qarqan He → *China* 39°30N 88°30E **78** D6
Qarqaraly *Kazakhstan* 49°26N 75°30E **78** B4
Qarshi *Uzbekistan* 38°53N 65°48E **87** B11
Qatar ■ *Asia* 25°30N 51°15E **87** E7
Qattâra Depression *Egypt* 29°30N 27°30E **95** C11
Qazvin *Iran* 36°15N 50°0E **86** B7
Qena *Egypt* 26°10N 32°43E **95** C12
Qeqertarsuaq *Greenland* 69°15N 53°38W **54** C5
Qeshm *Iran* 26°55N 56°10E **87** E9
Qiemo *China* 38°8N 85°32E **78** D6
Qijiaojing *China* 43°28N 91°36E **78** C7
Qikiqtarjuaq *Canada* 67°33N 63°0W **109** C13
Qilian Shan *China* 38°30N 96°0E **78** D8
Qingdao *China* 36°5N 120°20E **79** D13
Qinghai □ *China* 36°0N 98°0E **78** D8
Qinghai Hu *China* 36°40N 100°10E **78** D9
Qinhuangdao *China* 39°56N 119°30E **79** D12
Qinzhou *China* 21°58N 108°38E **78** G10
Qiqihar *China* 47°26N 124°0E **79** B13
Qira *China* 37°0N 80°48E **78** D5
Qitai *China* 44°2N 89°35E **78** C6
Qitaihe *China* 45°48N 130°51E **79** B15
Qom *Iran* 34°40N 51°0E **87** C7
Qostanay *Kazakhstan* 53°10N 63°35E **76** D7
Quadring *U.K.* 52°54N 0°10W **23** G8
Quang Ngai *Vietnam* 15°13N 108°58E **82** A3
Quantock Hills *U.K.* 51°8N 3°10W **24** D2
Quanzhou *China* 24°55N 118°34E **79** F12
Quaqtaq *Canada* 60°55N 69°40W **109** C13
Quartu Sant'Élena *Italy* 39°15N 9°10E **68** E3
Québec *Canada* 46°52N 71°13W **113** B12
Québec □ *Canada* 48°0N 74°0W **109** E12
Queen Charlotte Is. *Canada* 53°20N 132°10W **108** D6
Queen Charlotte Sd. *Canada* 51°0N 128°0W **108** D7
Queen Elizabeth Is. *Canada* 76°0N 95°0W **109** B10
Queen Maud G. *Canada* 68°15N 102°30W **108** C9
Queenborough *U.K.* 51°25N 0°46E **25** D10
Queensbury *U.K.* 53°46N 1°50W **23** E5
Queensland □ *Australia* 22°0S 142°0E **98** E7
Queenstown *N.Z.* 45°1S 168°40E **99** K12
Queenstown *S. Africa* 31°52S 26°52E **97** L5
Queimadas *Brazil* 11°0S 39°38W **122** B3
Quelimane *Mozam.* 17°53S 36°58E **97** H7
Quendale, B. of *U.K.* 59°53N 1°20W **18** C15
Querétaro *Mexico* 20°36N 100°23W **114** C4
Quesnel *Canada* 53°0N 122°30W **108** D7
Quesnel L. *Canada* 52°30N 121°20W **108** D7
Quetta *Pakistan* 30°15N 66°55E **84** D5
Quezaltenango *Guatemala* 14°50N 91°30W **114** E6
Quezon City *Phil.* 14°37N 121°2E **83** B6
Qui Nhon *Vietnam* 13°40N 109°13E **82** B3
Quibdó *Colombia* 5°42N 76°40W **120** B2
Quilán, C. *Chile* 43°15S 74°30W **121** G2
Quilon *India* 8°50N 76°38E **84** Q10
Quilpie *Australia* 26°35S 144°11E **98** F7
Quimper *France* 48°0N 4°9W **66** B1
Quincy *Ill., U.S.A.* 39°56N 91°23W **111** C81
Quincy *Mass., U.S.A.* 42°14N 71°0W **113** D12
Quito *Ecuador* 0°15S 78°35W **120** C2
Qujing *China* 25°32N 103°41E **78** F9
Qulsary *Kazakhstan* 46°59N 54°1E **71** E9
Qŭnghirot *Uzbekistan* 43°2N 58°50E **87** A9
Quorndon *U.K.* 52°46N 1°10W **23** G6
Qŭqon *Uzbekistan* 40°31N 70°56E **87** A12
Quseir *Egypt* 26°7N 34°16E **95** C12
Quzhou *China* 28°57N 118°54E **79** F12

R

Raahe *Finland* 64°40N 24°28E **63** E8
Raasay *U.K.* 57°25N 6°4W **18** H5
Raasay, Sd. of *U.K.* 57°30N 6°8W **18** H5
Raba *Indonesia* 8°36S 118°55E **83** F5
Rabat *Morocco* 34°2N 6°48W **94** B4
Rabaul *Papua N. G.* 4°24S 152°18E **99** C8
Rābigh *Si. Arabia* 22°50N 39°5E **89** C2
Race, C. *Canada* 46°40N 53°5W **109** E14
Rach Gia *Vietnam* 10°5N 105°5E **82** B3
Rackheath *U.K.* 52°45N 1°22E **25** A11
Radcliffe *U.K.* 53°34N 2°18W **23** E4
Radcliffe-on-Trent *U.K.* 52°57N 1°2W **23** G6

Radford *U.S.A.* 37°8N 80°34W **112** G7
Radley *U.K.* 51°41N 1°14W **24** C6
Radnor Forest *U.K.* 52°17N 3°10W **26** C7
Radom *Poland* 51°23N 21°12E **65** C11
Radstock *U.K.* 51°17N 2°26W **24** D4
Rae *Canada* 62°50N 116°3W **108** C8
Rae Bareli *India* 26°18N 81°20E **85** F12
Rae Isthmus *Canada* 66°40N 87°30W **109** C11
Rafaela *Argentina* 31°10S 61°30W **121** F3
Rafsanjān *Iran* 30°30N 56°5E **87** D9
Ragusa *Italy* 36°55N 14°44E **68** F6
Rahimyar Khan *Pakistan* 28°30N 70°25E **84** E7
Raichur *India* 16°10N 77°20E **84** L10
Raigarh *India* 21°56N 83°25E **85** J13
Rainbow Lake *Canada* 58°30N 119°23W **108** D8
Rainham *U.K.* 51°22N 0°37E **25** D10
Rainier, Mt. *U.S.A.* 46°52N 121°46W **110** A2
Rainworth *U.K.* 53°7N 1°7W **23** F6
Rainy L. *Canada* 48°42N 93°10W **108** E10
Raipur *India* 21°17N 81°45E **85** J12
Raj Nandgaon *India* 21°5N 81°5E **85** J12
Rajahmundry *India* 17°1N 81°48E **85** L12
Rajapalaiyam *India* 9°25N 77°35E **84** Q10
Rajasthan □ *India* 26°45N 73°30E **84** F8
Rajkot *India* 22°15N 70°56E **84** H7
Rajshahi *Bangla.* 24°22N 88°39E **85** G16
Rajshahi □ *Bangla.* 25°0N 89°0E **85** G16
Rakaia → *N. Korea* 39°0N 125°30E **79** D14
Raleigh *U.S.A.* 35°47N 78°39W **111** C11
Rame Head *U.K.* 50°19N 4°13W **27** G5
Ramgarh *India* 23°40N 85°35E **85** H14
Ramna Stacks *U.K.* 60°35N 1°24W **18** A15
Rampside *U.K.* 54°6N 3°9W **22** D2
Rampur *India* 28°50N 79°5E **84** E11
Ramree I. *Burma* 19°0N 93°40E **85** K19
Ramsbottom *U.K.* 53°38N 2°19W **23** E4
Ramsbury *U.K.* 51°26N 1°36W **24** D5
Ramsey *I. of Man* 54°20N 4°22W **29** C13
Ramsey *Cambs., U.K.* 52°27N 0°7W **25** B8
Ramsey *Essex, U.K.* 51°55N 1°13E **25** C11
Ramsgate *U.K.* 51°20N 1°25E **25** D11
Rancagua *Chile* 34°10S 70°50W **121** F2
Ranchi *India* 23°19N 85°27E **85** H14
Randalstown *U.K.* 54°45N 6°19W **29** B9
Randers *Denmark* 56°29N 10°1E **63** F6
Rangoon *Burma* 16°45N 96°20E **85** L20
Rangpur *Bangla.* 25°42N 89°22E **85** G16
Rankin Inlet *Canada* 62°30N 93°0W **108** C10
Rannoch *U.K.* 56°40N 4°20W **19** J9
Rannoch, L. *U.K.* 56°41N 4°20W **19** J9
Rannoch Moor *U.K.* 56°38N 4°48W **19** J8
Rantoul *U.S.A.* 40°19N 88°9W **112** E3
Rapa *French Polynesia* 27°35S 144°20W **103** K13
Rapallo *Italy* 44°21N 9°14E **68** B3
Raper, C. *Canada* 69°44N 67°6W **109** C13
Rapid City *U.S.A.* 44°5N 103°14W **110** B6
Rarotonga *Cook Is.* 21°30S 160°0W **103** K12
Ra's al Khaymah *U.A.E.* 25°50N 55°59E **87** E9
Rasht *Iran* 37°20N 49°40E **86** B7
Rat Islands *U.S.A.* 52°0N 178°0E **108** D1
Ratangarh *India* 28°5N 74°35E **84** E9
Rath Luirc *Ireland* 52°21N 8°40W **30** D5
Rathdrum *Ireland* 52°56N 6°14W **31** C10
Rathkeale *Ireland* 52°32N 8°56W **30** D5
Rathlin I. *U.K.* 55°18N 6°14W **29** A9
Rathmelton *Ireland* 55°2N 7°38W **28** A6
Rathkield *U.S.A.* 38°46N 112°5W **110** C4
Rathnew *Ireland* 52°56N 6°17W **31** C10
Ratlam *India* 23°20N 75°0E **84** H9
Ratnagiri *India* 16°57N 73°18E **84** L8
Raton *U.S.A.* 36°54N 104°24W **110** C6
Rattray Hd. *U.K.* 57°38N 1°50W **19** G14
Rauma *Finland* 61°10N 21°30E **63** E8
Raunds *U.K.* 52°21N 0°32W **25** B7
Raurkela *India* 22°14N 84°50E **85** H14
Ravenglass *U.K.* 54°22N 3°24W **22** D2
Ravenna *Italy* 44°25N 12°12E **68** B5
Ravenstonedale *U.K.* 54°26N 2°25W **22** D4
Ravi → *Pakistan* 30°35N 71°49E **84** D7
Rawalpindi *Pakistan* 33°38N 73°8E **84** C8
Rawlins *U.S.A.* 41°47N 107°14W **110** B5
Rawmarsh *U.K.* 53°27N 1°21W **23** F6
Rawson *Argentina* 43°15S 65°5W **121** G3
Rawtenstall *U.K.* 53°42N 2°17W **23** E4
Ray, C. *Canada* 47°33N 59°15W **109** E14
Rayleigh *U.K.* 51°36N 0°37E **25** C10
Rayong *Thailand* 12°40N 101°20E **82** B2
Raz, Pte. du *France* 48°2N 4°47W **66** C1
Ré, Î. de *France* 46°12N 1°30W **66** C3
Reading *U.K.* 51°27N 0°58W **25** D7
Reading *U.S.A.* 40°20N 75°56W **113** E10
Reay Forest *U.K.* 58°22N 4°55W **19** F8
Rebiana Desert *Libya* 24°30N 21°0E **95** D10
Recife *Brazil* 8°0S 35°0W **122** A3
Reconquista *Argentina* 29°10S 59°45W **121** E4
Red → *U.S.A.* 31°1N 91°45W **111** D8
Red Bluff *U.S.A.* 40°11N 122°15W **110** B2
Red Deer *Canada* 52°20N 113°50W **108** D8
Red Dial *U.K.* 54°49N 3°10W **22** C2
Red L. *Canada* 51°3N 93°49W **108** D10
Red L. *U.S.A.* 48°8N 94°45W **111** A8
Red Lake *Canada* 51°3N 93°49W **108** D10
Red Grande → *N. Amer.* 25°58N 97°9W **111** E7
Red River of the North → *N. Amer.* 49°0N 97°15W **108** D10
Red Sea *Asia* 25°0N 36°0E **89** C2
Red Wing *U.S.A.* 44°34N 92°31W **111** B81
Redbridge □ *U.K.* 51°35N 0°7E **25** C9
Redcar *U.K.* 54°37N 1°4W **22** C6
Redding *U.S.A.* 40°35N 122°24W **110** B2
Redditch *U.K.* 52°18N 1°55W **24** B5
Rede → *U.K.* 55°8N 2°13W **22** B4
Redesmouth *U.K.* 55°8N 2°13W **22** B4
Redhill *U.K.* 51°14N 0°9W **25** D8
Redlynch *U.K.* 50°59N 1°41W **24** E5
Redmile *U.K.* 52°54N 0°48W **23** G7
Redmire *U.K.* 54°19N 1°55W **22** D5
Redon *France* 47°40N 2°6W **66** C2
Redruth *U.K.* 50°14N 5°14W **27** G3
Ree, L. *Ireland* 53°35N 8°0W **28** D6
Reedham *U.K.* 52°34N 1°34E **25** A12

Reepham *U.K.* 52°46N 1°6E **25** A11
Reese → *U.S.A.* 40°48N 117°4W **110** B3
Reeth *U.K.* 54°23N 1°56W **22** D5
Regensburg *Germany* 49°1N 12°6E **64** D7
Réggio di Calábria *Italy* 38°6N 15°39E **68** E6
Réggio nell'Emília *Italy* 44°43N 10°36E **68** B4
Regina *Canada* 50°27N 104°35W **108** D9
Reichenbach *Germany* 50°37N 12°17E **64** C7
Reigate *U.K.* 51°14N 0°12W **25** D8
Reims *France* 49°15N 4°1E **66** B6
Reina Adelaida, Arch. *Chile* 52°20S 74°0W **121** H2
Reindeer L. *Canada* 57°15N 102°15W **108** D9
Remanso *Brazil* 9°41S 42°4W **122** A2
Remscheid *Canada* 45°30N 76°40W **112** C9
Renfrew *U.K.* 55°52N 4°24W **20** C7
Rennell *Solomon Is.* 11°40S 160°10E **99** C11
Rennes *France* 48°7N 1°41W **66** B3
Reno *U.S.A.* 39°31N 119°48W **110** C3
Repton *U.K.* 52°50N 1°33W **23** G5
Republican → *U.S.A.* 39°4N 96°48W **111** C7
Repulse Bay *Canada* 66°30N 86°30W **109** C11
Resistencia *Argentina* 27°30S 59°0W **121** E4
Resolute *Canada* 74°42N 94°54W **109** B10
Resolution I. *Canada* 61°30N 65°0W **109** C13
Reston *U.K.* 55°51N 2°10W **21** C11
Retford *U.K.* 53°19N 0°56W **23** F7
Rethimno *Greece* 35°18N 24°30E **69** G11
Réunion ☑ *Ind. Oc.* 21°0S 56°0W **91** J9
Reus *Spain* 41°10N 1°5E **67** B6
Reutlingen *Germany* 48°29N 9°12E **64** D5
Revda *Russia* 56°48N 59°57E **70** C10
Revelstoke *Canada* 51°0N 118°10W **108** D8
Revillagigedo, Is. de *Pac. Oc.* 18°40N 112°0W **114** D2
Rewa *India* 24°33N 81°25E **85** G12
Rexburg *U.S.A.* 43°49N 111°47W **110** B4
Rey Malabo *Eq. Guin.* 3°45N 8°50E **96** D1
Reykjavík *Iceland* 64°10N 21°57W **63** B1
Reynosa *Mexico* 26°7N 98°18W **114** B5
Rēzekne *Latvia* 56°30N 27°17E **63** F9
Rhayader *U.K.* 52°18N 3°29W **26** C7
Rheidol → *U.K.* 52°25N 4°5W **26** C5
Rheine *Germany* 52°17N 7°26E **64** B4
Rheinland-Pfalz □ *Germany* 50°0N 7°0E **64** C4
Rhine → *Europe* 51°52N 6°2E **64** C4
Rhinelander *U.S.A.* 45°38N 89°25W **112** C3
Rhinns Pt. *U.K.* 55°40N 6°29W **20** C3
Rhins, The *U.K.* 54°52N 5°3W **20** E5
Rhode Island □ *U.S.A.* 41°40N 71°30W **113** E12
Rhodes *Greece* 36°15N 28°10E **69** F13
Rhodope Mts. *Bulgaria* 41°40N 24°20E **69** D11
Rhondda *U.K.* 51°39N 3°31W **26** D6
Rhône → *France* 43°28N 4°42E **66** E6
Rhosllanerchrugog *U.K.* 53°1N 3°3W **26** A7
Rhossili *U.K.* 51°34N 4°17W **27** D5
Rhossili B. *U.K.* 51°32N 4°14W **27** D5
Rhum *U.K.* 57°0N 6°20W **18** J5
Rhum, Sound of *U.K.* 56°55N 6°14W **18** J5
Rhyl *U.K.* 53°20N 3°29W **26** A7
Rhymney *U.K.* 51°46N 3°17W **26** D7
Riau, Kepulauan *Indonesia* 0°30N 104°20E **82** D2
Ribble → *U.K.* 53°52N 2°25W **23** E4
Ribeirão Prêto *Brazil* 21°10S 47°50W **122** D1
Riberalta *Bolivia* 11°0S 66°0W **120** D3
Riccall *U.K.* 53°50N 1°3W **23** E6
Rice Lake *U.S.A.* 45°30N 91°44W **112** C2
Richards Bay *S. Africa* 28°48S 32°6E **97** K6
Richfield *U.S.A.* 38°46N 112°5W **110** C4
Richland *U.S.A.* 46°17N 119°18W **110** A3
Richland Center *U.S.A.* 43°21N 90°23W **112** D2
Richlands *U.S.A.* 37°6N 81°48W **112** G7
Richmond *U.K.* 54°25N 1°43W **22** D5
Richmond *Ind., U.S.A.* 39°50N 84°53W **112** F5
Richmond *Ky., U.S.A.* 37°45N 84°18W **112** G5
Richmond *Va., U.S.A.* 37°33N 77°27W **112** G9
Richmond-upon-Thames □ *U.K.* 51°27N 0°17W **25** D8
Rickmansworth *U.K.* 51°38N 0°29W **25** C8
Ridgecrest *U.S.A.* 35°38N 117°40W **110** C3
Ridgway *U.S.A.* 41°25N 78°44W **112** E8
Ridsdale *U.K.* 55°9N 2°9W **22** B4
Rievaulx *U.K.* 54°16N 1°7W **22** D6
Rift Valley *Africa* 7°0N 30°0E **90** G7
Riga *Latvia* 56°53N 24°8E **63** F8
Riga, G. of *Latvia* 57°40N 23°45E **63** F8
Rigestān *Afghan.* 30°15N 65°0E **87** D11
Rigolet *Canada* 54°10N 58°23W **109** D14
Rijeka *Croatia* 45°20N 14°21E **68** B6
Rillington *U.K.* 54°9N 0°42W **22** D7
Rímini *Italy* 44°3N 12°33E **68** B5
Rimouski *Canada* 48°27N 68°30W **109** E13
Ringmer *U.K.* 50°53N 0°5E **25** E9
Ringwood *U.K.* 50°50N 1°47W **24** E5
Rio Branco *Brazil* 9°58S 67°49W **120** C3
Rio Claro *Brazil* 22°19S 47°35W **122** D1
Rio Cuarto *Argentina* 33°10S 64°25W **121** F3
Rio de Janeiro *Brazil* 22°54S 43°12W **122** D2
Rio de Janeiro □ *Brazil* 22°50S 43°0W **122** D2
Rio Gallegos *Argentina* 51°35S 69°15W **121** H3
Rio Grande *Brazil* 32°0S 52°20W **121** F4
Rio Grande *Puerto Rico* 18°23N 65°50W **115** d
Rio Grande → *N. Amer.* 25°58N 97°9W **111** E7
Rio Grande de Santiago → *Mexico* 21°36N 105°26W **114** C3
Rio Grande do Norte □ *Brazil* 5°40S 36°0W **122** A3
Rio Grande do Sul □ *Brazil* 30°0S 53°0W **121** E4
Rio Largo *Brazil* 9°28S 35°50W **122** A3
Rio Muni □ *Eq. Guin.* 1°30N 10°0E **96** D2
Riohacha *Colombia* 11°33N 72°55W **120** A2
Ripley *Derby, U.K.* 53°3N 1°24W **23** F6
Ripley *N. Yorks., U.K.* 54°3N 1°34W **22** D5
Ripon *U.K.* 54°9N 1°31W **22** D5
Ripon *U.S.A.* 43°51N 88°50W **112** D3
Rishton *U.K.* 53°46N 2°26W **23** E4
Rishton *U.K.* 51°37N 3°5W **27** D7
Rivera *Uruguay* 31°0S 55°50W **121** F4
Riverhead *U.S.A.* 40°55N 72°40W **113** E11
Riverside *U.S.A.* 33°59N 117°22W **110** D3
Riverton *U.S.A.* 43°2N 108°23W **110** B5
Rivière-du-Loup *Canada* 47°50N 69°30W **109** E13
Rivière-Pilote *Martinique* 14°26N 60°53W **114** c

Rivière-Salée · **Santa Rosa**

Place	Region	Coordinates	Ref
Rivière-Salée	Martinique	14°31N 61°0W	114 c
Rivne	Ukraine	50°40N 26°10E	65 C14
Riyadh	Si. Arabia	24°41N 46°42E	86 E6
Rize	Turkey	41°0N 40°30E	71 F7
Rizhao	China	35°25N 119°30E	79 D12
Road Town	Br. Virgin Is.	18°27N 64°37W	115 e
Roade	U.K.	52°9N 0°53W	25 B7
Roanne	France	46°3N 4°4E	66 C6
Roanoke	U.S.A.	37°16N 79°56W	112 G8
Roanoke →	U.S.A.	35°57N 76°42W	111 C11
Roberton	U.K.	55°25N 2°54W	21 D10
Roberval	Canada	48°32N 72°15W	109 E12
Robin Hood's Bay	U.K.	54°27N 0°32W	22 D7
Robson, Mt.	Canada	53°10N 119°10W	108 D8
Roca, C. da	Portugal	38°40N 9°31W	67 C1
Rocester	U.K.	52°57N 1°50W	23 G5
Rocha	Uruguay	34°30S 54°25W	121 F4
Rochdale	U.K.	53°38N 2°9W	23 E4
Roche	U.K.	50°24N 4°50W	27 G4
Rochefort	France	45°56N 0°57W	66 D3
Rochester	Medway, U.K.	51°23N 0°31E	25 D10
Rochester	Northumberland. U.K.	55°17N 2°17W	22 B4
Rochester	Ind., U.S.A.	41°4N 86°13W	112 E4
Rochester	Minn., U.S.A.	44°1N 92°28W	111 B81
Rochester	N.H., U.S.A.	43°18N 70°59W	113 D12
Rochester	N.Y., U.S.A.	43°10N 77°37W	112 D9
Rochford	U.K.	51°34N 0°43E	25 C10
Rock Hill	U.S.A.	34°56N 81°1W	111 D10
Rock Island	U.S.A.	41°30N 90°34W	112 E2
Rock Springs	U.S.A.	41°35N 109°14W	110 B5
Rockall	Atl. Oc.	57°37N 13°42W	56 D3
Rockford	U.S.A.	42°16N 89°6W	112 D3
Rockhampton	Australia	23°22S 150°32E	98 E9
Rockingham	U.K.	52°31N 0°43W	25 A7
Rockingham Forest	U.K.	52°29N 0°42W	25 B7
Rockland	U.S.A.	44°6N 69°7W	113 C13
Rocky Mount	U.S.A.	35°57N 77°48W	111 C11
Rocky Mts.	N. Amer.	49°0N 115°0W	108 D7
Rodez	France	44°21N 2°33E	66 D5
Roding →	U.K.	51°31N 0°6E	25 C9
Rodrigues	Ind. Oc.	19°45S 63°20E	53 E13
Roe →	U.K.	55°6N 6°59W	29 A8
Roes Welcome Sd.	Canada	65°0N 87°0W	109 C11
Rogans Seat	U.K.	54°26N 2°7W	22 C4
Rogate	U.K.	51°0N 0°50W	25 D7
Rogers City	U.S.A.	45°25N 83°49W	112 C6
Rohri	Pakistan	27°45N 68°51E	84 F6
Rojo, C.	Mexico	21°33N 97°20W	114 C5
Rolla	U.S.A.	37°57N 91°46W	111 C81
Roma	Australia	26°32S 148°49E	98 F8
Romaine →	Canada	50°18N 63°47W	109 D13
Romania ■	Europe	46°0N 25°0E	65 F12
Romans-sur-Isère	France	45°3N 5°3E	66 D6
Rome	Italy	41°54N 12°28E	68 D5
Rome	Ga., U.S.A.	34°15N 85°10W	111 D9
Rome	N.Y., U.S.A.	43°13N 75°27W	113 D10
Romney	U.S.A.	39°21N 78°45W	112 F8
Romney Marsh	U.K.	51°2N 0°54E	25 D10
Romorantin-Lanthenay	France	47°21N 1°45E	66 C4
Romsey	U.K.	51°0N 1°29W	24 E6
Rona	U.K.	57°34N 5°59W	18 G6
Roncador, Serra do	Brazil	12°30S 52°30W	120 D4
Rondônia □	Brazil	11°0S 63°0W	120 D3
Rondonópolis	Brazil	16°28S 54°38W	120 D4
Ronge, L. la	Canada	55°6N 105°17W	108 D9
Ronne Ice Shelf	Antarctica	77°30S 60°0W	55 D18
Roosevelt →	Brazil	7°35S 60°20W	120 C3
Roosevelt I.	Antarctica	79°30S 162°0W	55 D12
Ropsley	U.K.	52°54N 0°30W	23 G8
Roquetas de Mar	Spain	36°46N 2°36W	67 D4
Roraima □	Brazil	2°0N 61°30W	120 B3
Roraima, Mt.	Venezuela	5°10N 60°40W	120 B3
Rosario	Argentina	33°0S 60°40W	121 F3
Rosario	Mexico	22°58N 105°53W	114 C3
Rosario de la Frontera	Argentina	25°50S 65°0W	121 E3
Roscommon	Ireland	53°38N 8°11W	28 D5
Roscommon □	Ireland	53°49N 8°23W	28 D5
Roscrea	Ireland	52°57N 7°49W	30 C7
Roseau	Dominica	15°17N 61°24W	115 D12
Roseburg	U.S.A.	43°13N 123°20W	110 B2
Rosedale Abbey	U.K.	54°21N 0°52W	22 D7
Rosehearty	U.K.	57°42N 2°7W	19 G13
Rosenheim	Germany	47°51N 12°7E	64 E7
Rosetown	Canada	51°35N 107°59W	108 D9
Roseville	U.S.A.	38°45N 121°17W	110 C2
Roslavl	Russia	53°57N 32°55E	70 D5
Ross Ice Shelf	Antarctica	80°0S 180°0E	55 E12
Ross-on-Wye	U.K.	51°54N 2°34W	24 C3
Ross River	Canada	62°30N 131°30W	108 C6
Ross Sea	Antarctica	74°0S 178°0E	55 D11
Rossall Pt.	U.K.	53°55N 3°3W	23 E2
Rossan Pt.	Ireland	54°42N 8°47W	28 B4
Rosses, The	Ireland	55°2N 8°20W	28 A5
Rossignol L.	Canada	44°12N 65°10W	113 C15
Rosslare	Ireland	52°17N 6°24W	31 D10
Rosslare Harbour	Ireland	52°15N 6°20W	31 D10
Rossosh	Russia	50°15N 39°28E	71 D6
Rostock	Germany	54°5N 12°8E	64 A7
Rostov	Russia	47°15N 39°45E	71 E6
Roswell	Ga., U.S.A.	34°2N 84°22W	111 D10
Roswell	N. Mex., U.S.A.	33°24N 104°32W	110 D6
Rothbury	U.K.	55°19N 1°58W	22 B5
Rothbury Forest	U.K.	55°19N 1°50W	22 B5
Rother →	U.K.	50°59N 0°45E	25 E10
Rotherham	U.K.	53°26N 1°20W	23 F6
Rothes	U.K.	57°32N 3°13W	19 G11
Rothesay	U.K.	55°50N 5°3W	20 C5
Rothwell	Northants., U.K.	52°25N 0°48W	25 B7
Rothwell	W. Yorks., U.K.	53°45N 1°28W	23 E6
Roti	Indonesia	10°50S 123°0E	83 F6
Rotorua	N.Z.	38°9S 176°16E	99 H14
Rotterdam	Neths.	51°55N 4°30E	64 C3
Rottingdean	U.K.	50°48N 0°4W	25 E8
Rotuma	Fiji	12°25S 177°5E	99 C14
Roubaix	France	50°40N 3°10E	66 A5
Rouen	France	49°27N 1°4E	66 B4
Round Mt.	Australia	30°26S 152°16E	98 G9
Rousay	U.K.	59°10N 3°2W	19 D11
Roussillon	France	42°30N 2°35E	66 E5
Rouyn-Noranda	Canada	48°20N 79°0W	109 E12
Rovaniemi	Finland	66°29N 25°41E	63 D9
Rovigo	Italy	45°4N 11°47E	68 B4
Rowanburn	U.K.	55°5N 2°55W	21 D10
Roxas	Phil.	11°36N 122°49E	83 B6
Roxburgh	U.K.	55°35N 2°28W	21 C11
Roxby	U.K.	53°38N 0°38W	23 E7
Royal Canal	Ireland	53°30N 7°13W	31 B8
Royal Leamington Spa	U.K.	52°18N 1°31W	24 B5
Royal Tunbridge Wells	U.K.	51°7N 0°16E	25 D9
Royale, Isle	U.S.A.	48°0N 88°54W	112 B3
Royan	France	45°37N 1°2W	66 D3
Royston	U.K.	52°3N 0°0	25 B8
Royton	U.K.	53°34N 2°8W	23 E4
Rub' al Khālī	Si. Arabia	19°0N 48°0E	89 D4
Rubery	U.K.	52°24N 2°1W	24 B4
Rubh a' Mhail	U.K.	55°56N 6°8W	20 C3
Rubha Hunish	U.K.	57°42N 6°20W	18 G5
Rubtsovsk	Russia	51°30N 81°10E	78 A5
Ruby L.	U.S.A.	40°10N 115°28W	110 B3
Rudnyy	Kazakhstan	52°57N 63°7E	76 D7
Rudston	U.K.	54°6N 0°20W	22 D8
Ruffling Pt.	Br. Virgin Is.	18°44N 64°27W	115 e
Rufford	U.K.	53°38N 2°50W	23 E3
Rufiji →	Tanzania	7°50S 39°15E	96 F7
Rugby	U.K.	52°23N 1°16W	24 B6
Rugeley	U.K.	52°46N 1°55W	23 G5
Rügen	Germany	54°22N 13°24E	64 A7
Ruhr →	Germany	51°27N 6°43E	64 C4
Ruki →	Dem. Rep. of the Congo	0°5N 18°17E	96 E3
Rukwa, L.	Tanzania	8°0S 32°20E	96 F6
Rumania = Romania ■	Europe	46°0N 25°0E	65 F12
Rumford	U.S.A.	44°33N 70°33W	113 C12
Runaway Bay	Jamaica	18°27N 77°20W	114 a
Runcorn	U.K.	53°21N 2°44W	23 F3
Rundu	Namibia	17°52S 19°43E	97 H3
Rungwe	Tanzania	9°11S 33°32E	96 G7
Ruoqiang	China	38°55N 88°10E	78 D6
Rupert →	U.S.A.	42°37N 113°41W	110 B4
Rupert →	Canada	51°29N 78°45W	109 D12
Ruse	Bulgaria	43°48N 25°59E	69 C12
Rush	Ireland	53°31N 6°6W	31 A10
Rushden	U.K.	52°18N 0°35W	25 B7
Rushville	Ill., U.S.A.	40°7N 90°34W	112 E2
Rushville	Ind., U.S.A.	39°37N 85°27W	112 F5
Ruskington	U.K.	53°3N 0°22W	23 F8
Russellville	U.S.A.	35°17N 93°8W	111 C8
Russia ■	Eurasia	62°0N 105°0E	77 C11
Rustavi	Georgia	41°30N 45°0E	71 F8
Rustenburg	S. Africa	25°41S 27°14E	97 K5
Rutherglen	U.K.	55°49N 4°13W	20 C7
Ruthin	U.K.	53°6N 3°19W	26 A7
Ruthwell	U.K.	55°0N 3°25W	21 E9
Rutog	China	33°27N 79°42E	78 E4
Ruvuma →	Tanzania	10°29S 40°28E	96 G8
Ruwenzori	Africa	0°30N 29°55E	96 D5
Rwanda ■	Africa	2°0S 30°0E	96 E5
Ryan, L.	U.K.	55°0N 5°2W	20 E5
Ryazan	Russia	54°40N 39°40E	70 D6
Rybachi Pen.	Russia	69°43N 32°0E	70 A5
Rybinsk	Russia	58°5N 38°50E	70 C6
Rybinsk Res.	Russia	58°30N 38°25E	70 C6
Rydal	U.K.	54°27N 2°59W	22 D3
Ryde	U.K.	50°43N 1°9W	24 E6
Rye	U.K.	50°57N 0°45E	25 E10
Rye →	U.K.	54°11N 0°44W	22 D7
Rye Bay	U.K.	50°52N 0°49E	25 E10
Ryhope	U.K.	54°53N 1°21W	22 C6
Ryton	U.K.	52°22N 1°25W	24 B6
Ryukyu Is.	Japan	26°0N 126°0E	79 F14
Rzeszów	Poland	50°5N 21°58E	65 C11
Rzhev	Russia	56°20N 34°20E	70 C5

S

Place	Region	Coordinates	Ref
Saale →	Germany	51°56N 11°54E	64 C6
Saar →	Europe	49°41N 6°32E	64 D4
Saarbrücken	Germany	49°14N 6°59E	64 D4
Saaremaa	Estonia	58°30N 22°30E	63 F8
Sabadell	Spain	41°28N 2°7E	67 B7
Sabah □	Malaysia	6°0N 117°0E	82 C5
Sabhā	Libya	27°9N 14°29E	95 C8
Sabinas	Mexico	27°51N 101°7W	114 B4
Sabinas Hidalgo	Mexico	26°30N 100°10W	114 B4
Sabine →	U.S.A.	29°59N 93°47W	111 E8
Sable, C.	Canada	43°29N 65°38W	113 D15
Sable, C.	U.S.A.	25°9N 81°8W	111 E10
Sable I.	Canada	44°0N 60°0W	109 E14
Sachsen □	Germany	50°55N 13°10E	64 C7
Sachsen-Anhalt □	Germany	52°0N 12°0E	64 C7
Saco	U.S.A.	43°30N 70°27W	113 D12
Sacramento	U.S.A.	38°35N 121°29W	110 C2
Sacramento →	U.S.A.	38°3N 121°56W	110 C2
Sacramento Mts.	U.S.A.	32°30N 105°30W	110 D5
Sado	Japan	38°0N 138°25E	81 D6
Safford	U.S.A.	32°50N 109°43W	110 D5
Saffron Walden	U.K.	52°1N 0°16E	25 B9
Safi	Morocco	32°18N 9°20W	94 B4
Saga	Japan	33°15N 130°16E	81 G2
Sagaing	Burma	21°52N 95°59E	85 J19
Sagar	India	23°50N 78°44E	84 H11
Saginaw	U.S.A.	43°26N 83°56W	112 D6
Saginaw B.	U.S.A.	43°50N 83°40W	112 D6
Sagua la Grande	Cuba	22°50N 80°10W	115 C8
Saguenay →	Canada	48°22N 71°0W	113 A12
Sagunt	Spain	39°42N 0°18E	67 C5
Sahara	Africa	23°0N 5°0E	94 D6
Saharanpur	India	29°58N 77°33E	84 E10
Sahel	Africa	16°0N 5°0E	94 E5
Sahiwal	Pakistan	30°45N 73°8E	84 D8
Saidpur	Bangla.	25°48N 89°0E	85 G16
St. Abb's Head	U.K.	55°55N 2°8W	21 C11
St. Agnes	Corn., U.K.	50°19N 5°13W	27 G3
St. Agnes	Corn., U.K.	49°54N 6°21W	27 H1
St. Agnes Hd.	U.K.	50°19N 5°15W	27 G3
St. Albans	U.K.	51°45N 0°19W	25 C8
St. Albans	Vt., U.S.A.	44°49N 73°5W	113 C11
St. Albans	W. Va., U.S.A.	38°23N 81°50W	112 F7
St. Alban's Head	U.K.	50°34N 2°4W	24 E4
St. Andrews	U.K.	56°20N 2°47W	21 B10
St. Ann's	U.K.	55°14N 3°28W	21 D9
St. Ann's Bay	Jamaica	18°26N 77°12W	114 a
St. Asaph	U.K.	53°15N 3°27W	26 A7
St-Augustin	Canada	51°13N 58°38W	109 D14
St. Augustine	U.S.A.	29°54N 81°19W	111 E10
St. Austell	U.K.	50°20N 4°47W	27 G4
St. Bees	U.K.	54°30N 3°35W	22 C1
St. Bees Hd.	U.K.	54°31N 3°38W	22 C1
St. Blazey	U.K.	50°22N 4°43W	27 G4
St. Brides B.	U.K.	51°49N 5°9W	26 D3
St-Brieuc	France	48°30N 2°46W	66 B2
St. Buryan	U.K.	50°4N 5°37W	27 G2
St. Catharines	Canada	43°10N 79°15W	112 D8
St. Catherine's Pt.	U.K.	50°34N 1°18W	24 E6
St. Charles	U.S.A.	38°47N 90°29W	112 F2
St. Clair, L.	N. Amer.	42°27N 82°39W	112 D6
St. Clears	U.K.	51°49N 4°31W	26 D4
St. Cloud	U.S.A.	45°34N 94°10W	111 A8
St. Columb Major	U.K.	50°26N 4°58W	27 G4
St. Croix	U.S. Virgin Is.	17°45N 64°45W	115 D12
St. David's	U.K.	51°53N 5°16W	26 D3
St. David's Head	U.K.	51°54N 5°19W	26 D3
St-Denis	France	48°56N 2°20E	66 B5
St. Dennis	U.K.	50°23N 4°53W	27 G4
St-Dizier	France	48°38N 4°56E	66 B6
St. Dominick	U.K.	50°29N 4°16W	27 G3
St. Elias, Mt.	U.S.A.	60°18N 140°56W	108 C5
St. Elias Mts.	N. Amer.	60°33N 139°28W	108 D6
St. Enoder	U.K.	50°22N 4°59W	27 G4
St. Erth	U.K.	50°9N 5°26W	27 G3
St-Étienne	France	45°27N 4°22E	66 D6
St-Félicien	Canada	48°40N 72°25W	113 A11
St-Flour	France	45°2N 3°6E	66 D5
St. Gallen	Switz.	47°26N 9°22E	64 E5
St-Gaudens	France	43°6N 0°44E	66 E4
St. George	U.S.A.	37°6N 113°35W	110 C4
St. George's	Grenada	12°5N 61°43W	115 E12
St. George's Channel	Europe	52°0N 6°0W	31 E11
St. Germans	U.K.	50°23N 4°19W	27 G5
St. Helena	Atl. Oc.	15°58S 5°42W	52 E9
St. Helens	U.K.	53°27N 2°44W	23 F3
St. Helens, Mt.	U.S.A.	46°12N 122°12W	110 A2
St. Helier	U.K.	49°10N 2°7W	27 J9
St-Hyacinthe	Canada	45°40N 72°58W	109 E12
St. Ignace	U.S.A.	45°52N 84°44W	112 C5
St. Issey	U.K.	50°30N 4°57W	27 G4
St. Ives	Cambs., U.K.	52°20N 0°4W	25 B8
St. Ives	Corn., U.K.	50°12N 5°30W	27 G3
St. Ives B.	U.K.	50°13N 5°27W	27 G3
St-Jean, L.	Canada	48°40N 72°0W	113 A12
St-Jérôme	Canada	45°47N 74°0W	113 C11
St. John	Canada	45°20N 66°8W	109 E13
St. John →	N. Amer.	45°12N 66°5W	104 E13
St. John I.	U.S. Virgin Is.	18°20N 64°42W	115 e
St. John's	Antigua & B.	17°6N 61°51W	115 D12
St. John's	Canada	47°35N 52°40W	109 E14
St. Johns	U.S.A.	43°0N 84°33W	112 D5
St. Johns →	U.S.A.	30°24N 81°24W	111 D10
St. Johns Chapel	U.K.	54°44N 2°10W	22 C4
St. John's Pt.	Ireland	54°34N 8°27W	28 B5
St. Johnsbury	U.S.A.	44°25N 72°1W	113 C11
St-Joseph	Martinique	14°38N 61°4W	114 c
St. Joseph	Mich., U.S.A.	42°6N 86°29W	112 D4
St. Joseph	Mo., U.S.A.	39°46N 94°50W	111 C8
St. Joseph, L.	Canada	51°10N 90°35W	109 D10
St. Just	U.K.	50°7N 5°42W	27 G2
St. Keverne	U.K.	50°3N 5°6W	27 G3
St. Kilda	U.K.	57°49N 8°34W	62 C2
St. Kitts & Nevis ■	W. Indies	17°20N 62°40W	115 D12
St. Lawrence →	Canada	49°30N 66°0W	109 E14
St. Lawrence, Gulf of	Canada	48°25N 62°0W	109 E13
St. Lawrence I.	U.S.A.	63°30N 170°30W	108 C3
St. Levan	U.K.	50°2N 5°41W	27 G2
St-Lô	France	49°7N 1°5W	66 B3
St-Louis	Guadeloupe	15°56N 61°19W	114 b
St. Louis	Senegal	16°8N 16°27W	94 E2
St. Louis	U.S.A.	38°37N 90°11W	112 F2
St. Lucia ■	W. Indies	14°0N 60°57W	115 f
St. Mabyn	U.K.	50°30N 4°47W	27 G4
St. Magnus B.	U.K.	60°25N 1°35W	18 B14
St-Marc	Haiti	19°10N 72°41W	115 D10
St. Margaret's-at-Cliffe	U.K.	51°9N 1°23E	25 D11
St-Martin ☑	W. Indies	18°0N 63°0W	115 D12
St-Martin, C.	Martinique	14°52N 61°14W	114 c
St. Martins	Barbados	13°5N 59°28W	115 g
St. Martin's	U.K.	49°58N 6°17W	27 H1
St. Mary Bourne	U.K.	51°15N 1°24W	24 D6
St. Mary's	Corn., U.K.	49°55N 6°18W	27 H1
St. Mary's	Orkney, U.K.	58°54N 2°54W	19 E12
St. Marys	U.S.A.	41°26N 78°34W	112 E8
St. Mary's Sd.	U.K.	49°54N 6°20W	27 H1
St. Matthew I.	U.S.A.	60°24N 172°42W	108 C2
St. Mawes	U.K.	50°10N 5°2W	27 G3
St. Merryn	U.K.	50°32N 5°1W	27 G3
St. Michael's Mount	U.K.	50°7N 5°29W	27 G3
St. Minver	U.K.	50°33N 4°53W	27 F4
St. Moritz	Switz.	46°30N 9°51E	64 E5
St-Nazaire	France	47°17N 2°12W	66 C2
St. Neots	U.K.	52°14N 0°15W	25 B8
St-Omer	France	50°45N 2°15E	66 A5
St. Osyth	U.K.	51°47N 1°5E	25 C11
St. Paul	U.S.A.	44°56N 93°5W	111 C8
St. Paul, Î.	Ind. Oc.	38°55S 77°34E	53 F13
St. Peter Port	U.K.	49°26N 2°33W	27 J8
St. Petersburg	Russia	59°55N 30°20E	70 C5
St. Petersburg	U.S.A.	27°46N 82°40W	111 E10
St-Pierre	Martinique	14°45N 61°10W	114 c
St-Pierre-et-Miquelon ☑	N. Amer.	46°55N 56°10W	109 E14
St-Quentin	France	49°50N 3°16E	66 B5
St. Stephen	Canada	45°16N 67°17W	113 C14
St. Stephen	U.K.	50°21N 4°53W	27 G4
St. Teath	U.K.	50°35N 4°45W	27 F4
St. Thomas	Canada	42°45N 81°10W	112 D7
St. Thomas I.	U.S. Virgin Is.	18°20N 64°55W	115 e
St-Tropez	France	43°17N 6°38E	66 E7
St. Tudy	U.K.	50°33N 4°45W	27 F4
St. Vincent, G.	Australia	35°0S 138°0E	98 G6
Ste-Anne	Guadeloupe	16°13N 61°24W	114 b
Ste. Genevieve	U.S.A.	37°59N 90°2W	112 G2
Ste-Marie	Canada	46°26N 71°0W	113 B12
Ste-Marie	Martinique	14°48N 61°1W	114 c
Ste-Rose	Guadeloupe	16°20N 61°45W	114 b
Saintes	France	45°45N 0°37W	66 D3
Saintes, Îs. des	Guadeloupe	15°50N 61°35W	114 b
Saintfield	U.K.	54°28N 5°49W	29 C10
Saintonge	France	45°40N 0°50W	66 D3
Saipan	N. Marianas	15°12N 145°45E	102 F6
Saitama	Japan	35°54N 139°38E	81 F7
Sajama	Bolivia	18°7S 69°0W	120 D3
Sakakawea, L.	U.S.A.	47°30N 101°25W	110 A6
Sakarya	Turkey	40°48N 30°25E	71 F5
Sakata	Japan	38°55N 139°50E	81 D6
Sakhalin	Russia	51°0N 143°0E	77 D15
Sakurajima	Japan	31°35N 130°39E	81 H2
Sala	Sweden	59°58N 16°35E	63 F7
Sala-y-Gómez	Pac. Oc.	26°28S 105°28W	103 K17
Salado →	La Pampa. Argentina	37°30S 67°0W	121 F3
Salado →	Santa Fe, Argentina	31°40S 60°41W	121 F3
Salālah	Oman	16°56N 53°59E	89 D5
Salamanca	Spain	40°58N 5°39W	67 B3
Salamanca	U.S.A.	42°10N 78°43W	112 D8
Salar de Uyuni	Bolivia	20°30S 67°45W	120 E3
Salavat	Russia	53°21N 55°55E	70 D10
Salaverry	Peru	8°15S 79°0W	120 C2
Salayar	Indonesia	6°7S 120°30E	83 F6
Salcombe	U.K.	50°14N 3°47W	27 G6
Saldanha	S. Africa	33°0S 17°58E	97 L3
Sale	Australia	38°6S 147°6E	98 H8
Salé	Morocco	34°3N 6°48W	94 B4
Sale	U.K.	53°26N 2°19W	23 F4
Salekhard	Russia	66°30N 66°35E	76 C7
Salem	India	11°40N 78°11E	84 P11
Salem	Ind., U.S.A.	38°36N 86°6W	112 F4
Salem	Mass., U.S.A.	42°31N 70°53W	113 D12
Salem	Ohio, U.S.A.	40°54N 80°52W	112 E7
Salem	Oreg., U.S.A.	44°56N 123°2W	110 B2
Salem	Va., U.S.A.	37°18N 80°3W	112 G7
Salerno	Italy	40°41N 14°47E	68 D6
Salford	U.K.	53°30N 2°18W	23 F4
Salford Priors	U.K.	52°10N 1°53W	24 B5
Salida	U.S.A.	38°32N 106°0W	110 C5
Salina	U.S.A.	38°50N 97°37W	110 C7
Salina Cruz	Mexico	16°10N 95°12W	114 D5
Salinas	Ecuador	2°10S 80°58W	120 C1
Salinas	U.S.A.	36°40N 121°39W	110 C2
Salinas →	U.S.A.	36°45N 121°48W	110 C2
Salinas Grandes	Argentina	30°0S 65°0W	121 E3
Salisbury	U.K.	51°4N 1°47W	24 D5
Salisbury	U.S.A.	38°22N 75°36W	113 F10
Salisbury I.	Canada	63°30N 77°0W	109 C12
Salisbury Plain	U.K.	51°14N 1°55W	24 D5
Salmon	U.S.A.	45°11N 113°54W	110 A4
Salmon →	U.S.A.	45°51N 116°47W	110 A3
Salmon Arm	Canada	50°40N 119°15W	108 D8
Salmon River Mts.	U.S.A.	44°50N 115°30W	110 B4
Salon-de-Provence	France	43°39N 5°6E	66 D5
Salsk	Russia	46°28N 41°30E	71 E7
Salt →	U.S.A.	33°23N 112°19W	110 D4
Salt Lake City	U.S.A.	40°45N 111°53W	110 B4
Salta	Argentina	24°57S 65°25W	121 E3
Saltash	U.K.	50°24N 4°14W	27 G5
Saltburn by the Sea	U.K.	54°35N 0°58W	22 C7
Saltcoats	U.K.	55°38N 4°47W	20 C6
Saltee Is.	Ireland	52°7N 6°37W	31 D9
Saltfleet	U.K.	53°25N 0°11E	23 F9
Saltfleetby	U.K.	53°23N 0°10E	23 F9
Saltillo	Mexico	25°25N 101°0W	114 B4
Salton Sea	U.S.A.	33°15N 115°45W	110 D3
Saltwood	U.K.	51°4N 1°2E	25 D11
Salvador	Brazil	13°0S 38°30W	122 B3
Salvador, El ■	Cent. Amer.	13°50N 89°0W	114 E7
Salween →	Burma	16°31N 97°37E	85 L20
Salyan	Azerbaijan	39°33N 48°59E	71 G8
Salzburg	Austria	47°48N 13°2E	64 E7
Salzgitter	Germany	52°9N 10°19E	64 B6
Samangān □	Afghan.	36°15N 68°3E	87 B12
Samar	Phil.	12°0N 125°0E	83 B7
Samara	Russia	53°8N 50°6E	70 D9
Samarinda	Indonesia	0°30S 117°9E	82 E5
Samarqand	Uzbekistan	39°40N 66°55E	87 B11
Sambalpur	India	21°28N 84°4E	85 J14
Sambhal	India	28°35N 78°37E	84 E11
Sambhar	India	26°52N 75°6E	84 F9
Samoa ■	Pac. Oc.	14°0S 172°0W	99 C16
Samos	Greece	37°45N 26°50E	69 F12
Samothraki	Greece	40°28N 25°28E	69 D11
Sampford Courtenay	U.K.	50°47N 3°58W	27 F6
Samsun	Turkey	41°15N 36°22E	71 F6
Samui, Ko	Thailand	9°30N 100°0E	82 C2
San →	Poland	50°45N 21°51E	65 C11
San Ambrosio	Pac. Oc.	26°28S 79°53W	103 K20
San Andrés, I. de	Caribbean	12°42N 81°46W	115 E8
San Andres Mts.	U.S.A.	33°0N 106°30W	110 D5
San Andrés Tuxtla	Mexico	18°27N 95°13W	114 D5
San Angelo	U.S.A.	31°28N 100°26W	110 D6
San Antonio	Chile	33°40S 71°40W	121 F2
San Antonio	U.S.A.	29°25N 98°29W	110 E7
San Antonio →	U.S.A.	28°30N 96°54W	111 E7
San Antonio Oeste	Argentina	40°40S 65°0W	121 G3
San Bernardino	U.S.A.	34°7N 117°19W	110 D3
San Bernardino Str.	Phil.	13°0N 125°0E	83 B6
San Bernardo	Chile	33°40S 70°50W	121 F2
San Blas, C.	U.S.A.	29°40N 85°21W	111 E9
San Carlos	Phil.	10°29N 123°25E	83 B6
San Carlos de Bariloche	Argentina	41°10S 71°25W	121 G2
San Carlos de Bolivar	Argentina	36°15S 61°6W	121 F3
San Cristóbal	Argentina	30°20S 61°10W	121 F3
San Cristóbal	Solomon Is.	10°30S 161°0E	99 C11
San Cristóbal	Venezuela	7°46N 72°14W	120 B2
San Cristóbal de las Casas	Mexico	16°45N 92°38W	114 D6
San Diego	U.S.A.	32°42N 117°9W	110 D3
San Felipe	Venezuela	10°20N 68°44W	120 A3
San Félix	Pac. Oc.	26°23S 80°0W	103 K20
San Fernando	Chile	34°30S 71°0W	121 F2
San Fernando	Spain	36°28N 6°17W	67 D2
San Fernando de Apure	Venezuela	7°54N 67°15W	120 B3
San Francisco	U.S.A.	37°46N 122°23W	110 C2
San Francisco, C. de	Colombia	6°18N 77°29W	117 C3
San Francisco de Macorís	Dom. Rep.	19°19N 70°15W	115 D10
San German	Puerto Rico	18°4N 67°4W	115 d
San Gottardo, P. del	Switz.	46°33N 8°33E	64 E5
San Ignacio	Bolivia	16°20S 60°55W	120 D3
San Joaquin →	U.S.A.	38°4N 121°51W	110 C2
San Jorge, G.	Argentina	46°0S 66°0W	121 G3
San José	Costa Rica	9°55N 84°2W	115 F8
San Jose	Phil.	12°27N 121°4E	83 B6
San Jose	U.S.A.	37°20N 121°53W	110 C2
San Jose →	U.S.A.	34°25N 106°45W	110 D5
San José de Chiquitos	Bolivia	17°53S 60°50W	120 D3
San José de Jáchal	Argentina	30°15S 68°46W	121 F3
San José de Mayo	Uruguay	34°27S 56°40W	121 F4
San Juan	Argentina	31°30S 68°30W	121 F3
San Juan	Dom. Rep.	18°49N 71°12W	115 D10
San Juan	Puerto Rico	18°28N 66°7W	115 d
San Juan →	Nic.	10°56N 83°42W	115 E8
San Juan →	U.S.A.	37°16N 110°26W	110 C4
San Juan de los Morros	Venezuela	9°55N 67°21W	120 B3
San Juan Mts.	U.S.A.	37°30N 107°0W	110 C5
San Lorenzo, Mte.	Argentina	47°40S 72°20W	121 G2
San Lucas, C.	Mexico	22°52N 109°53W	114 C3
San Luis	Argentina	33°20S 66°20W	121 F3
San Luis Obispo	U.S.A.	35°17N 120°40W	110 C2
San Luis Potosí	Mexico	22°9N 100°59W	114 C4
San Marcos	U.S.A.	29°53N 97°56W	110 E7
San Marino ■	Europe	43°56N 12°25E	68 C5
San Matías, G.	Argentina	41°30S 64°0W	121 G3
San Miguel	El Salv.	13°30N 88°12W	114 E7
San Miguel de Tucumán	Argentina	26°50S 65°20W	121 E3
San Nicolás	Argentina	33°25S 60°10W	121 F3
San Pedro	Ivory C.	4°50N 6°33W	94 H4
San Pedro de las Colonias	Mexico	25°45N 102°59W	114 B4
San Pedro de Macorís	Dom. Rep.	18°30N 69°18W	115 D11
San Pedro Sula	Honduras	15°30N 88°0W	114 D7
San Pietro	Italy	39°8N 8°17E	68 E3
San Rafael	Argentina	34°40S 68°21W	121 F3
San Remo	Italy	43°49N 7°46E	68 C2
San Salvador	El Salv.	13°40N 89°10W	114 E7
San Salvador de Jujuy	Argentina	24°10S 64°48W	121 E3
San Salvador I.	Bahamas	24°0N 74°40W	115 C10
San Sebastián	Puerto Rico	18°20N 66°59W	115 d
San Severo	Italy	41°41N 15°23E	68 D6
San Valentin, Mte.	Chile	46°30S 73°30W	121 G2
Sana'	Yemen	15°27N 44°12E	89 D3
Sanaga →	Cameroon	3°35N 9°38E	96 D1
Sanandaj	Iran	35°18N 47°1E	86 C6
Sancti Spíritus	Cuba	21°52N 79°33W	115 C9
Sancy, Puy de	France	45°32N 2°50E	66 D5
Sandakan	Malaysia	5°53N 118°4E	82 C5
Sanday	U.K.	59°16N 2°31W	19 D12
Sandbach	U.K.	53°9N 2°21W	23 F4
Sandgate	U.K.	51°4N 1°10E	25 D11
Sandhurst	U.K.	51°21N 0°48W	25 D7
Sandown	U.K.	50°40N 1°10W	24 E6
Sandpoint	U.S.A.	48°17N 116°33W	110 A3
Sandray	U.K.	56°53N 7°31W	18 J2
Sandringham	U.K.	52°51N 0°31E	25 A10
Sandusky	U.S.A.	41°27N 82°42W	112 E6
Sandwich	U.K.	51°16N 1°21E	25 D11
Sandy	U.K.	52°8N 0°17W	25 B8
Sandy	U.S.A.	40°32N 111°50W	110 B4
Sandy L.	Canada	53°2N 93°0W	108 D10
Sanford, Mt.	U.S.A.	62°13N 144°8W	108 C5
Sanghe, Pulau	Indonesia	3°35N 125°30E	83 D7
Sangli	India	16°55N 74°33E	84 L9
Sangre de Cristo Mts.	U.S.A.	37°30N 105°20W	110 C5
Sanikiluaq	Canada	56°32N 79°14W	109 D12
Sankt Pölten	Austria	48°12N 15°38E	64 D8
Sankuru →	Dem. Rep. of the Congo	4°17S 20°25E	96 E4
Sanliurfa	Turkey	37°12N 38°50E	71 G6
Sanlúcar de Barrameda	Spain	36°46N 6°21W	67 D2
Sanmenxia	China	34°47N 111°12E	79 E11
Sanming	China	26°15N 117°40E	79 F12
Sanquhar	U.K.	55°22N 3°54W	21 D8
Sant Feliu de Guíxols	Spain	41°45N 3°1E	67 B7
Santa Ana	El Salv.	14°0N 89°31W	114 E7
Santa Ana	U.S.A.	33°46N 117°52W	110 D3
Sant' Antíoco	Italy	39°4N 8°27E	68 E3
Santa Barbara	U.S.A.	34°25N 119°42W	110 D3
Santa Catarina □	Brazil	27°25S 48°30W	121 E5
Santa Clara	Cuba	22°20N 80°0W	115 C9
Santa Clarita	U.S.A.	34°24N 118°33W	110 D3
Santa Coloma de Gramenet	Spain	41°27N 2°13E	67 B7
Santa Cruz	Bolivia	17°43S 63°10W	120 D3
Santa Cruz	U.S.A.	36°58N 122°1W	110 C2
Santa Cruz de Tenerife	Canary Is.	28°28N 16°15W	94 C2
Santa Cruz Is.	Solomon Is.	10°30S 166°0E	99 C12
Santa Cruz Mts.	Jamaica	17°58N 77°43W	114 a
Santa Fé	Argentina	31°35S 60°41W	121 F3
Santa Fe	U.S.A.	35°41N 105°57W	110 C5
Santa Inés, I.	Chile	54°0S 73°0W	121 H2
Santa Isabel	Solomon Is.	8°0S 159°0E	99 B10
Santa Maria	Brazil	29°40S 53°48W	121 E4
Santa Maria	U.S.A.	34°57N 120°26W	110 D2
Santa María →	Mexico	31°0N 107°14W	114 A3
Santa Marta	Colombia	11°15N 74°13W	120 A2
Santa Marta, Sierra Nevada de	Colombia	10°55N 73°50W	120 A2
Santa Rosa	Argentina	36°40S 64°17W	121 F3
Santa Rosa	U.S.A.	38°26N 122°43W	110 C2

Santai   Soldotna

Santai *China* 31°5N 104°58E 78 E9
Santana do Livramento *Brazil* 30°55S 55°30W 121 F4
Santander *Spain* 43°27N 3°51W 67 A4
Santanilla, Is. *Honduras* 17°22N 83°57W 115 D8
Santarém *Brazil* 2°25S 54°42W 120 C4
Santarém *Portugal* 39°12N 8°42W 67 C1
Santiago *Chile* 33°26S 70°40W 121 F2
Santiago de Compostela *Spain* 42°52N 8°37W 67 A1
Santiago de Cuba *Cuba* 20°0N 75°49W 115 D9
Santiago de los Caballeros *Dom. Rep.* 19°30N 70°40W 115 D10
Santiago del Estero *Argentina* 27°50S 64°15W 121 E3
Santo Amaro *Brazil* 12°30S 38°43W 122 B3
Santo André *Brazil* 23°39S 46°29W 122 D1
Santo Antônio de Jesus *Brazil* 12°58S 39°16W 122 B3
Santo Domingo *Dom. Rep.* 18°30N 69°59W 115 D11
Santo Domingo de los Colorados *Ecuador* 0°15S 79°9W 120 C2
Santorini *Greece* 36°23N 25°27E 69 F11
Santos *Brazil* 24°0S 46°20W 122 D1
Santos Dumont *Brazil* 22°55S 43°10W 122 D2
Sanya *China* 18°14N 109°29E 79 H10
São Bernardo do Campo *Brazil* 23°45S 46°34W 122 D1
São Borja *Brazil* 28°39S 56°0W 121 E4
São Caitano *Brazil* 8°21S 36°6W 122 A3
São Carlos *Brazil* 22°0S 47°50W 122 D1
São Francisco → *Brazil* 10°30S 36°24W 122 B3
São Gonçalo *Brazil* 22°48S 43°5W 122 D2
São João da Boa Vista *Brazil* 22°0S 46°52W 122 D1
São João de Meriti *Brazil* 22°48S 43°22W 122 D2
São João del Rei *Brazil* 21°8S 44°15W 122 D2
São João do Piauí *Brazil* 8°21S 42°15W 122 A2
São José do Rio Preto *Brazil* 20°50S 49°20W 122 D1
São José dos Campos *Brazil* 23°7S 45°52W 122 D1
São Lourenço *Brazil* 2°39S 44°15W 120 C5
São Marcos → *Brazil* 18°15S 47°37W 122 C1
São Marcos, B. de *Brazil* 2°0S 44°0W 120 C5
São Mateus *Brazil* 18°44S 39°50W 122 C3
São Paulo *Brazil* 23°32S 46°38W 122 D1
São Paulo □ *Brazil* 22°0S 49°0W 120 E5
São Roque, C. de *Brazil* 5°30S 35°16W 120 C6
São Sebastião do Paraiso *Brazil* 20°54S 46°59W 122 D1
São Tomé *São Tomé & Príncipe* 0°10N 6°39E 90 F4
São Tomé & Príncipe ■ *Africa* 0°12N 6°39E 91 F4
São Vicente *Brazil* 23°57S 46°23W 122 D1
São Vicente, C. de *Portugal* 37°0N 9°0W 67 D1
Saône → *France* 45°44N 4°50E 66 D6
Sapele *Nigeria* 5°50N 5°40E 94 G7
Sapporo *Japan* 43°0N 141°21E 81 B7
Saqqez *Iran* 36°15N 46°20E 86 B6
Sar-e Pol *Afghan.* 36°10N 66°0E 87 B11
Saraburi *Thailand* 14°30N 100°55E 82 B2
Sarajevo *Bos.-H.* 43°52N 18°26E 69 C8
Saranac Lakes *U.S.A.* 44°20N 74°28W 113 C10
Saransk *Russia* 54°10N 45°10E 70 D8
Sarapul *Russia* 56°28N 53°48E 70 C9
Sarasota *U.S.A.* 27°20N 82°32W 111 E10
Saratoga Springs *U.S.A.* 43°5N 73°47W 113 D11
Saratov *Russia* 51°30N 46°2E 71 D8
Sarawak □ *Malaysia* 2°0N 113°0E 82 D4
Sarda → *India* 27°21N 81°23E 85 F12
Sardinia □ *Italy* 40°0N 9°0E 68 D3
Sargasso Sea *Atl. Oc.* 27°0N 72°0W 104 G13
Sargodha *Pakistan* 32°10N 72°40E 84 C8
Sarh *Chad* 9°5N 18°23E 95 G9
Sārī *Iran* 36°30N 53°4E 87 B8
Sariwon *N. Korea* 38°31N 125°46E 79 D14
Sark *U.K.* 49°25N 2°22W 27 J9
Sarlat-la-Canéda *France* 44°54N 1°13E 66 D4
Sarmiento *Argentina* 45°35S 69°5W 121 G3
Sarnia *Canada* 42°58N 82°23W 109 E11
Sarreguemines *France* 49°5N 7°4E 66 B7
Sarthe → *France* 47°33N 0°31W 66 C3
Sasebo *Japan* 33°10N 129°43E 81 G1
Saskatchewan □ *Canada* 54°40N 106°0W 108 D9
Saskatchewan → *Canada* 53°37N 100°40W 108 D9
Saskatoon *Canada* 52°10N 106°38W 108 D9
Sássari *Italy* 40°43N 8°34E 68 D3
Sassnitz *Germany* 54°29N 13°39E 64 A7
Satmala Hills *Andhra Pradesh, India* 19°45N 78°45E 84 K11
Satmala Hills *Maharashtra, India* 20°15N 74°40E 84 J9
Satna *India* 24°35N 80°50E 85 G12
Satpura Ra. *India* 21°25N 76°10E 84 J10
Satu Mare *Romania* 47°46N 22°55E 65 E12
Saudi Arabia ■ *Asia* 26°0N 44°0E 89 B3
Sault Ste. Marie *Canada* 46°30N 84°20W 112 B5
Saumur *France* 47°15N 0°5W 66 C3
Saurimo *Angola* 9°40S 20°12E 96 F4
Sava → *Serbia* 44°50N 20°26E 69 B9
Savai'i *Samoa* 13°28S 172°24W 99 C16
Savannah *U.S.A.* 32°5N 81°6W 111 D10
Savannah → *U.S.A.* 32°2N 80°53W 111 D10
Savannakhet *Laos* 16°30N 104°49E 82 A2
Savoie □ *France* 45°26N 6°25E 66 D7
Savona *Italy* 44°17N 8°30E 68 B3
Sawatch Range *U.S.A.* 39°0N 106°30W 110 C5
Sawbridgeworth *U.K.* 51°48N 0°9E 25 C9
Sawel Mt. *U.K.* 54°50N 7°2W 29 B7
Sawston *U.K.* 52°8N 0°10E 25 D9
Sawtry *U.K.* 52°27N 0°17W 25 B8
Sawu *Indonesia* 10°35S 121°50E 83 F6
Sawu Sea *Indonesia* 9°30S 121°50E 83 F6
Saxilby *U.K.* 53°16N 0°38W 23 F7
Saxlingham Nethergate *U.K.* 52°32N 1°18E 25 A11
Saxmundham *U.K.* 52°13N 1°30E 25 B12
Sayan Mts. *Russia* 54°0N 96°0E 77 D10
Saydā *Lebanon* 33°35N 35°25E 86 C3
Sayre *U.S.A.* 41°59N 76°32W 112 E9
Sázava → *Czech Rep.* 49°53N 14°24E 64 D8
Scafell Pike *U.K.* 54°27N 3°14W 22 D2

Scalby *U.K.* 54°18N 0°26W 22 D8
Scalloway *U.K.* 60°9N 1°17W 18 B15
Scalpay *Highl., U.K.* 57°18N 6°0W 18 H6
Scalpay *W. Isles, U.K.* 57°52N 6°40W 18 G4
Scamblesby *U.K.* 53°17N 0°5W 23 F8
Scandicci *Italy* 43°45N 11°11E 68 C4
Scandinavia *Europe* 64°0N 12°0E 56 C8
Scapa Flow *U.K.* 58°53N 3°3W 19 E11
Scarba *U.K.* 56°11N 5°43W 20 B4
Scarborough *U.K.* 54°17N 0°24W 22 D8
Scariff I. *Ireland* 51°44N 10°15W 30 E2
Scarning *U.K.* 52°41N 0°54E 25 A10
Scarp *U.K.* 58°1N 7°8W 18 F3
Schaffhausen *Switz.* 47°42N 8°39E 64 E5
Schelde → *Belgium* 51°15N 4°16E 64 C3
Schenectady *U.S.A.* 42°49N 73°57W 113 D11
Schiehallion *U.K.* 56°40N 4°6W 20 A7
Schleswig *Germany* 54°31N 9°34E 64 A5
Schleswig-Holstein □ *Germany* 54°30N 9°30E 64 A5
Schœlcher *Martinique* 14°36N 61°7W 114 c
Schreiber *Canada* 48°45N 87°20W 112 A4
Schwäbische Alb *Germany* 48°20N 9°30E 64 D5
Schwarzwald *Germany* 48°30N 8°20E 64 D5
Schwerin *Germany* 53°36N 11°22E 64 B6
Schwyz *Switz.* 47°2N 8°39E 64 E5
Scilly Is. *U.K.* 49°56N 6°22W 27 H1
Scioto → *U.S.A.* 38°44N 83°1W 112 F6
Scole *U.K.* 52°22N 1°10E 25 B11
Scone *U.K.* 56°25N 3°24W 21 B9
Scopwick *U.K.* 53°8N 0°24W 23 F8
Scotia Sea *Antarctica* 56°5S 56°0W 55 B18
Scotland □ *U.K.* 57°0N 4°0W 62 C5
Scott I. *Antarctica* 67°0S 179°0E 55 C11
Scottish Borders □ *U.K.* 55°35N 2°50W 21 C10
Scottsbluff *U.S.A.* 41°52N 103°40W 110 B6
Scottsburg *U.S.A.* 38°41N 85°47W 112 F5
Scrabster *U.K.* 58°36N 3°33W 19 E10
Scranton *U.S.A.* 41°25N 75°40W 113 E10
Scremerston *U.K.* 55°44N 2°0W 22 A5
Scunthorpe *U.K.* 53°36N 0°39W 23 E7
Scutari *Albania* 42°4N 19°32E 69 C8
Scutari *Turkey* 41°1N 29°0E 86 A2
Seaford *U.K.* 50°47N 0°7E 25 E9
Seaford *U.S.A.* 38°39N 75°37W 113 F10
Seaforth, L. *U.K.* 57°52N 6°36W 18 G4
Seaham *U.K.* 54°50N 1°20W 22 C6
Seahouses *U.K.* 55°34N 1°39W 22 A5
Seal → *Canada* 59°4N 94°48W 108 D10
Seamer *U.K.* 54°14N 0°26W 22 D8
Seascale *U.K.* 54°24N 3°29W 22 D2
Seaton *Cumb., U.K.* 54°40N 3°31W 22 C1
Seaton *Devon, U.K.* 50°42N 3°5W 27 F7
Seaton Delaval *U.K.* 55°5N 1°33W 22 B6
Seattle *U.S.A.* 47°36N 122°19W 110 A2
Sebastián Vizcaino, B. *Mexico* 28°0N 114°30W 114 B2
Şebinkarahisar *Turkey* 40°22N 38°28E 71 F6
Sedalia *U.S.A.* 38°42N 93°14W 111 C8
Sedan *France* 49°43N 4°57E 66 B6
Sedbergh *U.K.* 54°20N 2°31W 22 D3
Sedgefield *U.K.* 54°40N 1°26W 22 C6
Seend *U.K.* 51°21N 2°4W 24 D4
Segesta *Italy* 37°56N 12°50E 68 F5
Ségou *Mali* 13°30N 6°16W 94 F4
Segovia *Spain* 40°57N 4°10W 67 B3
Séguéla *Ivory C.* 7°55N 6°40W 94 G4
Sehore *India* 23°10N 77°5E 84 H10
Seil *U.K.* 56°18N 5°38W 20 B4
Seine → *France* 49°26N 0°26E 66 B4
Sekondi-Takoradi *Ghana* 4°58N 1°45W 94 H5
Selborne *U.K.* 51°6N 0°56W 25 D7
Selby *U.K.* 53°47N 1°5W 23 E6
Selebi-Phikwe *Botswana* 21°58S 27°48E 97 J5
Selenge Mörön → *Asia* 52°16N 106°16E 78 A10
Selkirk *Canada* 50°10N 96°55W 108 D10
Selkirk *U.K.* 55°33N 2°50W 21 C10
Selkirk Mts. *Canada* 51°15N 117°40W 108 D8
Sellafield *U.K.* 54°25N 3°29W 22 D2
Selma *U.S.A.* 32°25N 87°1W 111 D9
Selsey *U.K.* 50°44N 0°47W 25 E7
Selsey Bill *U.K.* 50°43N 0°47W 25 E7
Selvas *Brazil* 6°30S 67°0W 120 C3
Selwyn L. *Canada* 60°0N 104°30W 108 C9
Selwyn Mts. *Canada* 63°0N 130°0W 108 C6
Semarang *Indonesia* 7°0S 110°26E 82 F4
Semey *Kazakhstan* 50°30N 80°10E 78 A5
Semnān *Iran* 35°40N 53°23E 87 C8
Sena Madureira *Brazil* 9°5S 68°45W 120 C3
Sendai *Japan* 38°15N 140°53E 81 D7
Seneca L. *U.S.A.* 42°40N 76°54W 112 D9
Senegal ■ *W. Afr.* 14°30N 14°30W 94 F3
Sénégal → *W. Afr.* 15°48N 16°32W 94 E2
Senegambia *Africa* 12°45N 12°0W 90 E2
Senhor-do-Bonfim *Brazil* 10°30S 40°10W 122 B2
Senja *Norway* 69°25N 17°30E 63 D7
Senlis *France* 49°13N 2°35E 66 B5
Sennen *U.K.* 50°4N 5°42W 27 G2
Sens *France* 48°11N 3°15E 66 B5
Seoul *S. Korea* 37°31N 126°58E 79 D14
Seph → *U.K.* 54°18N 1°8W 22 D6
Sept-Îles *Canada* 50°13N 66°22W 109 D13
Seram *Indonesia* 3°10S 129°0E 83 E7
Seram Sea *Indonesia* 2°30S 128°30E 83 E7
Serang *Indonesia* 6°8S 106°10E 82 F3
Serbia ■ *Europe* 43°20N 20°0E 69 B9
Serdar *Turkmenistan* 39°4N 56°23E 87 B9
Seremban *Malaysia* 2°43N 101°53E 82 D2
Serengeti Plain *Tanzania* 2°40S 35°0E 96 E6
Sergipe □ *Brazil* 10°30S 37°30W 122 B3
Sergiyev Posad *Russia* 56°20N 38°10E 70 C6
Serhetabat *Turkmenistan* 35°20N 62°18E 87 C10
Serifos *Greece* 37°9N 24°30E 69 F11
Serov *Russia* 59°29N 60°35E 70 C11
Serowe *Botswana* 22°25S 26°43E 97 J5
Serpukhov *Russia* 54°55N 37°28E 70 D6
Serra *Brazil* 20°7S 40°18W 122 D2
Serra de Mesa, Barragem de *Brazil* 14°30S 49°10W 122 B1
Serrinha *Brazil* 11°39S 39°0W 122 B3

Sète *France* 43°25N 3°42E 66 E5
Sete Lagoas *Brazil* 19°27S 44°16W 122 C2
Sétif *Algeria* 36°9N 5°26E 94 A7
Settat *Morocco* 33°0N 7°40W 94 B4
Settle *U.K.* 54°5N 2°16W 22 D4
Settlement, The *Br. Virgin Is.* 18°43N 64°22W 115 e
Setúbal *Portugal* 38°30N 8°58W 67 C1
Setúbal, B. de *Portugal* 38°40N 8°56W 67 C1
Seul, Lac *Canada* 50°20N 92°30W 108 D10
Sevan, L. *Armenia* 40°30N 45°20E 71 F8
Sevastopol *Ukraine* 44°35N 33°30E 71 F5
Seven → *U.K.* 54°12N 0°52W 22 D7
Sevenoaks *U.K.* 51°16N 0°11E 25 D9
Severn → *Canada* 56°2N 87°36W 109 D11
Severn → *U.K.* 51°35N 2°40W 24 C3
Severn Beach *U.K.* 51°33N 2°39W 24 C3
Severn Stoke *U.K.* 52°5N 2°12W 24 B4
Severnaya Zemlya *Russia* 79°0N 100°0E 77 B10
Severodvinsk *Russia* 64°27N 39°58E 70 B6
Severomorsk *Russia* 69°5N 33°27E 70 A5
Sevier → *U.S.A.* 39°4N 113°6W 110 C4
Sevier L. *U.S.A.* 38°54N 113°9W 110 C4
Seville *Spain* 37°23N 5°58W 67 D2
Seward *U.S.A.* 60°7N 149°27W 108 C5
Seward Peninsula *U.S.A.* 65°30N 166°0W 108 C3
Seychelles ■ *Ind. Oc.* 5°0S 56°0E 91 G9
Seyðisfjörður *Iceland* 65°16N 13°57W 63 A3
Seydişehir *Turkey* 37°25N 31°51E 71 G5
Seymour *U.S.A.* 38°58N 85°53W 112 F5
Sfântu Gheorghe *Romania* 45°52N 25°48E 65 F13
Sfax *Tunisia* 34°49N 10°48E 95 B8
Shaanxi □ *China* 35°0N 109°0E 79 C10
Shabeelle → *Somali Rep.* 2°0N 44°0E 89 G3
Shache *China* 38°20N 77°10E 78 D4
Shaftesbury *U.K.* 51°0N 2°11W 24 D4
Shahjahanpur *India* 27°54N 79°57E 84 F11
Shakhty *Russia* 47°40N 40°16E 71 E7
Shaki *Nigeria* 8°41N 3°21E 94 G6
Shaldon *U.K.* 50°32N 3°31W 27 F6
Shaluli Shan *China* 30°40N 99°55E 78 E8
Shamo, L. *Ethiopia* 5°45N 37°30E 89 F2
Shan □ *Burma* 21°30N 98°30E 85 J21
Shandong □ *China* 36°0N 118°0E 79 D12
Shandong Pen. *China* 37°0N 121°0E 79 D13
Shanghai *China* 31°15N 121°26E 79 C13
Shangqiu *China* 34°26N 115°36E 79 C12
Shangrao *China* 28°25N 117°59E 79 D12
Shangshui *China* 33°42N 114°35E 79 C11
Shanklin *U.K.* 50°38N 1°11W 24 E6
Shannon → *Ireland* 52°35N 9°30W 30 C4
Shannon ✈ (SNN) *Ireland* 52°42N 8°57W 30 C5
Shannon, Mouth of the *Ireland* 52°30N 9°55W 30 D3
Shantou *China* 23°18N 116°40E 79 G12
Shanxi □ *China* 37°0N 112°0E 79 D11
Shaoguan *China* 24°48N 113°35E 79 G11
Shaoxing *China* 30°0N 120°35E 79 C13
Shaoyang *China* 27°14N 111°25E 79 F11
Shap *U.K.* 54°32N 2°40W 22 C3
Shapinsay *U.K.* 59°3N 2°51W 19 D12
Shaqrā' *Si. Arabia* 25°15N 45°16E 86 E6
Shaqrā' *Yemen* 13°22N 45°44E 89 E4
Sharjah *U.A.E.* 25°23N 55°26E 87 E8
Shark B. *Australia* 25°30S 113°32E 98 F1
Sharm el Sheikh *Egypt* 27°53N 34°18E 86 E3
Sharon *U.S.A.* 41°14N 80°31W 112 E7
Sharpness *U.K.* 51°43N 2°28W 24 C4
Sharya *Russia* 58°22N 45°20E 70 C8
Shashi *China* 30°25N 112°14E 79 E11
Shasta, Mt. *U.S.A.* 41°25N 122°12W 110 B2
Shatt al Arab *Asia* 29°57N 48°34E 86 D7
Shawano *U.S.A.* 44°47N 88°36W 112 C3
Shawbury *U.K.* 52°48N 2°39W 23 G3
Shawinigan *Canada* 46°35N 72°50W 109 E12
Shawnee *U.S.A.* 35°20N 96°55W 111 C7
Shebbear *U.K.* 50°51N 4°15W 27 F5
Sheboygan *U.S.A.* 43°46N 87°45W 112 D4
Sheelin, L. *Ireland* 53°48N 7°20W 28 D7
Sheep Haven *Ireland* 55°11N 7°52W 28 A6
Sheerness *U.K.* 51°26N 0°47E 25 D10
Sheffield *U.K.* 53°23N 1°28W 23 F6
Shefford *U.K.* 52°2N 0°20W 25 B8
Shehy Mts. *Ireland* 51°47N 9°15W 30 E4
Shelburne *Canada* 43°47N 65°20W 113 D15
Shelby *U.S.A.* 48°30N 111°51W 110 A4
Shelbyville *Ill., U.S.A.* 39°24N 88°48W 112 F3
Shelbyville *Ind., U.S.A.* 39°31N 85°47W 112 F5
Shelikhov G. *Russia* 59°30N 157°0E 77 D16
Shenandoah *U.S.A.* 40°49N 76°12W 113 E9
Shenandoah → *U.S.A.* 39°19N 77°44W 112 F9
Shendi *Sudan* 16°46N 33°22E 95 E12
Shenfield *U.K.* 51°38N 0°22E 25 D9
Shenyang *China* 41°48N 123°27E 79 C13
Shenzhen *China* 22°32N 114°5E 79 a
Shepparton *Australia* 36°23S 145°26E 98 H8
Sheppey, I. of *U.K.* 51°25N 0°48E 25 D10
Shepshed *U.K.* 52°47N 1°18W 23 G6
Shepton Mallet *U.K.* 51°11N 2°33W 24 D3
Sherborne *U.K.* 50°57N 2°31W 24 E3
Sherborne St. John *U.K.* 51°17N 1°7W 24 D6
Sherbrooke *Canada* 45°28N 71°57W 113 C12
Sherburn *N. Yorks., U.K.* 54°12N 0°32W 22 D7
Sherburn *N. Yorks., U.K.* 53°48N 1°15W 23 E6
Shere *U.K.* 51°13N 0°27W 25 D8
Sherfield English *U.K.* 51°1N 1°34W 24 D5
Sheridan *U.S.A.* 44°48N 106°58W 110 B5
Sheriff Hutton *U.K.* 54°5N 1°0W 22 D7
Sheringham *U.K.* 52°56N 1°13E 25 A11
Sherkin I. *Ireland* 51°28N 9°26W 30 E3
Sherman *U.S.A.* 33°38N 96°36W 111 D7
Sherston *U.K.* 51°34N 2°14W 24 C4
Sherwood Forest *U.K.* 53°6N 1°7W 23 F6
Shetland □ *U.K.* 60°30N 1°30W 18 B15
Shetland Is. *U.K.* 60°30N 1°30W 18 B15
Sheyenne → *U.S.A.* 47°2N 96°50W 111 A7
Shiant Is. *U.K.* 57°54N 6°22W 18 G3
Shibām *Yemen* 15°59N 48°36E 89 D4
Shiel, L. *U.K.* 56°48N 5°34W 18 J6
Shifnal *U.K.* 52°39N 2°23W 23 G4
Shihezi *China* 44°15N 86°2E 78 C6

Shijiazhuang *China* 38°2N 114°28E 79 D11
Shikarpur *Pakistan* 27°57N 68°39E 84 F6
Shikoku □ *Japan* 33°30N 133°30E 81 G3
Shilbottle *U.K.* 55°22N 1°40W 22 B5
Shildon *U.K.* 54°38N 1°38W 22 C5
Shiliguri *India* 26°45N 88°25E 85 F16
Shillelagh *Ireland* 52°45N 6°32W 31 C9
Shillingstone *U.K.* 50°53N 2°15W 24 E4
Shillong *India* 25°35N 91°53E 85 G17
Shimla *India* 31°2N 77°9E 84 D10
Shimoga *India* 13°57N 75°32E 84 N9
Shimonoseki *Japan* 33°58N 130°55E 81 G2
Shin, L. *U.K.* 58°5N 4°30W 19 F8
Shinyanga *Tanzania* 3°45S 33°27E 96 E6
Shipdham *U.K.* 52°38N 0°54E 25 A10
Shipley *U.K.* 53°50N 1°47W 23 E5
Shipston-on-Stour *U.K.* 52°3N 1°37W 24 B5
Shipton under Wychwood *U.K.* 51°51N 1°36W 24 C5
Shīrāz *Iran* 29°42N 52°30E 87 D8
Shire → *Africa* 17°42S 35°19E 97 H7
Shirebrook *U.K.* 53°12N 1°13W 23 F6
Shivpuri *India* 25°26N 77°42E 84 G10
Shizuishan *China* 39°15N 106°50E 78 D10
Shizuoka *Japan* 34°57N 138°24E 81 F6
Shoeburyness *U.K.* 51°32N 0°49E 25 C10
Shoreham by Sea *U.K.* 50°50N 0°16W 25 E8
Shreveport *U.S.A.* 32°31N 93°45W 111 D8
Shrewsbury *U.K.* 52°43N 2°45W 23 G3
Shrewton *U.K.* 51°12N 1°54W 24 D5
Shrirampur *India* 22°44N 88°21E 85 H16
Shrivenham *U.K.* 51°36N 1°38W 24 C5
Shropshire □ *U.K.* 52°36N 2°45W 23 G3
Shuangliao *China* 43°29N 123°30E 79 C13
Shuangyashan *China* 46°28N 131°5E 79 B15
Shule *China* 39°25N 76°3E 78 D4
Shumagin Is. *U.S.A.* 55°7N 160°30W 108 D4
Shumen *Bulgaria* 43°18N 26°55E 69 C12
Shwebo *Burma* 22°30N 95°45E 85 H19
Shymkent *Kazakhstan* 42°18N 69°36E 87 A12
Si Kiang = Xi Jiang → *China* 22°5N 113°20E 79 G11
Siahan Range *Pakistan* 27°30N 64°40E 84 F4
Sialkot *Pakistan* 32°32N 74°30E 84 C9
Šiauliai *Lithuania* 55°56N 23°15E 63 F8
Šibenik *Croatia* 43°48N 15°54E 68 C6
Siberia *Russia* 60°0N 100°0E 72 B11
Siberut *Indonesia* 1°30S 99°0E 82 E1
Sibi *Pakistan* 29°30N 67°54E 84 E5
Sibiu *Romania* 45°45N 24°9E 65 F13
Sible Hedingham *U.K.* 51°59N 0°37E 25 C10
Sibolga *Indonesia* 1°42N 98°45E 82 D1
Sibsey *U.K.* 53°2N 0°1E 23 F9
Sibu *Malaysia* 2°18N 111°49E 82 D4
Sibuyan Sea *Phil.* 12°30N 122°20E 83 B6
Sichuan □ *China* 30°30N 103°0E 78 E9
Sicily *Italy* 37°30N 14°30E 68 F6
Sicuani *Peru* 14°21S 71°10W 120 D2
Sidbury *U.K.* 50°42N 3°14W 27 F7
Sidi-bel-Abbès *Algeria* 35°13N 0°39W 94 A5
Sidlaw Hills *U.K.* 56°32N 3°2W 21 A9
Sidlesham *U.K.* 50°47N 0°47W 25 E7
Sidmouth *U.K.* 50°40N 3°15W 27 F7
Sidney *Nebr., U.S.A.* 41°8N 102°59W 110 B6
Sidney *Ohio, U.S.A.* 40°17N 84°9W 112 E5
Sidra, G. of *Libya* 31°40N 18°30E 95 B9
Siedlce *Poland* 52°10N 22°20E 65 B12
Siegen *Germany* 50°51N 8°0E 64 C5
Siena *Italy* 43°19N 11°21E 68 C4
Sierra Blanca Peak *U.S.A.* 33°23N 105°49W 110 D5
Sierra Leone ■ *W. Afr.* 9°0N 12°0W 94 G3
Sierra Madre *Mexico* 16°0N 93°0W 104 H10
Sierra Madre Occidental *Mexico* 27°0N 107°0W 114 B3
Sierra Madre Oriental *Mexico* 25°0N 100°0W 114 C5
Sierra Nevada *Spain* 37°3N 3°15W 67 D4
Sierra Nevada *U.S.A.* 39°0N 120°30W 110 C2
Sierra Vista *U.S.A.* 31°33N 110°18W 110 D4
Sifnos *Greece* 37°0N 24°45E 69 F11
Sighty Crag *U.K.* 55°7N 2°38W 22 B3
Sikar *India* 27°33N 75°10E 84 F9
Sikasso *Mali* 11°18N 5°35W 94 F4
Sikeston *U.S.A.* 36°53N 89°35W 112 G3
Sikhote Alin Ra. *Russia* 45°0N 136°0E 79 B16
Sikkim □ *India* 27°50N 88°30E 85 F16
Silesia *Poland* 51°0N 16°30E 64 C9
Silifke *Turkey* 36°22N 33°58E 71 G5
Siling Co *China* 31°50N 89°20E 78 E6
Silloth *U.K.* 54°52N 3°23W 22 C2
Silsden *U.K.* 53°55N 1°55W 23 E5
Silver City *U.S.A.* 32°46N 108°17W 110 D5
Silvermine Mts. *Ireland* 52°47N 8°15W 30 C6
Silverstone *U.K.* 52°5N 1°2W 24 B6
Silverton *U.K.* 50°49N 3°29W 27 F7
Simcoe, L. *Canada* 44°25N 79°20W 112 C8
Simeulue *Indonesia* 2°45N 95°45E 82 D1
Simferopol *Ukraine* 44°55N 34°3E 71 F5
Simi *Greece* 36°35N 27°50E 69 F12
Simonsbath *U.K.* 51°8N 3°46W 27 E6
Simonside *U.K.* 55°17N 1°59W 22 B5
Simplonpass *Switz.* 46°15N 8°3E 64 E5
Simpson Desert *Australia* 25°0S 137°0E 98 F6
Simpson Pen. *Canada* 68°34N 88°45W 109 C11
Sinai *Egypt* 29°0N 34°0E 95 C12
Sincelejo *Colombia* 9°18N 75°24W 120 B2
Sinclair's B. *U.K.* 58°31N 3°5W 19 E11
Sind Sagar Doab *Pakistan* 32°0N 71°30E 84 D7
Sindh □ *Pakistan* 26°0N 69°0E 84 G6
Sines *Portugal* 37°56N 8°51W 67 D1
Singapore ■ *Asia* 1°17N 103°51E 82 D2
Singaraja *Indonesia* 8°7S 115°6E 82 F5
Singida *Tanzania* 4°49S 34°48E 96 E6
Singkawang *Indonesia* 1°0N 108°57E 82 D3
Singleton *U.K.* 50°55N 0°46W 25 E7
Sinkiang □ *China* 42°0N 86°0E 78 C6
Sinop *Turkey* 42°1N 35°11E 71 F6
Sintra *Portugal* 38°47N 9°25W 67 C1
Sion *Switz.* 46°14N 7°20E 64 E4
Sion Mills *U.K.* 54°48N 7°29W 28 B7
Sioux City *U.S.A.* 42°30N 96°24W 111 B7
Sioux Falls *U.S.A.* 43°33N 96°44W 111 B7

Sioux Lookout *Canada* 50°10N 91°50W 108 D10
Siping *China* 43°8N 124°21E 79 C13
Sir James MacBrien, Mt. *Canada* 62°7N 127°41W 108 C7
Siracusa *Italy* 37°4N 15°17E 68 F6
Sirajganj *Bangla.* 24°25N 89°47E 85 G16
Sirsa *India* 29°33N 75°4E 84 E9
Sīstān *Asia* 30°50N 61°0E 87 D10
Sitapur *India* 27°38N 80°45E 85 F12
Sitges *Spain* 41°17N 1°47E 67 B6
Sitka *U.S.A.* 57°3N 135°20W 108 D6
Sittingbourne *U.K.* 51°21N 0°45E 25 D10
Sittwe *Burma* 20°18N 92°45E 85 J18
Sivas *Turkey* 39°43N 36°58E 71 G6
Sivrihisar *Turkey* 39°30N 31°35E 71 G5
Sīwa *Egypt* 29°11N 25°31E 95 C11
Siwalik Range *Nepal* 28°0N 83°0E 85 F12
Siwan *India* 26°13N 84°21E 85 F14
Six Cross Roads *Barbados* 13°7N 59°28W 115 g
Sixmilebridge *Ireland* 52°44N 8°46W 30 C5
Sizewell *U.K.* 52°12N 1°37E 25 B12
Sjælland *Denmark* 55°30N 11°30E 63 F6
Skagerrak *Denmark* 57°30N 9°0E 63 F5
Skagway *U.S.A.* 59°28N 135°19W 108 D6
Skeena → *Canada* 54°9N 130°5W 108 D6
Skegness *U.K.* 53°9N 0°20E 23 F9
Skeleton Coast *Namibia* 20°0S 13°0E 97 J2
Skellefteå *Sweden* 64°45N 20°58E 63 E8
Skellefteälven → *Sweden* 64°45N 21°10E 63 E8
Skellingthorpe *U.K.* 53°15N 0°37W 23 F7
Skelmersdale *U.K.* 53°33N 2°48W 23 E3
Skelmorlie *U.K.* 55°52N 4°53W 20 C6
Skelton *Cleve., U.K.* 54°34N 0°58W 22 C7
Skelton *Cumb., U.K.* 54°43N 2°51W 22 C3
Skerries, The *U.K.* 53°25N 4°36W 26 A4
Skiathos *Greece* 39°12N 23°30E 69 E10
Skibbereen *Ireland* 51°33N 9°16W 30 E4
Skiddaw *U.K.* 54°39N 3°9W 22 C2
Skien *Norway* 59°12N 9°35E 63 F6
Skikda *Algeria* 36°50N 6°58E 94 A7
Skipsea *U.K.* 53°58N 0°13W 23 E8
Skipton *U.K.* 53°58N 2°3W 23 E4
Skopelos *Greece* 39°9N 23°47E 69 E10
Skopje *Macedonia* 42°1N 21°26E 69 C9
Skovorodino *Russia* 54°0N 124°0E 77 D13
Skowhegan *U.S.A.* 44°46N 69°43W 113 C13
Skull *Ireland* 51°32N 9°34W 30 E3
Skye *U.K.* 57°15N 6°10W 18 H5
Skyros *Greece* 38°55N 24°34E 69 E11
Slaidburn *U.K.* 53°58N 2°26W 23 E4
Slaney → *Ireland* 52°26N 6°33W 31 D9
Slatina *Romania* 44°28N 24°22E 65 F13
Slave → *Canada* 61°18N 113°39W 108 C8
Slave Coast *W. Afr.* 6°0N 2°30E 94 G6
Slave Lake *Canada* 55°17N 114°43W 108 D8
Sleaford *U.K.* 53°0N 0°24W 23 F8
Sleat, Sd. of *U.K.* 57°5N 5°47W 18 H6
Sledmere *U.K.* 54°4N 0°35W 22 D7
Sleeper Is. *Canada* 58°30N 81°0W 109 D11
Sleights *U.K.* 54°27N 0°40W 22 D7
Slieve Aughty *Ireland* 53°4N 8°30W 30 B5
Slieve Bloom *Ireland* 53°4N 7°40W 31 B7
Slieve Donard *U.K.* 54°11N 5°55W 29 C10
Slieve Gamph *Ireland* 54°6N 9°0W 28 C4
Slieve Gullion *U.K.* 54°7N 6°26W 29 C9
Slieve League *Ireland* 54°40N 8°42W 28 B4
Slieve Mish *Ireland* 52°12N 9°50W 30 D3
Slievenamon *Ireland* 52°25N 7°34W 31 D7
Sligo *Ireland* 54°16N 8°28W 28 C5
Sligo □ *Ireland* 54°8N 8°42W 28 C4
Sligo B. *Ireland* 54°18N 8°40W 28 C4
Sliven *Bulgaria* 42°42N 26°19E 69 C12
Slough *U.K.* 51°30N 0°36W 25 D7
Slovak Rep. ■ *Europe* 48°30N 20°0E 65 D10
Slovenia ■ *Europe* 45°58N 14°30E 64 F8
Slovyansk *Ukraine* 48°55N 37°36E 71 E6
Słupsk *Poland* 54°30N 17°3E 65 A9
Slutsk *Belarus* 53°2N 27°31E 70 D4
Slyne Hd. *Ireland* 53°25N 10°10W 28 E1
Smallwood Res. *Canada* 54°5N 64°30W 109 D13
Smederevo *Serbia* 44°40N 20°57E 69 B9
Smerwick Harbour *Ireland* 52°12N 10°23W 30 D2
Smethwick *U.K.* 52°30N 1°57W 23 G5
Smithfield *U.K.* 54°59N 2°51W 22 C3
Smiths Falls *Canada* 44°55N 76°0W 113 C9
Smoky → *Canada* 56°10N 117°21W 108 D8
Smoky Hill → *U.S.A.* 39°4N 96°48W 111 C7
Smolensk *Russia* 54°45N 32°5E 70 D5
Snaefell *I. of Man* 54°16N 4°27W 29 C13
Snainton *U.K.* 54°14N 0°35W 22 D7
Snaith *U.K.* 53°42N 1°1W 23 E6
Snake → *U.S.A.* 46°12N 119°2W 110 A3
Snape *U.K.* 52°10N 1°30E 25 B12
Snettisham *U.K.* 52°53N 0°31E 25 A10
Snizort, L. *U.K.* 57°33N 6°28W 18 H5
Snohetta *Norway* 62°19N 9°16E 63 E5
Snow Hill *U.S.A.* 38°11N 75°24W 113 F10
Snowdon *U.K.* 53°4N 4°5W 26 A5
Snowdonia △ *U.K.* 53°7N 3°59W 26 A6
Snowy Mts. *Australia* 36°30S 148°20E 98 H8
Sobat, Nahr → *Sudan* 9°22N 31°33E 95 G12
Sobradinho, Represa de *Brazil* 9°30S 42°0W 120 C5
Sobral *Brazil* 3°50S 40°20W 120 C5
Soc Trang *Vietnam* 9°37N 105°50E 82 C3
Sochi *Russia* 43°35N 39°40E 71 F6
Société, Îs. de la *French Polynesia* 17°0S 151°0W 103 J12
Socorro *U.S.A.* 34°4N 106°54W 110 D5
Socotra *Yemen* 12°30N 54°0E 89 E5
Söderhamn *Sweden* 61°18N 17°10E 63 E7
Sofia *Bulgaria* 42°45N 23°20E 69 C10
Sognefjorden *Norway* 61°10N 5°50E 63 E5
Sohâg *Egypt* 26°33N 31°43E 95 C12
Soham *U.K.* 52°21N 0°21E 25 B9
Soissons *France* 49°25N 3°19E 66 B5
Sokhumi *Georgia* 43°0N 41°0E 71 F7
Sokodé *Togo* 9°0N 1°11E 94 G6
Sokoto *Nigeria* 13°2N 5°16E 94 F7
Solapur *India* 17°43N 75°56E 84 L9
Soldotna *U.S.A.* 60°29N 151°3W 108 C4

Soledad

Taunus

Soledad Colombia 10°55N 74°46W 120 A2
Solent, The U.K. 50°45N 1°25W 24 E6
Solihull U.K. 52°26N 1°47W 23 H5
Solikamsk Russia 59°38N 56°50E 70 C10
Solingen Germany 51°10N 7°5E 64 C4
Söller Spain 39°46N 2°43E 67 C7
Sologne France 47°40N 1°45E 66 C4
Solomon Is. ■ Pac. Oc. 6°0S 155°0E 99 B10
Solomon Sea Papua N. G. 7°0S 150°0E 98 B9
Solon China 46°32N 121°10E 79 B13
Solothurn Switz. 47°13N 7°32E 64 E4
Solway Firth U.K. 54°49N 3°35W 22 C1
Somali Pen. Africa 7°0N 46°0E 90 F8
Somali Rep. ■ Africa 7°0N 47°0E 89 F4
Somaliland □ Somali Rep. 9°0N 46°0E 89 F4
Sombrerete Mexico 23°38N 103°39W 114 C4
Somerby U.K. 52°42N 0°50W 23 G7
Somerset U.S.A. 37°5N 84°36W 112 G5
Somerset U.K. 51°9N 3°0W 24 D2
Somerset I. Canada 73°30N 93°0W 108 B10
Somersham U.K. 52°24N 0°1W 25 B8
Somerton U.K. 51°2N 2°43W 24 D3
Somme → France 50°11N 1°38E 66 A4
Songhua Hu China 43°35N 126°50E 79 C14
Songhua Jiang → China 47°45N 132°30E 79 B15
Songkhla Thailand 7°13N 100°37E 82 C2
Songpan China 32°40N 103°30E 78 E9
Sonid Youqi China 42°45N 112°48E 79 C11
Sonning U.K. 51°28N 0°54W 25 D7
Sonora → Mexico 29°5N 110°55W 114 B2
Sonoran Desert U.S.A. 33°40N 113°30W 110 D4
Sonoyta Mexico 31°51N 112°50W 114 A2
Sonsonate El Salv. 13°43N 89°44W 114 E7
Sopot Poland 54°27N 18°31E 65 A10
Sorel-Tracy Canada 46°0N 73°10W 113 C11
Soria Spain 41°43N 2°32W 67 B4
Sorocaba Brazil 23°31S 47°27W 122 D1
Søreya Norway 70°40N 22°30E 63 C8
Sosnowiec Poland 50°20N 19°10E 65 C10
Soufrière Guadeloupe 16°5N 61°40W 114 b
Soufrière St. Lucia 13°51N 61°3W 115 f
Soufrière Bay St. Lucia 13°51N 61°4W 115 f
Sound, The U.K. 50°20N 4°10W 27 G5
Souris → N. Amer. 49°40N 99°34W 108 E9
Sousse Tunisia 35°50N 10°38E 95 A8
South Africa ■ Africa 32°0S 23°0E 97 L4
South Australia □ Australia 32°0S 139°0E 98 G6
South Ayrshire □ U.K. 55°18N 4°41W 20 D6
South Bend U.S.A. 41°41N 86°15W 112 E4
South Benfleet U.K. 51°33N 0°36E 25 C10
South Brent U.K. 50°25N 3°51W 27 G6
South Carolina □ U.S.A. 34°0N 81°0W 111 D10
South Cave U.K. 53°47N 0°37W 23 E7
South Charleston U.S.A. 38°22N 81°44W 112 F7
South China Sea Asia 10°0N 113°0E 82 C4
South Dakota □ U.S.A. 44°15N 100°0W 110 B7
South Dorset Downs U.K. 50°40N 2°26W 24 E4
South Downs U.K. 50°52N 0°25W 25 E8
South East C. Australia 43°40S 146°50E 98 J8
South Esk → U.K. 56°43N 2°31W 19 J12
South Foreland U.K. 51°8N 1°24E 25 D11
South Georgia Antarctica 54°30S 37°0W 55 B1
South Harris U.K. 57°50N 7°0W 18 G4
South Hayling U.K. 50°47N 0°58W 25 E7
South I. N.Z. 44°0S 170°0E 99 J13
South Korea ■ Asia 36°0N 128°0E 79 C14
South Lanarkshire □ U.K. 55°37N 3°53W 21 C8
South Magnetic Pole Antarctica 64°8S 138°8E 55 C9
South Molton U.K. 51°1N 3°51W 27 E6
South Nahanni → Canada 61°3N 123°21W 108 C7
South Negril Pt. Jamaica 18°16N 78°22W 114 a
South Orkney Is. Antarctica 63°0S 45°0W 55 C18
South Ossetia □ Georgia 42°21N 44°2E 71 F7
South Petherton U.K. 50°57N 2°46W 24 E3
South Petherwin U.K. 50°36N 4°24W 27 F5
South Platte → U.S.A. 41°7N 100°42W 110 B6
South Pole Antarctica 90°0S 0°0 55 E
South Pt. Barbados 13°2N 59°32W 115 g
South Queensferry U.K. 56°0N 3°23W 21 C9
South Ronaldsay U.K. 58°48N 2°58W 19 E12
South Sandwich Is. Antarctica 57°0S 27°0W 55 B1
South Saskatchewan → Canada 53°15N 105°5W 108 D9
South Shetland Is. Antarctica 62°0S 59°0W 55 C18
South Shields U.K. 55°0N 1°25W 22 C6
South Tawton U.K. 50°44N 3°55W 27 F6
South Tyne → U.K. 54°59N 2°8W 22 C4
South Uist U.K. 57°20N 7°15W 18 H3
South Woodham Ferrers U.K. 51°39N 0°37E 25 C10
South Yorkshire □ U.K. 53°27N 1°36W 23 F5
Southam U.K. 52°18N 1°23W 24 B6
Southampton U.K. 50°54N 1°23W 24 E6
Southampton I. Canada 64°30N 84°0W 109 C11
Southborough U.K. 51°9N 0°16E 25 D9
Southend-on-Sea U.K. 51°32N 0°44E 25 C10
Southern Alps N.Z. 43°41S 170°11E 99 J13
Southern Indian L. Canada 57°10N 98°30W 108 D10
Southern Ocean Antarctica 62°0S 60°0E 53 H13
Southern Uplands U.K. 55°28N 3°52W 21 D8
Southery U.K. 52°31N 0°24E 25 A9
Southminster U.K. 51°40N 0°51E 25 C10
Southport U.K. 53°39N 3°0W 23 E2
Southwark □ U.K. 51°29N 0°6W 25 D8
Southwell U.K. 53°4N 0°57W 23 F7
Southwick U.K. 50°50N 0°13W 25 E8
Southwold U.K. 52°20N 1°41E 25 B12
Sovetsk Russia 55°6N 21°50E 63 F8
Sowerby U.K. 54°14N 1°21W 22 D6
Soweto S. Africa 26°14S 27°52E 97 K5
Spain ■ Europe 39°0N 4°0W 67 B4
Spalding U.K. 52°48N 0°9W 23 G8
Spanish Canada 46°12N 82°20W 112 B6
Spanish Town Br. Virgin Is. 18°43N 64°26W 115 e
Spanish Town Jamaica 18°0N 76°57W 114 a
Sparkford U.K. 51°2N 2°33W 24 D3
Sparks U.S.A. 39°32N 119°45W 110 C3
Sparta Greece 37°5N 22°25E 69 F10
Sparta U.S.A. 43°56N 90°49W 112 D2

Spartanburg U.S.A. 34°56N 81°57W 111 D10
Spartivento, C. Italy 37°55N 16°4E 68 F7
Speightstown Barbados 13°15N 59°39W 115 g
Speke U.K. 53°21N 2°52W 23 F3
Spencer U.S.A. 43°9N 95°9W 111 B7
Spencer G. Australia 34°0S 137°20E 98 G6
Spennymoor U.K. 54°42N 1°36W 22 C5
Sperrin Mts. U.K. 54°50N 7°0W 29 B7
Spey → U.K. 57°40N 3°6W 19 G11
Spilsby U.K. 53°10N 0°6E 23 F9
Spithead U.K. 50°45N 1°10W 24 E6
Split Croatia 43°31N 16°26E 68 C7
Spofforth U.K. 53°57N 1°27W 23 E6
Spokane U.S.A. 47°40N 117°24W 110 A3
Spooner U.S.A. 45°50N 91°53W 112 C2
Spratly Is. S. China Sea 8°20N 112°0E 82 C4
Spree → Germany 52°32N 13°12E 64 B7
Spring Hall Barbados 13°18N 59°36W 115 g
Springbok S. Africa 29°42S 17°54E 97 K3
Springfield Ill., U.S.A. 39°48N 89°39W 112 F3
Springfield Mass., U.S.A. 42°6N 72°35W 113 D11
Springfield Mo., U.S.A. 37°13N 93°17W 111 C8
Springfield Ohio, U.S.A. 39°55N 83°49W 112 F6
Springfield Oreg., U.S.A. 44°3N 123°1W 110 B2
Springhill Canada 45°40N 64°4W 113 C15
Springs S. Africa 26°13S 28°25E 97 K5
Sproatley U.K. 53°47N 0°11W 23 E8
Spurn Hd. U.K. 53°35N 0°8E 23 E9
Srebrenica Bos.-H. 44°6N 19°18E 69 B8
Sredinnyy Ra. Russia 57°0N 160°0E 77 D16
Sri Lanka ■ Asia 7°30N 80°50E 84 R12
Srikakulam India 18°14N 83°58E 85 K13
Srinagar India 34°5N 74°50E 84 B9
Stacks Mts. Ireland 52°20N 9°34W 30 D3
Staffa U.K. 56°27N 6°21W 20 B3
Stafford U.K. 52°49N 2°7W 23 G4
Staffordshire □ U.K. 52°53N 2°10W 23 G4
Staindrop U.K. 54°36N 1°47W 22 C5
Staines U.K. 51°26N 0°29W 25 D8
Stainforth U.K. 53°37N 1°0W 23 E7
Stainmore Forest U.K. 54°29N 2°5W 22 D4
Stainton U.K. 53°18N 0°24W 23 F8
Staithes U.K. 54°34N 0°46W 22 C7
Stakhanov Ukraine 48°35N 38°40E 71 E6
Stalbridge U.K. 50°57N 2°23W 24 E4
Stalham U.K. 52°47N 1°31E 25 A12
Stallingborough U.K. 53°35N 0°12W 23 E8
Stalybridge U.K. 53°28N 2°3W 23 F4
Stamford U.K. 52°39N 0°29W 23 G8
Stamford U.S.A. 41°3N 73°32W 113 E11
Stamford Bridge U.K. 54°0N 0°54W 23 E7
Stamfordham U.K. 55°3N 1°53W 22 B5
Standish U.K. 53°35N 2°41W 23 E3
Standish U.S.A. 43°59N 83°57W 112 D6
Stanford on Teme U.K. 52°18N 2°25W 24 B4
Stanhope U.K. 54°45N 2°1W 22 C4
Stanley Falk. Is. 51°40S 59°51W 121 H4
Stanley U.K. 54°53N 1°41W 22 C5
Stannington U.K. 55°7N 1°40W 22 B5
Stanovoy Ra. Russia 55°0N 130°0E 77 D13
Stansted, London ✈ (STN) U.K. 51°54N 0°14E 25 C9
Stansted Mountfitchet U.K. 51°52N 0°11E 25 C9
Stanwix U.K. 54°55N 2°56W 22 C3
Stapleford U.K. 52°57N 1°16W 23 G6
Staplehurst U.K. 51°9N 0°34E 25 D10
Stara Zagora Bulgaria 42°26N 25°39E 69 C11
Staraya Russa Russia 57°58N 31°23E 70 C5
Starbuck I. Kiribati 5°37S 155°55W 103 H12
Start B. U.K. 50°13N 3°39W 27 G6
Start Pt. U.K. 50°13N 3°39W 27 G6
Staryy Oskol Russia 51°19N 37°55E 71 D6
State College U.S.A. 40°48N 77°52W 112 E9
Staten, I. = Estados, I. de Los Argentina 54°40S 64°30W 121 H3
Staunton U.K. 51°57N 2°17W 24 C4
Staunton U.S.A. 38°9N 79°4W 112 F8
Stavanger Norway 58°57N 5°40E 63 F5
Staveley Cumb., U.K. 54°23N 2°48W 22 D3
Staveley Derby., U.K. 53°16N 1°21W 23 F6
Stavropol Russia 45°5N 42°0E 71 E7
Steiermark □ Austria 47°26N 15°0E 64 E8
Steinkjer Norway 64°1N 11°31E 63 E6
Stellarton Canada 45°32N 62°30W 113 C16
Stellenbosch S. Africa 33°58S 18°50E 97 L3
Stenhousemuir U.K. 56°2N 3°48W 21 B9
Stephenville Canada 48°31N 58°35W 109 E14
Steppe Asia 50°0N 50°0E 72 C7
Sterling Colo., U.S.A. 40°37N 103°13W 110 B6
Sterling Ill., U.S.A. 41°48N 89°42W 112 E3
Sterlitamak Russia 53°40N 56°0E 70 D6
Stettiner Haff Germany 53°47N 14°15E 64 B8
Stettler Canada 52°19N 112°40W 108 D8
Steubenville U.S.A. 40°22N 80°37W 112 E7
Stevenage U.K. 51°55N 0°13W 25 C8
Stevens Point U.S.A. 44°31N 89°34W 112 D3
Stevenston U.K. 55°39N 4°45W 20 C6
Stewart Canada 55°56N 129°57W 108 D6
Stewart → Canada 63°19N 139°26W 108 C6
Stewart I. N.Z. 46°58S 167°54E 99 K12
Stewarton U.K. 55°40N 4°32W 20 C6
Steyning U.K. 50°53N 0°18W 25 E8
Steyr Austria 48°3N 14°25E 64 D8
Stikine → Canada 56°40N 132°30W 108 D6
Stillington U.K. 54°6N 1°6W 22 D6
Stillwater U.S.A. 36°7N 97°4W 111 A8
Stiperstones U.K. 52°36N 2°55W 23 G3
Stirling U.K. 56°8N 3°57W 21 B8
Stirling □ U.K. 56°12N 4°18W 20 B7
Stobo U.K. 55°38N 3°17W 21 C9
Stockbridge U.K. 51°7N 1°29W 24 D6
Stockport U.K. 53°25N 2°9W 23 F4
Stocksbridge U.K. 53°29N 1°35W 23 F5
Stockton U.S.A. 37°58N 121°17W 110 C2
Stockton-on-Tees U.K. 54°35N 1°19W 22 C6
Stoer, Pt. of U.K. 58°16N 5°23W 18 F7
Stoke U.K. 51°26N 0°41E 25 D10
Stoke Ferry U.K. 52°34N 0°31E 25 A10
Stoke Fleming U.K. 50°19N 3°37W 27 G6

Stoke Mandeville U.K. 51°47N 0°47W 25 C7
Stoke-on-Trent U.K. 53°1N 2°11W 23 F4
Stoke Prior U.K. 52°19N 2°4W 24 B4
Stokesley U.K. 54°28N 1°12W 22 D6
Stone Bucks., U.K. 51°48N 0°52W 25 C7
Stone Staffs., U.K. 52°55N 2°9W 23 G4
Stonehaven U.K. 56°59N 2°12W 19 J13
Stonehouse U.K. 51°45N 2°16W 24 C4
Stonham Aspal U.K. 52°12N 1°8E 25 B11
Stony Stratford U.K. 52°3N 0°50W 25 B7
Stony Tunguska → Russia 61°50N 90°13E 77 C10
Stora Lulevatten Sweden 67°10N 19°30E 63 D7
Storavan Sweden 65°45N 18°10E 63 D7
Store Bælt Denmark 55°20N 11°0E 63 F6
Stormberge S. Africa 31°16S 26°17E 97 L5
Stornoway U.K. 58°13N 6°23W 18 F5
Storsjön Sweden 63°9N 14°30E 63 E6
Stort → U.K. 51°46N 0°2E 25 C9
Storuman Sweden 65°5N 17°10E 63 D7
Stotfold U.K. 52°1N 0°13W 25 B8
Stour → Dorset, U.K. 50°43N 1°47W 24 E5
Stour → Kent, U.K. 51°18N 1°22E 25 D11
Stour → Suffolk, U.K. 51°57N 1°4E 25 C11
Stour → Worcs., U.K. 52°21N 2°17W 24 B4
Stourbridge U.K. 52°28N 2°8W 23 H4
Stourport-on-Severn U.K. 52°21N 2°17W 24 B4
Stow U.K. 55°42N 2°50W 21 C10
Stow Bardolph U.K. 52°38N 0°24E 25 A9
Stow-on-the-Wold U.K. 51°56N 1°42W 24 C5
Stowmarket U.K. 52°12N 1°0E 25 B10
Strabane U.K. 54°50N 7°27W 28 B7
Stradbroke U.K. 52°19N 1°16E 25 B11
Stralsund Germany 54°18N 13°4E 64 A7
Strangford L. U.K. 54°30N 5°37W 29 C10
Stranraer U.K. 54°54N 5°1W 20 E5
Strasbourg France 48°35N 7°42E 66 B7
Stratford Canada 43°23N 81°0W 112 D7
Stratford St. Mary U.K. 51°58N 1°0E 25 C10
Stratford-upon-Avon U.K. 52°12N 1°42W 24 B5
Strath Avon → U.K. 57°18N 3°23W 19 H11
Strath Dearn U.K. 57°20N 4°0W 19 H9
Strath Glass U.K. 57°22N 4°42W 19 H8
Strath Halladale U.K. 58°30N 3°51W 19 F10
Strath Naver U.K. 58°24N 4°12W 19 F9
Strath of Kildonan U.K. 58°14N 3°56W 19 F10
Strath Spey U.K. 57°9N 3°49W 19 H10
Strath Tay U.K. 56°40N 3°48W 21 A8
Strathaven U.K. 55°40N 4°5W 20 C7
Strathbogie U.K. 57°25N 2°45W 19 H12
Strathmore Angus, U.K. 56°37N 3°7W 19 J11
Strathmore Highl., U.K. 58°22N 4°40W 19 F8
Strathpeffer U.K. 57°35N 4°32W 19 H8
Strathroy Canada 42°58N 81°38W 112 D7
Strathy Pt. U.K. 58°36N 4°1W 19 E9
Stratton U.K. 50°49N 4°32W 27 F4
Stratton St. Margaret U.K. 51°35N 1°44W 24 C5
Streatley U.K. 51°31N 1°8W 24 C6
Street U.K. 51°8N 2°44W 24 D3
Strensall U.K. 54°3N 1°2W 22 D6
Stretford U.K. 53°28N 2°17W 23 F4
Stroma U.K. 58°41N 3°7W 19 E11
Strómboli Italy 38°47N 15°13E 68 E6
Stromeferry U.K. 57°21N 5°33W 18 H6
Stromness U.K. 58°58N 3°17W 19 E11
Stronsay U.K. 59°7N 2°35W 19 D12
Stroud U.K. 51°45N 2°13W 24 C4
Stuart L. Canada 54°30N 124°30W 108 D7
Studland U.K. 50°39N 1°58W 24 E5
Studley U.K. 52°16N 1°53W 24 B5
Sturgeon Bay U.S.A. 44°50N 87°23W 112 C4
Sturgeon Falls Canada 46°25N 79°57W 112 B8
Sturminster Marshall U.K. 50°47N 2°5W 24 E4
Sturminster Newton U.K. 50°55N 2°18W 24 E4
Sturt Stony Desert Australia 28°30S 141°0E 98 F6
Sturton U.K. 53°19N 0°39W 23 F7
Stuttgart Germany 48°48N 9°11E 64 D5
Stuttgart U.S.A. 34°30N 91°33W 111 D8
Suakin Sudan 19°8N 37°20E 95 E13
Subā Si. Arabia 27°10N 35°40E 86 E3
Subotica Serbia 46°6N 19°39E 69 A8
Suceava Romania 47°38N 26°16E 65 E14
Suck → Ireland 53°17N 8°3W 30 B6
Sucre Bolivia 19°0S 65°15W 120 D3
Sudan ■ Africa 15°0N 30°0E 95 E11
Sudbury Canada 46°30N 81°0W 112 B7
Sudbury Derby., U.K. 52°54N 1°43W 23 G5
Sudbury Suffolk, U.K. 52°2N 0°45E 25 B10
Sûdd Sudan 8°20N 30°0E 95 G12
Sudeten Europe 50°20N 16°45E 65 C9
Suez Egypt 29°58N 32°31E 95 C12
Suez, G. of Egypt 28°40N 33°0E 95 C12
Suez Canal Egypt 31°0N 32°20E 95 B12
Suffolk □ U.K. 52°16N 1°0E 25 B11
Sugluk Canada 62°14N 75°38W 109 C12
Suḩār Oman 24°20N 56°40E 87 E9
Suihua China 46°32N 126°55E 79 B14
Suining China 30°26N 105°35E 78 E10
Suir → Ireland 52°16N 7°9W 31 D8
Sukabumi Indonesia 6°56S 106°50E 82 F3
Sukhona → Russia 61°15N 46°39E 70 C8
Sukkur Pakistan 27°42N 68°54E 84 F6
Sulaiman Range Pakistan 30°30N 69°50E 84 D6
Sulawesi Indonesia 2°0S 120°0E 83 E6
Sullana Peru 4°52S 80°39W 120 C1
Sullom Voe U.K. 60°27N 1°20W 18 B15
Sulu Arch. Phil. 6°0N 121°0E 83 C6
Sulu Sea E. Indies 8°0N 120°0E 83 C6
Sumare Brazil 22°49S 47°16W 122 D1
Sumatra Indonesia 0°40N 100°20E 82 D2
Sumba Indonesia 9°45S 119°35E 83 F5
Sumbawa Indonesia 8°26S 117°30E 82 F5
Sumburgh Hd. U.K. 59°52N 1°17W 18 C15
Summer L. U.S.A. 42°50N 120°45W 110 B2
Summerside Canada 46°24N 63°47W 109 E13
Sumqayıt Azerbaijan 40°34N 49°38E 71 F8
Sumter U.S.A. 33°55N 80°21W 111 D10
Sumy Ukraine 50°57N 34°50E 71 D5
Sun Valley U.S.A. 43°42N 114°21W 110 B4
Sunart, L. U.K. 56°42N 5°43W 18 J6

Sunbury U.S.A. 40°52N 76°48W 112 E9
Sunda, Selat Indonesia 6°20S 105°30E 82 F3
Sunda Is. Indonesia 5°0S 105°0E 102 H2
Sundarbans Asia 22°0N 89°0E 85 J16
Sunderland U.K. 54°55N 1°23W 22 C6
Sundsvall Sweden 62°23N 17°17E 63 E7
Sungaipenuh Indonesia 2°1S 101°20E 82 E2
Sunk Island U.K. 53°39N 0°6E 23 E8
Sunninghill U.K. 51°24N 0°39W 25 D7
Sunshine Coast Australia 26°30S 153°0E 98 F9
Superior U.S.A. 46°44N 92°6W 112 B1
Superior, L. N. Amer. 47°0N 87°0W 112 B4
Sūr Lebanon 33°19N 35°16E 86 C3
Sura → Russia 56°6N 46°0E 70 C8
Surabaya Indonesia 7°17S 112°45E 82 F4
Surakarta Indonesia 7°35S 110°48E 82 F4
Surat India 21°12N 72°55E 84 J8
Surgut Russia 61°14N 73°20E 76 C8
Surigao Phil. 9°47N 125°29E 83 C7
Suriname ■ S. Amer. 4°0N 56°0W 120 B4
Surrey □ U.K. 51°15N 0°31W 25 D7
Surt Libya 31°11N 16°39E 95 B9
Surtsey Iceland 63°20N 20°30W 63 B1
Susquehanna → U.S.A. 39°33N 76°5W 112 F9
Sussex Canada 45°45N 65°37W 113 C15
Sutherland U.K. 58°12N 4°50W 19 F8
Sutlej → Pakistan 29°23N 71°3E 84 E7
Sutterton U.K. 52°55N 0°6W 23 G8
Sutton □ U.K. 51°21N 0°11W 25 D8
Sutton Bridge U.K. 52°47N 0°10E 23 G9
Sutton Coldfield U.K. 52°35N 1°49W 23 G5
Sutton Courtenay U.K. 51°39N 1°16W 24 C6
Sutton in Ashfield U.K. 53°8N 1°16W 23 F6
Sutton-on-Sea U.K. 53°18N 0°16E 23 F9
Sutton Scotney U.K. 51°9N 1°20W 24 D6
Suva Fiji 18°6S 178°30E 99 D14
Suvorov Is. Cook Is. 13°15S 163°5W 103 J11
Suwałki Poland 54°8N 22°59E 65 A12
Suzhou China 31°19N 120°38E 79 E13
Svalbard Arctic 78°0N 17°0E 54 B8
Svealand Sweden 60°20N 15°0E 63 E7
Sverdrup Chan. Canada 79°56N 96°25W 109 B10
Sverdrup Is. Canada 79°0N 97°0W 109 B10
Svir → Russia 60°30N 32°48E 70 B5
Swadlincote U.K. 52°47N 1°33W 23 G5
Swaffham U.K. 52°39N 0°42E 25 A10
Swakopmund Namibia 22°37S 14°30E 97 J2
Swan Hill Australia 35°20S 143°33E 98 H7
Swan River Canada 52°10N 101°16W 108 D9
Swanage U.K. 50°36N 1°58W 24 E5
Swansea U.K. 51°37N 3°57W 27 D6
Swansea B. U.K. 51°32N 3°57W 27 D6
Swartberge S. Africa 33°20S 22°0E 90 K6
Swaziland ■ Africa 26°30S 31°30E 97 K6
Sweden ■ Europe 57°0N 15°0E 63 F7
Sweetwater U.S.A. 32°28N 100°25W 110 D6
Swellendam S. Africa 34°1S 20°26E 97 L4
Swift Current Canada 50°20N 107°45W 108 D9
Swilly, L. Ireland 55°12N 7°33W 28 A6
Swindon U.K. 51°34N 1°46W 24 C5
Swineshead U.K. 52°57N 0°10W 23 G8
Swinford Ireland 53°57N 8°58W 28 D4
Swinton Borders, U.K. 55°43N 2°15W 21 C11
Swinton Gt. Man., U.K. 53°31N 2°20W 23 E4
Swinton S. Yorks., U.K. 53°29N 1°20W 23 F6
Switzerland ■ Europe 46°30N 8°0E 64 E5
Swords Ireland 53°28N 6°13W 31 B10
Sydney Australia 33°52S 151°12E 98 G9
Sydney Canada 46°7N 60°7W 113 B17
Syktyvkar Russia 61°45N 50°40E 70 C9
Sylhet Bangla. 24°54N 91°52E 85 G17
Sylhet □ Bangla. 24°50N 91°50E 85 G17
Symington U.K. 55°36N 3°36W 21 C8
Symonds Yat U.K. 51°51N 2°38W 24 C3
Syracuse U.S.A. 43°3N 76°9W 113 D9
Syrdarya → Kazakhstan 46°3N 61°0E 76 E7
Syria ■ Asia 35°0N 38°0E 86 C4
Syrian Desert Asia 32°0N 40°0E 86 C4
Syston U.K. 52°42N 1°3W 23 G6
Syzran Russia 53°12N 48°30E 70 D8
Szczecin Poland 53°27N 14°27E 64 B8
Szczecinek Poland 53°43N 16°41E 65 B9
Szeged Hungary 46°16N 20°10E 65 E11
Székesfehérvár Hungary 47°15N 18°25E 65 E10
Szekszárd Hungary 46°22N 18°42E 65 E10
Szolnok Hungary 47°10N 20°15E 65 E11
Szombathely Hungary 47°14N 16°38E 65 E9

T

Tabas Iran 33°35N 56°55E 87 C9
Tablas Phil. 12°25N 122°2E 83 B6
Table B. S. Africa 33°35S 18°25E 97 L3
Table Mt. S. Africa 33°58S 18°26E 97 L3
Tabora Tanzania 5°2S 32°50E 96 F6
Tabrīz Iran 38°7N 46°20E 86 B6
Tabuaeran Kiribati 3°51N 159°22W 103 G12
Tacheng China 46°40N 82°58E 78 B5
Tacloban Phil. 11°15N 124°58E 83 B6
Tacna Peru 18°0S 70°20W 120 D2
Tacoma U.S.A. 47°14N 122°26W 110 A2
Tacuarembó Uruguay 31°45S 56°0W 121 F4
Tadcaster U.K. 53°53N 1°16W 23 E6
Tademaït, Plateau du Algeria 28°30N 2°30E 94 C6
Tadley U.K. 51°21N 1°7W 24 D6
Taganrog Russia 47°12N 38°50E 71 E6
Taguatinga Brazil 12°27S 46°22W 122 B1
Tagus → Europe 38°40N 9°24W 67 C1
Tahiti French Polynesia 17°37S 149°27W 103 J13
Tahoe, L. U.S.A. 39°6N 120°2W 110 C2
Tahoua Niger 14°57N 5°16E 94 F7
Tahta Egypt 26°44N 31°32E 95 C12
T'ai Hu China 31°5N 120°10E 79 E13
T'aichung Taiwan 24°9N 120°37E 79 G13
Taimyr Peninsula Russia 75°0N 100°0E 77 B11
Tain U.K. 57°49N 4°4W 19 G9
T'ainan Taiwan 23°17N 120°18E 79 G13
T'aipei Taiwan 25°4N 121°29E 79 F13
Taiping Malaysia 4°51N 100°44E 82 D2
Taitao, Pen. de Chile 46°30S 75°0W 121 G2

T'aitung Taiwan 22°43N 121°4E 79 G13
Taiwan ■ Asia 23°30N 121°0E 79 G13
Taiwan Str. Asia 24°40N 120°0E 79 G12
Taiyuan China 37°52N 112°33E 79 D11
Ta'izz Yemen 13°35N 44°2E 89 E3
Tajikistan ■ Asia 38°30N 70°0E 87 B12
Tak Thailand 16°52N 99°8E 82 A1
Takamatsu Japan 34°20N 134°5E 81 F4
Takaoka Japan 36°47N 137°0E 81 E5
Takasaki Japan 36°20N 139°0E 81 E6
Takeshima = Tokdo Asia 37°15N 131°52E 81 E2
Taklamakan Desert China 38°0N 83°0E 78 D5
Talara Peru 4°38S 81°18W 120 C1
Talaud, Kepulauan Indonesia 4°30N 126°50E 83 D7
Talavera de la Reina Spain 39°55N 4°46W 67 C3
Talca Chile 35°28S 71°40W 121 F2
Talcahuano Chile 36°40S 73°10W 121 F2
Taldyqorghan Kazakhstan 45°10N 78°45E 78 B4
Talgarth U.K. 52°0N 3°14W 26 D7
Taliabu Indonesia 1°50S 125°0E 83 E6
Tallaght Ireland 53°17N 6°22W 31 B10
Tallahassee U.S.A. 30°27N 84°17W 111 D10
Tallinn Estonia 59°22N 24°48E 63 F8
Taloyoak Canada 69°32N 93°32W 108 C10
Taltal Chile 25°23S 70°33W 121 E2
Tamale Ghana 9°22N 0°50W 94 G5
Tamana Kiribati 2°30S 175°59E 99 A13
Tamanrasset Algeria 22°50N 5°30E 94 D7
Tamar → U.K. 50°27N 4°15W 27 G5
Tambov Russia 52°45N 41°28E 70 D7
Tame → U.K. 52°44N 1°43W 23 G5
Tamerton Foliot U.K. 50°25N 4°11W 27 G5
Tamil Nadu □ India 11°0N 77°0E 84 P10
Tampa U.S.A. 27°56N 82°27W 111 E10
Tampa B. U.S.A. 27°50N 82°30W 111 E10
Tampere Finland 61°30N 23°50E 63 E8
Tampico Mexico 22°13N 97°51W 114 C5
Tamworth Australia 31°7S 150°58E 98 G9
Tamworth U.K. 52°39N 1°41W 23 G5
Tana → Kenya 2°32S 40°31E 96 E8
Tana → Norway 70°30N 28°14E 63 C9
Tana, L. Ethiopia 13°5N 37°30E 89 E2
Tanami Desert Australia 18°50S 132°0E 98 D5
Tanana → U.S.A. 65°10N 151°58W 108 C4
Tandil Argentina 37°15S 59°6W 121 F4
Tandragee U.K. 54°21N 6°24W 29 C9
Tanezrouft Algeria 23°9N 0°11E 94 D6
Tanga Tanzania 5°5S 39°2E 96 F7
Tanganyika, L. Africa 6°40S 30°0E 96 F6
Tanggula Shan China 32°40N 92°10E 78 E7
Tanggula Shankou China 32°42N 92°27E 78 E6
Tangier Morocco 35°50N 5°49W 94 A4
Tangshan China 39°38N 118°10E 79 D12
Tanimbar, Kepulauan Indonesia 7°30S 131°30E 83 F8
Tanjungbalai Indonesia 2°55N 99°44E 82 D1
Tanjungpandan Indonesia 2°43S 107°38E 82 E3
Tanjungredeb Indonesia 2°9N 117°29E 82 D5
Tanna Vanuatu 19°30S 169°20E 99 D12
Tannu Ola Asia 51°0N 94°0E 77 D10
Tanta Egypt 30°45N 30°57E 95 B12
Tanworth U.K. 52°20N 1°50W 24 B5
Tanzania ■ Africa 6°0S 34°0E 96 F6
Taolanaro Madag. 25°2S 47°0E 97 K9
Taos U.S.A. 36°24N 105°35W 110 C5
Tapachula Mexico 14°54N 92°17W 114 E6
Tapajós → Brazil 2°24S 54°41W 120 C4
Tapti → India 21°8N 72°41E 84 J8
Taquaritinga Brazil 21°24S 48°30W 122 D1
Tarakan Indonesia 3°20N 117°35E 82 D5
Taransay U.K. 57°54N 7°0W 18 G3
Táranto Italy 40°28N 17°14E 68 D7
Táranto, G. di Italy 40°8N 17°20E 68 D7
Tarawa Kiribati 1°30N 173°0E 102 G9
Taraz Kazakhstan 42°54N 71°22E 87 A12
Tarbagatay, Khrebet Kazakhstan 48°0N 83°0E 76 E9
Tarbat Ness U.K. 57°52N 3°47W 19 G10
Tarbela Dam Pakistan 34°8N 72°52E 84 B8
Tarbert Argyll & Bute, U.K. 55°52N 5°25W 20 C5
Tarbert W. Isles, U.K. 57°54N 6°49W 18 G4
Tarbes France 43°15N 0°3E 66 E4
Tarcoola Australia 30°44S 134°36E 98 G5
Taree Australia 31°50S 152°30E 98 G9
Tarfaya Morocco 27°55N 12°55W 94 C3
Târgoviște Romania 44°55N 25°27E 65 F13
Târgu Jiu Romania 45°5N 23°19E 65 F12
Târgu Mureș Romania 46°31N 24°38E 65 E13
Tarija Bolivia 21°30S 64°40W 120 E3
Tarim Basin China 40°0N 84°0E 78 D5
Tarim He → China 39°30N 88°30E 78 D6
Tarleton U.K. 53°41N 2°50W 23 E3
Tarn → France 44°5N 1°6E 66 E4
Tarnów Poland 50°3N 21°0E 65 C11
Taroudannt Morocco 30°30N 8°52W 94 B4
Tarporley U.K. 53°10N 2°40W 23 F3
Tarragona Spain 41°5N 1°17E 67 B6
Tarsus Turkey 36°58N 34°55E 71 G5
Tartu Estonia 58°20N 26°44E 63 F9
Tarțūs Syria 34°55N 35°55E 86 C3
Tashkent Uzbekistan 41°20N 69°10E 87 A12
Tasiilaq Greenland 65°40N 37°20W 54 C6
Tasikmalaya Indonesia 7°18S 108°12E 82 F3
Tasman Sea Pac. Oc. 36°0S 160°0E 99 H10
Tasmania □ Australia 42°0S 146°30E 98 J8
Tassili n' Ajjer Algeria 25°47N 8°1E 94 C7
Tatar Str. Russia 50°0N 141°0E 77 E14
Tatarstan □ Russia 55°30N 51°30E 70 D8
Tatnam, C. Canada 57°16N 91°0W 109 D10
Tatra Slovak Rep. 49°20N 20°0E 65 D11
Tatta Pakistan 24°42N 67°55E 84 G5
Tattenhall U.K. 53°7N 2°46W 23 F3
Tatui Brazil 23°25S 47°53W 122 D1
Tatvan Turkey 38°31N 42°15E 71 G7
Taubaté Brazil 23°0S 45°36W 122 D1
Tauern Austria 47°15N 12°40E 64 E7
Taunggyi Burma 20°50N 97°0E 85 J20
Taunton U.K. 51°1N 3°5W 24 D2
Taunton U.S.A. 41°54N 71°6W 113 E12
Taunus Germany 50°13N 8°34E 64 C5

Taurus Mts. *Turkey* 37°N 32°30E 71 G5
Tavan Bogd Uul *Mongolia* 49°10N 87°49E 78 B6
Tavistock *U.K.* 50°33N 4°9W 27 F5
Taw → *U.K.* 51°4N 4°4W 27 E5
Tawas City *U.S.A.* 44°16N 83°31W 112 C6
Tawau *Malaysia* 4°20N 117°55E 82 D5
Taxkorgan Tajik Zizhixian *China* 37°49N 75°14E 78 D4
Tay → *U.K.* 56°37N 3°38W 21 A8
Tay, Firth of *U.K.* 56°25N 3°8W 21 B9
Tay, L. *U.K.* 56°32N 4°8W 20 A7
Taylor, Mt. *U.S.A.* 35°14N 107°37W 110 C5
Taylorville *U.S.A.* 39°33N 89°18W 112 F3
Tayport *U.K.* 56°27N 2°52W 21 B10
Taz → *Russia* 67°32N 78°40E 76 C8
Taza *Morocco* 34°16N 4°6W 94 B5
Tbilisi *Georgia* 41°43N 44°50E 71 F7
Tebay *U.K.* 54°26N 2°35W 22 D3
Tébessa *Algeria* 35°22N 8°8E 94 A7
Tees → *U.K.* 54°37N 1°10W 22 C6
Teesdale *U.K.* 54°37N 2°10W 22 C4
Teesside *U.K.* 54°36N 1°15W 22 C6
Tegal *Indonesia* 6°52S 109°8E 82 F3
Tegucigalpa *Honduras* 14°5N 87°14W 114 E7
Tehrān *Iran* 35°41N 51°25E 87 C7
Tehuantepec *Mexico* 16°21N 95°13W 114 D5
Tehuantepec, G. de *Mexico* 15°50N 95°12W 114 D5
Tehuantepec, Istmo de *Mexico* 17°15N 94°30W 114 D6
Teifi → *U.K.* 52°5N 4°41W 26 D4
Teign → *U.K.* 50°32N 3°32W 27 F6
Teignmouth *U.K.* 50°33N 3°31W 27 F6
Tejen *Turkmenistan* 37°23N 60°31E 87 B10
Tekirdağ *Turkey* 40°58N 27°30E 71 F4
Tel Aviv-Jaffa *Israel* 32°4N 34°48E 86 C3
Tela *Honduras* 15°40N 87°28W 114 D7
Telegraph Creek *Canada* 58°0N 131°10W 108 D6
Teles Pires → *Brazil* 7°21S 58°3W 120 C4
Telford *U.K.* 52°40N 2°27W 23 G4
Tell City *U.S.A.* 37°57N 86°46W 112 G4
Tellicherry *India* 11°45N 75°30E 84 P9
Telpos Iz *Russia* 63°16N 59°13E 70 B10
Teluk Intan *Malaysia* 4°3N 101°0E 82 D2
Tema *Ghana* 5°41N 0°0 94 G5
Teme → *U.K.* 52°11N 2°13W 24 B4
Temirtau *Kazakhstan* 50°5N 72°56E 76 D8
Témiscaming *Canada* 46°44N 79°5W 112 B8
Temple *U.S.A.* 31°6N 97°21W 111 D7
Temple Combe *U.K.* 51°0N 2°24W 24 D4
Temple Ewell *U.K.* 51°8N 1°17E 25 D11
Temple Sowerby *U.K.* 54°38N 2°36W 22 C3
Templemore *Ireland* 52°47N 7°51W 30 C7
Temuco *Chile* 38°45S 72°40W 121 F2
Tenali *India* 16°15N 80°35E 85 L12
Tenbury Wells *U.K.* 52°19N 2°35W 24 B3
Tenby *U.K.* 51°40N 4°42W 26 D4
Tenerife *Canary Is.* 28°15N 16°35W 94 C2
Tengchong *China* 25°0N 98°28E 78 D8
Tengger Desert *China* 38°0S 104°0E 78 D9
Tennant Creek *Australia* 19°30S 134°15E 98 D5
Tennessee □ *U.S.A.* 36°0N 86°30W 111 C9
Tennessee → *U.S.A.* 37°4N 88°34W 111 C9
Tenterden *U.K.* 51°4N 0°42E 25 D10
Teófilo Otoni *Brazil* 17°50S 41°30W 122 C2
Tepic *Mexico* 21°30N 104°54W 114 C4
Teraina *Kiribati* 4°43N 160°25W 103 G12
Téramo *Italy* 42°39N 13°42E 68 C5
Teresina *Brazil* 5°9S 42°45W 120 C5
Termiz *Uzbekistan* 37°15N 67°15E 87 B11
Ternate *Indonesia* 0°45N 127°25E 83 D7
Terni *Italy* 42°34N 12°37E 68 C5
Ternopil *Ukraine* 49°30N 25°40E 65 D13
Terrace *Canada* 54°30N 128°35W 108 D7
Terrassa *Spain* 41°34N 2°1E 67 B7
Terre Haute *U.S.A.* 39°28N 87°25W 112 F4
Terschelling *Neths.* 53°25N 5°20E 64 B3
Teruel *Spain* 40°22N 1°8W 67 B5
Tesiyn Gol → *Mongolia* 50°40N 93°20E 78 A7
Teslin *Canada* 60°10N 132°43W 108 C6
Teslin → *Canada* 61°34N 134°35W 104 C6
Test → *U.K.* 50°56N 1°29W 24 E6
Tetbury *U.K.* 51°38N 2°10W 24 C4
Tete *Mozam.* 16°13S 33°33E 97 H6
Tetney *U.K.* 53°29N 0°1W 23 E8
Tétouan *Morocco* 35°35N 5°21W 94 A4
Tetovo *Macedonia* 42°1N 20°59E 69 C9
Teuco → *Argentina* 25°35S 60°11W 121 E3
Teutoburger Wald *Germany* 52°5N 8°22E 64 B5
Teviot → *U.K.* 55°29N 2°38W 21 D10
Teviotdale *U.K.* 55°25N 2°50W 21 D10
Teviothead *U.K.* 55°20N 2°56W 21 D10
Tewkesbury *U.K.* 51°59N 2°9W 24 C4
Texarkana *U.S.A.* 33°26N 94°3W 111 D8
Texas □ *U.S.A.* 31°40N 98°30W 110 D7
Texel *Neths.* 53°5N 4°50E 64 B3
Teynham *U.K.* 51°20N 0°50E 25 D10
Tezpur *India* 26°40N 92°45E 85 F18
Thabana Ntlenyana *Lesotho* 29°30S 29°16E 97 K5
Thabazimbi *S. Africa* 24°40S 27°21E 97 J5
Thailand ■ *Asia* 16°0N 102°0E 82 A2
Thailand, G. of *Asia* 11°30N 101°0E 82 B2
Thal Desert *Pakistan* 31°10N 71°30E 84 D7
Thame *U.K.* 51°45N 0°58W 25 C7
Thame → *U.K.* 51°39N 1°9W 24 C6
Thames → *Canada* 42°20N 82°25W 112 D6
Thames → *U.K.* 51°29N 0°34E 25 D10
Thanet, I. of *U.K.* 51°21N 1°20E 25 D11
Thanjavur *India* 10°48N 79°12E 84 P11
Thar Desert *India* 28°0N 72°0E 84 F7
Thargomindah *Australia* 27°58S 143°46E 98 F7
Thasos *Greece* 40°40N 24°40E 69 D11
Thatcham *U.K.* 51°24N 1°15W 24 D6
Thaxted *U.K.* 51°57N 0°22E 25 C9
The Everglades *U.S.A.* 25°50N 81°0W 111 E10
The Pas *Canada* 53°45N 101°15W 108 D9
The Wash *U.K.* 52°58N 0°20E 25 B9
The Weald *U.K.* 51°4N 0°20E 25 D9
Theale *U.K.* 51°26N 1°5W 24 D6
Thebes *Egypt* 25°40N 32°35E 95 C12

Thelon → *Canada* 64°16N 96°4W 108 C9
Thermopolis *U.S.A.* 43°39N 108°13W 110 B5
Thermopylæ *Greece* 38°48N 22°35E 69 E10
Thessalon *Canada* 46°20N 83°30W 112 B6
Thessaloniki *Greece* 40°38N 22°58E 69 D10
Thetford *U.K.* 52°25N 0°45E 25 B10
Thetford Mines *Canada* 46°8N 71°18W 109 E12
Thiers *France* 45°52N 3°33E 66 D5
Thiès *Senegal* 14°50N 16°51W 94 F2
Thika *Kenya* 1°1S 37°5E 96 E7
Thimphu *Bhutan* 27°31N 89°45E 85 F16
Thionville *France* 49°20N 6°10E 66 B7
Thira = Santorini *Greece* 36°23N 25°27E 69 F11
Thirlmere *U.K.* 54°32N 3°4W 22 C2
Thirsk *U.K.* 54°14N 1°19W 22 D6
Thlewiaza → *Canada* 60°29N 94°40W 108 D9
Thomasville *U.S.A.* 30°50N 83°59W 111 D10
Thompson *Canada* 55°45N 97°52W 108 D10
Thornaby on Tees *U.K.* 54°33N 1°18W 22 C6
Thornbury *U.K.* 51°36N 2°31W 24 C3
Thorndon *U.K.* 52°17N 1°9E 25 B11
Thorne *U.K.* 53°37N 0°57W 23 E7
Thorney *U.K.* 52°37N 0°6W 25 A8
Thornham *U.K.* 52°58N 0°35E 25 A10
Thornhill *U.K.* 54°37N 3°13W 22 C2
Thornton *U.K.* 53°52N 2°59W 23 E3
Thornton Dale *U.K.* 54°15N 0°42W 22 D7
Thorpe *U.K.* 52°38N 1°22E 25 A11
Thorpe le Soken *U.K.* 51°51N 1°11E 25 C11
Thrace *Turkey* 41°0N 27°0E 69 D12
Thrace, Sea of *Greece* 40°30N 25°0E 69 D11
Thrapston *U.K.* 52°24N 0°32W 25 B7
Three Gorges Dam *China* 30°45N 111°15E 79 E11
Threlkeld *U.K.* 54°37N 3°3W 22 C2
Threshfield *U.K.* 54°4N 2°1W 22 D4
Thunder B. *U.S.A.* 45°0N 83°20W 112 C6
Thunder Bay *Canada* 48°20N 89°15W 112 A3
Thüringer Wald *Germany* 50°35N 11°0E 64 C6
Thurlby *U.K.* 52°45N 0°22W 23 G8
Thurles *Ireland* 52°41N 7°49W 30 C7
Thurmaston *U.K.* 52°40N 1°5W 23 G6
Thursby *U.K.* 54°51N 3°2W 22 C2
Thurso → *U.K.* 58°36N 3°32W 19 E10
Thurso *U.K.* 58°36N 3°32W 19 E10
Thurston I. *Antarctica* 72°0S 100°0W 55 D16
Tian Shan *Asia* 40°30N 76°0E 78 C4
Tianjin *China* 39°7N 117°12E 79 D12
Tianmen *China* 30°39N 113°9E 79 E11
Tianshui *China* 34°32N 105°40E 78 E10
Tiaret *Algeria* 35°20N 1°21E 94 A6
Tibati, Sarīr *Libya* 22°50N 18°30E 95 D9
Tiber → *Italy* 41°44N 12°14E 68 D5
Tiberias, L. = Galilee, Sea of *Israel* 32°45N 35°35E 86 C3
Tibesti *Chad* 21°0N 17°30E 95 D9
Tibet = Xizang Zizhiqu □ *China* 32°0N 88°0E 78 E6
Tibet, Plateau of *Asia* 32°0N 86°0E 72 E10
Tiburón, I. *Mexico* 29°0N 112°25W 114 B2
Ticehurst *U.K.* 51°3N 0°25E 25 D9
Ticino → *Italy* 45°9N 9°14E 68 B3
Tickhill *U.K.* 53°26N 1°6W 23 F6
Ticonderoga *U.S.A.* 43°51N 73°26W 113 D11
Tideswell *U.K.* 53°17N 1°47W 23 F5
Tieling *China* 42°20N 123°55E 79 C13
Tierra de Campos *Spain* 42°10N 4°50W 67 A3
Tierra del Fuego, I. Grande de *Argentina* 54°0S 69°0W 121 H3
Tiffin *U.S.A.* 41°7N 83°11W 112 E6
Tighina *Moldova* 46°50N 29°30E 65 E15
Tignish *Canada* 46°58N 64°2W 113 B15
Tigris → *Asia* 31°0N 47°25E 86 D6
Tijuana *Mexico* 32°32N 117°1W 114 A1
Tikhoretsk *Russia* 45°56N 40°5E 71 E7
Tikhvin *Russia* 59°35N 33°30E 70 C5
Tikrīt *Iraq* 34°35N 43°37E 86 C5
Tiksi *Russia* 71°40N 128°45E 77 B13
Tilburg *Neths.* 51°31N 5°6E 64 C3
Tilbury *U.K.* 51°27N 0°22E 25 D9
Till → *U.K.* 55°41N 2°13W 22 A4
Tillicoultry *U.K.* 56°9N 3°45W 21 B8
Tilmanstone *U.K.* 51°12N 1°18E 25 D11
Tilt → *U.K.* 56°46N 3°51W 19 J10
Timaru *N.Z.* 44°23S 171°14E 99 J13
Timişoara *Romania* 45°43N 21°15E 65 E10
Timmins *Canada* 48°28N 81°25W 109 E11
Timor *Asia* 9°0S 125°0E 83 F7
Timor Leste = East Timor ■ *Asia* 8°50S 126°0E 83 F7
Timor Sea *Ind. Oc.* 12°0S 127°0E 72 K14
Tingewick *U.K.* 51°59N 1°2W 24 C6
Tinogasta *Argentina* 28°5S 67°32W 121 E3
Tinos *Greece* 37°33N 25°8E 69 F11
Tintagel *U.K.* 50°39N 4°46W 27 F4
Tintagel Hd. *U.K.* 50°40N 4°47W 27 F4
Tipperary *Ireland* 52°28N 8°10W 30 D6
Tipperary □ *Ireland* 52°37N 7°55W 30 C7
Tipton *U.K.* 52°32N 2°4W 23 G4
Tiptree *U.K.* 51°48N 0°46E 25 C10
Tiranë *Albania* 41°18N 19°49E 69 D8
Tiraspol *Moldova* 46°55N 29°35E 65 E15
Tirebolu *Turkey* 40°58N 38°45E 71 F6
Tiree *U.K.* 56°31N 6°55W 20 A2
Tiree, Passage of *U.K.* 56°30N 6°30W 20 B2
Tirich Mir *Pakistan* 36°15N 71°55E 84 A7
Tirol □ *Austria* 47°3N 10°43E 64 E6
Tiruchchirappalli *India* 10°45N 78°45E 84 P11
Tirunelveli *India* 8°45N 77°45E 84 Q10
Tiruppur *India* 11°5N 77°22E 84 P10
Tisa → *Serbia* 45°15N 20°17E 69 B9
Tisdale *Canada* 52°50N 104°0W 108 D9
Titchfield *U.K.* 50°50N 1°15W 24 E6
Titicaca, L. *S. Amer.* 15°30S 69°30W 120 D3
Titusville *U.S.A.* 41°38N 79°41W 112 E8
Tiverton *U.K.* 50°54N 3°29W 27 F7
Tivoli *Italy* 41°58N 12°45E 68 D5
Tlaxiaco *Mexico* 17°25N 97°35W 114 D5
Tlemcen *Algeria* 34°52N 1°21W 94 B5

Toamasina *Madag.* 18°10S 49°25E 97 H9
Toba, Danau *Indonesia* 2°30N 97°30E 82 D1
Toba Kakar *Pakistan* 31°30N 69°0E 84 D6
Tobago *Trin. & Tob.* 11°10N 60°30W 120 A3
Tobermory *Canada* 45°12N 81°40W 112 C7
Tobermory *U.K.* 56°38N 6°5W 20 A3
Tobol → *Russia* 58°10N 68°12E 76 D7
Tobolsk *Russia* 58°15N 68°10E 76 D7
Tocantins → *Brazil* 1°45S 49°10W 120 C5
Toddington *U.K.* 51°57N 0°32W 25 C7
Todmorden *U.K.* 53°43N 2°6W 23 E4
Todos os Santos, B. de *Brazil* 12°48S 38°38W 122 B3
Toe Hd. *U.K.* 57°50N 7°8W 18 G3
Togliatti *Russia* 53°32N 49°24E 70 D8
Togo ■ *W. Afr.* 8°30N 1°35E 94 G6
Tok *U.S.A.* 63°20N 142°59W 108 C5
Tokachi-Dake *Japan* 43°17N 142°5E 81 B8
Tokat *Turkey* 40°22N 36°35E 71 F6
Tokdo *Asia* 37°15N 131°52E 81 E2
Tokelau Is. *Pac. Oc.* 9°0S 171°45W 99 B16
Tokushima *Japan* 34°4N 134°34E 81 F4
Tokuyama *Japan* 34°3N 131°50E 81 F2
Tōkyō *Japan* 35°43N 139°45E 81 F6
Toledo *Spain* 39°50N 4°2W 67 C3
Toledo *U.S.A.* 41°39N 83°33W 112 E6
Toledo, Montes de *Spain* 39°33N 4°20W 67 C3
Toliara *Madag.* 23°21S 43°40E 97 J8
Tolima *Colombia* 4°40N 75°19W 120 B2
Tollesbury *U.K.* 51°45N 0°51E 25 C10
Toluca *Mexico* 19°17N 99°40W 114 D5
Tomah *U.S.A.* 43°59N 90°30W 112 D2
Tomakomai *Japan* 42°38N 141°36E 81 B7
Tomaszów Mazowiecki *Poland* 51°30N 20°2E 65 C10
Tombador, Serra do *Brazil* 12°0S 58°0W 120 D4
Tombigbee → *U.S.A.* 31°8N 87°57W 111 D9
Tombouctou *Mali* 16°50N 3°0W 94 E5
Tomini, Teluk *Indonesia* 0°10S 121°0E 83 E6
Tomintoul *U.K.* 57°15N 3°23W 19 H11
Tomsk *Russia* 56°30N 85°5E 76 D9
Tonbridge *U.K.* 51°11N 0°17E 25 D9
Tone → *U.K.* 52°40N 2°17W 23 G4
Tonga ■ *Pac. Oc.* 19°50S 174°30W 99 D16
Tonga Trench *Pac. Oc.* 18°0S 173°0W 99 D16
Tongareva *Cook Is.* 9°0S 158°0W 103 H12
Tongatapu Group *Tonga* 21°0S 175°0W 99 E16
Tongchuan *China* 35°6N 109°3E 79 D10
Tonghua *China* 41°42N 125°58E 79 C14
Tongliao *China* 43°38N 122°18E 79 C13
Tongling *China* 30°55N 117°48E 79 E12
Tongue → *U.K.* 58°29N 4°25W 19 F9
Tongue → *U.S.A.* 46°25N 105°52W 110 A5
Tonk *India* 26°6N 75°54E 84 F9
Tonkin, G. of *Asia* 20°0N 108°0E 78 H10
Tonle Sap *Cambodia* 13°0N 104°0E 82 B2
Tonopah *U.S.A.* 38°4N 117°14W 110 C3
Toowoomba *Australia* 27°32S 151°56E 98 F9
Topeka *U.S.A.* 39°3N 95°40W 111 C7
Topolobampo *Mexico* 25°36N 109°3W 114 B3
Topsham *U.K.* 50°41N 3°28W 27 F7
Tor B. *U.K.* 50°25N 3°33W 27 G6
Torbay □ *U.K.* 50°26N 3°31W 27 G6
Tornëalven → *Europe* 65°50N 24°12E 63 D7
Torneträsk *Sweden* 68°24N 19°15E 63 D7
Tornio *Finland* 65°50N 24°12E 63 D8
Toro, Cerro del *Chile* 29°10S 69°50W 121 E3
Toronto *Canada* 43°39N 79°20W 112 D8
Torpoint *U.K.* 50°23N 4°13W 27 G5
Torquay *U.K.* 50°27N 3°32W 27 G6
Torre del Greco *Italy* 40°47N 14°22E 68 D6
Torrejón de Ardoz *Spain* 40°27N 3°29W 67 B4
Torrelavega *Spain* 43°20N 4°5W 67 A3
Torremolinos *Spain* 36°38N 4°30W 67 D3
Torrens, L. *Australia* 31°0S 137°50E 98 G6
Torrent *Spain* 39°27N 0°28W 67 C5
Torreón *Mexico* 25°33N 103°26W 114 B4
Torres Strait *Australia* 9°50S 142°20E 98 C7
Torridge → *U.K.* 51°0N 4°13W 27 E5
Torridon, L. *U.K.* 57°35N 5°50W 18 H6
Torthorwald *U.K.* 55°6N 3°32W 21 D8
Tortola *Br. Virgin Is.* 18°19N 64°45W 115 e
Tortosa *Spain* 40°49N 0°31E 67 B6
Toruń *Poland* 53°2N 18°39E 65 B10
Torver *U.K.* 54°20N 3°6W 22 D2
Tory I. *Ireland* 55°16N 8°14W 28 A5
Toscana □ *Italy* 43°25N 11°0E 68 C4
Toshka Lakes *Egypt* 22°50N 31°0E 95 D12
Totland *U.K.* 50°41N 1°32W 24 E5
Totley *U.K.* 53°20N 1°32W 23 F5
Totnes *U.K.* 50°26N 3°42W 27 G6
Totton *U.K.* 50°55N 1°29W 24 E6
Tottori *Japan* 35°30N 134°15E 81 F4
Toubkal, Djebel *Morocco* 31°0N 8°0W 94 B4
Touggourt *Algeria* 33°6N 6°4E 94 B7
Toul *France* 48°40N 5°53E 66 B6
Toulon *France* 43°10N 5°55E 66 E6
Toulouse *France* 43°37N 1°27E 66 E4
Touraine *France* 47°20N 0°30E 66 C4
Tournai *Belgium* 50°35N 3°25E 64 C2
Tournon-sur-Rhône *France* 45°4N 4°50E 66 D6
Tours *France* 47°22N 0°40E 66 C4
Towanda *U.S.A.* 41°46N 76°27W 112 E9
Towcester *U.K.* 52°8N 0°59W 25 B7
Town Yetholm *U.K.* 55°33N 2°17W 21 C11
Townsville *Australia* 19°15S 146°45E 98 D8
Towraghondī *Afghan.* 35°13N 62°16E 87 C10
Towson *U.S.A.* 39°24N 76°36W 112 F9
Toyama *Japan* 36°40N 137°15E 81 E5
Toyohashi *Japan* 34°45N 137°25E 81 F5
Toyota *Japan* 35°3N 137°7E 81 F5
Trabzon *Turkey* 41°0N 39°45E 71 F6
Trafalgar, C. *Spain* 36°10N 6°2W 67 D2
Trail *Canada* 49°5N 117°40W 108 E8
Tralee *Ireland* 52°16N 9°42W 30 D3
Tralee B. *Ireland* 52°17N 9°55W 30 D2
Tramore *Ireland* 52°10N 7°10W 31 D8
Tramore B. *Ireland* 52°9N 7°10W 31 D8
Tranent *U.K.* 55°57N 2°57W 21 C10
Trang *Thailand* 7°33N 99°38E 82 C1

Transantarctic Mts. *Antarctica* 85°0S 170°0W 55 E12
Transylvania *Romania* 46°30N 24°0E 65 E12
Transylvanian Alps *Romania* 45°30N 25°0E 65 F13
Trápani *Italy* 38°1N 12°29E 68 E5
Trasimeno, L. *Italy* 43°8N 12°6E 68 C5
Traverse City *U.S.A.* 44°46N 85°38W 112 C5
Trawbreaga B. *Ireland* 55°20N 7°25W 28 A7
Trawsfynydd *U.K.* 52°54N 3°55W 26 B6
Tredegar *U.K.* 51°47N 3°14W 26 D7
Tregaron *U.K.* 52°14N 3°56W 26 D6
Treinta y Tres *Uruguay* 33°16S 54°17W 121 F4
Trelew *Argentina* 43°10S 65°20W 121 G3
Trent → *U.K.* 53°41N 0°42W 23 E7
Trentham *U.K.* 52°58N 2°11W 23 G4
Trento *Italy* 46°4N 11°8E 68 A4
Trenton *Canada* 44°10N 77°34W 112 C9
Trenton *U.S.A.* 40°14N 74°46W 113 E10
Tres Arroyos *Argentina* 38°26S 60°20W 121 F3
Três Corações *Brazil* 21°44S 45°15W 122 D1
Três Lagoas *Brazil* 20°50S 51°43W 120 E4
Três Pontas *Brazil* 21°23S 45°29W 122 D1
Três Puntas, C. *Argentina* 47°0S 66°0W 121 G3
Três Rios *Brazil* 22°6S 43°15W 122 D2
Tresco *U.K.* 49°57N 6°20W 27 H1
Treviso *Italy* 45°40N 12°15E 68 B5
Trevose Hd. *U.K.* 50°32N 5°3W 27 F3
Trichur *India* 10°30N 76°18E 84 P10
Trier *Germany* 49°45N 6°38E 64 D4
Trieste *Italy* 45°40N 13°46E 68 B5
Trim *Ireland* 53°33N 6°48W 29 D8
Trimdon *U.K.* 54°42N 1°24W 22 C6
Trimley *U.K.* 51°59N 1°20E 25 C11
Trincomalee *Sri Lanka* 8°38N 81°15E 84 Q12
Trindade *Atl. Oc.* 20°20S 29°50W 52 F8
Trinidad *Bolivia* 14°46S 64°50W 120 D3
Trinidad *Cuba* 21°48N 80°0W 115 C9
Trinidad *U.S.A.* 37°10N 104°31W 110 C6
Trinidad & Tobago ■ *W. Indies* 10°30N 61°20W 115 E12
Trinity → *U.S.A.* 29°45N 94°43W 111 E8
Trinity B. *Canada* 48°20N 53°10W 109 E14
Trinity Is. *U.S.A.* 56°33N 154°25W 108 D4
Tripoli *Lebanon* 34°31N 35°50E 86 C3
Tripoli *Libya* 32°49N 13°7E 95 B8
Tripolitania *N. Afr.* 31°0N 13°0E 95 B8
Tripura □ *India* 24°0N 92°0E 85 H18
Tristan da Cunha *Atl. Oc.* 37°6S 12°20W 52 F9
Trivandrum *India* 8°41N 77°0E 84 Q10
Trnava *Slovak Rep.* 48°23N 17°35E 65 D9
Trois-Rivières *Canada* 46°25N 72°34W 109 E12
Trois-Rivières *Guadeloupe* 15°57N 61°40W 114 b
Trollhättan *Sweden* 58°17N 12°20E 63 F6
Trombetas → *Brazil* 1°55S 55°35W 120 C4
Tromsø *Norway* 69°40N 18°56E 63 D7
Tronador *Argentina* 41°10S 71°50W 121 G2
Trondheim *Norway* 63°36N 10°25E 63 E6
Trondheimsfjorden *Norway* 63°35N 10°30E 63 E6
Troon *U.K.* 55°33N 4°39W 20 C6
Trossachs, The *U.K.* 56°14N 4°24W 20 B7
Trostan *U.K.* 55°3N 6°10W 29 A9
Trotternish *U.K.* 57°32N 6°15W 18 G5
Trou Gras Pt. *St. Lucia* 13°51N 60°53W 115 f
Trout L. *N.W.T., Canada* 60°40N 121°14W 108 C7
Trout L. *Ont., Canada* 51°20N 93°15W 108 D10
Trowbridge *U.K.* 51°18N 2°12W 24 D4
Troy *Turkey* 39°57N 26°12E 71 G4
Troy *Ala., U.S.A.* 31°48N 85°58W 111 D9
Troy *N.Y., U.S.A.* 42°44N 73°41W 113 D11
Troy *Ohio, U.S.A.* 40°2N 84°12W 112 E5
Troyes *France* 48°19N 4°3E 66 B6
Trujillo *Honduras* 16°0N 86°0W 114 D7
Trujillo *Peru* 8°6S 79°0W 120 C2
Trujillo *Venezuela* 9°22N 70°38W 120 B2
Truk *Micronesia* 7°25N 151°46E 102 G7
Trull *U.K.* 51°0N 3°6W 24 E2
Trumpington *U.K.* 52°10N 0°7E 25 B9
Truro *Canada* 45°21N 63°14W 109 E13
Truro *U.K.* 50°16N 5°4W 27 G3
Tsavo *Kenya* 2°59S 38°28E 96 E7
Tsetserleg *Mongolia* 47°36N 101°32E 78 B9
Tshikapa *Dem. Rep. of the Congo* 6°28S 20°48E 96 F4
Tsiigehtchic *Canada* 67°15N 134°0W 108 C6
Tsimlyansk Res. *Russia* 48°0N 43°0E 71 E7
Tskhinvali *Georgia* 42°14N 44°1E 71 F7
Tsna → *Russia* 54°55N 41°58E 70 D7
Tsuchiura *Japan* 36°5N 140°15E 81 E7
Tsugaru Str. *Japan* 41°35N 141°0E 81 C7
Tsumeb *Namibia* 19°9S 17°44E 97 H3
Tsuruoka *Japan* 38°44N 139°50E 81 E6
Tsushima *Japan* 34°20N 129°20E 81 F1
Tuam *Ireland* 53°31N 8°51W 28 D4
Tuamotu, Îs. *French Polynesia* 17°0S 144°0W 103 J13
Tuapse *Russia* 44°5N 39°10E 71 F6
Tubarão *Brazil* 28°30S 49°0W 121 E5
Tübingen *Germany* 48°31N 9°4E 64 D5
Tubruq *Libya* 32°7N 23°55E 95 B10
Tubuai, Îs. *French Polynesia* 25°0S 150°0W 103 K13
Tucson *U.S.A.* 32°13N 110°58W 110 D4
Tucumcari *U.S.A.* 35°10N 103°44W 110 C6
Tucupita *Venezuela* 9°2N 62°3W 120 B3
Tucuruí *Brazil* 3°42S 49°44W 120 C5
Tucuruí, Represa de *Brazil* 4°0S 49°30W 120 C5
Tuguegarao *Phil.* 17°35N 121°42E 83 A6
Tuktoyaktuk *Canada* 69°27N 133°2W 108 C6
Tula *Russia* 54°13N 37°38E 70 D6
Tulancingo *Mexico* 20°5N 98°22W 114 C5
Tulare *U.S.A.* 36°13N 119°21W 110 C3
Tulcán *Ecuador* 0°48N 77°43W 120 B2
Tulcea *Romania* 45°13N 28°46E 65 F15
Tulita *Canada* 64°57N 125°30W 108 C7
Tulla *Ireland* 52°53N 8°46W 30 C5
Tullamore *Ireland* 53°16N 7°31W 31 B7
Tulle *France* 45°16N 1°46E 66 D4
Tullow *Ireland* 52°49N 6°45W 31 C9
Tulsa *U.S.A.* 36°10N 95°55W 111 C7
Tumaco *Colombia* 1°50N 78°45W 120 B2
Tumbes *Peru* 3°37S 80°27W 120 C1
Tummel → *U.K.* 56°42N 4°5W 19 J9
Tummel, L. *U.K.* 56°43N 3°55W 19 J10

Tumucumaque, Serra *Brazil* 2°0N 55°0W 120 B4
Tunis *Tunisia* 36°50N 10°11E 95 A8
Tunisia ■ *Africa* 33°30N 9°10E 95 A7
Tunja *Colombia* 5°33N 73°25W 120 B2
Tunstall *U.K.* 52°9N 1°27E 25 B11
Tupaciguara *Brazil* 18°35S 48°42W 122 C1
Tupelo *U.S.A.* 34°16N 88°43W 111 D9
Tupiza *Bolivia* 21°30S 65°40W 120 E3
Turfan Basin *China* 42°40N 89°25E 78 C6
Turgutlu *Turkey* 38°30N 27°43E 71 G4
Turin *Italy* 45°3N 7°40E 68 B2
Turkana, L. *Africa* 3°30N 36°5E 96 D7
Turkey ■ *Eurasia* 39°0N 36°0E 71 G6
Türkmenabat *Turkmenistan* 39°6N 63°34E 87 B10
Türkmenbashi *Turkmenistan* 40°5N 53°5E 87 A8
Turkmenistan ■ *Asia* 39°0N 59°0E 87 B9
Turks & Caicos Is. ☑ *W. Indies* 21°20N 71°20W 115 C10
Turku *Finland* 60°30N 22°19E 63 E8
Turnberry *U.K.* 55°18N 4°49W 20 D6
Turneffe Is. *Belize* 17°20N 87°50W 114 D7
Turpan *China* 43°58N 89°10E 78 C6
Turriff *U.K.* 57°32N 2°27W 19 G13
Tuscaloosa *U.S.A.* 33°12N 87°34W 111 D9
Tuscany = Toscana □ *Italy* 43°25N 11°0E 68 C4
Tutbury *U.K.* 52°51N 1°41W 23 G5
Tuticorin *India* 8°50N 78°12E 84 Q11
Tutuila *Amer. Samoa* 14°19S 170°50W 99 C16
Tutume *Botswana* 20°30S 27°5E 97 J5
Tuva □ *Russia* 51°30N 95°0E 77 D10
Tuvalu ■ *Pac. Oc.* 8°0S 178°0E 99 B14
Tuxford *U.K.* 53°14N 0°54W 23 F7
Tuxpan *Mexico* 20°57N 97°24W 114 C5
Tuxtla Gutiérrez *Mexico* 16°45N 93°7W 114 D6
Tuz Gölü *Turkey* 38°42N 33°18E 71 G5
Tuzla *Bos.-H.* 44°34N 18°41E 69 B8
Tver *Russia* 56°55N 35°59E 70 C6
Tweed → *U.K.* 55°45N 2°0W 21 C11
Tweedmouth *U.K.* 55°45N 2°0W 22 A5
Tweedshaws *U.K.* 55°27N 3°29W 21 D8
Twenty *U.K.* 52°47N 0°17W 23 G8
Twin Falls *U.S.A.* 42°34N 114°28W 110 B4
Two Harbors *U.S.A.* 47°2N 91°40W 112 B2
Two Rivers *U.S.A.* 44°9N 87°34W 112 C4
Twyford *Hants., U.K.* 51°1N 1°19W 24 D6
Twyford *Wokingham, U.K.* 51°28N 0°51W 25 D7
Tychy *Poland* 50°9N 18°59E 65 C10
Tydd St. Mary *U.K.* 52°45N 0°7E 23 G9
Tyler *U.S.A.* 32°21N 95°18W 111 D7
Tyndrum *U.K.* 56°26N 4°42W 20 B6
Tyne → *U.K.* 54°59N 1°32W 22 C5
Tyne & Wear □ *U.K.* 55°6N 1°17W 22 B6
Tynemouth *U.K.* 55°1N 1°26E 22 B6
Tyrol = Tirol □ *Austria* 47°3N 10°43E 64 E6
Tyrone *U.K.* 54°38N 7°11W 29 B7
Tyrrhenian Sea *Medit. S.* 40°0N 12°30E 68 E5
Tyumen *Russia* 57°11N 65°29E 76 D7
Tywardreath *U.K.* 50°21N 4°42W 27 G4
Tywi → *U.K.* 51°48N 4°21W 26 D5
Tywyn *U.K.* 52°35N 4°5W 26 B5
Tzaneen *S. Africa* 23°47S 30°9E 97 J6

U

U.S.A. = United States of America ■ *N. Amer.* 37°0N 96°0W 110 C7
U.S. Virgin Is. ☑ *W. Indies* 18°20N 65°0W 115 e
Uaupés → *Brazil* 0°2N 67°16W 120 B3
Ubá *Brazil* 21°8S 43°0W 122 D2
Ubaitaba *Brazil* 14°18S 39°20W 122 B3
Ube *Japan* 33°56N 131°15E 81 G2
Uberaba *Brazil* 19°50S 47°55W 122 C1
Uberlândia *Brazil* 19°0S 48°20W 122 C1
Ubon Ratchathani *Thailand* 15°15N 104°50E 82 A2
Ucayali → *Peru* 4°30S 73°30W 120 C2
Uckfield *U.K.* 50°58N 0°6E 25 E9
Udagamandalam *India* 11°30N 76°44E 84 P10
Udaipur *India* 24°36N 73°44E 84 G8
Uddingston *U.K.* 55°49N 4°5W 20 C7
Údine *Italy* 46°3N 13°14E 68 A5
Udmurtia □ *Russia* 57°30N 52°30E 70 C9
Udon Thani *Thailand* 17°29N 102°46E 82 A2
Udupi *India* 13°25N 74°42E 84 N9
Uele → *Dem. Rep. of the Congo* 3°45N 24°45E 96 D4
Ufa *Russia* 54°45N 55°55E 70 D10
Uffculme *U.K.* 50°54N 3°20W 27 F7
Ufford *U.K.* 52°8N 1°23E 25 B11
Uganda ■ *Africa* 2°0N 32°0E 96 D6
Ugborough *U.K.* 50°22N 3°53W 27 G6
Uig *U.K.* 57°35N 6°21W 18 G5
Uinta Mts. *U.S.A.* 40°45N 110°30W 110 B4
Uitenhage *S. Africa* 33°40S 25°28E 97 L5
Ujjain *India* 23°9N 75°43E 84 H9
Ujung Pandang *Indonesia* 5°10S 119°20E 83 F5
Ukhta *Russia* 63°34N 53°41E 70 B9
Ukiah *U.S.A.* 39°9N 123°13W 110 C2
Ukraine ■ *Europe* 49°0N 32°0E 71 E5
Ulaangom *Mongolia* 50°5N 92°10E 78 A7
Ulaanjirem *Mongolia* 45°5N 105°30E 78 B10
Ulan Bator *Mongolia* 47°55N 106°53E 78 B10
Ulan Ude *Russia* 51°45N 107°40E 79 A10
Ulceby Cross *U.K.* 53°15N 0°7E 23 F9
Ulhasnagar *India* 19°15N 73°10E 84 K8
Uliastay *Mongolia* 47°56N 97°28E 78 B8
Ullapool *U.K.* 57°54N 5°9W 18 G6
Ulleungdo *S. Korea* 37°30N 130°30E 81 E2
Ullswater *U.K.* 54°34N 2°52W 22 C3
Ulm *Germany* 48°23N 9°58E 64 D5
Ulster □ *U.K.* 54°35N 6°30W 29 B9
Ulungur He → *China* 47°1N 87°24E 78 B6
Uluru *Australia* 25°23S 131°5E 98 F5
Ulva *U.K.* 56°29N 6°13W 20 B3
Ulverston *U.K.* 54°13N 3°5W 22 D2
Ulyanovsk *Russia* 54°20N 48°25E 70 D8
Uman *Ukraine* 48°40N 30°12E 71 E5
Umeå *Sweden* 63°45N 20°20E 63 E8
Umeälven → *Sweden* 63°45N 20°20E 63 E8
Umlazi *S. Africa* 29°59S 30°54E 97 L6
Umm al Qaywayn *U.A.E.* 25°30N 55°35E 87 E8
Umnak I. *U.S.A.* 53°15N 168°20W 108 D3

Umuarama · · · Wheatley Hill

Umuarama *Brazil* 23°45S 53°20W **121 E4**
Unalakleet *U.S.A.* 63°52N 160°47W **108 C3**
Unalaska *U.S.A.* 53°53N 166°32W **108 D3**
Unalaska I. *U.S.A.* 53°35N 166°50W **108 D3**
'Unayzah *Si. Arabia* 26°6N 43°58E **86 E5**
Uncía *Bolivia* 18°25S 66°40W **120 D3**
Ungava, Pén. d' *Canada* 60°0N 74°0W **109 D12**
Ungava B. *Canada* 59°30N 67°30W **109 D13**
Unimak I. *U.S.A.* 54°45N 164°0W **108 D3**
Union City *U.S.A.* 36°26N 89°3W **112 G3**
Uniontown *U.S.A.* 39°54N 79°44W **112 F8**
United Arab Emirates ■ *Asia* 23°50N 54°0E **87 F8**
United Kingdom ■ *Europe* 53°0N 2°0W **62 E6**
United States of America ■
 N. Amer. 37°0N 96°0W **110 C7**
Unst *U.K.* 60°44N 0°53W **18 A16**
Unzen-Dake *Japan* 32°45N 130°17E **81 G2**
Upavon *U.K.* 51°18N 1°48W **24 D5**
Upington *S. Africa* 28°25S 21°15E **97 K4**
'Upolu *Samoa* 13°58S 172°0W **99 C16**
Upper Heyford *U.K.* 51°56N 1°15W **24 C6**
Upper Klamath L. *U.S.A.* 42°25N 121°55W **110 B2**
Uppingham *U.K.* 52°36N 0°43W **23 G7**
Uppsala *Sweden* 59°53N 17°38E **63 F7**
Upton *U.K.* 53°13N 2°53W **23 F3**
Upton-upon-Severn *U.K.* 52°3N 2°12W **24 B4**
Upwey *U.K.* 50°39N 2°29W **24 E4**
Ur *Iraq* 30°55N 46°25E **86 D6**
Ural *→ Kazakhstan* 47°0N 51°48E **71 E9**
Ural Mts. *Eurasia* 60°0N 59°0E **70 C10**
Uranium City *Canada* 59°34N 108°37W **108 D9**
Uraricoera *→ Brazil* 3°2N 60°30W **120 B3**
Urbana *Ill., U.S.A.* 40°7N 88°12W **112 E3**
Urbana *Ohio, U.S.A.* 40°7N 83°45W **112 E6**
Ure *→ U.K.* 54°5N 1°20W **22 D5**
Urganch *Uzbekistan* 41°40N 60°41E **87 A10**
Urmia *Iran* 37°40N 45°0E **86 B6**
Urmia, L. *Iran* 37°50N 45°30E **86 B6**
Urmston *U.K.* 53°27N 2°21W **23 F4**
Uroyan, Mts. de *Puerto Rico* 18°12N 67°0W **115 d**
Uruaçu *Brazil* 14°30S 49°10W **122 B1**
Uruapan *Mexico* 19°24N 102°3W **114 D4**
Urubamba *→ Peru* 10°43S 73°48W **120 D2**
Ure *→ Brazil* 26°0S 53°30W **121 E4**
Uruguaiana *Brazil* 29°50S 57°0W **121 E4**
Uruguay ■ *S. Amer.* 32°30S 56°30W **121 F4**
Uruguay *→ S. Amer.* 34°12S 58°18W **117 G5**
Ürümqi *China* 43°45N 87°45E **78 C6**
Usa *→ Russia* 66°16N 59°49E **70 A10**
Uşak *Turkey* 38°43N 29°28E **71 G4**
Usakos *Namibia* 21°54S 15°31E **97 J3**
Usedom *Germany* 53°55N 14°2E **64 B8**
Ushant *France* 48°28N 5°6W **66 B1**
Ushuaia *Argentina* 54°50S 68°23W **121 H3**
Usk *→ U.K.* 51°33N 2°58W **27 D8**
Usolye Sibirskoye *Russia* 52°48N 103°40E **77 D11**
Uspallata, P. de *Argentina* 32°37S 69°22W **121 F3**
Usselby *U.K.* 53°26N 0°21W **23 F8**
Ussuriysk *Russia* 43°48N 131°59E **81 B2**
Ust-Ilimsk *Russia* 58°3N 102°39E **77 D11**
Ust-Kut *Russia* 56°50N 105°42E **77 D11**
Ústí nad Labem *Czech Rep.* 50°41N 14°3E **64 C8**
Ustica *Italy* 38°42N 13°11E **68 E5**
Usu *China* 44°27N 84°40E **78 C5**
Usumacinta *→ Mexico* 18°24N 92°38W **114 D6**
Utah □ *U.S.A.* 39°20N 111°30W **110 C4**
Utah L. *U.S.A.* 40°12N 111°48W **110 B4**
Utica *U.S.A.* 43°6N 75°14W **113 D10**
Utrecht *Neths.* 52°5N 5°8E **64 B3**
Utsunomiya *Japan* 36°30N 139°50E **81 E6**
Uttar Pradesh □ *India* 27°0N 80°0E **84 F12**
Uttaradit *Thailand* 17°36N 100°5E **82 A2**
Uttarakhand □ *India* 30°0N 79°30E **84 D11**
Uttoxeter *U.K.* 52°54N 1°52W **23 G5**
Utuado *Puerto Rico* 18°16N 66°42W **115 d**
Uusikaupunki *Finland* 60°47N 21°25E **63 E8**
Uvalde *U.S.A.* 29°13N 99°47W **110 E7**
Uvira *Dem. Rep. of the Congo* 3°22S 29°3E **96 E5**
Uvs Nuur *Mongolia* 50°20N 92°30E **78 A7**
Uyuni *Bolivia* 20°28S 66°47W **120 E3**
Uzbekistan ■ *Asia* 41°30N 65°0E **87 A10**
Uzhhorod *Ukraine* 48°36N 22°18E **65 D12**

V

Vaal *→ S. Africa* 29°4S 23°38E **97 K4**
Vaasa *Finland* 63°6N 21°38E **63 E8**
Vadodara *India* 22°20N 73°10E **84 H8**
Vadsø *Norway* 70°3N 29°50E **63 C9**
Vaduz *Liech.* 47°8N 9°31E **64 E5**
Váh *→ Slovak Rep.* 47°43N 18°7E **65 D9**
Vail *U.S.A.* 39°40N 106°20W **110 C5**
Vaila *U.K.* 60°12N 1°36W **18 B14**
Val-d'Or *Canada* 48°7N 77°47W **109 E12**
Valdai Hills *Russia* 57°0N 33°30E **70 C5**
Valdés, Pen. *Argentina* 42°30S 63°45W **121 G3**
Valdez *U.S.A.* 61°7N 146°16W **108 C5**
Valdivia *Chile* 39°50S 73°14W **121 F2**
Valdosta *U.S.A.* 30°50N 83°17W **111 D10**
Vale of Glamorgan □ *U.K.* 51°28N 3°25W **27 F7**
Valença *Brazil* 13°20S 39°5W **122 B3**
Valence *France* 44°57N 4°54E **66 D6**
Valencia *Spain* 39°27N 0°23W **67 C5**
Valencia *Venezuela* 10°11N 68°0W **120 A3**
Valencia □ *Spain* 39°20N 0°40W **67 C5**
Valencia, G. de *Spain* 39°30N 0°20E **67 C6**
Valencia I. *Ireland* 51°54N 10°22W **30 E2**
Valenciennes *France* 50°20N 3°34E **66 A5**
Valera *Venezuela* 9°19N 70°37W **120 B2**
Valladolid *Mexico* 20°41N 88°12W **114 C7**
Valladolid *Spain* 41°38N 4°43W **67 B3**
Valledupar *Colombia* 10°29N 73°15W **120 A2**
Vallejo *U.S.A.* 38°7N 122°14W **110 C2**
Vallenar *Chile* 28°30S 70°50W **121 E2**
Valletta *Malta* 35°54N 14°31E **68 G6**
Valley *U.K.* 53°16N 4°34W **26 A4**
Valley City *U.S.A.* 46°55N 98°0W **110 A7**
Valparaíso *Chile* 33°2S 71°40W **121 F2**
Van *Turkey* 38°30N 43°20E **71 G7**

Van, L. *Turkey* 38°30N 43°0E **71 G7**
Van Buren *U.S.A.* 47°10N 67°58W **113 B13**
Van Wert *U.S.A.* 40°52N 84°35W **112 E5**
Vanadzor *Armenia* 40°48N 44°30E **71 F7**
Vancouver *Canada* 49°15N 123°7W **108 E7**
Vancouver *U.S.A.* 45°38N 122°40W **110 A2**
Vancouver I. *Canada* 49°50N 126°0W **108 E7**
Vandalia *U.S.A.* 38°58N 89°6W **112 F3**
Vanderhoof *Canada* 54°0N 124°0W **108 D7**
Vänern *Sweden* 58°47N 13°30E **63 F6**
Vännäs *Sweden* 63°58N 19°48E **63 E7**
Vannes *France* 47°40N 2°47W **66 C2**
Vanrhynsdorp *S. Africa* 31°36S 18°44E **97 L3**
Vantaa *Finland* 60°18N 24°56E **63 E8**
Vanua Levu *Fiji* 16°33S 179°15E **99 D14**
Vanuatu ■ *Pac. Oc.* 15°0S 168°0E **99 D12**
Varanasi *India* 25°22N 83°0E **85 G13**
Varangerfjorden *Norway* 70°3N 29°25E **63 C9**
Varberg *Sweden* 57°6N 12°20E **63 F6**
Vardak □ *Afghan.* 34°0N 68°0E **87 C12**
Vardø *Norway* 70°23N 31°5E **63 C10**
Varese *Italy* 45°48N 8°50E **68 B3**
Varginha *Brazil* 21°33S 45°25W **122 D1**
Varna *Bulgaria* 43°13N 27°56E **69 C12**
Vasa Barris *→ Brazil* 11°10S 37°10W **122 B3**
Västerås *Sweden* 59°37N 16°38E **63 F7**
Västervik *Sweden* 57°43N 16°33E **63 F7**
Vaté *Vanuatu* 17°40S 168°25E **99 D12**
Vatersay *U.K.* 56°55N 7°32W **18 J2**
Vatican City ■ *Europe* 41°54N 12°27E **68 D5**
Vatnajökull *Iceland* 64°30N 16°48W **63 B2**
Vättern *Sweden* 58°25N 14°30E **63 F6**
Vaughn *U.S.A.* 34°36N 105°13W **110 D5**
Vava'u Group *Tonga* 18°40S 174°0W **99 D16**
Vega *Norway* 65°40N 11°55E **63 D6**
Vega Baja *Puerto Rico* 18°27N 66°23W **115 d**
Vegreville *Canada* 53°30N 112°5W **108 D8**
Vélez-Málaga *Spain* 36°48N 4°5W **67 D3**
Velhas *→ Brazil* 17°13S 44°49W **122 C2**
Velikiye Luki *Russia* 56°25N 30°32E **70 C5**
Veliko Tŭrnovo *Bulgaria* 43°5N 25°41E **69 C11**
Velikonda Range *India* 14°45N 79°10E **84 M11**
Vellore *India* 12°57N 79°10E **84 N11**
Velsk *Russia* 61°10N 42°5E **70 B7**
Vendée □ *France* 46°50N 1°35W **66 C3**
Vendôme *France* 47°47N 1°3E **66 C4**
Venézia, G. di *Italy* 45°15N 13°0E **68 B5**
Venezuela ■ *S. Amer.* 8°0N 66°0W **120 B3**
Venezuela, G. de *Venezuela* 11°30N 71°0W **120 A2**
Vengurla *India* 15°53N 73°45E **84 M8**
Venice *Italy* 45°27N 12°21E **68 B5**
Ventnor *U.K.* 50°36N 1°12W **24 E6**
Ventoux, Mt. *France* 44°10N 5°17E **66 D6**
Ventspils *Latvia* 57°25N 21°32E **63 F8**
Veracruz *Mexico* 19°11N 96°8W **114 D5**
Veraval *India* 20°53N 70°27E **84 J7**
Vercelli *Italy* 45°19N 8°25E **68 B3**
Verde *→ U.S.A.* 33°33N 111°40W **110 D4**
Verdun *France* 49°9N 5°24E **66 B6**
Vereeniging *S. Africa* 26°38S 27°57E **97 K5**
Verkhoyansk *Russia* 67°35N 133°25E **77 C14**
Verkhoyansk Ra. *Russia* 66°0N 129°0E **77 C13**
Vermont □ *U.S.A.* 44°0N 73°0W **113 D11**
Vernal *U.S.A.* 40°27N 109°32W **110 B5**
Vernon *Canada* 50°20N 119°15W **108 D8**
Vernon *U.S.A.* 34°9N 99°17W **110 D7**
Verona *Italy* 45°27N 10°59E **68 B4**
Versailles *France* 48°48N 2°7E **66 B5**
Vert, C. *Senegal* 14°45N 17°30W **94 F2**
Verviers *Belgium* 50°37N 5°52E **64 C3**
Verwood *U.K.* 50°52N 1°52W **24 E5**
Veryan *U.K.* 50°13N 4°56W **27 G4**
Veryan B. *U.K.* 50°13N 4°51W **27 G4**
Vesoul *France* 47°40N 6°11E **66 C7**
Vesterålen *Norway* 68°45N 15°0E **63 D7**
Vestfjorden *Norway* 67°55N 14°0E **63 D6**
Vesuvio *Italy* 40°49N 14°26E **68 D6**
Veszprém *Hungary* 47°8N 17°57E **65 E9**
Vianópolis *Brazil* 16°40S 48°35W **122 C1**
Viareggio *Italy* 43°52N 10°14E **68 C4**
Vicenza *Italy* 45°33N 11°33E **68 B4**
Vichada *→ Colombia* 4°55N 67°50W **120 B3**
Vichy *France* 46°9N 3°26E **66 C5**
Vickerstown *U.K.* 54°6N 3°15W **22 D2**
Vicksburg *U.S.A.* 32°21N 90°53W **111 D8**
Victoria *Canada* 48°30N 123°25W **108 E7**
Victoria *China* 22°17N 114°9E **79 a**
Victoria *U.S.A.* 28°48N 97°0W **111 E7**
Victoria □ *Australia* 37°0S 144°0E **98 H7**
Victoria, L. *Africa* 1°0S 33°0E **96 E6**
Victoria Falls *Zimbabwe* 17°58S 25°52E **97 H5**
Victoria I. *Canada* 71°0N 111°0W **108 B8**
Victoria Ld. *Antarctica* 75°0S 160°0E **55 D11**
Victoria Str. *Canada* 69°31N 100°30W **108 C9**
Victoriaville *Canada* 46°4N 71°56W **113 B12**
Vidin *Bulgaria* 43°59N 22°50E **69 C10**
Viedma, L. *Argentina* 49°30S 72°30W **121 G2**
Vienna *Austria* 48°12N 16°22E **64 D9**
Vienne *France* 45°31N 4°53E **66 D6**
Vienne *→ France* 47°13N 0°5E **66 C4**
Vientiane *Laos* 17°58N 102°36E **82 A2**
Vieques *Puerto Rico* 18°8N 65°25W **115 d**
Vierge Pt. *St. Lucia* 13°49N 60°53W **115 f**
Vierzon *France* 47°13N 2°5E **66 C5**
Vietnam ■ *Asia* 19°0N 106°0E **82 A3**
Vieux Fort *St. Lucia* 13°46N 60°58W **115 f**
Vigévano *Italy* 45°19N 8°51E **68 B3**
Vigo *Spain* 42°12N 8°41W **67 A1**
Vijayawada *India* 16°31N 80°39E **85 L12**
Vikna *Norway* 64°55N 10°58E **63 E6**
Vila Nova de Gaia *Portugal* 41°8N 8°37W **67 B1**
Vila Velha *Brazil* 20°20S 40°17W **122 D2**
Vilaine *→ France* 47°30N 2°27W **66 C2**
Vilhelmina *Sweden* 64°35N 16°39E **63 E7**
Vilhena *Brazil* 12°40S 60°5W **120 D3**
Vilkitskiy Str. *Russia* 78°0N 103°0E **77 B11**
Villa Bella *Bolivia* 10°25S 65°22W **120 D3**
Villa María *Argentina* 32°20S 63°10W **121 F3**
Villach *Austria* 46°37N 13°51E **64 E7**
Villahermosa *Mexico* 17°59N 92°55W **114 D6**
Villajoyosa *Spain* 38°30N 0°12W **67 C5**

Villarrica *Paraguay* 25°40S 56°30W **121 E4**
Villavicencio *Colombia* 4°9N 73°37W **120 B2**
Ville-Marie *Canada* 47°20N 79°30W **112 B8**
Villeneuve-sur-Lot *France* 44°24N 0°42E **66 D4**
Vilnius *Lithuania* 54°38N 25°19E **63 G9**
Vilyuy *→ Russia* 64°24N 126°26E **77 C13**
Vilyuysk *Russia* 63°40N 121°35E **77 C13**
Viña del Mar *Chile* 33°0S 71°30W **121 F2**
Vincennes *U.S.A.* 38°41N 87°32W **112 F4**
Vindhya Ra. *India* 22°50N 77°0E **84 H10**
Vineland *U.S.A.* 39°29N 75°2W **113 F10**
Vinnytsya *Ukraine* 49°15N 28°30E **65 D15**
Virden *Canada* 49°50N 100°56W **108 E9**
Vire *France* 48°50N 0°53W **66 B3**
Vírgenes, C. *Argentina* 52°19S 68°21W **121 H3**
Virgin *→ U.S.A.* 36°28N 114°21W **110 C4**
Virgin Gorda *Br. Virgin Is.* 18°30N 64°26W **115 e**
Virgin Is. (British) ☑
 W. Indies 18°30N 64°30W **115 e**
Virgin Is. (U.S.) ☑ *W. Indies* 18°20N 65°0W **115 e**
Virginia *S. Africa* 28°8S 26°55E **97 K5**
Virginia □ *U.S.A.* 37°30N 78°45W **112 G8**
Virginia Beach *U.S.A.* 36°49N 76°9W **111 C11**
Viroqua *U.S.A.* 43°34N 90°53W **112 D2**
Vis *Croatia* 43°4N 16°10E **68 C7**
Visalia *U.S.A.* 36°20N 119°18W **110 C3**
Visby *Sweden* 57°37N 18°18E **63 F7**
Viscount Melville Sd.
 Canada 74°10N 108°0W **109 B9**
Vishakhapatnam *India* 17°45N 83°20E **85 L13**
Vistula *→ Poland* 54°22N 18°55E **65 A10**
Vitebsk *Belarus* 55°10N 30°15E **70 C5**
Viterbo *Italy* 42°25N 12°6E **68 C5**
Viti Levu *Fiji* 17°30S 177°30E **99 D14**
Vitim *→ Russia* 59°26N 112°34E **77 D12**
Vitória *Brazil* 20°20S 40°22W **122 D2**
Vitória da Conquista *Brazil* 14°51S 40°51W **122 B2**
Vitoria-Gasteiz *Spain* 42°50N 2°41W **67 A4**
Vittória *Italy* 36°57N 14°32E **68 F6**
Vizianagaram *India* 18°6N 83°30E **85 K13**
Vladikavkaz *Russia* 43°0N 44°35E **71 F7**
Vladimir *Russia* 56°15N 40°30E **70 C7**
Vladivostok *Russia* 43°10N 131°53E **79 C15**
Vlissingen *Neths.* 51°26N 3°34E **64 C2**
Vlorë *Albania* 40°32N 19°28E **69 D8**
Vltava *→ Czech Rep.* 50°21N 14°30E **64 D8**
Voe *U.K.* 60°21N 1°16W **18 B15**
Vogelsberg *Germany* 50°31N 9°12E **64 C5**
Vohimena, Tanjon' i *Madag.* 25°36S 45°8E **97 K9**
Voi *Kenya* 3°25S 38°32E **96 E7**
Vojvodina □ *Serbia* 45°20N 20°0E **69 B9**
Volga *→ Russia* 46°0N 48°30E **71 E8**
Volga Hts. *Russia* 51°0N 46°0E **71 D8**
Volgodonsk *Russia* 47°33N 42°5E **71 E7**
Volgograd *Russia* 48°40N 44°25E **71 E7**
Volgograd Res. *Russia* 50°0N 45°20E **71 D8**
Vologda *Russia* 59°10N 39°45E **70 C6**
Volos *Greece* 39°24N 22°59E **69 E10**
Volsk *Russia* 52°5N 47°22E **70 D8**
Volta *→ Ghana* 5°46N 0°41E **94 G6**
Volta, L. *Ghana* 7°30N 0°0 **94 G6**
Volta Redonda *Brazil* 22°31S 44°5W **122 D2**
Volzhskiy *Russia* 48°56N 44°46E **71 E7**
Vorkuta *Russia* 67°48N 64°20E **70 A11**
Voronezh *Russia* 51°40N 39°10E **71 D6**
Vosges *France* 48°20N 7°10E **66 B7**
Vostok I. *Kiribati* 10°5S 152°23W **103 J12**
Votkinsk *Russia* 57°0N 53°55E **70 C9**
Vratsa *Bulgaria* 43°15N 23°30E **69 C10**
Vryburg *S. Africa* 26°55S 24°45E **97 K4**
Vryheid *S. Africa* 27°45S 30°47E **97 K6**
Vulcano *Italy* 38°24N 14°58E **68 E6**
Vung Tau *Vietnam* 10°21N 107°4E **82 B3**
Vyazma *Russia* 55°10N 34°15E **70 C5**
Vyborg *Russia* 60°43N 28°47E **70 B4**
Vychegda *→ Russia* 61°18N 46°36E **70 B8**
Vyrnwy, L. *U.K.* 52°48N 3°31W **26 B6**
Vyshniy Volochek *Russia* 57°30N 34°30E **70 C5**

W

Waal *→ Neths.* 51°37N 5°0E **64 C3**
Wabasca *→ Canada* 58°22N 115°20W **108 D8**
Wabash *U.S.A.* 40°48N 85°49W **112 E5**
Wabash *→ U.S.A.* 37°48N 88°2W **112 G3**
Waco *U.S.A.* 31°33N 97°9W **111 D7**
Wad Medanî *Sudan* 14°28N 33°30E **95 F12**
Waddeson *U.K.* 51°51N 0°55W **25 C7**
Waddingham *U.K.* 53°27N 0°32W **23 F7**
Waddington *U.K.* 53°10N 0°32W **23 F7**
Waddington, Mt. *Canada* 51°23N 125°15W **108 D7**
Wadebridge *U.K.* 50°31N 4°51W **27 F4**
Wadhurst *U.K.* 51°3N 0°20E **25 D9**
Wadi Halfa *Sudan* 21°53N 31°19E **95 D12**
Wager B. *Canada* 65°26N 88°40W **109 C11**
Wagga Wagga *Australia* 35°7S 147°24E **98 H8**
Wah *Pakistan* 33°45N 72°40E **84 C8**
Wahiawā *U.S.A.* 21°30N 158°2W **110 H15**
Waigeo *Indonesia* 0°20S 130°40E **83 E8**
Wailuku *U.S.A.* 20°53N 156°30W **110 H16**
Wainfleet All Saints *U.K.* 53°7N 0°15E **23 F9**
Wakayama *Japan* 34°15N 135°15E **81 F4**
Wake I. *Pac. Oc.* 19°18N 166°36E **102 F8**
Wakefield *Jamaica* 18°26N 77°42W **114 a**
Wakefield *U.K.* 53°41N 1°29W **23 E6**
Wakkanai *Japan* 45°28N 141°35E **81 A7**
Walbrzych *Poland* 50°45N 16°18E **64 C9**
Walbury Hill *U.K.* 51°21N 1°28W **24 D6**
Waldron *U.K.* 50°56N 0°13E **25 E9**
Wales □ *U.K.* 52°19N 4°43W **26 C4**
Walgett *Australia* 30°0S 148°5E **98 G8**
Walker L. *U.S.A.* 38°42N 118°43W **110 C3**
Walla Walla *U.S.A.* 46°4N 118°20W **110 A3**
Wallaceburg *Canada* 42°34N 82°23W **112 D6**
Wallachia *Romania* 44°35N 25°0E **65 F13**
Wallasey *U.K.* 53°25N 3°2W **23 F2**
Wallingford *U.K.* 51°35N 1°8W **24 C6**
Wallis & Futuna, Is.
 Pac. Oc. 13°18S 176°10W **99 C15**

Walls *U.K.* 60°14N 1°33W **18 B14**
Wallsend *U.K.* 54°59N 1°31W **22 C5**
Walmer *U.K.* 51°11N 1°25E **25 D11**
Walney, I. of *U.K.* 54°6N 3°15W **22 D2**
Walpole *U.K.* 52°45N 0°13E **25 A9**
Walsall *U.K.* 52°35N 1°58W **23 G5**
Walsenburg *U.S.A.* 37°38N 104°47W **110 C6**
Walsoken *U.K.* 52°41N 0°11E **25 A9**
Waltham *U.S.A.* 53°31N 0°7W **23 E8**
Waltham Abbey *U.K.* 51°41N 0°1E **25 C9**
Waltham Forest □ *U.K.* 51°35N 0°0 **25 C9**
Waltham on the Wolds *U.K.* 52°50N 0°48W **23 G7**
Walton-on-the-Naze *U.K.* 51°51N 1°17E **25 C11**
Walvis Bay *Namibia* 23°0S 14°28E **97 J2**
Wamba *Dem. Rep. of the Congo* 2°10N 27°57E **96 D5**
Wanborough *U.K.* 51°33N 1°42W **24 C5**
Wandsworth □ *U.K.* 51°27N 0°11W **25 D8**
Wanganui *N.Z.* 39°56S 175°3E **99 H14**
Wanleweyne *Somali Rep.* 2°37N 44°54E **89 G3**
Wansbeck *→ U.K.* 55°10N 1°32W **22 B5**
Wantage *U.K.* 51°35N 1°25W **24 C6**
Wanxian *China* 30°42N 108°20E **78 E10**
Wapakoneta *U.S.A.* 40°34N 84°12W **112 E5**
Warangal *India* 17°58N 79°35E **84 L11**
Warboys *U.K.* 52°24N 0°4W **25 B8**
Ward *Ireland* 53°26N 6°20W **31 B10**
Wardha *India* 20°45N 78°39E **84 J11**
Wardington *U.K.* 52°7N 1°17W **24 B6**
Wardle *U.K.* 53°7N 2°35W **23 F3**
Ward's Stone *U.K.* 54°1N 2°36W **23 D3**
Ware *U.K.* 51°49N 0°0 **25 C8**
Wareham *U.K.* 50°42N 2°9W **24 E4**
Wark *U.K.* 55°6N 2°14W **22 B4**
Warkworth *U.K.* 55°21N 1°37W **22 B5**
Warley *U.K.* 52°30N 1°59W **23 G5**
Warminster *U.K.* 51°12N 2°10W **24 D4**
Warrego *→ Australia* 30°24S 145°21E **98 G8**
Warren *Mich., U.S.A.* 42°28N 83°1W **112 D6**
Warren *Ohio, U.S.A.* 41°14N 80°49W **112 E7**
Warren *Pa., U.S.A.* 41°51N 79°9W **112 E8**
Warrenpoint *U.K.* 54°6N 6°15W **29 C9**
Warri *Nigeria* 5°30N 5°41E **94 G7**
Warrington *U.K.* 53°24N 2°35W **23 F3**
Warrnambool *Australia* 38°25S 142°30E **98 H7**
Warsaw *Poland* 52°14N 21°0E **65 B11**
Warsaw *U.S.A.* 41°14N 85°51W **112 E5**
Warsop *U.K.* 53°12N 1°9W **23 F6**
Warta *→ Poland* 52°35N 14°39E **64 B8**
Warwick *U.K.* 52°18N 1°35W **24 B5**
Warwick *U.S.A.* 41°42N 71°28W **113 E12**
Warwickshire □ *U.K.* 52°14N 1°38W **24 B5**
Wasatch Ra. *U.S.A.* 40°0N 111°30W **110 B4**
Wash, The *U.K.* 52°58N 0°20E **25 A9**
Washburn *U.S.A.* 46°40N 90°54W **112 B2**
Washford *U.K.* 51°9N 3°21W **24 D2**
Washington *U.K.* 54°55N 1°30W **22 C6**
Washington *D.C., U.S.A.* 38°53N 77°2W **112 F9**
Washington *Ind., U.S.A.* 38°40N 87°10W **112 F4**
Washington *Pa., U.S.A.* 40°10N 80°15W **112 E7**
Washington □ *U.S.A.* 47°30N 120°30W **110 A2**
Washington, Mt. *U.S.A.* 44°16N 71°18W **113 C12**
Washington I. *U.S.A.* 45°23N 86°54W **112 C4**
Wasilla *U.S.A.* 61°35N 149°26W **108 C5**
Waskaganish *Canada* 51°30N 78°40W **109 D12**
Wast Water *U.K.* 54°26N 3°18W **22 D2**
Watampone *Indonesia* 4°29S 120°25E **83 E6**
Watchet *U.K.* 51°10N 3°19W **24 D2**
Waterbeach *U.K.* 52°16N 0°12E **25 B9**
Waterbury *U.S.A.* 41°33N 73°3W **113 E11**
Waterford *Ireland* 52°15N 7°8W **31 D8**
Waterford □ *Ireland* 52°10N 7°40W **31 D7**
Waterford Harbour *Ireland* 52°8N 6°58W **31 D9**
Watergate B. *U.K.* 50°26N 5°4W **27 G3**
Waterloo *Canada* 43°30N 80°32W **112 D7**
Waterloo *Ill., U.S.A.* 38°20N 90°9W **112 F2**
Waterloo *Iowa, U.S.A.* 42°30N 92°21W **111 B81**
Watertown *N.Y., U.S.A.* 43°59N 75°55W **113 D10**
Watertown *S. Dak., U.S.A.* 44°54N 97°7W **111 B7**
Watertown *Wis., U.S.A.* 43°12N 88°43W **112 D3**
Waterville *U.S.A.* 44°33N 69°38W **113 C13**
Watford *U.K.* 51°40N 0°24W **25 C8**
Watlington *Norfolk, U.K.* 52°40N 0°24E **25 A9**
Watlington *Oxon., U.K.* 51°38N 1°0W **24 C6**
Watrous *Canada* 51°40N 105°25W **108 D9**
Watsa *Dem. Rep. of the Congo* 3°4N 29°30E **96 D5**
Watseka *U.S.A.* 40°47N 87°44W **112 E4**
Watson Lake *Canada* 60°6N 128°49W **108 C7**
Watton *U.K.* 52°34N 0°51E **25 A10**
Waukegan *U.S.A.* 42°22N 87°50W **112 D4**
Waukesha *U.S.A.* 43°1N 88°14W **112 D31**
Waupaca *U.S.A.* 44°21N 89°5W **112 C3**
Waupun *U.S.A.* 43°38N 88°44W **112 D3**
Wausau *U.S.A.* 44°58N 89°38W **112 C3**
Wautoma *U.S.A.* 44°4N 89°18W **112 C3**
Wauwatosa *U.S.A.* 43°2N 88°0W **112 D4**
Waveney *→ U.K.* 52°35N 1°39E **25 A12**
Waver *→ U.K.* 54°50N 3°15W **22 C2**
Wâw *Sudan* 7°45N 28°1E **95 G11**
Wawa *Canada* 47°59N 84°47W **112 B5**
Waycross *U.S.A.* 31°13N 82°21W **111 D10**
Wayne *U.S.A.* 38°13N 82°27W **112 F6**
Waynesboro *U.S.A.* 38°4N 78°53W **112 F8**
Waynesburg *U.S.A.* 39°54N 80°11W **112 F7**
Wazirabad *Pakistan* 32°30N 74°8E **84 C9**
Weald, The *U.K.* 51°4N 0°20E **25 D9**
Wear *→ U.K.* 54°55N 1°23W **22 C6**
Weardale *U.K.* 54°44N 2°5W **22 C4**
Wearhead *U.K.* 54°45N 2°13W **22 C4**
Weaver *→ U.K.* 53°17N 2°35W **23 F3**
Weaverham *U.K.* 53°16N 2°35W **23 F3**
Webster Springs *U.S.A.* 38°29N 80°25W **112 F7**
Weddell Sea *Antarctica* 72°30S 40°0W **55 D1**
Wedmore *U.K.* 51°13N 2°48W **24 D3**
Wednesbury *U.K.* 52°34N 2°1W **23 G4**
Wednesfield *U.K.* 52°37N 2°2W **23 G4**
Weedon Bec *U.K.* 52°15N 1°5W **24 B6**
Weifang *China* 36°44N 119°7E **79 D12**
Weihai *China* 37°30N 122°6E **79 D13**
Weipa *Australia* 12°40S 141°50E **98 C7**

Welch *U.S.A.* 37°26N 81°35W **112 G7**
Weldon *U.K.* 55°17N 1°45W **22 B5**
Welford *Northants., U.K.* 52°25N 1°3W **24 B6**
Welford *W. Berkshire, U.K.* 51°27N 1°24W **24 D6**
Welkom *S. Africa* 28°0S 26°46E **97 K5**
Welland *Canada* 43°0N 79°15W **112 D8**
Welland *→ U.K.* 52°51N 0°5W **23 G8**
Wellesley Is. *Australia* 16°42S 139°30E **98 D6**
Wellingborough *U.K.* 52°19N 0°41W **25 B7**
Wellington *N.Z.* 41°19S 174°46E **99 J13**
Wellington *Somst., U.K.* 50°58N 3°13W **24 E2**
Wellington *Telford & Wrekin,*
 U.K. 52°42N 2°30W **23 G3**
Wellington, I. *Chile* 49°30S 75°0W **121 G1**
Wellington Chan. *Canada* 75°0N 93°0W **109 B10**
Wells *U.K.* 51°13N 2°39W **24 D3**
Wells-next-the-Sea *U.K.* 52°57N 0°51E **25 A10**
Wellsboro *U.S.A.* 41°45N 77°18W **112 E9**
Wellsville *U.S.A.* 42°7N 77°57W **112 D9**
Welney *U.K.* 52°31N 0°15E **25 A9**
Wels *Austria* 48°9N 14°1E **64 D8**
Welshpool *U.K.* 52°39N 3°8W **26 B7**
Welton *U.K.* 53°18N 0°29W **23 F8**
Welwyn Garden City *U.K.* 51°48N 0°12W **25 C8**
Wem *U.K.* 52°52N 2°44W **23 G3**
Wembury *U.K.* 50°19N 4°6W **27 G5**
Wemindji *Canada* 53°0N 78°49W **109 D12**
Wemyss Bay *U.K.* 55°53N 4°53W **20 C6**
Wenatchee *U.S.A.* 47°25N 120°19W **110 A2**
Wendover *U.K.* 51°45N 0°44W **25 C7**
Wenlock Edge *U.K.* 52°30N 2°43W **23 G3**
Wensu *China* 41°15N 80°10E **78 C5**
Wensum *→ U.K.* 52°40N 1°15E **25 A11**
Wenzhou *China* 28°0N 120°38E **79 F13**
Weobley *U.K.* 52°11N 2°50W **24 B3**
Werrington *U.K.* 50°39N 4°23W **27 F5**
Weser *→ Germany* 53°36N 8°28E **64 B5**
West Antarctica *Antarctica* 80°0S 90°0W **55 D15**
West Auckland *U.K.* 54°38N 1°42W **22 C5**
West Bank ■ *Asia* 32°6N 35°13E **86 C3**
West Bend *U.S.A.* 43°25N 88°11W **112 D3**
West Bengal □ *India* 23°0N 88°0E **85 H16**
West Berkshire □ *U.K.* 51°25N 1°17W **24 D6**
West Bridgford *U.K.* 52°55N 1°8W **23 G6**
West Bromwich *U.K.* 52°32N 1°59W **23 G5**
West Burra *U.K.* 60°5N 1°21W **18 B15**
West Calder *U.K.* 55°51N 3°33W **21 C8**
West Coker *U.K.* 50°55N 2°40W **24 E3**
West Falkland *Falk. Is.* 51°40S 60°0W **121 H3**
West Fen *U.K.* 53°5N 0°5W **23 F8**
West Frankfort *U.S.A.* 37°54N 88°55W **111 C91**
West Grinstead *U.K.* 50°58N 0°19W **25 E8**
West Haddon *U.K.* 52°20N 1°3W **24 B6**
West Kirby *U.K.* 53°23N 3°11W **23 F2**
West Linton *U.K.* 55°46N 3°21W **21 C9**
West Lulworth *U.K.* 50°37N 2°14W **24 E4**
West Malling *U.K.* 51°17N 0°26E **25 D9**
West Meon *U.K.* 51°1N 1°5W **24 D6**
West Mersea *U.K.* 51°46N 0°56E **25 C10**
West Midlands □ *U.K.* 52°26N 2°0W **23 H5**
West Moors *U.K.* 50°49N 1°53W **24 E5**
West Palm Beach *U.S.A.* 26°43N 80°3W **111 E10**
West Point *U.S.A.* 37°32N 76°48W **112 G9**
West Rasen *U.K.* 53°23N 0°24W **23 F8**
West Seneca *U.S.A.* 42°51N 78°48W **112 D8**
West Siberian Plain *Russia* 62°0N 75°0E **72 B9**
West Sussex □ *U.K.* 50°55N 0°30W **25 E8**
West Virginia □ *U.S.A.* 38°45N 80°30W **112 F7**
West Yorkshire □ *U.K.* 53°45N 1°40W **23 E5**
Westbourne *U.K.* 50°52N 0°55W **25 E7**
Westbrook *U.S.A.* 43°41N 70°22W **113 D12**
Westbury *Shrops., U.K.* 52°41N 2°55W **23 G3**
Westbury *Wilts., U.K.* 51°15N 2°11W **24 D4**
Westbury-on-Severn *U.K.* 51°50N 2°25W **24 C4**
Wester Ross *U.K.* 57°37N 4°51W **18 G6**
Westerham *U.K.* 51°16N 0°5E **25 D9**
Western Australia □ *Australia* 25°0S 118°0E **98 F2**
Western Ghats *India* 14°0N 75°0E **84 N9**
Western Isles □ *U.K.* 57°30N 7°10W **18 G3**
Western Sahara ■ *Africa* 25°0N 13°0W **94 D3**
Westerwald *Germany* 50°38N 7°56E **64 C4**
Westfield *U.K.* 50°55N 0°35E **25 E10**
Westhill *U.K.* 57°9N 2°19W **19 H13**
Westhoughton *U.K.* 53°33N 2°31W **23 E3**
Westmeath □ *Ireland* 53°33N 7°34W **28 D6**
Westminster *U.S.A.* 39°34N 76°59W **112 F9**
Westmoreland *Barbados* 13°13N 59°37W **115 g**
Weston *U.K.* 52°51N 2°1W **23 G4**
Weston *U.S.A.* 39°2N 80°28W **112 F7**
Weston-super-Mare *U.K.* 51°21N 2°58W **24 D3**
Westport *Ireland* 53°48N 9°31W **28 D2**
Westray *U.K.* 59°18N 3°0W **19 D11**
Westruther *U.K.* 55°45N 2°35W **21 C10**
Westward Ho! *U.K.* 51°2N 4°15W **27 E5**
Wetar *Indonesia* 7°48S 126°30E **83 F7**
Wetaskiwin *Canada* 52°55N 113°24W **108 D8**
Wetherby *U.K.* 53°56N 1°23W **23 E6**
Wetwang *U.K.* 54°1N 0°35W **23 D7**
Wewak *Papua N. G.* 3°38S 143°41E **98 A7**
Wexford *Ireland* 52°20N 6°28W **31 D10**
Wexford □ *Ireland* 52°20N 6°25W **31 D10**
Wexford Harbour *Ireland* 52°20N 6°25W **31 D10**
Wey *→ U.K.* 51°22N 0°27W **25 D8**
Weybourne *U.K.* 52°57N 1°19E **25 A11**
Weybridge *U.K.* 51°22N 0°27W **25 D8**
Weyburn *Canada* 49°40N 103°50W **108 E9**
Weymouth *U.K.* 50°37N 2°28W **24 E4**
Wha Ti *Canada* 63°8N 117°16W **108 C8**
Whale Cove *Canada* 62°10N 92°34W **108 C10**
Whales, B. of *Antarctica* 78°0S 160°0W **55 D12**
Whalley *U.K.* 53°49N 2°24W **23 E4**
Whalsay *U.K.* 60°22N 0°59W **18 B16**
Whalton *U.K.* 55°8N 1°46W **22 B5**
Whangarei *N.Z.* 35°43S 174°21E **99 H13**
Whaplode *U.K.* 52°42N 0°3W **23 G8**
Wharfe *→ U.K.* 53°51N 1°9W **23 E6**
Wharfedale *U.K.* 54°6N 2°1W **22 D4**
Wheatley Hill *U.K.* 54°45N 1°23W **22 C6**

Wheeler Pk. U.S.A. 38°57N 114°15W 110 C4
Wheeling U.S.A. 40°4N 80°43W 112 E7
Whernside U.K. 54°14N 2°24W 22 C2
Whicham U.K. 54°15N 3°21W 22 D2
Whimple U.K. 50°46N 3°20W 27 F7
Whipsnade U.K. 51°51N 0°32W 25 C7
Whissendine U.K. 52°43N 0°46W 23 G7
Whitburn U.K. 55°52N 3°40W 21 C8
Whitby U.K. 54°29N 0°37W 22 D7
Whitchurch Devon, U.K. 50°32N 4°9W 27 F5
Whitchurch Hants., U.K. 51°14N 1°20W 24 D6
Whitchurch Hereford, U.K. 51°51N 2°39W 24 C3
Whitchurch Shrops., U.K. 52°59N 2°40W 23 G3
White → Ark., U.S.A. 33°57N 91°5W 111 D8
White → Ind., U.S.A. 38°25N 87°45W 112 F5
White → Utah, U.S.A. 40°4N 109°41W 110 B5
White Esk → U.K. 55°13N 3°11W 21 D9
White Horse, Vale of U.K. 51°37N 1°30W 24 C5
White Horse Hill U.K. 51°34N 1°33W 24 C5
White Mts. Calif., U.S.A. 37°30N 118°15W 110 C3
White Mts. N.H., U.S.A. 44°15N 71°15W 111 B12
White Nile → Sudan 15°38N 32°31E 95 E12
White Sea Russia 66°30N 38°0E 70 A6
Whiteadder Water → U.K. 55°51N 2°25W 21 C11
Whitecourt Canada 54°10N 115°45W 108 D8
Whitefish Pt. U.S.A. 46°45N 84°59W 112 B5
Whitehall U.S.A. 44°22N 91°19W 112 C2
Whitehaven U.K. 54°33N 3°35W 22 C1
Whitehorse Canada 60°43N 135°3W 108 C6
Whitesand B. U.K. 50°21N 4°18W 27 G5
Whitewater U.S.A. 42°50N 88°44W 112 D3
Whithorn U.K. 54°44N 4°26W 20 E7
Whitley Bay U.K. 55°3N 1°27W 22 B6
Whitney, Mt. U.S.A. 36°35N 118°18W 110 C3
Whitstable U.K. 51°21N 1°3E 25 D11
Whittington Derby, U.K. 53°16N 1°26W 23 F6
Whittington Shrops., U.K. 52°52N 3°0W 23 G3
Whittlesey U.K. 52°33N 0°8W 25 A8
Whittlesford U.K. 52°7N 0°9E 25 B9
Whitwell Derby, U.K. 53°17N 1°12W 23 F6
Whitwell I. of W., U.K. 50°36N 1°15W 24 E6
Whitwick U.K. 52°45N 1°22W 23 G6
Whitworth U.K. 53°39N 2°11W 23 E4
Wholdaia L. Canada 60°43N 104°20W 108 C9
Whyalla Australia 33°2S 137°30E 98 G6
Wiarton Canada 44°40N 81°10W 112 C7
Wiay U.K. 57°24N 7°13W 18 H3
Wichita U.S.A. 37°42N 97°20W 111 C7
Wichita Falls U.S.A. 33°54N 98°30W 110 D7
Wick U.K. 58°26N 3°5W 19 F11
Wickford U.K. 51°36N 0°33E 25 C10
Wickham U.K. 50°54N 1°11W 24 E6
Wickham Market U.K. 52°9N 1°23E 25 B11
Wicklow Ireland 52°59N 6°3W 31 C10
Wicklow □ Ireland 52°57N 6°25W 31 C10
Wicklow Hd. Ireland 52°58N 6°0W 31 C11
Wicklow Mts. Ireland 52°58N 6°26W 31 C10
Wicklow Mts. △ Ireland 53°6N 6°21W 31 B11
Wickwar U.K. 51°36N 2°23W 24 C4
Widdrington U.K. 55°15N 1°35W 22 B5
Widecombe U.K. 50°34N 3°49W 27 F6
Widemouth U.K. 50°47N 4°34W 27 F4
Widnes U.K. 53°23N 2°45W 23 F3
Wiener Neustadt Austria 47°49N 16°16E 64 E9
Wiesbaden Germany 50°4N 8°14E 64 C5
Wigan U.K. 53°33N 2°38W 23 E3
Wight, I. of U.K. 50°41N 1°17W 24 E6
Wight, Isle of □ U.K. 50°41N 1°17W 24 E6
Wigmore U.K. 52°19N 2°51W 24 B3
Wigston U.K. 52°35N 1°6W 23 G6
Wigton U.K. 54°50N 3°10W 22 C2
Wigtown U.K. 54°53N 4°27W 20 E7
Wigtown B. U.K. 54°46N 4°15W 20 E7
Wilhelm, Mt. Papua N. G. 5°50S 145°1E 98 B8
Wilhelmshaven Germany 53°31N 8°7E 64 B5
Wilkes-Barre U.S.A. 41°15N 75°53W 113 E10
Wilkes Land Antarctica 69°0S 120°0E 55 D9
Wilkins Ice Shelf Antarctica 70°30S 72°0W 55 D17
Willemstad Neth. Ant. 12°5N 68°55W 115 E11
Willenhall U.K. 52°36N 2°2W 23 G4
Willesborough U.K. 51°8N 0°56E 25 D10
Williams Lake Canada 52°10N 122°10W 108 D7
Williamsburg U.S.A. 37°16N 76°43W 112 G9
Williamson U.S.A. 37°41N 82°17W 112 G6
Williamsport U.S.A. 41°15N 77°1W 112 E9
Willingdon U.K. 50°47N 0°17E 25 E9
Williston U.S.A. 48°9N 103°37W 110 A6
Williston L. Canada 56°0N 124°0W 108 D7
Williton U.K. 51°9N 3°19W 24 D2
Willmar U.S.A. 45°7N 95°3W 111 A7
Willoughby U.K. 53°13N 0°12E 23 F9
Wilmington U.K. 50°47N 3°7W 27 F7
Wilmington Del., U.S.A. 39°45N 75°33W 113 F10
Wilmington N.C., U.S.A. 34°14N 77°55W 111 D11
Wilmslow U.K. 53°19N 2°13W 23 F4
Wilnecote U.K. 52°36N 1°39W 23 G5
Wilton U.K. 51°5N 1°51W 24 D5
Wiltshire □ U.K. 51°18N 1°53W 24 D5
Wimblington U.K. 52°31N 0°4E 25 A9
Wimborne Minster U.K. 50°48N 1°59W 24 E5

Wincanton U.K. 51°3N 2°24W 24 D4
Winchelsea U.K. 50°55N 0°43E 25 E10
Winchester U.K. 51°4N 1°18W 24 D6
Winchester Ky., U.S.A. 37°59N 84°11W 112 G6
Winchester Va., U.S.A. 39°11N 78°10W 112 F8
Wind → U.S.A. 43°12N 108°12W 110 B5
Wind River Range U.S.A. 43°0N 109°30W 110 B5
Windermere U.K. 54°23N 2°55W 22 D3
Windhoek Namibia 22°35S 17°4E 97 J3
Windrush → U.K. 51°43N 1°24W 24 C6
Windsor Canada 42°18N 83°0W 109 E11
Windsor U.K. 51°29N 0°36W 25 D7
Windward Is. W. Indies 13°0N 61°0W 115 E12
Windward Passage Caribbean 20°0N 74°0W 115 D10
Wing U.K. 51°53N 0°43W 25 C7
Wingham U.K. 51°16N 1°13E 25 D11
Winisk → Canada 55°17N 85°5W 109 D11
Winkleigh U.K. 50°50N 3°58W 27 F6
Winkler Canada 49°10N 97°56W 108 E10
Winneba Ghana 5°25N 0°36W 94 G5
Winnebago, L. U.S.A. 44°0N 88°26W 112 D3
Winnemucca U.S.A. 40°58N 117°44W 110 B3
Winona U.S.A. 44°3N 91°39W 111 B8
Winooski U.S.A. 44°29N 73°11W 113 C11
Winsford U.K. 53°12N 2°31W 23 F3
Winslow U.K. 51°57N 0°52W 25 C7
Winslow U.S.A. 35°2N 110°42W 110 C4
Winster U.K. 53°9N 1°39W 23 F5
Winston-Salem U.S.A. 36°6N 80°15W 111 C10
Winterborne Abbas U.K. 50°42N 2°33W 24 E3
Winterthur Switz. 47°30N 8°44E 64 E5
Winterton N. Lincs., U.K. 53°39N 0°37W 23 E7
Winterton Norfolk, U.K. 52°43N 1°41E 25 A12
Winton Australia 22°24S 143°3E 98 E7
Wirksworth U.K. 53°6N 1°35W 23 F5
Wirral U.K. 53°25N 3°0W 23 F2
Wisbech U.K. 52°41N 0°9E 25 A9
Wisborough Green U.K. 51°2N 0°30W 25 D7
Wisconsin □ U.S.A. 44°45N 89°30W 111 B9
Wisconsin Rapids U.S.A. 44°23N 89°49W 112 C3
Wishaw U.K. 55°46N 3°54W 21 C8
Wiske → U.K. 54°19N 1°27W 22 D6
Witham U.K. 51°48N 0°40E 25 C10
Witham → U.K. 52°59N 0°2W 23 G8
Withern U.K. 53°18N 0°8E 23 F9
Withernsea U.K. 53°44N 0°1E 23 E9
Witley U.K. 51°9N 0°39W 25 D7
Witney U.K. 51°48N 1°28W 24 C6
Wittersham U.K. 51°0N 0°43E 25 D10
Wiveliscombe U.K. 51°2N 3°19W 24 D2
Wivenhoe U.K. 51°51N 0°59E 25 C10
Wkra → Poland 52°27N 20°44E 65 B11
Wloclawek Poland 52°40N 19°3E 65 B10
Woburn U.K. 51°59N 0°36W 25 C7
Woburn Sands U.K. 52°1N 0°39W 25 C7
Wodonga Australia 36°5S 146°50E 98 H8
Woking U.K. 51°19N 0°34W 25 D7
Wokingham U.K. 51°24N 0°49W 25 D7
Wolf Rock U.K. 49°57N 5°49W 27 H2
Wolfsburg Germany 52°25N 10°48E 64 B6
Wolin Poland 53°50N 14°37E 64 B8
Wollaston L. Canada 58°7N 103°10W 108 D9
Wollaston Pen. Canada 69°30N 115°0W 108 C8
Wollongong Australia 34°25S 150°54E 98 G9
Wolsingham U.K. 54°44N 1°52W 22 C5
Wolstenholme, C. Canada 62°35N 77°30W 104 C12
Wolverhampton U.K. 52°35N 2°7W 23 G4
Wolverton U.K. 52°3N 0°47W 25 B7
Wolviston U.K. 54°38N 1°18W 22 C6
Wombwell U.K. 53°32N 1°25W 23 E6
Wönsan N. Korea 39°11N 127°27E 79 D14
Wonston U.K. 51°8N 1°18W 24 D6
Woodbridge U.K. 52°6N 1°20E 25 B11
Woodbury U.K. 50°41N 3°24W 27 F7
Woodhall Spa U.K. 53°10N 0°12W 23 F8
Woodhouse U.K. 53°22N 1°21W 23 F6
Woodley U.K. 51°27N 0°53W 25 D7
Woodroffe, Mt. Australia 26°20S 131°45E 98 F5
Woods, L. of the N. Amer. 49°15N 94°45W 108 E10
Woodstock N.B., Canada 46°11N 67°37W 109 E13
Woodstock Ont., Canada 43°10N 80°45W 112 D7
Woodstock U.K. 51°51N 1°20W 24 C6
Woodstock U.S.A. 42°19N 88°27W 112 D3
Wookey U.K. 51°13N 2°41W 24 D3
Wookey Hole U.K. 51°14N 2°40W 24 D3
Wool U.K. 50°40N 2°12W 24 E4
Woolacombe U.K. 51°10N 4°13W 27 E5
Wooler U.K. 55°33N 2°1W 22 A4
Woonsocket U.S.A. 42°0N 71°31W 113 E11
Wootton Bassett U.K. 51°32N 1°54W 24 C5
Wootton Wawen U.K. 52°16N 1°47W 24 B5
Worcester S. Africa 33°39S 19°27E 97 L3
Worcester U.K. 52°11N 2°12W 24 B4
Worcester U.S.A. 42°16N 71°48W 113 D12
Worcestershire □ U.K. 52°13N 2°10W 24 B4
Worfield U.K. 52°34N 2°21W 23 G4
Workington U.K. 54°39N 3°33W 22 C1

Worksop U.K. 53°18N 1°7W 23 F6
Worms Germany 49°37N 8°21E 64 D5
Wortham U.K. 52°21N 1°3E 25 B11
Worthing Barbados 13°5N 59°35W 115 g
Worthing U.K. 50°49N 0°21W 25 E8
Worthington U.S.A. 43°37N 95°36W 111 B7
Wotton under Edge U.K. 51°37N 2°20W 24 C4
Wragby U.K. 53°18N 0°17W 23 F8
Wrangel I. Russia 71°0N 180°0E 77 B19
Wrangell U.S.A. 56°28N 132°23W 108 D6
Wrangell Mts. U.S.A. 61°30N 142°0W 108 C5
Wrangle U.K. 53°3N 0°7E 23 F9
Wrath, C. U.K. 58°38N 5°1W 18 E7
Wrekin, The U.K. 52°41N 2°32W 23 G3
Wrentham U.K. 52°23N 1°40E 25 B12
Wrexham U.K. 53°3N 3°0W 26 A8
Wrexham □ U.K. 53°1N 2°58W 26 B3
Wrigley Canada 63°16N 123°37W 108 C7
Wrocław Poland 51°5N 17°5E 65 C9
Wroughton U.K. 51°31N 1°47W 24 C5
Wroxham U.K. 52°42N 1°24E 25 A11
Wu Jiang → China 29°40N 107°20E 78 F10
Wuhai China 39°47N 106°52E 78 D10
Wuhan China 30°31N 114°18E 79 E11
Wuhu China 31°22N 118°21E 79 E12
Wuppertal Germany 51°16N 7°12E 64 C4
Würzburg Germany 49°46N 9°55E 64 D5
Wushi China 41°9N 79°13E 78 C4
Wutongqiao China 29°22N 103°50E 78 F9
Wuwei China 37°57N 102°34E 78 D9
Wuxi China 31°33N 120°18E 79 E13
Wuyi Shan China 27°0N 117°0E 79 F12
Wuzhong China 38°2N 106°12E 78 D10
Wuzhou China 23°30N 111°18E 79 G11
Wye U.K. 51°10N 0°57E 25 D10
Wye → U.K. 51°38N 2°40W 24 C3
Wylye → U.K. 51°5N 1°51W 24 D5
Wymondham Leics., U.K. 52°45N 0°43W 23 G7
Wymondham Norfolk, U.K. 52°35N 1°7E 25 A11
Wyndham Australia 15°33S 128°3E 98 D4
Wyoming □ U.S.A. 43°0N 107°30W 110 B5
Wyre → U.K. 53°52N 2°57W 23 E3
Wyre Forest U.K. 52°24N 2°24W 23 H4

X

Xaçmaz Azerbaijan 41°31N 48°42E 71 F8
Xainza China 30°58N 88°35E 78 E6
Xalapa Mexico 19°32N 96°55W 114 D5
Xankändi Azerbaijan 39°52N 46°49E 71 G8
Xenia U.S.A. 39°41N 83°56W 112 F6
Xi Jiang → China 22°5N 113°20E 79 G11
Xiaguan China 25°32N 100°16E 78 F9
Xiamen China 24°25N 118°4E 79 G12
Xi'an China 34°15N 109°0E 79 C10
Xiang Jiang → China 28°55N 112°50E 79 F11
Xiangfan China 32°2N 112°8E 79 E11
Xianggang = Hong Kong □ China 22°11N 114°14E 79 a
Xiangtan China 27°51N 112°54E 79 F11
Xianyang China 34°20N 108°40E 79 C10
Xichang China 27°51N 102°19E 78 F9
Xigazê China 29°5N 88°45E 78 F6
Xilinhot China 43°52N 116°2E 79 C12
Xing'an China 25°38N 110°40E 79 F11
Xinghua China 32°58N 119°48E 79 C12
Xingu → Brazil 1°30S 51°53W 120 C4
Xining China 36°34N 101°40E 78 D9
Xinxiang China 35°18N 113°50E 79 D11
Xinyang China 32°6N 114°3E 79 E11
Xique-Xique Brazil 10°50S 42°40W 122 B2
Xizang Zizhiqu □ China 32°0N 88°0E 78 E6
Xuanhua China 40°40N 115°2E 79 C12
Xuanwei China 26°15N 103°59E 78 F9
Xuzhou China 34°18N 117°10E 79 E12

Y

Ya'an China 29°58N 103°5E 78 F9
Yablonovyy Ra. Russia 53°0N 114°0E 77 D12
Yabucoa Puerto Rico 18°3N 65°53W 115 d
Yacuiba Bolivia 22°0S 63°43W 120 E3
Yakeshi China 49°17N 120°43E 79 B13
Yakima U.S.A. 46°36N 120°31W 110 A2
Yakutat U.S.A. 59°33N 139°44W 108 D6
Yakutia □ Russia 66°0N 130°0E 77 C13
Yakutsk Russia 62°5N 129°50E 77 C13
Yala Thailand 6°33N 101°18E 82 C2
Yalong Jiang → China 26°40N 101°55E 78 F9
Yalta Ukraine 44°30N 34°10E 71 F5
Yalu Jiang → China 39°55N 124°19E 79 D13
Yamagata Japan 38°15N 140°15E 81 D7
Yamaguchi Japan 34°10N 131°32E 81 F2
Yamal Pen. Russia 71°0N 70°0E 76 B7
Yambol Bulgaria 42°30N 26°30E 69 C12
Yamethin Burma 20°29N 96°18E 85 J20
Yamoussoukro Ivory C. 6°49N 5°17W 94 G4

Yampa → U.S.A. 40°32N 108°59W 110 B5
Yamuna → India 25°30N 81°53E 85 G12
Yamzho Yumco China 28°48N 90°35E 78 F7
Yan'an China 36°35N 109°26E 79 D10
Yanbu 'al Baḩr Si. Arabia 24°0N 38°5E 86 E4
Yancheng China 33°23N 120°8E 79 E13
Yangambi Dem. Rep. of the Congo 0°47N 24°24E 96 D4
Yangjiang China 21°50N 111°59E 79 G11
Yangquan China 37°58N 113°31E 79 D11
Yangtze → China 31°48N 121°10E 79 E13
Yangzhou China 32°21N 119°26E 79 E12
Yanji China 42°59N 129°30E 79 C14
Yankton U.S.A. 42°53N 97°23W 111 B7
Yanqi China 42°5N 86°35E 78 C6
Yantai China 37°34N 121°22E 79 D13
Yaoundé Cameroon 3°50N 11°35E 96 D2
Yap Pac. Oc. 9°30N 138°10E 102 G5
Yapen Indonesia 1°50S 136°0E 83 E9
Yaqui → Mexico 27°37N 110°39W 114 B2
Yaraka Australia 24°53S 144°3E 98 E7
Yarcombe U.K. 50°51N 3°5W 27 F7
Yare → U.K. 52°35N 1°38E 25 A12
Yarkant He → China 40°26N 80°59E 78 C5
Yarkhun → Pakistan 36°17N 72°30E 84 A8
Yarm U.K. 54°31N 1°21W 22 C6
Yarmouth Canada 43°50N 66°7W 109 E13
Yarmouth U.K. 50°42N 1°29W 24 E5
Yaroslavl Russia 57°35N 39°55E 70 C6
Yarrow U.K. 55°33N 3°1W 21 C9
Yarumal Colombia 6°58N 75°24W 120 B2
Yate U.K. 51°32N 2°25W 24 C4
Yathkyed L. Canada 62°40N 98°0W 108 C10
Yatsushiro Japan 32°30N 130°40E 81 G2
Yatton U.K. 51°23N 2°49W 24 D3
Yauco Puerto Rico 18°2N 66°51W 115 d
Yavari → Peru 4°21S 70°2W 120 C2
Yaxley U.K. 52°31N 0°16W 25 A8
Yazd Iran 31°55N 54°27E 87 D8
Yazoo → U.S.A. 32°22N 90°54W 111 D8
Yazoo City U.S.A. 32°51N 90°25W 111 D8
Yealmpton U.K. 50°21N 4°1W 27 G5
Yecheng China 37°54N 77°26E 78 D4
Yelets Russia 52°40N 38°30E 70 D6
Yell U.K. 60°35N 1°5W 18 A15
Yell Sd. U.K. 60°33N 1°15W 18 A15
Yellow = Huang He → China 37°55N 118°50E 79 D12
Yellow Sea China 35°0N 123°0E 79 D13
Yellowhead Pass Canada 52°53N 118°25W 108 D8
Yellowknife Canada 62°27N 114°29W 108 C8
Yellowstone → U.S.A. 47°59N 103°59W 110 A6
Yellowstone Nat. Park △ U.S.A. 44°40N 110°30W 110 B5
Yemen ■ Asia 15°0N 44°0E 89 E3
Yenisey → Russia 71°50N 82°40E 76 B9
Yeo → U.K. 51°2N 2°54W 24 D3
Yeola India 20°2N 74°30E 84 J9
Yeovil U.K. 50°57N 2°38W 24 E3
Yerevan Armenia 40°10N 44°31E 71 F7
Yes Tor U.K. 50°41N 4°0W 27 F5
Yeu, Î. d' France 46°42N 2°20W 66 C2
Yevpatoriya Ukraine 45°15N 33°20E 71 E5
Yeysk Russia 46°40N 38°12E 71 E6
Yibin China 28°45N 104°32E 78 F9
Yichang China 30°40N 111°20E 79 E11
Yichun China 47°44N 128°52E 79 B14
Yinchuan China 38°30N 106°15E 78 D10
Yingkou China 40°37N 122°18E 79 C13
Yining China 43°58N 81°10E 78 C5
Yishan China 24°28N 108°38E 78 G10
Yixing China 31°21N 119°48E 79 E12
Yiyang China 28°35N 112°18E 79 F11
Yogyakarta Indonesia 7°49S 110°22E 82 F4
Yokkaichi Japan 34°55N 136°38E 81 F5
Yokohama Japan 35°27N 139°28E 81 F6
Yokosuka Japan 35°20N 139°40E 81 F6
Yonago Japan 35°25N 133°19E 81 F3
Yong'an China 25°59N 117°25E 79 F12
Yongzhou China 26°17N 111°37E 79 F11
Yonkers U.S.A. 40°56N 73°52W 113 E11
Yonne → France 48°23N 2°58E 66 B5
York U.K. 53°58N 1°6W 23 E6
York U.S.A. 39°58N 76°44W 112 F9
York, C. Australia 10°42S 142°31E 98 C7
York, Vale of U.K. 54°15N 1°25W 22 D6
Yorkshire Dales △ U.K. 54°12N 2°10W 22 D4
Yorkshire Wolds U.K. 54°8N 0°31W 22 D7
Yorkton Canada 51°11N 102°28W 108 D9
Yosemite Nat. Park △ U.S.A. 37°45N 119°40W 110 C3
Yoshkar Ola Russia 56°38N 47°55E 70 C8
Youghal Ireland 51°56N 7°52W 30 E7
Youghal B. Ireland 51°55N 7°49W 30 E7
Youlgreave U.K. 53°11N 1°40W 23 F5
Youngstown U.S.A. 41°6N 80°39W 112 E7
Yoxall U.K. 52°46N 1°47W 23 G5
Yoxford U.K. 52°16N 1°31E 25 B12
Yozgat Turkey 39°51N 34°47E 71 G5
Yreka U.S.A. 41°44N 122°38W 110 B2

Ystalyfera U.K. 51°46N 3°48W 26 D6
Ythan → U.K. 57°19N 1°59W 19 H14
Yu Jiang → China 23°22N 110°3E 79 G11
Yuan Jiang → China 28°55N 111°50E 79 F11
Yuba City U.S.A. 39°8N 121°37W 110 C2
Yucatán Mexico 19°30N 89°0W 114 D7
Yucatan Basin Cent. Amer. 19°0N 86°0W 104 H11
Yucatan Channel Caribbean 22°0N 86°30W 114 C7
Yueyang China 29°21N 113°5E 79 F11
Yukon → U.S.A. 62°32N 163°54W 108 C3
Yukon Territory □ Canada 63°0N 135°0W 108 C6
Yulin China 38°20N 109°30E 79 D10
Yuma U.S.A. 32°43N 114°37W 110 D4
Yumen China 39°50N 97°30E 78 D8
Yungas Bolivia 17°0S 66°0W 120 D3
Yunnan □ China 25°0N 102°0E 78 G9
Yurimaguas Peru 5°55S 76°7W 120 C2
Yushu China 33°5N 96°55E 78 E8
Yutian China 36°52N 81°42E 78 D5
Yuzhno-Sakhalinsk Russia 46°58N 142°45E 79 B17
Yuzhou China 34°10N 113°28E 79 E11
Yvetot France 49°37N 0°44E 66 B4

Z

Zāb al Kabīr → Iraq 36°1N 43°24E 86 B5
Zābol □ Afghan. 32°0N 67°0E 87 D11
Zabrze Poland 50°18N 18°50E 65 C10
Zacatecas Mexico 22°47N 102°35W 114 C4
Zadar Croatia 44°8N 15°14E 68 B6
Zagaoua Chad 15°30N 22°24E 95 E10
Zagazig Egypt 30°40N 31°30E 95 B12
Zagreb Croatia 45°50N 15°58E 68 B7
Zagros Mts. Iran 33°45N 48°5E 86 C7
Zāhedān Iran 29°30N 60°50E 87 D10
Zahlah Lebanon 33°52N 35°50E 86 C3
Zakynthos Greece 37°47N 20°54E 69 F9
Zalantun China 48°0N 122°43E 79 B13
Zambezi → Africa 18°35S 36°20E 97 H7
Zambia ■ Africa 15°0S 28°0E 97 G5
Zamboanga Phil. 6°59N 122°3E 83 C6
Zamora Mexico 19°59N 102°16W 114 D4
Zamora Spain 41°30N 5°45W 67 B3
Zamość Poland 50°43N 23°15E 65 C12
Zanesville U.S.A. 39°56N 82°1W 112 F6
Zanjān Iran 36°40N 48°35E 86 B7
Zanzibar Tanzania 6°12S 39°12E 96 F7
Zaouiet Reggâne Algeria 26°32N 0°3E 94 C6
Zaoyang China 32°10N 112°45E 79 E11
Zaozhuang China 34°50N 117°35E 79 E12
Zapala Argentina 39°0S 70°5W 121 F2
Zaporozhye Ukraine 47°50N 35°10E 71 E6
Zaragoza Spain 41°39N 0°53W 67 B5
Zaranj Afghan. 30°55N 61°55E 87 D10
Zárate Argentina 34°7S 59°0W 121 F4
Zaria Nigeria 11°0N 7°40E 94 F7
Zaskar Mts. India 33°15N 77°30E 84 C10
Zaysan, L. Kazakhstan 48°0N 83°0E 76 E9
Zeebrugge Belgium 51°19N 3°12E 64 C2
Zeil, Mt. Australia 23°30S 132°23E 98 E5
Zelenograd Russia 56°1N 37°12E 70 C6
Zenica Bos.-H. 44°10N 17°57E 68 B7
Zhangjiakou China 40°48N 114°55E 79 C11
Zhangye China 38°50N 100°23E 78 D9
Zhangzhou China 24°30N 117°35E 79 G12
Zhanjiang China 21°15N 110°20E 79 G11
Zhaoqing China 23°0N 112°20E 79 G11
Zhaotong China 27°20N 103°44E 78 F9
Zhejiang □ China 29°0N 120°0E 79 F13
Zhengzhou China 34°45N 113°34E 79 E11
Zhezqazghan Kazakhstan 47°44N 67°40E 76 E7
Zhigansk Russia 66°48N 123°27E 77 C13
Zhlobin Belarus 52°55N 30°0E 70 D5
Zhob Pakistan 31°20N 69°31E 84 D6
Zhongdian China 27°48N 99°42E 78 F8
Zhuhai China 22°17N 113°34E 79 a
Zhumadian China 32°59N 114°2E 79 E11
Zhytomyr Ukraine 50°20N 28°40E 65 C15
Zibo China 36°47N 118°3E 79 D12
Zielona Góra Poland 51°57N 15°31E 64 C8
Zigong China 29°15N 104°48E 78 F9
Ziguinchor Senegal 12°35N 16°20W 94 F2
Žilina Slovak Rep. 49°12N 18°42E 65 D10
Zimbabwe ■ Africa 19°0S 30°0E 97 H5
Zinder Niger 13°48N 9°0E 94 F7
Ziway, L. Ethiopia 8°0N 38°50E 89 F2
Zlatoust Russia 55°10N 59°40E 70 C10
Zlín Czech Rep. 49°14N 17°40E 65 D9
Zonguldak Turkey 41°28N 31°50E 71 F5
Zrenjanin Serbia 45°22N 20°23E 69 B9
Zug Switz. 47°10N 8°31E 64 E5
Zunyi China 27°42N 106°53E 78 F10
Zürich Switz. 47°22N 8°32E 64 E5
Zuwārah Libya 32°58N 12°1E 95 B8
Zvishavane Zimbabwe 20°17S 30°2E 97 J6
Zwelitsha S. Africa 32°55S 27°22E 97 L5
Zwickau Germany 50°44N 12°30E 64 C7
Zwolle Neths. 52°31N 6°6E 64 B4

Published in Great Britain in 2009 by Philip's, a division of Octopus Publishing Group Ltd, www.octopusbooks.co.uk 2–4 Heron Quays, London E14 4JP

An Hachette UK Company www.hachette.co.uk

www.philips-maps.co.uk Ninety-sixth edition

Copyright © 2009 Philip's

ISBN 978-1-84907-013-3 (PAPERBACK EDITION)

ISBN 978-1-84907-012-6 (HARDBACK EDITION)

A CIP catalogue record for this book is available from the British Library.
All rights reserved. Apart from any fair dealing for the purpose of private study, research, criticism or review, as permitted under the Copyright, Designs and Patents Act, 1988, no part of this publication may be reproduced, stored in a retrieval system, or transmitted in any form or by any means, electronic, electrical, chemical, mechanical, optical, photocopying, recording, or otherwise, without prior written permission. All enquiries should be addressed to the Publisher.

Details of other Philip's titles and services can be found on our website at: www.philips-maps.co.uk

Printed in Hong Kong

Philip's World Atlases are published in association with The Royal Geographical Society (with The Institute of British Geographers).
The Society was founded in 1830 and given a Royal Charter in 1859 for 'the advancement of geographical science'. Today it is a leading world centre for geographical learning – supporting education, teaching, research and expeditions, and promoting public understanding of the subject.
Further information about the Society and how to join may be found on its website at: www.rgs.org

PHOTOGRAPHIC ACKNOWLEDGEMENTS
Satellite images in the atlas are courtesy of the following: EROS pp. 8, 9, 12tl, 12tr, 14bl, 14br; China RSGS p. 14tl; ESA 10b, 15b; Fugro-NPA (www.satmaps.com) pp. 10t, 11t, 14tr, 15t, 17, 49, 88, 123. 130; GeoEye p. 16b; NASA pp. 11bl, 12b; Precision Terrain Surveys Ltd p. 16t.